MODERN
RUSSIAN HISTORY

MODERN RUSSIAN HISTORY

FROM THE AGE OF CATHERINE THE GREAT TO THE END OF THE NINETEENTH CENTURY

by

ALEXANDER KORNILOV

Onetime Professor at the Polytechnikum of Peter the Great in Petrograd

Translated from the Russian by Alexander S. Kaun
With a bibliography by John S. Curtiss

NEW YORK / RUSSELL & RUSSELL

CONTENTS: VOLUME I

CHAPTER I 3

The aim and the contents of the book.— The method of its structure.— General characteristics of the socio-political process of development of the Russian people and state up to the eighteenth century.— The struggle for territory, and its socio-political results.— The main features of the new developmental process in Russian history, as it began to appear by the end of the eighteenth century.

CHAPTER II 23

The situation of Russia on the eve of the nineteenth century, at the end of Catherine's reign.— State boundaries.— The importance of Catherine's territorial acquisitions.— Means of communication.— Population.— Its racial composition.— Its order- and class-composition.— The conditions of various peasant-classes.— Urban-classes.— The clergy.— The nobility.— The *Intelligentzia* and the masses.— The development of education in Russia and the origin of the *Intelligentzia*.— The ideology of the masses.— The schism.— The government and its organs.— The financial conditions in the eighteenth century.— General conclusions.

CHAPTER III 50

The reign of Paul I.— His place in history.— Biographical facts.— The general character of Paul's governmental activity.— The peasant question under Paul.— His attitude towards other classes.— Society's attitude towards Paul.— The financial state during his reign, and his foreign policy. — Results of his reign.

CHAPTER IV 64

The reign of Alexander I.— Its division into periods.— Biographical facts.— His education.— His marriage.— His position under Catherine and Paul.

CHAPTER V 77

Alexander's accession.— His purpose, and the degree of his equipment.— His first collaborators, and his early meas-

CONTENTS

ures.— The work of the Unofficial Committee.— Its composition.
— Discussion of political reforms.— The peasant question.—
The formation of ministries and the reformation of the
Senate.— The results of the Committee's works.

CHAPTER VI 96

Moods and political views of society at the beginning of
Alexander's reign.— Important periodicals in the years 1802–
1805.— The condition of the masses.— The law of Free Farmers, 1803.— The peasant reform in Ostsee district in 1804 and
1805.—Growth of population.— Colonisation of the southern provinces.— The Jewish question.— The Government's
attitude towards sects.— Russian finances and financial policy in 1801–1805.— The problem of state reforms in 1803.—
Educational activity of the government in 1802–1805.

CHAPTER VII 114

The second period of Alexander's reign (1805–1807).
— Russia's international position at the beginning of the
nineteenth century.— Rupture with Napoleon.— Czartoryski's
plans and Alexander's attitude towards the Poles in 1805.—
The failure of the campaign of 1805.— The war of 1806–
1807.— The defeat of Prussia.— Great preparations in Russia for the war with Napoleon.— The winter campaign of
1807.— The exhaustion of Russia's military forces.— The
treaty of Tilsit.— Alliance with Napoleon, keen disappointment in Russia.— The character of the opposition.

CHAPTER VIII 130

Alexander's resolution to resume internal reforms in 1809.
Speransky.— The plan of state reorganisation.— Steps to its
realisation: establishment of the State Council and reorganisation of the ministries.— The ukase about service-examina-
tions.— The desperate condition of Russian finances in 1809–
1810.— Speransky's financial plan. Karamzin's address on
Ancient and New Russia.— The fall of Speransky.— The conditions of popular education.— The establishment of academic
societies.

CHAPTER IX 146

The immediate causes of the war of 1812.— Rupture with
Napoleon.— The comparative forces of the antagonistic armies and the plan of the campaign.— The general course of the
war.— The mood of the Russian army and people.— Napoleon's position before and after Moscow.— The repulsion of
the invader.— Alexander's triumph.— The transference of the

CONTENTS

war into Western Europe.— The campaign of 1813–1814.—
The deposition of Napoleon. The congress in Vienna.—
Alexander's plans in regard to Poland and Prussia.— Talleyrand's intrigues and friction among allies.— The solution
of the Polish question.— Condition of affairs in the Duchy of
Warsaw and the question of its future organisation.— Alexander's mystic mood and the idea of the Holy Alliance.

CHAPTER X 165

Alexander's return to Russia in 1815.— The Polish constitution of 1815.—Russian affairs in 1812–1815.— Misery and
material sacrifices of the population.—The cost of the war
and the degree of devastation.— Russian finances.— The upheaval of the national spirit.— The state of industry and commerce in 1812–1815.— The influence of the returning army
on society.— Spread of enlightenment in the country.— The
hopes of the society in Alexander.— His mood in 1816.—
Cares for army maintenance in connection with the foreign
policy.— The idea of military settlements, its origin and realisation. Arakcheiev.— His characteristic. The course of
affairs in the Committee of Ministers and the revelation of
abuses in 1816.— The rôle of Arakcheiev in the Committee
of Ministers and in other institutions.

CHAPTER XI 181

The rôle of the State Council during the wars of 1812–1815.
The restoration of its significance with the return of Admiral
Mordvinov into its body.— Mordvinov's activity and the financial measures of 1816–1820.— The tariffs of 1816 and of
1819 and their bearing on the course of paper money and on
the factory industry in Russia.— The growth of factories
during Alexander's reign.— The peasant question in 1816–
1820.— The liberation of the serfs in the Ostsee district and
the attitude of the government and society towards the peasant question in Russia.— The development of education after
1812.— The rôle of the universities.— The infiltration of mystic currents.— The Biblical Society.— The ministries of religion and of popular education.— Prince Golitzyn and his
adherents: Sturdza, Magnitzky, and Runich.— The breaking
up of the universities.— Journalism after 1815 and the position of the press.— The rôle of the ministry of police.— Alexander's mood in 1818–1820.— His speech in the Polish diet,
1818.

CHAPTER XII 196

The appearance of secret societies after the Napoleonic
wars.— The Union of Salvation. Its constitution.— Pestel

CONTENTS

and Muraviov.— Muraviov's opposition and the reorganisation of the Union of Salvation into the Union of Prosperity. — Its constitution, organisation, and activity along the four "branches."— Political questions among the members of the Union.— Outburst of indignation against Alexander in 1817. — The question of a republic in 1820.— The influence of the "Semionov-affair," of the second Polish diet, and of the Neapolitan revolution on Alexander's mood.— The suspension of the Union of Prosperity. "The Southern Society." — The activity of Pestel and other members.— The Vassilkov Board.— The society of United Slavs.— The Northern Society.— The Constitution of N. Muraviov and the "Russian Justice" of Pestel.

CHAPTER XIII 209

Alexander's mood and activity after 1820.— His agreement with Metternich.— The rôle of the Holy Alliance at that time.— The Greek insurrection, and Alexander's attitude.— Alexander's internal policy 1820–1825.— Withdrawal of reforms.— The reign of obscurantism.— Fotiy and the dismissal of Golitzyn.— The reason for the hesitation in the Government's persecutions.— Alexander and the Polish constitution.— Financial affairs.— The tariff of 1822 and the appointment of Kankrin as minister of finance.

SUMMARY AND GENERAL VIEW ON THE EPOCH.

PART II

CHAPTER XIV 223

The reign of Nicolas I.— The conditions of his accession. — The question of throne-succession.— The unpublished manifesto of Alexander about the abdication of Constantine.— Confusion and interregnum from the death of Alexander to December 14, 1825.— Negotiations between Nicolas and Constantine.— Accession of Nicolas.— The insurrection of December 14.— Its suppression.— Personality of Nicolas I.— His biography.— Investigation of the secret societies.— The execution of the Decembrists, and the results of Nicolas' acquaintance with them.— The influence of Karamzin on the Tzar.

CHAPTER XV 241

The division of Nicolas' reign into periods.— First period (1825–1831).— Nicolas' assistants: Kochubey, Speransky, Kankrin, Benckendorf, Dibich, Paskevich.— The Committee of December 6, 1826; its composition and purpose; its activity.

CONTENTS

— The peasant question.— The military settlements.— Speransky's codificatory work. The formation of the Third Department of H. M.'s Private Chancery.— The tendency of the ministry of education.— Attitude towards the Polish constitution.— International policy.— The war with Turkey, 1828–29.— The end of the first period.

CHAPTER XVI 252

The second period.— Conservative principles in foreign policy.— The Eastern question.— The meeting in Muenchengraetz.— The leading principles in the internal policy.— The legislative work.— Speransky's activity in preparing and issuing the Code of Laws.— The significance of the event.— The peasant question.— The condition of the people.— The material factors that had brought about the abolition of serfdom.— The activity of the Government.— Secret committees.— The work of Kankrin and Kiselev in managing the state-peasants.— The establishment of the ministry of state estates.— Kiselev's work for the management of the bonded peasants.— The law of 1842 about the bondage-peasants.— Inventory-taking in the Western region.— The law of May 26, 1846, concerning Poland.

CHAPTER XVII 266

The development of industry under Nicolas I.— The fate of some industrial branches.— The competition of Polish industry. Complaints of merchants.— Kankrin's activity.— His principles and policy.— Protectionism and its influence on industry and commerce.— The decrease in the growth of the military budget.— The cost of the war of 1827–31.— The beverage-reform.— The financial reform of 1839–43.— The rôle of Nicolas in the introduction of that measure.— Kankrin's cares for the betterment of cultural conditions.

CHAPTER XVIII 279

The system of popular education under Nicolas.— The Tzar's views.— The ministry of Uvarov.— His principles.— The decrees of December 28, 1828.— The university-decree of 1835.— The university of Moscow under Stroganov.— The position and development of the *Intelligentzia* under Nicolas. — The significance of the catastrophe of December 14.— Two channels of ideas: the German and the French.— The decay of the latter, and the growth of the first.— Schellingianism in Russia.—" Mnemosina."—" The Lovers of Wisdom " and " The Moscow Messenger."— Polevoy's " The Moscow Telegraph."— Nadezhdin's " Telescope."— The idealists of the 30-ies.— The circle of Stankevich.— Bakunin and Bielin-

CONTENTS

sky.— The evolution of Bielinsky.—"The Annals of the Fatherland" and "The Contemporary."—"The Muscovite," and the system of "official nationalism."— The Slavophiles and the Westerners in the 40-ies.— Socialism and "left" Hegelianism.— Provincial society in the 40-ies.— Sects during Nicolas I.

CHAPTER XIX 299

The European revolutions of 1848 and their influence on the mood of Nicolas I.— The third period of his reign.— Foreign policy.— The manifesto of March 14, 1848.— The Hungarian campaign.— Internal policy.— The peasant question.— Measures against the press and the universities.— Other repressions.— The dismissal of Uvarov.— Prince Shirinsky-Shikhmatov.— The position of the *Intelligentzia* after 1848.— The circle of Petrashevsky.— Incidents with Samarin, Aksakov, Turgeniev, Dostoievsky.— The prohibition of Slavophile publications.— The Kiev Federalists.— The general mood of the *Intelligentzia*.— The war of 1853–56.— The inevitable crisis.— The death of Nicolas.— General conclusions about the reign of Nicolas.

CONTENTS: VOLUME II

CHAPTER XX I

The Crimean campaign and its significance.— Characteristics of Alexander II.— His education, political views and
tastes.— The influence of the Crimean campaign on the Tzar.
His first steps.— The attitude of society towards Alexander
in 1855–56.— The conclusion of peace and the manifesto of
March 19, 1856.— The address to the nobles in Moscow.—
Preparations for the peasant-reform.— The activity of Lanskoy and Levshin.— The relationship of the nobles.— Circulating monographs.— The formation of the Secret Committee.—
Rostovtzev.— The course of activities in the Secret Committee during 1857.— The petition of the Lithuanian nobles and
the Imperial Rescript to Adjutant-General Nazimov, November 20, 1857.— The programme of the government.— The
publication of the November Rescript.

CHAPTER XXI 20

The nobility and the reform-programme of the government.
— The differing interests of landowners in the agricultural
and industrial provinces.— The attitude of the *Intelligentzia;*
the articles of Chernyshevsky and Herzen; the Moscow Banquet.— The address of the nobility of Nizhni-Novgorod.— The
hesitation in Moscow.— Addresses of other provinces.—
Provincial committees. — The point of view of Unkovsky and
of the Tver committee.— The sanctioned programme of activities.— The attitude of the press.— The evolution of Rostovtzev's views.— The opening of the Zemstvo department.—
Miliutin.— The examination of the governmental programme
by the Main Committee and the opening of the Editing Commissions.— The composition of the commissions.— Rostovtzev's programme.— The first assembly of the delegates of the
provincial committees.— The addresses of the nobles.— The
death of Rostovtzev.— Panin.— The second assembly of the
delegates.— The inner struggle in the Editing Commissions.
— The summary of their work.

CONTENTS

CHAPTER XXII 42

The Course of work in the Main Committee and in the State-Council, the discussions of the projects of the Editing Commissions.— Their conflicts.— The manifesto of February 19, 1861.— Its analysis.— Its legal, administrative, and economic significance for the peasants, for the nobles, and for the country.

CHAPTER XXIII 55

The influence of the peasant-reform on society and the press.— The conditions of the press in 1855.— The exceptional position of Herzen, his prophecy in 1853, and his programme in 1855–1858.— The attitude of the liberals towards Herzen.— The rôle of the *Bell* in the work of reform and in the development of public opinion in Russia.— The differentiation of tendencies in society and press after 1858. — The position of various press-organs.— The radicalisation of the *Contemporary*, and its relation to Herzen in 1859–60.— The *Russian Messenger* and other liberal organs.— The position and rôle of the Slavophiles.— Social demands crystallized during 1859–61.— Their comparison with the government's views of that moment.

CHAPTER XXIV 65

The attitude of the peasants towards the reform of February 19, 1861.— Disturbances and uprisings accompanying the introduction of the new order of things.— The Besdna catastrophe.— The impression of these facts on society.— Reaction in governmental circles in 1861.— Valuiev's policy.— The relationship of the public and the government.— First appearances of Nihilism in 1861.— The *Russian Word*.— The oppositional tendencies of the nobility.— Its two wings.— The Tver incident of 1862.— The constitutional movement and the differing opinions in nobility circles.— The attitude of the industrial-commercial spheres.— The evolution of this class after the Crimean campaign and the reasons of its oppositional tendencies.

CHAPTER XXV 80

The development of a general opposition and the first manifestations of a revolutionary spirit.— The proclamations of 1861–62.—" Young Russia " and the conflagrations of 1862. — Arrests and exiles of radical writers.— The impressions of these facts on the public.— The schism between the liberals and radicals.— Herzen on the latter side.— The impression in Western Europe.— The circular of Gorchakov.—

CONTENTS

The Polish movement.— The policy of Marquis Velepolsky, its failure.— The uprising of 1863.— Its impression on the Russian public.— The significance of the intervention of foreign powers.— Its resultant outburst of patriotism in Russia.— The fall of the *Bell.*— The triumph of Katkov and the general reaction.— Continuation of reforms.— Tatarinov's financial reform.— The excise reform.— The university-movement and the decree of 1863.— Other reforms in the ministry of education.— Secondary schools, education of women, primary schools.— The statute of 1864.

CHAPTER XXVI 96

The Zemstvo-reform.— Its connection with the peasant-reform.— Its analysis.— The attitude of the public and press towards the zemstvo-reform.— Conditions under which the zemstvo-institutions had to function.— The judicial reform. — Its significance and content.— The first steps of the new courts.— Press legislation.— The vacillation of the government in this sphere.— Two commissions of Prince Obolensky. — The policy of Golovnin and Valuiev.— The temporary laws of 1865.— The mood of the nobles in 1865. The address of the Moscow nobles.— The position of the radical press and circles.— The attentate of Karakosov.— The end of the reform-epoch and general conclusions about it.

PART III

CHAPTER XXVII 111

The attentate of Karakosov. The subsequent reaction.— The internal development of Russia in spite of the reaction.— Continuation of certain reforms.— The completion of the peasant reform.— The general picture of land-ownership among various groups of the population after the reforms of 1861, 63, 66.— The amount of soil-property among the liberated peasants.

CHAPTER XXVIII 123

The immediate results of the peasant-reform.— The growth of population before and after the reform.— The distribution of population before and after the reform.— The growth of the urban population before and after the reform. — The industrial crisis and its causes.

CONTENTS

Chapter XXIX 136

The financial conditions during the reform-epoch and in the next years.— The financial policy and activity of Reitern.— The effort to raise the productive capacity of the country, and particularly the export commerce.— The question of railroad-building.— Its course up to the middle of the 70–ies.— Organisation of commercial credit.— Opening of private banks.— Deficits in the state budget.— The question of continuing internal reforms and the report of Reitern in 1866.

Chapter XXX 151

The new municipal statute.— Former legal and actual status of cities.— The measures of the 40-ies.— The statute of 1870. Its substance and criticism thereof.— The question of military reorganisation.— The reforms of Miliutin.— The abrogation of recruitments and the law of universal service, 1874.— The general educational significance of Miliutin's military reforms.

Chapter XXXI 163

The activity of the Ministry of Education after 1866.— Ccunt Dimitry Tolstoy and Miliutin as representatives of two antagonistic camps in the reign of Alexander II.— The views of Tolstoy.— Tolstoy and Katkov.— The question of the reform of the secondary school.— The struggle for the introduction of classicism.— The importance of the reform of 1871.— Tolstoy's plans and measures in regard to the universities.— The development of woman educaton in the period of 1866–78.— Primary education.— The statutes of 1864 and 1874.— The struggle of the ministry of education with the zemstvo.— History of the zemstvo-schools from 1866–1880.

Chapter XXXII 176

The development of zemstvo-institutions from 1866 to 1878.— The region of their activity.— Their aims and means.— Their budgets.— Their effort to tax commerce and industry, and conflict with the government on the question.— The zemstvo expenses and their growth.— Class interests within the zemstvo.— The question and natural taxation and its distribution.— The struggle of the government with the zemstvo and the limitation of the latter's activity.

CONTENTS

CHAPTER XXXIII 181

The establishment of new courts and their first steps.—
Valuiev's fight against them.— The reactionary activity of
Count Pahlen.— The beginning of the work of the new statutes.— The position and tendency of the procuratorship.—
Special order of deciding cases of crimes against the state.—
Changes in the institution of jurists, and exemption of certain
cases from the jurisdiction of juries.— The position of the
press in the post-reform period.— Leading organs and literary tendencies after 1866.— The public mood.

CHAPTER XXXIV 196

The conditions of the masses and of the rural communities in the 60-ies and 70-ies.— The course of the redemption-
process.— Poor portions.—" Cut-offs."— Rent in the southern and northern provinces.— Growth of rent.— Indebtedness
of landowners.— Intensive cultivation of the soil owing to the
increasing export and prices of grain.— Landownership in
the north and in the south.— Sale of land.— The buyers.
— The condition of peasant-estates.— Insufficient property.—
Burden of taxes and payments.— Lack of equity in taxation.
— The famine of 1868.— Investigations by the zemstvo.—
— Tax-arrears.— The condition of the peasant-estates in the
black-soil region.— The famine in Samara in 1872-73.— Pro-
vision-loans.— The conclusions of Yanson and Prince Vassilchikov about the status of the peasants in the 70-ies.

CHAPTER XXXV 207

The attitude of the government and of the public towards
the position of the masses.— Popular tendencies in literature.
— Student-disorders in 1869.— Niechaiev and Niechaievism.
— The circle of Chaikovsky in Petrograd; their ideas and
plans.— Bakunin and Lavrov abroad.— Lavrists and Baku-
nists.— *Forward.*— The beginnings of the movement " Into the
People."— Arrests.— The report of Pahlen.— The society
" Land and Freedom."

CHAPTER XXXVI 224

The government's policy in the borderlands.— Oppressions
in Little Russia and Poland.— Foreign policy.— The Eastern
question.— Rivalry between Russian and British interests in
Asia.— The conquest of the Caucasus and of Central Asiatic
Khanates.— Disorders in Turkey.— Balkan Slavs.— The
Servian war and the Bulgarian Atrocities.— The conven-

CONTENTS

tions of the Powers.— The Russo-Turkish War of 1877–78.
— Its course and outcome.— The congress in Berlin.— Economic and financial results of the war.— The resignation of Reitern.— The impression of the war and the Congress on the Russian public.— Slavophiles.— The zemstvo movement. — The revolutionary movement.— The appeal of the government to the public.— The declarations of the zemstvos.— The formation of the party "The Will of the People."

CHAPTER XXXVII 239

Series of revolutionary attempts to assassinate Alexander II.— Confusion and vacillation in the upper spheres.— The explosion in the Winter Palace and the establishment of the Supreme Commission under the leadership of Loris-Melikov. — Loris-Melikov's programme and its realisation.— Relations of liberals and revolutionists towards him.— The resignation of Tolstoy.— The reforms of Loris-Melikov.— Senatorial revisions and the peasant question.— The constitutional movement— Loris-Melikov's report about the appointment of a special preparatory commission.— The catastrophe of March 1, 1881.

CHAPTER XXXVIII 249

Alexander III. His education.— Public attitude towards him before his accession.— His views.— His first steps.— The conflict of two tendencies in the upper spheres.— The council of March 8, 1881.— Vacillation.— Katkov and Aksakov.— The agitation of Pobiedonostzev. The manifesto of April 29, 1881.— The resignation of Loris-Melikov and other ministers.— The ministry of Ignatiev.— His programme. — Measures for the improvement of the economic conditions of the people. Compulsory redemption.— Agitation of the nobles.— Lowering of redemption-payments.— The policy of Bunge.— The abolition of poll-tax.— The introduction of tax-inspectors.

CHAPTER XXXIX 256

Early measures of Alexander III for the solution of the land-dearth problem among the peasants.— The peasant-bank and its first steps under Bunge.— The facilitation of renting state land.— Organisation of peasant-migrations.— The rules of 1881.— The law of July 13, 1889.— The introduction of factory inspectors and the law for the protection of minors and women in factories.— Taxes on inheritance and bonds.— The question of administrative peasant-re-

CONTENTS

form.— The commission of Kokhanov.— Its participators and the liquidation of their work.— The collapse of Ignatiev's régime.

CHAPTER XL 260

The decisive turn towards reaction.— The rôle of Pobiedonostzev.— Count D. Tolstoy.— Reaction in the Ministry of Education.— Reactionary policy of the nobility in internal affairs.— The jubilee of the granting of the nobility-charter in 1885.— Pazukhin's programme.— The liquidation of the question of reorganising the peasant-institutions after the dismissal of Kokhanov's commission.— The law of July 12, 1889, about the Zemsky Chiefs.— The zemstvo-statute of June 12, 1890.— Judicial restrictions.— The new press-law of 1882.— Persecution of non-Orthodox Christians.— The Jewish question.— New orders in the army.

CHAPTER XLI 267

The financial policy in the second half of Alexander's reign. Vishnegradsky and his system.— Extreme protectionism in custom policies and in railroad-tariff legislation.— The results of this system.— Foreign policy of Alexander III. — Conquest of Turcomania.— Russo-British relations in Central Asia.— The Balkan affairs.— Bulgarian troubles.— The Franco-Russian alliance and its significance.

BIBLIOGRAPHY 273
INDEX . . . . . . *follows page* 284

VOLUME I

PREFACE

TO PARTS I AND II

This "History of Russia in the Nineteenth Century" is based upon a course of lectures which I have been delivering since 1909 before the senior students of the Politechnicum of Peter the Great in Petrograd. It appears now in three parts, of which the first, beside two introductory chapters that contain a rapid sketch of the developmental process of the Russian state and people before the nineteenth century, presents the general evolutionary course of national and political life in Russia in the first quarter of the nineteenth century, up to the accession of Nicolas I. The second part contains a general survey of the internal life in Russia during the reign of Nicolas I and during the first, reformatory, period of the reign of Alexander II (to the year 1866). The third part deals with the history of Russia in the last thirty-five years.

I consider it my duty to mention with the deepest gratitude the late Professor V. O. Kluchevsky, in whose works I have found enormous aid for the formation of my own views on the course of Russian history in modern times.

THE AUTHOR.

Petrograd, January, 1912.

PART ONE

MODERN RUSSIAN HISTORY

CHAPTER I

I SUPPOSE that for every conscious man, whether he adheres to the idealistic or to the materialistic point of view, his own life becomes meaningful and significant only after he has found for himself a place in that collective labour and struggle of humanity by which "man liveth." Of course, in defining one's place in social life a person is guided primarily by the general *Weltanschauung* he has already formed and adapted. I do not pretend to influence my readers in this respect in one direction or another, but I presume that it is of great value for every man, even for one with a quite definite outlook upon life, to acquire a clear conception about that historical process in one of whose stages he is destined to live and act consciously. I shall not enter here into a discussion of the rôle of the individual in history. However negligible this rôle may appear in the eyes of those who profess the point of view of economic materialism, yet, I think, not even they will deny the need of orientation in surrounding phenomena for one who intends to be a social worker and a conscientious citizen.

In order to orient ourselves in the process of a nation's evolving life, particularly in that stage of the process in which we are to act, we must clearly conceive this process by studying all the circumstances amidst which it is taking place. And one can know the circumstances of the evolutionary process of any human society, naturally, by learning its history.

A few words about the contents of this course and the method of its structure. Under the history of Russia, I understand the process of the development of the Russian state. The state, as it is generally known, consists of three elements: the territory, the population settled in that territory, and the supreme power which unites the population into a political whole. From the point of view of political science all these elements are tantamount and equivalent in the sense that all of them are equally necessary for the formation of the modern idea of state. But from the point of view of the historian the inner significance of the three elements is far from being homologous. For the historian the subject of history is always man, human society, people. The state itself is doubtless the product of human activity, of human life. It is undisputable that the territory exists for the population and not *vice versa,* and at present it is likewise beyond dispute that the state-power exists for the people, and not the people for the state-power; furthermore, that the state-power is the product of human activity and life in a larger degree than is the territory; for whereas the latter is a self-sufficient quantity regardless of its population, the state-power is a direct product of human activity. Consequently for us the subject of the historical process expressed in the creation and development of a commonwealth is human society — a people; in this case the people that have created the Russian state.

We conceive the population composing a state as a nation of a definite territory united by one supreme power. The Russian state is composed, as we know, not only of Russian people in the proper ethnological sense of the word, but of a large number of tribes and nationalities of which some have become partly Russified and some have preserved their national physiognomy in a more or less full measure. On the other hand, beside this so to say vertical subdivision into races, the population of the Russian state may be classified also horizontally, into various orders and classes, differing juridically, economically, and socially. Finally, we must distinguish out of the common national mass the so-called *intelligentzia,* the intellectual body composed of men of various orders and classes, standing apart by virtue of their education and consciousness of ideals as well as by their aim not only to build up consciously their own life, but to exercise their influence on the life-structure of the whole nation according to their ideas and views.

Concerning the vertical subdivision of the population (into races), I must say at the outset that in this necessarily brief course I shall not be able to trace the development of each nationality separately, but shall expound mainly the history of the Russian people, touching the history of other parts of the population only inasmuch as certain events, problems, and processes in the development of particular nationalities concern the interests of the Russian state in general. From this point of view I shall discuss the general problem of nationalism and non-Russian elements in the state, as well as the various local events, conflicts, and questions that have arisen or developed during the nineteenth century in the midst of diverse nationalities.

As to the horizontal subdivision (i.e., into orders, classes, *intelligentzia,* etc.), I feel obliged to give, difficult as it may be, a possibly full exposition of the history of the *whole* nation, not of one class or another, nor of the educated society only, but indeed of the entire people, else the aim of my course, as I stated it in the beginning, would not be attained.

Such is the subject-matter of this course. A question may arise, whether I shall analyse the external or the internal history of the Russian state and people; whether I shall expound mainly the social, cultural history of Russia, or the so-to-speak external pragmatic history of the Russian state. Of what I have already said you may probably expect an exposition not of the external history of Russia, but of its social, cultural, inner history. This does not mean, of course, that we shall absolutely ignore the international relations and situation of Russia, which have always, and particularly in the nineteenth century, influenced to a great extent the internal processes in which we are interested. It means only that we shall occupy ourselves not with battle courses, not with heroic deeds and biographies of generals, not with the skill of diplomats, but with the general trend of world events and with those results that have been reflected upon the internal life of the Russian state. As to the socio-political process through which the Russian people and state have passed during the nineteenth century, we shall study it thoroughly in all respects, i.e., in the *economic,* by which I have in mind the development of national wealth as well as the conflict of class interests; in the *political* — the history of state institutions, of the people's attitude towards the state-power, of the interrelations of orders and classes, and, in general, of the political evolution and struggle; and in the *ideational,* by which I mean the enlightenment-movement and the development of the national ideology. One may conclude from the aforesaid that I intend to give not a pragmatic (in the narrow sense of the word) exposition of historical events and of individual acts, but a general picture of the development of culture and socio-political life in Russia during the nineteenth century. Yet I must beg to observe that although I do not intend to offer a pragmatic history proper, this course is expounded not in form of general deductions and conclusions in regard to the character and direction of the forces active in the process under observation, but in the form of a minutely elaborate picture of the general course of events, as they have taken place in reality. Hence I shall endeavour to relate clearly and specifically all the big historical facts in their chronological connection with reality, striving to clarify at the same time their interrelation and their rôle in that socio-political process which interests us. I should like, at any rate, to give in this course not a finished system of conclusions, not an established theory, but chiefly carefully studied facts and a clear understanding of their mutual relation and of their importance in the development of Russia.

Therefore if I should employ the term " pragmatic history " in a somewhat broader sense, in contradistinction from that history without proper names, without events and dates, from that algebraic history to which some sociologists reduce the purpose of cultural history and historical sociology, then in this expanded sense the exposition of my course may be called pragmatic. I think this inevitable in a case where there are as yet but a few well-established data, and particularly where the course comprises not the history of mankind as a whole, and not even the history of one nation through all its extent, but the history of one century of one nation.

Before approaching the history of the nineteenth century I must characterise at least in most general terms the whole socio-political process of Russian development, of which the nineteenth century presents only one stage.[1]

The first nine centuries of Russian history, if we start from the early chronicles to the middle of the eighteenth century, or the first eleven centuries, if we reckon from the supposed beginning of the distribution of the northeastern Slavic tribes (i.e., approximately from the seventh century), had been occupied in the main with the settling process of the tribes that have eventually formed the Russian nationality, and with the formation of a national territory. The first historical data concerning the origin of the Russian state go back to the ninth century. After the centre of the then political life had been established in Kiev, the Dnieper-Russ in the tenth century began to blossom luxuriously as a formative military-commercial state which,

[1] For a more detailed and thorough study of Russian political and social development I recommend two excellent works: V. O. Kluchevsky, "Course of Russian History" in 4 parts, and P. N. Miliukov, "History of Russian Culture" in 3 parts. (The first work has been translated by Hogarth.)

as all states of a similar type, had based its rising culture and wealth on military plunder, on widely developed slavery, and on an armed, well-scattered trade in slaves and other objects of military booty. But this developing state was not destined to become a firm and enduring political body. Towards the end of the twelfth century under the pressure of the steppe-invaders, the Kiev principality fell into decay, and the population that had peacefully settled on the banks of the Dnieper and had attempted to establish there an agricultural state became a prey of wild marauders. The constantly recurring attacks of the steppe-raiders caused the growing migration of the Dnieper-Russians into the Susdal district of the Volga and its tributary, Oka, where at present we find the provinces of Moscow, Yaroslavl, Vladimir, Kostroma, and Nizhni-Novgorod. There the climate was more severe, and the soil less fertile, but the farmer could safely settle among the scattered peaceful Finnish tribes.

This region had become, according to the expression of Professor Kluchevsky, the cradle of the Great Russian tribe which had formed during the twelfth and thirteenth centuries. In the second half of the twelfth century it became the political centre of Russian life, and an attempt was even made to create a consolidated monarchy. The attempt was undertaken by Prince Andrey Bogoliubsky, and was followed up by Vsevolod Big Nest; both had failed, however. The dissensions of the Princes had not ceased, Russ had not been ready yet to accept a monarchical rule, and in the meantime the Mongols invaded the land, which they held for three hundred years. The appanage system was firmly established in the devastated land for two centuries, a period of incessant strifes and internecine warfare. At the same time the land was constantly pressed and robbed by preying neighbours: from the east and the south the Tartars, from the northwest, the Lithuanians, the Poles, the Livonian Knights, the Swedes. From the year 1228 to

1462, i.e., for the period of two hundred and thirty-four years, the land had borne, according to Professor Kluchevsky's calculation, ninety internal wars among the Princes and one hundred and sixty foreign invasions. Yet during that trying period, under the shadow of the Tartar yoke, the Great Russian tribe had become definitely formed and strengthened in the incessant struggle with nature and men, and synchronously in its consciousness had grown and matured the need of a firm and single state-power which could unite the people, and with thus united forces repulse the enemies. For this reason when after a series of favourable circumstances the principality of Moscow had succeeded in establishing a strong dynasty capable of the unification of Russia, all the classes of society with the higher clergy and *boyars* at their head willingly upheld the ambitions of the Moscow Princes. Ivan Kalita and his successors accomplished that for which Andrey Bogoliubsky had striven in vain; by the middle of the fifteenth century, at the accession of Ivan III, there were present in the Grand Principality of Moscow all the elements of a state united by a strong single power, although it had not yet been completely free from foreign rule.

But that state, if it was to endure and grow, was confronted with enormous tasks that demanded for their fulfilment centuries of time, heroic self-sacrifice, and a tremendous strain upon all national forces. First of all it had to acquire complete political independence, and to throw off definitely the already weakened Tartar yoke. The achievement of this task was facilitated by the internal dissensions of the Golden Horde, which finally brought its dissolution.

Much more difficult was the accomplishment of the other tasks, the consolidation and unification of the Russian lands, and the strengthening and protection of the national territory. Both aims were interdependent, and rooted in the consciousness of the people.

The situation of the young Moscow state in the fifteenth century was precarious. A glance at the map will make this clear.[2] From the east and the south, even after the overthrow of the Tartar rule, Moscow had been threatened by constant invasions and raids of nomad-hordes which were grouped after the fall of the Golden Horde in three Tzardoms, three rapacious restless nests, that of Kazan, of Astrakhan, and of Crimea. On the west and southwest was consolidated at that time the strong kingdom of Poland-Lithuania, which had absorbed the remnants of the Dnieper-Russ and of the West-Russ, and had threatened to swallow up the other Russian territories. The frontiers of that formidable neighbour almost touched Moscow in the fifteenth century. To the northwest of Moscow lay the dominions of its ardent foe and rival, the Grand Duke of Tver; on the north the Moscow territories bordered and merged with the territories and colonies of Great Lord Novgorod, the city-republic in which the masses strove for union with Moscow, while the upper classes intrigued against Moscow with Lithuania and Poland. Finally in the very centre of the Muscovite state lay territories that were appanages of the Princes of Rostov and Yaroslav. These last were peacefully annexed to Moscow by Ivan III. The enormous dominions of Novgorod, the principality of Tver, Pskov, Oriol, and Riazan (the last as late as 1520) were ultimately annexed after stubborn fighting.

The Tartar yoke was overthrown in 1480, but the subjugation of the Volga-Tartars took place only in the second half of the sixteenth century, and up to that time Ivan III, Vassily III, and Ivan IV had to undertake not less than ten expeditions against the Tzar of Kazan to keep off his raids. Kazan was conquered in 1552, Astrakhan in 1556, but the Khan of Crimea preserved his formidable sway over the whole south of Russia until the eighteenth century. More than once during the sixteenth and seventeenth centuries the Crimean Tar-

[2] See the map at the end of this volume.

tars appeared at the walls of Moscow, on which occasions they captured hundreds of thousands of men and women and filled the Eastern slave-markets with Russian captives.

The protection of Russian frontiers from Lithuania, and the reconquest of old Russian territories from Lithuania and Poland had occupied the whole of the sixteenth and seventeenth centuries, and were properly accomplished only at the end of the eighteenth century. During the reign of Alexis the annexation of the left shore of Ukraina brought the first long peace with Poland (1667); but the ancient lands that had formed parts of the Dnieper-Russ were restored to Russia only after the division of Poland under Catherine II. By straining the nation's forces to the uttermost Peter the Great succeeded at the beginning of the eighteenth century in conquering Lifland, Estland, and Ingermanland from Sweden and thus joined the Baltic coast to Russia. It was only after the conquest of Crimea and the division of Poland, i.e., towards the end of the eighteenth century, that the tasks which were put forth by the natural course of events in the time of Ivan III, could be considered accomplished. Only since Russia had pushed its boundaries towards the Black and the Caspian seas on the south and towards the Baltic on the west, could the formation of the state territory of the great Tzardom be considered finished, at least in its general features, and there came at last the time when the powers and means of the country could be concentrated toward the satisfaction of the needs of the people themselves.

At what expense was this formation of a state-territory accomplished, and what were the socio-political consequences of this centuries-long process?

We know that in modern times a few months' warfare swallows up the budget of a whole year. In the past the state budgets were not large, and the governments did not spend any big, in the modern scale, sums for either preparation or management of wars; but the very wars were not less but more devastating and ruinous than those of the present. Whereas now the enemy's attack is aimed mainly at armies, war-vessels, and armed fortresses, in those days the devastation of the land was inevitable, the civil population suffered mutilation and tortures and enslavement, cattle were slaughtered or carried away, buildings were set afire, property was destroyed or plundered. Russ suffered such consequences of war not only from raids of savage hordes, not only from Lithuanian invasions, but from their own Orthodox Christian brethren in times of internecine wars among the Princes, and especially during the struggles of the Muscovites with their most stubborn opponents, Tver and Novgorod. The annals of the fifteenth and sixteenth centuries abound in descriptions of bloody murders, atrocities, and systematic ravages promulgated by the armies of the Muscovite princes in the towns and villages of the Grand Principality of Tver and in the territories of Great Novgorod, until these lands had finally been brought under the dominion of the " Collectors of Russian Soil." It is needless to mention the havoc and chastisements inflicted by the Tartar invasions which occurred periodically during the fifteenth, sixteenth and seventeenth centuries, particularly on the part of the Crimean Tartars. The human loss on battlefields was not so great as the loss in men, women, and children who were captured and sold into slavery by the Mongols. In order to protect the frontiers from the steppe hordes the Government had to construct abatis and outposts for hundreds of versts along the southern border, from the shores of Oka and its tributaries about Riazan far to the west. Beside this it had to mobilise every spring thousands of soldiers for the defence of that frontier.[3] With the

---

[3] According to the testimony of Fletcher, the English ambassador to Russia in the sixteenth century, the yearly mobilisation for the southern frontier amounted to 65,000 men. Professor Kluchevsky gives the same number. P. N. Miliukov quotes the figures of the southern army in the seventeenth century as considerably smaller than those of Fletcher. At any rate the fact of yearly mobilisations of many

view of protection from the steppe raiders the Government of Moscow built more and more new cities, continuously pushing the chain of outposts farther to the south, settling military colonies there which were to serve as a living fence. Thus the colonisation of the fertile steppe region to the south of Moscow went on. In the same time in the west a stubborn struggle had taken place against Lithuania, Poland, the Livonian Knights, and the Swedes. From the end of the fifteenth to the end of the sixteenth century there were three great wars with Sweden and seven long exasperating wars with Poland and its temporary ally, the Livonian Order. These wars occupied on the whole fifty years. According to contemporaries the number of Russian men in operation reached at times two hundred to three hundred thousand, while the entire population of the Muscovite state at that time did not exceed several million souls of both sexes. National wealth was exclusively natural, hence a pecuniary upkeep of the army was out of question. In the words of Professor Kluchevsky, the Muscovite Government possessed a single capital acquired during the " Collection of Russian Soil "— enormous stretches of land, partly peopled by peasants, partly waste.

This capital was put into circulation for the maintenance of the large " serving " class which grew out of proportion. From this resulted at first the " estate system," and later the " bondage system." [4] The upkeep of the serving class had become the dominant interest in the Muscovite state at the expense of all other national interests, and it required the sacrifice of all the

thousands for the protection of the southern frontier from the Tartars has been documentally established.

[4] For the history of the " estate " and " bondage " systems the author recommends a number of works which are unfortunately inaccessible to non-Russian readers. The English reader will find helpful chapters on the question in the first two volumes of Kluchevsky's History, in the first volume of J. Mavor's " An Economic History of Russia," and in M. Kovalevsky's " Russian Political Institutions."— TRANSLATOR.

live forces of the land. The inevitable constant and durable strain of all the means of the country which was sparsely populated and forced to protect, guard, and extend the already too far extended boundaries, resulted in the compulsion of the whole populace to bear state-service in one way or another. The idea of general service, and its concomitant idea of " binding " the classes, were consequences of such a state of affairs. This continuous mobilisation of all the national forces for the formation and strengthening of the state territory brought along another political result — the enormous increase of the central authority. Under the stress of foreign invasions and internal strifes and dissensions the Russian people as far back as in the fourteenth century had extended a helping hand to the Muscovite princes in their struggle for a dictatorship over the disunited country. But with the course of events the interests of the central power fell more and more in line with the interests of the serving class, for whose sake the supreme authorities did not hesitate to sacrifice the freedom of the peasants. The serving men in their turn helped the central power to break down the *boyar* class who attempted to maintain certain political prerogatives.

The larger part of the arable soil, in the centre of the state, on the west, south, and southeast, had become the possession of the serving class, as military benefices or as hereditary estates. In the interests of this class the peasants were gradually bound to their land, and given over to their masters into personal bondage, partly in fact, and partly juridically.

In the meantime wars and military needs did not diminish, but on the contrary continually increased. The life and death struggle with the western neighbours forced Russia to follow closely their standard of military organisation. Expensive firearms and foreign instructors had to be imported in large numbers, to cite one instance. This sort of militarism demanded not only the maintenance of the serving class, but a considerable expenditure of money, for which again the nation's strength had to be strained to the utmost. In quest of financial sources there arose and gradually took root a peculiar fiscal system based on the idea of general *tyaglo* or tax, which in the absence of local state institutions necessitated the *mutual guarantee* system within each taxable group, and later the fixation of those groups as classes in the Muscovite state. This process took place in the rural as well as in the urban population.

By the beginning of the eighteenth century this process of the formation of state-classes and of the socio-political structure of the Russian commonwealth was practically accomplished in its general features. At the same time the strain of the national means and forces had reached its apogee, though the task of fixing and strengthening the national territory was far from completion. Until the middle of the seventeenth century, despite the tenacious struggles, the work of consolidating the Russian lands in the west had not progressed, and the western frontier still remained extremely precarious and indefinite. In the sixteenth and seventeenth centuries the Muscovite state could hardly resist the aggressive moves of the Polish-Lithuanian kingdom and of Sweden. At the beginning of the seventeenth century by the peace of Stolbovsk the outlet into the Baltic Sea was affixed to Sweden, and this at the time when Russian oversea commerce had become especially important and was badly needed, since the natural wealth could no longer satisfy the growing needs of the state.

Towards the time of the reign of Peter the Polish-Lithuanian kingdom, owing to internal causes, had begun to lose its power, and thus Russia was enabled to concentrate its western forces on the struggle with Sweden. This struggle, lasting two whole decades and complicated by a hard war with Turkey, almost drained the nation.

Peter finally succeeded in fulfilling his task, or rather the task bequeathed to him by the preceding centuries: Sweden was defeated, Ingria, Korelia, and Estland, conquered by Ivan III and subsequently lost by Ivan IV, were reannexed together with Lifland, thus giving Russia the coveted outlet to the Baltic. Petersburg was founded. Russia, hardly known to the West in the time of Ivan III, became a European Power, while its ancient rival, Poland, descended to the degree of a second-rate state patronised by its neighbours and rent by internal dissensions.

Peter's success in his conflict with Sweden has borne enormous consequences for Russia, but that success was gained at a terrible price. According to Miliukov, Russia paid for her promotion to a European Power with the ruination of the country. Indeed such an impoverishment, such a drainage of national means and sources, Russia had not experienced even during the Interregnum period.[5] For the war, for the construction of Petersburg, for the building of the navy, there were needed not only enormous financial means, but also men. Long before — early in the seventeenth century, the forces of the serving class proving insufficient for carrying on the struggle with the western neighbours, standing regiments were formed of the *Streltzy* (musketeers), and later *Reiter* (cavalry) and dragoons, and artillery of a foreign model. These armies were composed not only of the nobility and their retinues, but also of new cadres specially recruited from the population in time of war. Under Peter, beginning with 1701, the recruitments had become a yearly contribution of the people, not only for the ranks of the reformed army, but also for the construction of Petersburg and for other state works. These recruitments and the enormously increased taxes were responsible for the fact that during the period of time between the eighties of the seventeenth century and the twenties of the next century one-fifth of Russian households disappeared. One part of

[5] From the death of Boris Godunov — 1605 — to the accession of the first Romanov — in 1613.— TRANSLATOR.

this unusual human loss was a direct victim of war, another part consisted of those who fled from the burden of unbearable taxation. It is possible, even probable, that the actual depopulation during those thirty years was less; a part of the dissolved households had doubtless been somehow redistributed among the remaining households, but at any rate the fact of the destruction of twenty per cent. of those units is beyond question.

Peter's government had simultaneously to fight his enemies and to preserve the land from total ruination. It had to sharpen its wits in hunting the fugitive citizen who tried to evade the immense state burdens, and at the same time it had to seek means for the upholding and developing of industry and trade in the impoverished country. In the first decade of the eighteenth century two hundred thousand labour-men were drawn out of the sparse population, and at least half of them had perished. The state budget exceeded many times that of the end of the seventeenth century, and three quarters of it went for the upkeep of the army and navy, while all the other needs of the great state had to be satisfied with the remaining one-fourth. All the poll-taxes from the non-exempt classes, which at that time formed the lion's share of the state income, were exclusively spent on the maintenance of the army; all the indirect taxes, on the navy expenditures. In his struggle with fugitives and evaders Peter had definitely fixed the bondage system, and had equalised the bonded peasants with the *Kholopy*,[6] while the brunt of the heavy military duty was borne no longer by the serving class alone, but by the tax-paying population. Military service had become an additional heavy burden on the back of the people.

Such was the strain of national resources under Peter. Yet his success proved permanent. In spite of the profligacy and disorderliness of his incapable and casual successors up to Cath-

[6] Personal property of the owner, practically slaves.—TRANSLATOR.

erine II, and owing to a large extent to happy conjectures in foreign affairs, the national borders established by Peter remained and even somewhat extended to the south and southwest.

By the time of Catherine II Poland was quite ripe for dissolution, and Russia received without much effort not only the ancient regions that had formed parts of Dnieper-Russ, but also Lithuania and Curland. Turkey likewise grew steadily weaker, and after two successful wars Russia conquered at length Crimea, its old menace, and the northern coast of the Black Sea. On the southwest its border line was the river Dniester, on the south, the Black Sea, on the southwest, the rivers Kuban and Terek. The international situation of the great empire was mightier and more brilliant than that of any contemporary European Power.

The task of forming and strengthening the national territory, which had stood before the Russian nation since Ivan III and which had absorbed and drained all its forces and means during many centuries, could at length be considered accomplished.

That moment appeared to be the turning point in the development of Russia. A quite new historical process began and with it modern Russian history. If before Catherine the main slogan of the state-power had been the consolidation of the old lands, the protection of the national territory, and the imperial aggrandisement, during her reign new tendencies appeared in the consciousness of the nation and of the Government itself. The chief aim of the state was no longer the expansion of the country, but the well-being of the subjects. Catherine definitely formulated that principle at her very accession to the throne. In her desire to acquire the love and loyalty of her subjects she declared in one manifest after another her intention to devote all her time and energy to the improvement of internal conditions rather than to promote external grandeur.

We may regard critically the fulfilment of her promises, though it is impossible to deny the great cultural importance of her reign, but it is worth noticing, at any rate, the change in the formulation of the fundamental state problems.

Under Peter *all* national forces were still directed toward territorial formation; from Catherine on problems of national welfare, of material and spiritual well-being, were moved to the foreground. Alongside with these began the gradual unbinding of the classes that had been bound during the territorial struggles. The process of unbinding was slow and long, growing complicated and obstructed by a mass of concomitant phenomena and circumstances, but it began at once, as soon as there came a possibility of releasing the strain of the nation's forces in the incessant struggle for territory. Then, concurrently with the unbinding of classes began the general liberation of the people from oppression and burdens that had been accumulated through centuries of tension, and finally the gradual loosening of the basis of the supreme dictatorship, which originated in the time of the Muscovite Tzars owing to the constant perils of struggle.

This complex process of the unbinding of classes, of the liberation of the people, and of the relaxation of the monarchical power, becomes the history of Russia in the nineteenth century. Its culmination is taking place in our own days, but its starting point belongs to the end of the eighteenth century, to the moment when the lasting struggle for the formation of the national territory came to an end.

At first the questions of popular welfare and enlightenment came to the front. In fact those questions were not new. The idea of the nation's welfare and even of its enlightenment was not foreign to the pre-Petrine Muscovite governments, but this idea was completely pushed to the background by current urging needs in the tense struggle for territory.

We should be quite unjust to Peter if we did not acknowledge that he was particularly interested in the weal and education of his people. But that mighty titan, engulfed more than any of his predecessors in territorial struggle, was able to give but little attention to popular needs, and even that by fits and starts. Owing to the demands and exactions of the exhausting, all absorbing struggle, the questions of internal welfare had in his eyes a dependent, subservient importance. Hence even those measures which he undertook for the encouragement of commerce and industry, and for the dissemination of education, had an official, technical character. The Petrine factories and foundries served in the main fiscal interests, and produced primarily things that were needed for the equipment of the army and navy. The Petrine schools were chiefly professional, technical, e.g., those of navigation, of artillery, of engineering, and the lower " cipher " schools. Even the Theological Academy he, evidently, had intended to turn into a peculiar politechnicum which would furnish men for clerical service, for civil offices, and for military, architectural, and medical professions.

Under Catherine the questions of common weal and enlightenment were placed in principle above all other tasks. Unfortunately common weal was conceived in a quite peculiar way; in its conception one felt the influence of the preceding historical process under which the socio-political structure of the nation had been formed. Moreover, Catherine herself perhaps exaggerated her dependence on the nobility who had elevated her to the throne and whose support she sought and maintained. For this reason she was bound to regard the problems of popular welfare from the point of view of the nobles, which view she skilfully tried to combine with the theoretical teachings borrowed from the coryphæi of European political thought in the eighteenth century. In the first years of her reign Catherine dreamt somewhat naïvely to establish, in her expression, the "beatitude" of the people by the aid of a rational legislation. In her summons to the famous Legislative Commission she outlined a programme of an all-embracing national reorganisation along lines chiefly adapted from Montesquieu and Beccaria.

No direct results followed from the work of that Commission which was dissolved one year and a half after its assembling, and Catherine, disappointed in the possibility of promulgating the grand reform in that way, made use of the Commission's discussions that reflected the opinions of various groups of the population, and started on the way of partial solution of separate internal problems. She had endeavoured to establish legal principles in the life of the people, in the relations of the classes to one another and to the Government, and her legislators codified for the first time the principle of personal and property security of the citizens.

Catherine succeeded in carrying through some measures for the protection of public health and for the security of public alimentation. Finally she succeeded in seriously stimulating the work of popular enlightenment and in placing on a firm basis the internal organisation of the classes and the formation of local administrations in the provinces and districts.

The class-unbinding began from the nobility, and owing to the actual prevalence of that class no practical measures were undertaken for the unbinding of the peasants, but on the contrary the legal condition of the peasants on the nobles' estates grew worse, and the bondage-right reached its culminating point. Yet at the same time the abnormality of the bondage system was admitted in principle, and it was then that the idea of serf-liberation began to circulate publicly, not without the influence of the Empress. The abolition of excessive repressions and regulations in regard to commerce and industry, and the granting of civil rights and guarantees to the third estate, were also ripening during that period. Towards the end of Catherine's reign the status and general tendencies of the further development of the Russian state and people were marked in quite definite features.

CHAPTER II

U NABLE to trace here in detail the development of Russia under Catherine, I shall endeavour only to formulate in brief terms the conditions of the country at the time of Catherine's death, i.e., at the very end of the eighteenth century.

The state boundaries differed from those of the present day only in these instances: of Finland not more than the province of Viborg formed a part of the Russian Empire; the kingdom of Poland proper had not yet belonged to the tzars; Bessarabia was still a Turkish possession; of the Caucasus the province of Stavropol and parts of the districts of Kuban and Terek belonged to Russia; the Central Asiatic possessions and the Amur region were not conquered till far into the nineteenth century. Thus the territory of European Russia included all the ancient Russ-lands for which centuries of struggle had taken place, and its well-protected boundaries expanded northward, westward, and southward to four seas that wash the shores of the Russian plain in Europe.

The international position of Russia was such that not only could no anxiety arise concerning the safety of its frontiers, but, enjoying the status of a great Power and exploiting the weakness of its neighbours, the Empire was able to wield a tremendous influence upon the international relations of the whole civilised world. During the second half of her reign Catherine occupied herself with definite plans for the expulsion of the Turk from Europe and the restoration of the Greek Empire; the imperial crown was to be placed on the head of Catherine's grandson, Constantine.

23

From the economic viewpoint Catherine's territorial acquisitions had an enormous, one may say a colossal, significance for the future development of Russia. The conquest of black-soil expanses in the south and southwest, and the resultant establishment of perfect safety on the southern frontier and the intensive colonization of those lands, have brought a new factor of great importance into the economic state of the country.

Thenceforward Russia became an agricultural country not only by name, but one of Europe's granaries, in fact. Indeed, already in 1779 the corn export from the chief ports (except those of Ostsee, i.e., the Baltic) exceeded the export of 1776 more than ten times. In spite of the rapid spread of agriculture in the South, the prices on grain remained quite firm, owing to the development of the grain-trade, which circumstance in its turn encouraged further growth of agriculture in the South simultaneously with its increasing colonization.

As to means of communication, of great importance in the eighteenth century had been the waterways, particularly the canals that connected the river-systems, two of which — the Vyshnevolotzk and the Ladoga — had been constructed under Peter. Catherine had considerably improved the Vyshnevolotzk system connecting Volga with the Baltic Sea. Other canals planned and partly opened during her reign, as those of Siask, Novgorod, Beresina, Schluesselburg, the Oginsky, and Maryinsky, were completed under Paul and Alexander in the nineteenth century.[1]

The population, whose decrease was reported after the first census in 1724, grew continually in the second half of the eighteenth century when the strain for territorial struggle had

[1] The adequate work of increasing and improving the water-ways began properly in 1782, when by the advice of Sivers a special body of hydraulicians was established in the department of water-way communications. Cf. the historical sketch of the development of that department for the century (1798–1898) issued in Petrograd by the Ministry of Ways of Communications in 1898.

ceased. In 1763 (the third census) the population of both sexes did not exceed twenty million; at the end of Catherine's reign the same regions had twenty-nine million, and with the newly acquired territories the total population amounted to thirty-six million (according to the figures of Academic Storch). The racial composition of the nation was even then quite varicoloured, if we may judge by the description of Russian nationalities in those days made by a contemporary, Georgy, who gave no numbers, however, nor information about the degree of Russification in one case or another. Certainly the numerical prevalence of Russians, even of the Great Russian tribe, was more decisive at that time than now, for the Empire had not yet absorbed the populations of Poland, the Caucasus, Finland, and Bessarabia. Catherine favoured foreign immigration and encouraged the colonization of New Russia and the Saratov province by Germans and western and southern Slavs. She issued about fifty ukases inviting back Russian fugitives who had fled abroad on account of religious persecutions and other oppressions; on their return and settlement they received considerable privileges.

In regard to the order- and class-composition of the population, we may form some idea from the figures worked out by Academic Storch on the basis of the fourth census, 1783. The male population in Russia, not counting that of the then conquered provinces, amounted to 12,838,529 souls.[2] Of them:

Landowners' private peasants		6,678,239
State-peasants	4,674,603	5,448,259
One-yarders [Free-holders] and freedmen..	773,656	
Burghers		293,743
Merchants		107,408
Tax-exempted, i.e., nobles, clergy, and state-officials..		310,880

12,838,529 males.

[2] Till the middle of the nineteenth century the census considered only the male population, since the Government was interested in the num-

Total rural population ....12,126,498 or 94.5 per cent.
Total urban population .... 401,151 or 3.1 per cent.
Total privileged classes .... 310,880 or 2.4 per cent.

Of the rural population about 45 per cent. were state-peasants and one-yarders (free-holders), and about 55 per cent. landowners' bondage-peasants. The development of the serfdom-institution reached at that time its climax. Legally the serfs had no rights whatever. The landowners concentrated in their hands not only the right to dispense freely with the labour of their bonded-peasants, whom they could transfer from the soil to house-service, could sell singly and with the families, could lend to others into service, whose status they could change, assigning them to factories, etc.; they also had the power to punish them: by putting them into domestic or other prisons, by appointing them to perform some extra work, and by inflicting upon them corporal punishment (rods, whips, knuts) for relatively unimportant transgressions and even just for "insolent" behaviour.

From the time of Empress Elizabeth, landowners were permitted to hand over their "insolent" serfs to the Government for exile to Siberia. As a matter of fact, however terrible that word may sound to us, to many serfs the exile appeared as a liberation from unendurable suffering. But under Catherine the landowners were allowed to exile their serfs to hard-labour prisons as well. The masters had from old days appropriated the right to interfere with the family life of their serfs, to marry them by force, to dispense with their property. Abuses and maltreatment reached unbelievable dimensions. At the same time the serfs were forbidden to complain against their masters, except in cases of state treason. As a matter of fact, the serfs did not quietly accept such a state of affairs, and they reacted to their most heavy oppressions, not only by sending

ber of taxpayers exclusively. We can only approximately construct the total number of the population by multiplying the given figures by two.

complaints to the Government, but also by uprisings, assassinations of landowners and their managers, and by flights. At times, particularly at every accession of a new monarch, rumours circulated among the peasants about fantastic liberation-ukases; then the unrest would embrace considerable territories, and would only be quelled by military repressions, executions, whipping, and exile.

At Catherine's accession about 150,000 peasants took part in disturbances. But the chief elemental and formidable protest against serfdom, which grew to enormous dimensions threatening the existence of the state, burst out in 1773 in the Pugachov-insurrection.

The condition of the serfs depended upon whether they were *barshchina*-peasants or *obrok*-paying peasants. The first had to do obligatory labour for the lord, usually three days in the week. But this custom had not become a law until the time of Paul I, and in some cases the masters exacted from their serfs more than three days labour. Besides the field-work the peasant had to perform various winter services for his owner, and paid natural tribute in the form of fowls, sheep, pigs, berries, and mushrooms, while the women had to bring a certain amount of flax and hemp yarn and texture, and even home-spun cloth.

On the *obrok*-estates the entire plough-land, and at times also the forest, were given over to the peasant community who were obliged to pay a certain amount of money or kind according to the arbitrary will of the owner. The *obrok*-peasants were better off than their *barshchina*-brothers, for, although they had to pay very often exorbitant tribute, they enjoyed a certain degree of freedom and self-government. By the end of the eighteenth century the number of *obrok*-estates had increased in connection with the development of industry and commerce, so that in the northern, not black-soil provinces, they exceeded half of the estates, amounting in the province of Yaroslavl to 78 per cent., in Nizhni-Novgorod to 82 per cent., in Kostroma to 85 per cent., in Vologda to 83 per cent.; while in the fertile black-soil region their number was very slight and did not exceed 8 per cent. in the governments of Kursk and Tula.

The state-peasants presented a variegated mass. Not less than two-sevenths of them were formerly church-peasants who were secularised and managed by an Economic Collegium, for which reason they had been known as Economical peasants. About one-seventh of the state-peasants constituted the Court-serfs. Catherine had considerably improved their lot by sup-planting *barshchina* with *obrok* in the court estates, the pay-ments being made quite moderate; they had another advantage over landowners' peasants in that they could not be sold with-out their soil. At the beginning of Catherine's reign there were in the northern, central, and eastern provinces over half a million male state-peasants, including the so-called " Tzar's peasants " (about 62,000), who belonged to various members of the Imperial family, and the " Stable peasants," who per-formed very hard labour for the court stables.

Then followed the groups of the Fiscal peasants, whose labour was exploited for various state needs. There were about 330,000 male persons assigned to factories, state (241,-253) and private (70,965). They were known as " Posses-sional peasants," and they carried on a vigorous fight for their privileges as compared with the bonded peasants. The factory owners strove to enslave not only the " ascribed " peasants, but even the free, hired labourers. In the same class we must consider the peasants ascribed to the admiralty forests (112,357) and the coachmen (about 50,000) who were settled at important highways for the maintenance of post-stations.

All these groups of Fiscal peasants, though not bonded pri-vate slaves in the sense that they could not be sold without

soil, still were state-serfs by the character of their rights and labour.

A greater freedom and independence among the Fiscal peasants was enjoyed by the " black-ploughmen " in the North, who paid the state definite money-*obroks* and taxes, and filled certain natural obligations of a public nature; they had a comparatively broad form of self-government. In the seventies of the eighteenth century there were more than 627,000 such peasants. Another free group of rural population in the South and in some central provinces presented the " Freeholders " and the " Old service serving people," who were not only free from bondage, but at times possessed bonded serfs. They were formed from among the lower ranks of those who had borne frontier service for the Muscovite state and had received in possession small portions of free land. Storch placed their figures, together with the figures of some other free rural groups of an indefinite character, close to 773,656 males at the end of the eighteenth century.

We have already seen that the total number of peasants in the eighteenth century amounted to about 94.5 per cent. of the population. For this reason Russia has of old been known as an exclusively agricultural country. But this definition cannot be accepted without some reserve for the eighteenth century. The fact of the matter is that not all persons classed as peasants were agriculturists. First of all we must exclude not less than 10 per cent. of peasants of the Fiscal groups, who were ascribed to various factories; then the *obrok*-peasants, who formed at least one-half of the landowners,' court-, and Economical peasants, could not be considered as pure agriculturists, since a large part of them, especially in the industrial, not black-soil provinces, did not earn a living from agriculture. Finally various branches of home-industry were considerably developed even among the agricultural population in certain regions. Generally speaking, commerce and small industry had been very popular in the Muscovite state as well as in Imperial Russia; until the acquisition and settlement of the black-soil South the grain produced in the original Russian provinces was hardly sufficient for the provision of the local population.

The eighteenth century marked a considerable growth of the urban population which had developed rather slowly up to that time. Whereas from 1630 to 1724, i.e., for almost a whole century, the number of city-dwellers increased from 292,000 to 328,000, in the period between 1724 and 1796 the number increased almost four times, reaching 1,301,000. The merchant-class that formed a part of the urban population had also increased, consisting of 240,000 members towards the end of Catherine's reign; their business had grown complex and large in view of the development of industry and foreign trade. In pre-Petrine Russ there hardly existed any factories or big industry; the largest transactions consisted in buying up and re-selling the products of small *kustarny*-industry (home work). Under Peter the Government gave a mighty stimulus for the development of factories and mills which were necessary for the production of army and navy equipment. The Government founded factories and assigned to them peasants who became the property of the factory-owners, even if the latter were not of noble origin. (Only nobles were allowed to own serfs.— TR.) Later the factories, together with the ascribed working-men established by the Government, were given over to private persons.

Considerable capital accumulated earlier through commerce was attracted by Peter towards manufacturing industry. Although Catherine in her desire to favour the nobility patronised small industry, factories grew rapidly during her reign and made use of free hired workers alongside with the ascribed peasants. The nobles were hostile to this development. It was to their interest to uphold the small peasant industry and commerce which enabled them to draw enormous *obroks* from their peasants. In the commission appointed by Catherine for the discussion of this question the struggle between the two classes burst forth for the first time. Ultimately the nobles, with the aid of the Empress, prevailed against the merchants. The Government began to observe strictly that the merchants should not possess peasants illegally; while the nobles began to build their own factories based exclusively on bondage-labour.

The number of factories and mills increased from 984 to 3,161 (not counting the mines) under Catherine, according to Tugan-Baranovsky. The figures of Lappo-Danilevsky, on the other hand, show that their number grew from 500 to 2,000 during her reign. At any rate the number of the most important factories and mills increased not less than 40 per cent. The foreign trade was greatly enhanced by the abolition of various limitations and regulations introduced in the first half of the eighteenth century, also by the opening of credit associations, by the development of merchant marines, establishment of consulates abroad, and by the conclusion of foreign trade-agreements. The export grew from thirteen million to fifty-seven million rubles, and the import increased from eight million to thirty-nine million rubles during the reign of Catherine. These facts were largely due to Catherine's first two tariffs, the quite liberal one of 1776, and that of 1782, which was slightly protectionist.

The legal position of the merchants was changed by Catherine who had exempted them from the poll-tax and taxed them instead with 1 per cent. of their capital, the amount of capital to be " conscientiously " declared by the merchants themselves. The merchants valued highly this reform which freed them, as they said, from " a state of slavery." Yet the obligation of performing fiscal duties was not removed from the merchants (except those of the first guild. Russian merchants are to this day classified into three grades or guilds, according to their wealth and privileges.— Tr.), thus retaining a somewhat subjected character for this class.

The charter granted to cities originated municipal self-government among the urban population. It was divided into six classes, and each sent representatives to the city-*Duma*. Those were:

1. Merchants (of three guilds).
2. *Tzekhs,* i.e., trade groups and artisans.
3. Townspeople.
4. Houseowners.
5. Prominent citizens.
6. Foreign merchants and free artisans.

Catherine's municipal regulations remained in power until the reforms of Alexander II.

The secularisation of the church lands changed the status of the clergy radically. Together with the estates were freed from the power of the bishops more than 30,000 lower clerks who had been bondmen to their superiors. This reform, as Lappo-Danilevsky justly remarks, has deprived the church of its position of an independent corporation within the state; the higher clergy has lost a part of its power and importance, while the lower parish-clergy has been freed from a peculiar bondage.

As I said above, the most conspicuous change under Catherine took place in regard to the legal position of the nobility. Practically, the "unbinding" of the nobles had begun even before her accession, by the ukase of Peter III of February 18, 1762,[3]

[3] Many events in Russian modern history are known by their dates, e.g., the insurrection of December 14 (1825). Since Russia still employs the Julian calendar the dates throughout this book are of the Old Style. The Gregorian calendar is in advance of the Julian 11 days in the eighteenth century, 12 days in the nineteenth, and 13 days in the twentieth century.— Tr.

which released the nobles from obligatory service. The charter granted them in 1785 summarised all their privileges, allowed self-government for the nobility of each province, exempted them from corporal punishment, and gave them the right to bring petitions concerning social questions and needs. The nobles had the exclusive property right to their peopled estates, to the soil, its surface and depth.

The statute about the provinces in 1775 had made the nobles the ruling local class. Thus the nobility, although exempted from obligatory service, still retained the privileges of state-service and the important right of electing provincial officials. After the introduction of the statute more than 10,000 men were elected to provincial and district offices. In this way the landowner, beside being actually an independent monarch on his estate, had acquired after Catherine's reform an enormous socio-political influence on national life through his power of electing officials for important provincial boards and courts.

In order to become an all-powerful political class and influence the fate of the Russian people and state, the nobility needed one more thing — limitation of the monarchical autocracy and their participation in legislation and state administration. This they failed to obtain. Catherine had guarded skilfully and successfully the inviolability of absolutism both from the constitutional aspirations of the nobles, whose typical representative was the famous historian, Prince Shcherbatov, and from the assaults of the aristocracy in the person of Nikita Panin, and, of course, from the " arrogant " ambitions of the constitutionalists-democrats, such as Radishchev.

To summarise all that has been said about the class-composition of the Russian people at the end of the eighteenth century, — we have seen that 94.5 per cent. constituted peasantry, economically a variegated mass and by no means an exclusively agricultural class, while juridically it presented a series of grades and groups, from the totally disabled landowners' bondmen to the comparatively free groups of the black-ploughmen in the North and the freeholders in the South. Alongside with the latter groups stood the lower ranks of the urban population, about 300,000 male persons, or 2½ per cent. Above them stood the merchants — 107,000 or less than 1 per cent. of the population. Next came the parish-clergy freed from the bishop-bondage by the secularisation act of 1764. The clergy constituted not more than 1 per cent. of the population. Finally, superior to all classes by their privileges and wealth loomed the nobles, numerically not more than 1 per cent. of the population, or 1¼ to 1½ per cent., if we include the personal (not hereditary) noblemen and the officials. This was the one class that had become during the eighteenth century not only completely "unbound," but had acquired important rights and privileges.

It behooves us now to characterise the mental state of the people. In this respect we must bear in mind the division of the nation into the *intelligentzia* and the people, the schism that had begun in Peter's days and still, as a matter of fact, exists at present.

In ancient Russ there was no such division. In Kiev-Russ general culture evidently grew synchronously with material wealth, a culture quite high for those days, though the opinions of the investigators differ on this question. However it might be, that Kiev-Byzantine culture was not handed over to the next epoch, but disappeared almost entirely during the Tartar invasion, the internecine appanage-wars, and other internal troubles.

During the fifteenth and sixteenth centuries, when the Muscovite state had already been formed, ignorance was almost general. In this respect we have authentic information; for instance, the testimony of Gennady, the bishop of Novgorod, about the frequent consecration of illiterates as priests by force of necessity. The Muscovite Government had taken but a few timid steps toward the education of the people; it feared Western heresies, and its enlightening measures had been paralysed by the reactionary efforts of the obscurantists who reigned supreme, especially at the court of Tzar Feodor. Beginning with Peter the Government undertook some serious measures for spreading education among the people. As I have remarked before, the characteristic peculiarity of Peter's educational measures had been their definitely practical nature: he needed technically educated men to help him in his gigantic struggle, and with this view he established schools. There were opened forty-two "cipher" or primary schools with an attendance of about two thousand pupils of various classes; Peter had no class-scruples when his great task was concerned. According to Miliukov the composition of the pupils was as follows: 45 per cent. children of the clergy; 19.6 per cent. soldiers' children; 18 per cent. children of *prikaz*-clerks, more than 10 per cent. of commoners, 4½ per cent. of towns-people, and only 2½ per cent. from the nobility. In 1716 Peter ordered the nobles to send their children not to the " cipher "-schools but to higher special institutions; in the lower classes of the latter there were many commoners also.

Peter's successors were indifferent to education, and the people were no longer forced to send their children to the " cipher "-schools. In 1732 under Empress Anna the " cipher "-schools were partly supplanted by the so-called Garrison-schools for the regiments; although these schools were organised primarily for soldiers they had nevertheless a general cultural importance.

Under Peter originated also the diocesan schools; in 1727 there were forty-six of them with three thousand pupils. Some of them were soon reorganised into provincial seminaries. In Catherine's time there were eleven thousand students in the diocesan schools and about six thousand in the twenty-six seminaries.

Peter also restored the Moscow theological academy which

was established by Tzar Feodor after the Kiev model with the aid of the two Greeks, the brothers Likhud, and had fallen into decay subsequently by reason of persecution. In restoring it Peter had peculiar purposes, as I have mentioned before: he expected the academy to produce all sorts of specialists, to be a kind of a politechnicum. For the nobility Peter founded the schools of navigation, of engineering, and of artillery. Under Anna to these three schools was added another, the " Szlakhta Corpus," which had become in course of time the highest and most favourite school for children of the nobles. Peter made the first experiment with establishing a university at the Academy of Sciences; he imported professors from abroad, but their number exceeded that of the students, who had to be forcibly recruited from among the academies and seminaries. More successful proved the Gymnasium opened at the Academy: in 1728 it had more than two hundred students, mostly from the commoners.

Such were the main facts of Peter's educational activity. His schools, in spite of their professional character, had a great cultural significance; they were secular, free from the former fear of heresy and novelty, and they brought up and created the first generation of the Russian *intelligentzia*. That *intelligentzia,* having donned European garments, differed from the people no longer in appearance only; it was at that time that the moral schism between the people and the *intelligentzia* began and it has continued to our day. The newly-formed *intelligentzia* produced as early as in the thirties of the eighteenth century a brilliant expounder of new ideas and views in the person of Tatishchev, historian, author, and active administrator. And in the forties began the glorious career of the great Russian scholar and reformer of the Russian language, Lomonosov.

The young *intelligentzia* had feathered quite rapidly. By the middle of the eighteenth century reading of books became general, particularly of novels, translated in most cases; somewhat later there appeared original novels. Under Elizabeth a European theatre was founded, and later the first literary periodical, *The Monthly Writings,* issued at the Academy of Sciences under the editorship of Mueller. In 1755 began to appear the first private magazine, published by Sumarokov.

Finally, in 1755, Shuvalov founded the university of Moscow with two gymnasia (one for nobles, another for commoners). True, the new university did not become at once the disseminator of education in the country, and in the beginning it appeared to be as much a failure as Peter's university; but Shuvalov did not become discouraged and planned a wide net of schools for a systematic spread of knowledge, at least among the nobility.

With Catherine the work of education received a definite turn. Enlightenment had come to be considered necessary for its own sake, with the aim of ennobling man and developing " good morals," rather than producing useful men for the state. On the other hand the need for education was found equal for all classes. For some time Catherine even advocated the education of women as tantamount in importance to that of men. At the end of her reign Emperor Joseph sent to Russia by her request the experienced pedagogue Yankovich-de Mirievo, a Serb by origin, who introduced the Austrian system of schools. Austrian text-books, considered the last word in pedagogy at that time, were translated and distributed among the teachers of the new schools.

In the second half of the eighteenth century, particularly after the Seven Years' War, the second generation of Russian *intelligentzia* began to manifest an independent striving for education and for working out its own ideology. These strivings were enhanced by the growing contact with Western Europe and the constant influx of Western ideas, through two channels: the ideas of French encyclopedists, materialists, and such thinkers as Voltaire, Montesquieu, Rousseau, and Mably, on one hand, and the ideas of the German idealists — Masons (the Martinists and Rosenkreizers). They were represented by Novikov and Schwarz who organised the famous " Friendly Society " which rendered great services in the work of disseminating enlightenment and awakening self-consciousness in Russian society.

Catherine had not expected such a rapid and independent development of public opinion; in the early years of her reign she had considered the necessity of cultivating social feelings through literature. With this view she undertook in 1769 the publication of the magazine *Motley*. But this attempt to direct public opinion by the aid of a literary organ had convinced her that the public was far more advanced than she had supposed: *Motley* was forced to resent the attacks of other magazines, which went considerably further and assumed more independence than the Empress desired.

Under Catherine permission was given to establish private printing-houses, and owing to the labours of Novikov and Schwarz the publication of books advanced rapidly. During the eighteenth century there were issued, according to Sipovsky's figures, 9,513 books; of them 6 per cent. in the reign of Peter (i.e., 24 years), 6.7 per cent. during the forty years between Peter and Catherine, 84½ per cent. during the thirty-four years of Catherine's reign, and 2½ per cent. during the four years of Paul's reign. Book-publishing had reached its apogee in the eighties of the eighteenth century, before the crash of Novikov's " Friendly Society " and his other undertakings in the nineties, when Catherine, under the influence of the terrors of the French Revolution, fell into a reactionary mood.[4]

[4] Miliukov distributes Sipovsky's figures in periods of ten and five years:

1698–1710 .... 149 books; yearly, 12 books.
1711–1720 .... 248 books; yearly, 25 books.

The growth of social consciousness manifested itself in the differentiation of public circles; this was conditioned, on one hand, by the difference in the channels through which entered the Western ideas (the materialistic — French, and the idealistic — German), and, on the other hand, by the growing class-consciousness. A by no means negligible rôle was played in this regard by the foreign travels of young nobles, and particularly by their long life abroad during the Seven Years' War.

Thus we see that the development of the Russian *intelligentzia* by the end of the eighteenth century had reached considerable dimensions, if we consider the state of Russian society at the beginning of that century. As to the ideology of the masses, we must analyse it separately in view of the schism which I have already mentioned.

For the first six centuries after the Christianisation of Russia the people were quite indifferent to the teachings of Christianity, and the clergy represented Christian enlightenment only as long as they came from Byzantium. After the transference of the centre from Kiev to the northeast and the subsequent Mongol conquest of Russ, connections with Byzantium weakened and the influx of their priests had ceased; the native Russian clergy gradually descended in their cultural status to the level of the masses, instead of lifting them up.

1721–1725	182	} 215	yearly, 36 books.
1726–1730	33		yearly, 7 books.
1731–1740	140 books;		yearly, 14 books.
1741–1750	149 books;		yearly, 15 books.
1751–1760	233 books;		yearly, 23 books.
1761–1770	1050 books;		yearly, 105 books.
1771–1775	633	} 1466	bks. yearly, 126 books.
1776–1780	833		yearly; 166 books.
1781–1785	986	} 2685	yearly, 197 books.
1786–1790	**1699**		yearly, 366 books.
1791–1795	1494	} 2660	yearly, 299 books.
1796–1800	1166		yearly, 233 books.

In the number 9513 were not included liturgical books, newspapers, and magazines.

In the first six centuries after the conversion Russia had become, to use Miliukov's happy expression, " Holy Russ, the land of numerous churches and incessant chimes, the land of long ' standing ' services, pious prostrations and severe fasts, as it had been pictured by the foreign travellers of the sixteenth and seventeenth centuries." In the sixteenth century, and particularly in the seventeenth, there appeared in Russia for the first time a fermentation of ideas, which was caused by the infiltration of certain Western heresies and also by the correction of the liturgical books and ceremonies after the Greek model. This correction of books and customs brought about the Schism which, combined with the bloody disturbances of a sociopolitical nature that took place at that time, stirred the minds of the masses to such an extent that the Schismatic movement could not only not be eradicated by ruthless persecutions, but on the contrary actually throve because of them.

By Catherine's time the Schismatics had already gone through a period of bloody persecutions; with the new reign began a policy of comparative toleration. This toleration brought about the internal differentiation of the Schismatics into various sects, which process went on alongside with the formation of numerous other religious sects among the people. The latter developed mainly in the nineteenth century, and we shall have to return to this subject later. To estimate the number of Schismatics in the eighteenth century is impossible. Their majority officially figured as Orthodox; many others avoided registration, and the number of Schismatics grew and developed without the knowledge of the Government. In the middle of the nineteenth century the officers of the General Staff published the results of an investigation of the country, in which the official number of Schismatics was declared to be 806,000 as against 56,000,000 of Orthodox; but the same publication explained that the figures did not correspond with the facts, and that the actual number of Schismatics was not less than 8,000,000, i.e., 15 per cent. of the population. At the end of the eighteenth century the percentage was hardly lower. At any rate we may say that during that epoch whatever was alive and creative in the people went over to the side of the Schism, and if we want to follow up the movement of the nation's thought we shall have to look for it chiefly among the Schismatics, and later among the other sects that had formed during the eighteenth and nineteenth centuries, for within the " spiritual fence " of the official church there remained for the most part the passive and indifferent elements of the masses.

I have characterised the position of the population by its classes and the educational stage of the country at the end of the eighteenth century; it remains for me now to examine the position of the sovereign-power on the eve of the nineteenth century. I have pointed out that in the Muscovite state that power had become despotic under the influence of the territorial struggle; true, the character of the supreme power had vacillated more than once even under the Muscovite tzars, especially under the Romanovs who had ascended the throne, not by force of heritage, but by election, after the deliverance of the country from foreign enemies by the aid of the extreme upheaval of the nation's powers. Whenever the finances were in straits the sovereign-power was forced to appeal to the people, by summoning the *zemski sobory* (assemblies of the men of the land). On the other hand, the *boyars* (higher nobility) and the *Boyars' Duma* that had been established in Moscow had attempted to strengthen and broaden their influence on legislation and on the national administration. Those attempts were finally frustrated, and under Peter the autocratic despotism had reached its climax and even received an official theoretic sanction in " The Truth of the Monarchical Will," written by Feofan Prokopovich when Peter ordered him to find reasons justifying the Tzar's elimination of his son Alexis from the throne succession.[5] This document, based mainly on the theory of the English Monarchist Hobbes, was later incorporated in the Complete Code of Laws, as an act of the Government. Although Peter had always endeavoured to popularise the idea of legality among his subjects and had preferred the collegiate principle to the individualistic, as a guarantee against the wilfulness of the officials, his personal power he considered as absolutely unlimitable.

Under Peter's weak successors there had been more vacillations in the position of the sovereign power, and once, at the accession of Empress Anna Joannovna, the ambitious courtiers almost succeeded in limiting the autocracy in favour of a secret oligarchical council, and later in favour of the Senate. But their effort failed in view of the opposition of the provincial nobles who happened to assemble at that time in Moscow. Upon the request of the provincial nobility Anna Joannovna publicly tore to pieces the limiting " Points," to which she had previously consented.

Catherine believed in the principle of unlimited autocracy, yet she admitted the need of mitigating the despotism of the sovereign authority. Theoretically she tried to distinguish between a just monarchy and a despoty; in practice she alleviated the governmental cruelties that had been customary, especially under Peter, and mitigated judicial penalties. She advocated autocracy as an indispensable form of government in the vast Russian Empire composed of variegated parts. It is curious to note that she instructed her grandson Alexander with the help of the Republican La Harpe in principles of liberalism and conscious acknowledgement of the rights of man and citizen.

[5] The reader will find a powerful treatment of this incident and of that epoch in general in Merezhkovsky's novel " The Anti-Christ or Peter and Alexis." Merezhkovsky's fiction is of great historical value, based as it is on original documents.— TR.

As to the administrative organs, the old Muscovite local units that were formed for lack of a powerful central authority began to decay at the very beginning of the eighteenth century. Peter's impetuous policy dealt the old organs a death blow before, occupied as he had been with foreign wars and travels, he could supplant them with new ones. In 1711, leaving for the war with Turkey, he hastily organised the Senate, which was to act in the place of the absent Monarch in internal affairs. Since those absences were frequent and lengthy the authority of the Senate was considerable.

When the war cares had somewhat diminished there came to the front the question of conserving and maintaining the army. As a result of this exigency it was quartered throughout the country which was for this purpose divided into eight *gubernii* or provinces. The entire provincial administration was adapted to the satisfaction of a single need — the maintenance of the army.

For several years there were no intermediary departments between the Senate and the provincial administration. In 1715 Peter, somewhat released from cares of war, betook himself to carry out internal reforms. Instead of the decayed *prikazy* (boards) he established after the Swedish model *collegia,* which corresponded to the present ministries with the difference that in the Collegium the power was not in the hand of a single minister, but in the hands of from three to twelve persons. There were nine, and later twelve Collegia; at first they were subjected to the supervision of the Senate.

Under Peter's successors the position of the Senate as the highest administrative organ had changed: though the Senate was not abolished, it became subservient to the Supreme Secret Council, and later to the Cabinet (under Anna) — institutions composed of favourites and temporary rulers who used their personal influence to rise above the Senate. Then, beside these casual institutions, some Collegia — the Military, the Naval, the Foreign — were exempted from subjection to the Senate and placed on the same level with it.

Elizabeth had partly rehabilitated the Senate, but the three above-mentioned Collegia remained independent. Owing to Elizabeth's dislike for tedious state affairs the Senate assumed during her reign even more authority than under Peter.

At her accession Catherine, imbued with the philosophical tendencies of the "enlightenment epoch," intended to grant Russia an ideal, rational legislation. With this aim she summoned the Code Commission. She soon grew disappointed in her hope of reorganising at once the legislation, and she started out on a gradual reform of the administration from below, guided by the complaints against provincial disorders, which had been discussed by the Code Commission. As a result she worked out an adequate plan of the province-reform. She had transferred to the local administration a considerable part of the power that had been in the hands of the central Collegia. There were established local Fiscal Chambers as branches of the Chamber-Collegium (corresponding to the present Ministry of Finance). Then all Collegia, except the first three, were dismissed, and all local administrative and financial management passed into the hands of the Fiscal Chambers; all police powers were concentrated in the Provincial Boards; care for public health and general safety was in the hands of Provincial Boards of Public Safety, but the latter received no appropriations, and their activity remained only on paper. All the power in the new institutions fell into the hands of the provincial nobility, who had been granted the right to elect the officials, while these were elected mainly from among the nobility themselves.

Having reformed the provinces Catherine did not succeed, however, in adequately reorganising the central institutions. The abolished Collegia were not succeeded by anything permanent. The Senate appeared again to be the single supervising and administering body; but in reality the only power was in the

hand of the Procurator-General of the Senate, who had the right
to report personally to the Empress on all the questions that
came before the Senate. He played the part of a prime-minister
and minister of justice (to this day the Minister of Justice is at
the same time the Procurator-General) and minister of finance
combined. The position of the Senate was deplorable. Beside the
Procurator-General Catherine intrusted with important functions various individuals, her favourites, or some persons who
had won her confidence. Such a state of affairs, the absence of
a definite central power, and the cupidity and insolence of the
favourites, had led to flagrant abuses, sheer robbery and spolia-
tion of the State treasury on a gigantic scale. Besides, the country remained without any code of laws, since Catherine had not
carried through her original intention of granting a " rational "
legislation; judges and administrators used their own discretion in choosing for their decisions some legal basis out of the
mass of laws, ukases, and decrees that filled the bureaucratic
archives. It can be easily understood what a broad field for
abuse such conditions offered. The question of codification
passed into the nineteenth century.

Concerning the finances in the eighteenth century we may
say that in general the means of the Government were extremely meagre. I have already pointed out how Peter had
to scheme. During his reign the disproportion between the
growing requirements of the State and the paying capacity
of the nation had completely drained the land, and considerably
decreased the population.

In the meantime the budget grew with unbelievable rapidity.
Before the accession of Peter, in 1680, the expenses of the State
did not exceed one million and a half rubles (one must remember that the ruble was worth fifteen to seventeen times more
than at present) ; in 1724 they were eight and a half million
rubles (the ruble equal to our nine to ten rubles), consequently
in forty-four years the nominal budget had increased six-fold.

Even if we should take into account the fall in the value of the ruble for that period and translate both budgets in our money, there will still be an increase of the budget about three and a half times.[6]

Under Peter's immediate successors, in spite of the court's profligacy and its desire to spend without limit, the budget did not increase very much because there were no draining wars. During those forty years (from Peter to Catherine) it only doubled.

Upon her accession Catherine found the finances terribly entangled. At that time the Seven Years' War was taking place, in which Russia, for some unknown purpose, participated; the soldiers had not received pay for a whole year. When the Empress appeared before the Senate she was informed that there was need for the immediate expenditure of fifteen million rubles, but that the Treasury was empty. Catherine made skilful use of the exigency and demonstrated her magnanimity in the opportune moment by granting immediately a considerable sum of money from the Imperial Private Cabinet for the state needs; whereby she at once gained popularity.

Then she carried out a very happy reform — the lowering of the salt-tax; in order to acquire national sympathy which

[6] In comparing the financial budgets of the seventeenth and eighteenth centuries one must bear in mind the change in the purchasing power of the silver ruble and later of the surrogates (copper coins under Peter, assignations under Catherine). From the beginning of the sixteenth century down to our time the value of the ruble has almost steadily fallen for two reasons: the cheapening of silver (ab. 15–18 times), and the decrease in the weight of the coin (7 times). The silver ruble of the fifteenth century was equivalent to our 100–130 rubles, toward the end of the sixteenth century it fell to 24–25 of our present rubles; at the beginning of the seventeenth century, to 12, but at the end of that century it rose to 17 rubles; under Peter it fell to 9, and toward the end of Catherine's reign to 5 present rubles. Regardless of this, the course of the copper money and of the assignations had been fluctuating in its turn, depending on the size of the issue and the general trade-conjunctures.

she needed badly in her abnormal position, Catherine decided to cut down considerably that most exasperating tax, at the same time assigning 300,000 rubles from her Cabinet-money to cover the possible deficit. But the lowering of the tax brought an increase in consumption (especially for fisheries), and as a result the income of the fiscal salt monopoly even increased.

But despite her first successful steps Catherine had after all not introduced a regulated financial system; the financial conditions remained almost as deplorable as before. True there was not such a strain on the nation's strength as under Peter, and the country's industry grew fast and profitable owing to the economic advantages of the conquered territories. In emergency cases when large expenditures appeared necessary (beginning with the first Turkish war), Catherine made use of the Assignational bank, founded before her accession. No foreign loans had existed yet. During the Seven Years' War Elizabeth attempted to transact a foreign loan of only two million rubles, but her attempt suffered a complete fiasco. By the aid of the Assignational bank Catherine had received a means for making quite large internal loans. At first this operation proved successful. In 1769 there were issued assignations for 17,841,000 rubles, and their course remained at par, i.e., the paper-ruble was equivalent to the silver one. The subsequent loans, comparatively small in size, also passed fairly well. Even when after the declaration of the second Turkish war there was issued a loan for 53,000,000 rubles, almost equal to the then yearly budget, the course of the assignations did not fall in a marked way; the total amount of assignations at that time had reached one hundred million rubles at the course of ninety-seven silver kopecks for one assignation-ruble. But the next issues caused a growing fall of the course. During the whole reign of Catherine assignations were issued for one hundred and fifty-seven million rubles, and at the end the course had fallen below seventy kopecks. Such a state of affairs threatened the State with bankruptcy in the future. At the same time expenses continued to grow with great rapidity. During her reign the state expenditures had increased (nominally) five-fold; at her accession they equalled sixteen and a half million; at her death — seventy-eight million.

This financial situation was made worse by the terrible thievery of the higher officials, which aroused a cry of despair in the letter of the young Grand Duke (later Emperor) Alexander to La Harpe: "What takes place is beyond conception; all rob, you can hardly meet an honest person."

We may make a résumé of all that we have said about the position of Russia at the end of Catherine's reign in the following fundamental points:

1. On the eve of the nineteenth century Russia presented a powerful state united by a single strong authority on an enormous and definite territory, with firm and safe borders, containing a population of thirty-six million. This population, though composed of various races, was dominated by the prevalence of the Russian nationality.

2. In regard to the class-composition of that political organism, its differentiation into separate fixed or "bound" classes and orders had come to an end at the beginning of the eighteenth century, as a result of a long process. Under the influence of new national conditions, and mainly because of the cessation of the former territorial struggle, the higher classes had begun to "unbind," while the liberation of the lower strata, the peasantry, had come to be considered, at least in principle, as a question to be solved in the more or less near future.

3. Mentally the population was divided at the beginning of the eighteenth century into the *intelligentzia* and the masses. Among the latter arose a strong fermentation of ideas, caused by the stirring effect of the Schism. The *intelligentzia* had been from the very start a body consisting if not of all classes, at least of various orders and classes, and it appeared as the most

active, progressive, and conscious element in the state; ideas of limiting the autocratic power and of demanding greater freedom had already begun to develop among that body in the fifteenth century.

4. About that time began to appear some elements of the future capitalism — the centralisation of the merchants' capital and the first experiments in its application to big industry; then also originated the struggle between the interests of the land-owning class of nobles and the representatives of the commercial-industrial capital.

5. The supreme power remained autocratic, but the autocracy was manifested in milder forms. As to the administration itself Catherine had succeeded in organising the local provincial governments quite firmly along lines rather rational for those days, but she had not reorganised the central Government, and by the end of her reign there was complete chaos in the central management of the state affairs.

A weak place in the organisation of the Russian state was its financial system and the national economy in general.

CHAPTER III

ON the border-line between the eighteenth and nine-teenth centuries took place the four years' reign of Paul I. This period, until recently under the seal of censorship, has always aroused public curiosity, as something mysterious and forbidden, while the attention of historians, psychologists, biographers, dramatists, and novelists has nat-urally been attracted by the original personality of the crowned psychopath and by the exceptional circumstances under which his drama was enacted and ended so tragically.

From the point of view of our attitude towards historical events, this reign has but a secondary importance. Though it lies between two centuries and separates the " age of Catherine " from the " age of Alexander," it can by no means be considered as a transitional period. On the contrary, in the historical process of the development of the Russian people, which in-terests us, that reign appears as a sudden intrusion, as an un-expected squall that, coming from the outside, confused every-thing, caused a temporary topsy-turvy in the national life, but which could not have interrupted for long or radically changed the natural course of the functioning process. In view of this nature of Paul's reign, Alexander upon his accession had noth-ing else to do but erase everything committed by his father, and having healed the not deep, but painful wounds inflicted by him upon the state-organism, to proceed further from the point at which Catherine's age-weakened and shaky hand had stopped.

For us the reign of Paul is interesting not on account of its tragi-comic phenomena, but because of the changes that took place in the position of the people during that time, and the mental movement among the public aroused by the governmental terror. Still more important for us are the international relations conditioned, on one hand, by Paul's idiosyncrasies, and on the other, by the great events that had taken place in Western Europe.

I do not intend therefore to give here a detailed biography of Paul; those interested in it will turn to Schilder's great work, or to the brief compilation of that work, issued by Shumigorsky. For our purposes proper the following brief biographical facts will suffice. Paul was born in 1754, eight years before Catherine's accession. His childhood passed under most abnormal conditions: Empress Elizabeth took him away from his parents immediately after his birth, and placed him into an unhealthy, hot-house atmosphere of a variety of nurses and governesses. Later he fell under the care of Count Nikita Panin, a man of great distinction for that time. He was a wise statesman, but not a conscientious pedagogue, and did not pay sufficient attention to his task.

Catherine had no confidence in Panin, but she feared to dismiss him in view of the rumours that she intended to remove Paul altogether, and she yielded to the public opinion that Paul would be safe as long as he remained under Panin's care. The grown-up Paul inspired no affection in Catherine; she did not admit him to state affairs, and even removed him from the military department for which he felt a special inclination. Paul's first marriage was unhappy and of short duration; his wife, who died during her confinement, aggravated still more the tense relations between Paul and his mother. When he married for the second time, Catherine assigned the new couple Gatchina where they were to lead a private life. Their children Catherine treated as Elizabeth had treated hers, i.e., she took them from their parents immediately after their birth and educated them herself. Paul's removal from state affairs, and his impertinent treatment by the favourites of the Empress, especially by Potiomkin, poured oil on the fire and aroused in Paul hatred for all the court of Catherine. For thirty years he waited impatiently for the moment when he would begin to reign and exercise his own power.

We must add that towards the end of Catherine's reign Paul began to suspect that his mother would deprive him of the throne, and we know that such a plan had indeed been considered but failed of realisation only because Alexander refused to ascend the throne before his father, thus frustrating Catherine's intentions.

On his accession Paul gave vent to the hatred that had accumulated in his mind against all his mother's acts. Having no definite plan of action and not even a clear conception of state matters and needs, Paul began to set aside indiscriminately whatever his mother had enacted. In some respects he restored old forms. For instance he reinstalled some Collegia, but gave them no proper authority, while their old authority had passed over to the Fiscal Boards. He had invented a plan for the reorganisation of the entire central administration; but in fact the plan consisted in the abolishment of all state institutions and the concentration of the whole administration in the hands of the Tzar — an unrealisable plan. His particular effort was expressed in the abolition of all the rights and privileges granted by Catherine to certain classes. Thus he withdrew the charters given to cities and to the nobility, and not only abolished the rights of the nobles for offering petitions concerning their needs, but even set aside the exemption of the nobles from corporal punishment by court decisions.[1]

There exists a view that Paul, negatively inclined towards

[1] Let us remark that there were some just revocations of Catherine's measures under Paul. Such were: The liberation of Novikov from Schluesselburg, the recall of Radishchev from his exile, and the solemn release with special honours of Kosciusco and the other captive Poles who had been kept in Petrograd.

privileges for the upper classes, favoured the liberation of the people from the oppression of the landowners. He might have had some good intentions, but we can hardly ascribe to him any seriously thought out system in this regard. In support of that proposition one usually brings forward the Manifesto of April 5, 1797, which established Sunday rest and three days-*barshchina;* but the Manifesto is not quite correctly interpreted. Only holiday-work for the landowner was categorically forbidden, and there was an additional " supposition " that three days-*barshchina* might be sufficient for the upkeep of the landowner's estate. The very form of expressing that desideratum, in the absence of any sanction, shows that there was no law establishing a three days-*barshchina,* although later it came to be so interpreted. Furthermore one must mention that in Little Russia, for instance, the three days-*barshchina* was not favourable for the peasants, since there had prevailed a custom for two days-*barshchina.* Another law issued by Paul upon the request of Bezborodko, prohibiting the sale of bondsmen without soil, affected only Little Russia (Bezborodko's birth-place. Tr.).

Paul's attitude towards peasant-disturbances and their complaints against oppressions by their landowners, is quite characteristic. At his accession there burst out disturbances in thirty-two provinces. Paul sent for their suppression enormous regiments under the command of Fieldmarshal-General Prince Riepnin, who rapidly quelled the unrest by the employment of ruthless means. At the suppression of twelve thousand peasants of the landowners Apraksin and Prince Golitzin in the province of Oriol, a regular battle took place, in which the peasants lost twenty dead and about seventy wounded. Riepnin ordered the dead peasants buried outside of the cemetery fence and put an epitaph over their grave: " Here lie criminals before the Lord, the Tzar, and the landowners, justly punished according to God's law." The houses of those peasants were destroyed and levelled with the ground. Paul not only approved of these measures, but issued a special manifesto on January 29, 1797, in which he threatened with similar punishments all peasants who would not strictly obey their masters.

In another instance certain house-serfs in Petrograd had attempted to complain before Paul of their cruel oppression. Without investigating the case, Paul ordered the peasants led out on the public square and flogged with the knut " as much as their owners will desire."

Thus Paul was hardly guilty of a serious effort to improve the condition of the peasants. He considered the landowners as gratis-police-chiefs, and deemed the peace of the country secure as long as Russia had 100,000 such police-chiefs. He was not averse to increasing that number, granting Fiscal peasants to private persons with a generous hand: in four years he gave away 530,000 Fiscal peasants of both sexes to various landowners and officials, earnestly arguing that he did so for the good of the peasants, and for the improvement of their lot, which was not true. Consider that Catherine, who had lavishly rewarded her favourites and other persons with peasants, gave out in all 800,-000 peasants, while Paul distributed in four years 530,000.

Of all classes the clergy had most reasons to be satisfied with Paul, who as a religious person and as one who assumed to be the head of the Church, cared for the welfare of the clergy; but even in that case the results were at times strange. Some of his cares had an ambiguous character, so that the Metropolitan Platon, Paul's early religious instructor and greatly respected friend, was forced to join those who protested against certain of his measures. The protest concerned the introduction of a queer novelty — the bestowing of orders upon the clergy. Platon thought that from the canonic point of view the rewarding of church-ministers by lay authorities was not to be allowed. The Metropolitan besought Paul on his knees not to honour him with the order of Andrey the First Called, but finally he had to submit and accept it. This incident may appear unimportant in itself, but it is characteristic of the attitude of Paul towards the class which he had particularly respected.

Of a greater, positive importance was Paul's relation to religious schools, for which he did a good deal; he appropriated for them a considerable sum of money from the income of the secularised church-estates. Here we should note also Paul's tolerant attitude towards non-Orthodox and even non-Christian churches, especially his favourable relation towards Catholicism. The reason lies perhaps in his personal religiousness and high estimate of clerical duties; as to the Catholic church, there Paul's place in the Order of the Knights of Malta played an important rôle. He not only accepted the supreme protectorate of that order, but even permitted a special priorate of it to open in Petrograd. This circumstance, which was due to the Tzar's quaint fantasies, had very important consequences on the course of international relations, as we shall see later.

Another prominent fact in the sphere of church affairs under Paul was his rather tolerant attitude towards the Schismatics. In this respect he followed the policy of Catherine, the traces of whose reign he had so energetically tried to destroy with all his other measures. Upon the request of Platon the Tzar consented to take an important step, namely to permit public worship to those old believers who did not belong to the so called pernicious sects, who were thus for the first time equalised with other non-Orthodox creeds.

As to Paul's treatment of secular education, his activity in that direction was most reactionary, one may say destructive. Even at the end of Catherine's reign private printing-houses were forbidden, so that the publishing of books had greatly decreased; but under Paul, particularly in his last two years, the number of published books was reduced to a negligible quantity, while the nature of the books had also changed — there were issued exclusively books for schools or of some practical contents.[3] The

2 The first volume of Storch's work, *Gemaelde des Russischen*

import of books published abroad was entirely prohibited at the end of his reign, and from the year 1800 everything printed abroad, regardless of contents, even music-notes, had no access into Russia.

Of still greater importance was another measure — the recall of Russian students from foreign universities (there were 65 in Jena, and 36 in Leipzig), and the forbidding of Russian youths to go abroad for educational purposes.

In his hatred for revolutionary ideas and for liberalism in general, Paul persecuted with the stubbornness of a maniac every manifestation of free tendencies. Hence his war against round hats and top-boots which had been worn in France, against frock-coats and tricoloured ribbons. For these crimes peaceful citizens were severely persecuted, officials were dismissed, private persons were arrested, many were exiled from the capital. Similar punishments were inflicted upon those who failed to observe the prescribed etiquette upon meeting the Tzar (at the sight of the Imperial carriage passers-by were required to stop and remain on their knees until the Despot had passed them. Tr.) In view of that etiquette the people considered a meeting with the Tzar as a great calamity; at the sight of his approach they tried to hide themselves in courtyards, behind fences, and so forth. The number of persons exiled and imprisoned for utter trivialities reached thousands, and there were 15,000 (or more than 12,000, according to other sources) such persons rehabilitated by Alexander upon his accession.

The yoke of Paul's régime was felt most heavily by the army, from the orderlies to the generals. Endless mustering, severe penalties for the slightest fault in the front-line, senseless ways of instruction, most uncomfortable uniforms, which proved par-

Reichs, appeared in Riga in 1797, while the other volumes had to be printed abroad; yet Storch was a *persona grata* at the court — he occupied the position of personal reader to the Empress Maria Feodorovna, and had his first volume dedicated to Paul.

ticularly annoying during the marching, which was required to be of almost as high a standard as the art of ballet; finally the compulsory wearing of locks and braids that were smeared with lard and powdered with flour or brick-dust — all these complicated the difficulty of military service which lasted at that time twenty-five years. The officers and generals had to fear for their fate hourly, since the slightest imperfection of any of their subordinates might provoke the most cruel consequences, in case the Emperor was in bad humour. (Paul was a devout worshipper of the Prussian system of militarism. Tr.)

Such were some of the terrors of Paul's régime. It is interesting to read the opinion of the staunch conservative and advocate of autocracy, N. M. Karamzin, in his "Paper on Ancient and Modern Russia," which he presented in 1811 to Alexander I as an argument against the projected liberal reforms. Though antagonistic to the liberal Emperor, he thus characterised the reign of Paul: "Paul ascended the throne at a time very favourable for autocracy, when the terrors of the French Revolution had cured Europe of the dreams about civil liberty and equality; but what the Jacobines had done for the republic Paul did for the autocracy: he forced hatred against its abuses. In his miserable fallacy of mind, and because of his numerous personal bitter experiences he wished to be an Ivan IV (The Terrible. Tr.); but the Russians had already had Catherine II, had known that the monarch not less than the subjects was bound to fulfil his sacred duties, the neglecting of which destroys the ancient covenant between rule and obedience and hurls the people from the heights of civilism into the chaos of individual natural rights. The son of Catherine could have both remained a strict monarch and deserved the gratitude of his country; but to the great astonishment of the Russians he began to dominate by force of general terror (ising?), following no statutes save his own whims; he considered us not as subjects, but as slaves; executed for no guilt, rewarded for no merits, deprived punishment of shame, reward —

of its glory, humiliated ranks and ribbons by lavishing them without limit; he frivolously destroyed results of years-long state-wisdom out of hatred for his mother's enactments; he killed in our army the heroic spirit cultivated by Catherine, and supplanted it with corporalship. The heroes who had been accustomed to victories, he taught how to march; reverted the nobility from military service; while despising the soul, he respected caps and collars; although of a natural human inclination to do good, he nourished himself on the gall of evil: day after day he invented means for terrifying people, and was himself afraid most of all; he had intended to erect for himself an inaccessible palace — and erected a tomb . . . Let us note," Karamzin added, " a curious feature: in the opinion of foreigners the Russians were afraid even to think during that reign of terror; nay! they spoke openly, became silent only out of ennui and frequent repetition, confided in one another and were not deceived. A spirit of sincere brotherhood reigned in the capitals; the common misfortune had united all hearts, and the magnanimous indignation against the abuses of the Crown had drowned the voice of personal safety." Analogous information may be found in the writings of Wiegel and Grech, also avowed conservatives.

We must, however, say that the " magnanimous indignation " was not expressed in any action. The public had not even tried to demonstrate its attitude towards Paul through some general protest; it hated in silence, but that general mood gave the few conspirators of the coup d'état of March 11, 1801, sufficient encouragement for the removal of Paul.

The economic condition of the country could not have altered considerably under Paul, in view of the brief duration of his reign; as to the financial position of Russia, it had depended largely upon his foreign policy and the whimsical changes that had taken place in it during his time. Paul began with a conclusion of peace with Persia and the revocation of the recruitment-conscription decreed by Catherine; he declined to send an army of forty thousand men against the French republic, to which Catherine had consented owing to the pleadings of the British ambassador, Witworth, and recalled the Russian vessels that had been sent to help the English fleet. Then he started on the extinguishing of the Assignational loan. The Government decided to withdraw a portion of the issued assignations; in the presence of Paul there took place a solemn burning of assignations for the sum of six million rubles. Thus the total amount of issued assignations fell from 157 million to 151 million, i.e., a decrease of less than 4 per cent., but even that slight difference was significant as indicating the Government's intention to pay debts rather than accumulate them. At the same time steps were taken for the strengthening of the course of the silver money; a permanent weight of the silver ruble was established, to be equivalent to the weight of four francs. Then of great importance was the restoration of the liberal custom-tariff of 1782, a measure taken by Paul not because of his belief in free trade but from his desire to annul the tariff introduced by Catherine in 1793.

The new tariff helped to develop national trade. For big industry a great service was played by the discovery of coal in the basin of the Donietz. This discovery, made in southern Russia, a region poor in forests, immediately influenced the conditions of industry in the New-Russia district. Of great significance for the growth of internal trade relations and for the transportation of certain products to ports was the opening of new canals under Paul; some of them had been begun under Catherine. The Oginsky Canal connecting the basin of the Dnieper with the river Niemen was begun in 1797 and finished in the same reign; a canal was dug (by Sivers) around lake Ilmen; one of the lake Ladoga canals, the Siassky, was started; the works for the Maryinsky canal were continued. Under Paul was also established a free-port system in the Crimea, which proved an enlivening stimulus for the South.

But the improvement of economic conditions in the country did not endure long, and the national finances soon experienced new vacillations. In 1798 the peaceful course of events was suddenly interrupted. At that time Napoleon Bonaparte on his way to Egypt captured the island of Malta. The island had an impregnable fortress, but the Grand Master of the Order for some unknown reason (treason was even suspected) surrendered it without battle, removed the archives and treasures and departed for Venice. The Petrograd priorate declared him deposed, and some time after, to the general astonishment, Paul, the head of the Orthodox church, accepted the title of Grand Master of that Catholic order, subject to the Pope. There exists a theory that in Paul's mind that strange step was connected with a fantastic undertaking — the ubiquitous eradication of revolutions by way of uniting all the nobles of the world under the Maltian order. Whether this was so, is hard to say; but certainly the idea was not realised. Having declared war against France, and being unwilling to fight single-handed, Paul assisted Pitt in creating a strong coalition against the Republic. He entered into an alliance with Austria and England, then into the coalition came the Sardinian kingdom and even Turkey, which had suffered from Napoleon's invasion into Syria. Following the counsel of the emperor of Austria, Paul appointed Suvorov commander of the allied armies of Russia and Austria. Suvorov had been under ban, and stayed in his estate surveyed by the police; he disliked Paul's military changes, and had let him feel it through masqued jokes and frolics, for which he paid with disgrace and exile. But now Paul appealed to Suvorov in his own name and in the name of the emperor of Austria. Suvorov accepted the commandership with joy. His campaign was signified by brilliant victories over the French in Northern Italy and by the famous crossing of the Alps. But when Northern Italy had been cleared of the French Austria was satisfied and refused to support Suvorov in his further plans.

Suvorov was unable to carry through his plan of proceeding to Paris. This " Austrian treachery " caused the defeat of General Rimsky-Korsakov's regiment by the French. Paul was infuriated and recalled his army, thus bringing to an end the war with France. At the same time the Russian corps sent to Holland against the French was not adequately supported by the British, who failed, besides, to keep the agreement about paying proper wages to the soldiers; again Paul was indignant.

In the meantime Napoleon returned from Egypt to carry out his first coup d'état: on Brumaire 18 he overthrew the Directory, and became First Consul, actually the lord of France. Seeing that things were leading to the restoration of the monarchy, even if by the " usurper," Paul changed his attitude towards France, expecting Napoleon to do away with the last vestiges of the revolution. Napoleon, in his turn, skilfully flattered him by releasing and sending back with gifts the Russian prisoners, without any demand of exchange. This impressed the knight-spirit in Paul, and in the hope of gaining Napoleon's co-operation in other questions, he entered with him into a discussion of terms of peace and of an alliance against England, whom he held responsible for the defeat of his army in Holland. It was not difficult for Napoleon to array Paul against the English, for about that time the latter had taken Malta from the French, and did not give it back to the Order.

Immediately, ignoring all international treaties, Paul placed an embargo on all the English merchant-vessels, put through radical changes in the customs-tariff, and finally forbade altogether the export and import of goods to and from England and Prussia, which was then on the side of the British. By these measures directed against the English Paul shook the entire Russian trade. Not satisfied with the custom repressions Paul ordered arrested all English goods in the stores. Evidently encouraged by Napoleon, Paul decided to strike England on its sore spot: he determined to conquer India, a task that seemed quite easy to him. Forty regiments of Don-Cossacks went to take India, equipped with double sets of horses, but without provender, with no good maps and with impassable steppes to pass through. The army was naturally doomed to perish. The folly of that act appeared so obvious to his contemporaries that the Princess Lieven, wife of the Tzar's closest adjutant-general, stated in her memoirs that Paul undertook the plan in order to abolish deliberately the Cossack army, which he suspected of excessive love for freedom. The suggestion was not true, of course, but it shows the sort of intentions ascribed to Paul by his entourage. Happily that march began two months before Paul's death and Alexander hastened on the very night of the overthrow to send a courier for the return of the unlucky Cossacks; it was found that they had not yet reached the frontier, but had already lost half of their horses. . . .

This fact illustrates Paul's madness and the horrible consequences which his measures could have had. The finances were naturally painfully affected by his campaigns and expeditions. We have seen him burning six millions' worth of assignations early in his reign, but his wars required extra expenses, and he was forced to issue assignations again, since there was no other source for money. By the end of his reign their sum rose from 151 to 212 millions, which definitely devalued the paper-ruble. Such were the results of Paul's international policy.

In summarising Paul's reign we see that the territorial boundaries remained intact. The tzar of Gruzia, pressed by Persia, declared in January, 1801, his desire to become a Russian subject; but the formal annexation of Gruzia took place under Alexander.

As to the condition of the people, Paul's measures, however pernicious they had been, could not cause any profound effects in four years. The most disastrous change in the peasant-life was the transference from the state-class into private bondage of 530,000 persons distributed by Paul among private citizens.

In the realm of commerce and industry, despite the numerous favourable conditions at the beginning of the reign, towards the end the foreign trade was annihilated, and the internal trade in the most chaotic state. A still greater chaos reigned in the national and provincial administration.

Such was the situation of Russia when Paul ceased to exist.[3]

[3] The personality of the half-demented Tzar and the circumstances of his assassination are vividly and truthfully pictured by Merezhkovsky in his play, " Paul I."— TR.

CHAPTER IV

WITH March 12, 1801, begins the history of Russia in the nineteenth century. I deem it not useless to cast a preliminary view at its contents, and to say a few words about its possible division into periods. At this I recall the words which I heard twenty-five years ago in a lecture by Professor V. I. Sergeyevich: " If history has to do with the developmental laws of human societies, then its division into periods reflecting the consequentiality of that development has an essential significance: in the division of history into periods is its whole sense, the entire philosophy of its course and changes."

It is clear from my preceding exposition that I share this view on the rôle of the periodical division of history. I have characterised the first long period of Russian history, and have pointed out the advent of a new period under Catherine and those changes which accompanied the process that formed the contents of the history of Russia in the nineteenth century. This new period, of the nineteenth century, may in its turn be divided into two large parts. The process of the " unbinding " of all classes and the mitigation of the autocratic despotism has been carried on by the way of inter-class struggle and by the way of a struggle between the Government and the most conscious and progressive representatives of the public. The course and outcome of that struggle were influenced by internal as well as by foreign events taking place during that time; all these phenomena and facts compose the subject of this book. If we shall bear in mind only the most general course of the historical process in the development of which those phenomena took place,

we may point out from the outset the two epochs into which
the process is naturally divided by the chief event of internal
Russian history in the nineteenth century — the abolition of
serfdom.

From this point of view to the first period of the nineteenth
century belong the reigns of Alexander I and Nicholas I, characterised by preparations for the fall of bondage — the event
that has served as a starting point for the liberation of the
whole population. To the next period we must assign the following four decades of the nineteenth century, when the results
of the abolition of serfdom had developed the further process of
the substitution by a constitutional of the autocratic state.

These are the two main stages in the history of the last century, but in the detailed study of the events and facts that have
taken place in the course of the process we shall have to observe
considerably more stages and periodical subdivisions.

In Russia only the first years of the nineteenth century passed
peacefully; the external peace and the progressive tendencies of
the Government helped the regular course of the internal life
and the calm evolution of the historical process for which preceding history had prepared. Then the general course of events
in Western Europe, which had grown very stormy and threatened to engulf the whole universe into its whirlpool, had influenced resolutely the tempo and direction of Russian affairs.
It had influenced the tendency of the Russian Government and
the change in the nature of its task; the participation in the universal struggle had checked the peaceful trend of evolution, but
it had also accelerated the tempo of events, quickening the beat
of the pulse in the national organism and drawing Russia resolutely into the sphere of European social life. The reign of
Alexander was full of great events, and the progress of Russian
life went on rapidly and turbulently under external shocks, but
with marked vacillations, making, so to say, considerable zigzags.
These zigzags are the fractional periods or stages into which the

reign of Alexander must be divided. I count six such stages in the first quarter of the last century.

The first stage of Alexander's reign — 1801–1805 — is characterised by the Emperor's ardent and sincere reformatory activity, taken up on his own initiative — the period of most rosy though indefinite expectations on the part of the people. The next two years (1805–1807) stand sharply apart: they are the years of the first wars with Napoleon, wars that were carried on without any visible relation to Russian interests, heavily impressed the position of the people, and temporarily interrupted the reforms of the Government.

The third period (1808–1811) is marked by Alexander's alliance with Napoleon, and in connection with this, by the Continental System which had an enormous significance, disastrous for Russian trade, and provoked the first friction between the Government and the people. At the same time those four years saw the second attempt to introduce reforms, less ardent and important, but undertaken in connection with the public dissatisfaction, and therefore symptomatic. Society began to regard Alexander's policy consciously and critically.

Then followed the fourth period (1812–1815), when not only the Government but the whole country took part in the greatest universal events of that time.

The fifth period (1816–1820) passed for Alexander largely in international congresses, and for the public in expectation of reforms and reorganisations which they regarded more consciously, putting forth definite demands, but still not breaking completely with the Government and not losing hope for its reformatory activity.

The sixth period (1821–1825) was quite definitely reactionary in the ruling spheres, showed despair on the part of the people, and the formation of a revolutionary movement, subterranean but very keen and of definite political ideals.

Before discussing the events of his reign I shall define the personality of Alexander, a personality that greatly influenced the internal and external development of Russia and of contemporary Europe.

Alexander was the eldest grandson and personal pupil of Catherine, who with much energy, and revealing a remarkable pedagogical talent, endeavoured to make out of him if not an ideal man, at least an ideal ruler. The Imperial grandmother took him away immediately after his birth, and had closely observed to the slightest details his nourishment and education, personally inspecting his nursery, composing an alphabet and fairy-tales for her little grandson, and later not sparing her time in digging out old chronicles and first sources in order to write for him a history text-book. In her letters to Baron Grimm she expressed her views on physical and mental education and on the application of her views to the bringing up of Alexander; in them she showed not only a profound intellect but such energy, tenderness, and love for her grandson, as one could hardly have suspected in that woman accustomed to spend her time upon either state affairs or personal pleasures — sensual and intellectual.

Later Catherine carefully thought out a plan for the further education and development of her grandson, and she drew up her instructions for the staff of teachers and governors, whose chief was Count Saltykov. One of the teachers, Masson, sarcastically remarks in his memoirs that the main and exclusive function of Saltykov consisted in guarding Alexander and his brother from draught and indigestion. But the choice of that ordinary individual as chief educator of the Grand Duke was explained by the fact that Catherine intended to use Saltykov as a screen for her personal interest in the high pupil. Besides, Saltykov in his rank of court-steward in Paul's household had shown his skill as mediator between the Empress and her son and smoothed over many frictions and difficulties. Catherine had evidently hoped to be able to use his services in the future relations between Paul and Alexander.

The real teachers were indeed remarkable persons. First among them was the Swiss, La Harpe, whose discovery and selection Catherine owed to her connection with the best intellectual forces of contemporary Europe. Grimm recommended him for a travelling companion to Lanskoy, the younger brother of Catherine's favourite. In 1782, when Alexander was barely five years old, La Harpe was invited to remain with him as Chevalier and to teach him French. Two years later La Harpe presented a memorandum about the education of the future emperor, expressing lofty views on the duties of the monarch to his subjects. Catherine approved of his views and plans and gave him full liberty to imbue Alexander with his own ideas, which corresponded to the ideas of the foremost people of his age.

La Harpe was brought up on republican and democratic ideas; he had a high education, and professed lofty views not only in theory, but was in real life scrupulously honest, straightforward, sincere, and incorruptible. These moral qualities had as much influence on Alexander as the knowledge which La Harpe transmitted to him.

La Harpe remained Alexander's tutor and educator eleven years, from 1784 to 1795, and Alexander had frequently declared afterwards in public that whatever was good in him he owed to La Harpe.

The selection of a religious instructor for Alexander and Constantine (his brother) was quite characteristic. The Archpresbyter Somborsky was married to an Englishwoman, lived in England a long time, and had become so accustomed to conditions of Western Europe that Catherine was forced to permit him to wear secular garments and shave his beard and moustache, to the confusion of the entourage. (Orthodox clergy do not cut or trim their hair and whiskers. Tr.) Somborsky remained with Alexander not less than nine years, and had a favourable influence on his pupils, inspiring them with the belief that they must " find in every human being their neighbour in order to fulfil the law of God." He also taught Alexander English (which Alexander knew from his infancy, his nurse being an Englishwoman).

His instructor in Russian language and history was Mikhail Muraviov, one of the best Russian writers at the end of the eighteenth century, who later collaborated with Karamzin in his researches into Russian history. He was the father of the famous Decembrist, Nikita Muraviov. Alexander preserved for him respect and gratitude all his life. One should mention also Masson, his instructor in mathematics, Pallas, the well known traveller who taught him geography, and the professor of physics, Kraft. His tutor, General Protasov, who had left a curious diary, had a considerable influence over him. He was a man of old regulations, but undoubtedly conscientious and honest; being a patriot and a conservative he did not approve of La Harpe's political views, but admitted his merits, valuing his honesty and incorruptibility. Protasov's rôle consisted mainly in watching Alexander's behaviour, in reprimanding him for the slightest fault, to which Alexander reacted patiently and kindly.

Such was Alexander's education until the age of sixteen. Unfortunately the broad educational plans of Catherine and La Harpe were not brought to a conclusion, but were twisted in the end, when in her last year new state-plans had taken hold of the Empress. Definitely convinced of Paul's incapacity for the throne, she decided to set him aside and proclaim Alexander her heir. At the same time, having in mind her old age, she determined to hasten the education of her grandson. To make him appear grown-up in the eyes of the court she found nothing better than marrying him before he was yet sixteen. La Harpe had fallen into disgrace: the Empress had expected that he would sympathise with the idea of substituting Alexander for Paul and assist her in preparing his pupil for the plan. But the straight and strict La Harpe suspected a court-intrigue, and although Paul's attitude towards him was hostile he categorically refused to take part in Catherine's plan. The irritated Empress dismissed him immediately after Alexander's wedding under the pretext that the married Grand Duke was no longer in need of a tutor. Thus Alexander was deprived of his chief guide and instructor and at the same time entered into a position which did not in the least correspond with his age.

The plans for his education were in this way confounded. True, he continued reading books according to the programme of La Harpe, who had left, upon Alexander's request, a detailed instruction about his behaviour on all occasions. To be sure the ten years' teaching of La Harpe could not have remained without influence; but the premature interruption of his regulated and systematic education had a very bad effect on Alexander. La Harpe instilled into Alexander a number of high ideas and noble strivings, but he had not had time to give him a sufficient amount of positive knowledge, the acquisition of which was to begin just at the moment when his education was stopped. In regard to his liberal ideas and humanitarian views, Catherine herself, though quite reactionary at the end of her reign, continued in her conversations with Alexander to side with the liberal ideas of the Enlightenment epoch. Curiously enough, she read and explained to him the famous Declaration of Rights, thus strengthening in him his liberal ideas and even republican dreams.

But all this did not make up for the lack of positive knowledge, which, according to the memoirs of Prince Adam Czartoryski, was responsible for the excessive dreaminess of Alexander's intentions.

The development of Alexander's character was unfavourably influenced by the abnormal family conditions and by the unhealthy court atmosphere in which he grew up, and which could not be paralysed by any educational plans.

Towards Catherine Alexander had always expressed a tender feeling, not at all times, however, sincere. With the growth of consciousness in the sensitive youth he could not overlook the mass of contradictions between the ideas preached to him and the facts round about him. Neither could he help observing the abnormal relations that existed between him and his parents, and between the latter and Catherine. The more he grew and developed the more his eyes opened to the negative sides of Catherine's court and to the unpleasant features of Catherine herself. He could hardly as yet appreciate her state-merits and brilliant gifts, but he could certainly observe or at least feel quite early the atmosphere of falsehood and intrigues that had surrounded her. La Harpe and Protasov did their duty in implanting in their pupil good feelings for his father, while Paul himself could not or would not conceal his negative attitude towards the "big court." At any rate Alexander felt, if he did not know definitely, that his grandmother was responsible for the tense relations between her and his father, and that the latter was the suffering and persecuted victim. Under such conditions it appears very probable that in spite of the savage and unattractive manners in Gatchina there grew up in the heart of the youthful Alexander some sympathy for the position of his father and a concealed condemnation of Catherine. Little by little he began to express in secret to his friends his negative attitude towards his grandmother and her entourage. Openly he could not speak it, trained as he was from his childhood to tell his grandmother only respectful and flattering phrases. No wonder that under such circumstances there developed in him early dissimulation and hypocrisy. It is quite probable that he had received instructions in that spirit at the "little court," if not from his father then from his mother. All the flagrant, and in his eyes revolting, contradictions between the ideas preached to him from his childhood and the surrounding reality, aroused in Alexander a natural disgust for the court life and the atmosphere of falsehood, intrigues, lewdness, and cupidity that reigned there. By nature reserved, mild, disinclined to sharp forms of protesting, and at the same time greatly inclined towards dreaming and idealisation, owing to the peculiarities of his education, he began to form plans of a peaceful existence as a private person somewhere on the Rhine, and gradually came to the conviction of the possibility and necessity of abdicating from his future high but unpleasant position. Alexander's young wife, Elizabeth, the Princess of Baden, who was barely fourteen at her marriage, shared these plans and maybe took part in their formulation and development. According to the unanimous testimony of her contemporaries, the Grand Duchess Elizabeth was an extremely attractive and fascinating person, of an honest mind and developed intellect open for all the lofty ideas and conceptions that had then inspired her husband. During the years preceding Alexander's accession the young couple lived in perfect harmony; one may even suppose that Elizabeth, more passionate and outspoken than her husband, had exercised a certain influence on the further development of the principles they worked out together.

In the last year of Catherine's reign Alexander's plans, directly opposed to her plans, had evidently ripened definitely, and he described them in his letters to La Harpe and to his young friend Kochubey, then ambassador at Constantinople, and later in a conversation with the young Polish aristocrat and patriot, Prince Adam Czartoryski, with whom he became acquainted not long before. It is not known what La Harpe and Kochubey replied (if they did reply), but Czartoryski testifies in his memoirs that however impressed he was with the mood of the youthful Alexander, however he admired the sincerity, enthusiasm, and simplicity with which Alexander confided to him his thoughts, he even then was able to discern in them dreamy and egoistic elements, which opinion he did not conceal from his exalted friend.

The convictions of Czartoryski and of his other young friends — Stroganov and Novosiltzev — impressed Alexander, and he admitted that he had no right to decline the burden which was descending upon his shoulders at a moment of difficulty for the country, and he soon changed his original decision. Several months after his conversation with Czartoryski he declared that he saw himself obliged to ascend the throne, when the time came, and that he must first grant the land a firm, free, political structure before he might abdicate and retreat into private life.

Later events proved the last decision of Alexander also a dream that was not realised. But before he could bear the test he had to live through the four years of his father's reign — the most trying period in Alexander's life.

Those four years were morbidly reflected in the final formation of his character and on his subsequent fate. His own position and the position of all Russia at that time were passionately described by him in a letter to La Harpe secretly sent with Novosiltzev, who fled abroad from the horrors of Paul's reign in September, 1797. " To state briefly," he wrote in that letter, " the welfare of the state plays no rôle in the management of affairs. There exists only an unlimited power which does everything topsy-turvy. It is impossible to relate all the madnesses that have taken place here. Add to it severity which lacks the slightest justice, not a small amount of partiality, and absolute inexperience in matters (of state). The choice of executives is based on favouritism, merits are of no account. In a word, my unhappy country is in an indescribable state. The farmer is abused, trade is oppressed, freedom and personal security are abolished. Such is the picture of Russia — you may judge how my heart suffers. Obliged to comply with all the details of military service, I waste all my time in fulfilling the functions of a sub-officer, and have no possible chance to devote myself to my studies, which used to be my favourite pastime . . . I have become the most unfortunate man . . ."

This extract shows how Alexander felt as early as the first year of his father's reign. In the same letter he informed La Harpe about the formation of that friendly circle which eventually played such an important rôle in the first years of his reign, and consisted of Czartoryski, Stroganov, Novosiltzev, and Kochubey. Then the young liberals found all roads closed for them, and it was left for them only to translate foreign books, which could not be published. Soon they were forced to give up even that innocent occupation and to disperse in different directions to await a better future.

The position of Alexander grew worse as Paul showed increasing ferociousness in his treatment of his subjects. During those four years he went through a school that was to leave its fatal traces on his whole life. Paul compelled him to be not only a witness, but not infrequently a participant in all his follies and cruel undertakings. At the very beginning of the reign Alexander was appointed Chief Military Governor of Petrograd, which made him the main police official in the capital. Through him had passed thus the mass of punitive measures which Paul had showered upon his subjects. In this position Alexander had to serve with such persons as Arkharov, one of the most revolting Gatchina-men. After Arkharov his fellow-official was Count Pahlen, the one who eventually became the soul of the conspiracy that brought about the murder of Paul. He was a man of strong will, lustful for power, and of a big mind, but also a cynicist who was unscrupulous about his means.

At times Alexander had to live through tragic moments which left deep morbid traces in his sentimental soul; this took place when Paul wished to emphasise their unanimity. Paul actually made him sign decrees about shooting innocent people in order that all might see, as he had said, that " you and I breathe with the same spirit." One can easily imagine how these facts impressed the twenty year old pupil of La Harpe, after all the idyllic plans he had formed during the last years of Catherine.

Finally Alexander was forced against his will to take part in the conspiracy against his own father. The conspirators did not spare Alexander; they reckoned that by drawing him into the affair they would secure their own safety. Palen and Panin argued with Alexander for months, and at last persuaded him to consent to the removal of Paul and the establishment of a regency.[1] There was no doubt of the need for the welfare and security of Russia of removing the mad Paul. Alexander made Pahlen swear to him that Paul's life would be spared and then gave his consent for the overthrow.

But when the oath was broken, and the tragic death of Paul took place, Pahlen explained to Alexander that there had been no other way out. The naïve Alexander had not expected such a tragic result, although one could not have imagined the removal of Paul without the taking of his life. The violent death of his father made a despondent, depressing impression on him, the traces of which remained through all his life. Some of his biographers claim, perhaps not without reason, that the heavy, mystic mood of Alexander in his last years had its roots on one hand in the horrors of Paul's reign, and, on the other, in his indirect participation in his father's assassination.

Under such heavy influences and exceptional conditions had been formed the character of Alexander, which has baffled both his contemporaries and his later biographers. His early childhood passed in the apparently rational and brilliant care of his grandmother, but even then he could not have escaped the harmful influence of the unhealthy atmosphere of Catherine's court and of the strange relations between his parents and the Empress. His further education under La Harpe was suddenly interrupted by his premature marriage and the dismissal of his tutor. Then came a period very unfavourable for a normal course of study; his continued reading after La Harpe's plan

[1] Panin evidently sincerely believed that such was the purpose.

was not accompanied by an acquisition of positive knowledge. Hence — lofty and noble aspirations, but deprived of soil and stability. This inclination to flirt with high plans without considering the methods of their realisation and their consequences, remained with Alexander for ever, and caused those contradictions which we shall observe all through his reign. Finally the horrible four years' schooling under Paul, with its climatic tragedy, had put the finishing touch to the formation of his character.

CHAPTER V

ASCENDING the throne in his twenty-third year, Alexander was no longer the naïve dreamer of the letters to La Harpe in the years 1796–97. True, he had not given up his quest for the good, but he had considerably lost his confidence in people and his former enthusiasm.

In spite of his participation in administrative affairs under Paul he still remained inexperienced and ignorant about Russian conditions. Yet we must not take his despondency and the apparent helplessness he manifested in the first days of his reign as showing lack or weakness of will-power. He proved later that he had a perseverant will and was able to achieve what he wished to, but he wanted, especially at first, positive knowledge, a definite programme and experience. He was well aware of these shortcomings, and for this reason he hesitated, not knowing what to undertake immediately.

At the same time outside of a few old statesmen who did not understand his aims he had no one at his side on whom he could depend and in whom he could confide absolutely. There were clever men of the sort of Palen and Panin, but he could not trust them entirely in view of their rôle in the conspiracy against Paul; it is probable even that they were repulsive to him though he had to conceal the feeling of disgust. The Catherinian lords were dispersed by Paul, the most distinguished among them had died (e.g., Bezborodko), and those who remained inspired no confidence. Alexander was very glad, however, when on the very night of the overthrow there came to his call one of the " old servers," D. P. Troshchinsky, whom he had known as a man honest and experienced in affairs. He then appointed another "old server," Bekleshev, as Procurator-General in place of the dismissed Obolianinov. Both of these were naturally clever and honest, but not well educated, of no definite ideas or principles, and they managed state-matters according to the usual routine and "common sense."

Of course there were immediately recalled from abroad Alexander's personal friends: Czartoryski, Novosiltzev, Kochubey, but they could not come at once on account of the slow means of communication.

Some are inclined to explain by the weakness of the young tzar the fact that he did not arrest the conspirators, that he retained Count Pahlen at his post and recalled Count Panin, who had been dismissed by Paul. But knowing at present all the circumstances of the plot we may say that he could have hardly done otherwise, since the two counts did not take direct part in the murder of Paul, and as to actual participation in the conspiracy, Alexander would have had to arrest himself as well. For reasons of state, and because of lack of men around him, Alexander had to appreciate every capable statesman. In the hands of Pahlen were concentrated all the threads of administration, and he was the only person who knew all the ins and outs of the Government, which was then in a state of chaos. The situation was very difficult and even dangerous, at least externally, so far as foreign relations were concerned. At the end of his reign Paul had seriously enraged England, who was forced to undertake a naval expedition against Russia and its ally, Denmark. A week after Paul's death Nelson bombarded Copenhagen, and having destroyed the Danish fleet, prepared to bombard Cronstadt and Petrograd. Quick action was necessary to stop the English without hurting the national prestige. Pahlen was the only available member of the Collegium of Foreign Affairs at Petrograd. He performed the task quickly and successfully, perhaps owing to the fact that the British Government had been initiated into the significance of the coup d'état by the ex-ambassador, Witworth, who knew closely the conspirators. At any rate the English were entirely appeased, and Nelson departed from Reval with apologies.

As to Count Nikita Panin, he was one of the few experienced and gifted diplomats, and his return to affairs was quite natural. Alexander invited him from his Moscow estate to Petrograd, and immediately entrusted him with the management of all foreign affairs.[1]

Despite his depressed mood Alexander demonstrated from his first days great energy in matters that appeared clear to him. On the very night of the overthrow he did not forget to

---

[1] The relations of Alexander to Palen and Panin are differently described in the memoirs of the Decembrist Von Visin (nephew of the famous author). According to him Palen and Panin demanded from Alexander a solemn promise to grant a constitution immediately after his accession, but the commander of the Petrograd garrison, General Talyzin, persuaded Alexander not to consent to the demand, and promised him the support of all the Guards in the capital in case of need. Alexander heeded Talyzin and rejected the offer of Palen and Panin, whereupon the infuriated Palen ordered Talyzin poisoned (as a matter of fact Talyzin did suddenly die just at that time). The legend claims that those circumstances were responsible for the dismissal of Palen and Panin. Nobody to-day doubts the incorrectness of that story.

Panin was not even in Petrograd then; he came only several weeks after. Besides, if the story were true, Alexander would have dismissed Palen at once and would not have appointed Panin, whereas both of them resigned months after, when they were no longer needed. The facts of Palen's dismissal are known. He was dismissed on the demand of the Dowager Empress Marie, who had a sharp collision with him in June, 1801, on account of the ikons presented to her by the Old Believers and exhibited by her command in the court chapel; one of the ikons had an inscription in which Palen saw a hint at the desirability of inflicting a severe punishment upon the murderers of Paul. Palen allowed himself to remove the ikon and even complained to Alexander about the matter. The Empress in her turn demanded his discharge. Alexander not only took his mother's side and discharged him, but even banished him from Petrograd.

Panin managed foreign affairs from April to September, 1801. It is well known to-day that Panin did not agree with Alexander's views, and tried his own against the will of Alexander, which proved to be

issue an order for the recall of the Cossacks who were sent to conquer India.

On the same night Troshchinsky formed a hasty, but happy, project for the Manifesto of Accession, in which Alexander solemnly promised to govern the people " after the laws and heart of his grandmother, Catherine the Great." The reference to Catherine was very clever, as it signified in the eyes of the contemporaries the promise to annul all that had been decreed by Paul and a return to the age of Catherine, which appeared then to all in rosy colours.

On the first day Alexander ordered the release of the numerous victims of the Secret Expedition from prison and exile.

Then he began a careful change in personnel; the first to be discharged were: Procurator-General Obolianinov, who performed the rôle of supreme inquisitor under Paul; the equerry Kutaysov, one of Paul's most despicable sycophants, who started as the heir apparent's barber and had attained during Paul's reign the highest rank and distinctions, orders and decorations, and enormous wealth, but was generally hated; the Supreme Chief of Police at Moscow, Ertel, who had terrified the inhabitants of the first Capital.

Then followed a series of ukases annulling the hateful obscurantist and prohibitive measures of Paul: from twelve to fifteen thousand adminstratively discharged clerks and officers were recalled; an amnesty was declared for all fugitives (except homicides) ; the Secret Expedition was abolished, and it was declared that every offender must be accused, tried, and punished according to the general system of law; officials were strictly warned not to mistreat the citizens; the prohibition of foreign

stronger than Panin had expected. He had to resign. It is no wonder that there were a multitude of various legends concerning the unusual accession of Alexander, which had been veiled in mystery for many years; many important materials illuminating that event were published only very recently.

books was removed, private printing-houses were reopened, the embargo was set aside, and Russians were permitted to go abroad; then the granted charters to the nobility and the cities were restored, and the more liberal tariff of 1797 was reintroduced. The soldiers were exempted from wearing the hated locks, but the somewhat shortened braids remained till 1806. Finally the peasant-question was touched upon: the Academy of Sciences which issued public announcements was enjoined from accepting announcements about sales of serfs without soil. These were the most important measures taken during the first week of Alexander's reign.

All these measures introduced no new radical changes, but merely did away with Paul's tyrannical follies. As to organic changes, Alexander felt that he could not promulgate them without having a definite plan and without preliminary work. Still he made a few early steps in the direction of fundamental reorganisations. Troshchinsky worked out the reformation of the Court Council, which was established by Catherine and had degenerated under Paul into a committee for censoring foreign and Russian books. This Council was dismissed on March 26, and four days later was established the Permanent Council (consisting of twelve high officials least mistrusted by Alexander), which was to act as an advisory board to assist the Tzar in his management of state-affairs. Troshchinsky was one of the members and the Chief of the Council's chancery.

The next important step was the ukase of June 5, 1801, to the Senate, ordering that institution to present a report about its rights and duties for incorporation into the laws of the state. At that moment Alexander was evidently inclined to restore to the Senate its power as the highest organ of government, and to assure it by law an independence of judgments and orders.

Another ukase of the same date instituted " under the Emperor's personal supervision " and under the direct management of Count Zavadovsky, a " Commission for the Constitution of

Laws." The Commission was not to work out any new laws but to clarify and adjust the existing old laws. In his rescript to Zavadovsky Alexander said: " Basing the people's welfare on the uniformity of our laws, and believing that various measures may bring the land happy times but that only the law may affirm them forever, I have endeavoured from the very first days of my reign to investigate the conditions of this department of the state. I have known that since the edition of the *Ulozheniye* (the Code of Laws under Tzar Alexis, in 1649) to our days, i.e., during one century and a half, the laws issuing from different and often contradictory sources and published more for occasions than from general state-considerations, could have neither connection, nor unity of purpose, nor permanence of function. Hence the general confusion of rights and duties, darkness enwrapping both the judge and the defendant, the impotence of the laws in their performance, and the convenience of changing them by the first move of whim or despotism. . . ."

These ukases had an enormous demonstrative importance in their day. After the despotism of Paul the intention of Alexander to augment law above everything had gained for him popularity and sympathy among wide strata of the population.

Such were Alexander's steps in the first three months of his reign.

As early as April 24, 1801, Alexander expressed in a conversation with Stroganov his intention of reorganising the State along radical lines. He agreed with Stroganov, however, that before limiting the autocracy the administration should be reformed.[2]

---

[2] Let us say a few words about Stroganov and Alexander's other young friends recalled from abroad. Stroganov was the only son of the richest Catherinian lord, Count A. S. Stroganov. His instructor was a French mathematician, Romm, who subsequently was a member and even a temporary president of the Convention of 1793; he died on the scaffold. Romm, a stauncher republican than La Harpe, travelled in 1790 with young Stroganov through Europe, and arriving in Paris during the revolution, both entered the Jacobine club, of

In May, 1801, on the basis of the aforementioned April conversation, Stroganov presented to Alexander a memorandum in which he proposed the institution of an unofficial committee for the discussion of the plan for reorganisations. Alexander approved of the idea, and appointed as members of the Committee Stroganov, Novosiltzev, Czartoryski, and Kochubey. In view

which the Russian became a librarian, and grew intimate with the famous revolutionary, Mlle. Théroigne de Méricourt. Catherine recalled Stroganov and sent him to his village under his mother's supervision; Romm was forbidden to enter Russia. Soon, however, Stroganov was permitted to return to court where he became a friend of Alexander (through Czartoryski), and gradually familiarised himself with Russian conditions. Of his former radicalism and Jacobinism remained a rectilinearity of character and a tendency to realise even liberal reforms in a Jacobine way; but his views were not more than liberal, with a marked democratic tint. From his instructor Romm he adopted a remarkable exactness of thought and a habit of formulating his ideas with absolute definiteness.

Among Alexander's young advisors Stroganov was if not the most gifted, the most steadfast, with a definite plan of action in his mind. Stroganov was five years Alexander's senior, and considered the Emperor a man of noble intentions but lazy and weak. He endeavoured to hold Alexander under the influence of his circle, lest he fall under other influences.

Another member of that circle, N. N. Novosiltzev, was a cousin of Stroganov, appeared considerably more clever than Stroganov, and possessed a brilliant literary style for the exposition of his ideas. He was five years older than Stroganov, consequently much older than Alexander, less passionate, more cautious, though he lacked Stroganov's exactness of thought and consciousness of plan.

A third member of the circle was Prince Adam Czartoryski, a man of remarkable gifts, an ardent native Polish patriot, a subtle diplomat, a sober observer, who understood best of all Alexander's character. In his time he had been also attracted by the revolutionary ideas of 1789, but all his cravings and efforts were directed toward the restoration of a strong, independent Poland. Describing the members of the circle in his memoirs, Czartoryski calls himself the most disinterested, since he took part in a matter foreign to him. He never concealed from Alexander his real intentions and aims, and in 1802, before accepting the post of Deputy-Minister of Foreign Affairs, he warned Alexander that as a Polish patriot he would side with Polish interests in case of their collision with Russian interests.

The fourth person, originally not a member of the triumvirate, but of the absence of the last three, the work was postponed till June 24, 1801.

At the first session of the Committee plans and purposes were definitely formulated. They found it necessary first of all to learn the actual state of affairs, then to reform the governmental mechanism, and finally to secure the existence and independence of the renewed institutions by a constitution granted by the autocratic power in accordance with the spirit of the Russian people. The formulation voiced the sentiment of Stroganov, but did not entirely satisfy Alexander, who was preoccupied with the idea of issuing some demonstrative declaration, a sort of " Declaration of Rights."

Novosiltzev was appointed to gather information about the internal state of affairs and to submit reports and opinions on various branches of the administration. Unfortunately this matter was not considered profoundly, but was reduced to the study of the governmental apparatus and the observation of its faults, and it was not a study of the conditions of the people. Novosiltzev's programme embraced the following points: (1) questions of national defence on land and sea; (2) questions of foreign relations; (3) questions of internal affairs of the country in the statistic and administrative respects. By the " statistic respect " one could perhaps understand the study of the conditions of the people, but according to the plan this term meant only: trade, means of communication, agriculture, and industry; the administrative point — which was to be the *clef*

added to it by Alexander, was Count V. P. Kochubey, a distinguished diplomat, a nephew of Bezborodko, who began his career under Catherine, and at the age of 24 occupied with success the post of ambassador at Constantinople. A sincere liberal, he was more moderate than Stroganov and even than Alexander. He was brought up in England, and knew it better than Russia. He took part in the internal reforms of Russia, for which he willingly gave up his brilliant diplomatic career (he had the rank of Vice-Chancellor under Paul).

de la voute of the plan,— comprised: justice, finances, and legislation.

Statistics in our modern sense did not exist at that time; besides, the sessions of the Committee were secret, and a consensus gentium could not take place. The only statistic data in the possession of the Committee were those received through the Permanent Council, or through the Emperor, or some private sources in the governmental spheres. The members could have made use of their own information, but only Stroganov had some acquaintance with internal affairs, owing to his life in a village, while Kochubey and Czartoryski had some knowledge of international matters.

The discussion of the first point of the programme, the defence of the country, did not occupy much time, and the question was handed over to a special commission of military and naval experts. The discussion of the second point, of foreign relations, revealed Alexander's complete unpreparedness and ignorance in matters of foreign policy. Kochubey and Czartoryski, on the other hand, had quite definite knowledge and views in the matter. Alexander, who had just signed a friendly treaty with England, suddenly expressed his opinion before the Committee about the need of forming a coalition against England. The members felt confused and uneasy, all the more since they knew the Emperor's inclination to converse personally with foreign representatives and thus entangle matters. The Committee insistently counselled Alexander to ask the opinion of old experienced diplomats on the question, and they pointed out Count A. R. Vorontzov.

This first flaw strongly impressed Alexander, and he came to the next session better prepared. He asked Kochubey to expound his view on the foreign policy. Kochubey in his turn expressed his desire first to get acquainted with the views of the Emperor. An exchange of opinions took place. All agreed with the views of Czartoryski and Kochubey that England was Russia's natural ally, receiving almost all her export.

At the same time they pointed out the need for checking the over-ambitious aspiration of the French Government. These views were in direct opposition to Alexander's original views; but soon he demonstrated his remarkable talents in the field of diplomacy, and succeeded not only in orienting himself in foreign affairs, but in working out an independent outlook on those questions.

At the next sessions of the Committee internal affairs were discussed with numerous digressions. Alexander was interested most of all in two problems that appeared interdependent in his mind; the first was the granting of some " charta " or declaration of rights, and in connection with this the second — the reorganisation of the Senate, in which he saw at that time the guarantor of civil rights. In the latter question Alexander was supported even by the old senators, by liberals as well as by conservatives. Prince P. A. Zubov (the last favourite of Catherine) presented a project for making the Senate an independent legislative body, consisting of highest officials and highest nobles. Derzhavin proposed that the Senate be composed of persons elected by the officials of the first four ranks from their midst. The Committee had no difficulty in proving that those projects had little in common with a popular representation.

The third project handed over to the Committee by Alexander was planned by A. R. Vorontzov, and it had to do not with the reorganisation of the Senate but with the Emperor's idea about a charta. Vorontzov's project for granting the people a charter resembled in form Catherine's charters granted to the nobility and the cities, and in substance it expanded over the whole people, giving them serious guaranties of civil rights not unlike the English Habeas Corpus Act. At the discussion of the project by the Committee Novosiltzev expressed his doubt whether such promises could be given under the conditions of that time, and his fear that if given they would have to be withdrawn in a few years. Alexander hastened to agree with Novosiltzev's opinion, and the Committee decided that the publication of the charter at the time of the coronation would be inopportune.

This incident is very characteristic, showing how careful were those members of the Committee whom their enemies labelled Jacobines. The " old server " Vorontzov demonstrated on many occasions that he could be more liberal than the " Jacobines " assembled in the Winter Palace.

The same moderate and conservative views were expressed in regard to the peasant-question. The Committee touched the question for the first time in connection with Vorontzov's charter, which had a clause about giving the peasants the right to own real estate. Alexander found it at that time too dangerous a right. Later, after the coronation, in November, 1801, Alexander informed the Committee that a number of persons, among them La Harpe, invited by the Emperor to return to Russia, and Admiral Mordvinov, a convinced constitutionalist of the type of an English Tory, had declared the need of doing something for the peasants. Mordvinov proposed a practical measure, apparently having little to do with the peasant-question proper, which consisted in extending the right of real estate ownership to merchants, burghers, and state-peasants. Mordvinov had his own logic, however.

He considered that the limitation of the autocratic power could be best secured by the presence of an independent nobility, hence his desire to create such an independent aristocracy in Russia. He advocated the transference of a considerable part of fiscal lands (by sale or gift) to the nobles, so as to increase their material security and independence. As to the peasant-question and the abolition of serfdom, he thought that the supreme authority had no right to meddle with those matters, but that the liberation of the serfs from bondage should be de-

cided by the nobles alone. Having this point of view, Mordvinov intended to create an economic state in which the nobles
would find bondage-labour unprofitable and would willingly
resign their rights. He hoped that on the lands owned by commoners there would develop farms on the basis of hired labour,
which would compete with the bondage-system and compel the
landowners to abolish that system. Thus Mordvinov had in
mind a roundabout way for preparing the abolition of serfdom,
instead of any legislative restrictions in that field. Such was
the status of the peasant-question even among liberal and enlightened men like Mordvinov.

Zubov, who had no principles but simply tried to meet Alexander's liberal ideas, also presented a project about the peasant-
question, even more liberal than that of Mordvinov: he proposed to forbid the sale of serfs without soil. We have seen
that Alexander had already enjoined the Academy of Sciences
from publishing announcements about such sales; but Zubov
went further: desiring to lend the institution of serfdom a character of ownership of estates to which permanent labourers were
assigned (glebæ adscripti), he proposed to forbid ownership
of house-serfs, transferring them into tzekhs and guilds and
recompensing the landowners with money for the loss they sustained.

In the Committee the first to oppose categorically Zubov's
project was Novosiltzev. He pointed out that, first, the State
had no money for the redemption of the house-serfs, and, next,
that it was uncertain what could be done with such a mass of
men incapable of helping themselves. There was further expressed an opinion that it was inadvisable to take at once several
measures against serfdom for fear of irritating the nobles. Nobody shared Novosiltzev's ideas; but Alexander was evidently
shaken by them. Czartoryski spoke passionately against serfdom, arguing that it was such a revolting institution that in
the struggle against it there should be no fears or hesitations.

Kochubey maintained that in case of the acceptance of Mord-vinov's project the bonded peasants would consider themselves overlooked, since the other classes would get important rights while their lot would not be alleviated. Stroganov delivered a long, brilliant speech which was directed mainly against the idea that it was dangerous to irritate the nobles; he showed that politically the Russian nobles were zero, that they were in-capable of protesting, that they could be only slaves of the Monarch; in proof he pointed to the reign of Paul when the nobles had shown that they were unable to protect their own honour when it was trampled by the Government with the aid of other nobles. At the same time he asserted that the peasants still considered the Tzar as their only defender, that the loyalty of the people to the Tzar depended upon their hopes in him, and that to shake those hopes was indeed dangerous. Therefore he believed that if apprehensions should be enter-tained at all, the last ones should be considered most of all.

His speech was listened to with great attention, and it had an effect, but it did not shake either Alexander or Novosiltzev. Zubov's project was rejected. In the end they accepted Mordvinov's plan; thus persons of not-noble classes were per-mitted to buy unpopulated lands. Novosiltzev asked permis-sion to consult La Harpe and Mordvinov concerning Zubov's project; the two shared Novosiltzev's apprehensions. It is re-markable that La Harpe who was considered a Jacobine and a democrat remained in the peasant-question as undecisive and timid as the rest. He saw Russia's chief need in education and stubbornly emphasised that without education nothing could be accomplished, yet though he admitted the difficulty of spreading education under conditions of bondage, he feared the danger of seriously affecting the institution of serfdom under such condi-tions of education. A peculiar enchanted circle.

The members of the Committee proposed that in the course of time they might, by a slow and gradual process, come to the abolition of serfdom, but even the course of that process remained obscure.

Trade, industry, and agriculture were not investigated, although the state of those branches of national economy was such that it required the serious attention of the Government. The most important work of the Committee consisted in the reorganisation of the central administrative organs. The need of this had been evident since Catherine had reformed the local organs, but had not had time to reorganise the central institutions, except to abolish the larger part of the Collegia. The members of the Committee saw the pressing need for the reorganisation of the central organs, where the confusion was so great that in cases of great disturbances or calamities, as for instance when in Siberia people died from famine, there was no way of obtaining information about the state of affairs. Under the influence of such an occasion Alexander expressed his desire that the question of the differentiation of the jurisdiction among the central organs should be advanced in the work of the Committee. In the absence of Novosiltzev the Emperor instructed Czartoryski to present a report on the question. On February 10, 1802, Czartoryski read his clear and orderly report, in which he pointed out the necessity of dividing the jurisdiction of the supreme administrative organs, the supervisory, judiciary, and legislative, and of clearly defining the rôle of each. In his opinion the Senate should be independent from its chancery; as it was, the real ruler of the Senate appeared to be the Procurator-General who as head of the chancery had the privilege of personally reporting to the tzar. Then Czartoryski advocated the exact definition of the jurisdiction of the Permanent Council, and the differentiation of the jurisdiction of the Senate and the Permanent Council. He suggested that the Senate should deal only with contestable matters both administrative and judicial, while the Permanent Council should be an advisory institution discussing matters and projects of a legislative nature. The supreme administration should be divided among separate de- partments, each with a strictly defined sphere of work; at the head of each department should be, not a Collegium, but one responsible minister. He aptly explained how in the Collegia any personal responsibility necessarily disappeared.

We see thus that the merit of introducing the question of ministries belongs to Czartoryski. At one time this was ascribed to La Harpe, but since the publication of the Committee's minutes which were accurately written down by Stroganov, there have been no more doubts in this respect. In the report another measure was advocated, touching the part of the judiciary. Czartoryski wished to copy the system introduced in France after the Revolution, which divided the courts into three classes: criminal, civil, and police. The highest appeal for all judiciary matters should be to the Supreme Court of Cassations. This part of Czartoryski's plan was not thoroughly examined by the Committee but his idea about the institution of ministries was accepted unanimously. The work of the Committee became concentrated on the development of that idea; on the basis of that work there were established September 8, 1802, the Ministries of Foreign Affairs, of War, and of the Navy, which corresponded to the three then still existing Collegia, and entirely new Ministries of the Interior, Finances, Popular Education, and Justice. Upon Alexander's initiative there was formed also the Ministry of Commerce, on the institution of which he insisted for absolutely casual reasons, as he wished to give the rank of Minister to Count N. P. Rumiantzev, who had been in charge of the waterways.

The establishment of ministries was, properly speaking, the only original and accomplished work of the Committee. The reorganisation of the Senate took place in accordance with Czartoryski's ideas and with the report of the Senate about its rights. The Senate was to be an organ of state supervision over the administration and at the same time the highest judiciary body.

The following points were accepted in regard to the reformed Senate: (1) The Senate was to be the supreme administrative and judiciary institution in the Empire; (2) the power of the Senate was to be limited only by the power of the Emperor; (3) the Emperor was to preside in the Senate; (4) the ukases of the Senate were to be fulfilled by all, as the ukases of the Tzar himself, who alone could stop their fulfilment; (5) the Senate was to be permitted to present an opinion concerning such Imperial ukases as it might appear impossible to carry out, or which seemed to be opposed to other laws, or not clear; but if after the Senate's presentation no changes were made in the protested ukase, it was to remain valid; (6) the ministers were to submit to the Senate their yearly accounts for examination; the Senate could require from them information and explanations and should report to the Tzar about any faults and abuses it found; (7) in case of disagreement between certain decisions of the general assembly of the Senate and the opinion of the Procurator-General or the Super-Procurator, the matter should be submitted to the Tzar; (8) in criminal cases involving deprivation of nobility and rank the confirmation of the Tzar should be sought; (9) for unjust complaints against the Senate before the Tzar offenders should be tried by court; (10) senators impeached in a crime should be judged by the general assembly of the Senate.

On the whole these fundamental points of the senatorial jurisdiction did not contradict the fundamental statutes of Peter's Reglament.

The sixth point of the Reglament aroused at the session of the Committee sharp opposition on the part of Alexander who was afraid that the Senate would hamper his reformatory activities by displaying control over the ministers. The obstinacy with which he protested against that point showed the superficiality of his liberal views; at the first practical attempt to submit to control not even his own acts, but those of his assistants, he at once demonstrated a stubborn opposition to the plan in which he now saw but aggravating negative sides. Not without foundation did he fear that the Senate, composed of " old servers," would try to check his reformatory activity, but it is curious that in view of that apprehension Alexander was unable to hold to his principle.

The superficiality of his political views was still more clearly demonstrated on another occasion, in connection with the fifth point of the Reglament, which gave the Senate the right to protest against Imperial ukases if they did not correspond with the laws, or were not clear, or for some reason or other inconvenient. This right corresponded with the *droit de remontrance,* the privilege of the old French parlements.

Soon after the publication of the new Reglament there came an occasion for the application of that privilege. Upon the report of the Minister of War the Emperor declared that all the nobles of the sub-officer rank had to serve twelve years in the army. One of the senators, Count Severin Potocky, justly found in it an infringement of the granted Charter, and he suggested that the Senate make use of its right to protest. The Procurator-General, G. R. Derzhavin, was so astounded by the idea of protesting that without placing the protest before the Senate he reported to Alexander. The Emperor was disconcerted at the news, but he ordered action to proceed according to the law. On the next day Derzhavin appeared before Alexander and reported: " Sire, the entire Senate is against you on the question raised by Potocky." The Emperor, according to Derzhavin (in his memoirs), changed in countenance, but only said that the Senate should send him a deputation with a report on the motives of their protest. Alexander received the deputation very dryly, accepted the written report, and promised to consider it. After a long time, in March of 1803, he issued an ukase which declared that the Senate had misinterpreted its rights, that the right of protest was extended only in regard to old ukases, but not to new ukases; these the Senate was to accept promptly.

It is difficult to comprehend how Alexander with the *idea* of limiting the autocratic power could justify such contradictions in practice. Alexander's behaviour in the above case was the stranger since the disputed right of the Senate did not limit his power in fact, for according to the Reglament the Senate was to accept the protested ukase if the Emperor refused to consider the protest. But such were the superficial political views of Alexander at that time.

Thus the chief results of the work of the Committee were the establishment of the Ministries and the issue of the new Reglament for the Senate. In May of 1802 the sessions of the Committee in the Winter Palace were practically discontinued; Alexander left for a meeting with the King of Prussia, and upon his return did not summon the Committee. At the end of 1803 the Committee was assembled several times again, but for the discussion of private questions unrelated to the work of reorganisation. Actually, then, the Committee was in existence for one year.

Let us summarise its activity. The conservatives of the time, " old servers " and inveterate serf-owners of Derzhavin's type, called the members of the Committee " a band of Jacobines." But we have seen that if they could be accused of anything, it was of timidity and of the inconsequentiality with which they pursued the course of liberal reforms. The two chief problems of the day — the bondage and the autocracy — were reduced to nought. The only important result of its work was an administrative reform, quite daring in the technical sense; the " old servers " attacked the institution of the Ministries as an arrogant blow at Peter's collegiate principle. The critics also pointed out the unfinished form of the law, its lack of harmony in defining the jurisdiction of the Senate and the Permanent Council, and their relation to the Ministries; the chief point of attack was the want of a regulation for the inner composition of the Ministries, of a separate instruction for each Ministry, and of a clear statement about the relation of the Ministries to the provincial institutions.

The reproach for mistreating Peter's legislation had no foundation, for we have seen that the Collegia had been abolished by Catherine, and Alexander's task consisted not in supplanting the existing Collegia with ministries, but in erecting a new building on a vacant place. As to the flaws in the law, they were numerous indeed. The law embraced in one statute all the Ministries, there were no separate instructions, the inner order was not worked out, the relation of the Ministries to the provincial institutions was not clear. But admitting all this, we must say that the establishment of the Ministries was the means of doing away with a considerable portion of those faults; they were new institutions, and had to be given a chance for a gradual, empirical development of their inner order and for the regulation of mutual relations among various departments.[3]

Such were the tangible results of the Committee's work.

But for Alexander himself work on the Committee with its educated and talented members was a very useful school which had made up to some extent for his lack of positive knowledge. Having made use of the lessons he had received in the Committee, and having accepted as a gift from it an excellent instrument for the further development of his internal policy, in the form of the Ministries and the Committee of Ministers, Alexander undoubtedly felt firmer and more conscious in his intentions and was better equipped for the promulgation of his political plans than he had been a year before. This may certainly be said also with respect to his foreign policy in which he soon manifested great originality.

[3] All the mentioned faults of the first ministerial law were soon observed by V. P. Kochubey, as it can be seen from his report to Alexander on March 28, 1806.

CHAPTER VI

FROM the study of the state measures we shall now turn to an examination of the position of society at the time of Alexander's accession and during the first years of his reign, and of the changes in the conditions of the country and its economic and social life that took place during that time. All historians agree as to the general mood that reigned in the country after the death of Paul.

"All is calm and peaceful," wrote the Empress Elizabeth to her mother, " unless we speak of the mad joy that has taken possession of everybody, from the last muzhik to the highest ranks of society . . . I breathe peacefully together with all Russia."

Wiegel, eye-witness of the Moscow reception of the accession-manifesto, wrote in his memoirs: " This is one of those reminiscences which time can never erase: a silent general joy illumined by a bright spring sun. . . . Common embraces, as on the day of Easter-Sunday; not a word about the deceased, so as not to darken even for a moment the hearty gladness that burned in all eyes; not a word about the past, but only about the present and the future . . ."

The public rejoiced over their deliverance from the terrors and tribulations of Paul's régime; at once there reappeared the forbidden hair-dresses, hats, carriages, for even such miserable privileges had been taken away by the despot. More earnest patriots rejoiced not so much over the passing of the terror as over the advent of a new epoch with which they connected the most rosy hopes. They saw a confirmation of their hopes in the energetic activity of the young Monarch who tried from the outstart to erase and smoothe over all the morbid traces of his father's reign, and to revoke all his oppressive and hateful measures.

The progressive elements had good reasons for expecting radical reforms from the new Tzar whose political views had been known even before he had declared them in his early ukases. It is curious, however, to note that all these liberals associated their constitutional expectations with the manifesto of March 12, in which Alexander promised to reign according to the heart and will of his grandmother. But Catherine was a convinced autocrat, with no thoughts about granting a constitution! The public had evidently suffered so much under Paul that it looked back to the time of Catherine as to the golden age. Generally speaking there were many young men who had dreamt about limiting the absolutism, but most of them were poorly informed as to the real foundations of a constitutional order.

For the time being they felt satisfied with the chance to breathe freely and to get a respite from the mad governmental terror; even such enlightened and scholarly men as Academic Storch, the investigator of Adam Smith, in his chronicle of Alexander's early reign considered all the young Monarch's measures for the first five years as direct steps toward a constitutional state. Even the incident with Potocky and the wilful interpretation of the rights of the Senate that followed, aroused no criticism of Alexander among his contemporaries. The nobles organised ovations in honour of Potocky and hostile demonstrations against Derzhavin and Viazmitinov (the minister of war and author of the circular that had caused the whole imbroglio), but nobody thought of accusing Alexander, or of questioning the sincerity of his constitutional intentions.

The liberal-rosy mood of the public was reflected also in the periodical press which reappeared immediately after the unsealing of the private printing-houses. The first magazine to have gained great importance after 1802 was the *European Messenger,* issued by Karamzin, the most popular and favourite publication of the time, as may be seen from the fact that Karamzin earned six thousand rubles a year from subscriptions only. Karamzin himself no longer belonged to the young generation; he had lived through his " Sturm und Drang Periode " back in the nineties of the eighteenth century, when he wrote his *Letters of a Russian Traveller.* At the beginning of the nineteenth century he was already a well-balanced writer of ultra-sentimental tendencies, author of such works as *Poor Lize* over which our grandmothers raved so much.

Karamzin asserted in 1802 that all the nations had grown convinced of the necessity of a firm government after a decade of revolutionary wars, and that all governments had become convinced of the importance of public opinion, of the need of popular loyalty and of the necessity of eradicating abuses. He saw then the pledge for the aggrandisement of Russia's prestige and glory in the development of civil consciousness and the spread of education in the country; for this reason he sympathised at that time with Alexander's mild rule and with his liberal and enlightening measures. He had not yet become that extreme conservative who later condemned Alexander's liberalism and fiercely opposed Speransky. In the *European Messenger* Karamzin lauded the human policy of the Government. " Russia sees on her throne a beloved Monarch who zealously desires her happiness, guided by the rule that virtue and enlightenment should be the basis of national welfare . . ."

" Through our zeal for education we shall prove that we do not fear its consequences, and wish to enjoy only such rights as agree with the general well-being of the state and with love for mankind."

The magazine had an abundance of sentimental novels partly original and partly translated; in its publicistic department was preached a sentimental and haughty patriotism, and very opti-

mistic views were expressed on Russian reality, including serfdom, which was described idyllically, the landowners figuring
in most cases as benefactors of their peasants. Praising Alexander's first reforms and greeting the establishment of ministries, Karamzin found it opportune to emphasise the formation
of an intelligent public opinion that had taken place in Russia.
" The time has passed," he wrote, " when the Monarch's grace
and a peaceful conscience could be the reward of a virtuous
minister. . . . Now it is glorious to deserve together with the
Monarch's grace also the love of the enlightened Russians."

By the success of the *European Messenger* we may judge
that it corresponded to the tastes and requirements of the public. There was a number of other sentimental-idyllic magazines; one should mention the *Moscow Mercury,* which was
the first to introduce a critical department where at times negative views about other publications were expressed. This magazine was also the first to raise the woman-problem in the most
energetic manner; in the very first number it advocated the
need of woman-education and her participation in the social life
of the country; it pointed out the rôle of the French salons in
enlightening the public. The reign of sentimentalism in the
tastes of that time was responsible for the appearance of such
revolting magazines as the *Magazine for Lovers,* or the *Moscow
Observer* and similar frivolous publications that offered empty
anecdotes and dubious stories. Those magazines had also
a reactionary character: they attacked the free-thinkers who
doubted the usefulness of orders and ranks, and so forth. In
the *Friend of Enlightenment* appeared attacks against the new
reforms, written by Derzhavin and Shishkov.

The progressive elements united in 1804 around the *Magazine of Russian Letters,* published by Brusilov with the active
co-operation of the talented publicist, I. P. Pnin. Pnin had
there an imaginary dialog between a censor and an author in
China, in which he expressed a definite liberal view on the

necessity of freedom of the press and the futility of any censorship; in his verses, which were very popular, Pnin also discussed personal freedom and the abnormality of serfdom. Still more radical was Pnin's pamphlet "An Essay on Education," which was published in 1804, but the second edition of which was forbidden by the censor. It is curious that although Pnin was a liberal, his educational ideas were based on a class-point of view. In his opinion there should be special schools for each class — for peasants, commoners, merchants, and nobles; the children of the lower classes should study a cycle of subjects corresponding to their needs, and only the nobles were to acquire the higher sciences and abstract knowledge.

Not less remarkable was another liberal organ, the *Northern Messenger,* published by I. I. Martynov, director of the chancery of the Ministry of Education. The magazine was financially supported by the Government, and carried on a polemic with all reactionaries. In its educational programme it agreed with the views of Pnin. Politically it tried to prepare the minds for constitutional ideas. It considered England as the ideal country in the political sense. In one article it advocated an aristocratic constitution of the type that corresponded with the views of Mordvinov, mentioned above, and one may assume that the article was inspired by Mordvinov.

Another liberal magazine was published from 1804 to 1806, *Periodical Publication of the Society of Lovers of Letters,* the editor and chief publicist of which, Popugaiev, lent it an outspoken democratic tendency, in contrast to the *Northern Messenger.*

In 1804 a censorship-statute was issued, copied from that of Denmark, which established preliminary censorship of all publications. Though the statute was not liberal in substance, it recommended the censors to be lenient with authors. In view of the liberal views of the Government the press enjoyed in fact considerable freedom; it could print what it wanted to, but one must say that it did not want overmuch.

The existence of all these magazines shows how strongly the public interest in political thought had been cultivated at that time, with the direct co-operation of the Government.

Besides magazines there appeared during that period a mass of new.books, economic, political, juridical, and philosophical treatises, of which the majority presented expositions and translations of European works of the later eighteenth century. For this purpose Alexander generously offered subsidies, which amounted to more than sixty thousand rubles in five years. The translator of Adam Smith received five thousand rubles, and about the same sum was given to the publishers of Bentham and Tacitus. Among the published works were the political tractates of Beccaria, Montesquieu, Mably, and others. A detailed account of the books published then occupies a considerable part of the ninth volume of Storch's *Russland unter Alexander dem Ersten*.

Such was the mood of the Government, of the public, and particularly of the metropolitan *intelligentzia* and press during the first five years of Alexander's reign.

As to the masses, no essential changes in their condition had taken place since the time of Catherine, and my sketch of the position of the peasants under Catherine holds true also concerning the first years of the nineteenth century. One should note, however, that the peasants, who usually manifested restlessness at each new accession, remained calm at Alexander's accession.

The most prominent act of Alexander's early reign in regard to the peasant question was the ukase of February 20, 1803, concerning the Free Agriculturists. The law was issued on the basis of Count Rumiantzev's memorandum, and it allowed serf-owners to liberate their bondmen individually or by whole villages not otherwise than with land-allotments under conditions arrived at by mutual agreement between the owners and their serfs; the agreement was to be presented to the Emperor for sanction, after which it became a legal enactment. The peasants thus liberated were called Free Agriculturists, and the Government could not dispose of their land as it did of that of the Fiscal peasants.

The serfdom-advocates considered the ukase extremely harmful, not without reason, seeing in it the first symptom of hostility toward the bondage system. Derzhavin made many efforts to prevent the enactment of that law, but he achieved only an Imperial reprimand. In the years immediately following the publication of the ukase there were concluded on its basis a very few agreements, by which the peasants had to pay as much as five hundred rubles in assignations per person. One may judge how high that price was by the fact that in the fifties the value of the landowners' estates (with the land and buildings) divided by the number of bondmen did not exceed two hundred to three hundred rubles per soul.

Altogether there were made during the reign of Alexander one hundred and sixty agreements about Free Agriculturists, the total number of liberated peasants amounting to 47,153 male souls; in seventeen cases the liberation was transacted without redemption (the number of freely liberated peasants was 7,415, of which 7,000 were liberated without land by the bequest of one landowner). In other cases the peasants bought their freedom; the average redemption sum for the whole reign equalled three hundred and ninety-six rubles in assignations per soul, or about one hundred rubles in silver (according to the course established after the year 1809). In single cases the Government helped the peasants to pay out their redemption-fees.

The next peasant-measure was the regulation of February 20, 1804, concerning the peasants of the Lifland province. The initiative in this case belonged to the landowners of the province themselves, as a result of the liberation movement that had started under Catherine. The regulations were worked out by a special committee that consisted of Kochubey, Stroganov, Kozodavlev, and two representatives of the Lifland nobility, and according to them, (1) it was forbidden to sell or pledge peasants without land; (2) the peasants received personal rights, self-government and *volost*-courts;[1] (3) the peasants became hereditary owners of their land portions, which they could lose only by the verdict of the court, or for profligacy; (4) the *barshchina* was limited to two days; (5) in the *obrok*-estates the money dues established by a special revision-commission could not be raised by the landowners, while the curtailment of the peasants' portions could take place only for a special compensation; (6) the houseworkers and journeymen remained under the disciplinary authority of the landowners, but the peasants could be punished only by verdict of the *volost*-court.

In 1805 similar regulations were worked out for the province of Estland, though on conditions somewhat less favourable for the peasants. These regulations later played a certain part in the course of the peasant-question, as we shall see.

Alexander's personal attitude toward the peasant-question at that time was characterised by his attention to peasant-complaints against their landowners and by his inflicting severe punishments upon guilty owners, usually depriving them of the management of their estates.

Economically the land underwent no radical changes during that period. The population increased normally in the absence of wars or other extraordinary calamities. The general increase of the population for the years 1801–1805 equalled 2,655,000.

The first five years of Alexander's reign saw a rapid development of the colonisation of southern Russia. At the same

[1] A *volost* is a district consisting of several villages.— Tr.

time the immigration of foreign colonists continued to grow owing to the rumours about the improved conditions of administration, and also to the privileges offered the colonists by the manifesto of 1763. From 1803 to 1805 five thousand male colonists settled in New Russia (Germans, Czechs, and various southern Slavs).

In the meantime there began to appear a dearth of land in densely populated regions, such as the provinces of Tula and Kursk, where the extensive system of agriculture predominated and industry was slightly developed. The Government began to transport Fiscal peasants from those places to New Russia, and encouraged privately organised immigration of peasants, allotting them land on favourable conditions. The Government was forced to change its attitude toward foreign immigration in view of the need of land in Russia proper, and also because of the numerous disorders in the foreign colonies that had taken place during Catherine and Paul. In 1804 Kochubey presented a report on the question to the Committee of Ministers, after which it was decided, (1) to make use of the southern steppes primarily for the colonisation of Russians, and (2) to handle more cautiously foreign immigration by discontinuing the practice of inviting masses from abroad and by allowing only such immigrants as had means for defraying their travel-expenses and for establishing themselves on the new place, and who would at the same time be capable of introducing better methods in agriculture, or be skilled in some craft.

In spite of numerous errors, failures, and abuses of various authorities, the colonisation of New Russia developed intensely. Empty expanses became peopled with Russians as well as with foreigners: Germans, German Mennonites, southern and western Slavs (especially since disturbances had begun in Turkey), and Jews from White Russia. The cultivation of the fertile southern fields was markedly reflected on the productivity of

Russian grain, the export of which had grown thirty times since the middle of the eighteenth century and five to six times since the eighties. The, lion share of the export consisted of corn that was raised in the newly cultivated southern steppes.

Caring for the rapid economic development of the South, the Government granted various privileges to the colonists in regard to the payment of dues and taxes, and also trade privileges, by establishing free ports at first in Crimea (under Paul) and later in Odessa. Odessa, established by Catherine, was administered at that time by the French émigré, Duke Richelieu (ultimately minister of Louis XVIII), and rapidly grew into a large commercial city and port.

In connection with the colonisation-policy of the Government we should mention here two big problems of internal life that had come to the front about that time: that of the Jews and of the Sectarians.

The first was directly connected with the annexation at the end of the eighteenth century of the vast Polish-Lithuanian provinces that contained one million Jews. Up to that time the question had only a limited importance, touching mainly the permission for Jewish merchants to appear at Little Russian fairs. This permission was regulated by a ukase of Catherine I (in 1727), and was later greatly curbed by Elizabeth. Under Catherine II, after the annexation of Crimea, New Russia, and the partitions of Poland, there was introduced for the first time the idea of a Jewish Pale of Settlement, which consisted of the provinces of Little Russia, New Russia, Crimea, and the territories included in the three partitions of Poland. The Jews were forbidden to enter other parts of the Empire, but within the Pale they were given all civil rights of the "middle sort." Only at the end of Catherine's reign, by the law of 1794, were the Jews required to pay double taxes in comparison with the taxes of Christian commoners and merchants. Under Paul the law remained intact; in his last years Derzhavin, who had performed a senatorial revision of White Russia in view of its failure of crops and famine, presented a special report on the Jewish question, which was disregarded by Paul and remained in the Senate until 1802, when the question came under discussion. A special committee was organised to examine " the complaints of the inhabitants of those provinces where Jews lived, about various abuses and disorders detrimental to agriculture and industry." As a result of the committee's work came the " Statute concerning the Jews " of 1804. The Jews were as before forbidden to settle outside of the Pale, but the Pale itself was somewhat expanded; to the provinces of Lithuania, White Russia, Little Russia, Kiev, Minsk, Volhyn, Podolsk, Kherson, Ekaterinoslav, and Tavrida (Crimea), were added the provinces of Astrakhan and the Caucasus; in view of complaints against Jew-smugglers, they were not allowed to settle within fifty versts of the frontier. Within the Pale the Jews were to enjoy " the protection of the law on equal basis with the other Russian subjects." The Statute, however, specified the civil rights of the Jews, setting forth a double purpose: to encourage their assimilation with the rest of the population and to direct them to useful work that they might abandon such occupations as exploited the local population, especially the lower class, whose frequent complaints to the Government had brought about the discussion of the Jewish question. The Jews were divided by the Statute of 1804 into four classes: (1) agriculturists, (2) factory-owners and artisans, (3) merchants, and (4) commoners. They were encouraged to take up farming and were forbidden to keep taverns in villages. The Statute endeavoured to secure for the Jews all means of education, in which respect it differed favourably from the later policy of the Government in the same question. Their children could attend all primary schools, gymnasia, and universities, and were granted the same degrees as other subjects

of the Empire. For the Jews who in view of their religious exclusiveness were unwilling to send their children to common
schools, the Government ordered special schools established, for
the maintenance of which an extra tax was levied on the Jews.
According to Prof. A. D. Gradovsky the Statute of 1804 has
been the starting point for all the subsequent legislation concerning the Jews, and one should note that the further measures have developed by no means favourably for the Jews, so
that the Statute of 1804 is in many respects much better disposed toward them than the later policy of the Government.

More favourable and human was the attitude of the Government, and particularly of the Emperor himself, towards the
various Russian and foreign sects. Such sects as the *Dukhobory* and *Molokane* were granted toleration, while under Catherine the *Dukhobory* were sentenced to be burned, and only
through the intercession of the Empress were they exiled instead
to Siberia. Alexander protected all rationalistic sects and considered useless not only repressive measures against Sectants
and Schismatists, but even the missionary activity of the Orthodox church.

The rapid growth of the fertile South was reflected on the
industrial life of the northern, not black-soil, provinces. Unable to compete with the South in the production of cereals,
particularly of corn, they concentrated their activity on the
production of flax and hemp and their fabrics, which was
greatly aided by the removal of the commercial restraints in the
relations with England, the chief consumer at that time of
flax and hemp for its fleet. The restoration of the liberal
tariff of 1797 and the abolition of Paul's restrictions in regard
to foreign lands, had benefited the Russian foreign trade, and
the temporary trade-balance had in its turn favourably impressed the course of the paper-money, notwithstanding the new
issues of assignations for the extinction of the yearly deficits.
This favourable financial situation after the depressed state of

affairs under Paul had aroused in governmental circles an excessive optimism and carelessness in financial management, the results of which were quite painful; but at the same time it allowed the progressive government to spend generously on various productive purposes, and first of all on education. Of a similar productive importance were the enormous subsidies given for the building of waterways, mainly begun under Catherine and Paul and finished during the first years of Alexander,[2] and the expenses for the colonisation of the South. Yet the lion-portion of the budget was even at that time absorbed by the army and navy (30–40 per cent.). About 10 per cent. went for the court expenses; Alexander had tried to cut down the extravagant court expenditures, so that the courtiers, used to the prodigality of Catherine and Paul, loudly accused him of parsimony. In view of the broadened progressive activity of the Government, the income from the earlier established taxes could not cover the new expenses, and the budgets brought yearly deficits of about 20–25 per cent. Instead of revising the tax-system by a simple proportional increase of the direct taxes, the Government covered the deficit year after year by issues of assignations, the course of which had not fallen, but had, on the contrary, risen, owing to the rapid development of foreign commerce and to a favourable balance of trade. By the end of Catherine's reign the course of the assignations

[2] In 1805 was the Beresina canal opened for navigation. It joined the Dnieper with Western Dvina; in 1804 the Oginsky canal for the connection of the rivers Shara and Yatzolda was opened; in the same year Sivers finished the canal around lake Ilmen, connecting the rivers Msta and Volkhov; the work for the Maryinsky canal was intensified by the great sums offered by Empress Marie Feodorovna (the Dowager), for which reason the canal finished in 1810 has borne her name. At the same time were finished the Svirsky and Siassky canals around lake Ladoga. Among the works of secondary importance one may consider the Mytishchinsky aqueduct in Moscow, which was brought up to the Kuznietzky Bridge (the centre of Moscow) in 1805 at the cost of 1,164,000 rubles.

(their total was 157 million) fell to 70 copecks per ruble; by the end of Paul's reign, when the number of assigrations had reached 212 million, the course fell below 50 copecks and threatened to fall further, owing to the mad measures of Paul in regard to foreign trade; but after the revocation of all Paul's restrictions the course began to rise, despite the new yearly issues of assignations, so that in 1803–1804, when their number in circulation exceeded 300 million rubles, their course still stood above 80 copecks per ruble. The war that began in 1805 completely destroyed these favourable financial conditions.

The work of fundamental state reorganisation, that had been planned by Alexander, progressed with a slow tempo after the cessation of the Committee sessions. The discussion of important state affairs and questions was now concentrated in the Committee of Ministers which consisted of all the members of the Committee who had become ministers and deputy-ministers. The working out of further administrative reforms was centred mainly in the Ministry of the Interior, at the head of which stood Kochubey and his deputy Stroganov and the talented young assistant of Troshchinsky, M. M. Speransky, destined to play a prominent rôle in the reorganisation of Russian state-institutions. The views of Speransky on the necessary caution in promulgating fundamental reforms were clearly expressed in a memorandum presented by him in 1803.

"In the present state of affairs," he wrote there, "we do not find the first elements necessary for the establishment of a monarchical order (by monarchical Speransky understood constitutional). Indeed, how is it possible to introduce a monarchical (i.e., constitutional) order after the plan expounded above, in a land where half of the population is in complete slavery, where that slavery is bound with almost all parts of the political organisation and with the military system, and where that system is indispensable in view of the expansion of the frontiers and the political situation? How is it possible to organise a monarchical state without a code of laws? How is it possible to establish a code of laws without separating the legislative power from the executive? How is it possible to separate the legislative power without an independent institution for its maintenance and support? How introduce such an independent institution without overthrowing the whole existing order of things, with the existence of slavery and in the absence of education? How develop a public opinion, create a national spirit without freedom of the press? How introduce or allow freedom of the press in the absence of education? How establish a real ministerial responsibility where the planning and execution of measures are combined in one person? How can the observance of the laws be secured in the absence of responsibility? How can the laws be observed without education and an abundance of executors? . . ."

All these questions, in Speransky's opinion, had to be solved before granting a constitution. For this reason he insisted that the fundamental reorganisation of the state should be postponed, and the immediate future should be devoted to regulating the existing order. He suggested the following: (1) the autocracy to be preserved for the time being, (2) to strengthen public opinion which should wield an influence on the authorities, (3) to aim at an approach toward a constitutional order, for which purpose the existing order should contain institutions capable of "adapting the national spirit" to the new ideas.

Speransky's considerations resembled in substance those of Stroganov, but they were formulated more practically and categorically. It is characteristic that for Speransky in 1803, as for the members of the Committee, a constitutional order was the fundamental ideal, but an ideal unrealisable in the near future. The chief obstacle to its realisation appeared in the eyes of the most earnest progressives of that period to be the institution of serfdom, but to abolish serfdom was considered dangerous — in the absence of education; and to spread edu-

cation under conditions of serfdom was difficult; hence the
enchanted circle, from which they hoped to get out by the way
of slow and persistent efforts.

The immediate task was the care for education, to which
the whole attention of the Government was directed during
the first five years of the nineteenth century. The Ministry of
Education produced very effective results. Though at its head
stood the lazy Catherinian aristocrat, Count Zavadovsky, he had
the co-operation of an entire committee (the Chief Management of Schools) which consisted of enlightened and devoted
workers. Some of them were appointed Curators over five
educational districts: the Curator of the Moscow district was
Michail Muraviov, the former teacher of Alexander (at the
same time he remained Deputy-Minister), of the Petrograd
district — N. N. Novosiltzev (at the same time Deputy-Minister of Justice), of the Vilna district (to which belonged all
Lithuania, White Russia, and the South-Western Region) —
Prince Czartoryski (Deputy-Minister of Foreign Affairs), of
the Kharkov district — Count Severin Potocky (the Senator
who protested in 1802), of the Kazan district — Academic Ru-
movsky, one of Lomonosov's favourite pupils, quite senile at the
time of his appointment, and finally, of the Dorpat district
(Livonia) — the enlightened General Klinger. All the Curators lived in Petrograd, visited their districts from time to time,
and took part in collegiate discussions of all problems related
to the spread of education in Russia. One of the members of
the Chief Management of Schools was Yankovich de Mirievo,
the Austrian pedagogue, who had laid a foundation for a net
of schools in Russia under Catherine. The secretary of the
Management was Vassily Karazin, the young enthusiast whose
address of welcome to Alexander immediately after his accession had become the leit-motive of the progressives. South
Russia owed to the energy of Karazin the establishment of the
university of Kharkov: he induced the Kharkov nobility to col-

lect 400,000 rubles for that purpose, and the university was founded in 1804. At the same time were founded the university of Kazan and the Petrograd Institute of Pedagogy, later reorganised into a university. Thus Russia, up to that time in possession of one university at Moscow, had now six high educational institutions (that of Vilna was Polish, and that of Dorpat — German). The Government actively set out to plant education from above; for most of all there was need of forming a cadre of teachers, for which reason in Petrograd was founded not a university, but an Institute of Pedagogy, divided into departments.

One may judge of the dimensions of the governmental educational activity by comparing the following figures: whereas the highest assignment for education under Catherine reached 780,000 rubles a year, in 1804 there was assigned for the purpose 2,800,000 rubles — an enormous sum, considering the low cost of living at that time and the remuneration of the personnel, which, compared with modern salaries, was negligible. During 1803–1806 the Government assigned sums for the support of educational institutions; each university received 130,000 rubles, each of the 42 gymnasia (not counting those of the districts of Vilna and Dorpat) 5,500–6,500 rubles, and each of the District-Schools (there were 405) — 1250–1600 rubles. Besides the state institutions there were formed during that period by private means the Demidov Lyceum in Yaroslavl and the Gymnasium of Higher Sciences of the Name of Bezborodko in Niezhin.

The first University Statute was issued in 1804. It was based on the principle of respect for knowledge and for freedom of instructions, and gave autonomy to university Councils, which was greatly limited and almost destroyed by the end of Alexander's reign, and entirely abolished by Nicolas I. By the Statute of 1804 the university Councils were placed at the head of all educational institutions of the districts; they enjoyed full power for spreading and directing education in their districts, while the Curators were not administrators in the proper sense of the word, but dignitaries who lived in Petrograd and represented the needs of each district.

I have already mentioned the generous subsidies of the Government for the publication of books and magazines. To this one should add the pensions that the Government appointed for persons who devoted themselves to the pursuit of knowledge outside of state-service; Karamzin, for instance, received a pension of 2,000 rubles a year, a sum that allowed one at that time to live comfortably and devote oneself entirely to study. On the whole we may consider those years as the best and most productive in the history of Russian education. Unfortunately the government of Alexander I could not long continue in the same way, for first of all there were not sufficient financial resources for the purpose. As soon as in 1805 the war with France broke out, the sums assigned for education, which had been continually increasing up to that time, not only ceased to increase, but were diminished by force of need.

CHAPTER VII

THE next period of Alexander's reign was signified by two wars with Napoleon. The relations, however, which brought the war of 1805 had begun to take form long before that year.

Let us recall that at the moment of Paul's death war with England seemed imminent, and the English fleet was about to bombard Cronstadt. Immediately after Alexander's accession peace was concluded, and the disputable questions of sea-rights which had long impeded the good relations between Russia (and other powers) and England were solved. Although all the sympathies of the youthful Alexander lay on the side of France, he yielded, nevertheless, as we have seen, to the pressure of his close advisors and formed an alliance with England. At the very first sessions of the Committee it was decided in principle not to meddle with any internal affairs of foreign countries, and although they looked with suspicion upon France in view of the ambitious designs of Bonaparte, there prevailed the pacifist principle in foreign relations. Thus Russia was free from foreign entanglements, which was quite in line with Alexander's desire to turn all his attention to internal affairs. This pacifism was not limited to Western Europe alone, but expanded to the Eastern frontier as well, so that when Gruzia, pressed by Persia, appealed to Russia for annexation, the question was decided negatively by the Committee; in view of the insistence of the Permanent Council, however, Alexander had to revise his decision, but he prescribed that all the income from the population of Gruzia should be spent for local needs, and that Gruzia should be

governed according to native customs. Unfortunately the good
intentions of the young Tzar did not prevent the Russian
representatives in Gruzia — Knorring and Kovalensky — from
arousing against Russia the entire public opinion of Gruzia by
their revolting abuses and the violence of the first few months
of the Russian administration.

The relations with Napoleon, that had been quite favourable
at the beginning and were confirmed by a treaty in the fall of
1801, became tense by the end of the same year, partly because
of the hostile attitude toward Napoleon taken by the Russian
ambassador at Paris, the supercilious Count Morkov, and partly
because of Napoleon's resolution to wipe out the king of Sardinia, in defiance of his previous agreement with Alexander
on the matter. Besides, Alexander became more and more
inclined to think it necessary to curb the ambitions of Bonaparte. At the same time, having grown better acquainted with
international relations, and coming in personal contact with
foreign representatives at Petrograd (in spite of his friends'
efforts to prevent him from doing so), Alexander had evidently
discovered in himself — not without foundation — a diplomatic
talent and a great predilection for diplomatic negotiations; he
was probably attracted by the very technique of diplomatic relations. One may assume that even then he was guided by a
vague idea of liberating in the future Europe from the growing despotism and limitless lust for power of Napoleon.

In spite of the warnings of his friends Alexander decided to
take an active part in European affairs, and for a beginning he
arranged a meeting with the king of Prussia in Memel, in 1802.
In the same year he was completely convinced of Napoleon's
vulgar aspirations, when after another coup d'état he proclaimed
himself Consul for life. " The veil has fallen," wrote Alexander to La Harpe; " Napoleon has deprived himself of the
best glory which a mortal may achieve, the glory of proving
that he worked disinterestedly for the good of his country, and

remaining loyal to the constitution to which he swore allegiance, after ten years resign his power. Instead he has preferred to emulate monarchical courts, breaking thereby the constitution of his land. Henceforth he is the most prominent of the tyrants that we find in history."

At the same time the rights of the king of Sardinia were absolutely trampled down, and his possessions annexed to France. In 1803, on the renewal of his war with England, Napoleon seized Hanover and ostensibly threatened to become the dictator of the destinies of Central Europe. The personal relations of Napoleon and Count Morkov had become so unpleasant that Napoleon demanded his recall. Alexander did not meet the demand at once, and finally when recalling Morkov he rewarded him demonstratively with the highest Russian order, of Andrey the First Called, in which decoration Morkov appeared to take his leave from Napoleon. Russia did not appoint another ambassador to France, and the temporary management of the embassy's affairs was entrusted to a minor official, Oubri. The proclamation of Napoleon as emperor and the preceding execution of the Duke d'Enghien served as the last causes for a rupture.

From the aforesaid we see that the interests of Russia had in fact nothing to do with the story; in the whole affair Alexander acted not as a representative of Russian interests proper, but as a head of one of the European Powers. Having broken with Napoleon, Alexander became active in forming a coalition against him.

The management of foreign affairs was at that time in the hands of Prince Adam Czartoryski, since the Chancellor, Count A. R. Vorontzov, whom Alexander did not like, had resigned. Czartoryski sympathised with the idea of a coalition against Napoleon, in his hope that as one of the war's results might be the restoration of Poland. He tried to persuade Alexander that an armed resistance to Napoleon was not sufficient, that in view of his extraordinary genius and prestige of invincibility, it was necessary to arouse in the European nations a strong enthusiasm for a struggle against him. As an idea that might arouse such an enthusiasm Czartoryski put forth the principle of restoring the independence of nationalities. Alexander evidently agreed with such a formulation of the question, although in the mouth of Czartoryski the restoration of the Polish nationality meant the wresting from Russia of such ancient Russian lands as Volhynia and Podolia, for Czartoryski dreamt of Poland before the partition of 1772. At such a formulation of the question the war of 1805 against Napoleon was not only not aroused by Russian interests, but threatened to involve Russia in the future into a new territorial struggle, a struggle which had conditioned in the past centuries her backwardness and darkness. Pretending to share all the views of Czartoryski, Alexander, however, made peculiar use of the hopes of the Polish patriots. He encouraged them, though not binding himself with any definite promises, mainly with the view of compelling the vacillating king of Prussia to join the coalition against Napoleon under the threat of a Polish insurrection in Prussian Poland; as soon as he coerced Friedrich Wilhelm of Prussia into signing a treaty with him (it was not carried out after all), he declined to encourage the inflamed hopes of the Poles and indefinitely postponed the solution of the Polish question. By this reckless and incorrect behaviour Alexander aroused a bitter disappointment in the Poles and pushed them into the arms of Napoleon, who made good use of them.

In the war of 1805 Russia had to mobilise a considerable army, for on the Continent only Austrian and Russian troops actually fought against Napoleon. Three consecutive recruitments were required to get 150,000 men (ten recruits from every thousand males, but since the recruits were taken from among those of the age of twenty to thirty-five, the relation of the number of recruits to the number of that group of the population equalled 10:225). Besides, a new and considerable deficit had to be allowed in the budget, which had to be covered with a new issue of assignations.

Alexander acted in this case as a true autocrat who knew no obstacles to his will and was not responsible before any one. But we should note that Russian public opinion was all against Napoleon, and a war with him did not appear unreasonable, except to a few of his worshippers; Czartoryski's scheme was not generally known, and as to the people — they had been accustomed to bear even heavier burdens.

As it is well known, the war of 1805 ended very badly for Russia and Austria, chiefly because of the stupidity of the Austrian generals, and partly because of the inexperience and self-confidence of Alexander, who forced the chief commander Kutuzov to act against his convictions, but in accordance with the plan of the Austrian theoretic strategist, the doctrinaire Weiroter. After the capitulation of the Austrian army at Ulm and the subsequent defeat of the Russians in the Battle of Austerlitz — which was fought against the will and advice of Kutuzov, the Russian army had to retreat quickly towards the frontier, and the war was at an end. Austria concluded in Presburg a humiliating peace, while Prussia signed an offensive and defensive alliance with Napoleon.

Nevertheless Alexander began to make preparations for the continuation of the war; the defeat of the army created a patriotic mood in society, which Alexander tried to fan by direct appeals to the people. Desiring to reach the masses he employed a strong means, in the form of appeals of the Holy Synod, which were read in all churches. In those appeals Napoleon was declared an enemy of mankind, who intended to proclaim himself a Messiah, and arouse the Jews to annihilate the Christian Church.[1] Foreseeing the transference of the war into Russian territory, Alexander in addition to the mobilisation of recruits gave orders for calling a militia, which according to the original plan was to consist of 612,000 men. One can imagine the cost of such preparations. They were

[1] " The furious enemy of peace and blessed calm," thus began the proclamation of the Synod, " Napoleon Bonaparte, who wilfully usurped the royal crown of France and by force of arms, but mainly by treachery, has spread his power over numerous neighbourly states and has devastated their towns and villages with fire and sword, dares in the madness of his fury to threaten God protected Russia with an invasion of her territory, with destruction of her well-being which she alone in the whole world enjoys at present under the mild sceptre of by God blessed and by all beloved most pious Tzar Alexander the First, and with shocking the Orthodox Greco-Russian Church in all purity and sanctity blossoming in this Empire. . . ."

After an appeal to all shepherds of the church the Synod continued: " The whole world knows his Godless intentions and deeds by which he has trampled law and truth.

" Yet in the times of national disturbances that reigned in France during the Godless revolution, disastrous for mankind, which brought down the heavenly curse upon its instigators, he rejected the Christian faith, celebrated in popular assemblies pagan festivities instituted by evil-minded heretics, and in company with evil-doers he paid homage, due only to the Almighty, to statues, human creatures, and whores that served them as idols.

" In Egypt he associated with the persecutors of the Christian Church, preached the Alkoran of Mahomet, proclaimed himself defender of the creed of the followers of that false prophet, and solemnly demonstrated his contempt for the shepherds of the Holy Church of Christ.

" Finally to the greater shame of France he assembled there Jewish synagogues, ordered to pay honour to the Rabbins, and established a new great Jewish Synedrion, that same Godless congregation which once dared condemn to crucifixion our Lord and Saviour Jesus Christ, and now he attempts to unite the Jews scattered by Divine wrath over the whole earth, and to direct them for the overthrow of Christ's Church and for (O horrible impudence overstepping all his wickedness!) the proclamation of a false Messiah in the person of Napoleon. . . ."

After various vigorous curses and threats borrowed from the book of Deuteronomy, the proclamation reiterated in the end:

accompanied, especially in the western provinces, with the tax of carts by means of which munitions and provisions were brought to the front.

Although Prussia soon after the first treaty concluded a second with Napoleon, Alexander did not lose hope of arousing her against Bonaparte, who kept his army on German territory, refused to evacuate, and at the same time did not give his consent to the formation by the king of Prussia of a North-German union out of the states that were not included in the Rhenish Confederation. Prussia's rupture with Napoleon did take place, and sooner than Alexander had expected it. The weak Friedrich Wilhelm hesitated a long time, then suddenly sent an ultimatum to Napoleon, demanding the immediate evacuation of the French army and his non-interference in the organisation of the North-German union. All this happened so unexpectedly that Alexander did not have time for bringing his army to Prussia's aid. Napoleon gave no answer to the ultimatum, but began at once military activities, and after eight days delivered Prussia a terrible defeat at Jena. The main Prussian army was destroyed there, and after their second defeat at Auerstaedt almost all Prussia was occupied by the French. The Prussians held only two fortresses in the north-eastern corner of the kingdom — Danzig and Koenigsberg — behind which Friedrich Wilhelm had to seek refuge, in the little

" Having rejected the thought of God's judgement, Napoleon in his madness dreams about appropriating (the thought of which is horrible!) the holy name of Messiah with the aid of the enemies of Christ, the Jews; show him that he is a creature consumed by conscience and deserving scorn. . . ." In the same tone was the proclamation by the Catholic Metropolitan of Mohilev, Sestrentzevich, sent out to the Catholic priests of the western provinces. The local administration in western Russia was ordered to watch the Jews from communicating with the Paris Synedrion, and the Jews were persuaded that the Synedrion attempted to change their religion. It is curious that in 1812 the Jews of the western provinces remained absolutely loyal to Russia, in spite of all apprehensions.

town of Memel on the Niemen, on the very frontier of Russia. Poland had become the zone of the war, and Napoleon, wishing to counterpoise his own intentions to the hopes of the Poles in Alexander, made clever use of their disappointment caused by the treachery of 1805, and began to spread rumours that he would restore Poland as a bulwark against Russia.

The commander of the Russian army was the old Fieldmarshal Kamensky, who lost his reason immediately after his arrival at headquarters, and almost destroyed the army by his senseless orders; happily he withdrew voluntarily after one week, leaving an order to retreat with the utmost rapidity. The generals, however, decided to disobey him, and Benigsen concentrated the army at one point and successfully repulsed the French advance-guard under Pultusk, fifty versts from Warsaw, east of the Vistula. Benigsen was appointed commander-in-chief. In the battle of Eylau that followed soon, despite the loss of 50,000 men on both sides, both the French and the Russian armies retained their positions; the fact that a battle with such an opponent as Napoleon was not lost greatly uplifted the spirit of Benigsen's army. But five months after Napoleon decidedly defeated the Russian army at Friedland, with a loss of 15,000 men, after which the Russians could not continue the war. There was no hope of reinforcements, except for one division of infantry under Prince Lobanov-Rostovsky, which consisted entirely of fresh recruits; in the meantime war was declared against Turkey, and a part of the army had to withdraw to assist Michelson's army which had occupied Moldavia and Wallachia. As to the militia, in spite of its great numbers it proved quite useless; it might give great resistance in case of the enemy's invasion of Russia, in a guerrilla-war, but for the regular army the untrained and poorly armed militiamen were of no use.[2] It was particularly difficult to fill

[2] Bogdanovich states that only one-fifth of the militiamen could be equipped with rifles; the rest were to be armed with pikes. After

the enormous loss of officers and generals; of the latter there remained a very few good ones, and as to officers there had always been a dearth of them, so that their ranks had to be filled with unprepared students or with mere " fledglings " from among the nobility who consented to go through some instruction in the Cadet-Corpuses. Thus Russia was unable to continue the war alone; England took part in it only by subsidies, and even those were not too large — 2,200,000 pounds a year for all her continental allies. Alexander was forced to start peace negotiations in which he was met half way by Napoleon, who was also in great difficulties after the bloody battles of Eylau and Friedland.

The two emperors met at Tilsit, on the Niemen. There Alexander demonstrated for the first time his remarkable diplomatic talent, since Napoleon suggested carrying on the negotiations without the participation of their ministers, to which Alexander willingly consented. He had to employ strenuous efforts to dissuade Napoleon from completely annihilating Prussia. Still Prussia suffered unprecedented humiliation; she lost half of her territory, and from a Great Power was reduced temporarily to a dependency of Napoleon, with the right to maintain an army of not more than 42,000 soldiers, while the fortresses she retained were occupied by the French (until the payment of the war-contribution).

During the Tilsit negotiations Napoleon took into account no one except Alexander, with whom he intended to share for

the Pultusk battle Alexander ordered the militia decreased to 252 thousand. Roustam in his memoirs published in *Revue Retrospective* brings out the following fact: After the disorderly retreat of the Russians from the battle-field of Friedland, the French having reached the Niemen at Tilsit saw a quaint sight: " A horde of barbarians with Asiatic faces, Kalmucks and Siberians (?), without rifles, ran about the plain, shooting arrows and trying in vain to frighten us. This was the reserve-army under Prince Lobanov, of which Russia had boastfully announced to the world."

the time being the domination of the world. Alexander, seeing the impossibility of an immediate continuation of the struggle, decided to meet temporarily the desires of his rival, who
offered quite honourable conditions of peace. But as the *con-
ditio sine qua non* of the peace Napoleon demanded that in case
of England's refusal to accept his conditions — and that she
would not accept them was beyond doubt — Alexander had to
declare war against her, and at the same time to accept the
famous Continental System, which forbade Napoleon's allied
and dependent countries of Europe to have any trade relations
with England, or to admit to their ports English vessels. Besides this, Alexander obligated himself to compel Sweden and
Denmark to break with England and enter the Continental
System; one could have foreseen that Sweden, being absolutely
defenceless from the attack of England, would not consent,
and, moreover, King Gustave IV had manifested a fanatical
hatred for Napoleon. Thus one could have foretold even then
the inevitability of a joined attack of England and Sweden
against Russia both from sea and land in the vicinity of
Petrograd. The northern shore of the Gulf of Finland belonged at that time to Sweden, and Napoleon pointed out to
Alexander the strategic necessity for its conquest. In Tilsit,
then, was planned the annexation of Finland to Russia, for
which the latter had to carry on for two years a difficult war
with Sweden.

In regard to Turkey Napoleon offered his mediation for
a conclusion of peace on conditions favourable for Russia, and
in a verbal agreement he promised to uphold Alexander even
unto the partition of European Turkey, should the latter refuse
to surrender the principalities of Moldavia and Wallachia; but
as a preliminary condition for an armistice and for beginning
peace negotiations Napoleon required the evacuation of the
principalities by the Russian army, with the understanding that
they were not to be occupied by the Turks either. In fact

the war with Turkey did not cease, and although Napoleon continued to tempt Alexander with brilliant prospects of driving out the Turk from Europe and of undertaking a joint invasion of India, Russia had to carry on a fruitless war with Turkey until 1812.

Napoleon's intrigues and undertakings in regard to the Poles did Russia considerable harm; he refused to return to Prussia the conquered Polish districts, and formed out of them the Grand Duchy of Warsaw under the rule of the king of Saxony and under the protectorate of the French emperor. Thus Napoleon established a military post on the Russian frontier.[3] At the same time he placed Alexander in a difficult situation concerning the Poles, as he was forced to act in contradiction to his former declarations, and oppose the restoration of an independent Poland. This circumstance brought the final disappointment of the Poles in Alexander, and transferred all their hopes to Napoleon.

In Tilsit and after Tilsit Alexander manifested his admiration for the genius of Napoleon and his friendship with him. His contemporaries reproached him in having been hoodwinked by the sly Corsican who failed to fulfil many of his promises. But in fact Alexander was not infatuated with Napoleon; he skilfully played his part both in Tilsit and later in Erfurt, so that Napoleon called him later " the Talma of the North " (Talma was a well-known dramatic actor at that time) and " a Byzantine Greek."

It is difficult to say who was more deceived in that diplomatic tournament, for Napoleon's advisors told him later more than once that he was deceived by Alexander. From the point

---

[3] Napoleon's adorer, Albert Vandal, in his work "Napoleon and Alexander I" speaks on this matter: " Not intending to augment the victim of the triple partition into a strong power, he wishes to create in Europe — I do not say a Polish nation — but a Polish army, since he considers the projected state only as a big military force on the guard of France " (! — on the shores of the Vistula).

of view of the international relations of that time, and considering the actual conditions of the moment, we must admit that Alexander's policy in Tilsit and a year later in Erfurt was very clever. In those negotiations Alexander appeared for the first time in the rôle of a keen and far-seeing diplomat, and we may now presume that diplomacy was his real sphere, where he was able to cope with the most prominent statesmen of Europe.

The influence of those wars on the conditions of the population was grave. We have spoken about the burdens of recruitments, calling of militia, transportation of provision, etc. Of great importance was also the cessation of the Government's legislative activity on account of the war. Finally the disastrous state of the finances under the influence of the war-expenditures had greatly affected the Government's plans in the field of popular education which had so well advanced until then. As a consequence of the wars of 1805–7 and of the complete failure of crops in 1806, the financial conditions grew worse from year to year. In 1806 the income and the expenditures were 100 million and 122 million, in 1807 — 121 and 171 million, in 1808 — 111.5 million and 240 million, of which 140 million were spent on the army. The enormous deficits were again covered by new paper-issues, the total of which amounted in 1806 to 319 million rubles, in 1807 to 382 million, in 1808 to 477 million rubles. In the meantime foreign trade, under the influence of the war, and later of the Continental System and of the prohibition of exporting grain from the western provinces on account of the crop-failure of 1806, had diminished considerably; the export of raw material had suffered especially, and this caused an unfavourable turn in the balance of trade, hence an outflow of metal-money, to the further fall of the course of the paper-money. The paper-ruble, quite firm from 1802 to 1805, now began to depreciate rapidly: in 1806 its value fell to seventy-eight copecks, in

1807 — to sixty-six, in 1808 — to forty-eight copecks.   In the meantime taxes were paid in assignations, while a considerable portion of the state-expenses (for the maintenance of the army and for subsidies to the ruined king of Prussia) had to be paid in metal-money.   The situation was difficult, and after the Peace of Tilsit and the acceptance of the Continental System it became unbearable.   The Treaty of Tilsit had a depressing effect on all parts of Russian society and the masses; many considered it more ignominious than all the lost battles.   Alexander's popularity was greatly dimmed after his peace with Napoleon.   The people who not long before had heard in the churches anathemas hurled at Napoleon, could not understand how the Russian tzar so demonstratively showed his friendship for the "enemy of mankind" who had schemed to annihilate Christianity.

The dissatisfaction became general when the Continental System had completely destroyed the export trade, brought many firms to bankruptcy, ruined many estates that used to send raw material abroad (particularly flax and hemp in various forms), and raised the cost of living.[4]   According to his contemporaries Alexander's unpleasant and difficult rôle in his relations with Napoleon began to affect his temper; his customary politeness and evenness was supplanted by an irritable and often gloomy mood, while his natural obstinacy was manifested in a quite disagreeable form.   It is noteworthy that already in 1805, leaving for the war, Alexander confidentially ordered the secret-police system restored, by establishing a special temporary committee of three persons for the surveillance of public opinion. After the Treaty of Tilsit he made the committee official and permanent, and by a secret instruction gave it the right of mail-

[4] Especially the prices of colonial wares that had been imported up to that time from England rose tremendously. In 1808 a pud (a little over thirty-six pounds) of sugar was priced in Petrograd at one hundred rubles.

perlustration and other means of police supervision which during the first years of his reign he had abhorred.

At the head of those who opposed Alexander's " friendship " with Napoleon was the Dowager Empress Marie; Alexander had to play his part without being able to reveal his real intentions to any one. His closest friends — Kochubey, Czartoryski, Novosiltzev — resigned, and the last two went abroad, while Stroganov entered the army in order not to meddle with politics. Even his court-marshal, Count N. A. Tolstoy, expressed his disapproval of Alexander's friendship with Napoleon by refusing to wear alongside with the ribbon of the Legion of Honour given to him by the French emperor the ribbon of the highest Russian order — of Andrey the First Called — which Alexander wished to bestow upon him. The opposition of the higher circles of Petrograd society was most strongly manifested when there arrived Napoleon's military agent, General Savary, who had been personally connected with the execution of the Duke d'Enghien. The Petrograd salons shut their doors to him; he was received nowhere outside of the Winter Palace, and nobody called on him, until Alexander personally interceded and demanded from the courtiers a politer treatment of his ally's representative. Savary, eventually Napoleon's Minister of Police, decided to employ his police-talent right then and there. He carefully collected and fabricated all sorts of gossip and careless phrases dropped by persons dissatisfied with Alexander's policy, and even invented a story about a gigantic plot and attempted coup d'état, all of which he tried to communicate to the Tzar in his endeavour to bring friction between him and the public, and to fan the mutual mistrust that began to appear at that period between the young ruler and his subjects.[5]

[5] It is curious that other foreign diplomats in Petrograd (e.g., Baron Steding) and Canning in London (in his conversation with the Russian ambassador, Alopeus) repeated alarming rumours about

In wider circles dissatisfaction appeared in stronger forms, was expressed in literature and in theatres where the audience applauded vehemently patriotic passages and places that derided or attacked the French. Still stronger was the opposition in Moscow where the ardent patriot, S. N. Glinka, began to publish an anti-Napoleonic magazine, the *Russian Messenger*. Between the meetings at Tilsit and Erfurt, the very period when Alexander displayed before the world his friendship for Napoleon, Glinka wrote that the Peace of Tilsit was only a temporary armistice, that during the inevitable next war the Russians would strain all their efforts to repulse the power-fiend, Napoleon. The French ambassador called the attention of the Tzar to those writings, and as a result the patriot and conservative Glinka was the first to suffer from censorship-persecutions during Alexander's reign. About the same time Count Rastopchin, one of Paul's dignitaries, issued in Moscow a pamphlet under a pseudonym, in which the same ideas were put in a popular form, to attract the masses. In Petrograd Admiral Shishkov, an Old Believer, founded a patriotic literary society "Discourse," to which belonged Old Believers, conservatives like Derzhavin and Karamzin, and even liberals like Mordvinov.

It is worth noting that this opposition which had united quite broad circles and was so patriotic bore by no means a chauvinistic character. It was directed solely against Napoleon and the Tilsit Treaty with its disastrous effects on Russian trade, industry, and public life. Russia carried on four wars at that time, and in every case society remained quite indifferent, even hostile to the success of the Government's plans. Two of those wars (with weak Persia and with Austria; against the latter Alexander fought *à contre cœur* as an ally of Napoleon) [6]

attempted plots and revolutions in Petrograd. It is quite possible that those were results of Savary's intrigues and inventions.

[6] In 1809 after the Erfurt meeting, when Alexander saw the futility of his efforts to keep Austria from war with France in which he had

were comparatively easy, although they had also required considerable expenditures. But the other two wars were difficult and demanded enormous quantities of money and men. The war with Turkey continued with interruptions but with no peace conclusion from 1806 till the spring of 1812; the war with Sweden came after the Tilsit Treaty as a direct result of it, and after heroic heavy fighting it ended in 1809 with the conquest of Finland as far as the river Torneo.

Alexander determined to attract the hearts of his new subjects by magnanimity, and even before the conclusion of peace he summoned the Diet in Borgo and affirmed in a special charter the ancient rights and privileges of the Finnish population. Thus the legal conditions of Finland did not grow worse after the annexation, while the economic conditions of the province even improved at first, owing to the abolition of the tax which Finland had to pay for the extinction of the Swedish debt, and the abrogation of internal custom-houses.

But the Russian public disapproved of the peace of Friedrichsham, and there were even expressed condolences for Sweden. The war with Turkey also aroused opposition. In 1810 Mordvinov presented a memorandum in which he proved the uselessness of territorial acquisitions for Russia, whose frontiers were already too extended, and insisted on the necessity of an immediate cessation of the war with Turkey.

Such was the mood of the public after the Treaty of Tilsit.

formally agreed to aid Napoleon, said to the Austrian ambassador, Prince Schwarzenberg: ". . . My position is so strange that although we stand on opposite sides I cannot help wishing you success! . . ." The Russian public in 1809 openly rejoiced at every victory of their "enemies," the Austrians, and at every defeat of their "ally," Napoleon. (In the "Memoirs" of Wiegel, a contemporary of very moderate views.)

CHAPTER VIII

ALEXANDER was troubled by the general dissatisfaction of the people after the Treaty of Tilsit. He understood that the public mood could not be altered by police measures, and decided to regain the common goodwill by a nobler and more reasonable means — by returning to the work of internal reforms which had begun so promisingly at his accession. This time his chief co-operator came to be a new statesman, Mikhail Speransky, by intellect and talent undoubtedly the greatest man of Alexander's epoch, and perhaps the most remarkable statesman in all modern Russian history.

A son of a village-priest and a student of a theological Seminary, Speransky succeeded without any protection in rising to a prominent position, and acquiring a thorough knowledge of the best French political, economic, and juridical works. In four years he rose from a private secretaryship to Prince Kurakin to the rank of Imperial State-Secretary. The ministers Troshchinsky and Kochubey fought for Speransky, each desiring to have him in his department.

I have already mentioned Speransky's memorandum worked out by the request of Kochubey in 1803. Practically the same principles were laid as a basis for his famous plan for the re-organisation of the state, although, as we shall see, under the influence of his journey abroad (in 1808 to Erfurt) and in connection with Alexander's mood, Speransky's views had become more optimistic in regard to the readiness of the country for a constitutional order.

Although Alexander gave up his plan for an immediate constitutional reorganisation in 1802, he continued to keep others occupied with the idea. In 1804 he commissioned for this purpose Baron Rosenkampf who, by the way, knew no Russian at that time. His plan, called " Constitutional Cadre," was then handed over to Novosiltzev and Czartoryski, but in view of the war that broke out in 1805 the plan lay motionless until 1808, when among other materials it was brought before Speransky who received after his return from Erfurt an order from Alexander to work out a general plan for the reorganisation of the state. Korf relates, and Schilder repeats an anecdote about a conversation that supposedly took place between Alexander and Speransky in Erfurt, where Speransky became acquainted with Talleyrand and other notables of Napoleon's entourage. Alexander asked Speransky about his impression of Europe, and Speransky is alleged to have answered: " We have better men, but they have better institutions." Alexander agreed with him and added: " On our return we shall discuss the matter." In direct connection with this conversation they place the new reform-activity of 1809.

I hardly believe that the conversation took place. In Prussia there was no constitution at that time; her entire structure lay in ruins, and the Prussians had a task of building it up anew; in France there was only a ghost of a constitution, and all her " constitutional " institutions bore a charlatanic character. Alexander and Speransky knew it quite well, and we can hardly ascribe to Speransky the expression " We have better men, but they have better institutions "; besides he had no reason to give such a flattering opinion about the Russian men of affairs. It is much more probable to assume that Alexander intended to win back the lost sympathy of the people by way of renewing his former activity for the improvement of internal conditions. It is important to note the change in Speransky's own views since 1803: then he considered the radical reorganisation of the state unrealisable, while now he regarded it as quite feasible. This change could perhaps have occurred under the influence of his conversations with Talleyrand and others, and particularly under the influence of Alexander's new mood. Later, in his defence-letter from Perm, Speransky emphasised the fact that the fundamental idea about the reorganisation of the state had been given to him by Alexander himself.

In his " Plan," in the chapter on " The wisdom of state laws " Speransky discussed in detail the question of the timeliness of a radical reconstruction of the state. He observed that while in the West constitutions were wrested in " chunks " after cruel revolutions, the Russian constitution would owe its existence to the beneficial grace of the supreme authority, which consequently had the right to choose the proper time and forms for the reform. He examined the " timeliness " of the moment, and let himself dwell at length on historical-political investigations; he reduced all the existing political systems to three main forms: republic, feudal monarchy, and despoty. The Western European states since the crusades had gone through a process of struggle in the result of which the feudal form yielded more and more to the republican. As to Russia Speransky considered that she had already emerged from the purely feudal forms, since all her portions had been united under a single power. Regarding the constitutional attempts at the accession of Anna Joannovna and under Catherine II as " untimely," Speransky thought the present moment opportune for such a reform, in contradiction to his view in 1803. The presence of serfdom did no longer trouble him, for he considered a constitutional structure co-existable with unequal rights. For this reason his plan was based on a system of different class-rights, the distinct right of the nobility being the possession of bondage-estates. Thus the bondage-right appeared as one of the essential elements of the reorganised order. Political rights he allowed only for those citizens who had property.

Speransky considered as important preparatory steps for intro-

ducing the preparatory constitution, the permission for all classes
to buy land, the establishment of the class of Free Agriculturists,
the law concerning the Lifland peasants, and the founding of responsible ministries (though he knew well the value of that
responsibility, as we have seen). Of more importance is Speransky's admission of the significance of public opinion. As
symptoms of the ripeness of the moment he recognised the dis-
appearance of respect for ranks, orders, and other external signs
of authority, the fall of the moral prestige of the authorities,
the growing spirit of criticism in regard to the Government's
activity. He observed that under such conditions it would be
impossible to promulgate partial improvements of the existing
system, and came to the conclusion that the moment had arrived
for a change of the old order of things. These considerations of
Speransky, approved by Alexander himself, are of great value
for us; they testify to the consciousness of the Government that
there had developed elements intent to participate in the management of the state.

Speransky recommended two ways out of the situation: one
insincere, fictitious, and another, sincere,— a radical way. The
first consisted in lending the autocracy an external form of legality, leaving its essential power intact; the other way recommended " not only to conceal the autocracy behind external
forms, but to limit it by an intrinsic and substantial force of
statutes, and to base the ruling power on law not only in words
but in very deed." Speransky insisted that at the very approach to carrying out the reforms they had to choose definitely
one way or the other. For the fictitious reform use could be
made of institutions which, possessing an apparent freedom of
legislative power, would in fact remain under the influence and
complete dependence of the autocracy. At the same time the executive power could be so instituted that " by the *wording* of the
law it would bear responsibility, but by its *sense* it would be absolutely independent." The judicial power would be given all

advantage of *visible* freedom, but *in essence* it would be always subject to the autocracy. As an example of such a fictitious-constitutional state Speransky pointed out Napoleon's France.

If, on the contrary, the second alternative was to be chosen, the appearance of the state-structure would be entirely different. In the first place the legislative institutions would in that case have to be so built that although they could not carry through their enactments without the confirmation of the Monarch, yet their judgments would be free and really express the popular opinion; in the second place the judicial department would have to be so formed that its existence would be based on free election, and the Government would only supervise the fulfilment of its decisions; in the third place the executive power would have to be responsible before the legislative power.

" Comparing these two systems," explained Speransky, " we can see beyond doubt that the first has only an appearance of law, while the second is its very essence; the first — under the pretence of a single authority — introduces complete absolutism, while the second seeks indeed to limit and moderate it. . . ."

Thus the question was put so clearly and straight that Alexander was unable to proceed with his customary dreamy indefiniteness, and he had to make a serious choice. He chose the second system. Speransky worked out a corresponding plan of reorganisation, and after two months of almost daily discussion between the two Alexander ordered in the fall of 1809 the beginning of its realisation.

According to the Plan the fundamental territorial units were based on the administrative division of the country, i.e., provinces were subdivided into districts, and districts into *volosts*. Each *volost* was to have a *Volost Duma* composed of delegates from Fiscal peasants (one from five hundred) and of private landowners. The *Duma* would be renewed once in three years. The chief objects of the *Volost Duma* would be (1) the election of officers for the *volost* administration, (2) the control of the *volost* income and expenditures, (3) the election of delegates for the District-*Duma*, (4) the presentation of *volost*-needs before the District-*Duma*. The District-*Duma* was to consist of delegates elected by the *Volost-Dumas;* its jurisdiction corresponded with that of the *Volost-Duma*, but it concerned the affairs of the district; it elected delegates to the Provincial *Duma*, the District-Court, and the District-Council. The Provincial *Duma* was proposed to have an analogous jurisdiction, and to send delegates to the State-*Duma* which was to assemble every year in Petrograd. According to Speransky's plan the sessions of the State-*Duma* could be postponed by the Monarch for one year; but its prorogation could take place only upon the election of delegates for the next *Duma*. The chairman of the State-*Duma* was to be the State-Chancellor, i.e., an appointed person; the work was to be performed by commissions. The right of legislative initiative was to belong exclusively to the Monarch, with the exception of presentations about national needs, about the responsibility of officials, and about decrees that might infringe upon the fundamental state-laws. The Senate was to become the supreme court and consist of life-members to be elected by the Provincial *Dumas* and confirmed by the Monarch.[1]

Above the State-*Duma* the Plan proposed to institute the State Council out of the highest dignitaries selected by the Monarch, which was to be not a second legislative chamber, as it is at present, but an advisory institution under the Monarch for the discussion of new projects presented by the ministers and of proposed financial measures before bringing them to the State-*Duma*.

Such were the general features of Speransky's plan approved in principle by Alexander. We shall not discuss its weak sides, for it was not put into practice. Alexander admitted its de-

---

[1] Compare Speransky's Plan with the Duma-statutes of Nicolas II, in the supplementary chapters to volume two.— TR.

sirability and usefulness, but he decided to introduce it only in parts. At first was published the new statute about the ministries and the State Council as an advisory institution. The State Council did not receive its preparatory character as originally designed by Speransky, which could take place only after the realisation of the whole Plan; it was divided into four departments — the department of civil and church affairs, the departments of laws, of war, and of national economy. Each department had at its head a state-secretary. Speransky was appointed Imperial Secretary; in his hands were concentrated besides the matters of the State Council all the threads of the reform-measures and of the whole legislative activity.

The project of the State Council was shown before its publication to several influential dignitaries, such as Zavodovsky, Lopukhin, Kochubey, and others, and all of them approved it, not knowing the ultimate purpose of Speransky with regard to the rôle of the State Council. But despite Speransky's efforts to remain outside of any parties, there was formed against him a strong opposition among the officials, nobles, and courtiers. The hostility was aggravated after the issue of two ukases, April 3, and August 6, 1809 — which were credited to Speransky's influence. The first ukase prescribed that all persons with court-titles chose some state-service; thenceforward court-titles were considered only as honourable distinctions and gave no service-rights. The other ukase, with a view of improving the personnel, required that the titles of Collegiate Assessor and Councillor of State were given only to those who had passed a certain examination and had presented a university diploma.

The bureaucratic and court-circles were indignant about those ukases, and they began a campaign of intrigue against Speransky, finally succeeding in overthrowing that remarkable statesman. The nobles blamed him for the deplorable state of the finances, which was due, of course, not to Speransky's policy, but to the growing budgets and increasing paper-issues connected with the results of the Continental System.

I have said that after the Treaty of Tilsit in 1808 the income of the state equalled one hundred and eleven million rubles in assignations or about fifty millions in silver, while the expenses reached two hundred and forty-eight million rubles in assignations. The deficit was covered by a new issue of assignations the course of which in that year was below fifty copecks per ruble, and during the summer months it fell below forty copecks. In the next year, 1809, the course in the average did not exceed forty copecks, and by the end of the year it descended to thirty-five copecks; the income of that year equalled one hundred and ninety-five million rubles in assignations (less than eighty million in silver), and the expenses — two hundred and seventy-eight million rubles in assignations (about one hundred and fourteen million in silver). The deficit was again covered by a new issue of assignations, but they had no circulation; the market refused to accept such a quantity of paper-money. Toward the end of 1810 their course fell below twenty copecks. The country faced bankruptcy. In this difficult situation Alexander turned to Speransky in 1809.

We have seen the influence of the limitation of the market and of the diminished trade-turnover on the fall of the course of the paper-money. The limitation of the market was conditioned by the Continental System which stopped the export of flax and hemp to England, which formed then about half of the Russian export trade. At the same time the custom tariff was very unfavourable for the development of the big industries, since in view of the insignificant duties on foreign commodities the Russian manufacturers could not compete with the foreigners. Besides, owing to the prevalence of import over export, the balance of trade was very unfavourable: Russia had to pay for the imported commodities with metal-money, while the small export brought an insignificant sum of metal-money.

Hence there was an enormous outflow of money abroad, and at home remained only assignations which continually depreciated. Then, the Russian court gave big subsidies to the king of Prussia. Finally Russia carried on four wars during those years: a long war with Persia (from 1804 to 1813) ; with Turkey the war spasmodically fell and rose for six years (from 1806 to 1812); the war with Sweden, which ended with the annexation of Finland (1808–1809) ; finally by virtue of her alliance with Napoleon Russia had to take part in the war against Austria (1809). True the last war was a bloodless farce (by orders from above the Russian troops evaded the Austrians), yet it cost considerable money.

These causes — the unfavourable balance of trade and the necessity of maintaining an army abroad on metal-money — were responsible for the difficult conditions of the treasury.

Nominally the budget increased from year to year, but in fact it constantly fell. For instance, the maintenance of the court in 1803 cost eight million six hundred thousand rubles, or in silver — seven million eight hundred thousand rubles; in 1810 the expenses of the court equalled fourteen million five hundred thousand rubles in assignations, but in silver it amounted only to four million two hundred thousand rubles; thus the actual budget of the court decreased in those years by forty-five per cent. Below are the figures of the budget of the Ministry of Popular Education (in millions of rubles) :

Years	In assignations:	In silver:
1804	2.8	2.3
1809	3.6	1.144
1810	2.5	0.727

Thus the budget of the Ministry of Education had diminished almost four times in six years. Under such circumstances there could be no question about opening new schools: even the old ones could scarcely exist, and that only by way of paying the teachers in assignations, as all officials were paid then; imagine their position when the cost of all commodities increased four times, and some (colonial wares) even considerably more!

The national treasury faced a collapse, and the country grew alarmed and dissatisfied. It was then that Speransky, who had just finished his plan for the general reorganisation of the state, received the order of the Tzar to take up immediately the financial question. Speransky had long ago become interested in financial affairs, and now he made a thorough study of them with the aid of the young scholars, Professors Balugiansky and Jacob, who had been recently invited from abroad. Soon he presented an exhaustive memorandum on the state of finances and on the necessary improvements, which he submitted for a preliminary discussion to an unofficial assembly of all those statesmen who had some financial knowledge. Among them were Count Severin Potocky, Admiral Mordvinov, Kochubey, State-Comptroller Kampfenhausen, and Speransky's close assistant, Balugiansky.

Towards the first of January, 1810 — the opening of the State-Council — Speransky presented to Alexander a complete plan for a financial reorganisation, the essence of which consisted in the finding of measures for making the state income correspond with the state expenditures. Since the fiscal income had actually decreased owing to the fall of the course of paper-money, Speransky proposed first of all to discontinue the further issue of assignations, to recognise those already issued as a state-debt, and to take steps for the gradual extinction of that debt by way of redemption. He offered the following measures for getting the necessary means: (1) to decrease the deficit by cutting the current expenses, even for such useful needs as popular education, improving ways of communication, and so forth; (2) to introduce a new tax for the exclusive purpose of extinguishing the national debt; (3) to make an internal loan under the pledge of state-property; a part of the state-property he even proposed to sell. He asserted that such a loan, made for a certain length of time and secured by definite property, would not play the rôle of an assignation loan. But as all those measures were not sufficient, the more so since the wars with Turkey and Persia still continued, Speransky proposed a special tax of fifty copecks from every soul on the landowners' and state-estates, for one year only. In general he claimed that deficits should be covered as much as possible by percentage additions to the existing taxes, so that the people could immediately cover the current deficits without leaving their burdens for the coming generations. For the improvement of credit-conditions and the regularisation of political economy Speransky proposed to introduce regulated reports and publicity in the management of national economy. The last reform was carried through only as late as in the sixties. Seeing one of the main reasons for the fall of the paper-course in the unfavourable balance of trade, Speransky, with the energetic support of Mordvinov, president of the department of national economy, insisted on the revision of the custom tariff. He argued that the conditions accepted in Tilsit concerning the Continental System should be interpreted in a limited sense, since Napoleon had intended to ruin England, not Russia, whereas the contrary was the result. In accordance with the suggestion of Speransky and Mordvinov it was decreed in 1810 that all Russian ports were free for vessels under neutral flags, regardless of whose goods they carried. On the other hand, by the new tariff of 1810 the import of luxuries was forbidden, and high duties were placed on other foreign manufactures; that tariff was to decrease the import, while the opening of the ports at once renewed the export of raw materials and certain manufacturers (flax and hemp cloth) to England, whose ships were not long in arriving under the Teneriffe flag. Both these circumstances brought about a very favourable balance of trade for Russia, and if Speransky's plan had been followed in toto, the course of the paper ruble would undoubtedly have risen. Unfortunately in 1810 were issued new assignations for the sum of forty-three million rubles. Although that issue was made on the basis of a previous decree it nevertheless fundamentally destroyed all Speransky's measures and the confidence of the public, so that the course continued to fall: during 1811 it never rose above twenty-three copecks, while at certain months it fell below twenty copecks. But the tariff played an enormous rôle in the economic life of the country; one may say that it had saved Russia from complete ruination. Yet the measures that were taken by the State Council not only did not bring Speransky the gratitude of his contemporaries, but even enhanced the hatred of wide circles of nobles and officials for him.

The conclusions which the public had drawn from Speransky's financial plans were quite discouraging. It had become clear (1) that the condition of the finances was deplorable, (2) that the treasury had been involved in considerable internal loans (it was news for many, since few had understood before that the issues of assignations were equivalent to loans), and (3) that there were no means for the ordinary expenditures in 1810, in view of which new taxes and loans had to be applied. The last conclusion was the most disagreeable, as the position of the tax-payers, especially of the landowners, was unenviable even if no new burdens had been lain upon them. This dissatisfaction was stupidly directed not against those who had caused the financial ruin, but against the one who had opened the eyes of the public to the real state of affairs. The irritation of the nobles at the new taxes on their estates grew more bitter when it appeared that in spite of all burdens the course of the assignations continued falling. The tax that had been intended for the extinction of the debt was used for current expenses which increased greatly in view of the expected war with Napoleon, so that the public had a plausible reason for accusing the State Council and the author of its plan in having simply deceived them.

As I said, Speransky was blamed for the failure of his plan, the carrying out of which fell into the hands of the inefficient Minister of Finances, Guriev; there were even rumours that Speransky had invented his plan with the purpose of irritating the opposition, and that he was in criminal relations with Napoleon. Alexander was unable to hold out against the attack of Speransky's enemies. He deemed it necessary at that time to raise the patriotic sentiment of the people, regardless of the form in which it was expressed, for he hoped to repulse Napoleon only in case the war had a popular character; he saw no way of entering into explanations and decided to sacrifice his best co-operator to the wrath of the privileged mob. In March of 1812 Speransky was discharged and exiled to Nizhni-Novgorod, and later on the basis of a new insinuation, to Perm, although Alexander could not have doubted that Speransky had committed no serious crime. His only guilt consisted in having received through a certain official copies of all important secret papers of the Ministry of Foregin Affairs, which in his position he could have easily received by getting the Tzar's permission.

The hatred of the public for Speransky had found a strong expression in the famous memorandum of Karamzin " On ancient and modern Russia," which was presented to Alexander through the Grand Duchess Catherine Paulovna. In it Karamzin gave a brief picturesque sketch of Russian history, praised Catherine II to heaven, spared no dark colours for the reign of Paul, as we have seen already, and vigorously condemned the reforms of Alexander. " Russia is seething with dissatisfaction," he wrote, " they grumble in palaces and in huts; there is no confidence, no loyalty to the Government; its aims and measures are severely condemned. An astonishing phenomenon! It is customary for a successor of a cruel monarch to gain general approval upon mitigating his predecessor's régime; how explain the deplorable state of minds among the people pacified by Alexander's mildness, enjoying all civil rights, fearing neither the Secret Chancery nor Siberia? — By the unfortunate circumstances in Europe, and by the important, in my opinion, mistakes of the Government; for even with good intentions one may err in the means for bringing happiness. . . ."

The main fallacy of Alexander's inexperienced law-givers, according to Karamzin, consisted in their undertaking organic reforms instead of perfecting Catherine's institutions. Karamzin had no mercy for the State Council or for the new ministries, or even for the educational measures of the government, which he had praised some time before in his *European Messenger*. In place of all reforms he recommended the appointment of fifty good governors and the securing for the people of adequate spiritual shepherds. In regard to the ministerial responsibility he wrote: "Who selects the ministers? — The Tzar. Then let him reward the deserving ones with his grace and remove the bad ones without noise. A bad minister is a monarchical error: such errors should be corrected, but secretly, in order that the people have confidence in the Tzar's personal selection. . . ."

In the same way Karamzin argued against the uncalled for confessions of the Government regarding the bad financial conditions. Concerning the superabundant issue of assignations in former years he remarked: "When an inevitable evil has been done, one should deliberate and take measures quietly, not whimper, not beat the tocsin, which increase the evil. Let the ministers be sincere before the Tzar alone, but not before the people; God beware if they will follow a different rule: to deceive the Tzar and reveal the truth to the people. . . ." (!) Karamzin agreed to the redemption of assignations, but the declaration of the assignations as a state-debt he considered the height of thoughtlessness. The naïveté of Karamzin's argument is remarkable: as if he did not understand that if secrecy in the management of affairs existed it would be easiest for the ministers to deceive the Monarch.

A curious feature of Karamzin's memorandum is its noble's point of view. Not of course the point of view of the constitutionalist-nobles, not that of the liberals of his time, from the noble Mordvinov to the commoner Speransky, but the point of view followed and promulgated by Catherine, namely that the nobility was the first class in the state and its relations to other classes, among them to bonded peasants, were inviolable, while in regard to the autocracy of the sovereign the nobles had to be submissive and loyal servants.

The presence of general dissatisfaction in the country Speransky ascribed to the ripeness of the public for a radical reorganisation of the form of government; whereas Karamzin explained it by the failure of the new reforms. Both of them were wrong: the dissatisfaction had more real reasons — it was rooted in the fallacious foreign policy that brought about the unnecessary, at least from the point of view of the contemporaries, war of 1805–1807, the Continental System and its resultant ruination of the country, and finally the Tilsit humiliation which offended the national honour and aroused a keen patriotic opposition to the friendship of Alexander with Napoleon. Karamzin did mention those circumstances in passing, but he did not allow them the primary significance which they undoubtedly had.

It is curious that Speransky's enemies tried, and one must say not without considerable success, to spread the information that he intended to introduce in Russia the Code of Napoleon, that he was an admirer of Napoleon, if not his agent. The success of those insinuations can be explained by the strength of the patriotic protestantism that dominated society at that time.

Before passing to the next period I must say a few words about the condition of popular education at that time. The activity of the Ministry of Education, which had well developed in the preceding period, especially in the years 1803-4, came to a standstill for lack of means. Yet private societies and literature continued to grow. A number of literary and philanthropic societies were founded. Besides Shiskov's "Russian Discourse" we should mention the "Society of Lovers of Russian Letters" founded by Yazykov at the university of Moscow; the "Society of Lovers of Mathematics," founded by Mikhail Muraviov at the age of fifteen, which later developed into a free school and served as the cradle of the Russian General Staff; many of the members of the secret societies in the twenties were educated in that school. At the university of Moscow was opened by Professor Chebotarev a "Society of Russian History and Antiquities"; at the same university was founded in 1804 by Count A. K. Razumovsky the "Society of Nature Experimentators," which still enjoys a deserved fame. Such societies were opened even in the provinces; for instance, in Kazan was founded in 1806 a "Society of Lovers of Russian Letters," which had in 1811 a membership of thirty-two.

CHAPTER IX

WE have observed the conditions in Russia after the Treaty of Tilsit — the third period of Alexander's reign. The alliance with Napoleon was intolerable for Russia not only because it conflicted with national consciousness and pride, but also because it destroyed the economic forces and the welfare of the Russian state and people. Napoleon, while forcing Russia to waste her forces fruitlessly in wars with England, Sweden, Turkey, and Austria, sharpened at the same time the Polish question in a way quite dangerous for Russia. The relations of the Poles to Alexander became increasingly unhappy, while as devoted allies of Napoleon in his war against Austria in 1809 they received by the treaty after the battle of Wagram a considerable territorial addition to the Grand Duchy of Warsaw at the expense of Galicia, with a population of over one and a half million; at the same time Russia received but a small portion of Galicia, the district of Tarnopol, with a population of only four hundred thousand. True, Alexander was in no need of territorial acquisitions; but the Russian Government could not remain indifferent to the growth of the hostile Duchy, the more so since it learned the secret views and plans of Napoleon from the confidential report of Duroc, obtained from the French Ministry of Foreign Affairs by Ambassador Prince Kurakin. Duroc had definitely declared in his report that Napoleon's domination of Europe would not be firmly based as long as even in one country there reigned a Bourbon, as long as Austria was not excluded from the German Empire, and as long as Russia was not weakened and repulsed beyond the Dnieper and Western Dvina. With equal definiteness Duroc condemned the acquiescence of the former French government in the partition of Poland, and recommended the restoration of the frontiers of 1772, as a necessary bulwark against Russia. The report naturally alarmed the Russian Ministry of Foreign Affairs; but since it could not refer to a stolen document, the Russian Government based its apprehensions and complaints concerning the Polish question on the territorial aggrandisements of the Duchy of Warsaw in formal violation of one of the statutes of the Tilsit Treaty. To appease Alexander on this point Napoleon agreed to a special treaty with Russia, by which both emperors mutually guaranteed to oppose the restoration of an independent Polish state. But when such a treaty was concluded by the French representative, Caulaincourt, and the Russian Minister, Rumiantzev, Napoleon declined to ratify the document, alleging that Caulaincourt had overstepped his powers. His refusal came immediately after the failure of his negotiations for marrying one of Alexander's sisters, Anna Paulovna; some historians see an inner connection between those two events. But the reason evidently lay not in the unsuccessful wooing which had not even begun formally, but in the fact that Napoleon was decidedly unwilling to alter his policy in regard to the Polish question, and simply tried to gain time, since in view of his failures in Spain he was not ready for a war with Russia. At the same time he drove out the Duke of Oldenburg from his own territory, on account of the Duke's failing to observe strictly the Continental System. The house of Oldenburg had received that territory from their older line, the house of Holstein-Gotorp, after the latter had become connected with the Russian reigning dynasty, beginning with Peter III. Alexander, as a representative of that house, considered himself personally insulted, and after failing in his negotiations for the compensation of the Duke with some other territory, he sent a protesting circular to all European courts. Napoleon took the protest as a *casus belli,* and if he did not immediately declare war, it was because he was still not ready for it. Finally Russia's violation of the Continental System by the acceptance of Speransky's plan, and particularly the tariff of 1810, which directly affected the pockets of the French merchants and manufacturers, appeared to be the most important circumstances in which Napoleon could not acquiesce.

By the beginning of the year 1812 the war between France and Russia was inevitable. It was clear that in that "last struggle" between Alexander and Napoleon, Austria, and especially Prussia, not to mention the other states that were subjected by France, could not remain neutral. Prussia might side with Russia in case Russia led an offensive campaign and threw her armies across the Niemen before Napoleon had time to draw there sufficient forces. But Russia was not in position to do it, as the Poles would have given an energetic opposition from the very first, while the Prussian fortresses had remained in the hands of the French since 1806, so that Napoleon could have definitely destroyed Prussia before Alexander had time to come to her help. Besides, the war with Turkey had not come to an end until the spring of 1812, and on the whole, the forces which Russia could move against Napoleon were considerably inferior to those that he was able to draw to the Vistula, even not counting the Austrian and Prussian armies. Thus a Russian offensive was unthinkable.

Before the outbreak of the war, however, Napoleon suffered two important diplomatic fiascoes. He failed to draw into the coalition against Russia either Sweden or Turkey.

He failed to win over Sweden — in spite of his promise to restore Finland and even the Baltic (Ostsee) provinces — first of all because Sweden was unable to fight against England, who of course renewed her alliance with Russia immediately after Russia had broken away from France; besides, the provoking actions of Napoleon's agents in Swedish Pomerania

strongly aroused the Swedes against France; finally Berna-
dotte, Sweden's heir-elect, being of old Napoleon's rival, refused to enter into an alliance with him. On the contrary,
after a meeting with Alexander in the summer of 1812 Berna-
dotte concluded with him a friendly agreement by which the
Russian emperor promised to assist in the annexation of Nor-
way to Sweden as a compensation for Finland. Owing to this
treaty Alexander was not only relieved from apprehensions
about an attack from that side (which would have threatened
Petrograd), but he was enabled to withdraw his troops from
Finland and employ them against Napoleon.

As to Turkey, the new Russian commander, Kutuzov, succeeded early in 1812 in decisively defeating the Turks, after
which and in view of the continued internal disturbances in
Turkey they were unable to continue the war. In May,
1812, Kutuzov signed in Bucharest a peace with Turkey, at a
most opportune moment — two weeks before the entrance of
Napoleon's army into Russia. Although now there could no
longer be any chance of the annexation of Moldavia and Wallachia — to which Napoleon gave his conditional consent at
Tilsit and Erfurt — still by that peace Russian territory was
enlarged by the addition of Bessarabia, with the river Prut.
True, in making the treaty Kutuzov neglected some of Alexander's instructions: Alexander had insisted on demanding
from Turkey as an indispensable condition of peace its conclusion of a defensive and offensive alliance with Russia, or at
least a secure passage for the Russian army through Turkish
territory to Napoleon's Illyria. Kutuzov's relinquishment of
those demands was of great service, since less than one month
after the peace with Turkey Napoleon's army was on Russian
territory.

To such an experienced general as Kutuzov it was clear
even then that the coming war was to be defensive, not offensive: one had to think not of sending troops to Illyria, ac-

cording to the dreams of Alexander and the ambitious Admiral Chichagov who was sent to the Southern army in place of Kutuzov, but of concentrating all defensive forces against the enormous enemy whom, even then, many considered it possible to defeat only by drawing him far into the depths of Russia. The " Scythian " plan, which consisted in evading serious battles, but in fighting off attacks, and constant retreating, leaving behind devastated and ruined places,— had been in many minds before the war of 1812. There was nothing new about the method which was known in ancient times (since Darius of Persia); but for the realisation of such a plan it was necessary that the war became national, for only the people could burn their own houses, not the army, which in doing so against the wish of the population would acquire a new enemy in them.

Alexander understood this well. Aware of the danger and responsibility of a war with Napoleon, and at the same time of its inevitability, he hoped that the war on Russian territory would become not less popular than that in Spain. The importance of a popular war Alexander appreciated even before the Spanish failure of Napoleon: he tried even in 1806, as you remember,— and not without success — to arouse the population against Napoleon, not scrupling about means. Yet a " Scythian " war was well adapted for Scythians; while in a land that stood even on such a stage of culture as Russia of those days, such a war was combined with terrible sacrifices. Moreover, the devastation had to begin from the western region, the most cultured and populated, and but recently annexed to Russia. Finally the necessity and inevitability of a " Scythian " war, in spite of its popularity, was not understood by all.

Towards the beginning of the year 1812 Napoleon was in a position to concentrate on the Russian frontier with the aid of all his allies and vassals about four hundred thousand men, and could add soon after one hundred and fifty thousand more. Russia was able to draw to the border not more than two hundred thousand men. This alone made an offensive war impossible, even disregarding Napoleon's genius and the talents and experience of his generals. Yet Alexander did not lose hope of prevailing in the long run over his enemy. On the very eve of the war he frankly said to one of Napoleon's messengers, General Narbonne, that he appreciated all the advantages of the French, but that he reckoned on his side *space and time;* his words ultimately came true, and " space and time," combined with his own firmness and perseverance and those of all Russia, did give him a complete triumph.

The original plan of the campaign consisted in slowly retreating before Napoleon, retaining him at positions convenient for giving resistance, and at the same time attempting to attack his flanks and rear. For this reason the Russian forces were divided into two armies, of which one under the command of the Minister of War, Barclay de Tolly, one of the heroes of the Finland campaign, was to retreat, to resist at fortified positions, and to draw Napoleon gradually into the heart of the country; the other army, commanded by Bagration, one of Suvorov's generals, was to harass the enemy's flanks and rear. The army of Barclay was concentrated more to the north (in the province of Vilna), and that of Bagration, more to the south (south of Grodno). But about half of Bagration's army — nearly forty thousand men — had to be sent at once against the Austrians and other allies of the French, who invaded Volhynia through Galicia. At the same time Barclay had to set aside a considerable corps under the command of Witgenstein for the defence of the Ostsee (Baltic) provinces and the road to Petrograd. For this reason, and in view of the fact that the Drissa fortifications on the Western Dvina were found to be in wretched condition, Barclay's forces were quite insufficient for checking Napoleon's advance.

After the separation of Witgenstein's corps from Barclay, and of several divisions of Bagration for the aid of Tormasov, Barclay's army consisted of eighty thousand, Bagration's of less than forty thousand, and Napoleon by cutting the communications between the two armies could defeat them singly, one after the other. Towards this were directed his efforts after his moving out of Vilna early in July. In view of this danger the Russian armies had to unite as soon as possible, and to give up their original plan. To prevent this Napoleon attempted to outflank Barclay under Vitebsk. Barclay understood Napoleon's intention, and endeavoured to unite with Bagration at Vitebsk. Napoleon's plan failed owing to the quick march of Barclay from Drissa to Vitebsk and to the brave resistance of a small corps under the command of Count Osterman-Tolstoy that was ordered to keep off the main forces of the French; but Barclay did not succeed in uniting with Bagration at Vitebsk, since under the furious attack of Davout, Bagration had to withdraw to Smolensk, where the Russian armies finally came together. A considerable battle took place there; the Russians evacuated Smolensk only after the enemy's cannonade had reduced it to a heap of burning ruins. Immediately after Smolensk Napoleon attempted to repulse the Russian army from the Moscow road to the north, and thus cut it off from the fertile southern provinces, but in this attempt he also failed and was forced to abandon his idea after a bloody battle at the Valutin Hill on the Moscow road.

In spite of the swift, aggressive attack of Napoleon's army and the almost uninterrupted retreat of the Russians who left behind them burned and devastated lands, the position of Napoleon grew with every step more difficult and perilous. After the battle at the Valutin Hill Napoleon even considered stopping for the winter at Smolensk; but the waste land around the ruined city did not appeal to him, and he determined to move on to the heart of Russia, Moscow, where he hoped to

dictate terms of peace to the defeated enemy. In the meantime his army melted. Already at Vilna he had about fifty
thousand sick soldiers. His main army, which had consisted —
with the subtraction of the corps of Macdonald and Oudinot,
later enforced by the division of St. Syr, that were to march
against Petrograd and the Ostsee provinces — of three hundred thousand men, had lost by the time of entering Vitebsk
nearly one hundred thousand in battles and from sickness, i.e.,
the army was diminished by one-third; after Smolensk and
the Valutin Hill not more than one-half of the original number remained in the ranks.

The Russians retreated in good order, fighting furiously.
Their resistance was costly both for them and for Napoleon.
When under the attack of Napoleon's enormous army Osterman-Tolstoy was asked by his adjutants, what there remained
to do, he answered: "To stand and die!" Such was the
mood of the army. The heroic resistance of Nievierovsky's
division of recruits, which held back the entire cavalry of Murat
during the retreat of Bagration, and Raievsky's short but
glorious defence of Smolensk against Napoleon's main forces
are well known. One must bear in mind that while Napoleon's
losses were irretrievable, the losses of the Russians who retreated into the country could be considerably replenished by
reserves.

If Alexander understood clearly the responsibility of the
war, Napoleon had also foreseen all the difficulties in store,
particularly in regard to forage and provision, and for this
reason he had stored up early in 1812 an enormous amount
of provisions at Danzig, which should have kept his army for
a whole year. But these provisions required a train of ten
thousand carts, a big burden for the marching army; the train
had to be constantly guarded from Cossack-raids. Having
prepared provisions for the soldiers Napoleon nevertheless could
not start the campaign till the middle of May, and remained

motionless on the Russian border for lack of provender for his horses that amounted to more than one hundred and twenty thousand; he had to wait till the middle of May, when the fields could offer some forage. This forced delay eventually proved very costly.

Thus the difficulties did not surprise Napoleon; he knew them and yet determined to achieve his purpose. One must say he did reach his purpose: he took Moscow. But there disappointment awaited him. He had underrated the force of popular resistance; he understood it when in Moscow, but it was too late for making repairs.

Looking back with the eye of a historian upon the war of 1812 and its outcome, one can easily see that Napoleon's chances began to fall at the very start, and fell constantly; but contemporaries did not understand this at once; they only knew that Napoleon was advancing, and the Russians retreating. Such a course of affairs aroused despondency in the population and grumbling in the army, which craved a general battle. The grumbling grew also from the fact that at the head of the army stood a German; the generals intrigued against Barclay de Tolly, and even gossiped about his being a traitor. The matter was complicated by unfriendliness between Barclay and Bagration; although formally Bagration submitted to Barclay, he commanded his army independently. Finally under the pressure of public opinion Alexander determined to appoint a new commander for both armies. The general voice was for Kutuzov. Personally he was disagreeable to Alexander ever since Austerlitz and his disobedience at the conclusion of the Bucharest Treaty, yet he yielded to the popular demand. Convinced of the need of a *national* war with Napoleon, Alexander had been very attentive to the public voice at that time, as we have observed. For this reason he sacrificed Speransky, appointed to the post of Imperial Secretary Admiral Shishkov, a "true-Russian" patriot of the ancient calibre, but in no way a statesman; for the same reason he appointed as Governor-General of Moscow the madcap Rastopchin who had been famous by his patriotic pamphlets and placards. For the same considerations he appointed Prince Kutuzov chief commander of all his armies.

At first Alexander intended to remain with the army, and he arrived at the headquarters in Vilna, but Shishkov, who accompanied him, had observed at the right moment that the Emperor's presence was a great inconvenience, embarrassing the actions of the Chief Commander. He persuaded Adjutant-General Balashov and Count Arakcheiev to sign with him a letter to Alexander, in which they entreated the Tzar to leave the army and go to Moscow for the support and upheaval of the patriotic spirit.

Reluctantly Alexander followed Shishkov's advice. In Moscow he was met with an outburst of general enthusiasm which exceeded all his expectations. The nobility of the province of Moscow offered at once three million rubles, an enormous sum for that time, and volunteered to bring ten recruits from every hundred souls, which meant almost half of the working population capable of bearing arms. The Moscow merchants offered ten million rubles. Similar unusual offers were made by the nobles of the provinces of Smolensk, Estland, Pskov, Tver, and others. Towards autumn the total amount of the contributions exceeded one hundred millions. The war was becoming truly national. Never before or after had such colossal sums been contributed.

Kutuzov assumed the commandership of the army at the village Tzarevo-Zaymishche, the place where Barclay had intended to give Napoleon a general battle, yielding to the persuasions of his staff and the desire of the whole army. After the observation of the positions by Benigsen, who had arrived with Kutuzov, it was decided to retreat still farther, and the general battle took place at Borodino, one hundred and thirty versts from Moscow, ten versts from Mozhaysk.[1]

The general course of that battle is well known, and I shall not describe it. It was the bloodiest of all Napoleonic battles; both armies lost half of their men, the number of killed and wounded officers alone exceeded two thousand. The Russians lost over twenty generals, among them Bagration and Tuchkov; Napoleon lost forty-nine generals.

Military historians are of the opinion that Napoleon could have won the battle if he had employed his Guards; but he refused to risk his Guards at a distance of three thousand versts from France, and he said so himself during the battle in answer to the advice of his staff.

Kutuzov, despite the fact that he had maintained all his positions, upon the review of his army after the two days' fighting came to the conclusion that it was necessary to retreat to Moscow, and not finding a good position for a new battle around Moscow he moved on beyond Moscow, at first on the road of Riazan, and then on the Kaluga road. Moscow was surrendered without fighting.[2] Napoleon's army,

[1] A verst is equivalent to 0.6629 of a mile, or 1.067 of a kilometer.

[2] The impression of the surrender of Moscow upon the public was reflected in numerous memoirs of that time, some of which have been used in later-day fiction, with particular artistic truthfulness in Tolstoy's " War and Peace." Recently was published the curious correspondence of Alexander with his favourite sister, Catherine Paulovna (issued by Grand Duke Nicolay Mikhailovich, Petrograd, 1910), which well illustrates the general indignation of the public at the first news about the evacuation of Moscow. On September 6 Catherine Paulovna, who mingled with patriots of the type of Karamzin and Rastopchin, wrote to her brother from Yaroslavl: " The occupation of Moscow by the French has overfilled the cup of despair in all minds, dissatisfaction has spread to an extreme degree, and even you (i.e., the Tzar) are not spared in the condemnations. . . . You are loudly blamed for the misfortunes of your empire, for the general ruination, in a word for the loss of the country's and of your own

"smashed at the Russians," in the expression of Yermolov, entered Moscow and encamped there for a long rest. That standstill reduced the French army to a definite decay and demoralisation. In the depopulated Moscow there began continuous conflagrations which could not be extinguished — Rastopchin had wisely withdrawn all pipes. There was nothing to eat; the remainder of the provisions was soon plundered. Astounded by the sight of the empty, burning Moscow, in which he had expected to find comfortable and well provided quarters, Napoleon remained five weeks without action in the "conquered" city among heaps of burning ruins. All his peace preludes were rejected. After five weeks Napoleon left Moscow with the single desire of returning home with his army. But Kutuzov blocked his way to the south, and he had to return by the old, devastated road of Smolensk. A cruel guerrilla war began, severe frost came earlier than usually, and the Grande Armée was fast reduced to a big frozen, starving mob, beaten and captured not only by peasants, but even by women. The escape of Napoleon in a native carriage, wrapped up in shawls and furs, but without his army, was due only to the negligence of Admiral Chichagov, who overlooked him. At Warsaw Napoleon said: "From the sublime to the ridiculous is only one step. . . ."

Alexander was in a position to raise his head high; he had not only fulfilled his promise "not to make peace as long as there remained one armed enemy in Russia," but there was no one to negotiate with.

Napoleon, however, though he had lost his army, did not

dignity." She reminded him of his determination not to conclude peace even if he had to retreat to Kazan.

Alexander, touched to the quick by that sharp letter, replied a few days later at his first moment of leisure in a long epistle, in which he expressed a firm and sober view of his own position and that of Russia, and his opinion about the persons in whose hands was at that time held to a considerable extent the fate of the army and Russia.

lose his spirit and self-confidence, and hastened to France to gather new troops; he foresaw that with the collapse of his army all his subjected nations would attempt to throw off his yoke.

Before Alexander appeared the question: Should he be satisfied with the repelling of the enemy from Russia, or should he make use of Napoleon's desperate plight and undertake the liberation of Europe from his power?

Alexander chose the latter. For three whole years he had been the " Agamemnon " of Europe, the king of kings, as they said then. One cannot deny that the task was of great importance for Russia also, as there could be no doubt that if Napoleon was given time to recuperate he would not fail to attempt eventually a *revanche*.

Alexander's activity in Europe during 1813–15 was undoubtedly the most brilliant phase in his life, but it forms the contents of universal, not Russian history. In regard to the socio-political process which we are studying, that activity has but an indirect and, moreover, a negative significance. For this reason we shall discuss only those circumstances of that period which have some bearing on the process under our observation.

The struggle with Napoleon was far from easy even after 1812. Still more difficult was the struggle that Alexander had to carry on against the mistrust and vacillations of his allies, Austria and Prussia. Finally after the defeat of Napoleon in the " battle of the nations " at Leipzig, Germany was freed from the French, and the allies, urged and led by Alexander (though formally the commander of the allied armies was not he, but an Austrian general — the weak wavering Prince Schwarzenberg), had passed by the beginning of the year 1814 the French border, and in April of the same year they entered Paris; Napoleon signed his abdication and withdrew to the island Elbe. The Bourbons were restored, and

Louis XVIII, to a great measure under the influence of Alexander, granted a constitutional charter.

At the Vienna Congress the map of Europe had to be rearranged once more; it was proposed to give some autonomy and representative governments to the nationalities that had taken part in the wars against Napoleon. The Congress restored the old frontiers of France (as before 1792), added a considerable slice to Austria, and remapped Germany without special difficulties. One of the most difficult questions was that of Poland. On the one hand Austria, England, and France feared a too strong Russia, and did not want to give her Poland; on the other hand complications arose in connection with the necessary compensation of Prussia for her losses by the Tilsit Treaty. Alexander did not want to offend the king of Prussia, who was now his faithful ally; but at Tilsit the Grand Duchy of Warsaw had been formed out of Prussian possessions. Alexander had intended to make use of Saxony for the compensation of Prussia, without destroying the new Polish state. The king of Saxony was Napoleon's most devoted ally, and was therefore treated almost as a traitor to the German nation; the Saxon people cared nothing about depriving their king of his dominion, since they were indignant over his anti-German policy; Frederick William of Prussia was pleased to receive so many German subjects in place of hostile Poles. But the king of Saxony found an unexpected and energetic champion in Talleyrand, who represented the interests of Louis XVIII at the Congress. Of course Talleyrand was not interested in Saxon affairs, but he endeavoured to uphold the interests of the small German states in order to preserve the weakness and disunion of Germany; besides, he hoped to arouse hostile feelings among the allies in connection with that question, and particularly to provoke mistrust in regard to Alexander. Indeed, he succeeded in drawing on his side England and Austria, and the three Powers refused to give Saxony to Prussia and the Duchy of Warsaw to Russia. As a matter of fact Alexander wanted to receive the Duchy not for the sake of enlarging Russia's territory, but in order to fulfil his old promise to the Poles; he had intended to transform the Duchy of Warsaw into a Kingdom of Poland, which would have a liberal constitution under the sceptre of the Russian Tzar.

Affairs in Poland were at that moment very difficult. As soon as the Russians had crossed the frontier in 1813 and entered the Duchy, they established there a temporary government in the form of a commission of five, with V. S. Lanskoy at the head; the members of the commission were N. N. Novosiltzev, Prince A. A. Czartoryski, and two former ministers of the Duchy. The Poles had tightly knit their fate with that of Napoleon; they had fought bravely and vigorously in his ranks both in Spain and in Russia. In the meantime the Polish lands were reduced to complete ruin, since they had become the zone of war; this circumstance had completed the financial and economic destruction of the country which had been groaning under the burden of maintaining an army of sixty-five thousand men.

When Napoleon's army entered Russia in 1812, it was joined by many Poles who had been Russian subjects, especially from the Lithuanian provinces; they had thus broken their oath of allegiance to Alexander. Yet Alexander granted them all an amnesty after the war of 1812, and besides published a very friendly proclamation to the population of the Duchy of Warsaw. This prompted Czartoryski to present to the Tzar a new proposition about the restoration of Poland according to the frontiers of 1772 under the sceptre of Alexander's youngest brother, Grand Duke Mikhail. Alexander categorically refused, declaring that to restore Poland with its frontiers of 1772 and not have it under the sceptre of the emperor of Russia would be contrary to the national feelings of his subjects who could not sympathise with the relinquishment of ancient Russian lands for which there had been centuries of struggle between Russia and Poland.

In this case Alexander understood correctly the sentiments of his people and army whose hostility towards the Poles was obvious; even some of the members of the Commission that governed Poland were not free from that feeling. Novosiltzev, for instance, called Alexander's attention to the Poles' opposition to everything Russian; Lanskoy vigorously protested against giving Poland an autonomy, particularly against preserving a separate Polish army which would, in his words, "become a snake spouting its venom at us." The diplomats and statesmen who surrounded Alexander at that time, Russians as well as foreigners, were all against the restoration of Poland, not to mention Metternich, who considered all the liberal plans of Alexander as dangerous dreams. The Russian ambassador to France, Count Pozzo di Borgo, expressed himself sharply against restoring Polish independence, and in a detailed memorandum he tried to prove on the basis of numerous historical analogies that Poland should not be restored, that she was not capable of a separate political existence, and that her restoration would be detrimental to Russia. Also Baron Stein, the famous Prussian reformer, one of the most honest statesmen of that epoch, considered that the maximum of what Poland should receive was a well organised local self-government. Even Capo d'Istria, subsequently the first president of liberated Greece, thought that Poland should not be given a constitution, since she had no developed middle class, but only a *szlachta* (nobility) and an enslaved peasantry.

In spite of all these opinions Alexander remained firm in his intentions. Though he refused in 1814 to restore to Poland her frontiers of 1772, he resolved not to return to Prussia the original Polish lands that formed the Duchy of Warsaw, but to found out of them an independent Polish state under his sceptre. In view of the sharp opposition of France, England,

and Austria, Alexander was forced to compromise: the king of Saxony retained his throne, and only a part of Saxony was given to Prussia; the king of Prussia received besides, the rich Rhenish provinces and the Duchy of Posen with the city of Thorn, which had formed a part of the Duchy of Warsaw before 1815.

Then Alexander had to give back to Austria all of Galicia, the part that was annexed by Napoleon to the Duchy of War- saw and the part that was given by Napoleon to Russia. Thus the Tzar succeeded in forming a Polish kingdom only out of the lands that form at present [3] the ten provinces of the " Vis- tula Region." The agreement of the Powers on all dis- putable questions was accelerated by the news of Napoleon's flight from Elbe and his arrival at France. After his final defeat at Waterloo by the British and Prussians Napoleon ab- dicated for the second time and was exiled to the island of St. Helena.

Alexander left Vienna in 1815, not waiting for the end of the work of the Congress. To that time belongs his ac- quaintance with an elderly lady raving with mystical nonsense, Baroness Juliane Krüdener. Many historians and biographers of Alexander have ascribed a great importance to that ac- quaintanceship in regard to the growth of Alexander's religious mysticism; Alexander himself considered his meeting with her of great significance. But we must say that his inclination for mysticism had developed even before his meeting with the Baroness, which circumstance, in my opinion, had given Mme. Krüdener an access to him. A definite impulse to Alexander's mysticism was given evidently by the great and formidable events of 1812, but even before 1812 he had eagerly conversed with monks and " holy men." We read in Shishkov's memoirs that in 1813, among his reports on important state-questions Shishkov — the Imperial Secretary — read to Alexander se-

[3] I.e., before the outbreak of the Great War in 1914.— TR.

lections from the Hebrew prophets, the text of which, it appeared to them, well fitted the contemporary events; at this both shed " tears of overcharged emotion." Since 1812 the New Testament had always been with Alexander, and he often used it as an oracle, opening pages at random and pondering over passages that had some relation to the facts of surrounding life. However, such mysticism was common in Europe at that time; the application of some expressions from the Apocalypse to Napoleon was particularly in vogue. The considerable spread of Freemasonry and the Masonic orders also caused the growth of mysticism. The colossal revolutions of that epoch contributed evidently to such an alarmed state of the contemporary mind. In any case the mystic mood of Alexander was not in any marked way reflected in 1815 upon his socio-political views and measures. But the far seeing La Harpe even then felt despondent about Alexander's new predilection.

In his foreign policy this inclination found expression, not without the influence of Baroness Krüdener, as it is asserted, in his at first quite innocent proposal to his allies about forming a Holy Alliance of the European monarchs for the promulgation of the ideas of peace and brotherhood in international relations. According to the idea of that Alliance the European monarchs were to treat one another as brothers, and their subjects, as children; all international misunderstandings and disputes were to be solved in a peaceful way. The king of Prussia expressed some sympathy with the idea; the emperor of Austria, Francis, a pietist who had been all his life in the hands of Jesuits, signed the agreement only after he had consulted Metternich, who said that although it was an empty chimera, it was yet an absolutely harmless one. The king of England could not sign the agreement without the approval of Parliament, but he expressed his sympathy in a personal letter to Alexander. Later into the Alliance had gradually entered all European monarchs except the Sultan and the Pope. In the hands of Metternich this institution had ultimately degenerated into an alliance of rulers against revolting nationalities, but in 1815 the Alliance did not have such a character, and Alexander was still a sincere advocate of liberal institutions. Yet his struggle with Napoleon and with the remains of the Revolution acquired after 1812 a growing mystical and sacramental aspect, which caused his old tutor, La Harpe, to express his apprehension.

CHAPTER X

IN the autumn of 1815, after considerable travelling through Europe Alexander departed at last for Russia, and on his way stopped at Warsaw, where a special commission consisting exclusively of Poles was at that time busy working out the constitution of the Kingdom of Poland, according to Alexander's instructions. The constitution had some features that resembled Speransky's Plan and many features in common with the Charter of Louis XVIII; the members of the commission had in mind also the constitution given by Napoleon to the Duchy of Warsaw in 1807. At any rate, contemporaries, even such radicals as Carnot who then lived at Warsaw, considered that constitution very liberal, not only for an autocrat, but even much better than the Charter of Louis XVIII, which was given to France largely under the pressure of Alexander. The constitution of 1815 guaranteed freedom of the press, the limits of which were to be determined by the Diet, and personal inviolability; abolished confiscation of property and administrative banishment, instituted the use of the Polish language in the governmental institutions of the Kingdom, and the obligatory occupation of all administrative, judicial, and military positions by subjects of the Kingdom of Poland. It even instituted the oath to the constitution on the part of the Tzar of Poland, i.e., the Russian Emperor, a point that is not found in the present Russian constitution. The Diet was to be the legislative apparatus; it consisted of the king and two chambers. The lower chamber had seventy-one members elected by the landowning nobility, and fifty-one members from the cities. The right of suffrage was given to persons not below the age of thirty, who paid in direct taxes not less than one hundred *zloty* (fifteen rubles in silver). The upper chamber consisted of "Princes of the blood," i.e., members of the Imperial Russian house during their abode in Warsaw, several Catholic bishops, one Uniate [1] bishop, and several Voivodes [2] and Castellans.[3] The membership of the upper chamber was half that of the lower chamber; the members were appointed by the Emperor, one from every two candidates recommended by the Senate out of persons who paid direct taxes of not less than two thousand *zloty* (three hundred rubles).

The Diet assembled once in two years for thirty days, during which time it had to discuss all the legislative projects brought in by the ministry responsible before it. The Diet had no legislative initiative, though it could present petitions to the Tzar and raise questions about ministerial responsibility. All the projects presented to the Diet by the ministry were first discussed in the State-Council whose rôle in this instance corresponded with that given it by Speransky's original Plan. The entire power in the land was given by that constitution to the *szlachta,* while certain administrative and judicial positions were to be occupied *only* by landowners.

Alexander at once ratified the constitution at Petrograd on December 12, 1815. In his speech on that occasion Prince Adam Czartoryski remarked that "Emperor Alexander could dominate by sheer force, but, led by the inspiration of virtue, he rejected such a domination. He has based his power not on external right alone, but on the feeling of gratitude, on the feeling of loyalty, and on that moral might which originates in place of terror — a feeling of obligation, in place of compulsion — devotion and voluntary sacrifices."

However, Czartoryski himself was for the second time of-

[1] The Uniates are a small sect professing a creed which is a compromise between Roman Catholicism and Greek Catholicism.— Tr.

[2] Polish administrative officials. The Poles employed also the equivalent title of *palatinus.*— Tr.

[3] Originally, castle-managers. Later — councillors.— Tr.

fended and disappointed in his expectations by Alexander. For the post of *Namiestnik* (viceroy) was appointed not he, but an old Polish general, Zayoncheck, a former Republican, who had commanded a division under Napoleon. The Council included besides five ministers who divided among them the spheres of administration, and besides the president (the viceroy) — an Imperial Commissary, and that position was given to Novosiltzev, whose attitude towards the restoration of Poland was quite sceptical. As commander of the Polish army — forty thousand men — was appointed Grand Duke Constantine, an excited, violent man who was considered responsible for the subsequent downfall of the Polish constitution.

During his stay at Warsaw Alexander received a deputation of Lithuanian nobles with Prince Oginsky at their head, but on the condition that they should not even mention the annexation of the Lithuanian provinces to Poland, and that the deputation did not include representatives of Volhynia and Podolia.[4]

In Russia Alexander was awaited by a mass of cares for the internal reconstruction of the country and the restoration of its welfare, which had been destroyed by the wars. The year of 1812 was accompanied with unparalleled misery, and the splendid defeat of the powerful enemy was accomplished at a big

[4] In his memoirs Prince Oginsky describes his conversation with Alexander at Warsaw in 1815, and the reception of the deputation from three Lithuanian provinces: Vilna, Grodno, and Minsk. In his conversation with Oginsky Alexander clearly hinted at his intention to join those provinces to Poland, figuring that through such a measure they would become closer united with the Russian Empire, since their population would have no more reason for dissatisfaction. But at the same time he forbade the delegates to ask him about it, fearing that this would sharpen the hostility of Russian public opinion toward the question. That hostility was keenly expressed in Karamzin's memorandum "An opinion of a Russian citizen" presented to Alexander in 1819, and in his notes "For posterity"; it is also illustrated in the memoirs of the Decembrist Yakushkin who observed the attitude of the progressive military circles towards the Polish question in the years 1817–18.

cost not only for the enemy, but also for Russia. Eyewitnesses relate unbelievable pictures of horror and death, that presented themselves to travellers on the big Smolensk road at the beginning of 1813. The mass of unburied corpses infected the air along the entire line from Vilna to Smolensk, and even far aside from that tract. Shishkov says that in February, 1813, the Minister of Police, Balashov, who accompanied him, had received a report from two provinces — Smolensk and Minsk — that there had been gathered and burned ninety-six thousand corpses, and that numerous more still remained on the ground. No wonder that various epidemics had spread in those provinces. In 1813 the population of the Smolensk province decreased by fifty-seven thousand, and that of Tver, which touched the war-zone only on its southern end, had lost twelve thousand. Similar losses were sustained by other provinces in the vicinity of the war-zone. Outside of the epidemics, the loss in human life was caused by direct consumption of the war-operations. During those years about one million men and nearly three thousand militia-men were recruited, which constituted almost one-third of the able-bodied population of the country. On the whole, in 1813 the population, instead of the normal increase of six hundred to six hundred and fifty thousand, suffered a loss of two thousand seven hundred men (according to the incomplete birth-registration of that year), and the general number of human lives lost during the last Napoleonic wars should be put at not less than one million and a half.

The provinces of Kovno, Vitebsk, Grodno, Mohilev, Volhynia, Vilna, Smolensk, and Moscow suffered most of all, and then the provinces of Kurland, Pskov, Tver, Kaluga. The material losses of the province of Moscow alone were figured out by the English who subsidised the campaign against Napoleon and therefore carefully gathered information about conditions in Russia, as two hundred and seventy million rubles. The provinces adjacent to the war-zone had also suffered greatly, owing to epidemics and the cart-tax. In the province of Tver that tax required at times one cart from every two and a half persons, i.e., an amount of carts that did not exist there at all. The provinces of Novgorod, Tver, Vladimir, and Yaroslavl were once ordered to contribute one hundred and forty-seven thousand carts at the fiscal price of four million six hundred and sixty-eight thousand rubles, whereas the peasants had to pay in addition about nine million rubles more. This order had to be recalled, but only after it had begun to be carried out, and the population was already ruined. Such examples were numerous.

As early as in April, 1812, the Minister of Finance, Guriev, proposed to raise provender and provisions for the army through requisitions from the population, who were to receive notes with a definite date of payment. These so called "obligations" did not lower the course of the assignations, being of a fixed date. But the Government's settlements of those notes were so extended, in spite of Alexander's sharp reprimands to the Committee of Ministers, that they had not been executed even towards the end of his reign, and the landowners who were the chief creditors of the Government on those notes lost all hope of recovering their money and relinquished their claims, involuntarily turning them thus into new contributions.

The general cost of the war of 1812-15 is very difficult to gauge at present. According to the report of Barclay de Tolly, composed by Kankrin, the fiscal expenses were expressed in an astonishingly small sum — one hundred fifty-seven and a half million rubles for the four years. But the enormous expenses of the population itself are hardly estimable. In his secret memorandum Minister Guriev moderately estimated the expenses of the people as early as 1812 above two hundred million rubles. The upheaval of patriotism caused by the in-

vasion of the enemy was expressed in voluntary direct contributions which in 1812 exceeded one hundred million rubles
and enabled the Government to bring the campaign of 1812 to
an end without special difficulties. The general sum of Russia's material loss during those years probably exceeded one
billion rubles.

The population had borne those expenses without complaints
and even with sincere enthusiasm, in spite of the gross abuses
by the ministerial and commissariat-officials. But the paying
capacity of the population was entirely drained, and in many
places the payment of all taxes had ceased already in 1815.
The treasury was then almost constantly empty. When in
1813 Alexander decided to transfer the war abroad Barclay
de Tolly reported that for the maintenance of the army of
two hundred thousand men for the next two months there
were needed fourteen and a half million rubles in coin, whereas
the total amount of coin in possession of the treasury at that
moment was not more than five and one-fourth million rubles,
so that it was short of nine million. An issue of assignations
would be of no help, as there was required only metal-money;
a loan was unattainable: Arakcheiev wrote then to Count Nesselrode about the Government's apprehensions that the course
of the paper ruble would fall to ten copecks.

Under such conditions the continuation of the war with
Napoleon was made possible only through the big subsidies
of England.

To a great extent Russia was saved from total bankruptcy
owing to her favourable balance of trade, which had been
established after the tariff of 1810. The exports considerably
exceeded the imports, in spite of the war. In 1812 the im-
portations were less than ninety million rubles, while the export rose to one hundred and fifty million. This was due to
the alliance with England and the unmolested trade with her
through Petrograd and Arkhangelsk.

It is remarkable that in 1812 the course of the ruble on the London Exchange was at its highest at the moment of Napoleon's entry into Moscow. At the same time the trade with China and Central Asia continued to develop; considerable quantities of cotton were imported from the Central Asiatic Khanates. Minister Guriev began to work out a plan for the return to a more liberal tariff, seeing that Russian manufactures had been sufficiently supported; his intention aroused wailing among the Moscow manufacturers who had just started to stand firmly on their feet, and their views were upheld by the Minister of Interior, Kozodavlev, and even by the Chancellor, Count N. P. Rumiantzev, who despite his fame as an admirer of the French and Napoleon, considered the claims of the Moscow manufacturers just. Count Guriev suffered a fiasco in 1813: the revision of the tariff was found untimely.

The rise of national feeling in the years 1812–1815 was shown also in the energetic activity of private persons for support of the families that had suffered from the war; in general the public had for the first time demonstrated initiative and voluntary action.

Of equal interest is the rapidity with which Moscow and other burned cities were rebuilt; the Government gave for this purpose some subsidies, altogether about fifteen million rubles. The cities began to revive at the beginning of the twenties, but the landowners' estates could not recuperate so soon from their ruination, and their indebtedness had assumed enormous dimensions and continued growing to the very time of the abolition of serfdom.

The vigorous work that was manifested throughout Russia after the war showed that the nation had come out of the terrible calamity renewed and ready for further growth and cultural development. High spirits were sustained also by the military successes that had brought Russia to the peak of fame. These together with the reforms of the first years of Alexander's reign gave assurance that after the happy end of the war and with the advent of peaceful times the socio-political forms of the country which required radical changes, especially in the eyes of those Russians who had been abroad and observed the different life there, would be rapidly improved.

It is obvious how important had been the influence of those men on the public, not only in the capitals and large cities, but even in remote provincial corners. The army-officers who had returned from France affected the nobility, the merchants, and the commoners, and this influence combined well with the early liberal tendencies of the Government.

True, the educational activity of the Government had come to a standstill after 1805 owing to lack of funds. But the progressive work of the Government was later renewed in the reforms of Speransky, and it appeared clear to the public that at the end of the war Alexander would take up again his early reforms, enriched with experience and knowledge.

It seemed that Alexander's activity in Paris, and later in Poland, gave good reasons for the confirmation of those hopes. True, the sporadic rumours about Alexander's infatuation with mysticism, and the manifesto which he issued on January 1, 1816, soon after his return to Russia, would have served as warnings for those who had been over-optimistic; but mystic moods could not alarm the progressive elements of that time, when mysticism was common and a considerable portion of society belonged to various Masonic orders or had close friends among the Masons. As to the manifesto of January 1, 1816, which was written by Shishkov back in 1814 on the occasion of the entry of the allied armies into Paris, and contained many loud phrases against the " Godless " French and the " abominable " revolutionists, without however attacking constitutional ideas,— it had made a very bad impression abroad, but passed without special notice in Russia, and was soon forgotten.

In any case Alexander in 1816 was still a sincere and convinced constitutionalist, and we must observe that he had realised his ideas in actual life — by granting constitutions to Finland and Poland, and by helping France and some secondary European states to secure constitutions.

Even his closest assistants were convinced then of his intention to give Russia a constitution.[5] Among the papers of General Kiselev were preserved notes about a detailed report that he made before Alexander in 1816 about the state of affairs in south Russia. Kiselev had been requested to find men fitted for the new administrative work, but having journeyed through the South he discovered not so many capable men as a mass of abuses, which he reported to Alexander. After hearing the report, Alexander remarked: " One cannot do everything at once: circumstances have not allowed us to take proper care of internal affairs, but at present we are engaged in reorganising. . . ." Discussing the administrative abuses in the South the Emperor said: " I know that the majority of the administrative officials should be dismissed, and you are right in holding that the evil comes both from the higher officials and from the poor selection of lower officials. But where can you get them? I am unable to choose fifty-two governors, and there are needed thou-

[5] However, one of the early co-operators of Alexander's reforms, Count V. P. Kochubey, who had held quite moderate views while on the famous Committee, now expressed his desiderata with still greater caution. After Alexander's death among his papers was found a memorandum presented by Kochubey at the very end of 1814. Among other things he wrote: " The Russian Empire is an autocratic state, and whether we consider its dimensions or its geographic position, the degree of its education and many other circumstances, we must admit that this form of government is the only one that will be proper for Russia for many years; but this form cannot prevent the Tzar from choosing all possible ways for the best government, and as it is proven that a monarch, however far seeing he may be, cannot alone embrace all branches of the government, he is obliged to seek firm state institutions which, bringing the empire nearer to other best ordered states, would present to the subjects the advantages of a just, mild, and enlightened government. . . ."

sands. . . ." " The army, the civil administration, everything, is not as I would have it — but what can you do? You cannot do everything at once; there are no assistants. . . ."

From that conversation, copied by Kiselev with a photographic exactness, we learn that Alexander was particularly interested in questions of military reorganisation, while he considered questions of civil administration of secondary importance. For instance, when Kiselev depicted the bacchanalia of abuses in Bessarabia, and suggested that its whole administration must go, and recommended that General Inzov be sent there, Alexander quickly remarked that he could not sacrifice such a good general for civil service.

In view of his European policy at that time, Alexander's position was not an easy one. In 1816–17 he set aside the earlier proposed recruitment, but at the same time he did not want to diminish the numbers of his standing army. When it was reported to him that the population was grumbling, since though the war was over the military expenditures did not decrease, Alexander replied with irritation that he could not maintain an army smaller than those of Prussia and Austria combined. In answer to the remark that those states had already dismissed part of their armies, Alexander said that he also " intended " to do so. To his generals who advised him to decrease the army Alexander pointed out that Russia needed a *prépondérance politique,* and that there could be no thought of diminishing the military forces. He was greatly interested, on the other hand, in the question of contracting military expenses and improving the status of the soldiers; he watched closely the military reform in Prussia after she was obliged by the Treaty of Tilsit to maintain not more than forty-two thousand men under arms. As is well known, General Scharnhorst found a clever way out of the difficulty; according to his system every Prussian served three years in the army, after which he was registered in the reserve, to be called from time to time for military exercises;

in this way the population was trained in a short time, and could easily be mobilised in case of need. Thus he increased the actual army several times. Alexander was greatly interested in that idea, but he soon figured out that it was not applicable to Russia, in view of her enormous territory, sparse population, and the total absence of good roads, which would make a rapid mobilisation impossible. In his constant preoccupation with that problem he came in 1810 upon a French work of a certain Servane, which advocated the idea of military colonies on the frontier, engaged in agriculture and at the same time bearing service. The idea appealed to him so much that he at once ordered P. M. Volkonsky to translate the brochure into Russian, in order that Arakcheiev, to whom he decided to entrust the matter, might become acquainted with it. Thus originated the system of military colonies which ultimately brought so much distress. The system consisted in transferring certain territories from the civil to the military department, exempting them from all taxes and dues, and obliging them in lieu of taxes to complete and maintain definite military units. The first application of the system was made in 1810–11 in the province of Mohilev, one of whose *volosts* was settled by the Yeletz infantry regiment, while the native population was transferred to New Russia. In order to lend the colony at once an agricultural character, a special battalion was formed of the married soldiers of the regiment, and their wives and children were arbitrarily brought to them. These married soldiers were to form the basic population of the *volost;* among their houses were distributed the unmarried soldiers who were turned into farmworkers and received their pay from the married soldiers in the form of complete maintenance, like members of their families.

Such was the idea that attracted Alexander in 1810. The first Mohilev colony did not succeed, because at the outbreak of the war of 1812 the Yeletz regiment went to the front, and the whole idea was smothered during the Napoleonic wars.

But in 1816 Alexander decided to renew his attempts to realise that idea. This time the experiment was made in the province of Novgorod in which Arakcheiev had an estate and could therefore better observe the course of affairs in the colonies. An order was given not to transplant the native population, but to transform it directly into military colonists. A whole *volost* was given over to the colony, all its peasants were declared military colonists, and a regiment was distributed among their homes. An incident helped the construction of the colony after a military model: the central village of the *volost* Vysokoie had burned down. Arakcheiev ordered the reconstruction according to a definite plan. The former inhabitants were installed in the mathematically symmetrical farmhouses; their beards were shaved off, they were donned in uniforms, and were ordered to maintain a regiment. Care was taken of their material well-being; they received cattle, horses, and were allowed subsidies and privileges. Among these soldier-farmers were settled prescribed battalions who had become farm-labourers. When bachelor-soldiers married they received separate households, but marriages required the permission of the military authorities. All widows and marriageable girls were kept on record, and marriages were prescribed by the authorities.

Large sums were spent to establish those colonies firmly and in an orderly manner. The life of the colonists was chained by a deadening, pedantic, military system; every household was under the incessant supervision of the authorities; a careless colonist might lose his household and even be banished from the *volost*. Not only the men were subject to military discipline, but even women; at a certain age the children were taken away and schooled as *cantonists* (soldiers' children). In spite of material advantages the population hated the system, for it was bondage, worse than serfdom-bondage.

One must say that Arakcheiev himself was honest in his transactions, and the enormous sums that had passed through his hands were properly employed; he strictly watched his subordinates. I must warn the reader that there does not exist an impartial biography of Arakcheiev; his rôle and significance are depicted only externally, and the gloomy legends that have gathered around his ominous name are hardly just. Too much hatred, too many bloody memories are connected with that name. Besides, it has been convenient to blame Arakcheiev for everything that was done by the will of Alexander. This was partly due to the censorship conditions under which, until recently, historical works have been written in Russia. Many ascribe to Arakcheiev a pernicious influence on Alexander, and endeavour to explain by that influence the dark features of the last years of his reign; they present Arakcheiev not only as a friend of the Tzar, but as the only friend towards whom Alexander had never changed. In fact Arakcheiev was not so much Alexander's friend, in the true sense of the word, as a faithful slave, regardless of whether his master was Paul or Alexander. He was not stupid, but uncultured; a man of action, diligent, very honest — he did not steal, a rare virtue at that time, and always tried to save a copeck for his master. With all his dog-like devotion — even his fatherland appeared to him as a trifle in comparison with the interests of his master — he had, nevertheless, a sense of honour and ambition. He was merciless, unhuman in his readiness to obey orders; but he also could foretell his master's desires. He was vainglorious, but the chief object of his ambition was to enjoy the unlimited confidence of his master. Of course such a servant is a real treasure for an autocrat, especially one like Alexander who, having grown tired of the tribulations of his reign, was in need of a faithful man capable of looking at things with the eyes of his master. But we can hardly call Arakcheiev a friend of Alexander, and still less may we ascribe to him a moral and political influence on the latter. He was but the executive of the Tzar's policy, and in regard to the military colonies he asserted more than once that it was not his idea, that he opposed them in the beginning, but since he had undertaken the work he carried it out conscientiously, to the end.

We must say that the military colonies grew and developed with great rapidity, so that by 1825 their Corpus consisted of ninety battalions of infantry in the province of Novgorod and of thirty-six battalions of infantry and two hundred and forty-nine cavalry-squadrons in the Little-Russian colonies. The historian Schilder calls attention to the fact that the work of the military colonies had been carried on in secret, without the interference of the State Council, i.e., against the legal order. Materially the undertaking was apparently a success; the population seemed to thrive, the colonies were self-sustaining and did not buy anything from the outside for the provisioning and clothing of their members. Owing to this Arakcheiev succeeded in saving up a reserved capital of nearly fifty million rubles (Capital of Military Colonies), and he liked to boast of his orderly management. It is noteworthy that many authoritative and relatively independent men of the time gave quite flattering reports about the colonies. Such were the opinions of Count Kochubey after his personal inspection, of the State Comptroller, Baron Kampfenhausen, and even of Speransky, who after his recall from Siberia visited the Novgorod colonies, and finally, of Karamzin. In spite of strict supervision, however, there were later discovered flagrant abuses in some colonies. But what chiefly undermined their importance from the economic point of view, was the account of the fiscal expenditures on that undertaking. In the very first years nearly one million rubles were spent, and one must besides take into consideration the exemption of the colonists from taxes. The very experiment of that peculiar type of state-Socialism deserves a serious, exhaustive study; such a study has not been made as yet. Most of the information we find in literature concerns the uprisings that took place in the colonies at various times. Among the people, at any rate, there has remained a gloomy memory of that monstrous attempt to place a considerable portion of the country under military bondage.

Alexander's chief care after the Napoleonic wars consisted in the reorganisation of the army by the aid of the colonies-system. In spite of his words to Kiselev in 1816, which he had probably repeated to many persons, about his intention to undertake internal reforms, those words were fulfilled, if at all, by fits and starts, and on an insignificant scale.

Since the Napoleonic wars all the higher administration and even the higher police were concentrated in the Committee of Ministers which, according to Alexander's repeated orders, had to act independently in the absence of the Tzar, and could carry through the most important measures without the monarch's sanction, and with only the confirmation of the president of the Committee. For the post of president N. I. Saltykov was appointed; he whom Catherine had chosen as the chief supervisor of Alexander's education. Now he was a quite infirm old man, and the actual ruler was the director of the Committee, Molchanov.

After the war cases of gross thievery were discovered, mainly in the commissariat, not so much in the army where at the head of this department stood Kankrin, a man of energy and sterling honesty, as in the Ministry of War and in the Committee of Ministers. Alexander, who had been long dissatisfied with the disorder and indolence of the Committee, became indignant at the revelation of spoliations, and ordered a prosecution of Molchanov and the whole Ministry of War with Prince Gorchakov at the head. At the same time he appointed, as an aid to Saltykov, Arakcheiev, who was to report to him personally on the affairs of the Committee. He remained in this position even when after the death of Saltykov, Lopukhin, a person far from senile, was appointed president of the Committee. Thus Arakcheiev had become something like a prime minister, although he had no portfolio. A strange order was established: Alexander no longer received the ministers with their reports, and never attended the sessions of the Committee. Most of his time he spent in travels through Russia or in attending international congresses abroad. All the matters that required the Emperor's sanction were brought by the ministers before the Committee, and the brief journal of the Committee with the concluding resolutions of Arakcheiev were presented to Alexander. Almost without exception the Tzar agreed with all of Arakcheiev's resolutions. This circumstance made Arakcheiev appear a powerful favourite who was responsible for all the obscurantist measures and repressions of the age. But a close study of the mass of those documents (e.g., in the *Historical Review of the Activity of the Committee of Ministers,* by Seredonin) convinces us that the greater part of them were of secondary importance, and that Arakcheiev's resolutions were not always cruel or repressive; we can rather discover in them a wide-awake watchfulness for the conservation of the fiscal coffers and for the strict fulfilment of the Emperor's ideas. Among Arakcheiev's resolutions were even such that recommended quite just decisions, often more human than those of the Committee. He always tried to decide in a way which would correspond to Alexander's mood. It is natural that under such conditions Alexander trusted the man who relieved him from such affairs as no longer interested him, his mind being occupied with other matters. On this chiefly was based Arakcheiev's reputation as a man who had had an unusual influence on Alexander.

Besides these positions Arakcheiev was chairman of the special committee for the construction of roads, and there he also demonstrated great activity and strict watchfulness, though the results were not brilliant. Then he was chairman of the department of military affairs at the State Council from the moment of its establishment (1810), resigning at that time his post of Minister of War.

CHAPTER XI

AFTER the removal of Speransky and the resignation of the president of the Department of State-Economy, Mordvinov, in 1812, the State Council remained almost idle during the Napoleonic wars; as we know, the Committee of Ministers was the only ruling body. In the absence of any other activity the State Council occupied itself with the discussion of Speransky's plan concerning the new civil and criminal code, his least successful work, as he later himself admitted. The code was based on French models, without sufficient investigation of the history of Russian legislation and of Russian needs. After Speransky's exile the State Council felt freer in criticising his project; they rejected point after point, and finally gave the matter over to a special committee where it remained till the reign of Nicolas I, when it again fell into the hands of Speransky.

In 1816 Admiral Mordvinov was once more invited to the post of president of the Department of State-Economy,[1] and only then the regular work of the State Council, at least in the matter of state-budgets, began. Mordvinov immediately after his reappointment harshly criticised the work of the Minister of Finance, Guriev, especially his financial reports, which lacked clearness and abounded in befogging accounts. About the same time he presented to the State Council his opinion concerning the economic condition of the country, with a detailed criticism of the financial system and suggestions for the improvements. He severely attacked the immoderate issues of assignations which the Committee of Ministers put through secretly during the war, an act

---

[1] At the same time Speransky was recalled and appointed governor of the province of Pezna.

absolutely against the law; he further appealed for the need of strict economy in every phase of national life, pointing out that the whole country was dissatisfied with the deplorable state of finances, the high cost of living, and general impoverishment. Mordvinov recommended measures analogous to those of Speransky in 1810.

Under the pressure of those attacks Guriev carried through the State Council a series of projects, quite substantial, externally at least, about the renewal of the work of the commission for the extinguishing of state-debts, about the establishment of a special council for credit transactions with the participation of representatives of the merchant-class, and about the founding of a commercial bank. For the first mentioned committee were assigned big sums, and in 1817 for the first time under Alexander, they burned assignations for the sum of thirty-eight million rubles. But the amount of the remaining assignations was still eight hundred million rubles, and the total state-debt exceeded one billion — an enormous sum for that time. Alongside with the payment of debts the Ministry of Finance abolished in 1817 private beverage-contracts, supplanting them with a state-monopoly, but this resulted only in the development of unusual thievery among the officials of that department. At the same time the free-port system was renewed for Odessa, and Berd was granted the privilege of establishing the first steam-ship line in Russia.

All these measures impressed the public favourably, although the cost of living remained very high owing to the low course of the paper-ruble. This last circumstance depended to a large degree upon the liberal changes in the tariff, that were made in 1816, and especially in 1819. I have mentioned that the Minister of Finance had intended to change the tariff in 1813, but the Moscow merchants successfully opposed it. At the Vienna Congress Alexander gave promises to representatives of various Powers to mitigate or abolish tariff-restrictions in Russia. The first mitigating measures were carried through in 1816. The new tariff removed all prohibitions from foreign trade, and lowered many customs dues, not so much on manufactured goods as on raw material not found in Russia; thus the tariff could not shake the position of Russian industry, but it undoubtedly affected the balance of trade, since imports increased while exports remained stationary. This circumstance kept the course of the paper-money low. In 1819 new serious changes were made in the tariff, lowering customs dues on some manufactured commodities, which caused many Russian factories to reduce or to discontinue their activity.

I have already mentioned that until the nineteenth century the Russian manufacturing industry had satisfied mainly fiscal needs, and most of the factories produced either iron and arms, or cloth and linen for the army and navy. The Possessional cloth-factories were not allowed to sell to private persons, and all their work was limited to supplying the army. Alexander's government hesitated a long time about removing that restriction, in view of the growing needs of the army, but in 1816 the factories were freed from that burden, and the results proved very favourable for the development of industry.

From the beginning of the nineteenth century cotton-mills began to develop. Before the Continental System Russia had imported thread from England, but upon its installation cotton-thread was made in Russia from Central-Asiatic cotton. The cotton-mills appeared to be dangerous competitors for the linen- and canvas-mills; back in 1818 the learned statistician, K. I. Arseniev, considered as the most profitable industry for Russia the manufacture of flax and hemp, i.e., of linen and canvas, which had been largely exported to England for the needs of her fleet.

The tariff of 1819 aroused the vehement opposition of the manufacturers, and they succeeded in bringing forth in 1822 a new protectionist tariff which established for a long time the protectionist principle in the state legislation.

During the first half of the nineteenth century the iron industry remained undeveloped; investigators explain it by the forced labour in the Possessional factories where the bonded workers could not be very productive; another circumstance must be added — the lack of good ways of communication: the transportation of iron from the Ural Mountains was then costlier and more difficult than from abroad.   Below are interesting figures about the state of industry during the reign of Alexander, worked out by Professor Tugan-Baranovsky.

In 1804 the number of factories was two thousand four hundred and twenty-three; in 1825 — five thousand two hundred and sixty-one.   The number of workers in 1804 was ninety-five thousand two hundred and two; of them forty-five thousand six hundred and twenty-five (48 per cent.) were free workingmen, not bonded and not Possessional.   In 1825 there were two hundred and ten thousand five hundred and sixty-eight workers, among them one hundred and fourteen thousand five hundred and fifteen (54 per cent.) free workingmen.   The increase in the number of free workers shows that there existed a tendency toward free hired labour among the manufacturers, a circumstance that had played a not unimportant rôle in undermining the bondage-institution by proving it detrimental to the interests of Russian industry.

With the return of society to peaceful occupations the attempts to solve the peasant-question were renewed.   In 1816 the question was definitely settled in the Ostsee provinces, very disadvantageously for the peasants.   In 1804–5 the conditions had been much more favourable for them, as the landowners were restricted in their power over the peasants' property and of raising their dues.   The Ostsee nobility were greatly dissatisfied with the laws of 1804 and 1805, tried to hinder the materialisation of those laws, and in 1811 the Estland nobles presented a new project in which they proposed to free the peasants from bondage altogether, but to deprive them also of their land.   The

Government took the bait. After the war Alexander signed the law for the abolition of serfdom in the government of Estland (1816); all the land remained in the hands of the nobles. The peasants became personally free, but were forced to become the economic slaves of their landowners. In 1817 a similar law was decreed for Kurland, and in 1819 for Lifland.

The results greatly tempted the nobles of certain provinces to free their peasants on the same basis. Fortunately the majority of the landowners had not been prepared for such reasoning; in some places (as in the province of Penza) the bondage-system was the most convenient for the exploitation of the estates, and the nobles dreaded the rumours about innovations.

The Government continued to vacillate on the peasant-question. For instance, Alexander gave his own money for the French publication of Academic Storch's course of political economy, which he read to the Grand Dukes, and in which was decisively condemned any forced labour, in particular the bondage system in Russia. But when Storch intended to issue his work in Russian, the censor forbade it. At the same time the learned Professor of the university of Kharkov, Schad, who was recommended to Uvarov by Goethe and Schiller, published in Latin a book in which he expressed views similar to those of Storch; for this he was banished from Russia. In the same year (1816) was issued a very intelligent though reservedly written book by Gribovsky on the position of the landowners' peasants; the book was dedicated to Arakcheiev, and passed the censor safely.

The most popular magazine of the time, *The Spirit of Journals,* had often discussed the question of liberating the peasants, and sharply opposed their liberation without land. But when that magazine printed in 1818 the speech of the Governor-General of Little Russia, Prince Riepnin, in which he urged the nobles of the provinces of Poltava and Chernigov to give their peasants the same conditions that had been proposed for the Ostsee region in 1804, the speech aroused considerable indignation, and the editor was reprimanded.

Alexander himself undoubtedly continued to think about peasant-reform. When he received through Miloradovich Pushkin's poem, *The Village,* he ordered Pushkin thanked for disseminating noble feelings and views, but the censor again without ceremonies forbade its publication. Alexander was interested in the memorandum of N. I. Turgeniev about rational methods for peasant-reform; he advocated their liberation with land. Another practical plan for the gradual extinction of serfdom was offered by Kankrin, who as Intendant-General of the army had observed the hard conditions of the peasants during his trips through various provinces; Kankrin was also a learned economist, and he prefaced his memorandum with a review of the liberation of the serfs in Western Europe. It is possible that the last memorandum induced Alexander in 1818 to request Arakcheiev for a project concerning the gradual liberation of the peasants; Alexander required that the project should not include " any measures oppressive for the landowners, and particularly that those measures should not appear forced by the Government." Arakcheiev fulfilled his order within those limits. He proposed a simple measure: to spend five million rubles yearly for the redemption of estates from those owners who would be willing to sell them; the peasants were to get two *desiatins* [2] of land per person. Of course Arakcheiev understood that this was not enough, but it was his intention to allow the peasants an incomplete security in order to secure thereby hired labour for the landowners.

There had been many unofficial attempts to accelerate the solution of the peasant-problem. It is worth noting an attempt to form an all-Russian union of landowners for the liquidation of serfdom; among the initiators were Count M. S. Vorontzov, Prince Vassilchikov, the brothers A. I. and N. I. Turgeniev.

[2] A desiatin equals 2.7 acres.— TR.

Alexander received the founders of the union very dryly, and remarked that there was no use in establishing an all-Russian undertaking; let the landowners act individually on their own estates, but the general treatment of the question belonged to the autocracy.   In the official spheres there reigned a marked reactionary attitude towards the peasant-question; it had been manifested in the sessions of the State Council, of the Free Economic Society, and in the utterings of such liberals as Admiral Mordvinov.

The symptoms of the growing reactionary mood after the Napoleonic wars appeared first of all in the activity of the Ministry of Education.

The impulse given in the years 1803–1804 had been strong and fruitful.   In 1804 the Government opened five new universities in the country where there had been only one university and almost no primary schools.   The aim of the universities was not only to give their students an advanced education, but also to care for the general education in the districts under their supervision.   The university Councils enjoyed considerable autonomy, and they successfully carried on the work of organising adequate school systems, and choosing the right personnel.   The pedagogical personnel was then quite high, chiefly owing to the invitation of foreign professors (about sixty), although they had to lecture in Latin, French, or German; only half of the professors lectured in Russian.

In view of lack of funds the number of schools did not increase considerably after 1805, but they continued to improve qualitatively.   The development of schools was enhanced by abundant private contributions.   Such institutions as the Richelieu Lyceum in Odessa, later transformed into a university, or the Lazarev Institute for Oriental Languages in Moscow, were founded on private capital.   The state founded in those years the Lyceum in Tzarskoie-Selo, which has played an important rôle in the history of Russian literature and education.   That

Lyceum was established as a counter-balance to the prevailing system among the nobles of that time to give their children a domestic education with the aid of private teachers, mostly French emigrants, among whom there had been Jesuits carrying on an active propaganda for Catholicism. The Government tried to prevent that influence by requiring the teachers to hold examinations and by founding the Lyceum as a rival to private pensions.

In the provincial schools the body of pupils was quite democratic. The nobles, accustomed to use the services of foreign tutors, did not favour the state-schools, and therefore were able to accept into their schools commoners' children, and even some of peasant origin, which was against the law. In fact the reluctance of the nobles to make use of the state-schools, which greatly distressed the Ministry of Education, played perhaps a beneficial rôle in spreading education among the lower classes.

The further free development of education was impeded by the infection of the Ministry of Education with mystic tendencies. Among the public the mystic inclination was manifested in infatuation with Freemasonry. But in the governmental spheres those tendencies were expressed in a different form, namely in the energetic activity after the war of the Biblical Society, whose development was largely due to Alexander's sympathy with the views of that quaint institution.

The Bible Society was founded in England in 1804, and its chief aim was the translation of the Bible into all languages, and its sale at a very low price, which was possible owing to the lavish contributions given for the purpose. A branch of the Society was opened in Russia in 1812, and its head soon became the Super-Procurator of the Synod, Prince A. N. Golitzin, a boyhood friend of Alexander, at first a free thinker, but later a believing mystic of approximately the same nature as Alexander had been in the epoch of the Holy Alliance. Like Alexander, Golitzin was impressed with the Baroness Krüdener and with her exalted dim mysticism, with the Quakers, with the Jesuit

Joseph de Maistre, and with Russian "saints" and ascetics of that time. When Golitzin became the head of the Bible Society the governors of the provinces hastened to establish such societies throughout Russia. Golitzin attracted to the Society the heads of the Orthodox church, and when a translation of the Bible into Russian was undertaken its editor became Bishop Philaret, subsequently the famous Metropolitan of Moscow. The aims of the Society, modest and not reactionary in themselves, had acquired a different aspect in Russia, spreading ideas of nebulous mysticism and hypocrisy, particularly among the officials. However, the spread of branches over the country, especially in remote districts, far from the direct supervision of the centre, had some beneficial results, since in their endeavour to popularise the Scripture the branches were inevitably confronted with the problem of preliminary spread of education. The idea of the need of popular education for the understanding of the Bible, originated in the provincial branches, had come to be shared by Golitzin, who decided to establish a net of primary schools and almost succeeded in getting the Government's assignment of two million rubles a year for the purpose, a sum that nearly equalled the whole budget of the Ministry of Education. But soon Golitzin was appointed to replace the Minister of Education, Count A. K. Razumovsky, and one year after the Ministry of Education was merged with the Ministry of Public Worship, according to the project of the Prince.[3] Golitzin surrounded himself with desirable members of the Chief Management of Schools, and added to them a Scholastic Committee, into which entered such persons as the famous Sturdza, the author of the pamphlet against the German universities that

[3] In the manifesto of October 24, 1817, about the establishment of the new Ministry, was said:
"Desiring to have Christian piety as the permanent basis of true enlightenment, we have deemed it useful to unite the work of education with the work of all creeds into one department under the name of the Ministry of Public Worship and Popular education."

served as a signal for their persecution in 1819. Alongside with Sturdza there appeared such hypocrites and bigots as Magnitzky and Runich, who became District Curators and completely smashed the educational system that had recently been introduced with the aid of foreign professors. Soon the obscurantist tendencies were enhanced by the reaction in Germany, that took place after the assassination of Kotzebue by the student Sand, which with the influence of Metternich had deeply impressed Alexander. We must say, however, that Magnitzky's activity in Kazan had preceded the measures of the German reactionaries.[4]

Magnitzky had been one of Speransky's assistants in the Law Committee, and together with him suffered banishment as a dangerous person in 1812, but upon his return from Siberia in 1816 and appointment as governor of Simbirsk he soon showed himself as a thorough reactionary, Mystic, and hypocrite. In 1819 as a member of the Chief Management of Schools he was appointed inspector, and then Curator of the school-district of Kazan. Upon his demand eleven out of the twenty-odd professors were dismissed, and he proceeded to reorganise the whole state of the university of Kazan, interfering with the programme of every course and putting forth absolutely impossible demands. For instance, the course of political economy had to be constructed on the fundamental teachings of the Scripture; the students were transformed into half-*cantonists* (pupils of Arakcheiev's military schools. Tr.), half-novices: they were forced to march, to read and sing prayers in

[4] In fact the first attempts of the Russian reactionaries to turn the tendency of the Ministry of Education in the direction of obscurantism had been made even in the time of the Ministry of Count Razumovsky. The famous Catholic clerical, Count Joseph de Maistre (the former minister from Sardinia, who lived then in Petrograd as a private person), made great efforts in 1810–11 to influence Razumovsky and Golitzin (then the Super-Procurator of the Synod). In the same reactionary spirit though less cleverly and less audaciously, acted the Moscow Curator, P. I. Golenishchev-Kutuzov (1810–1813).

chorus; those who disobeyed were put in cells and wore plates with the inscription "Sinner," after which they had to do penance. Such was the state of affairs in Kazan, but throughout Russia there was marked a sharp reaction in educational institutions, especially in the Scholastic Committee, which was instructed by Sturdza to revise all text-books and inspect the entire pedagogical personnel. Among the exempted books was " Common Moral, or a Book about the Duties of Man," which appeared in 1783 and ran through eleven editions; its authorship has been ascribed to Catherine. Later even such a retrograde as Shishkov, when he became Minister of Education, interceded for the rehabilitation of that book. Even most innocent text-books were put under suspicion.

After the University of Kazan came the turn of Kharkov. There the reoganisation took place after the same manner by the Curator Karnieev, although on a smaller scale: one of the best Russian professors, the mathematician Osipovsky, was discharged, and Professor Schad, as mentioned, was banished abroad; the latter was removed as a follower of a dangerous philosophical doctrine (he was a Schellingian), and for his opposition to serfdom.

This reaction, however, did not at once affect all educational districts; the district of Petrograd, for instance, presented an exception. Its Curator, Count S. S. Uvarov, for a time quite liberal and at any rate a very learned man, had attempted to oppose the reaction, and even carried through in 1819 the reorganisation of the Pedagogic Institute into a university. The fact that Uvarov, an admirer of Karamzin, whose views he later advocated as Minister of Education, appeared as the chief representative of the opposition in the Ministry of Public Worship and Popular Education, shows how extreme had been the reactionary activity of that Ministry. Uvarov, however, had to resign, and his place was taken by the mad obscurantist Runich, also a member of the Scholastic Committee, who began to do in Petrograd what Magnitzky had done in Kazan. In 1821 he started a persecution of the Professors Raupach, Hermann, Arseniev, and Galich. The first two were foreigners, and they were to be banished abroad, as in the case of Schad; Arseniev was a remarkable statistician, and Galich a distinguished philosopher. The nonsensical persecution of the Professors was prolonged, however, for several years, and it remained for Nicolas in 1827 to order their rehabilitation.

Among the magazines published after the Napoleonic wars the most important was *The Spirit of Journals* issued by Yatzenkov; another popular magazine was *The Son of the Fatherland,* edited by Grech, which supplanted Glinka's *Russian Messenger.* Yatzenkov had been a censor, and he knew how to get by the censorship. Under the rubric of *Thoughts and Judgments by Empress Catherine* he carried on an indirect criticism of contemporary events. The censor pursued him for his attitude towards the old order of government, for his financial and administrative views and especially for his opposition to serfdom.

Formally the Censorship Statute of 1804 was in force, but beginning with 1807 the special censorship of the secret police began to function, parallel with the official censorship of the Ministry of Education. The Secret Committee established in 1807 was to examine all newspapers and magazines, and the newly founded Ministry of Police had the right to confiscate even publications that had been passed by the official censor. Beginning with 1815 the censor did not allow any new publications before getting a preliminary sanction of the Ministry of Police. Razumovsky, who took the place of Zavadovsky as Minister of Education in 1810, expressed views analogous with those of the Ministry of Police, and held that no criticism of persons in the service of the state was permissible; the director of the Ministry of Police, Viazmitinov, demanded on this basis that even criticism of actors on the Imperial stage should be forbidden. Yet while under Razumovsky the censorship had a prohibitive, negative character, under Golitzin it began to manifest positive tendencies toward promulgating through books and periodicals a definite reactionary and obscurantist spirit.

However dark was the picture of the condition of education and of the press in the years that immediately followed the end of the Napoleonic wars, still during the years 1816–1820 one could definitely distinguish the tendencies and actions of obscurantists who had triumphed in separate departments, from the ideas of Alexander himself, who in spite of his growing mysticism remained moderately liberal in his attitude towards political questions.

In his speech at the opening of the first Polish Diet in 1818 Alexander requested the representatives of Poland to prove to Europe that " free institutions whose sacred principles some attempt to confuse with destructive teachings are not a dangerous dream; that on the contrary such institutions established with a pure heart for the achievement of a useful and salutary aim are in perfect accord with social order and confirm the well-being of nations." " It is for you," he said, " to prove by experience this great truth. May concord be the soul of your assemblies, and may dignity, coolness, and moderation signify your discussions. . . . In so acting your assembly will gain the approval of your country and those feelings of general respect which are inspired by such institutions when the representatives of a free people do not distort the sacred calling bestowed upon them. . . ."

In the beginning of that speech Alexander said: " The former existence of this order (constitutional. Tr.) in your country has enabled me to grant you at once that which has not ceased to be the object of my cares, and the beneficial influence of this free institution I hope, with the aid of God, to expand on all countries entrusted to my care. Thus you have given me a means to demonstrate to my country that which I have been preparing for it since long, and which it will enjoy as soon as the foundations for such an important matter will reach the necessary ripeness . . ."

The sessions of the Diet lasted, according to the Constitution, exactly thirty days.   In violation of the Constitution, Alexander postponed the presentation of the budget, relying on the confidence of the people, giving as a reason the impossibility of introducing a new financial system before knowing definitely the figures of the national debt, the investigation of which had not yet been finished.   The Chamber did not oppose the postponement.   Also the Criminal code presented to the Diet by the Government was accepted without discussion.   But the Chamber rejected by a large majority the bill concerning marriage and divorce, which disagreed with the established law of the land.   In this connection Alexander said in his speech at the closing of the Diet: "Of the bills presented to you only one was disapproved by the majority votes of both Chambers.   Inner conviction and frankness dictated this decision.   It gratifies me, as I see in it the independence of your opinions.   Those who are freely chosen must deliberate freely.   Through you I hope to hear a sincere and full expression of public opinion, and only an assembly similar to yours can serve for the Government as a pledge that the published laws are in accordance with the essential needs of the people."

The Warsaw speeches, reprinted and commented upon by the Russian periodicals — the censor was unable to forbid them as they were the speeches of the Emperor himself [5]— made an enormous impression on the Russian reading public.   Karamzin, who regarded them negatively, wrote to Dmitriev: "The War-

[5] What had been impossible for the Russian censor in 1818 was actually done in the next century by a more audacious censor.   About 1906 there appeared a brochure under the title: "Speeches and toasts by Emperor Nicolas II."   There was not a single word by way of comment in the pamphlet.   A few days after its publication the censor ordered its confiscation.— TR.

saw speeches have been strongly re-echoed in the hearts of the
young.   They see the constitution while asleep and awake; they
talk, discuss, even write about it — in *The Son of the Fatherland,* in the speech of Uvarov . . ."   Grech's publication had
had no stable, definite views, and belonged to the category of
newspapers which were later characterised by Shchedrin by the
slogan: "What is your request?"   Uvarov was then the Curator of the Petrograd district, and in the speech he delivered on
the occasion of the reorganisation of the Pedagogic Institute
he called political freedom "the latest fair gift of a god," and
declared that the dangers and storms which accompany that
freedom should not frighten the people: the great gift of
freedom is "accompanied with enormous sacrifices and losses,
it is gained slowly and is preserved only by steady firmness."   As
we see, Uvarov understood better than Alexander the inevitable connection between political disturbances and political
freedom.   On another occasion he remarked about those who
hoped to grant enlightenment and at the same time to tender
it "harmless," that "they desired fire which should not scald."

Such was the complicated internal policy of Alexander during
the fifth period of his reign, when under the influence of the
great events the public had developed a profound demand for
a radical reconstruction of the social and political order of the
state; the period that appeared so trying and unbearable for
those who had been imbued with the liberal doctrines of the
age and had seen with their own eyes the beginnings of the re-
nascence of Germany and the more democratic structure of the
Western European countries.   Those ideas found expression in
secret societies that had risen since 1816, secret because along with
the liberal declarations of Alexander there existed the Ministry
of Police which did not permit any criticism of internal affairs.
But the impression of Alexander's Warsaw speeches was such
that many of the founders of the secret societies hoped that before
long their societies would be declared open, legal organisations.

CHAPTER XII

THE aspiration for social activity which appeared among the young army-officers after their return from abroad in the years 1813–14, was manifested in the formation of various organisations, clubs, Masonic orders, literary and educational circles, like the " Arzamas," the " Green Lamp," and others, whose significance in the history of Russian literature is generally known. Soon there appeared also political organisations. In Petrograd two such undertakings were formed at the same time. On one hand, the twenty-four-year-old colonel, Alexander Muraviov, a young man inclined towards mysticism (he occupied a high degree in a French Masonic order), founded a society among the officers of the Semionovsky regiment; on the other hand, a young, brilliant general who had performed important diplomatic tasks during the war of 1814, Mikhail Orlov, made an attempt to attract to the formation of a political Masonic society Count Mamonov (a representative of the old Catherinian Freemasonry which had pursued political aims during Novikov and Schwarz) and Nicolay Turgeniev, who undertook the mission of talking the matter over with several persons, among them with the generals of the Guards, Benkendorf and Vassilchikov. In the provincial towns, among the infantry and artillery regiments, an analogous movement had taken place. Thus Junker Borisov founded a circle of " Lovers of Nature " for young officers, which later developed into the " Society of United Slavs " that subsequently joined the " Southern Society "—the most significant secret organisation in the twenties.

Orlov's attempt had failed, the circle of " Lovers of Nature " had no importance at the beginning, but the undertaking of Muraviov was destined to play a great historical rôle. Here is an outline of its history.

In 1816 several officers of the Semionovsky regiment came together — Lieutenant I. D. Yakushkin, the brothers Sergey and Matvey Muraviov-Apostol, Colonel Alexander Muraviov, and Nikita Muraviov (the son of Mikhail Muraviov, one of the teachers of Alexander I), and decided to form a political organisation. The organisation grew, but had no definite programme or aim, until a new member entered — Pavel Pestel, a young, clever, and energetic adjutant of Prince Witgenstein, who at once gave the society a definite platform. Its aim became the achievement of a constitutional form of government; Pestel borrowed its organisation from the Italian secret societies, the *Carbonari*. The Society, founded by Muraviov and organised by Pestel, was named " The Union of Salvation, or of the Faithful and True Sons of the Fatherland." In general two main types of secret societies were known in Europe at that time: one, the more peaceful, cultural organisation, of the kind of the German *Tugendbund,* whose aim had been the cultural and political revival of Germany, and which worked with the approval of the Government since it had been directed chiefly against the enemy of Germany — Napoleon; on the other hand, in southern Europe worked the *Carbonari,* or as they were called in Greece, the *Hetæriæ,*— typical organisations of conspirators. Pestel chose the type of the *Carbonari,* which corresponded better with his personal character and principles. Most of the founders of the " Union of Salvation " were liberal-minded men who sought better forms of political and social life, but to some degree they were mystics and dreamers; many of them were not yet twenty years of age. Pestel, although also young (he was not yet twenty-four), was a man with quite formed views and definite convictions, and of extraordinary ability and will-power. He was greatly respected not only by his comrades and friends, but also by his superiors and by all who knew him. His chief superior, the commander-in-chief of the Southern army, Prince Witgenstein, declared that Pestel might the very next day become a minister, or an army-commander, and that he would not fail in any post. Of the same opinion was General Kiselev, then Chief of the Staff of the Southern army. His close comrades — Prince Volkonsky, Yakushkin, and other Decembrists, who left memoirs or testified at the trial of Pestel, spoke about him, of course, with still greater enthusiasm. In a word Pestel was the most remarkable personality among the members of the secret societies. He possessed a big mind, and at the same time also a corresponding temperament; he had an iron will and a colossal ambition which had evidently been one of the moving springs in him alongside with his sincere ideals for common welfare.

It was natural that such a person could sway the vague dreamers on his side, and he had no difficulty in getting the members to accept the *Carbonari* constitution. One of the quaint points of that constitution was the ceremony of terrible oaths that had to be taken at the initiation, not unlike most of the Masonic orders. A more interesting point was the division of the members into various degrees unequal in their rights. At the head of the Society stood the *Boyars,* who were not even to be known (in principle) to the other members; the constitution of the Society was known only to the *Boyars* and to the next degree, the *Men,* but not to the third degree, the *Brothers,* who had to obey blindly the orders of the Society. Finally there was a fourth degree, not members, but sympathisers, *Friends,* who were registered as desirable material, could be recruited into active membership, but might not know either about their registration or their connection with the Society. Such an organisation corresponded with Pestel's Jacobine views which he had developed in himself as an admirer of the epoch of the Convention and of the revolutionary government in France of 1793.

Pestel had to leave soon after the acceptance of the Constitution for the place of his service, at first in the Ostsee Region, where Witgenstein had been in command of a corps, and from 1818, with the appointment of Witgenstein as commander-in-chief of the Southern army, at Tulchin, a small town on the Moldavian frontier, the headquarters of the army. Among the remaining members of the Society a fermentation soon took place, especially after the acceptance of a new member, Mikhail Muraviov, a man of strong will, who disagreed with Pestel's views and sharply opposed the Jacobine form of the organisation. He categorically refused to bring the oaths at his initiation, and upon reading the Constitution he declared that it was fit for forest-brigands, but not for a cultural society with political aims. There rose discussions and negotiations. About that time a considerable part of the Guards gathered at Moscow on the occasion of erecting a cathedral in memory of the last war, and long debates took place among the members of the Society concerning the differences of opinion that had risen on account of Mikhail Muraviov.

Muraviov and his adherents finally prevailed upon the members to let them work out a new constitution, for which they took as a model that of the *Tugendbund,* published in *Freimüthige Blätter.* Muraviov and his circle translated and adapted it for Russian circumstances, and after many debates it was accepted, and the Society was named instead of "Union of Salvation," "Union of Welfare" (1818). The platform was extremely moderate; the Society was to co-operate with the Government for the betterment of the condition of the people, materially and spiritually; it appealed to the Government for confidence, quoting for the purpose some of Catherine's early liberal aphorisms. In fact the Society acted almost openly, and the Government did not persecute it.

Some suggest that these aims were put forth only for appearance, and that there was a second part of the constitution, of a purely political nature. But that second part, the preparation of which was turned over to Nikita Muraviov, had not been finished; it had been discussed by some of the leaders, but had not been accepted by the Union, or even by the central organ. As they did not propose to pursue any conspiratory aims, the members acted openly along cultural-educational lines, and all knew their constitution, the so-called " Green Book."

The activity of the " Union of Welfare " was grouped in four branches. The first was *philanthropic,* i.e., it comprised succour for needy mankind. In practice this activity could be then expressed particularly in the improvement of peasant-conditions, the more so since most of the members (if not all) were landowners. But although the constitution of the *Tugendbund* forbade the members to have slaves, the constitution of the " Union of Welfare " advocated only a kind treatment of one's serfs. The chief worker for the improvement of the serfs in the Union had been N. I. Turgeniev.

The second branch of activity was *educational,* and in this respect the members worked chiefly among the army. The most active in that field had been General M. F. Orlov, the one who had long ago dreamt about founding a secret political society. As a commander of a division he aided the wide spread of Lancasterian schools both among his regiments and among the population with which his division had come in contact. Orlov contributed personally and collected large sums for the educational work. In 1818 he wrote, for instance, that he had collected sixteen thousand rubles. N. I. Turgeniev asserted that Orlov had given all his salary for education.

The third branch consisted in the work for *the betterment of justice* in Russia. In this respect the activity of the Society could be best expressed in the working out of projects for the new courts. This work fell also to Turgeniev who served as a state-secretary at the State Council. Many members had the idea that in order to effect an immediate improvement of justice they should have resigned their military positions and entered the service in lower courts, e.g., in Aulic courts. Some of them did so. Pushkin's close Lyceum-friend, I. I. Pushchin, accepted the post of Aulic judge at Moscow. Ryleiev did likewise, even before his becoming a member of the Society.

Finally, the fourth branch, the *economic,* cared for the economic and financial improvement of national affairs. The work consisted largely in publishing books on the question. As a monumental work of that activity we have Turgeniev's remarkable *Essay on the Theory of Taxation.* Turgeniev had intended together with Professor Kunitzin to issue a monthly, but he was not allowed to do so, in spite of his being a state-secretary at the State Council and a director of one of the departments in the Ministry of Finance.

In spite of the increase in membership (in 1819 the Society had two hundred members), the activity of the Union was rather indolent and appeared to many as too lukewarm, considering the growing dissatisfaction with the Government's policy of repressions, obscurantism, and the hateful Military Colonies. There was felt a need for a more revolutionary organisation. Some of the members had long been inclined toward more vigorous action. Thus in 1817, Yakushkin volunteered to assassinate Alexander, when the "Union of Salvation" had received a letter from Prince Trubetzkoy about the circulating rumours of Alexander's intention to move his throne to Warsaw, and similar nonsense. The question of regicidism was not carried out in practice, but the episode illustrates certain moods among the members.

In 1820 Pestel was in Petrograd, and took part in a gathering at the house of F. N. Glinka, the adjutant of the Governor-General of Petrograd, Miloradovich. The discussion turned to the question, Which form of government was preferable: a republic or a constitutional monarchy? Pestel categorically advocated a republic, and finally had the question voted upon; all but one expressed themselves for a republic. True the decision had only a theoretical value, but Pestel considered it more serious, and later tried to ascribe to it the significance of a formal resolution.

In the same year there took place in Petrograd an event which, although not caused by the activity of the " Union of Welfare," was reflected in the fate of all secret societies (among them the Masonic orders) ; this was the mutiny among the soldiers of the Semionovsky regiment, which was not influenced by the officers. The regiment had been treated before quite humanly; most of the officers were liberals, and belonged to the " Union of Welfare "; the commander was a good-hearted man, General Potiomkin. In 1820 the commandership passed to Colonel Schwarz, a rude despot, inclined to harsh reprisals; in his intention to bring the regiment under his subjection, he ordered flogged several cavaliers of the order of St. George, who were exempt by law from such punishment. Several companies rose in mutiny. It had a rather mild form: the soldiers wished to ask Schwarz not to employ such measures in the future. The officers — among them S. I. Muraviov-Apostol — tried to dissuade them, understanding that the soldiers would achieve no results; but their arguments were of no avail, and in the end the whole regiment was imprisoned in the fortress. This circumstance made an enormous impression on Alexander. He was at that time at the Leibach Congress. The mutiny took place synchronously with another unpleasant event — the sessions of the second Warsaw Diet in 1820, which rejected all the bills introduced by the Government after a series of sharp, oppositional speeches. To these were added the news about the revolution in Naples, which formed the subject of discussions at the Congress. All these circumstances worked on Alexander's mood, so that the "mutiny" of the Semionovsky regiment made a tremendous impression upon him, the more so since he had personally commanded it at one time, and had been very fond of it. He refused to believe that the regiment rose up without the agitation of secret leaders. The regiment was dispersed among various military parts. The event had two consequences. On one hand the scattered officers and soldiers formed excellent cadres of revolutionary propagandists throughout the Empire; on the other hand, in view of the tense mood of the Government, the " Union of Welfare " decided to disband, and in January, 1821, the chairman of the Moscow sessions of the Union, N. I. Turgeniev, sent out circulars to all the members about the closing up of the Society.

An opinion exists that the Society decided to disband only for the sake of appearance, in order to deceive the Government's vigilance, and to continue their activity in a more conspirative form. This could hardly have been the idea of the majority of the members. At any rate, in Petrograd the Society actually ceased to exist.

Upon his return from abroad Alexander received a detailed report about the activity of that Society through the treacherous Vassilchikov. True the Emperor remarked that he would not punish individuals who held the same liberal ideas which he had himself advocated in the first years of his reign, but he remained nevertheless greatly distressed over the state of mind among the Guards, and ordered them sent to the western frontier in 1821, and then purposely prolonged their stay for one year and a half in Lithuania, evidently believing that the Petrograd atmosphere acted detrimentally upon the young officers. Thus the main elements of the Society were removed from the capital.

But when the delegates of the Moscow conference arrived at Tulchin with the report about the disbandment of the Society, the southern members, headed by Pestel and Yushnevsky (the Intendant-General of the Southern army), declared that they would not disorganise, and their branch became an independent Society which reintroduced Pestel's former constitution of the " Union of Salvation," and put forth definitely political and revolutionary aims. The Society strove for the establishment of a republic in Russia by Jacobine means.

The Southern Society was organised in the form of three boards. The central board was at Tulchin under the management of Pestel and Yushnevsky, who were elected as the chief directors of the Society; the whole power was actually in the hands of Pestel. Then there were two branches, one in Kamenka under the management of a local landowner, a retired colonel, V. Davidov, and of the commander of the infantry brigade that was stationed there, General Prince S. G. Volkonsky; and another branch at Vassilkov under the management of Sergey Muraviov-Apostol who acted somewhat independently of Pestel, and made his chief assistant a young officer (also of the Semionovsky regiment), Mikhail Bestuzhev-Riumin.

Pestel had constantly put before his comrades the necessity not only of regicide but of the annihilation of the entire Imperial family; on this question dissensions always took place between him and Muraviov-Apostol. The conferences of the leaders occurred once a year at Kiev during the fair, in 1822, '23, '24, and 1825; the question about means for the destruction of the reigning House was discussed every time, but the final resolution had been postponed from conference to conference.

Although Pestel had put forth such radical aims, he acted coolly and cautiously, weighing and discussing every step with much deliberation. Sergey Muraviov-Apostol was, on the contrary, impatient and inclined to be enthusiastic and quick; though he could not bear the thought of annihilating a whole family, he yet demanded a prompt beginning of action, and always aspired to raise a revolt, even for insignificant causes, as the dismissal of an officer. His assistant, Bestuzhev-Riumin, was of a still more ardent and quick temperament. He actively propagated his views, and succeeded in accomplishing two big things. He discovered the existence of an independent " Society of United Slavs," whose aim was the establishment of a federative republic of all Slav nations; he persuaded them to join the " Southern Society." He also entered into negotiations with the Polish revolutionary organisations, and discussed with them at length whether they would consent to be guided by the Russian revolutionary plans, and whether they would arrest or kill, if so demanded, Grand Duke Constantine. The Poles answered those questions rather evasively, evidently not trusting the firmness and discreetness of the Russian organisations very much. Bestuzhev tried to throw dust into their eyes by exaggerating the dimensions of the Russian plot. Pestel interfered, and took part in the discussions about the limits within which Poland should be restored. The Poles of course demanded the frontiers of 1772, but Pestel declared definitely for the restoration of an ethnographical Poland only (not including, i.e., the Little-Russian and Lithuanian elements).

At the same time Pestel employed energetic measures for the revival of the secret Society in Petrograd. He kept sending his emissaries (Prince S. G. Volkonsky, Matvey Muraviov, Alexander Podgio, and others) there, and in 1824 he went there himself. With his efforts the Society did come to life again, but he was unable to make the members of that " Northern Society " follow his plans and obey his will: the Northerners had by that time developed independent views, which differed greatly from Pestel's. The " Northern Society " was resurrected in 1822, upon the return of the Guards. A new board was elected consisting of Nikita Muraviov, Prince S. P. Trubetzkoy, and N. Turgeniev, but the latter declined and was supplanted by a young officer, Prince Eugene Obolensky. Nikita Muraviov worked out a constitution which differed in many points from that of Pestel.

Muraviov's Constitution, on one hand, and Pestel's Constitution, under the name of "Russian Justice"[1] or "State Testament," on the other, presented two rival currents among the revolutionary circles. Pestel demanded a republican form of government; he had been influenced by Destutt de Tracy, the famous French commentator of Montesquieu's *L'esprit des lois,* and advocated his view about the incompatibility of a monarchical régime with the will of the people. Admitting that Russia was not ready for a republic, Pestel intended to overthrow the existing order by a military *coup d'état,* and to organise a military dictatorship as a temporary government which would prepare Russia for a republican order in some eight or ten years. This would naturally lead to a military-despotic régime, since the realisation of the plan would involve the suppression of a series of contre-revolutions.

Moreover, the very republic projected by Pestel was of a clearly Jacobine type, with a strong centralised administration. The legislative power was to belong to a *vieche* (a common council), but the whole administration was to be concentrated, after the model of the French Directory, in the hands of five Directors. Pestel did not allow any local autonomy, but desired to unite all the Empire into one politically uniform whole; he intended to incorporate Finland, and to allow Poland to separate only under the condition of establishing a socio-political order similar to that in Russia. Pestel did not consider linguistic or religious differences: the Russian language and Church were to be dominating. He intended to interfere with the internal life of the Mahomedans, and to abolish the subordination of their women. The Jews Pestel considered harmful exploiters of the peasants, and planned to transplant them all to Palestine, for which purpose he was to give them military aid.

[1] He borrowed that name from the ancient code of laws established in Russ early in the eleventh century by Prince Yaroslav. The word *pravda* signifies in Russian both justice and truth, or right and verity. — Tr.

Thus Pestel's views were not too liberal; but his democratic principles were deeply promulgated in his plan, especially in the economic region. His agrarian plan was original, democratic, and consequential. He planned to divide all lands into two categories: one, social, should be in communal possession of the people, the other, fiscal, could be exploited by the state or be distributed by the Government to private persons. At any rate Pestel considered that land could not be an object of private property, but should serve primarily for the provision of the masses.

As to the Constitution of the " Northern Society," worked out by Nikita Muraviov, it was monarchical. Many of their members, and Nikita himself, admitted that a republic was better than a monarchy, but they saw no hope for accomplishing such a form of government. This Constitution included the principles of the most radical constitutions of that time; as its model the Spanish constitution of 1812 had evidently served. The first paragraph of Muraviov's Constitution definitely declared that the Russian Empire could not be the property of a certain family. The will of the people was to be supreme. The Monarch's power was very limited. The *vieche* was to have not only all legislative powers, but could even declare war, peace, and amnesty — usually monarchical privileges. Another distinct feature of Muraviov's Constitution was Federalism, with a large provincial autonomy, as against Pestel's centralised republic. Muraviov's monarchy was divided into thirteen (fifteen, in the second edition of the Constitution) autonomous provinces, each of which was to have its own *Duma,* subject, of course, to the direction of the central authority.

Such were the two main currents that existed at that time among the revolutionary societies in Russia. Their difference lay not so much in the question of republic or monarchy, as in the means for the accomplishment of the aim: whether by a Jacobine way, or by way of submitting to the will of the people.

Ryleiev, who became at the beginning of the year 1825 the dominant force in the "Northern Society," declared that in principle one might prefer a republic, provided the people consented to it. Thus the chief opposition of the "Northern Society" to Pestel's plans was directed against his intention to establish a republic by all means, even against the will of the people. In this sense Ryleiev and Nikita Muraviov were true *Narodovoltzy*.[2] The views of the revolutionary circles found reflection, naturally, in the views of the broad layers of society.

[2] The revolutionary party, "The Will of the People," which operated during Alexander II's reign, and by whose decree that Tzar was assassinated in 1881.— TR.

CHAPTER XIII

TURNING to the activity of the Government in the last years of Alexander's reign, we must first of all admit that it was one of the darkest periods in Russian history. The Government decidedly repudiated any idea of liberal reforms.

Alexander's own mood had definitely changed after 1820. We have seen that up to that time despite his growing mysticism and increasing hatred for any form of revolution, he still had a warm sympathy for liberal institutions and for a constitutional order. Metternich, in whose eyes there had always existed a close connection between liberalism and revolutions, vigorously opposed Alexander's views at all international congresses, considering him a Utopianist and a romantic, and at times ascribed Alexander's liberalism to his masqued ambitious plots.

But in 1820 the incident with the Semionovsky regiment occurred, and Alexander falsely interpreted it as a result of revolutionary propaganda; then came the oppositional attitude of the Polish Diet; and finally the revolutionary fermentation in Western Europe had broken out in the Neapolitan and Spanish revolutions. All these events combined had shaken Alexander's conviction that liberal institutions and revolution were different matters; he observed how in the Twenties liberals and revolutionists worked hand in hand against reactionary governments which had broken their obligations and promises to the people.

In view of these changes, there was formed a complete *entente cordiale* between Alexander and Metternich, a perfect concord in their hostility to all the popular movements of that time. It was then that the " Holy Alliance," formed by Alexander in 1815, had become a union of monarchs against freedom-craving nations. Alexander tried to be extremely consequential in that policy, and for this reason he formally sided with the Sultan against his rebellious subjects, the Greeks, despite his personal sympathies and public opinion in Russia and the views of his mystical friends, such as Baroness Krüdener. This was demonstrated so sharply that Alexander's chief assistant in foreign affairs, Count Capo d'Istria, a Greek by origin, had to resign his post, while General Prince Alexander Ypsilanti who took active part in the Greek revolt was formally excluded from Russian service, although inwardly Alexander approved of Ypsilanti's activity, and did not conceal his opinion from his entourage. If, in spite of such a policy, the relations between Russia and Turkey were quite unstable at that time — one moment war was but a hair's distance away, and the Russian ambassador thought best to ask for his papers and depart — it was due to the fanatical actions of the Porte instigated by the British ambassador, Stratford.

In his internal policy Alexander demonstrated his new mood only negatively — in his rejection of all liberal undertakings and his absolute indifference to any reforms. He concentrated his interests in military administration, particularly in the Military Colonies which continued to grow rapidly, against public opinion and in spite of the protests of the peasants who were turned into Colonists. At the same time Alexander's mysticism reached its climax; he was gloomy and sought self-forgetfulness in frequent and rapid travels over Russia. He fell under the influence of persons far inferior to Baroness Krüdener and the English Quakers — of such black bigots as Archimandrite Fotiy, who had risen from the position of a bible-instructor in a military school by the aid of his devoted admirer, Countess Orlov-Chesmensky, and partly also by the aid of Arakcheiev and Prince Golitzin, the famous Minister. In regard to Golitzin, Fotiy, perhaps urged by Arakcheiev, displayed in the end insolent hostility, anathematising him for his alleged leniency towards non-Orthodox creeds and mystic sects.   In spite of Alexander's personal friendship for him, Golitzin was forced to resign.   The Ministry then fell apart; ecclesiastical matters were again transferred to the Super-Procurator of the Synod, Prince Meshchersky; Admiral Shishkov, the man who carried on a controversy with Karamzin about the inviolability of the ancient Russian style, and who later composed patriotic manifestoes in the name of Alexander, and read for him passages from the Prophets, was appointed Minister of Education.   Under Shishkov, Magnitzky and Runich remained in power for some time.   Magnitzky, having accomplished the ravage of the university of Kazan, undertook the working out of a new censorship-statute for which he strained all his reactionary inventiveness.   The Statute was published during the next reign and did not last long.

Still, in spite of the domination of reactionism at that period, the Government undertook no persecution of the revolutionary organisations, which led many to believe that it had been ignorant of their existence.   It is well established at present that from 1821 Alexander had been informed about every step of the secret Societies.   We have noted his argument against persecuting those who held his own former views, in his answer to the information of Vassilchikov.   Evidently his conscience was against taking strict measures to suppress the growing unrest.   Espionage had rapidly developed by that time, but it bore an academic aspect; the Government knew that the " Southern Society " was plotting against it, yet the conspirators were not disturbed.   Only in his last year Alexander gave some attention to the information of the sub-officer, Sherwood, about the " Southern Society "; Sherwood was instructed by Arakcheiev to obtain additional information.   When already in Taganrog Alexander became somewhat alarmed by Sherwood's additional information, and by the new report of Captain Maiboroda, one of Pestel's subordinates.   General Chernyshev was sent to the

Southern army with an order to arrest the leaders of the Society and begin an investigation. It is hard to say what would have happened had Alexander not died then, but we may presume that the persecution of the conspirators would not have had the cruel forms in which it was expressed under Nicolas, after the insurrection of December 14.

In regard to Poland Alexander's reactionary mood was expressed in his failure to convene the Diet for five years, and in another anti-Constitutional act — his ordering the sessions of the Diet of 1825 to be closed to the press and the public, except the opening and closing sessions. He said at that time that he considered the Constitution of 1815 an experiment, and evidently felt at liberty to withdraw it at any moment. The Diet of 1825 passed more quietly than that of 1820, externally at least; but the revolutionary ideas had developed in Poland as strongly as in Russia, and if they found full expression only in the insurrection of 1830, their fermentation undoubtedly had taken place under Alexander.

The only branch of the administration where order began to rule at that time, was the Ministry of Finance, after the appointment, by the recommendation of Arakcheiev, of Kankrin in place of Guriev. The activity of the honest, economical, and learned Kankrin was displayed mainly during the reign of Nicolas; when he was appointed, in 1823, financial affairs were in a deplorable state. The economic condition of the population was at its worst; taxes were collected with great difficulty; landowners, who were responsible for their peasants, were frequently placed under "wardship" (receivership) for failing to pay the taxes, and Fiscal peasants suffered forced sales of their houses and property. In the last years of Alexander's reign the western region suffered from crop-failures and famines, with which it was difficult to cope in view of the bad roads. The building of roads went on without any plan or system, by way of "natural obligation" that lay hard on the back of the

peasantry. Sometimes whole villages were driven out to perform the "natural obligation" hundreds of miles from their
homes, very often in summer, during field-labour time.

The taverns flourished under the fiscal monopoly; the people
left there their last copecks. Yet the beverage-income of the
state had decreased, owing to the extraordinary thievery of the
officials; this feature — official thievery and abuses — had
reached its climax in those years, according to the unanimous
testimony of all contemporaries.

Thus ended the reign that in its beginning had aroused such
bright hopes.

In casting a retrospective glance at the epoch we have now
passed, we cannot help being astonished — at least from the first,
superficial examination, at the comparatively meagre results of
the enormous expenditures and sacrifices of the whole nation:
Russia at the end of Alexander's reign seemed — externally —
not far advanced in the conditions of her state and social life
from the times of Catherine, of Novikov, and Schwarz. There
still remained the autocracy above, serfdom below, and the reign
of anarchy among administrators and landowners. Military
Colonies had come to be; popular education that had progressed
so well at the beginning of the reign, was now suppressed, distorted, and maimed by obscurantist and reactionary measures of
clericalists and fanatical mystics; the press was reduced to zero,
and it appeared that all legal and peaceful ways for the free
development of society were cut off. . . .

But such a conclusion about the results of Alexander's reign
would be true only from the external, formal, side; a careful
retrospective view at the inner meaning of the events we have
been studying and at their inner connection, will prove the incorrectness of such a conclusion.

By the time of Alexander's accession the process of the formation of a state-territory had been accomplished, at least in its

general features. The struggle for territory no longer presented an essential task of the Russian state, consequently the Government was able to turn its attention to the internal needs of the population. Even under Catherine there began to take form a considerable centre of thinking society, in which aspirations for working out independent views and some political ideals were manifest. Towards the end of her reign liberals and democrats stood in opposition to the Government, and suffered persecution. Under Paul those persecutions and the unbridled despotism of the authorities had reached unbelievable dimensions, and gave the whole of Russian educated society an impulse to think and feel the importance of practical guarantees against governmental despotism. Upon the removal of Paul the public fell into careless joy and rosy optimism, full of confidence in the new Monarch who declared his intention of granting his land " legally-free " institutions, and of later withdrawing to private life. But he was an inexperienced youth who knew neither the country nor himself; by the aid of his friends — councillors whom the conservatives of the time unjustly named " a Jacobine band "— Alexander became convinced of the great difficulty of realising his dreams and political plans. At the same time he became interested in the great events of Western Europe, and discovered in himself an inclination and vocation for diplomacy. As a result, the state-reforms of his first five years did not go further than the institution of the ministries and the very moderate reform of the Senate. The most important obstacles for a progressive movement were found to be: Serfdom, the liquidation of which was difficult without preparation, and the almost total absence of education among the people. For the removal of the last obstacle much had been done in the first years of Alexander's reign which are justly considered the most brilliant epoch in the history of Russian education in the nineteenth century. During the same period, owing to external and internal peace, Russian commerce and industry flourished very markedly. The first measures for the improvement of the peasant-life were also inaugurated and, in the Ostsee region — for the limitation of the landowners' power.

The wars of 1805–07, the defeat of the Russian armies, and the complete subjugation of their allies by Napoleon, had enormous consequences for the further course of Russian affairs: Russia could no longer stand aloof from the events that took place in Western Europe, and was forced by Alexander's policy to participate to the end in those affairs. The Treaty of Tilsit placed Alexander in a difficult position. He was not so vain as to be flattered for a moment with the rôle of the only equal ally and friend of the great conqueror of Europe. He was little attracted by Napoleon's proposal to divide between them the dominion of the world; moreover, he knew how to value Napoleon's words and suggestions, and the necessity of concluding a close alliance with a man whom a few months before he had declared from church pulpits to be the enemy of Christendom and of all mankind, was not very pleasant for him. At Tilsit he acted in direct opposition to the thoughts and aspirations of his people; the Continental System had added to Russia's moral humiliation also material ruination. Those conditions weakened and almost destroyed the popularity which Alexander had theretofore enjoyed in his country; they had also forced many minds to turn for the first time to political questions, and to stand in conscious opposition to the Government. Men of such opposite views as Karamzin and Speransky testified alike about the dissatisfaction of Russia. The unrealised reconstruction of Speransky could not improve matters, and his financial plan, also, in a large measure, not carried out, with all its merits, only helped to open the public's eyes to the evils of the former and subsequent financial policy, and on the inevitability of further ruin, from which the country could no longer be saved either by the abrogation of the Continental System or by the beneficial tariff of 1810.

This extremely tense and difficult situation was relieved by the War of 1812. Although the terrible sufferings and sacrifices caused by that war had devastated the most developed part of the country and had ruined almost irretrievably a large portion of the landowners' wealth, the results appeared redeeming in the eyes of the population. The people stood the test heroically, and the War of 1812 proved the power of Russia's national consciousness and firmness. If the consequences of the Tilsit Treaty and of the Continental System had been important for the formation of a critical and oppositional attitude in the public, the consequences of Russia's participation in the Napoleonic wars and in the overthrow of Napoleon were immeasurably more important for all the further development of Russian life. They were enormous, appeared in various spheres and currents, and have in various ways helped the acceleration of the decay and liquidation of the established social and political order. Later in the matter of the abolition of serfdom we shall see more clearly the importance of the ruin and indebtedness of the landowners. On the other hand, I have already noted the significance of the fact that a mass of young, educated, and susceptible representatives of Russian society had been present in Western Europe at the very moment of the reorganisation of that society, and had had an opportunity of getting acquainted with all sides of European life, owing to the length of their stay there; many had stayed on even after the conclusion of peace, during the three years' stay of Vorontzov's occupational corps in France. That circumstance had prepared the formation of the secret societies of the first and second decades of the nineteenth century. We have seen how after the wars the public once more put their hopes in Alexander's reformatory activity, the more so since he had confirmed his liberal views through the constitutions that were given by him or by his intercession to Poland, Finland, France, and Sweden. We have also seen how Alexander had for the second time disappointed those expectations, expectations no longer of the naïve nature that they possessed at the beginning of his reign; we have seen how, carried away by his rôle in the destinies of all nations, he was unable to devote sufficient attention to the needs and interests of Russia's internal life, where the activity of the Government expressed itself now in the establishment of Military Colonies, and in the distortion of the whole system of popular education.

In the last period of Alexander's reign, when he became disappointed in the possibility of a peaceful development of liberal institutions and constitutional principles, and when between him and Metternich had been established a complete *entente cordiale* in foreign affairs, while in the internal affairs there had grown a deep gulf between him and the thinking public,— then the last hope for achieving a mitigation of the Government's despotism in a peaceful way had disappeared, and the secret societies which had had no definitely revolutionary character at their formation, grew rapidly outspokenly revolutionary.

Alexander's biographer, Schilder, asserts that had not Alexander died on November 19, 1825, at Taganrog, one could have expected by some imperceptible signs a new turn in his views and mood, and that he would perhaps have been able to bring Russia out of the state of internal disruption into which he had hurled her in the end. I do not think so. In my opinion Alexander had accomplished all he could, and in this respect he died in time. Had he not died he would have abdicated rather than launch out on a new course. In a fatal way he had destroyed for himself the possibility of a consequential and regulated leadership of Russia on the way of progress and fundamental improvement of her state, destroyed it by being carried away with the chance for participation in the world-events of his time. But it is very probable that had he not done so, had he not dragged Russia into war with Napoleon in 1805, had he been able to continue the peaceful (in fact, hesitating) way in which he led the country at the beginning of his reign — he would have after all not accelerated but rather retarded the process of internal development in Russia. With his unpreparedness, inexperience, lack of faithful co-workers, and under the conditions in which Russia had been then, that process would have taken a very long time. The shocks that followed the wars of 1805–1807, and that aroused the public from its former passive-optimistic state; the economic and material jolts that came as a result of the Tilsit Treaty and the War of 1812; the great moral acquisitions which Russian society had made during the Napoleonic wars — served, I think, as more potent factors in the socio-political process of Russia's development in the nineteenth century. Great changes took place in the course of that process after the Napoleonic wars under the influence of the events of Alexander's reign; the importance of those changes will appear clearer to us when we shall get acquainted with the circumstances of Russia's development in the following thirty years.

In summarising the reign of Alexander, it may be not useless to consider a few facts and figures.

In regard to the state-territory, in spite of the fact that the country did not need any territorial expansion, of which Alexander himself was well aware, during his reign the territorial acquisitions were enormous. First of all, Gruzia came voluntarily under Russian dominion, trying to save herself from Persia. This peaceful annexation provoked, however, a war with Persia and with the warlike mountaineers of the Caucasus; as a result, by the end of Alexander's reign there were conquered considerable lands west and east of Gruzia, which pushed the frontiers of Russian Trans-Caucasia to the shores of the Black and Caspian seas. This occasioned a long war for the complete conquest of the Caucasus, that was ended only under Alexander II.

Next there were annexed the Kirghiz lands, namely, Ust-Urt (between the Caspian and Aral seas) and the enormous Akhmolinsk region, in space as large as any secondary European Power.

Then Bessarabia was annexed; strictly speaking, its possession was by no means necessary for Russia. Earlier still Finland had been conquered. Possibly this conquest, especially of the shores of the Gulf of Finland, was indeed necessary strategically for the organisation of an adequate defence of Petrograd in case of war with Sweden or England; but Finland was annexed as far as the Arctic Ocean, i.e., in absolutely superfluous limits.

Finally the Kingdom of Poland, whose fate has been so closely knit with the course of Russian social movements, was annexed.

Thus we see that the territorial acquisitions were very large. The annexation of those frontier-lands has brought out during the nineteenth century the race-question, which had not existed to any marked degree before. Even in Alexander's time the national question had been widely discussed and differently solved among intellectual circles, particularly among radicals: Pestel decided it centralistically, while Nikita Muraviov was inclined toward Federalism. Naturally enough, Karamzin considered the question from a nationalistic point of view, undoubtedly the most popular view at that time.

In regard to ways of communication which should unite the enormous territory, at the beginning of Alexander's reign much had been done for the development and improvement of waterways, by a net of canals; this circumstance has had a great importance for the development of the transportation of raw material to ports for export abroad, but for internal communication the canals had but a secondary significance.

Land-roads were built without system; the slowness of communications remained as before: for instance, the news of Alexander's death reached Petrograd only on the eighth day, with all the hard riding of couriers.

As to the population, its growth, as we have seen, had vacillated considerably. During the first five years of the century there was an increase of two million six hundred thousand per-

sons of both sexes; in the next five years, an increase of two
million one hundred thousand, but in the following five years, in
view of the wars and epidemics, the increase amounted only to
one million four hundred and ninety-five thousand; in the five
years after the war the population increased by three million one
hundred and forty-nine thousand, and in the following five
years, by three million one hundred and seventy-four thousand.
In the last five years the growth of the population was checked
by the failure of crops, which caused epidemics and famines.

Industry developed, on the whole, considerably, though it
often met with strong obstacles. The brilliant period of its development was in the first years of the reign, when it breathed
freely after the régime of Paul. Then came the time of the first
Napoleonic war and the Continental System which destroyed the
normal course of the industrial development, although it aided,
in part, the development of cotton-thread production, since in the
absence of thread imported from England Russia began to produce it from cotton imported from Central-Asiatic Khanates.

After the tariff of 1810 the manufacturing industry began to
develop quite rapidly, but later it was checked by the liberal
tariffs of 1816 and 1819, and only after the tariff of 1822 the
protectionist legislation again aided its development.

As to commerce, as a consequence of those constant changes in
the custom-tariffs, that occurred in connection with the Government's cares for a favourable balance of trade, and because of
the wars,— it underwent big shocks, from which foreign trade
suffered most.

PART TWO

CHAPTER XIV

B Y the time of the accession of Nicolas, the Government was in a quite complicated and even threatening situation. We have seen that from the beginning of Alexander's reign a mass of problems had accumulated, the solution of which was impatiently awaited by that part of Russian society which, after the Treaty of Tilsit and the Continental System, had become accustomed to an oppositional attitude, and had acquired definite political views after the contact with Western Europe during 1813–15. Those views were in direct opposition to the reactionary-obscurantist tendency of the Government at the end of Alexander's reign. We have observed how bitter dissatisfaction had developed among the progressive *intelligentzia,* and how it was expressed in the form of a conspiracy which had radical revolutionary aims.

Owing to casual circumstances, that revolutionary movement ended in the premature and unprepared explosion of December 14, 1825 — an explosion which allowed the government of Nicolas to liquidate and suppress the movement by cruel repressive measures. As a result the land was deprived of the best, most alive and original representatives of its progressive, thinking society, the remaining members of which were intimidated and terrorised by the repressions, while the Government throughout the reign of Nicolas found itself entirely divorced from the intellectual forces.

More important and difficult than the political and administrative tasks that loomed before Nicolas, were the socio-economical tasks that under the influence of the general development of the social process in Russia, whose course was sharpened and accelerated by the Napoleonic wars, had ripened by the time of his accession. The development of that process continued to advance and grow acute during the reign of Nicolas, and brought it in the end to a crisis, under the influence of a new external stimulus — the unhappy Crimean Campaign, which moved to the front with a fatal inevitability the period of the great reforms of the Fifties and Sixties.

We are now to study the events and facts in which the course of that process had been manifested.

The accession of Nicolas took place under quite exceptional conditions caused by the unexpected death of Alexander and by his strange orders in regard to the succession. By the law of 1797, issued by Paul, if the emperor left no son he was to be succeeded by his next brother. As Alexander left no children at his death, the throne should have been occupied by his brother, Constantine. But in the first place Constantine had a natural dislike for reigning, as he had declared on many occasions; then his family circumstances placed some obstacles in the way of his accession. In 1803 his first wife left him and Russia, and after having obtained a divorce, Constantine married for the second time, the Polish Countess, Jeannette Grudzinsky, who received the title of Illustrious Princess Lovich. The marriage was morganatic, and Constantine in contracting it acted as if he gave up his rights of succession. The circumstances had thus pointed out the possibility of the transference of the throne-rights to Constantine's younger brother. Yet Constantine had kept up to the death of Alexander the title of heir and Tzesarevich. Although Nicolas in later years often remarked that he had not expected to reign, the probability of his succession had been quite evident to all. Alexander himself openly hinted to Nicolas in 1812 that he would have to reign, and in 1819 he frankly declared it to him, warning him about the possibility of his own abdication before very long.

In 1823 Alexander formally arranged the matter, not so much in the event of death as in case he should abdicate, which he had been seriously thinking of doing at that time. Even in 1822 Alexander received from Constantine a written abdication, and had a manifesto prepared, in which Constantine's abdication was declared correct, and Nicolas was " appointed " as his successor. This was in full accord with the circumstance that in the oath of allegiance to Alexander there were the words, " and to the heir who will be appointed." But for some reason that manifesto was not published; instead Alexander ordered Prince Golitzin to make three copies of it, then the original was given to Metropolitan Philaret to be placed and kept in strictest secrecy on the altar of the Cathedral of Assumption at Moscow; the three copies were distributed among the State Council, the Senate, and the Synod, in sealed envelopes, on one of which, given to the State Council, was an inscription in Alexander's own hand: " To keep until recalled, and in case of my death be opened before taking any other measure, in extra session." Similar inscriptions were made on the other two envelopes. The manifesto was known only to the Dowager Empress Marie, to Constantine, who did not see it but knew about its existence, to Golitzin, and Philaret. The only plausible explanation for such conduct may be the fact that Alexander made the arrangement mainly with his abdication in view, and since that act would have been voluntary he hoped that the whole matter would remain in his hands.

When on November 27, 1825, the news of Alexander's death reached Petrograd, Nicolas did not deem it proper to make use of an unpublished document, and knowing from Miloradovich that the Guards in the capital were by no means disposed towards him, he decided not to ascend the throne until Constantine had formally and solemnly abdicated in his favour. For this reason he took an oath of allegiance to Constantine as the legal Sovereign, and not heeding Golitzin who advised him to open the sealed envelope containing the copy of the manifesto, which had been kept in the State Council, ordered all the troops of the Petrograd district swear allegiance to the Emperor Constantine. Then he sent a special courier to Constantine with a report about the administered oath and with an expression of his loyal feelings.

Constantine replied through his brother Mikhail who had been visiting him at Warsaw, that he had abdicated long ago; but he wrote this in a personal letter, without giving the act any official character. Nicolas considered such a letter insufficient, the more so since the Governor-General of Petrograd, Count Miloradovich, advised him to act with the utmost caution, in view of the indisposition of the Guards towards him.

To avoid misunderstandings, Nicolas despatched another courier, requesting Constantine to come to Petrograd and personally confirm his abdication. But Constantine again answered in a private letter that he had abdicated during Alexander's lifetime, that he could not come personally, and that if his arrival were insisted upon, he would take himself still farther away. Then Nicolas decided to bring these negotiations which had lasted two weeks to an end, and to declare his own accession. The manifesto, written by Speransky and Karamzin, was ready on December 12, but it was not published until December 14, which day was appointed for the general oath-taking to the new Emperor.

By the end of that unusual interregnum Nicolas had received alarming information from various sources about the state of mind in Petrograd and throughout Russia; but Miloradovich, though recommending caution, denied the possibility of a serious mutiny.

In the meantime the members of the Secret Society, who were in Petrograd, decided to make use of the unique confusion for their own purposes; it appeared to them that there could not be a mote favourable moment for raising a revolt and demanding a constitution.

On December 14, when a manifesto was issued regarding the abdication of Constantine and the accession of Nicolas, the members of the Northern Society, chiefly officers of the Guard and of the Navy, who gathered daily at Ryleiev's, made an attempt to persuade the soldiers that Constantine had not abdicated, that Nicolas acted against the law, and that they had to keep to their first oath to Constantine, and demand a constitution. The conspirators succeeded, however, in persuading only one regiment of the Guards — the Moscow regiment; its example was followed by several companies of the Guard-Marines, and by single officers and soldiers from various parts. The rebels gathered on the Senate Square, declared that they considered Constantine the lawful Emperor, refused to swear allegiance to Nicolas, and demanded a constitution.

Nicolas regarded the matter as serious; still he wanted to undertake measures for ending it if possible without bloodshed. With this view he at first sent Miloradovich who enjoyed a great prestige in the army as a war-general, and was especially loved by the soldiers, to talk to the mutineers. But when Miloradovich approached the rebels and began to speak to them, Kakhovsky, one of the conspirators, fired at him, and Miloradovich fell from his horse, deadly wounded. As the rebels were joined in the meantime by several artillery-batteries, Grand Duke Mikhail, the Chief of Artillery, offered to come out to them for negotiations, but he was also fired at by Wilhelm Küchelberg, and had to withdraw. Nicolas ordered an attack by the Cavalry Guards, under the command of Alexey Orlov, brother of the former member of the Union of Welfare. Orlov moved his men, but their horses were not shod properly, and could not speed over the rimed ground. The Generals then pointed out to Nicolas that it was necessary to bring a prompt end to the matter, since the civil population was beginning to join the rebels. Nicolas ordered a charge; after a few volleys of grape-shot the crowd was turned to flight; but the firing at the people continued and they fled over the Isaac Bridge to the Basil Island. A considerable number of dead and wounded were left.

As a matter of fact that was the end of the Petrograd uprising. The other troops took the oath promptly, and the incident was closed. Nicolas ordered all corpses and traces of the event to be removed by the next day, and the obedient Chief of Police, Shulgin, ordered the corpses thrown into the ice-holes on the Neva; rumours circulated that in the haste with which the work was done, wounded were thrown into the river along with the dead. It was discovered later that a number of corpses had frozen to the ice, on the Basil Island side; an order was issued not to use the water on that side during the winter, and not to cut ice there, since parts of human bodies were found in it. Such was the dark event with which the new reign opened.

Searches and arrests throughout Petrograd followed. Among the several hundred arrested there were many not connected with the affair, but the main leaders were apprehended.

Yet on December 10 Nicolas received the first warning from the young lieutenant Rostovtzev about the threatening disturbances among the Guards, and about the same time he received from Dibich (the Chief of His Majesty's Staff in Taganrog) a copy of the reports about the conspiracy of the Southern Society; an attempt was also made to bring about an uprising in January, 1826, by Sergey Muraviov, at Bielaia-Tzerkov. Nicolas ordered an investigation of all secret societies at once, and this work occupied the first months of his reign.

But before we deal with the first actions of Nicolas, it is necessary to give some information about his personality. He was the third son of Paul, and was in his fifth year at his

father's death. The Dowager Empress took over his education, and Alexander from false delicacy did not interfere, though
it would seem that the education of a possible heir to the throne
was not a private but a state-affair. Most of Nicolas' biographers assert that he was brought up not as a future heir, but as
an ordinary Grand Duke being prepared for military service.
This view is not correct, as the members of the Imperial family
could not have been ignorant of the probable accession of
Nicolas, and moreover, Empress Marie knew that Constantine
did not want to reign, and that neither he nor Alexander
had children. Nicolas was brought up as an heir to the throne,
but his education was quite different in every respect from that
of Alexander.

Although Empress Marie had endeavoured to keep Nicolas
from becoming attached to military service, he revealed quite
early militaristic inclinations. Instead of La Harpe his mother
entrusted his education to an old German routinist, General
Lamsdorff, whom the Empress called in intimate conversations
and in her letters, *" papà Lamsdorf."* Nicolas was a rude,
obstinate, arrogant boy; Lamsdorff tried to eradicate those defects by corporal punishments which he employed in liberal
doses. His games with his younger brother usually took on a
military character, and ended in most cases in a fight, owing to
Nicolas' pugnaciousness and wilfulness. The court atmosphere
was also such as deprived the education of family-intimacy. His
teachers were of a casual and poor selection. For instance, his
governor, a French émigré, Du-Pouge, taught him French and
history, without being adequately prepared for either subject.
All his instruction was reduced to inspiring the boy with hatred
for revolutionary and liberal views. Nicolas was a poor pupil;
all his teachers complained that he showed no progress, except in
drawing. Later, however, he manifested quite brilliant abilities
in military science.

When he passed the age of childhood, he was placed in care

of respectable and learned instructors. Academic Storch lectured to him on political economy; Professor Balugiansky, Speransky's instructor in financial science, taught him history and the theory of finance. But Nicolas himself confessed later that during those lectures he yawned, and managed to remember nothing of them. Military science was taught him by General-of-engineering, Opperman, and by various officers recommended by Opperman.

Empress Marie had intended to send Nicolas and Mikhail to the university of Leipzig, but Alexander interfered unexpectedly with his *veto,* and suggested instead that they be sent to the projected Lyceum in Tzarskoie Selo, but when that Lyceum was opened in 1811, the Grand Dukes were not sent there, and their education came thus to an end.

In 1812 Nicolas, then sixteen years old, begged Alexander to allow him to take part in active service, but the Emperor refused, and hinted that in the future he might play a more important rôle which did not permit him to risk his life, and obliged him to put more effort in preparing himself for his high and difficult mission.

In 1814 Alexander allowed his brothers to take part in the war, but they arrived late, when the Allied armies had already entered Paris. Nicolas was also late in 1815 when Alexander gave him permission to go to the front against Napoleon. Thus Nicolas did not see a real battle during the Napoleonic wars, and was present only at the brilliant reviews and manœuvres that followed the campaigns of 1814 and 1815.

In order to complete the characterisation of Nicolas' education, we must mention that in 1816 he undertook a journey through Russia, with the view of getting acquainted with his country, and after this he was allowed to travel in Western Europe. But those trips were performed with dizzying speed, so to speak, and the young Grand Duke was able to see Russia only superficially — its external side. In the same way he travelled through Europe. Only in England he stayed somewhat longer, visited the Parliament, clubs, meetings — which filled him with disgust — and even called at New Lanark on Robert Owen, whose attempts to improve of labour-conditions made a very favourable impression upon him.

It is curious that Empress Marie feared lest the young Grand Duke become infatuated with the constitutional forms of England, and she requested the Minister of Foreign Affairs, Count Nesselrode, to compose a proper memorandum for Nicolas, with the purpose of restraining him from such infatuations. But the impressions which Nicolas had carried out from his English voyage proved that the memorandum was absolutely superfluous: his previous education had evidently insured him against any liberal temptations.

His European travels ended with his wooing the daughter of the King of Prussia, Princess Charlotte, whom he married in 1817; she accepted the Orthodox creed and the name of Alexandra Feodorovna. In 1818, at the age of 21, Nicolas became a father of the future emperor Alexander II. The last years of Alexander I's reign were spent by Nicolas in family-happiness and in military service, though Alexander warned him and his consort in 1819 that he was feeling tired and might abdicate, and that Constantine would not reign. Then in 1820 Alexander called Nicolas out to the Congress of Leibach, arguing that his brother ought to be acquainted with the course of foreign affairs, and that the representatives of the European Powers should become accustomed to seeing in him the successor of Alexander and the follower of his policy.

In spite of those conversations no changes took place in Nicolas' life. In 1817 he was promoted to the rank of General, and almost to the end of his reign he remained commander of a Guard-brigade. The work was tedious and hardly instructive for the future ruler of a great empire; at the same time it was combined with unpleasant duties, since the main task of the Grand Duke consisted in restoring in the army that external discipline which had been greatly weakened during the foreign campaigns where the officers were accustomed to obey military regulations only at the front, while outside of it they considered themselves free citizens, and even wore civil garments. With these habits they returned to Russia. Alexander, who particularly cared for the preservation of the military spirit in the army, desired to " pull up " the officers, especially those of the Guards. In this matter of " pulling up " Nicolas appeared to be a most ardent and energetic missionary. In his reports he complained about the difficulties in accomplishing his task, in view of the dissatisfaction and even protests on the part of the officers who belonged to the highest society and were " infected " with free thoughts. In his activity Nicolas often met with the disapproval of his superiors, and soon with his pedantry and strictness he aroused the general hatred of the Guards to such an extent that during the interregnum in 1825 Miloradovich felt obliged, as we have seen, to warn him about the prevailing mood among the Guards, and to recommend caution.

Alexander, strangely enough, did not try to prepare him for the management of state-affairs, and did not introduce him to the work of the State Council and other institutions, so that Nicolas ascended the throne unprepared either in theory or in practice, although there exists an opinion that after the numerous admonitions of Alexander, Nicolas began to interest himself theoretically with state-matters.

His home-entourage, on the other hand, showed that he was not always the unpleasant, severe pedant of the brigade. Among the people who stood close to his family circle was Vassily Zhukovsky, the famous poet, who was at first invited to teach Russian to the Grand Duchess Alexandra, and later became the tutor of their eldest son. Nicolas' chief friend in service was General Paskevich, a strict, soulless, vain militarist, who later played an important rôle in reorganising the Russian army.

Having ascended the throne under conditions described above, Nicolas determined to investigate first of all the causes and threads of the " sedition " which in his conception nearly destroyed the State on December 14. He undoubtedly exaggerated the importance and number of the secret societies, and was always fond of speaking in lofty tones about those events and his rôle in them, presenting them in a heroic light, although the Petrograd mutiny was numerically a quite impotent affair. The numerous arrests throughout Russia brought a total of five hundred suspects, of whom only one hundred and twenty were finally tried. To Nicolas the conspiracy appeared enormous and monstrous, and he firmly believed that on December 14 he had saved Russia from inevitable perdition. Such was also the opinion of his flatterers and sincere admirers. At his coronation in the Cathedral of Assumption, the Metropolitan of Moscow, Philaret, who was known as a liberal churchman, called Nicolas the Tzar who had saved his country.

With this idea of securing his personal and the country's safety, Nicolas neglected all other affairs in the first half year of his reign for the investigation of the conspiracy. He took active part in examining the prisoners, and frequently displayed rudeness, impatience, and bad temper. In a letter to Constantine he naïvely wrote that by the establishment of a supreme court for the trial of the Decembrists he had shown almost constitutional tendencies; from the point of view of modern jurisprudence, his words are sheer mockery. The whole process was reduced to an inquisitorial examination by a special committee directed by Nicolas, which committee decided the verdict in advance. The Supreme Court was merely a solemn comedy. It consisted of senators, members of the State Council, three members of the Synod, and thirteen personal appointees of Nicolas, but no trial, in the modern sense of the word, took place there: no examination, no arguments, not always even a brief questioning of the accused; they were brought singly before the Court, and some only heard their sentence read to them, as a verdict of some secret Inquisition. Nicolas manifested great cruelty and callousness toward the defendants, although he sincerely believed that he was displaying justice and civil virility. One must admit that however his personal views differed regarding individual defendants, he sentenced them all with equal mercilessness; Pestel, whom he considered "a hell born fiend," and a most pernicious creature, received the same punishment as Ryleiev, in whom Nicolas saw the purest and loftiest personality, and whose family he generously supported later. By the verdict five men were sentenced to be quartered — Nicolas mitigated this by hanging; thirty-one men were sentenced to ordinary execution, i.e., to be shot — Nicolas commuted this to hard labour for life, in some cases for fifteen or twenty years. In the same proportion he commuted all sentences; but most of the accused were exiled to Siberia (some of them after long years of imprisonment in fortresses), and only a very few were reduced to soldiers for life — the mildest penalty.

For the subsequent course of the Government another side of that trial had been of no small importance. In his desire to fathom the sedition, Nicolas made the investigation extremely exhaustive. He wished to find out all the causes of dissatisfaction, to discover all the hidden springs, and thanks to this there was revealed to him a complete picture of the disorders in Russian social and official life, the dimensions and significance of which he had not before suspected. He understood at length that these disorders were enormous, that the dissatisfaction of many had good foundations, and he early admitted the need for radical reforms. "I have distinguished, and shall always distinguish," he said to the French Ambassador, "those who desire just reforms and expect them to emanate from the legal authority, from those who want to undertake them by themselves, employing God knows what means."

By Nicolas' order, one of the secretaries of the Investigating Committee, Borovkov, worked out a special memorandum of all the plans and notes received from the Decembrists during the inquiry, some of which were written by the imprisoned men upon their own initiative, some by request of Nicolas. The Tzar, then, quite consciously borrowed from the Decembrists everything that might serve as useful material for the State-activity.

Borovkov's memorandum had in the end definite conclusions only a few of which were inspired by the testimony of the Decembrists, while most of them were drawn directly from the general state of internal affairs as revealed to Nicolas. Borovkov made the following résumé of the essential needs for the state-management: "It is necessary to grant clear, positive laws; to establish justice through fastest court proceedings; to elevate the moral education of the clergy; to support the nobility which has deteriorated and become completely ruined by loans in credit-associations; to resurrect commerce and industry on immutable foundations; to direct education in accordance with the status of the pupils; to improve the conditions of the farmers; to abolish the humiliating sale of men; to rebuild the navy; to encourage private persons for sea-faring; in short, to rectify the innumerable disorders and abuses." Nicolas had selected for consideration those facts and conclusions that most astonished him.

At any rate he saw among the Decembrists not a majority of inexperienced youths infatuated with dreams, but a large number of persons who had been connected before with the local or central administration. Such was N. I. Turgeniev, state-secretary of the State Council and director of one of the departments of the Ministry of Finance; Krasnokutsky — Super-Procurator of the Senate; Batenkov — one of the close assistants of Speransky, and one time of Arakcheiev; Baron Steingel — Chief of the chancery of the Moscow Governor-General. Needless to say, Nicolas saw the opportunity of making use of such extraordinary minds as Pestel and Nikita Muraviov.

After the end of the trial of the Decembrists and the execution of the five men who were considered the chief conspirators, Nicolas hinted as to his views and intentions in the Coronation Manifesto of July 13, 1826: " Not by impertinent, destructive dreams, but from above, are gradually perfected the statutes of the land, are corrected the faults, are rectified the abuses. In this order of gradual improvement, every modest desire for the better, every thought for the strengthening of the power of the law, for the spread of true enlightenment and of industry, in reaching us by a legal way, open for all — will always be received by us with grace: for we have not, cannot have any other desire but to see our country on the highest grade of happiness and glory, by Providence predestined."

The Manifesto, issued immediately after the punishment of the Decembrists, showed undoubtedly the Monarch's intention of introducing a series of reforms, the nature of which depended upon his views on the essence and aims of the Sovereign's power. These views were made clear to him at his very accession by the aid of Karamzin who appeared at the difficult moment as the true guide and intimate counsellor of the young, inexperienced ruler. If from the Decembrists Nicolas had received the first surprising information about the disorder and abuses in the administration, he owed to Karamzin a general programme for his reign, which pleased his taste so much that he was willing to do everything for that, in his eyes unequalled, counsellor who stood already with one foot in the grave.[1]

Karamzin, as you know, had not occupied any official post under Alexander, which did not prevent him from coming out at times as a sharp critic of the Government's undertakings, as at the moment of the energetic reforms of Speransky, or later, when he openly opposed the Polish policy, the Military Colonies, the obscurantist activity of the Magnitzkys and the Runiches in the sphere of popular education and censorship. At the accession of Nicolas, Karamzin's days were drawing to an end; on the day of December 14 he caught a cold while on the Palace Square, and although he struggled on for two months, he finally became confined to his bed, and died half a year later, unable to make use of the frigate that was furnished by the Tzar to take the sick historian to Italy. From the first day of the interregnum which began on November 27, 1825, Karamzin appeared daily at the Palace to consult with the Monarch, whom he tried to imbue with his views on the rôle of the autocrat, and on the national problems of the moment. Karamzin's talks made a profound impression on Nicolas. Preserving deep respect and even admiration for the recently deceased Tzar, Karamzin at the same time mercilessly criticised his governmental policy, so mercilessly that the Empress Marie, who had been present at all those conversations and who was probably responsible for their taking place, exclaimed once during Karamzin's attacks on the measures of the former reign: " Have mercy, have mercy on the heart of a mother. . . ." To which Karamzin answered: " I am speaking not only to the mother of the deceased Monarch, but also to the mother of the Monarch who is going to reign."

[1] Not long before his death Karamzin was granted a pension of fifty thousand rubles a year, to be continued after his death for his family.

We know what Karamzin thought of the rôle of Russian autocracy from his memorandum "On Ancient and New Russia," presented to Alexander in 1811. Nicolas could not have known that memorandum, since its only copy was given by Alexander to Arakcheiev, among whose papers it was found after his death, in 1836. But Karamzin had developed the same views later (1815), in his introduction to the "History of the Russian Dominion," which was certainly known to Nicolas. Karamzin's views had not changed to his very death; he had borrowed them from Catherine who considered that autocracy was necessary for the country, that without autocracy Russia would perish.

At the same time he considered the rôle of the autocrat as a sacred mission, as a constant service for Russia. He was far from exempting the Monarch from obligations, and strictly condemned such actions of the Tzars as did not correspond with the interests of Russia, but were based on personal despotism, whims, or even on ideological dreams (Alexander). It appeared to Karamzin that the subject in an autocratic state should be not a mute slave, but a brave citizen who owes absolute obedience to the Monarch, but is at the same time obliged to declare freely and frankly his opinions and views concerning the affairs of the state. Karamzin's political views, with all their conservatism, were undoubtedly utopian, but were nevertheless not devoid of a certain exaltation and noble feeling; they endeavoured to lend autocracy some idealism and beauty, and allowed absolutism, towards which Nicolas had been inclined by nature, to base itself on a lofty ideology. The immediate, half-conscious aspirations of Nicolas had gained a principle and a system perfectly fitting the young Monarch's tastes and inclinations. On the other hand, Karamzin's practical conclusions were so elementary and simple that they appealed to the direct, militaristic mind of Nicolas.

Karamzin's views did not exclude the possibility, even the necessity of undertaking the rectification of the abuses and mismanagement in Russian life, that had become clear to Nicolas through his contact with the Decembrists. With all his conservatism, Karamzin was neither a reactionary nor an obscurantist. After December 14 he said to one of his friends (Serbinovich) that he was " an enemy of revolutions," but admitted the necessity of peaceful evolutions which in his opinion were " most convenient under a monarchical régime."

Nicolas' confidence in Karamzin's wisdom was so great that he had evidently intended to give him a permanent post; but the dying historian was unable to accept any appointment, and in place of himself he recommended to the Tzar younger exponents of his ideas from the former members of the literary society "Arzamas": Bludov and Dashkov, to whom soon was added a third prominent Arzamasian, Uvarov, who later definitely formulated that Nationalism, of which Karamzin was the father.[2]

[2] Pushkin, one of the former Arzamasians, was recalled from his village to the capitals, and did complete penance in 1826. He was recalled to Moscow during the Coronation, and was allowed to come in his own carriage, i.e., not as one under arrest. The Emperor received him personally, and was favourably impressed with Pushkin's frank and straightforward talk. Nicolas undoubtedly wished to utilise Pushkin's great mind for the good of the State. He requested him to prepare a memorandum about the means for the improvement of popular education. Pushkin undertook the work reluctantly, only after the repetition of the request through Benckendorff. The poet was unaccustomed to such work, yet he performed it, and promulgated the idea that education might be useful even for the establishment of " desirable " tendencies, but that for its development some freedom was necessary. Nicolas did not like it evidently, as is seen from Benckendorff's note to Pushkin: " One should prefer morality, diligence, loyalty, to inexperienced, immoral, and useless education. On such principles should well-intended education be based."

(NOTE. Pushkin, the greatest Russian poet, had to submit his works to Nicolas and Benckendorff for approval. Upon reading Pushkin's drama. " Boris Godunov," Nicolas inscribed on the MS.: " Mr. Pushkin would achieve his aim if he wrote a historical novel, in the style of Sir Walter Scott." Happily Pushkin did not go too far in his compromising, and refused to prostitute his art. But minor artists were not strong enough to hold their own during that depersonalising régime, and the situation was well characterised in the naïvely-earnest admission of a popular contemporary writer, Kukolnick: "If the Government so orders — I shall be a midwife."— Tr.)

CHAPTER XV

KARAMZIN'S views served as the basis of Nicolas' internal policy. He considered himself the first servant of the state, and devoting his person entirely to the state he felt justified in demanding the same of others, expecting them to follow his directions. From his militaristic point of view he could not conceive of a service not regulated by a supreme authority and directed by a strict discipline and an official hierarchy. This conviction formed the foundation for his absolutism which developed *crescendo* during his reign, becoming more and more sheer despotism.

In this respect we may divide his reign into three periods; the first, from 1826 to 1831, the second — from 1831 to 1848, and lastly, the third — from 1848 to 1855. This division one should make only for the demarcation of the consecutive changes in the course of Nicolas' governmental activity, but in regard to the history of the Russian people and society the whole reign presents one important stage during which the moving factors of the socio-political process had accumulated and grown acute, and had found expression partly in the epoch of the Great Reforms, during the next reign, partly in an incomplete form in our own days.

The first period may be characterised as *quasi*-reformatory, and, at least externally, not opposed to Progress. But the very personality of Nicolas, his personal tastes, character, and growing absolutism, proved an essential obstacle for any progressive action, however moderate. He had evidently struggled with himself, trying to subdue his character and meet the urgent needs that had been so palpably revealed to him, but he succeeded

rather poorly, and for this reason that period was full of astonishing contradictions and vacillations caused not by the lack
of decisiveness on the part of the redoubtable ruler of Russia —
his character was quite decisive — but by the inner contrast
between his nature and tastes, and the measures he undertook.
Those vacillations were noticeable in his internal as well as in
his foreign policy.

Many of Nicolas' biographers present his situation at that
time as very difficult, since he did not inherit from Alexander
any adequate assistants, aside from Arakcheiev. This is not
true. In the first place Arakcheiev resigned his post of Reporter
for the Committee of Ministers as early as December 10, 1825;
for some time he still managed the Military Colonies, but soon
he went abroad, and definitely abandoned even his pet Colonies.
In the second place, under the influence of Karamzin and perhaps of Zhukovsky who had become an intimate member of his
family circle from the year 1817, Nicolas determined to have
no connection with the reactionaries of the preceding reign.
Beside setting aside Arakcheiev, Nicolas treated the obscurantists
of the Ministry of Education severely; Magnitzky was removed
from the post of Curator of the Kazan university, and later in
view of his intrigues against the new Curator, he was arrested
and transported to Reval. The Curator of the Petrograd university was also discharged and brought to trial for financial
abuses. The influential Fotiy received a set-back, and was forbidden to leave his monastery. Of Alexander's reactionaries
there remained only the Minister of Education, Shishkov, who
in the absence of Magnitzky and Runich, was quite harmless.
Of greater importance for the future was the retainment, and
even promotion of one of Arakcheiev's worst assistants, General
Kleinmichel, a rude, cruel, hypocritical person.

On the whole, in the main spheres of administration a greater
rôle was played by the representatives of the more moderate
Conservatives, of the Karamzin type. Of Alexander's chief

assistants who continued their activity under Nicolas we should mention Count (later Prince) Kochubey, and Mikhail (later Count) Speransky. But Kochubey had grown old and had changed many of his former liberal views; yet in 1814 in the memorandum he presented to Alexander he expressed views very akin to those of Karamzin, and definitely stated that the conservation of autocracy was indispensable for Russia. Speransky had also changed many of his views since the catastrophe of 1812. He was no longer an ideologue of political liberalism, but decisively entered the road of political opportunism, devoting all his gifts and diligence for secondary technical improvements of the existing order instead of advocating its radical reorganisation. At the accession of Nicolas Speransky was no more the opponent of Karamzin, but his modest co-worker, and the two worked out by the order of the Tzar the first manifesto. Somewhat later Nicolas' confidence in Speransky wavered for a moment in view of his information about the plans of the Northern Society for appointing in case of the success of the revolution a temporary government with Speransky, Mordvinov, and Yermolov at the head. Soon, however, Nicolas convinced himself that these persons knew nothing about their candidatures, and had no relations with the revolutionary organisations.[1] Speransky regained Nicolas' complete trust in him after a long, frank conversation; the Tzar wrote about it to Dibich, and mentioned in his letter that Speransky had " done penance " for

[1] For Yermolov, however, Nicolas always preserved a hostile feeling. This was caused by a letter of Prince S. G. Volkonsky to Pestel, found during the searches. Volkonsky expressed his view on the state of mind among the Caucasian Corps under the command of Yermolov, which he had visited; he asserted that the revolutionary mood was so general in that Corps that one might hope for its joining the uprising in a body. Nicolas took the information seriously, and even feared that the Caucasian Corps would not take the oath. Although this did not happen, and after a careful investigation the words of Volkonsky had proved unfounded, the Tzar retained an unfriendly attitude toward Yermolov.

his former views. It is not known for what he repented, but in any case Nicolas' momentary mistrust had disappeared, and as early as January, 1826, Speransky was appointed head of the Commission of Laws which was soon reorganised into the Second Department of His Majesty's Own Chancery.

Nicolas did not allow Admiral Mordvinov to partake in his activities. Although he understood that there was no basis for suspecting Mordvinov in having had any relations with the Secret Society, he could not agree with the Admiral's views and policy. During Nicolas' reign Mordvinov with his always interesting and original opinions seldom appeared in the State Council.

Another person inherited by Nicolas from the preceding reign was Yegor Kankrin, a man of great originality and statesmanship, who then occupied the post of Minister of Finance. He was a man of a firm will and definite principles; his financial system consisted mainly in handling economically the people's money, and he always opposed most bitterly such of Nicolas' plans as required considerable expenditures. Later Nicolas jocosely remarked to his last Minister of Finance, the incapable and submissive Brock, that it was very agreeable to have such an obedient Minister, " Whereas Kankrin," recalled the Tzar, " would come to me in his slippers (he suffered from rheumatism), warm his back at the fireplace, and interrupt me every minute: ' Impossible, your Majesty, absolutely impossible.' . . ."

To Nicolas' credit we should mention that he kept Kankrin at his post for seventeen years, until he considered himself sufficiently trained by his Minister to manage the finances personally.

From letters of contemporaries we learn that from the very beginning Nicolas had shown great diligence and readiness to devote himself unreservedly to the service of the state, but at the same time he demonstrated an utter incapacity for selecting assistants, a fault that played great importance as an obstacle for the promulgation of those moderate changes that appeared necessary in his own eyes.

Beside the persons recommended to him by Karamzin, Nicolas employed for the management of internal affairs those who had distinguished themselves in the organisation of the Process of the Decembrists. Foremost among them was General Benckendorff who had tried in vain since 1821 to call Alexander's attention to the spread and growth of secret societies in Russia. Along with him were promoted Generals Chernyshev and Levashov, investigators in the case of the Decembrists.

In the military sphere the young Tzar respected the authority of Generals Dibich and Paskevich. The first had been the Chief of Staff, and at the moment of Alexander's death all the threads of the Conspiracy were concentrated in his hands. His energetic activity in investigating the affair inspired Nicolas with confidence for him. Paskevich had been an old friend and direct superior of Nicolas since 1814. Both were considered by Nicolas as highly gifted generals, although their military talents were later questioned by military writers.

For the working out of a general plan for the intended reforms, a special Committee was formed under the chairmanship of Kochubey, on December 6, 1826. Speransky, Prince A. N. Golitzin, and Generals Count P. A. Tolstoy, Dibich, I. V. Vassilchikov, entered the Committee; the young state-secretaries, Bludov and Dashkov, were appointed as secretaries. In a short memorandum given to Kochubey at the beginning of the Committee's work, Nicolas pointed out that this should consist first of all in the examination of the papers found in the chancery of the late Emperor, secondly in the revision of the statutes of the existing state, and thirdly in expressing their opinions as to what had been planned during the preceding reign, what had been accomplished and what remained to be finished, and finally what was good in the existing order and what was not to be retained, and in that case by what it should be supplanted.

Such were the indefinite features of the proposed work of the Committee which carried on its regular activity from December 6, 1826, to April, 1830; in the two years following there were a few sporadic sessions, and although the Committee was not officially closed, its work was discontinued in 1832.

The mission of the Committee was so broadly outlined that its work could apparently acquire the same character as the famous Unofficial Committee at the beginning of Alexander's reign. As a matter of fact there was nothing in common between the two institutions: Alexander's Committee consisted of idealistic representatives of the advanced tendencies of the age, whereas Nicolas' secret Committee contained men of the older generation, sated and disappointed with life (as Speransky, Kochubey, Golitzin), or young career-hunters and doctrinaires (as Bludov and Dashkov), who did not even propose any novel measures, and whose whole activity was reduced to the examination of the statutes of the central and provincial institutions, and of the then existing " class-laws " in which they suggested some changes in the status of the nobility and the middle class, in the elections among the nobles, and in the management of the Fiscal peasants. In passing they touched upon the peasant-question, but so hesitatingly and indolently that the Emperor remained utterly displeased with their work in that field.

In the peasant-question, the importance of which Nicolas admitted after the first peasant-disturbances that took place during his reign, he proved more progressive and firm than in all his other undertakings. The question was constantly under discussion till the year 1848; ten consecutive Committees were instituted for the exhaustive investigation of the problem, and we may say that during his reign was done more for the peasant-question than during that of the liberal Alexander I. We shall discuss this in the exposition of the second period of Nicolas' reign, when the question received most attention from the Government.

From the very beginning Nicolas regarded the Military Colonies sceptically, but he was unable to liquidate at once so great an undertaking, and unwilling to undermine the authority of his late brother, so that the Colonies not only continued to exist to the end of his reign, but were even enlarged on various occasions. Their final liquidation took place under Alexander II.

His particular ideas about the rôle and duties of an autocrat, on one hand, and his mistrust for the public and for the officials, on the other hand, were reflected in Nicolas' treatment of measures that appeared to him especially important and difficult, and which he desired to exclude from the ordinary matters entrusted to his regular Ministers. For this purpose Nicolas from the very beginning of his reign established separate departments of his own Chancery, at the head of which he placed persons in whom he had special confidence; he ranked them as Ministers, and they were officially known as Chief Directors. The first new Department was opened in January, 1826, and was named the Second Department of His Majesty's Own Chancery, under the directorship of Speransky who was transferred from the Commission of Laws which was abolished; the secretary of the Department was State-Secretary Balugiansky. The codificatory work concentrated in that Department was quite successful, as we shall see, and was accomplished in 1832 and 1833.

In the same way Nicolas desired to organise the management of the political and secret police. After the insurrection of December 14 he considered this activity as one of the most important in the state. He decided to leave the general overt police-work in the hands of the Ministry of Interior, but for the observation of the state of mind, opinions and tendencies of the population he created a special Corps of Gendarmes, with Adjutant General Benckendorff as its Chief (June 25, 1826); a few days later (July 3) the special Chancery of the Minister of Interior, in which had been concentrated the affairs of the

Secret police, was abolished, and its former jurisdiction transfered to the newly organised Third Department of His Majesty's Own Chancery, the Chief of which was the same General Benckendorff.

The following matters were included in the sphere of activity of the Third Department which subsequently acquired such a dark reputation:

(1) All orders and information about matters of Higher Police (political matters); (2) intelligence as to the number of existing sects and dissents in the state; (3) information about discoveries of assignation-forgers, coin-forfeiters, etc., the finding and further care of whom remained in the hands of the Ministers of Finance and of the Interior; (4) information and orders about persons under police-surveillance; (5) exile and transportation of suspicious and harmful persons; (6) supervision of all " political " prisons; (7) all regulations regarding foreigners; (8) information about all events and occurrences, without exception; statistical information of concern to the police.[2]

---

[2] Here are some of Benckendorff's views as to the purpose of that institution, with which Nicolas undoubtedly fully agreed:

. . . "The Chief of Gendarmes will be able to make use of opinions of honest persons who may desire to warn the Government about some conspiracy, or impart some interesting news. Criminals, intriguers, and simple persons, having repented of their sins and being desirous of redeeming their guilt by giving information, will at least know where to turn.

"Toward the Chief will flow information from all Gendarmes-Officers scattered throughout Russia and in the army: this would enable us to fill those places with honest and capable men who often despise the rôle of secret spies, but when wearing the uniform of governmental officials will zealously perform their function.

"Rank, decorations, crosses, serve as higher rewards than money for an officer, but for secret agents they are of no importance, and thus frequently they work as spies for and against the Government.

"The Chief will have to travel every year, to visit the big fairs, where he could contract connections and attract persons avariciously inclined.

From the very beginning Nicolas had given particular attention to the question of popular education. With the view of eradicating the spirit of "sedition," he intended to direct the education of the people in such a way that it should form desirable citizens, loyal and meek servants of the state among all classes, and should thus guarantee a firmer stability to the order of things than the one that had existed theretofore. The leading principle was to give each class such education as would not arouse any hopes and aspirations for rising from one class into a higher class. It was proposed first of all to limit the education of peasant children, lest they develop ideas about changing their conditions. Nicolas had intended to issue a law concerning this even before the formation of the Committee of December 6, but Kochubey opposed the idea, considering that such a law would lower the Government in the opinion of the foreign Powers; instead he recommended that a rescript on the name of the Minister of Education be published in which he should be directed to accept peasant children only into primary schools. Nicolas consented and issued such a rescript on the name of Minister Shishkov, in May, 1827. The Ministry of Education proceeded to act in this way in the future. In 1828 under the chairmanship of Shishkov a committee was formed for the revision of the statutes and programmes of all primary and secondary schools; among the members of that committee were two subsequent Ministers of Education: Prince Lieven and S. S. Uvarov.

In December, 1828, a new Statute for District-schools and Gymnasia was carried through. The Statute separated the District-schools from the Gymnasia; before that time, the former served as preparatory schools for the latter, but by the new

"His shrewdness should warn him against trusting even the director of his office; not even he must know all his assistants and agents. . . ."
General (later Count) Benckendorff enjoyed to his very death the complete confidence and favour of Nicolas.

Statute the Municipal and District-schools were made separate primary schools with no connection with the Gymnasia which were open thenceforward only to children of nobles and officials. Strict measures were undertaken for the prohibition of education by means of private teachers, since it had been observed that a large number of the Decembrists had been educated by private French teachers.

In closing our exposition of the main events and circumstances of the first period of Nicolas' reign, we must mention his attitude towards Poland. The Tzar had to act as a constitutional monarch and comply with the Constitution of 1815; it went much against his grain, yet he forced himself to overcome his personal aversion, and in 1829 came to Warsaw where he took the oath in a Catholic church, and assembled the Diet — as soon as the cessation of hostilities with Turkey permitted him to do so. On the whole we may say that up to the insurrection of 1830 Nicolas, in spite of his personal tastes, conducted himself more correctly as a constitutional monarch than did Alexander, the creator of the Constitution of 1815.

In his international relations Nicolas demonstrated in the first years of his reign the same vacillation that characterised his internal policy. Obeying the voice of the people he found it necessary to defend the Greeks from the atrocities of the Turks, while in his letters to Constantine he called the Greeks base and impertinent rioters who deserved no sympathy and should have been forced to submit to the Sultan. But the forced championship of the Greeks brought him to war with Turkey. The Russian fleet together with the British and French fleets destroyed the Turkish fleet at Navarino, and the Sultan considered Russia chiefly to blame. In the war that broke out in 1828 Nicolas strove to make Turkey accept his demands, but he tried not to bring upon her any crushing defeats, since he did not wish the destruction of the Turkish monarchy. Owing to this hesitation the first year of the war ended quite unfavourably, and only in 1829 when Nicolas took the advice of General Vassilchikov and did not go to the theatre of war, but granted freedom of action to the new commander-in-chief, Dibich, was the campaign ended successfully.   But the world was astonished by the moderateness of the conditions of peace presented to Turkey.

This first period of Nicolas' reign came to an end after the first days of the July revolution in France.   The banishment of his friend, Charles X, from France, and the subsequent fall of the Netherlands monarchy (where the queen was Nicolas's sister, Anna Paulovna), inspired Nicolas to stand rigorously for legitimistic principles in European affairs.   As early as 1830 he was about to send his army to the Rhine in defence of those principles; but instead he was forced to use it for the suppression of the Polish uprising.   That insurrection brought an end to any toleration of liberal ideas on the part of the Tzar, and was the cause of the abolition of the Constitution of 1815.

CHAPTER XVI

AFTER the July revolution in France and the Polish insurrection of 1830–1831, the first, *quasi*-reformatory period, of Nicolas' reign came to an end. Having abandoned all attempts to reorganise the state-institutions, the Tzar, one may say, found himself. He took a new, strictly conservative course, from which he never deviated. Thenceforth he considered it his main task to fight against revolutionary ideas in Western Europe as well as at home, although Russia seemed to have given no reasons for such activity, since everything had been quiet and obedient after the cruel punishment of the members of the secret societies.

The new firm course in international affairs appeared definitely in 1833, after the meeting of the Tzar with the Austrian emperor, Franz, at Münchengrätz, where there were established those good relations between the two countries that so heavily impressed the entire course of European affairs to the very time of the Crimean Campaign. Before that meeting a favourable moment had come for Russia's relations in the East, when Turkey was on the verge of destruction as a result of the revolt of the Egyptian Pasha, Mehmed Ali, whose son, Ibrahim, had crushed the Turkish army. The fall of Turkey was averted at that moment through the intervention of Russia. Nicolas offered Turkey military help and sent her a corps under General Muraviov. The Russian ships were permitted to enter the Bosphorus, and the Unkiar-Skelessi Treaty was concluded, which gave Russia a protectorate over Turkey — one of the most distinguished achievements of Russian diplomacy. The Tzar endeavoured to keep decaying Turkey alive, desiring to have such a weak neighbour under his protectorate.   Austria, however, looked upon that protectorate with suspicion, but she could not interfere in the East since after the July revolution considerable fermentation was going on among the various nationalities of the Hapsburg monarchy.

In the meantime Nicolas, fearing a general revolutionary movement in Europe under the influence of liberal England and revolutionary France, sought a close alliance with Austria and Prussia in order to counteract the free aspirations of the West. Metternich was the gladder to meet the proposal of Nicolas, since Austria by herself was quite impotent.   The position of Russia in Europe at that time was well characterised later by Ivan Aksakov who named the period the epoch of Russia's " police-chiefery " in Europe.   Indeed, Nicolas with his army of a million strong firmly occupied a position threatening any popular movement against the *status quo* established at the Vienna Congress; it was with his support that Austria and Prussia were able to carry on their reactionary policy until 1848.

In his internal policy Nicolas gave up all liberal reforms after the revolution of 1830, and his slogan became the safeguard of the original Russian order based on " Orthodoxy, Autocracy, and Nationality "— the formula invented by Uvarov who was then Minister of Education, and which was in complete accord with Karamzin's programme.   Nicolas endeavoured to preserve the Russian order from any political temptations, and blocked all connections with the revolutionary West.

Yet the repair of some institutions, of especially crying need, continued without, of course, any radical reorganisation.   Thus the issue of a legislative code, a century old problem, was safely brought to an end during this period.

This matter, as I have mentioned, was handed over to Speransky in the year 1826, and he started upon the work with more practical aims than he did during his earlier activity, when he worked on the basis of theoretic principles of foreign legislations.

Now he carefully consulted the old Russian codes, beginning with the *Ulozhenie* of Tzar Alexis. In a few years he performed the colossal work of collecting and issuing all the laws that had been promulgated by the Government since 1649; under his direction that task was accomplished in 1832, and published in forty-seven large volumes of the *Complete Collection of Laws*.

On the basis of this Collection, after a careful comparison, expurgation, and scientific classification, the *Code of Laws* was issued in 1833 in fifteen volumes. There was nothing reformatory, in the proper sense of the word, in that work, but it was beyond doubt an event of extraordinary importance. The absence of such a Code had been one of the main sources of abuses by various court officials and archaic solicitors in the epoch when the folk-saying was formed: *Zakon chto dyshlo: kuda poverniosh tuda y vyshlo* (the law is like a wagon-tongue, wherever you turn it, there it goes).

Another, still more important question which had not been definitely solved during that whole reign, was the peasant-problem. It had uninterruptedly occupied the mind of the Government till the year 1848. Nicolas was first moved to attempt its solution by the peasant-uprisings which broke out in the first year of his reign, and had constantly recurred, not allowing the Government to nap or to close their eyes on the crying wounds in the institution of serfdom.

The fact of the matter is that by that time there were formed in the internal national life such material conditions which undermined serfdom and prepared the way for its downfall more forcibly than any idealistic demands. First of all such a circumstance was the increased density of the population, especially in some of the central black-soil provinces, which rendered the bondage-labour under the *barshchina* system very unprofitable for the landowners, since there was a surplus of hands for the primitive farming of those days, while the forced labour did not allow any real intensification of the productivity of the soil.

The growth of the bonded population increased particularly in the period between 1816 and 1835. By the fifth census of the entire bonded population, including Siberia and the Ostsee region, there were nine million eight hundred thousand male persons; by the seventh census — nine million seven hundred and eighty-seven thousand (owing to the human loss during the Napoleonic wars); and from 1816 to 1835 the bonded population increased to ten million eight hundred and seventy-two thousand, i.e., by more than a million souls, in spite of the fact that during that period four hundred and thirteen thousand Ostsee serfs were freed. The superabundance of serfs greatly embarrassed the landowners who could do nothing but transfer the peasants into the class of house-serfs whose number had been always greater than necessary.

The *barshchina*-estate presented not only an agricultural unit, but a sort of a domestic factory, for every landowner endeavoured to buy only such commodities as iron or salt, and to have all other necessaries produced on the estate by bondage-labour. For this reason the number of house-serfs reached in those days enormous dimensions: before the ninth census out of ten million bondmen there was over one million house-serfs, i.e., a landless population occupied either with house work or with work in the domestic factories. By the tenth census the number of house-serfs had reached one million four hundred and seventy thousand. The landowners treated them without any ceremonies: in poor years many of them drove their serfs out to beg. Some landowners tried to employ their surplus hands in the estate-factories which had developed at the end of the eighteenth century, but in this direction the landowners met with the insurmountable competition of the growing and developing merchant-factories. The technical improvements in the latter factories were inaccessible for the landowners, first because of absence of capital, and second because it was quite difficult to adapt forced labour to the improved means of production. The professional factory-owners had come to the conclusion that forced labour was not profitable, and even owners of Possessional factories began to reject Possessional peasants, so that in 1847 a law was issued permitting those factory-owners to liberate their peasants. No wonder that the estate-factories were unable to cope with that competition, and that during the Thirties and Forties many of them had closed.

But outside of the increased density of the population, the landowners suffered from the enormous indebtedness that had hung over them since 1812. The voluntary and involuntary contributions and sacrifices during the wars amounted to hundreds of millions, and if we consider that the entire income of the estates did not exceed one hundred million rubles a year, we shall be able to form some idea of the enormous indebtedness of the landowners. By 1843 more than fifty-four per cent. of the estates were mortgaged to credit-institutions. The average indebtedness of the landowners was sixty-nine rubles per bonded peasant, while the average value of a serf was not above one hundred rubles, so that the greater part of the serfs did not in reality belong to the landowners. The mortgage-loans required high interest, and to this we should add that the majority of the land-owners had accumulated also " private " debts on which they paid much higher interest.

Acquaintance with the life of Western Europe during the Napoleonic wars had brought big changes in the status of the landowners: they were no longer satisfied with the standard of living that existed under patriarchal natural conditions, but had acquired new tastes, habits, and required a more luxurious and comfortable life which demanded a buying capacity. This circumstance necessitated new loans.

All these conditions combined caused increasing deficits in the landowners' budgets, and their deteriorating affairs were reflected mainly on the situation of their serfs, greatly aggravat-

ing the relations between the peasants and their masters.　In the
black-soil provinces, particularly in the densely populated ones,
conditions became unbearable.　During the Forties among many
landowners, especially in the provinces of Tula, Riazan, Oriol,
the idea had grown that such conditions could not endure, and
that the liquidation of serfdom with the retention of the land
by the gentry would be more profitable than the existing state.
These ideas were expressed in various declarations presented to
the Government in the Forties.　Some landowners of Tula, followed later by some of Riazan and Smolensk, were willing to
liberate their serfs, and even to allot them one desiatin per soul
on condition that the peasants took over a large portion of the
landowners' debts.　A lengthy correspondence took place with
the Government, a Committee was formed, deputations were
sent to the Tzar, but after 1848 all talk about changing the
order of things had to stop in view of the severe reaction that
had come to reign.

Such were the circumstances that had been in, so to speak, an
inner, organic way undermining the institution of serfdom, and
made its liquidation inevitable even from the point of view of the
nobles.　On the other hand, the peasants had not remained quiet.
There were five hundred and fifty-six peasant-disturbances during Nicolas' reign, uprisings of whole villages and *volosts,* not
ordinary local misunderstandings.　Of them forty-one disturbances took place during the first four years of his reign, before
1830; their highest number occurred in the period between 1830
and 1849 (three hundred and seventy-eight disturbances) ; the
last seven years of his reign saw one hundred and thirty-seven
disturbances.　About half of those uprisings had to be quelled
not by ordinary police measures, i.e., by the arrival of a police
squad for a mere flogging of the rioters, but by military force,
with frequent bloodshed.　The peasant-question demanded the
attention of the state, and it occupied a prominent place in the

discussions of the Committee of December 6, 1826; the work of the Committee, though it had some significance, did not bring any substantial results.

For example, in connection with the work of the Committee there was issued a law in 1827 prohibiting the landowners from depriving their peasants of soil by selling out lands without serfs. Earlier the question had been put about the sale of serfs without land, but now it was required that the estates were big enough to possess a minimum of four and a half desiatins per soul. In practice this law had no substantial value, for it was not carried through, but it received a legal sanction: in theory if a landowner sold more land than the law permitted, his estate could be confiscated by the state.

Another law connected with the work of the Committee of December 6, 1826, was the prohibition of transferring serfs to mines, which had been one of the heaviest forms of serf-exploitation. At the same time renting serfs to persons who did not have the right to own them was forbidden. These were all the measures of the Committee for the regulation of serfdom. After the cessation of its work the most important factor in regulating the conditions of the serfs was the publication of the Code of Laws. Its importance lay in the fact that all the various decrees and orders concerning the limitation of the landowners' power over their peasants had been normalised as general, obligatory laws.

In the ninth volume of the Code these laws were expounded in detail; on one hand they limited the authority of the landowners over their peasants, and on the other, they placed certain obligations upon the landowners. In this respect is important the prohibition — mentioned above — of selling too much land in congested estates. There was furthermore a series of regulations placing on the landowners the care for provisioning their serfs. This was an important measure, for during Nicolas' reign several failures of crops had taken place. But in practice the landowners tried to evade the provisioning law, and let the peasants starve. There was a law in the Code, punishing the landowners for begging on the part of their peasants (one and a half ruble for every case of begging discovered). This law also existed only in theory. The crop failures occupied the attention not only of the landowners, but of the Government, as they led in places to sheer famine which at times took on devastating dimensions owing to the bad roads. In 1833 the increase of the population in some districts was half of the normal, owing to a recent famine. In the western provinces there were numerous disturbances in those years on account of lack of provisions. The Government gave out considerable subsidies, at times millions, to the landowners for provisioning the peasants, but in most cases those subsidies were made use of for the needs of the landowners rather than for the starving peasants. The attempt of the Government to control the distribution of those subsidies was frustrated, since the local authority was in the hands of officials elected by the nobles.

After the publication of the Code of Laws, the next important step of the Government in regard to the peasant-question was the formation of the Secret Committee of the year 1835. The question was posed there categorically — to examine the means for the liquidation of the serfdom relations. The sessions of the Committee were held in strict secrecy, and only recently did their minutes become accessible in the Archives. The Committee found it convenient to divide the course of solving the serfdom problem into three tentative stages, without indicating the time for the succession of the stages. The first stage, then in existence, presented the regulation of the serfdom-rights by the statutes introduced into the Code of Laws. During the second stage was to enter the system of " Inventories," or the regulating of the economic and legal conditions of the peasants without however abolishing serfdom; this situation would correspond to that of the Ostsee provinces in the years 1804–5, before the new statutes of 1816–19. The third stage was presented by the Committee as the period of personal liberation of the serfs, without soil.

The work of the Committee brought no practical results. Among its members was Kiselev, the same Kiselev who as Chief of Staff in the Southern Army had been friendly with some Decembrists — with Pestel among them — for which reason he did not at first inspire Nicolas with confidence. Soon, however, at a personal meeting with the Tzar, Kiselev explained straightforwardly and loyally his political convictions, after which Nicolas no longer suspected him. In 1829 he was appointed head of the temporary management of the Principalities of Moldavia and Wallachia, then occupied by the Russian troops (until the payment of the war-contribution by Turkey). The peasant-question came there to the front; the relations between the *boyars* and the peasants became extremely acute. Kiselev's method of dealing with the problem — a method similar to the Ostsee statute of 1804 — pleased Nicolas greatly, and after reading Kiselev's report on the management of the Principalities he decided to make use of him for the solution of the peasant-question in Russia. He appointed him member of the State Council in 1834, and told him that since he did not hope for the sympathy of his Ministers in the matter, he would personally take care of the peasant-question, and invited Kiselev to become, so to speak, his Chief of Staff on peasant-affairs.

Kiselev gladly undertook the work, for the question had interested him from his youth, and even as an Adjutant of Alexander he had presented to the Tzar a memorandum about the peasant-question. At first he occupied himself with the Fiscal peasants who were under the management of the Department of State Domains, subject to the Minister of Finance; the Committee of December 6, 1826, already approved of Speransky's idea that the Government should show an example to private owners.

The Minister of Finance was Kankrin whose attitude towards the peasants was not less favourable than that of Kiselev. Although Kankrin was not a Physiocrat and opposed the principle of *Laissez faire,* he could also have inserted in his coat-of-arms the words: *pauvre paysan — pauvre royaume; pauvre royaume — pauvre roi.* His main purpose had been to improve the condition of the population, by regulating the finances, lessening expenditures, avoiding loans and other national burdens. We shall have later to speak of his economical and cultural activity. In regard to the Fiscal peasants Kankrin intended to regulate the system of collecting their dues and save them from the abuses of the police-officers who acted as locusts in their relations with the people. As an experiment he proposed to separate the Fiscal peasants of the provinces of Petrograd and Pskov from the general administration, and to establish Districts (as in the case of the Tzar's peasants) under the management of special officers appointed by the Minister of Finance. Of course that reform was a purely bureaucratic palliative: the peasants were transferred from the jurisdiction of one class of officials to that of another, but Kankrin had undoubtedly desired to come in closer contact with the peasants and try to alleviate their conditions. In 1834 Kankrin proposed to expand the new order on ten more provinces. But Nicolas, dissatisfied with the slowness of the work, and ascribing it to the fact that Kankrin had too many other cares, handed the work over to Kiselev who was appointed Chief of the new, Fifth, Department of His Majesty's Own Chancery, for the management of peasant affairs. Kiselev first of all inspected the position of the Fiscal peasants in four provinces, and revealed a mass of abuses not only on the part of the local administration, but on the part of the Department of State Domains, whose Chief, Senator Dubensky, was put on trial. Then, after a few collisions with Kankrin, Kiselev declared that he felt uncomfortable in managing the affair in the name of the Tzar, while it remained in the jurisdiction of the

Minister of Finance, who was unable to devote much time to the peasant-question. As a result, a new, independent institution was founded, the Ministry of State Domains, which was to take care of all fiscal estates, forests, and mines.

The new Ministry was founded in 1837, with Kiselev as its head. He followed the way indicated by Kankrin: established local Chambers of State Domains, and District Boards. The Fiscal peasants received some autonomy in their Communes and *Volosts,* but they were under the care of District Chiefs who had an unlimited right to interfere with their agricultural and domestic affairs. True Kiselev endeavoured to select good men for District Chiefs, but in the long run it became apparent that the new system had placed the peasants under a worse bondage than before, for whereas the former dishonest officials, the Rural Commissaries, could but seldom visit the Fiscal estates, having many other duties to perform, the new officials had only one special function to perform — the " protection " of the peasants. That system brought no good results.

Although Kiselev was given the management only of Fiscal peasants he actually remained what Nicolas called him — Chief of his Staff for peasant-affairs, and took active part in the development of the whole question.

The Committee of 1835 achieved nothing, and by 1839 a new Committee was formed, with more modest aims, and as a result of its work a new Statute about " Obligatory peasants " appeared in 1842. The Statute allowed landowners to free their peasants from personal bondage and transfer them into the class of Obligatory peasants; by mutual agreement between the landowners and their former bondmen the latter were given some land, not in property but in use, for which they " obliged " themselves either to bear a certain *barshhina* or to pay a definite money-*obrok,* the amount of those obligations to remain unchanged. Some degree of self-government was given with it to the village, of the kind that had already existed in some *obrok-*

estates. The peasants thus came into a situation similar to that of the Ostsee peasants in 1804–5. The Statute in itself was not bad, but the fact that the initiative was granted only to the landowner reduced the act to next to nothing.

When this reform was discussed in the State Council, Prince D. V. Golitzin, Governor-General of Moscow, told Nicolas that in his opinion the measure might have some sense only in case the transfer of the serfs into Obligatory peasants became obligatory upon the landowners. Nicolas replied that although he was an autocratic ruler, he could not decide to violate the privileges of the landowners in such a way. This answer shows how far peasant-reform could have been carried under Nicolas. But he acted more determinedly in the western provinces where the gentry was Polish, and the peasants Russian, and where, after the insurrection of 1831 he considered himself justified in not being over scrupulous about the property of the Polish nobles. There his policy was in complete accord with the principle: " Orthodoxy, Autocracy, Nationality."

And so in the Forties quite severe " Inventory Regulations " were issued for the landowners of the West; they were based on the ideas of Kiselev, and were ardently upheld by the Governor-General of Kiev, Bibikov, who had shown himself as a rabid Russificator. The Regulations defined the amount of land that the landowners had to allot to the peasants, and the amount of the peasants' dues. In 1847 those Regulations were introduced in the provinces of Kiev, Volhynia, and Podolia, and later in Lithuania and White Russia. In Lithuania similar rules had existed for a long time, but the landowners had had more freedom; the Lithuanian nobles vigorously protested against the new, Bibikovian, Regulations, and the question was alive until the Fifties. In 1849 Bibikov, then Minister of the Interior, wanted to introduce the Regulations by force, but the Lithuanian nobles found a defender in the person of the Heir (subsequently Alexander II), who had become reactionary after the revolu-

tions of 1848, and considered that it was necessary to uphold the
" sacred " rights of the gentry.   Thus the Inventory Regulations were not introduced in Lithuania and White Russia during
Nicolas' reign.

In 1846 an analogous structure was established in the Kingdom of Poland.   The Polish peasants had been personally freed
by a decree of Napoleon in 1807, but they had not received any
land.   The landowners did not drive the peasants away, and
allowed them to work on their former lands for *barshchina* or
obrok.   They occupied large tracts of land, but legally the landowners could expel them at any moment, and making use of this
advantage they exploited the peasants not less than if they were
bondmen.   In the same year, 1846, a terrible slaughter of landowners took place in adjacent Galicia, which terrified the gentry
of the Kingdom of Poland and the Viceroy, Prince Paskevich.
Improvement of the conditions of the peasants was admitted to
be urgently needed.   On May 26, 1846, a ukase was issued, introducing *Tables,* perfectly analogous to the Inventory Regulations in the western provinces.   The agrarian relations that had
existed before were confirmed, and the landowners were forbidden to diminish the peasants' allotments or to increase their
obligations.

Finally in 1847 upon the proposal of Baron M. A. Korf a
ukase was published permitting the peasants in Russia (as it had
been earlier permitted in Gruzia) to buy themselves out with
land by whole villages in cases when landowners' estates were
sold by auction for debts.   The peasants thus received a loop-
hole through which to creep out of bondage, the more so since,
owing to the terrible indebtedness of the landowners their estates were frequently sold by auction.   Among the nobility arose
bitter protests against that ukase; Governors reported that it
disturbed the public.   After 1848 it was actually annulled
through the addition of numerous amendments.   From that year

on Nicolas acquired an uncompromising reactionary attitude towards any novelties, and all attempts to regulate serfdom ceased.

Such were the peasant-measures undertaken during the second
period of Nicolas' reign.

CHAPTER XVII

IN outlining the second period of Nicolas' reign we must consider alongside with the course of the peasant-question the development of industry and commerce during the Thirties and Forties of the nineteenth century, and also in this connection, the policy of the Ministry of Finance.

As I have already mentioned, the cotton industry had developed most rapidly in the first half of the nineteenth century and this has been ascribed by many to the influence of the tariff of 1822, which had launched the Russian customs policy on the road of constant protectionism. The profoundest investigator of that question, Professor Tugan-Baranovsky, has shown that the situation was due not so much to the protectionist tariff as to the changes in the cotton industry, which had taken place in England during the very time of its development in Russia.

Up to the Forties the Russian cotton-spinning industry had existed mainly on English yarn; true, during the Continental System, when all connections with England had ceased the Russian factory-owners made an attempt to utilise Central-Asiatic cotton for the production of yarn, but still until the Forties the larger part of yarn came ready-made from England, because the arrangement of cotton-mills was not an easy matter. The custom dues on cotton were not very high, while the prices of yarn and tissue had been falling continually in England, in connection with the recurring crises. It has been statistically proven that every crisis in England was followed by technical improvements which immediately caused a fall in the value of the product. For this reason the cost of cotton-stuffs had been decreasing also in Russia, thus increasing the spread of cotton-mills. The vacillations in the English cotton industry had aroused vacillations in Russia, in view of the cheapening of the imported products and fabrics. The competition induced Russian manufacturers also to introduce improvements which consisted mainly in buying new costly machines, a measure possible only to large capitalists. Owing to these peculiarities in the development of Russian cotton industry, during the Forties many small and mediocre cotton-mills had perished, and production had become concentrated in the hands of the big manufacturers.

As an important consequence of the development of the cotton industry came the fall of the hemp and canvas industry, particularly in the Forties. The development of those factories which had mainly supplied the English fleet, had had the following course: in 1762 their number was one hundred and thirty-five, in 1804 — two hundred and seventy-five, and by the time of the accession of Alexander II the number fell to one hundred. The cheapening of the production of cotton had made competition impossible for hemp and harl producing regions, as in the province of Kaluga, where the number of such factories had fallen from seventeen to four.

As to cloth factories, their number began to increase considerably after the removal of restrictions from the Possessional factories, but toward the Forties that industry began to fall, owing to the competition of the Polish manufacturers. The Polish cloth industry was better situated because sheep-raising was more highly developed there, and because they had no custom-tariff for Silesian wool, so that having an abundance of cheap raw material they were able to produce cloth cheaper than the Russian manufacturers. Later Prussian manufacturers succeeded in obtaining privileges for the import of their cloth, and when those privileges were withdrawn, many Prussians migrated with their factories to the Kingdom of Poland, in order to sell their products to Russia and through Russia to China; thus the cloth industry in Poland was still further enhanced. This competition of Poland played a big rôle in the tariff measures of the Government.

In the cotton industry there was marked a concentration of production, owing to the fact that only big manufacturers were able to compete with foreign imports. But during the Forties there began to appear a reverse situation not only in cotton industry, but in all manufacturing industry. Statistics show that although the number of factories continued to grow, the increase in workingmen began to slacken, and if we should estimate the number of workingmen in each factory it will appear that production was becoming smaller. This was caused by the development not of the middle-sized industry, but of small *kustarny* (home work) production. I have already said that in the beginning of the nineteenth century in view of the greater productivity of hired labour in comparison with bonded labour, and because of other conditions unfavourable for the landowners, estate-factories began to disappear; but the merchants'-factories unexpectedly created a new competitor for themselves in the rural population. With the spread of cotton-spinning industry the manufacturers were not satisfied with the number of looms that they could put up in their factories, but in addition they gave out work for the peasants to do at home. But when the peasants found that they could easily buy (for cash or in credit) looms and yarn, they started an independent spinning industry, thus competing with the factories, and quite successfully, owing to the inexpensiveness of home production. This explains the fact that the number of factories grew, while the number of their workingmen diminished.

Let us observe that the *kustarny* industry, which originated in times immemorial, developed very rapidly in the nineteenth century in those productions that do not require particular outputs, as in the textile industries — cotton, hemp, silk, wool, etc. The *kustarny* production has been developing alongside with big industries, in contrast to conditions in other countries. The dimensions of the *kustarny* production were so large in the Forties that in the province of Vladimir, for instance, in the district of Shuisk, there were one thousand two hundred looms in the factories, while in the peasant-huts there were about twenty thousand of them; and throughout the province of Vladimir there were eighteen thousand looms in the factories and eighty thousand in the villages. The manufacturers complained to the Government, and petitioned for the curtailment of the petty industry. But the Government was not inclined to heed the complaints, since it sided with the gentry who were glad to see their bondmen earning considerable money, thus enabling the masters to raise high *obroks*.

In the history of the tariff-legislation during that period the most active worker had been the Minister of Finance, Count Y. F. Kankrin, whom we have mentioned before, and who had occupied his responsible post almost twenty-one years (from 1823 to 1844).[1]

---

[1] Kankrin was a man of an original and remarkable mind. He was German by origin; his father was invited by Catherine to come to Russia and manage the salt business. The young Kankrin was educated in a good German university, and had arrived in Russia by the end of the eighteenth century. For some time he had no definite occupation, but during the Napoleonic wars he came to the front, when, as an officer in the Commissariat he appeared to be an unusual phenomenon, since he was perhaps the only honest and educated person there. On one hand he naturally attracted bitter opposition and attacks, but on the other hand he won the attention of the superior authorities and even of Alexander.

The Tzar soon appreciated the value of Kankrin who proved to be well informed not only in the provision of the army, but in military administration, in general. In 1812 Kankrin was made General-Provision-Master of one army, and then of the entire army. He showed extraordinary ability not only in that branch of activity, but also in military tactics, and in the Council of War he greatly influenced the author of the Scythian plan, General Pful. Later Kankrin published a book on the theory of war, which again attracted the attention of Alexander.

When the war was transferred to Western Europe, Kankrin soon distinguished himself even there as the most resourceful and efficient

On the very eve of Kankrin's appointment as Minister of Finance the liberal tariff of 1819 was annulled, and the Government returned for a long time to protectionism. The new tariff of 1822 was worked out with Kankrin's aid. The protectionist system remained in power during his entire administration, which led the public to believe that he was a rabid and narrow protectionist, and hated free trade. This view is not just. Kankrin understood well the advantages of free trade, but he claimed that at the given moment Russia was in need of national independence, that with its low stage of culture the country would fall an easy prey to foreign industry (particularly to the interests of such a developed and aggressive country as England) under a free trade system.

From this point of view he considered it necessary to protect

Provision-Master, and acquired a universal reputation as the most competent of war-economists.

Upon the discovery of enormous abuses in the military department in Russia, and when the Minister of War, Prince Gorchakov, was arraigned before a court, the general expectation was that Kankrin would succeed to his place; but Alexander evidently had forgotten him. In 1818, however, Kankrin once more came to the Tzar's notice, by presenting to Alexander a capable memorandum about the liberation of the serfs, a memorandum that served, in the opinion of many, as the impulse that caused the latter to commission Arakcheiev to work out a plan for the gradual extinction of serfdom.

In 1822 Alexander finally decided that he could no longer keep in office Minister of Finance, Guriev, the secret of whose influence (he kept his position eleven years) is to be found in his faculty of making friends with the powerful spheres through distributing big sums of money under various pretexts. In 1822 there was a famine in White Russia; Guriev considerably curtailed the sums assigned for the starving peasants, but at the same time he allowed seven hundred thousand rubles for the purchase of an estate from an influential landowner who was in need of money. Upon the discovery of this Guriev was discharged, and by Arakcheiev's advice Alexander offered the post to Kankrin.

Even earlier than Arakcheiev, Kankrin was appreciated by Speransky, who said during his exile in Perm that in his opinion, Kankrin was the only man capable of managing the Russian finances.

the development of Russian production.   Yet he never allowed too high privileges for native manufacturers by the aid of exorbitant custom duties; on the contrary, he watched to see that Russian industry did not fall asleep, and he constantly regulated the customs system in order to force the Russian manufacturers to pay attention to all improvements in the technique of production, under the threat of foreign competition.   For this reason his conditionally protective tariff was modified many times with this view in mind.   In certain commodities the custom dues had been constantly lowered, especially when Kankrin deemed it necessary to encourage Russian industry from the " other end," threatening it with foreign competition.   Thus his protectionism was quite moderate and wise.

On the other hand, his tariff policy was dictated also by fiscal considerations.   We must bear in mind that when he accepted the portfolio of Minister of Finance, the finances were at a very low ebb; the treasury in 1822 was almost empty; no loans could be made on tolerable conditions, and the course of the paper-money did not rise in spite of the fact that in the last years of Guriev's administration, owing to his system of extinguishing the assignation-debt, that debt had decreased from eight hundred to five hundred and ninety-five million rubles.   This decrease was accomplished at the price of loans arranged for very heavy interest, so that the non-interest-bearing assignation-debt had become a debt with the obligation of paying out constant high interest.   Kankrin came to the conclusion that under such conditions there was no sense in extinguishing the assignations, but he strove to make no more loans and to issue no more assignations. His principle was that the aim of a financial policy should be not the growth of fiscal income, but the increase of national welfare, under which he understood mainly the welfare of the masses.

With this aim in view, Kankrin was strictly economical and opposed loans and heavy taxation.   In his practical activity he avoided the increase of taxes, but tried to lower the budgets of various departments, worrying but little about the numerous enemies that he made among the higher bureaucracy by such measures. I have already mentioned how unrelenting he had been even with Nicolas. His system of economy gave noticeable results in the very first years of his administration, and created on the European money-markets a far different attitude towards the Russian credit than the one that had existed during Guriev.

Kankrin applied the same principles of national economy to the tariff question. He considered that custom dues should be raised on objects of luxury and on commodities consumed by the richer classes, and in this direction he constantly raised the tariff. Under him the customs income rose from eleven million to twenty-six million rubles, i.e., two and a half times.

In order to bring to an end the tariff question, we shall take up the history of the Russo-Polish commercial and customs relations. Poland, more developed culturally, especially in respect to industry which could better flourish there than in Russia for the reasons cited above, looked upon Russia as a desirable market for her products, and moreover, she wanted to exploit the Asiatic markets, which could be made possible only by free transit through Russia. In 1826 Prince Lubetzky, Minister of Finance for the Kingdom of Poland, arrived at Petrograd with the special aim of obtaining tariff privileges for Poland; ignoring the Constitution of 1815, he pointed out that Poland was in fact a part of Russia. Kankrin put forth weighty arguments against the Prince. In his opinion even the existing customs system between the two countries was detrimental for the Russian population. At the formation of the Kingdom of Poland it was agreed that the raw materials of both countries were to be exchanged free of duty; as to manufactured commodities, those produced from native raw material were taxed with a negligible duty, not more than one per cent. of the cost of the ware, while for manufactures from foreign material there was a three per cent. duty *ad valorem,* but for certain commodities special duties were arranged, for instance, products of the cotton industry were taxed at fifteen per cent., sugar at twenty-five per cent. The chief commodity of Polish manufacturing industry — cloth — was taxed at three per cent., while Russian cotton manufactures were taxed at fifteen per cent.

The Moscow manufacturers naturally complained vehemently against such an order of things, and Kankrin in his arguments against Lubetzky indicated that not only did he not consider the abolition of internal customs possible, but that he intended to raise the duties on certain commodities the competition of which hurt Russian manufacturers. After the insurrection of 1831, when Poland had ceased to exist as an independent state, and the Government considered the complete incorporation of Poland, the custom-tariff between Russia and Poland appeared to be an anomaly. The question aroused lengthy discussions and was settled only toward the Fifties, after the death of Kankrin, by a special Commission. Trengoborsky, the learned Polish economist, who was recommended, it appears, by Lubetzky, took active part in the work of that Commission. In the Fifties the frontier line between Russia and Poland was abolished, while in regard to foreign trade differentiated duties were introduced, which were adapted to the conditions of both countries, and varied according to whether the imported goods were sent to Poland or to Russia.

An important question of the financial policy at that time, as it is also at present, was the military budget. Kankrin had attained a considerable economy in the *ordinary* expenses on the army during the first twelve years of his administration. But during that period alongside with the decrease in the ordinary expenses Russia had gone through a number of wars which demanded *extraordinary* expenses; these, in spite of Kankrin's opposition, had to be covered by loans. The war with Persia broke out soon after the accession of Nicolas, and in 1828–29, came the war with Turkey, which cost over one hundred and twenty million rubles in silver; then finally the Polish campaign of 1831 proved quite expensive. The war-loans in the first years reached four hundred million rubles in silver. But we must say that those loans were much better than the former assignations-issues. In general, as I have said, the reputation of Russian finances so improved under the management of Kankrin, that in the Thirties Russian papers were quoted on foreign exchanges almost at par, which had never happened before.

Almost all investigators of the history of Russian finances reproach Kankrin for the indisputably negative measure which he carried through in 1826 — the Beverage Reform. As we remember, under Guriev private contracts were abolished, and a system of fiscal beverage-monopoly was introduced, which continued to exist also under Kankrin until 1826. The wine-income increased in the beginning, but soon began to fall tremendously, owing to disorders in the fiscal management and to the unbelievable thievery that reigned there.

It had become clear that it was impossible to carry on the business in the absence of a staff of officials who would be to some extent honest and prepared. In 1826 Nicolas ordered Kankrin to prepare a report about the regulation of the wine-income. This report was very objective. It expounded the ways existing in various countries of exploiting the wine-income, and indicated the possibility of three systems: the fiscal system, then in existence in Russia, which monopolised all wine-trade; the system of wine-contracts, which had existed till the beginning of the Twenties, and consisted in giving over to private contractors the right to exploit the wine-monopoly; and lastly, the system of free trade in wine under an excise collected from every bottle or other vessel. The last system was upheld by Mordvinov, but Kankrin pointed out that it might be good in theory, while in practice it required some culture, and mainly an organisation under strict control, which, in the absence of efficient officials, was impossible. For the same reason he considered the existing fiscal system impracticable. He indicated the possibility of a fourth system — the distribution of the wine-income among provinces which would be taxed with a certain amount and would collect it by the aid of local institutions. But Kankrin mistrusted the local organs, and asserted that the tempting wine-income would prove the nobility to be as easily corrupted as the officials.

Since the State could not relinquish the exploitation of the large wine-income, Kankrin came to the conclusion that the least detrimental system was that of private contracts; he admitted that the lessees would accumulate enormous sums at the people's expense, but he argued that if such accumulation of money should be allowed at all, preference should be given to the contractors who would utilise that capital for industry, to the people's advantage, whereas from the thievery of the officials there was no gain even for industry.

Such were the considerations which led him to restore the contracts-system. The new measure proved a great evil; not only did the contractors wax rich, but they bribed and corrupted the entire local administration. All the provincial officials received from the contractors additional salary, not smaller than the regular salary. It is natural that when the interests of the contractors collided with others, the interests of the former were always given preference both by the administrative and by the judicial authorities. The evil of that system was not redeemed by the considerations of Kankrin in 1826.

Perhaps the most significant of Kankrin's undertakings was the currency-reform. The reform brought about the devaluation of the assignations and their redemption at lowered prices, but its chief aim was not in fiscal interests; Kankrin's idea was to facilitate commercial intercourse. The course of the paper-ruble had always vacillated, and as a matter of fact several courses existed: there was a bill-course used in transactions with foreign merchants, a taxation-course by which assignations were accepted by the Treasury, finally there existed a common-people-course used arbitrarily at private transactions. The last course was the most wavering; at the very same time it might vary in places from three hundred and fifty to four hundred and twenty copecks in assignations for one silver ruble. This was caused by the fact that in view of the constantly falling course of the assignations it had become customary to indicate a much lower course in transactions for future delivery or purchase, so that in certain cases the course would be artificially lowered to four hundred and twenty copecks per ruble instead of the normal course of three hundred and fifty or three hundred and sixty copecks. As a result the buying public (especially peasants) had often to pay much more than the actual course required, and in the general mistrust of the unstable assignations and search for constant metal-money, it had become customary to import foreign coins and sell them to the people. These private transactions brought further confusion. In view of these conditions Kankrin decided to have a law issued, calling for the conducting of all transactions in silver, for which purpose the assignations were to be given a definite obligatory course by which the Treasury would redeem them. After an exchange of opinions with Speransky, who left a memorandum on this question shortly before his death, Kankrin determined to place the course at three hundred and fifty copecks per ruble. The law was issued in June, 1839, and it had splendid results; an end came to all the frauds and confusions in the common-people-course transactions. A few years later Kankrin issued the so-called *depositki,* paper certificates for twenty-five rubles given by the Treasury as receipts for deposited metal-money or gold and silver bars; it was declared that the deposits would be kept intact and handed back upon demand. The *depositki* at once acquired popularity; in a few months, toward the end of 1842, more than twenty-five million rubles in coin were thus deposited. In two years the Government was in a position to issue more than forty million rubles' worth of paper-money, at par with the silver course.

Thus the national system had three kinds of circulating money—coin, *depositki,* and assignations. Soon Kankrin decided to issue credit bills, as in other countries, which would not be secured by an equivalent amount of metal-money, but only by a certain fund required for uninterrupted exchange. The *credit-bills* were issued, with a fund of one-sixth. of their amount in metal-money. The operation proved successful, the new bills circulated freely, and their course remained at par.

Then came the idea of supplanting all assignations with one form of paper-money exchangeable for coin. Kankrin had apprehensions that with the introduction of paper-money on such a scale there would arise in the course of time, especially after his death or resignation, a temptation to overissue such money, and in the result the old assignation story would repeat itself. But Nicolas, at his accession completely ignorant in financial affairs, had gradually acquired from Kankrin some knowledge of the subject, and considered himself an experienced financier; when Kankrin hesitated Nicolas presented his own project in which he argued with his Minister, and advocated the possibility of supplanting all assignations and *depositki* with credit-bills. At this he proposed to redeem all assignations at the price fixed in 1839, i.e., at three hundred and fifty copecks per silver ruble. As the total amount of assignations was equal to five hundred and ninety-five million rubles, it was necessary to have a fund of one hundred and seventy million silver rubles for their redemption; this amount required in security for an equivalent number of credit-bills one-sixth, i.e., the State Treasury was to have a constant sum of about twenty-eight and a half million rubles in coin. Nicolas believed in the possibility of realising that plan at once; for this reason he determined to discontinue the further issue of *depositki,* but in the course of their return to the Treasury to destroy them, take a corresponding sum from the depository fund, and issue for that sum new credit-bills; one-sixth of the metal fund should be kept as a security for the credit-bills, and the rest should be placed in a reserve fund, for new issues. In Nicolas's view the whole operation was to take not more than five years.

Although Kankrin showed a stubborn opposition, Nicolas' views, naturally upheld by all Ministers, were finally adopted. The operation passed very successfully; after the deposit of twenty-eight million rubles in coin as the fund of one-sixth the amount of the issued credit-bills, there still remained in the Treasury about sixty-six million rubles in coin, which sum was solemnly transported to the fortress of Peter and Paul, counted over and deposited. Thus the Government was in possession of a reserve-fund that held up the course of the paper-money until the war of 1853.

A few words should be said about Kankrin's general cultural activity, which was manifested in founding educational institutions for the spread of technical knowledge. In 1828 he established the Technological Institute; he reorganised and, so to speak, put on their feet the Forestry and Mining Institutes. He was the first to introduce industrial exhibitions which occurred periodically at Moscow. An agricultural periodical was founded by him, which he supplied with his articles, and an Institute of Agriculture, in Gory-Goretzk. Petrograd still bears the stamp of Kankrin's activity — in the numerous buildings erected by him, like the Bourse, and other governmental and educational edifices.

CHAPTER XVIII

WE shall now examine the course of education and the development of the mental and political movement among the *intelligentzia* during the Thirties and Forties.

Admiral Shishkov, inherited by Nicolas from the preceding reign, remained at his post as Minister of Education until 1828; from 1828 to 1833 the post was occupied by the Pietist, Prince Lieven. S. S. Uvarov, the most famous of all Russian Ministers of Education, retained the post from 1833 till the beginning of Nicolas' third period — 1849. It was Uvarov who had laid the peculiar Nicolaievian stamp on the educational activity of that epoch, although in fact he was only a talented executor of Nicolas' orders. Uvarov's rôle in the Ministry of Education was by the significance of his reforms as important as the rôle of Kankrin in the history of Russian finances and as the rôle of Kiselev in the history of peasant-legislation.

We have seen that from the beginning Nicolas had turned his attention to the question of education which he intended to base on the principle of preservation of the youth from revolutionary tendencies. The conservative programme received a definite stimulus after 1831, and the chief promulgator of those views came to be the successor of the weak Lieven, S. S. Uvarov, recommended by Karamzin. We remember Uvarov's opposition to the reactionary activity of Prince Golitzin before the Twenties, and his radical utterances about freedom and education; Uvarov of the epoch of Nicolas was a completely changed person. He had become an obedient servant of his master, and agreed with him that the population needed just as much education as was

279

required for the technical needs of the state, and that the public should be carefully guarded against the infiltration of pernicious political ideas.

The statutes of the primary and secondary schools were revised from this point of view by the Committee of December 6, 1826; in accordance with Nicolas' views, the net of schools introduced by Yankovich de Mirievo was discarded, and new statutes were issued December 28, 1828. This reactionary measure was carried through during the period which I have characterised as not opposed to Progress.

When Deputy Minister under Lieven, Uvarov had been ordered to investigate the University of Moscow and other provincial institutions. On his return the clever careerist presented a written report, in which his views so skilfully coincided with those of Nicolas, that the latter was bound to appoint him Minister. In his impressions of the University of Moscow, Uvarov indicated the pernicious influence of Western European ideas, and added: "I firmly believe that we shall be able to avoid those mistakes, and shall succeed in gradually capturing the minds of the youth and bringing them to that point where there must merge together — a regulated, fundamental education with a deep conviction and warm belief in the true-Russian conservative principles of *Orthodoxy, Autocracy, and Nationality,* which present the last anchor of our salvation and the surest pledge of the strength and majesty of our country."

The Emperor saw in Uvarov an assuring means for the promulgation of those ideas which he considered salutary and necessary for the young mind. As Minister, Uvarov definitely declared that he considered the main purpose of his Ministry — the damming of the influx of new ideas into Russia; he wished to prolong Russia's youthfulness, and if he could keep back the development of the country for about half a century, he "would die in peace."

In his above mentioned Report Uvarov jesuitically advocated

the "multiplication of mental dikes for the struggle with destructive notions." This principle became the foundation of the subsequent policy of the Ministry of Education, at the head of which stood the most learned man of his age, who intended to implant "true enlightenment" and at the same time preserve the youth from imported revolutionary ideas. One is inclined to presume that Uvarov had been converted to profess what he used to mock at: to believe in "fire which does not scald."

Discussions had been going on yet in Shishkov's Committee about the desirable programme for Gymnasia. It was decided to introduce the Classical method with Latin as a compulsory subject, and with both Latin and Greek in several Gymnasia in the Capitals. At the beginning the Classical programme did not exclude other studies, but the longer that system lasted, the longer Uvarov remained Minister, the more subjects were thrown overboard from the curriculum; in 1844 statistics was excluded, in 1847 — logic, in 1846 the course of mathematics was abridged, and by the end of the Forties the programme of studies for secondary schools was considerably shortened.

At that time the nobles sent their children quite willingly to the Gymnasia. This was conditioned on one hand by the necessity of having a diploma for State service, and also by the exhaustion of the contingent of domestic teachers that had been furnished by the French émigrés. Thus the Government finally saw its plans carried out, and the demand for Gymnasia grew. Accordingly, in 1826 there were forty-eight Gymnasia, while in the Fifties — seventy-four; at the beginning of Nicolas' reign the number of students was seven thousand, and by its end, eighteen thousand. The number of District Schools also increased, but the quality of their instruction deteriorated. This was due to the reorganisation of the school-management. By the Statute of 1804, which had signified the most brilliant epoch in the history of Russian education, the universities stood at the head of the provincial school-management. But the Statute was radically changed in 1835, the organisation of the universities was greatly modified, and the primary and secondary schools passed from their jurisdiction to that of the District Curators, who were now in many cases local Governor-Generals, and in Siberia — Governors.

The Statute of 1835 deprived the universities of autonomy. True they preserved the right to elect Rectors and place professors in vacancies, but at the same time the Minister of Education had the right not to approve of the elected functionaries, and to appoint his own candidates. We must, however, mention that there still existed a tendency toward developing good professors, and during the Thirties it was a practice to send young candidates abroad, the results of which were splendid. During the Forties a whole pleiad of young Russian scholars who had been abroad appeared, and they contributed greatly to the education of the following generation of the *intelligentzia*. To mention a few names: Granovsky, Riedkin, Kriukov, Buslaiev (in Moscow), Meyer (Kazan), Nievolin, Kutorga (Petrograd). The Moscow Curator, Count S. G. Stroganov, a well educated man, made many efforts to improve the quality of the personnel, but he liked to interfere with the system of instruction and even with the programmes of individual professors, dictated desirable tendencies to them, and in general managed the university as an exemplary boss.

The number of universities did not increase; the University of St. Vladimir, opened in Kiev in 1834, took the place of the University of Vilna, which was closed after the insurrection of 1831.

As to the position of the *intelligentzia,* their ranks were greatly depleted after December 14, 1825. The flower of the *intelligentzia,* if we understand by it the independently thinking society, was cut down by the ruthless hand of the victor, and exiled to Siberia. Those who remained were terrorised and prevented from expressing their ideas.

" Thirty years ago," wrote Herzen in the Fifties, " Russia of
the future existed exclusively among a few boys who had just
passed their childhood; in them lay the heritage of universal
knowledge and of purely national Russ. This new life vege-
tated as grass trying to grow on the lips of a crater which has
not yet cooled." When those boys grew up, the young generation was split in the same two currents by which Western ideas
had been flowing into Russia since the days of Catherine. Again
there appeared on one side those who had absorbed the French
ideas of the end of the eighteenth century, the ideas of the French
Revolution, and the ideas of the Decembrists who had also been
brought up on the French ideology; on the other side there appeared the followers of German thought, German Idealism, and
of the Post-Kantian metaphysics which had deeply penetrated
the Russian thinking society of the Twenties and Thirties. The
followers of the second current were now in the majority, as
was clearly demonstrated by the nature of the university circles
around which the young generation of the Thirties concentrated.
At the end of Alexander's reign the French ideas, reflected in
the plans of Pestel and Nikita Muraviov, were undisputably
dominant; but even then followers of German philosophers, particularly of Schelling began to form circles. Already in 1804
an ardent expounder of Schelling's philosophy appeared in Petrograd in the person of Vellansky, a professor at the Medical
Academy. Schelling's monistic-idealistic philosophy which tried
to reconcile the objectivity of the existence of nature with the
possibility of its speculative contemplation, had brought him to
his *Naturphilosophie,* which appealed to natural scientists and
medical students. This explains the fact that in Russia Schellingianism was first introduced by Vellansky, Professor at the
Medical Academy, and by M. G. Pavlov, professor of physics
and mineralogy at the University of Moscow. Herzen relates
in his *Past and Meditations* the significance of Pavlov's lectures
for his (Herzen's) student-generation during the first course in

the Physico-Mathematical department. Pavlov would at once startle his students with the question: "You want to know Nature, but what is Nature, and what is To know?" Thus before expounding physics he would explain the theory of Consciousness according to Schelling. Later, however, that philosophy was preached by professors of the history of philosophy (Galich), of the theory of literature and æsthetics (Davidov, Nadezhdin), and others, and also in literature where the forerunners were grouped around the circle of the Moscow "Lovers of Wisdom," founded in the Twenties by Prince D. V. Odoievsky and D. V. Venevitinov, who began to issue in 1824 a literary almanach, *Mnemozina,* with the co-operation of Wilhelm Küchelberg and Professor Pavlov. To the "Lovers of Wisdom" belonged also the future Moscow Slavophiles, the brothers Kireievsky and Khomiakov, also Pogodin and Shevyrev, who undertook in 1826 the publication of the *Moscow Messenger.* Through Venevitinov and Küchelberg Pushkin was attracted to the publications of the "Lovers of Wisdom."

Mnemozina was devoted to the struggle with the ideas of the French Encyclopedists of the eighteenth century, and to the spread of the ideas of German Idealism. The direct successor of *Mnemozina* was the *Moscow Messenger,* but in spite of its gifted contributors this publication soon died, owing to the inexperience of its young editors. In 1831 the chief organ of Schellingianism in Russia was the *Telescope,* published by Nadezhdin, Professor of Æsthetics at the University of Moscow. Parallel with this strictly philosophical magazine there had been published at Moscow since 1825 the *Moscow Telegraph,* founded by the many-sided journalist, N. A. Polevoy [1] at first with the close co-operation of Prince P. A. Viazemsky, one of the Arzamasians. The *Moscow Telegraph* was char-

[1] The first Russian writer in the nineteenth century who was not a nobleman by birth. Pushkin, in one of his virulent epigrams, called him "plebeian."—TR.

acterised by its publishers as an Encyclopedic organ; it preached Romanticism, and struggled with the Pseudo-Classicism of the old *European Messenger* that was edited then by Professor Kachenovsky.

In spite of their theoretic differences, both the *Telescope* and the *Moscow Telegraph* were progressive organs, and advocated the liberal views then predominant in Western Europe. But the *Telegraph,* an eclectic and more superficial publication, was more acceptable to the unprepared readers, while the *Telescope* had a more select audience, among the university *intelligentzia.* For this reason the Censorship Department, whose actual head had been Uvarov, as Deputy Minister, since 1832, looked with suspicion on Polevoy's popular magazine, and stopped its publication in 1833. Nadezhdin's *Telescope,* in view of its smaller circle of readers, was treated by the Government with more tolerance, and it appeared unmolested until 1836, when the famous " Philosophical Letter " of Chaadaiev appeared.

The author of that letter, P. J. Chaadaiev, was a remarkable personality, and has left an important impression in the history of the Russian *intelligentzia.* Although his activity belonged to the Thirties and Forties, by his age, and particularly by his education and connections, he belonged to the preceding generation, which was removed from the scene after December 14, 1825. Together with Pushkin they were the only fragments of that generation of Russian *intelligentzia* saved by accident from the catastrophe. A brilliant Guard-officer, an aristocrat by birth (he was a grandson of the historian, Prince Shcherbatov), brought up as most of his contemporaries on the ideas of the end of the eighteenth century, he nevertheless early separated himself from his friends, and lived a solitary life. After the famous incident in the Semionovsky regiment, when he was sent with a report to Alexander at Leibach, he resigned, lived alone, and concentrated his thoughts on Mysticism. In his infatuation with Christian Mysticism (in its Catholic form), Chaadaiev rejected Hegel whose system did not agree with Christian revelation, but became an ardent adherent of Schelling, when the latter came in his second period to the reconciliation of the conclusions of the Idealistic philosophy with the dogmas of the Christian faith; in this respect Chaadaiev agreed perfectly with the subsequent founder of the Slavophil doctrine, I. I. Kireievsky. He had another point of contact with his later opponents, the Slavophils, in that he also admitted a radical difference between the development of Western Europe and Russia, on a religious basis; but that difference was not in his opinion in favour of Russia. In the Catholicism of Western Europe he saw a mighty and faithful guard of the principles of Christianity and Christian civilisation, while Russia appeared to him in the gloomiest light, a mediocrity which stood on the parting of the ways between East and West, and had neither great traditions nor a strong religious foundation for her development. Russia's only salvation he saw in her immediate and complete adoption of the religious and cultural principles of the West. He undertook the mission of propagating his views among the Moscow salons of the Thirties; he could not appear in the press because of the censorship conditions. His " Philosophical Letter," which belonged to a series of other Letters (they were published recently, with the exception of a few that have been lost), had not been intended for publication, but was written to a private person. He read those letters to his acquaintances, however, and Nadezhdin asked him to place them in his *Telescope*. The appearance of the first Letter produced the impression of an exploded bomb.

It was the sharpest and most daring protest against the system of " official Nationalism " that had been proclaimed by the Government with the aid of Uvarov. In contrast to the Government's praise of Russian historical principles and Russian reality, Chaadaiev's view on Russian history was stated thus: " At the very beginning we had savage barbarism, later rude superstition, then a cruel, humiliating domination of the conquerors, a domination the traces of which have not been erased from our mode of living to this day. Such is the sad history of our youth; we have not had that age of boundless activity, of the poetical display of the nation's moral forces. The epoch of our social life, corresponding to that age, was filled with a dark, colourless existence, without power, without energy.

" We have no charming memories, no strong, instructive examples in popular legends. Cast a glance at all the centuries of our existence, at all the expanse that we are occupying now, and you will not find a single reminiscence which would arrest you, a single monument which would tell you about the past in a strong, vivid, picturesque way.

" We live in indifference to all, in a narrow horizon, with no past or future . . ."

A strange fate has separated Russia from the universal life of mankind, and in order to become like other nations, she must — according to Chaadaiev —" begin over again the whole education of man. For this purpose we have before us the history of nations and the results of movements of ages. . . ."

The impression made by that Letter can be easily imagined: the *Telescope* was discontinued, Nadezhdin was exiled to Vologda, and Chaadaiev was officially declared insane.

In the Capitals and in the provinces the Letter produced an impression of a scandal, and aroused general confusion. Even the most progressive minds felt offended by Chaadaiev's tone of utter contempt for the Russian past. In the Moscow circles hot discussions took place, and among Chaadaiev's main opponents were his friends, the subsequent Slavophils, Kireievsky and Khomiakov. One year later Chaadaiev wrote — naturally not for publication — his *Apologia of an Insane,* in which he practically reiterated his former views, but asserted that nobody loved his country more than he did, and that the voice of the people is not always the voice of God. His decent opponents, like Kireievsky, etc., refused to take issue with a man whose teachings were officially condemned; but the former publishers of the *Moscow Messenger,* Shevyrev and Pogodin, did not scruple about the delicate situation, and in their desire to gain the favour of Uvarov they rudely attacked the man who had been ordered to keep silence. In Pogodin's *Muscovite* for the year 1841 there appeared an article under the title "A view of a Russian on European Education," in which Western Europe was diagnosed as a decaying, infectious organism, from which Russia should be guarded. Accepting Uvarov's Trinity — Orthodoxy, Autocracy, and Nationality, as a sound foundation for the life of Russia, the author of the article declared his perfect agreement with the views of the Government, and ended with the following exclamation: "By these three cardinal feelings our Russ is powerful, and our future is sure. A man of the Tzar's counsel, to whom our growing citizens are intrusted, has already expressed them in a profound thought, and has made them the basis of the education of the people."

Personally Count Uvarov did not, however, consider his position quite firm, and he was well aware of the existence among the *intelligentzia* of living forces ready to fight; the suppression of those forces formed his main purpose. In his report on the decenary of his management of the Ministry of Education he wrote (in 1843): "The direction dictated by Your Majesty to the Ministry, and its triple formula were bound to arouse the opposition of all those who had still preserved the stamp of Liberal and Mystical ideas: of the Liberals, because the Ministry, proclaiming Autocracy, declared its firm desire to return to the Russian Monarchical principle; of the Mystics — because the word Orthodoxy clearly indicated the intention of the Ministry to hold fast to the teachings of Christianity, and to do away with all the Mystical ghosts that had often obscured the clarity of the Holy traditions of the Church; finally the word Nationality has provoked our enemies' animosity for the daring assertion that the Ministry considered Russia mature and worthy of marching not behind, but at least alongside with the other European nationalities."

Indeed, about that time, the beginning of the Forties, a new Westernising movement was formed among the public, which opposed the "official Nationalism," rejected the point of view of the Slavophiles, and which soon became, in spite of repressions and persecutions, the leader of the young generation. This movement, unlike that of Chaadaiev and the Slavophiles, was based not on theological principles, but on their rejection. In order to follow through the origin and fate of that movement, and also of its antipode — Slavophilism, we must turn to the history of the circles of the Thirties, in which lay, in the words of Herzen, "Russia of the future."

At the beginning of the Thirties the thinking students of the University of Moscow were grouped around two circles: that of Stankevich and that of Herzen. Stankevich's circle consisted of persons interested chiefly in questions of philosophy and ethics, and who were under the influence of Schellingians, like Pavlov and Nadezhdin. To that circle belonged: Bielinsky, on one end, and Constantine Aksakov, on the other. Later they were joined by Bakunin, Botkin, Katkov, Granovsky (from abroad), and partly Samarin (with the aid of Aksakov) — all stars of first magnitude in the subsequent history of the Russian *intelligentzia*.

The men of Herzen's circle were interested mostly in political and social problems; among them were Ogarev, Satin, Ketcher, Passeck, and others. The most brilliant personality in the circle was, of course, Herzen, who remained a life friend of Ogarev. The circle considered themselves direct heirs of the Decembrists and through them of the ideas of French philosophy and the French Revolution. Of contemporary thought they adhered most of all to the socialistic doctrines of Saint-Simon and his followers.

The circle of Herzen was soon disbanded; the members sang revolutionary songs at a party arranged on their graduation from the university, were arrested, spent several months under arrest, and were then exiled to various remote provinces. From 1833 to 1839 Herzen lived in Perm, in Viatka, and later in Vladimir. Upon his return to Moscow he found Hegel's philosophy in full domination of the upper *intelligentzia* circles, and he had to take up its study and join the men who had been brought up in the circle of Stankevich (the latter was at that time dying abroad, in his twenty-seventh year).

Monistic Idealism in Western philosophy had passed from Kant through Fichte to Schelling; but in Russia, as we have seen, the acquaintance with German Idealism began with Schelling, while Kant received no audience. The members of the circle of Stankevich were attracted more by Fichte, however, especially one of them, Mikhail Bakunin, who although he received only a domestic education and was a graduate of the School of Artillery, had a natural gift for dialectic reasoning and philosophy in general. He had become interested in this when still in the Military school under the influence of Venevitinov's articles and of La Harpe's " History and Theory of Rhetoric," at the end of which were expounded the theories of Locke and Condillac. Stankevich and Bakunin, little attracted by Kant's *Critique of Pure Reason,* became interested in the conclusions of Fichte's Idealistic philosophy, which he applied for the solution of German and universal ethical and political problems of his age. Bakunin imparted his interest in Fichte to Bielinsky who, not knowing German, absorbed Schelling and Fichte from discussions with his friends. Bielinsky's articles in the *Telescope* for 1836 bore the stamp of Fichte's exalted Idealism which considered moral problems of paramount importance. From Fichte, Bakunin, Bielinsky, and their friends soon passed to Hegel, and the advent of the new philosophy had marked the end of the Thirties.

Bielinsky had also to depend on what he had been told about Hegel by Bakunin and Katkov. For this reason Bielinsky like

many of his contemporaries not only in Russia, but even among
the German Hegelians, misinterpreted Hegel's logical maxim,
"All reality is reasonable," as "everything that exists has a
reasonable purpose." As many other Hegelians, Bielinsky observed the life about him from a conservative point of view, tried
to justify existing institutions, and came out with a panegyric
for the Russian social and political order (his articles in 1838–
1840).

Of course such a sensitive and noble mind as Bielinsky's could
not long remain under that influence, and he soon passionately
rejected his former beliefs, and went to the other extreme: instead of examining the philosophy which he misunderstood, he
decided that German Idealism was bound to draw one to absurd
conclusions, and that one should better turn to the positive
political teachings of the contemporary French. This new turn
in Bielinsky was enhanced by his meeting with Herzen who
had recently come back to Moscow from his exile. Herzen's
influence was reflected in Bielinsky's subsequent activity which
was transferred to Kraievsky's monthly *Annals of the Fatherland*
in Petrograd. Soon Bielinsky was glad to hear that Bakunin,
with whom he had quarrelled before leaving Moscow, had
changed his conception of Hegelianism after a thorough study
of his philosophy in Berlin, and having joined the Left Wing
of the Hegelians, he became a prominent expounder of Materialistic Monism.

Bielinsky's further literary activity has an enormous significance in the history of the Russian *intelligentzia;* the magazines
Annals of the Fatherland and the *Contemporary* became the
most read publications in the country, and during the Forties
Bielinsky was the real intellectual leader of the young generation. He no longer advocated the ideas of German philosophy,
but promulgated the ideas of those social and political doctrines
which he had adapted with the aid of Herzen from French literature. His attitude became sharply hostile to the "official Na-

tionalism " which was expressed by the *Muscovite,* issued by Pogodin in co-operation with Shevyrev; but the *Muscovite* was not his only enemy at that time.

About the middle of the Forties the Moscow Slavophiles definitely formulated their views. Some of them, like the brothers Kireievsky, Khomiakov, Koshelev, were of the former Lovers of Wisdom; others, like Constantine Aksakov and Yuriy Samarin, were from Bielinsky's comrades in the circle of Stankevich. They were all pure, noble minds, who had worked out an original, solid, and well-proportioned system, their own historiosophy, which like that of Chaadaiev was based on theological principles, and they had also emphasised the contradictions and contrasts in the development of the two different worlds of contemporary mankind: the Western — Latin-German, and the Eastern — Byzantine-Slav, or Greco-Russian. But in direct opposition to Chaadaiev the Slavophiles idealised extremely the whole course of development of the Russo-Slavic world, and regarded negatively the entire Western-European culture.

In their conception the Orthodox faith and the Russian people had preserved the ancient principle of spiritual Christianity in all its purity, while in the West it had been distorted by the casuistry of Catholicism, by the Papal authority, and by the prevalence of material culture over spiritual. The consequent development of those circumstances had brought, in their opinion, at first Protestantism, and later the modern Materialism, and the denial of the Revelation and of all the truths of the Christian faith. The Slavophiles asserted that in Russia the state and society had developed on principles of freedom, on the domination of democratic, *communal,* elements, while in the West the state and society developed on principles of violence, of enslaving one class or nation by other classes or nations, which resulted in the Feudal, aristocratic form of personal ownership of land, and the landlessness of the masses.

Although there were points of contact between the teachings

of the Slavophiles and the " official Nationalism," they also had fundamental differences; the Slavophiles demanded complete freedom of speech and of creed, and full independence from the state of personal, communal, and church life — the ideas that were formulated later by Constantine Aksakov in his Memorandum to Alexander II, in which he proclaimed the famous Slavophile political formula: " The power of government — to the Tzar; the power of opinion — to the people."

Bielinsky attacked the Slavophiles as sharply and passionately as he did the representatives of " official Nationalism," especially after the attempt (which failed) of the Slavophiles to take over Pogodin's *Muscovite,* in 1845. Regarding the Slavophiles with utter intolerance, Bielinsky reproached his comrades — the Moscow Westerners, Granovsky and Herzen — for their mild treatment of them, and particularly for their willingness to contribute to their publications. Bielinsky himself decisively rejected the thought of such participation in his enemies' organs, and he used to say: " I am a Hebrew by nature, and will not eat at the same table with a Philistine."

The censorship conditions allowed the Westerners to carry on their ideals only between the lines, and the Slavophiles were unable to organise any stable organ of their own, so that most of their debates took place either in private houses or in sporadic almanachs; the *Moscow Almanach* appeared in 1846 and in 1847, and again in 1852, but by that time any discussion of political and social questions had become impossible. In this respect the revolutions of 1848 had played a decisive rôle.

With the accession of Nicolas the attitude of the Government had radically changed towards the Schismatics and particularly toward the Sectarians. The position of certain sects had become worse in the last years of Alexander under the influence of the bigoted and fanatic tendencies in the sphere of Public Worship, expressed by Archimandrite Fotiy and by the Metropolitan of Petrograd, Seraphim.

Although Fotiy was treated unfavourably by the new Monarch who in general did not sympathise with Orthodox fanaticism, Nicolas from the very beginning regarded the Schismatics and other dissenters very negatively, first because in his eyes they were rebels against the established Church, and secondly because of their anti-governmental tendencies. From the latter point of view the Government estimated the degree of perniciousness and dangerousness in various sects. At the same time the position of the Spiritual Christians, the *Dukhobory* and *Molokane,* whom Alexander had protected, and settled in the province of Tavrida (Crimea) changed to the worse. Under Nicolas the *Dukhobory* and *Molokane,* because of their anti-state tendencies, were declared pernicious sects. It is curious that these sects were regarded by the Government as more dangerous than such morbid sects as the *Khlysty* and the *Skoptzy;* the reason is that the latter masqued their practices behind superficial adherence to the Church, and not only prayed for the Tzar, but owing to their wealth they were able to buy the protection of corruptible officials. Whereas the *Dukhobory* and *Molokane* refused to compromise, led an irreproachably pure peasant life, and appearing as a state within a state they finally drew upon them the persecutions of the Government, in which the agents of the Third Department of His Majesty's Own Chancery played a large rôle. Back in 1826 Nicolas expressed his belief that the Sectarians (at least the most stubborn and active) should be transferred as soldiers to the Caucasus, and those incapable of military service should be exiled to Siberia. These measures were executed during the second period of his reign; in 1839, 1840, and 1841 the settlements of the *Dukhobory* and *Molokane* were abolished, and they were transported to Trans-Caucasia, while the most active of them were exiled to Siberia and put into military service. In 1841 Nicolas announced in an Imperial ukase that he considered the safeguard of the " inviolability of the forefathers' Orthodox Church " among his subjects as one of the duties imposed on him by Providence, and he gave warning that severe repressions would be inflicted upon dissenters, and that the children of those who would be exiled for religious reasons would be taken care of by the Government.

The Government had become convinced by that time that in spite of all repressions, and the external conversion of many dissenters to the Orthodox creed, the number of sects continued to grow. It was decided to make a special study of the Schism and the sects, in order to employ more adequate measures for their eradication. The matter was entrusted confidentially to several learned persons, among whom were Yuriy Samarin (in Riga), Ivan Aksakov (in the province of Yaroslavl and in the South), and at the centre of the work was placed the ex-Professor Nadezhdin, who had been the editor of the *Telescope,* passed through a period of exile in Vologda, and then entered into the service of the Ministry of the Interior, under L. A. Perovsky. The materials collected had a great value, as for the first time they furnished the Government with more or less substantial information. Before that time the information had been accidental and quite inaccurate. For instance, in the former records the number of Schismatics in the province of Yaroslavl was put at fourteen to fifteen thousand, whereas the special investigators stated that about one-half of its population were " infected " with Schism and various sects; in the province of Vologda the former official figures of the Schismatics showed about three and a half thousand, while the special investigators counted about one-third of the population (nearly two hundred thousand), who had dissented from Orthodoxy; in the province of Chernigov numerous towns and villages were discovered completely belonging to the Schism; in the province of Kostroma, in addition to twenty thousand overt Schismatics twenty-seven thousand four hundred and eighty-five secret, and fifty-seven thousand five hundred and seventy-one "infected" with the Schism were found. An enormous number of *Molokane* and Spiritual Christians were discovered in the provinces of Tambov and Saratov — about two hundred thousand in the first, and tens of thousands in the second.

It is no wonder, then, that while the official data about Schismatics and Sectarians showed their figures between the years 1826 and 1855 as seven hundred to eight hundred thousand, and only once (in 1837) the figures showed one million and three thousand,— a competent statistician who had access to confidential governmental data, General N. N. Obruchov, asserted that their number could not be less than eight million persons. According to the Government's classification of 1842 the Schismatics and Sectarians were divided into *most pernicious, pernicious,* and *less pernicious.* Less pernicious were the *Popovtzy,* i.e., those who accepted priests; their numbers were officially larger because they were less secret. The *Bez-popovtzy,* i.e., those who did not accept priests, but prayed for the Tzar and admitted marriage were considered pernicious. In regard to both those groups the Government decided not to destroy them but to prevent their further spread. Those *Bezpopovtzy* who refused to pray for the Tzar and did not admit marriage, and all sorts of sects, like the *Molokane, Dukhobory, Ikonobortzy, Khlysty, Skoptzy,* and others were considered most pernicious. The number of Sectarians in the Forties was probably not less than one million. In spite of the Government's decision to exterminate the "most pernicious," their numbers did not diminish and their hostility against the Government and its agents grew stronger. The latter phenomenon was true also in regard to the "least pernicious," as the *Popovtzy.* Catherine had permitted them to keep their own monasteries and hermitaries along the river Irghiz, in the province of Saratov. In the absence of their own Bishops, the *Popovtzy* had difficulty in obtaining priests, and were forced to make use of "fugitive" priests or of "unfrocked" Orthodox priests. Nicolas rigorously persecuted the "fugitive" priests. Then the agitation grew among the Schismatics for obtaining their own Bishops who would ordain priests from their midst. There exists a story that this idea was suggested or hinted to them by the Chief of Gendarmes, Benckendorff. When they had after many efforts succeeded in obtaining from Constantinople the supernumerary Metropolitan, Amvrosiy, and had him installed with the permission of the Austrian emperor at Bielaia Krenitza, in Bukovina (1847), the Russian Government demanded that Austria dismiss and banish Amvrosiy (at that time Austria had respect for Russian demands), and had the Patriarch of Constantinople depose him. But Amvrosiy had already ordained several Bishops who were now in a position to ordain priests for the Schismatics. The Government hunted the new Bishops and priests as "fugitives," and imprisoned them in monastic prisons, which intensified the hostility of the Schismatics towards the authorities, and while some of them formally joined the official Church, the more stubborn elements joined, on the contrary, the more pernicious branches and sects. The persecutions of the Schismatics brought about new, irreconcilable sects, as the *Pilgrims,* for example, whose principle had been to use no passports and to show no obedience to the authorities, whom they regarded as the servants of Satan. Thus by the end of Nicolas' reign, owing to the ruthless struggle which the Government had carried on against the Schismatics and Sectarians, their numbers not only did not decrease, but their hostility toward the authorities and toward any sort of government had become more acute.

The number of trials and severe penalties inflicted upon dissenters of all categories grew from year to year; according to official data, between 1847 and 1852 there were over five hundred verdicts a year against them, and the number of persons tried for belonging to the Schism during those five years was twenty-six thousand four hundred and fifty-six.

The gulf between the ideology of the Government and that of the people grew and broadened during that reign in perhaps greater dimensions than even the gulf between the Government and the *intelligentzia*.

CHAPTER XIX

THE third and last period of Nicolas' reign began after the revolution of February, 1848, in France and the subsequent revolutionary outbursts in other European countries; those events marked the third period with a ruthless reactionism.

The first news about the proclamation of a republic in France greatly disturbed Nicolas. A contemporary asserts that the Emperor appeared with the telegrams in his hand at the palace of his Heir, where a ball was going on, and coming to the centre of the salon stood amidst the dancing couples, and exclaimed: " Saddle your horses, gentlemen: a republic has been proclaimed in France." At the same time, however, he rejoiced at the fall of Louis Philippe whom he considered a justly punished usurper. " Serves him right. . . . Fine, splendid," he uttered to his entourage in the study of his Heir. To prevent an attack on the part of the French upon the neighbouring states, and in order to restrain the German Communists and Socialists who might emulate the French, Nicolas wanted on the spur of the moment to move an army three thousand strong to the Rhine. He was supported in his bellicose mood by Paskevich who was then in Petrograd. But his other advisers (Volkonsky, Kiselev) proved to him without difficulty that even if he had enough troops, he did not have enough money. Hence the pugnacious and indignant mood of Nicolas had to be relieved at first merely in a queer manifesto issued March 14, 1848, which was full of threats for the Western enemies and rebels (although there was no evidence of an attempted attack against Russia), and ended with this self-reliant outburst: " God is with us! Take heed, O nations, and submit, for God is with us! "

Soon, however, events in Austria where part after part of the Empire had begun to break off, and the appeal of the youthful Franz Joseph to Nicolas, induced the Tzar to employ more vigorous action which saved the Monarchy of the Hapsburgs from what generally appeared its inevitable decomposition and ruin. Some assert that Nicolas extended his aid to Franz Joseph not only out of a desire to uphold legal authorities against revolting nationalities, but also out of practical, selfish considerations which were supported especially by Paskevich who insisted that unless the Hungarian revolt were suppressed it would inevitably spread over the Kingdom of Poland, and in that case the events of 1831 would be repeated. The Hungarian uprising was quickly quelled by the much superior Russian forces led by Prince Paskevich whose stupid actions, however, had considerably shaken his reputation of a talented general.

After the suppression of the Hungarian uprising Nicolas became for a time the supreme dictator of Central and Eastern Europe. He forced the weak, vacillating king of Prussia to reject all plans about a " United Germany " and about the annexation of the Danish provinces which Nicolas considered belonged by right to Austria. At the same time he demanded from Friedrich Wilhelm more rigorous penalties for the revolutionary elements in Prussia, especially in Prussian Poland. By his constant interference in German affairs and by his threats to all enemies of the established order, Nicolas acquired such a reputation that German mothers frightened their children with the name of the Tzar.

The revolutionary outbursts of 1848 aroused an extreme reactionism not only in the Emperor, but in all his family and court circle. The Heir particularly was imbued with that spirit; he agreed perfectly with the views his father expressed in the manifesto of March 14, 1848, and even approved of the tone in which

it was composed. Immediately upon its publication, Tzesarevich Alexander called all the commanders of the Guard-regi-
ments together and read the manifesto to them; this was met
with enthusiastic ovations. The officers of that time little resembled those of the last years of Alexander I — in this respect
the twenty-five years' labours of Nicolas had been crowned with
great success; but one can not fail noticing that the eradication
of liberal ideas among the army was accompanied with a considerable lowering of its quality. The mechanical weeding out
of all independent thought caused the Russian army, when it
had to fight with European troops, to feel a dire lack of chiefs
with an initiative, of educated officers and generals capable of
independent thinking. . . .

The reactionary mood was immediately reflected on the internal policy. The Government tried to concentrate all conservative forces. In receiving a deputation of Petrograd nobles
on March 21, 1848, the Tzar said: " Let us forget mutual
grievances. Give your hand to one another, as brothers, as
children of our mother-country, so that the last hand may reach
me, and then, under my leadership, rest sure that no earthly
power can disturb us." Articles about the firmness of the
Bondage-Right began to appear in Governmental publications,
and Kiselev himself said to his nephew, Miliutin, that " the
peasant-question had burst." The same was categorically stated
to a representative of the Smolensk nobility by Olsufiev, Court-
Marshal of the Heir.

Entirely different was the reaction of the *intelligentzia* toward the stormy events of 1848. By that time the propaganda
carried on under the direction of Bielinsky in Kraievsky's *Annals of the Fatherland,* and from 1847 — in the *Contemporary*
of Panaiev and Nekrasov, had shown considerable results. In
the Capitals, especially in Petrograd, and partly in the provinces,
circles of progressive young men began to appear, peculiar salons
where political, literary, and social problems were discussed; the

discussions could not take place in the press. Such were the famous Fridays at the home of M. B. Butashevich-Petrashevsky, the evenings at the homes of Durov, Kashkin, Mombelli, Pleshcheiev, and others. Petrashevsky's Fridays since 1845 served as a meeting place for numerous young men from the provinces and capitals, and they were the most popular gatherings among the *intelligentzia*. Petrashevsky himself was a Socialist (a Fourierist), but at his evenings all varieties of questions were brought up, most often the peasant-question, also questions of the judiciary — juries, publicity and independence of courts, of the Censorship and freedom of press, in a word, the very questions that were solved a few years later, during the epoch of the Great Reforms; at the same time they discussed literary and political news from Western Europe, and read such productions as could not appear in the press, as, for instance, the famous letter of Bielinsky to Gogol concerning the latter's *Selections from the Correspondence with My Friends.*

At Kashkin's assembled persons especially interested in social problems, young Socialists and Communists, followers of Saint-Simon, Leroux, Lamennais, Louis Blanc, Cabet, and particularly of Fourier. At Durov's more moderate thinkers gathered.

All those circles were known to one another, and kept up mutual relations. In the provinces embryos of similar organisations existed among admirers of *Annals of the Fatherland,* the *Contemporary,* and of their inspirer — Bielinsky. It is interesting that Ivan Aksakov who travelled through all Russia in the Forties, taking part in various revisions and investigations, and often serving in provincial courts, testified in his letters that on the gloomy background of the provincial life, amidst the society that consisted of all sorts of grafters, cheats, serf-drivers, scoundrels, and trivial nonentities,— the only bright exceptions were the followers of Bielinsky, the readers and admirers of the progressive Petrograd magazines. The Slavophils were little known in the provinces, their Almanachs were not read; provincial book-sellers directly declared to Aksakov that they did not buy those Almanachs because the *Annals of the Fatherland* and the *Contemporary* did not praise them. " Both Polevoy and Bielinsky," wrote Aksakov in 1856, " had an enormous influence on the public, though a bad, harmful influence (from his Slavophil point of view). I have been all over Russia: the name of Bielinsky is known to every youth who does any thinking, to every one who craves fresh air amidst the stagnant mire of provincial life. There is not one Gymnasium teacher who does not know Bielinsky's letter to Gogol by heart; in the remote corners of Russia his influence only begins to penetrate, increasing the number of proselytes. . . . ' We owe our salvation to Bielinsky,' honest young men in the provinces tell me. . . . And if you want an honest man, capable of compassion for ills and misfortunes, an honest physician, an honest coroner who would fight for truth, look for such in the provinces, among the followers of Bielinsky. Here one does not hear about Slavophilism, and if one hears — it is from a hostile side. . . ."

This testimony is valuable, as it comes from Ivan Aksakov who, although he had some differences with his brother, Constantine, about that time, was yet a devoted member of the Slavophils, and personally regarded Bielinsky quite negatively.

It can be understood how the progressive Russian society at the end of the Forties, who were for the most part Bielinsky's followers, were agitated and moved at the first news about the revolution of 1848. Aksakov himself admitted that the year 1848 " threw him out of his rut." Bakunin and Herzen were then abroad and were taking active part in the formidable events. Bakunin played a distinguished part in the popular insurrection at Dresden and in the Slav movement directed against the empire of the Hapsburgs.

The Government regarded the state of mind of the Petrograd *intelligentzia* with alarm, and doubtless exaggerated its political significance and possible consequences. It pounced first of all upon the press. Had Bielinsky not died in May, 1848, he would have been arrested and punished not less severely than the Petrashevsky-circle were a year later.[1] With the first alarming news from the West the authorities took notice of the radical magazines. Admiral Prince Menshikov called the attention of the Heir to the bad influence of the universities and the press, and under his chairmanship a secret committee for the investigation of the matter was formed. Soon additional declarations in the same direction were received from Count Stroganov who was in disagreement with Uvarov, and from Baron Korf who had his eye on Uvarov's post. The secret committee was transformed into a permanent institution, under the chairmanship of the rabid reactionary and obscurantist, Count Buturlin; this so-called Buturlin-Committee was authorised by Nicolas to keep a watchful eye upon the press, and to call his attention to undesirable works even though they had passed the preliminary censorship. Buturlin had made the position of the press unendurable. Uvarov himself was regarded with suspicion, and when he inspired Professor Davidov to write an article in favour of the universities, in view of the rumours in circulation concerning their possible closing, Buturlin's Committee officially demanded his explanation for having let such an article pass through. Uvarov had to resign in October, 1849.

For some time Nicolas hesitated about the choice of his successor. In January, 1850, the Deputy-Minister, Prince Shirinsky-Shikhmatov presented a Memorandum to the Tzar in which he advocated the view that instruction in the universities should be based on religious truths, in connection with theology, and not on "philosophising." On reading that Memorandum Nicolas exclaimed: "Why look for a Minister of Education?

---

[1] Bielinsky was breathing his last, surrounded with his friends and wife, when a gendarme appeared at his rooms with an order for his arrest. Benckendorff raged when he found that his victim had escaped him.— TR.

Behold, he has been found." Jokers whispered on the occasion of his appointment that he would give education not only " check," but " mate " (a play of words in chess terms — Shikhmatov: shakh, i.e., check, and mat — mate).

But it was not a matter of joking for the universities. " It drives one insane," wrote Granovsky in 1850. " Good for Bielinsky who died in time." As early as May, 1849, the number of students in every university was limited to three hundred, outside of the medical and theological departments. Shirinsky-Shikhmatov opined that " the use of philosophy has not been proven, while its harm is probable," hence philosophy and metaphysics were eliminated, and the teaching of logic and psychology was handed over to professors of theology.

The censorship raged mercilessly, but the Buturlin-Committee was not satisfied with the present, and endeavoured to discover past sins on the part of individual censors, in which cases they were put under arrest, regardless of age, rank, and profession. Thus Professor Kutorga, who was no longer a censor, was arrested for having long before passed some ambiguous German verses. Signs of " sedition " were discovered not only in the universities, but even among privileged institutions, like the School of Law, or the Alexandrine Lyceum, whose suspected pupils were recruited into the army, expelled, severely penalised. In those years many writers suffered punishment. Saltykov was exiled to Viatka, to serve with the Governor. Turgeniev was arrested in 1852 and kept at a police-station for a successful attempt to evade the watchfulness of the censor. Yuriy Samarin was imprisoned for a few days in a fortress for sharp remarks about the actions of the Ostsee administration, while Ivan Aksakov for certain expressions in a letter to his relatives concerning the arrest of Samarin, was arrested at the Third Department. The arrests of Samarin and Aksakov ended quite graciously for both. Nicolas had a personal " instructive " conversation with Samarin, and wrote out some curious " resolutions " for Aksakov in a laconic order to Prince Orlov: " Call (him), read (this), exhort (him), release (him)." But the mild ending of those affairs did not prevent the Government from forbidding Ivan Aksakov from editing any publications, after the appearance of the most innocent Slavophil " Almanach " in 1852, and enjoining the contributors of the Almanach, Constantine Aksakov, Yuriy Samarin, Khomiakov, Koshelev, and others, from submitting their writings for publication. The Government acted considerably more severely and ruthlessly in cases of outspoken " sedition," as in the case of the Petrashevsky-group, twenty men of which were sentenced to hard labour, exile to Siberia, and reduction of rank to private; for the purpose of " frightening " them they had to go through fictitious preparations for execution. Yet the affair, although called a " conspiracy," offered no grounds for incriminating the members with any actions, so that even Baron Korf who bitterly disliked the Petrashevsky-circle, said that it was a " conspiracy of ideas." Among those condemned in that process was F. M. Dostoievsky who was sentenced to hard labour. The Government punished the members of the Kiev " Society of Cyril and Methody," which had shown federalistic tendencies, with equal severity; among them were: Shevchenko, Kostomarov, Kulish, Bielozersky, Markovitch, and others.

Beside the obscurantist measures of the Government in the field of popular education, against the press and the universities, we may mention the following of its reactionary undertakings: the prohibition to go abroad without the personal permission of the Tzar, which was given only in very rare cases, and the introduction of the so-called Third paragraph into the Civil Service Statute, by which the authorities were empowered to dismiss officials considered " untrustworthy " (politically), without trial or even explanation.

" The heart aches at the thought of what we had been, and what we have become now," wrote Granovsky to Herzen in

1853. The public prostration and the consciousness of their impotence in face of the terrible oppression of the reaction were so strong among the educated classes, that even such patriots as the Slavophil Koshelev admitted later that the defeats of the Russian troops in the war with Turkey, which broke out in 1853, did not grieve them much. On the contrary, they felt that the graver the foreign situation became the weaker grew the oppression at home.

When in 1853 the war with Turkey began, which was unsuccessful from the very start, and later complicated by the intervention of France, England, and Sardinia, and by the constant threats of ungrateful Austria, though she had been saved by Nicolas only five years before; when Russia's backwardness and unpreparedness, and complete lack of faithful and talented generals were revealed — the self-reliance of the Tzar, so defiantly expressed in his manifesto of March 14, 1848, and in his address to the Petrograd nobility, began to flag, and his proud spirit was unable to bear the unprecedented humiliation.

The foreign storm gradually softened the iron régime within Russia. Although all the reactionary measures promulgated after 1848 remained intact to the very end of the reign, sensitive men felt even in 1853 the approach of a thaw. "It seemed," A. I. Koshelev wrote in his memoirs, "as if out of a depressing, dark dungeon we were emerging if not into God's light, at least into an ante-chamber where we could sense refreshing air."

In society, even among conservative circles an indicting, oppositional attitude toward the Government awakened, and even Pogodin, who in the Forties had edited the *Muscovite,* now wrote daring letters of challenge addressed to the Tzar. Khomiakov wrote his virile poems breathing with religious denunciation of the sinful Government. The mood of the masses was also alarming. On one hand, the people showed heroic self-sacrifice in the struggle with the enemy, on the other hand, the mobilised militia, considering that service for the Tzar and the country freed them from bondage (by the very statutes recruits were excluded from the class of bondmen), refused to obey their landowners and police officials, and committed disturbances and riots.

For many it had become evident that the hour for the abolition of serfdom had struck, and that the entire system had inevitably to be reorganised. It is uncertain what would have been the policy of Nicolas after the unfortunate Crimean War of 1853–1856. He did not live to see its end. Death delivered him from the necessity of liquidating his own governmental policy, the inefficiency of which had been amply demonstrated by the time of his passing away.

In summarising these remarkable thirty years, we must admit that the governmental system of Nicolas I was one of the most consequential of attempts to realise the idea of enlightened absolutism. Nicolas did not in his views resemble Louis XIV; he would not have said, *L'état — c'est moi;* on the contrary, he declared many times that he considered himself the first servant of the state; but to the will of the first servant all others had unreservedly to submit. In his intentions Nicolas was rather akin to such representatives of enlightened despotism as Joseph II and Friedrich the Great. He endeavoured, as we have seen, to realise the system recommended by Karamzin in his Memorandum, " On Ancient and New Russia." If Karamzin had lived through the reign of Nicolas, he would have had to admit that his system had been given a trial, and he would have become convinced to what that system inevitably led, especially in such an enormous, sparsely populated, and rapidly developing country as Russia.

To Nicolas' mind every Governor should have been the master of his province, and he, the Emperor, the master of the empire;

just such a master as Friedrich the Great had been in his comparatively diminutive Prussia, where he was able to know how almost every peasant lived and worked.

For the very size of the Russian Empire, and because of the relatively meagre means in the hands of the Government, in spite of its apparently full authority, such a task could not possibly be realised.   As a brilliant illustration of the impotence of the bureaucratic administration, take the famous story about a certain order of the Tzar, which had not been fulfilled despite the twenty-three confirmations it had received.   The weaker and slower the means, the cruder were the forms in which the authorities expressed their power, and the more striking their abuses.   The best Ministers of Nicolas' reign — Kankrin and Kiselev — particularly resemble the men of the epoch of enlightened despotism; but the majority of his other assistants, especially those of his later years, were incapable men, often covetous and false lackeys, with no convictions or views of their own.

At the same time it was one of the most important epochs in the development and ripening of national life in Russia.   The rapidly increasing density of the population in the central black-soil provinces, the destruction of the former foundations of the landowners' bondage-estates after the Napoleonic wars, the growing antagonism between the bondmen and their masters, the new demands and needs of commerce and industry in connection with the altered universal conjunctures — all these placed before the Government a number of difficult tasks which required for their fulfilment not only the presence of remarkable statesmen, but the broad participation of the entire *intelligentzia* of the country, and the free and fast growth of education in the land. This was prevented by the administrative system that had developed in a consequential *crescendo* during the whole reign of Nicolas.

The wounds of Russia, revealed by the Crimean Campaign, became so evident, that the advent of an epoch of reforms appeared inevitable.   It fell upon the shoulders of Alexander II to realise those reforms.

VOLUME II

PREFACE

TO PART III

In my preface to the first part of my " History of Russia in the Nineteenth Century " I announced that the third part would contain the internal history of Russia for the last thirty years. But the abundance of material which I have come upon in the course of my taking up that period has forced me to change my mind.   The decisive turn in the national outlook that has taken place after the famine of 1891–92, and also a series of new factors and circumstances in the economic and social life of the country which had been crystallised at that time and had in their turn conditioned new tendencies and aspirations in our national policy and in the governmental activity (e.g., the construction of the Siberian railroad and the Far-Eastern policy),— these facts form a sufficient basis for the treatment of the last eight years of the nineteenth century together with the first years of the twentieth century as a separate period serving as a direct prelude to the great events that were displayed before our very eyes in 1904–1906.

Whether this period will form the contents of a fourth part of my work, I cannot state definitely at present.   But, at any rate, the construction of such a fourth part appears to me as a logical possibility.

This third part of the history expounds the reactionary period of our internal modern history, which began in 1866 and continued till the famine of 1891–92, with a brief, bright intermission in 1880–81.   No systematic investigations of that epoch have been made thus far, and for this reason the composition of this part has been for me a far more difficult and responsible task than that of the first two parts.

Petrograd, 1914. A. KORNILOV.

PART II: CONTINUED

MODERN RUSSIAN HISTORY

CHAPTER XX

THE military failures experienced by Russia in the Crimean Campaign, which revealed to all the inadequacy of Nicolas' policy, had been foretold by Nicolas Turgeniev back in 1847, a prediction that required considerable perspicacity and a profound understanding of the general course of affairs in Russia and in Europe. Until the Crimean Campaign the might of the Russian Government appeared colossal, and the strength of Nicolas' system seemed undisputable not only in his own eyes, but in the eyes of all his entourage, including the Heir. After the quick suppression of the Hungarian uprising by Paskevich's superior forces, the military power of Russia was deemed enormous even in Western Europe, and it is astonishing how rapidly that power vanished at the first collision with regular troops of civilised countries, though those forces were not very considerable. Moreover, Russia's unpreparedness had begun to appear even in her war with Turkey, and that unpreparedness was made still more apparent when Turkey was joined by England, France, and later by Sardinia.

Properly speaking, despite the apparent formidableness of the Coalition, the Allies did not disembark a very big army; in view of the sea-transport facilities of that time they were not able to bring ashore more than seventy thousand men. Yet although Nicolas possessed an army of a million men he proved unequal to those seventy thousand — partly because of the chaotic conditions of the military equipment and to the backwardness of Russian ammunition, partly because of the lack of convenient roads of communication, partly because of the astonishing absence of military leaders and generals accustomed to independent action. The provision of the Sebastopol army was carried on by the same means and methods as in 1812; the amount of the requisitioned carts, of transporting accommodations, of oxen and horses, was enormous and out of proportion to the amount of supplies delivered. The southern provinces groaned under the burden of that obligation and were ruined, while the army suffered want in every respect. The disorder was augmented by the terrible theft and all sorts of abuses which greatly increased the expenses of the State.

Medical and sanitary affairs were equally unsatisfactory, and the struggle with the diseases that spread in the South was very inadequately carried on. The strategic plans were below criticism. The most powerful man in the upper spheres at that time was Paskevich, and he brought great harm by delaying the sending of reinforcements to Crimea, as he feared an invasion by Austria who, in gratitude for Nicolas' aid in 1849, had mobilised her army and held it in readiness to join the Allies. Prince V. I. Vassilchikov, the former Chief of Staff at Sebastopol, definitely stated that had Paskevich sent the reinforcements without delay, Sebastopol could have been saved. The actions of other land-commanders also proved to be below criticism; they showed no initiative, no independence. The troops alone appeared above reproach in regard to endurance and bravery, and some naval commanders, educated in the school of Admiral Lazarev, demonstrated sufficient heroism and enterprise. The aggravation of the defeats was emphasised the more when with such an excellent spirit in the army, and with comparatively small forces of the enemy, the Russians could not defend their own territory. The glory of Russian arms, renowned since the days of Catherine, was dimmed with unusual rapidity. Nicolas I who used to like to end his manifestoes with self-confident exclamations, as, for instance, in 1848: " God is with us! Take heed, O nations, for God is with us!" was forced to see the inadequacy of that system which he had considered absolutely faultless, to which he had devoted all his powers, and by virtue of which he was wont to deem himself a great historical personality. Nicolas felt that he was bequeathing his son a deranged heritage; his last words to him on his death-bed were: " I am not handing over the command to you in good order." We may say that Nicolas died at the right time, for had he had to reign after the Sebastopol Campaign he would have been bound first of all to relinquish his thirty years' system, and to renounce his system would have meant to renounce himself.

But the Heir, Alexander II, was also completely unprepared for the reformatory activity that awaited him. In this respect there are a great many false legends and conceptions in Russian historical literature.

Generally the personality of Alexander II, the Tzar-Liberator, appears in the writings of panegyrical historians and naïve contemporary memoirists as that of an ideal reformer, humanistically inclined, who wished, so to speak, by virtue of his inner impulses and motives, to promulgate those reforms which he carried out. This is entirely untrue, and to dispose of these false notions appears to me in this case particularly important. True, Alexander's tutor, Zhukovsky, was a humanist, and he wished to imbue his pupil with humanistic ideas; but it is a mistake to consider Zhukovsky a liberal. He was an honest, good-hearted man, and hoped to make out of Alexander a good monarch, of the type of Henry IV, as he pictured him.[1] Zhukovsky acted quite courageously in his

[1] Vassili Zhukovsky was the father of the short-lived German pseudo-Romanticism in Russian literature. In spite of his sentimental leanings toward Western liberal minds, he remained all his life a

sphere: he straightforwardly declared to his parents that if they intended to make out of Alexander not a military commander but an enlightened Monarch who would see in his fatherland not a barrack but a nation, he must be set free from the " military parade " atmosphere which prevailed at the Court. Alexander's mother sympathised with Zhukovsky's views, and even Nicolas allowed him to express them freely, but in the end Nicolas' views prevailed: he wanted the future Emperor to be first of all a military man, in the *real* sense of the word. However, the " parade "-ideals triumphed in Alexander's education. From an early age he had a liking for display; he was greatly flattered at being able when ten years old to caracole splendidly, to command well, to ride past his grandfather, the king of Prussia, in a ceremonial march at Berlin. Those inclinations and feelings had become deeply rooted in his nature. It may be that he had received from Zhukovsky a general predilection for the good, but on the whole he emulated his father, and when he was admitted in the forties to state-affairs, he felt deep respect for Nicolas' system, and never attempted to criticise it. The more power Nicolas allowed him in managing various state-matters, the more strictly he adhered to the former's ideas. The reaction that took hold of the Government after 1848 was shared by Alexander not less than by his father. A great part of the reactionary measures of that time were carried through with the participation and even at times upon the initiative of Alexander. Thus, for instance, the famous Buturlin-Committee was founded with his direct co-operation. In the peasant-question Alexander was even more conservative than Nicolas, and in all the committee-

staunch Conservative and upholder of Autocracy. In a letter to Pushkin he reproached the Poet for having had connections with " the despicable scoundrels and villains "— the Decembrists. At the end of his life he plunged into pietistic Mysticism, and was one of the few who sided with Gogol's obscurantist views.— TR.

meetings concerning peasant-matters he invariably upheld the rights and interests of the landowners.

When he ascended the throne, persons who stood close to court circles thought that a real " gentry-era " had come to stay. The antagonists of serfdom regretted that now all hope for progress in the peasant-problems was gone (as may be seen from the correspondence between Miliutin and Kavelin); on the other hand, the proserfdom nobles were ready to celebrate their triumph: they knew that Alexander was opposed to the " Inventories " introduced in the southwestern region; they knew that he was responsible for the exemption of the Lithuanian provinces in 1853 from Bibikov's " Inventory Regulations," in spite of the fact that Bibikov was then Minister of Interior, and that those regulations had been confirmed for Lithuania by Nicolas on December 22, 1852. This incident aroused a disagreement between Alexander and Bibikov, and at the former's accession the latter was the first minister to go. The victim had been an adherent of Nicolas' system and a very contumacious person, but in the eyes of the public he had lost his post not as such, but as one who sided with the peasants against the views of the new Tzar.

Thus we see that Alexander's personal tastes and prejudices had shown little promise of his carrying through reforms, particularly the main reform — the abolition of serfdom. It seems to me important to emphasise this circumstance, for it illustrates the power, inevitableness and unavoidableness of the course events were taking; it is very important to make clear that the reforms took place not because of the Tzar's inclination for them, but rather in spite of his convictions; he had to yield to the developing socio-political process, since he saw that if he should struggle against that process, as his father did, Russia might be brought to disruption. Those reforms, then, began not by virtue of the humanistic ideas implanted in him by Zhukovsky; he did not side with the reforms because he

sympathised with the Men of the Forties who had announced
their Hannibal-oaths against serfdom,[2] but by reason of the
conviction that had grown up within him during the Crimean
War, that the Russian State, if it was to be preserved and
strengthened, had need of fundamental reforms. Of course
this does not in the least diminish Alexander's merits, but makes
them more significant and valuable inasmuch as he succeeded
in carrying through the great work staunchly, bravely, and
honestly, disregarding all difficulties, and not considering his
personal inclinations and sympathies, but retaining exclusively
the point of view of the exigency of the State.

But the first problem that confronted Alexander on his
accession, February 19, 1855, was the Crimean War; all the
thoughts of the Government and society were directed towards its ending and the conclusion of peace, which were
finally made possible by some Russian successes on the Caucasus, and particularly by the perseverance of the army in
Sebastopol. The Allies also were tired, and after the capture
of Kars by the Russians, peace was concluded in March, 1856,
not quite as humiliating for Russia as one might have expected from her defeats.

During the war Alexander was able to take only a few steps
on the road of internal reforms. These were such as did not
require particular efforts and yet demonstrated to all his new
progressive tendencies. To them belonged the dismissal of
the Buturlin-Committee, the permission to issue passports for
going abroad, and the abolition of the university restrictions

---

[2] The author refers to Turgeniev who, in his own words, "took a
Hannibal oath not to rest until serfdom would disappear from Russia."
The Men of the Forties is a name applied to the idealistic, altruistic
intelligentzia brought up on the teachings of Bielinsky and other cham-
pions of freedom during the iron régime of Nicolas I. In Russian
literature the Man of the Forties, or the Superfluous Type, is most
characteristically presented in Turgeniev's *Rudin* and in Herzen's
Who Is To Be Blamed? — TR.

introduced after 1848. The public regarded these first rays of a liberal policy with the same enthusiasm as it did the first steps of Alexander I. An optimistic, unusually rosy mood reigned. For thirty years society had experienced terrible repression, and having been weakened at the very beginning through the annihilation of its best representatives — the Decembrists, it was naturally humble and incapable of expressing its thoughts. The dominating feeling was that of liberation from the heavy Nicolaievian régime, and an expectation of a more liberal policy, supported by Alexander's first measures.

Alexander at once achieved the reputation of being a sincere friend of liberal reorganisations. Every hesitation or change in the activity of the Government was ascribed not to the young Monarch, but to the intrigues and hostility of his functionaries. At first the people manifested very little inclination for self-action and initiative; having become accustomed to expect everything from above, they now as well awaited everything from the progressive Government, and did not in the least try to secure for themselves some rights to participate in national affairs. It is curious that all the programmes that emanated at that time from the public were quite unanimous, whether they were composed by moderate liberals of the type of Granovsky (who died in October, 1855), or by subsequent radicals like Chernyshevsky, or by such free and experienced European revolutionists as Herzen who lived in London, outside of the pressure of Russian conditions. All those programmes, as formulated by Chernyshevsky in 1856, aspired for the following desiderata: the spread of education, the increase of the number of students and teachers, the improvement of censorship conditions (about the complete abolition of censorship nobody dared even dream), the building of railroads, as an important means for the development of industry, and finally, a " rational distribution of the economic forces," by which was understood the abolition of serfdom — the question was not allowed as yet to be openly discussed.

In written memoranda the matter was argued more directly; it was indicated that one of the immediate needs was the abolition of bondage, but the idea was expressed rather moderately; namely it was recommended to do away with the institution gradually, without "shocking the country," as Granovsky expressed himself in a Memorandum published in 1856 by Herzen in *Voices from Russia*. Herzen himself spoke considerably more openly and vigorously, in the inspired tone which he had been accustomed to employ, being free from the oppression of the censorship in London. But even his programme was quite moderate; it was expressed in his famous letter to Alexander II, published in the first number of the *Polar Star,* in 1855. Herzen considered as the most urgent needs of Russia: the liberation of the peasants from the land-owners, the liberation of the tax-paying classes from corporal punishment, and the liberation of the press from censorship. Further Herzen did not go; he only desired the mitigation of the oppression, and for the time being did not even demand constitutional guarantees.

Such was the mood of the Russian public at the beginning of Alexander's reign, during 1855–56. As a matter of fact, the Tzar himself had at that moment no definite programme of reforms, and the final words in his peace-Manifesto, which had attracted general attention, was his only declaration of any programme at all.

As the Treaty of Paris was concluded after an unfortunate campaign for Russia, which had revealed her internal disorder, one could have expected considerable concessions on the part of the defeated party, but after all they were not so very big. The Russian diplomats succeeded in obtaining quite honourable terms, utilising the disagreements and misunderstandings that had arisen between Napoleon III and England.

Napoleon, who had started the war with the idea of weakening Russia, considered that the Campaign should have a definite, practical purpose, and as such he placed the liberation of Poland, or at least her return to a semi-independent constitutional order. He based his argument on the Congress of Vienna and on the Constitution of 1815, and had logically figured that if Poland would be restored by the will of the European Powers, dictated to Russia, it would serve as an important political precedent for the intervention of European Powers in the internal affairs and relations of Russia, which circumstance would signify the political decline of Russia. But when Napoleon noticed that England was not disposed to intervene energetically in favour of Poland, he quickly moderated his bellicose spirit, and began to seek round-about ways for inducing Russia to start peace negotiations. Prince Gorchakov, at that time Ambassador at Vienna, wittily characterised the state of his Government's mind, remarking that although Russia was by necessity dumb, she would not remain deaf, meaning that while Russia, as the defeated party, would feel awkward about opening peace conversations, she would by no means decline to take part in them. The negotiations progressed quite favourably, in view of Napoleon's attitude, but here Austria again interfered, and continuing to ignore the services rendered her by Nicolas in 1849, she lowered Russia's international chances. At any rate the Congress of Paris, assembled in 1856, treated Russia comparatively mildly, and of the two chief demands of the Russian diplomats — that there should be no war-contribution and no decrease of territory — the first was granted; as for the second, Russia had to yield the estuary of the Danube to Roumania.

Declaring the terms of the Treaty, Alexander remarked in his Manifesto that the concessions were not important in comparison with the burdens of war and with the advantages of peace, and ended the Manifesto with the following significant words: "With the aid of the Divine Providence, forever gracious to Russia, may her internal welfare be established and perfected; may truth and kindness reign in her courts; may the aspiration for enlightenment and for all useful activities develop all over with new force, and may every one peacefully enjoy the results of honest labour under the shelter of laws equally just for all, equally protecting all. . . ."

The programme of internal reforms hinted in those words perfectly corresponded with the hopes and aspirations of the public, that had been awakened with the advent of the new reign. The last words of the sentence quoted clearly implied the equalisation of all classes, and could naturally be interpreted as hinting at the liberation of the serfs. The adherents of bondage became greatly alarmed. One of them, Count Zakrevsky, Governor-General of Moscow, asked Alexander during his stay at Moscow to reassure the nobles in regard to the disquieting rumours. Alexander consented, but his speech to the nobles was of a nature quite unexpected either by them or by Zakrevsky. He said that he did not intend to abolish serfdom at once, with one stroke of the pen, but that he considered it impossible to continue the existing conditions, so that " it would be better to abolish serfdom from above than wait till it will begin to liberate itself from below," and he ended his speech with a request that the gentry should " deliberate on the way by which this can be accomplished."

That speech was such a general surprise that even the Minister of Interior, Lanskoy, did not at first believe it, until Alexander himself assured him that he had not only actually delivered it but that he had no regrets for what he had said. Then a hurried preparation began in the Ministry of Interior for the elaboration of the peasant-reform, since Lanskoy was convinced that the Government had given out a watch-word, from which it was impossible to retreat.

Lanskoy began his Ministerial career in 1855 with a strange

circular on the name of the Marshals of Nobility, in which
he had spoken in the name of the Tzar about the sacred
rights of the nobles, granted to them by the crowned predecessors of the reigning Monarch; the nobles naturally interpreted the Circular as a promise that the institution of serfdom
would not be touched. But Lanskoy himself was not an upholder of serfdom; on the contrary, in his youth he belonged to
the liberal movement of the Tenths and Twenties, and was
probably a member of the Union of Welfare. He undoubtedly
sympathised with the idea of liberating the serfs, and was glad
to direct the activity of the Ministry of Interior in the preparation of the reform; but he had no definite views, and he
warned Alexander that it was a question of such a nature
that once started it could not be stopped, and he therefore
recommended the working out in the first place of a definite
programme which should be followed to the end. He invited
as an assistant A. I. Levshin, who was considered well prepared through his work in the Ministry of State Domains;
but Levshin also had no definite views, and was furthermore
very undecisive and timid in matters of such national importance. For this reason all the work under his direction was
reduced to gathering materials about the peasant-projects presented during the preceding reigns, and about the opinions
and memoranda that were then circulating in public. We
should remember that until 1857 the censorship had not allowed
the slightest mention of the bondage-problem, and when Constantine Aksakov hinted in the newspaper *Molva* at the advantages of free over forced labour, in reference to American
slavery, he was reprimanded in a friendly way by the Deputy-
Minister of Education, Prince P. A. Viazemsky, himself a
writer who had been known some time before as a great liberal.

Yet unofficial memoranda continued to circulate freely, especially in regard to the peasant-question, and under the influence of those memoranda the Ministry of Interior came to

the conclusion that there were three ways in which to solve the problem.

One was to abolish serfdom in one general ukase, without alloting any land to the peasants.

Or serfdom might be abolished with the retention by the peasants of their portions, through redeeming them by some financial operation, as it appeared clear that the peasants were not in a position to pay at once to their landowners the price of the allotments, and the landowners would not be willing to postpone the payments for many years. Theoretically this way was feasible.

The Ministry of Interior, however, considered both those ways hardly realisable, and at any rate combined with great difficulties and dangers for the State. It argued that the landless liberation of the peasants would gravely threaten the peace of the country; on the other hand, any financial measure for the redemption of the peasants' allotments with the aid of the Treasury would, in view of the deplorable state of the finances at that moment, threaten the country with bankruptcy. The Government could pay out at once to the landowners the redemption price, which was about one billion rubles, and collect it from the peasants in the form of delayed payments, only by making a special loan. But after the Crimean Campaign, because of the enormous issues of paper-money, Russian funds were extremely low, and such a big loan appeared almost impossible.

Thus there remained only a third way out — a series of preparatory measures which would convert the peasants into Obligatory Peasants for a definite or indefinite term (similar to the Ostsee Statute of 1804, or according to the system introduced by Kiselev in Moldavia and Wallachia, or like Bibikov's Inventory Regulations in the western provinces). The Ministry favoured the last system most of all, as it led to a

liquidation of serfdom without any expenditures on the part
of the Government.

The Ministry had to consider, however, what would be the
results of the reforms in different provinces. Levshin, who
possessed estates in various provinces, could dimly prevision
that if the peasants were freed and became Obligatory, those
landowners who had been getting the larger part of their income not from agriculture but from the side-earnings of their
serfs, would fall into a difficult position, as the obligation of
the peasants to perform some *barshchina* or to pay certain
obrok for their lands would by no means compensate the landowners for the exploitation of the side-earnings of their bondmen. Levshin sought means for the elimination or at least
mitigation of such difficulties which were bound to arise in the
industrial, not black-soil provinces. The Ministry of Interior
and Alexander himself considered that the redemption of the
personal freedom of the peasants was out of question, that
the person of the peasant should be freed without any compensation.

For this reason Levshin proposed a " covert " compensation
for the landowners of the industrial provinces, in the form of
obliging the peasants of those provinces to redeem their abode
on the estates on the basis of a special estimation of the industrial
advantages connected with their place. Under such a pretext
it was possible to include in the redemption a compensation for
the loss of the landowners' right to exploit the person of the
peasant. Such were the original propositions of the Ministry
of Interior.

But Alexander II did not want to consider those propositions before first hearing from the nobles, whose initiative he
preferred to that of the Government. He had been aware of
the movement among the nobles in the black-soil provinces, who
even during the preceding reign had pointed out the disad-

vantages of serfdom in densely populated regions. On the other hand he could see from the circulating unofficial memoranda that among the gentry elements ready to show an initiative in the matter existed. Negotiations with the nobles began, which were referred to the time of the Coronation, when the Marshals of Nobility assembled at Moscow.

In his first negotiations Lanskoy suffered a complete fiasco. Not one official representative of the nobility was willing to demonstrate any initiative; they said that they did not know the intentions of the Government, and had no plans of their own to suggest,— as a matter of fact they feared that the Government would make use of their initiative for promulgating the measure to their disadvantage, not to mention the fact that to the mass of the nobility the limitation of the bondage-right appeared as an extremely dangerous measure in every respect.

This, however, did not prevent individual progressive representatives of the nobility from expressing their views in private memoranda, as I have already mentioned. Most conspicuous among these was the memorandum of Kavelin, a well known professor, and at the same time a landowner in the province of Samara, a historian and a jurist, who knew well the economic condition of the country, and was inclined to a quite radical handling of the peasant-question. He advocated the second way, the redemption course. His idea was that the landowners should be compensated for the losses they would suffer through the liquidation of serfdom, whether those losses would result from the transfer of land to the peasants, or from the discontinuation of the exploiting of the serfs' earnings. In order to equalise the chances of agricultural and industrial estates, Kavelin proposed to base the redemption not on the estimation of the land value, but on the estimation of the selling value of the estates.

One of the memoranda was presented by Yuriy Samarin,

the famous Slavophile, a man who undoubtedly stood for the peasants' interests. Sharing the apprehensions of Levshin in regard to the financial side of the question, Samarin advocated the third way. He desired first of all the limitation of the power of the landowner over the peasant, especially over the person of the peasant; he insisted on retaining of his land by the peasant and on the compensation of the landowner either through regulated *barshchina*-work, or through definite *obroks,* according to local conditions. Of the same nature was the memorandum of another Slavophile, Prince Cherkassky. A memorandum presented by a landowner from the province of Poltava, a certain Posen, enjoyed serious consideration among governmental circles. He manipulated skilfully with liberal phrases, and even mentioned redemption, but his whole plan was actually reduced to voluntary agreements between landowners and peasants. Posen personally presented his memorandum to Alexander, and was supported by General Rostovtzev who was impressed with his financial and economic erudition.

The memorandum of Grand Duchess Yelena Paulovna, his aunt, and a very enlightened woman, made a strong impression on Alexander. She upheld the liberation of the peasants. Her memorandum was worked out with the aid of N. A. Miliutin and with the co-operation of Kavelin; it was, properly speaking, a project for the liberation and establishment of the peasants on her big estate, Karlovka, in the province of Poltava.

Grand Duchess Yelena Paulovna asked the Government for definite instructions as to how she should carry out her idea, and requested permission for organising councils with the landowners of adjacent provinces. Alexander answered that he awaited the initiative of the nobles, and while giving her no instructions expressed his approval of her intention to organise regular consultations among the landowners of the neighbouring provinces. At the same time a special secret committee was formed in January, 1857, for the examination of the projects presented; the members consisted largely of ministers and dignitaries of the preceding reign.

Among the members of the Committee Minister Lanskoy was unconditionally in favour of the reform. Of the same standing was General Rostovtzev, chief of the military schools, personally devoted to Alexander; he was quite inexperienced in the peasant-question, and when he was appointed with two other members, Baron M. A. Korf and Prince P. P. Gagarin, to examine the memoranda and projects which circulated among the public, he even tried to elude the appointment. On the other hand Rostovtzev was not an attractive figure in the eyes of the public: on his name lay a spot — a rumour existed that he had informed upon and betrayed the Decembrists. The truth of the matter was distorted. In 1825 Rostovtzev was a twenty-two years old officer, very friendly with the influential leaders of the Conspiracy of December 14 — Ryleiev, and particularly Prince Obolensky, with whom he shared rooms. During the interregnum in 1825 Rostovtzev not only was able to hear accidental phrases from the conspirators about their intentions, but he was evidently directly solicited by Ryleiev and Obolensky to join them. Rostovtzev, however, was absolutely loyal in his views and did not sympathise with the plans of the Decembrists or with any secret political societies. He categorically refused to take part in the conspiracy, even tried to dissuade Ryleiev and Obolensky from their intentions, and finally warned them that if they would not give up their plans he would consider it his duty to inform the Government of the threatening danger. Seeing that the plot was proceeding, Rostovtzev fulfilled his threat, came to Nicolas and told him that there was an opposition to his accession, that something was brewing, and pleaded with Nicolas either to abdicate himself or to persuade Constantine to come to Petrograd and publicly abdicate. Rostovtzev mentioned no names, and after his meeting with Nicolas (on December 10) he immediately informed Ryleiev and Obolensky, neither of whom had changed their attitude of respect for him, about it; on his return from exile Obolensky at once renewed his friendship with him.   But at that time the details were not generally known; Rostovtzev was suspected, and Herzen systematically pursued him to his very death, in his *Bell.*

Rostovtzev's real rôle in the peasant-question began later; his participation in the works of the Secret Committee was neither decisive, nor important.   The other members of the Committee were either indifferent or hostile towards the reform, although they dared not openly oppose Alexander's statement that the time had ripened for the limitation of the landowners' rights.   The work progressed very slowly; only the Ministry of Interior made active progress, owing to its chief, Lanskoy, and to its possession of collected materials.

In the summer of 1857 Levshin presented a definite plan for the reform, which consisted in declaring the peasants personally free, but bound to the soil, under a temporary or indefinite obligation to perform their duties for their allotments, the latter to be eventually bought by the peasants into personal property; the landowners of not black-soil provinces were allowed to add "industrial advantages" to the value of their lands.

Dissatisfied with the slow work of the Committee whose chairman, Prince Orlov, was opposed to the reform, Alexander introduced his brother, Constantine, well known for his liberal views, into the Committee.   Indeed, he enlivened the spirit of the Committee, but in view of his inexperience he was inclined too readily for compromises in order to accelerate the business. Among other measures he suggested publicity, claiming that the declaration of the Government's views would reassure the peasants and would give the public a chance to co-operate in the working out of the details of the reform.   The Committee decisively rejected the idea of giving publicity to the Government's views, and resolved to carry on the work gradually and deliberately, dividing it into periods, the first period to be devoted to the collecting of materials, and so forth. Competent persons, Levshin for example, asserted that the Committee intended to prolong the matter indefinitely, in the hope that it would finally be tabled.

But soon after this decision of the Secret Committee the Government found at last that initiative on the part of the nobility for which it had sought so long. It came from the Lithuanian nobles who had been under the sword of Damocles every since the Inventory Regulations were postponed in 1853; that question rose again in the Ministry of Interior, and the Lithuanian landowners in a declaration to the Governor-General of Vilna, Nazimov, declared that they would be glad to raise the question of the complete abolition of serfdom on condition that for the landowners be preserved the ownership of the soil. Nazimov presented the opinion to the Secret Committee where the discussions were prolonged for three weeks. Alexander lost his patience, and ordered Lanskoy in three days to prepare an answer to the Lithuanian nobles in co-operation with Muraviov, Minister of State Domains, who did not sympathise with the reform but dared not contradict the Tzar. On November 29, 1857, Alexander signed the rescript in the name of Nazimov, which had made a great impression and had played an important rôle in the development of the work. The Government proposed to form provincial committees in the three Lithuanian provinces from delegates of the nobles, one delegate from each district, under the chairmanship of Marshals of the Nobility, for the discussion of methods for the emancipation of the serfs. The Government indicated, however, the fundamental principles on which the reform could be carried out, and those principles did not agree with the views of the Lithuanian nobles.

It was indicated to the nobles that although the land would be considered the property of the landowners, the peasants should be given the right to purchase their allotments during a certain term of time, and should in addition be given sufficient appendaged land by the landowners to secure their subsistence and the payment of their taxes, for which they would have to pay in *barshchina* or *obrok,* in definite amounts.   During the transitory stage the landowners were to preserve the right of estate-policing.   The peasants were to be divided into village- or *volost*-communities.   The provincial committees were to take care of the regular payment of taxes to the Government.

CHAPTER XXI

IN the preceding chapter I expounded the basic principles on which the reform was proposed to be carried out. Not only the principles themselves, which at any rate rejected a landless liberation of the peasants, but also in particular the fact that the Rescript was sent out a few days after its sanctioning to all Governors and Marshals of Nobility, with the request that the nobles of other provinces express their views in regard to an analogous solution of the peasant-question, had a great significance for the further course of the reform. Later the Government decided to publish the Rescript for general information, in spite of the opposition of the members of the Secret Committee, especially of its chairman, Prince Orlov, who were against the sending of it even to the Governors.

The publication of the Rescript was a very important event; the Government could not turn back the course even had it wanted to, without running the risk of arousing great disturbances. On the other hand, since the peasants had become informed about the Government's proposal to the nobles, it was only a question of time before all provinces would participate in the work, for the landowners understood the necessity of hastening the presentation of their addresses concerning the desirability of establishing provincial committees, lest the delay provoke disturbances among the peasants.

Some delay in the presentation of those addresses was caused by the almost general dissatisfaction of the landowners with the principles proposed by the Government. In this case appeared first of all the economical difference between various provinces, of which the Government had been aware (Levshin, to wit), but had not appreciated sufficiently. Lanskoy received reports from local representatives of the administration concerning the reception of the Rescript by the nobles, and it appeared that it had aroused general criticism. All admitted the timeliness and inevitableness of the reform, but in not a single province did the nobles completely agree with the Government's programme. In the black-soil provinces the landowners derived their wealth exclusively from agriculture; the land was divided in two almost equal parts, one allotted to the peasants, and one cultivated by the landowner with the aid of the serfs' *barshchina.* In most of those provinces there existed no side earnings of a non-agricultural nature. In the most densely populated provinces, as in Tula, Kursk, Riazan, there was a surplus of hands, as we have seen, and in many places unpopulated lands were sold at higher prices than peopled estates, which showed what a burden the bondmen presented in comparison with the value of the soil. It is natural therefore that in such regions the landowners considered the liberation of the peasants with land very disadvantageous, and they preferred to free the peasants without compensation provided the masters retained the most valuable asset of the estates — the land.

In the Northern, not black-soil provinces, on the contrary, the conditions were quite different. There the landowners seldom lived on their estates, and the peasants themselves cultivated the soil very little, but payed their masters *obrok* from their various earnings — in commerce and industry. We see also at present that of the one million inhabitants of Petrograd in 1897 one hundred thousand were ascribed to the province of Yaroslavl, about the same number to Tver, and so forth, which shows how the population of those provinces are occupied with various city-industries, commercial and artisan. Even during the bondage-state numerous peasants were developing profitable occupations in Petrograd and Moscow; many kept inns and post-stations at high-ways and river-harbours, which was very profitable in the absence of railroads. For the land-owners of those provinces it appeared desirable to liberate the peasants with considerable land-allotments, but on condition that the redemption sum should cover the loss of the masters' income from the high *obroks*.

In view of this difference in the conditions of the various provinces there appeared two distinct theories among the gentry of that time; the most conscious and progressive elements in the Northern provinces desired a quick and complete liquidation of serfdom, but on the basis of high compensation for their estimated losses; the most conscious and progressive elements in the black-soil provinces, on the other hand, were willing to admit even a gratuitous liberation of the peasants, but on condition that they retained ownership of the land. The point of view of the first appeared very dangerous even in the eyes of such friends of the reform as Lanskoy and Levshin, since, in their opinion, it was apt to shake the financial position of the country.

At the time the advanced *intelligentzia* regarded the publication of the Rescript very enthusiastically. The permission of the Government to discuss the matter in the press brought forth congratulatory articles addressed to Alexander by all the progressive organs, even by the representative of the subsequent radical movement, the *Contemporary,* and by the free London publication of Herzen, the *Bell*. Chernyshevsky lauded the Tzar above Peter the Great, while Herzen dedicated to him an article with the epigraph: "Thou hast conquered, O Galilean!" The representatives of the universities, of literature, and of the highest *intelligentzia* of both Capitals gave a public banquet in Moscow, an unusual event in those days; sympathetic speeches were delivered concerning Alexander, and a warm ovation took place in front of his portrait. That loyal banquet naturally displeased the Governor-General of Moscow, Zakrevsky, and other proserfdom fanatics, but they were not in position to turn the course of the great movement once it was started.

But in spite of public sympathy the programme of the rescript of November 20 caused a delay in the formation of provincial committees. The Government hastened to open a provincial committee in Petrograd, under the pretext that the nobles there had long ago brought up the question of reorganising the condition of the peasants. Indeed, they had raised that question under Nicolas, and later at the accession of Alexander; with no intention, however, of abolishing serfdom, but with a desire to reorganise it on feudal-emphyteutic principles (i.e., the peasants should be ascribed to the landowners' estates with the right of perpetual-hereditary use of allotted lands); but the rescript of December 5, 1857, in the name of the Governor-General of Petrograd, Ignatiev, arranged the opening of a provincial committee on the same basis as those of the Lithuanian provinces.

The first gentry to present an address concerning the opening of a committee, was that of Nizhni-Novgorod; its governor, A. N. Muraviov, the founder of the Union of Salvation in 1817, succeeded in inspiring the nobles of Nizhni-Novgorod — with which patriotic traditions have been connected since the Troubled Time and the days of Kozma Minin-Sukhoruky [1] — to be the first to join the emancipatory steps of the Government. During the assembly of the nobles Muraviov collected a sufficient number of signatures, and sent a deputation to Petrograd; but his opponents aroused an agitation, and soon

[1] During the Interregnum, or Troubled Time, early in the seventeenth century, a patriotic butcher, Kozma Minin, induced his fellow-citizens at Nizhni-Novgorod to contribute men and money for the organisation of a national militia to repulse the Poles who had invaded Russia and were besieging Moscow. Alexander I also referred to Minin in his appeal to the people in 1812.— TR.

after the departure of the first deputation they sent to Petrograd a contra-deputation. The Government forged the iron while it was hot, and on December 24, 1857, before the arrival of the second deputation a rescript was issued in the name of Muraviov in answer to the address of the nobles. In Moscow the delay was due to the fact that the province of Moscow was one of the industrial, not black-soil provinces; only after a remark from above that the Government was expecting prompt action on the part of the First Capital did the Moscow nobles present an address about the opening of a committee. It pointed out the desirability of changes in the programme of activity in accordance with special local needs. The Government, however, insisted on its programme, and the committee was opened on the general basis. After this other provinces began to join, so that by the end of 1858 committees on the peasant-question were opened in all provinces.

The nobles of each district elected two members to the provincial committee, and for the defence of the interests of the peasants the Government appointed to every committee two members from among the local landowners, known to be in sympathy with the abolition of serfdom. In the majority of the committees there was marked from the very beginning an attempt to introduce some changes into the programme prescribed by the rescripts. The committee of the province of Tver expressed its opposition to the Government's programme more sharply than any other committee; its chairman was the Marshal of the Tver Nobility, A. M. Unkovsky, a man of the younger generation, who combined emancipatory ideas with the care for the interests of the local nobles. He considered himself obliged to guard the interests of the nobles whom he represented, so that they should not find themselves in worse condition that nobles of other provinces at the moment of the liberation of the peasants. At the same time he desired that the period of the reorganisation of the whole Russian life should not come to an end with the completion of the peasant-reform.

In a memorandum presented to the Minister of Interior even before the opening of the committee, he argued from the point of view of the progressive landowners of the industrial provinces that the palliatives offered in the rescripts, particularly the method of the gradual extinction of serfdom and the transitory Obligatory stage, did not solve the question at all; that the peasants would not be satisfied with a half-freedom and the landowners would be ruined, and that, finally, no regular collection of taxes could take place when the peasants were without property and the landowners had no right to manage their property. As the only true way to liberate the peasants " not in words, but in deed, not gradually, but at once, simultaneously and universally, without infringing any one's interests, without arousing dissatisfaction on any side, and without risking the future of Russia "— Unkovsky considered the *redemption* of the bondage-right, i.e., of the person of the peasant with a full land allotment. He demanded that this operation be performed with the aid of the Government, that the landowners receive *at once* the *entire* redemption-sum, at least in the form of obligations bringing a certain income and realisable on the money-market. He also insisted that the price of the land only should be paid by the peasants, and in installments, whereas that part of the compensation which should correspond with the loss of the right to exploit the working power of the peasants should be paid by the State, with the co-operation of all classes, for the bondage-right had been so instituted and it should be so abolished — in the name of national needs and considerations. Unkovsky succeeded in imbuing the landowners of Tver and of other provinces with his views, and when the work of the Tver committee began, his plan was accepted by a majority of votes, in contradiction to the literal sense of the rescripts and of the appended instructions of the Minister.

In the meantime the Government, which at first had intended to allow the provincial committees complete freedom in the internal organisation of their work within the frame of the rescripts, had become alarmed by the information about the dissensions and contradictions in the various interpretations of the meaning of the rescripts, and it decided to give the provincial committees a definite programme of action and a fixed form for their projects. This mission fell into the hands of a cunning man, a landowner in the fertile and densely populated province of Poltava, M. P. Posen, who in the guise of a Liberal enjoyed at that time the full confidence of Rostovtzev. Posen's programme was to place definitely the dots on the i's and to govern the work of the provincial committees by a uniform set of rules. With the interests of the landowners of the fertile black-soil provinces in view, Posen suggested the idea that the plan should provide for a *transitory Obligatory period* during which the peasants should use their allotments, but after that period (twelve years. Tr.) the allotments would *return to the landowners in absolute property,* and the peasants would receive personal freedom, *without land.*

Posen's programme met with the strenuous opposition of the nonblack-soil regions. The Tver committee sent a deputation under·the leadership of Unkovsky to Lanskoy and Rostovtzev with a decisive declaration that if the Government expected the nobility of Tver to co-operate in the liquidation of the bondage-right it must provide for the granting of land to the peasants, entire annihilation of all bondage-relations, and compensation to the landowners for their losses. Should this not be allowed, the committee would resign, and the Government might entrust the work of its officials who "would write down whatever they would be told to." This determined declaration of the

Tver committee took place in October, 1858, when both Lanskoy and Rostovtzev had been already considerably shaken in their views on the necessity of a transitory Obligatory period and on the impossibility of redemption.

We should mention here that the approval of the redemption idea was shared not only by some other committees of the non black-soil provinces, but by a considerable part of the progressive press. As soon as permission was granted to discuss the peasant-question, the *Contemporary* published an article by Chernyshevsky, the second part of which included Kavelin's project *in extenso,* and which on the whole advocated the view of the Tver committee. The *Russian Messenger* of Katkov declared redemption to be the only correct solution of the question, since it was impossible to free the peasants without land and equally impossible to liberate them with land except by means of redemption, for the peasants were not in position to pay for the land at once, and the landowners would not be willing to sell on the basis of delayed installments. The same stand was taken by Herzen's *Bell* in which his closest friend, Ogarev, published long articles on the peasant-question.

In the summer of 1858 Rostovtzev, during his vacation abroad, carefully studied various projects for the emancipation of the peasants, among them some projects worked out by foreign bankers (Frenkel and Homberg). He gradually came to the conviction that the " transitory Obligatory period " would not prevent disturbances and misunderstandings, but would make them inevitable, for the peasants having become personally free and yet obliged to pay *barshchina* and *obrok* to the landowners would not easily submit to their demands and not appreciate the legitimacy of the measure. For this reason he worked out with the aid of the Imperial Secretary, Bludov, a plan for the introduction of extreme police-measures for that transitory period, in the form of specially authorised District-Chiefs and temporary Governor-Generals. But this plan met with the strong opposition of the Ministry of Interior and of many private persons, who argued that such an order would be not a " transitory Obligatory," but a " state of siege," and life in the provinces would become unbearable. Rostovtzev understood the justness of those arguments and withdrew his plan despite the energetic support it had received from Alexander II who was much annoyed by sharp criticism of it in a memorandum presented to him by Lanskoy on behalf of the Ministry of Interior (the memorandum was drawn by the Governor of Kaluga, Artzimovich, although it had been ascribed for a long time to Miliutin).

The more deeply Rostovtzev went into the matter during his vacation abroad the more clearly he saw the difficulties of the original plan of the Government. He expressed his ideas in personal letters to the Tzar from Wildbad and Dresden. In his fourth (last) letter he pointed out that the shorter the transitory Obligatory period was made the better it would be for the peace of the country, and that in order to preserve authority and calm in the provinces, the power should be concentrated in the peasant-*mir* (village commune with mutual guarantee and responsibility. Tr.) and its representatives, leaving the landowner to deal not with individual peasants, but with the *mir*. At the same time Rostovtzev had already adopted the idea of redemption as a general financial measure; but he would not agree to force the measure on both parties, for he considered that the policy of redemption by aid of the Government should be voluntary and by means of mutual agreements.

At the same time the possibility and feasibility of redemption had been heartily endorsed in the ministry of Interior by N. A. Miliutin and Y. A. Soloviov, who exercised a direct influence on the course of the reform through the *Zemsky* (land-) Department formed in the Ministry of Interior on March 4, 1858, under the chairmanship of Deputy-Minister

Levshin. The activity of Levshin had come to an end with the publication of the Rescript; he did not sympathise with the rapid and energetic measures in the matter of the reform, and he considered the publication and dissemination of the rescripts a dangerous *salto mortale* for the State. Feverish activity began in the *Zemsky* Department and Levshin yielded his place to the younger and more capable workers — Soloviov and Miliutin; the latter soon supplanting him as Deputy-Minister.

Soloviov was an excellent worker in the preparation and elaboration of the materials necessary for the reform. The post of Miliutin was still more responsible and important. Rostovtzev later said that Miliutin was the nymph Egeria of the Editing Commissions. He performed the same rôle in the Ministry of Interior. He entered that Ministry in 1835 as an inexperienced youth of seventeen, immediately after his graduation from the Noble Pension at the Moscow University. Perhaps he was noticed more than the ordinary petty clerks owing to the fact that he was a nephew of the Minister of State Domains, Count Kiselev, but it is beyond doubt that his advancement was due mainly to his remarkable gifts which had been manifested from the first years of his service. Under Count Perovsky he occupied the position of director of the Economy Department, and in spite of his age (he was only thirty then) he was a distinguished figure in the Ministry. During the Forties he undertook an investigation of the economic conditions of the Russian cities; he attracted to this work such men as Yuriy Samarin and Ivan Aksakov, and in 1846 he carried through the reform of the public management of the city of Petrograd, approximately on the same principles on which the subsequent city-reform of 1870 was based.

During the years 1856–57 Miliutin, with the co-operation of his old friend, Samarin, and his new friend, Kavelin, thoroughly prepared himself for participation in the peasant-reform. In 1857 he was able to advocate his views in his conversations with Levshin, and at the same time he inspired Grand Duchess Yelena and Grand Duke Constantine with the idea that a basic and radical reform, in the form of an emancipation of the peasants with sufficient land-allotments, was necessary. He pointed out the way to make use of the nobles' initiative, but at the same time not to allow the nobles too great a share in the work, lest the aroused interests and appetites of the nobles paralyse the beneficial significance of the measure for the masses. His activity was soon noticed by the court-reaction-aries, who hastened to compromise him in the eyes of the Tzar, accusing him of radical political views, and even of revolu-tionary aspirations. Their attack succeeded, and Miliutin would have been dismissed in 1857, but for the energetic inter-cession of Lanskoy, Prince Gorchakov (Foreign Minister), and Grand Duchess Yelena. In spite of all the intrigues of his enemies, Miliutin was appointed early in 1859 to the post of Deputy-Minister, in place of Levshin, and although he bore the title of " temporary functionary," he retained the post till the issue of the statutes of February 19, 1861.

Miliutin shared the views of Samarin on the peasant-reform. Both admitted their preference for a radical solution of the question by means of compulsory redemption under the condi-tion of granting the peasants those allotments which they had been using under the bondage-system; but they were aware of the difficulties and dangers connected with such a solution, for the State Treasury which had been drained by the war and was in the weak and incapable hands of such ministers as Brock and (later) Kniazhevich. Miliutin and Samarin considered as the most important part of the reform the libera-tion of the peasants with a sufficient land allotment, and they regarded with mistrust the majority of the provincial com-mittees. Yet in the demands of the majority of the Tver committee Miliutin could not help seeing a desire to find a conscientious and radical solution of the question, with the preservation of the advantages and interests not only of the landowners, but also of the peasants.

Eventually Lanskoy and Rostovtzev found it necessary to allow the Tver committee to carry through their plan to its end, and they were permitted to work out a special redemption-project for an immediate and simultaneous liberation of the peasants with land, as against the projects based on Posen's programme, which considered the plan of a transitory Obligatory period. Soon a similar permission was granted to the Kaluga committee, and to fifteen other committees which had not finished their works by that time.

At the same time Rostovtzev, by the order of the Tzar, brought for discussion before the Main Committee extracts from his letters to Alexander written from abroad. The discussion caused very important changes and additions to the original programme of the Government. These influenced the whole further course of the reform, especially the works of the Editing Commissions, the institution established in March, 1859, in aid of the Main Committee for the examination of the projects of the provincial committees and for the working out of general statutes for the State and local units. The chairman, or according to the Imperial decree — the "chief," of the Editing Commissions was Rostovtzev. The Commissions were composed of representatives of various departments connected with the peasant-affairs and with the codificatory works, and also of "expert-members"— landowners who had attracted attention by their projects and work in the provincial committees. The suggestion for "expert-members" was offered by Miliutin to Alexander and to Rostovtzev, and was approved by both. In spite of Miliutin's apprehensions, good relations were at once established between Rostovtzev and him, and Rostovtzev showed his complete confidence in Miliutin, by asking his assistance in selecting members for the Editing Commissions. Miliutin made use of the invitation, and introduced some members who had been most active in the realisation of the reform. Among them were Y. F. Samarin, Prince V. A. Cherkassky, V. V. Tarnovsky, G. P. Galagan, not to mention Y. A. Soloviov, who was appointed by the Ministry of Interior, upon the advice of Miliutin.

With these friends of the reform, however, there came to the Commissions members with whom Miliutin's circle had to carry on a stubborn and bitter fight. They were: the Marshals of Nobility of Petrograd — Count P. P. Shuvalov, and of Oriol — V. V. Apraksin, Adjutant-General Prince Paskevich, the Poltava landowner, Posen, the editor of the *Journal of Landowners*, A. D. Zheltukhin, and a representative of the Ministry of State Domains, Bulygin, who obdurately advocated the views of his principal, M. N. Muraviov. Originally there were formed two Editing Commissions: one for the working out of a general project, and one for that of local projects; but Rostovtzev merged them into one, and then subdivided it into departments — administrative, juridical, and economical, to which was added later a financial department for the compensation question. These departments served as sub-commissions which worked out reports for the general meeting of the Commissions. Over the two most important sub-commissions — the economical and financial — Miliutin presided. But his activities were not limited by this. Not in vain did Rostovtzev name him the Egeria of the Editing Commissions. He actually was the central person of the whole work, the manager of the internal policy of the Commissions, and the leader of its progressive members in the fight with the hostile forces who acted within and without the Commissions. He succeeded at the very beginning in bringing together a united group of convinced, talented, and industrious advocates of the reform, in the persons of Samarin, Cherkassky, and Soloviov, who were joined in most cases by Tarnovsky, Galagan, Peter Semionov, and others. This group had gained the complete confidence of Rostovtzev. Miliutin eliminated the bad influence of Posen upon Rostovtzev, by revealing Posen's masqued intentions and forcing him to admit at the sessions of the Editing Commissions that he was in favour of a landless emancipation of the peasants.

From the very first the Commissions had to combat the advocates of the feudal aspirations of the Petrograd nobility. Count Shuvalov and Prince Paskevich, who based their arguments on the literal meaning of the Rescripts, and insisted on the perpetual conservation of the property right to all lands for the landowners, rejected all forms of redemption except individual voluntary agreements, and particularly insisted on the conservation by the landowners of the *votchina* (hereditary estate)-power and *votchina*-jurisdiction on their lands as an inviolable seignioral right. The fight began at the first sessions of the Editing Commissions in connection with those changes in the Government's programme which had been accepted upon the discussion of Rostovtzev's views expressed in his letters from abroad to Alexander. The new Governmental programme presented to the Commissions at the very opening of their sessions was later formulated by N. P. Semionov (in his " History of the Liberation of the Peasants during the Reign of Alexander II ") as follows:

1. To free the peasants *with land*.

2. The final outcome of the liberation to be the *redemption* by the peasants of their allotments in property.

3. The Government to *facilitate the process of redemption* through mediation, credit, guarantee, and financial operations.

4. To avoid if possible a transitory Obligatory period, and if inevitable, to *make the period short*.

5. *Barshchina must be abolished* within three years by legislation, by transferring the peasants to an *obrok* basis, except in cases where the peasants did not desire such a change.

6. The peasants to be *given autonomy* in their village-life.

This programme was received sympathetically by the members of the Editing Commissions, and was made the basis of their work.

But having accepted that programme, the Commissions had to take up a position contrary to the majority of the projects of the provincial committees, which had been worked out on the basis of the rescripts and of Posen's programme. The Editing Commissions decided not to take into account the opinions of the nobles expressed in the projects of the committees, but to use them only as material for their own judgments. Three thousand copies of the Commissions' reports were printed and widely distributed throughout the country, by the order of Rostovtzev. In the summer of 1858 the Tzar made a tour through various provinces, spoke to marshals of the nobility and to members of the committees, expressed his gratitude for their initiative, and promised to invite delegates from every committee to participate in the final discussion of the reform in Petrograd. The nobles understood that they would be admitted to the *Main Committee* for participation in the final decision of the question. Miliutin appeared determinedly opposed to such an interpretation of the Tzar's promise, and persuaded Rostovtzev and Lanskoy that the admission of the nobles to the Main Committee even with only an advisory voice would overturn the whole work and distort the result of the reform. It was finally decided to allow the delegates of the provincial committees to criticise the projects of the Editing Commission at its sessions, but not to vote on the questions.

The work of the Commissions was divided by Rostovtzev's plan into several periods. During the first period the projects of the first twenty-one provinces which had finished their work earlier than the rest were examined, and delegates from those provinces were invited to join in the discussions. After the criticism and revision of these projects, delegates of other provinces were called out, and after further criticism and discussion, the final projects were worked out. The arrival of the first group of delegates was awaited with some uneasiness by the members of the Editing Commissions, as their opponents considered the appearance of the delegates the most opportune moment for a general battle which might distort the course of the work.

The main objections of the nobles were directed, first, against the rejection of all those provincial projects which recommended the return of the land to the landowners after the termination of the transitory Obligatory period of eight to twelve years; next they objected to the lowering of the estimation of the value of the estates, and finally to the elimination in one form or another of the *votchina*-right of the landowners to be the " chiefs " of the village-communities, proposed by the programme of Posen.

Miliutin decided to counteract the attack of the hostile elements by proving the selfish and greedy motives of the majority of the provincial committees, and to accomplish this he wrote out a memorandum (presented to the Tzar through Lanskoy) in which he tersely criticised the activity of the provincial committees of the first summons, and expressed the opinion of the Ministry of Interior that the delegates should not be allowed to present any general decisions, but should only be invited to present their opinions on the work of the Editing Commissions at its special sessions. The Tzar approved of this view, and corresponding instructions were given to the delegates. The latter naturally grew indignant; at first they intended to present an address to the Tzar, protesting against the actions of the hateful bureaucracy, but when the address was not accepted, they petitioned Rostovtzev to allow them to assemble and work out general decisions for presentation to the " supreme Government." They were allowed to have private gatherings, without the right to make decisions, and they were promised in the name of the Tzar that their

considerations would reach him through the Main Committee.
The delegates proceeded then with their comments on the work
of the Commissions, and filled two thick volumes with sharp
and merciless criticism.

We should note that the majority of the delegates of the
first summons were liberally inclined, and with the exception
of a few persons were not proserfdom. Most of them belonged to the committees of the non black-soil or semi-black-
soil provinces, and definitely stood not only for the liberation
of the peasants, but for land allotment. Yet all of them opposed the granting of land to the peasants in perpetual possession under once for all fixed obligations. They feared, not
without reason, that the performance of *barshchina* after the
abolition of the landowners' authority would actually be impossible, while they considered unjust, in view of the constant rise
in land values, the fixation of *obroks* with no right for raising them. The majority demanded obligatory simultaneous redemption with the aid of a special credit operation. Very few
preferred the system of perpetual possession with the right of
periodical revision of the *obroks,* and only a few persons favoured the retention of all the land by the landowners after the
expiration of the temporary Obligatory period.

With absolute unanimity the delegates attacked the project
of the administrative organisation of the peasants; they did not
directly defend the *votchina*-power of the landowners, but
sharply criticised the intention of the Commissions to subordinate the proposed organs of peasant-autonomy to the local
district-police, whereby the very principle of autonomy was
annulled. In this part of their objections the delegates stood
on liberal and even democratic principles, and their arguments
made a strong impression on many members of the Commissions and on all progressives in the country. The delegate
from Tver, Unkovsky, formulated these ideas best of all and
went further in his criticism, attacking the whole existing

system of local district administration, against which he proposed his own project endorsed by the Tver committee. Unkovsky demanded a fundamental reorganisation of the local administration on the principles of decentralisation and autonomy, of which the smallest unit was to be an all-class *volost*.

The delegates came to the conclusion, however, that their comments could hardly be considered by the Tzar, if only because of their voluminosity. For this reason they decided before their departure to try once more to address the Tzar with a petition to admit them to the Main Committee at the time of the final discussion of the reform. But the idea of a general address was not realised, and the delegates broke into groups. Eighteen of them presented a very moderately composed address in which they petitioned that their comments be admitted before the Main Committee. The delegate from Simbirsk, Shidlovsky, presented a separate address with vague demands in an oligarchic spirit. Finally five delegates headed by Unkovsky appeared with a criticism of the bureaucratic régime, a demand for an obligatory redemption, and a general statement on the necessity of a reorganisation of the juridical and administrative order of the State. Simultaneously with those addresses a memorandum was presented to the Tzar by a Petrograd landowner, M. A. Bezobrazov, an aristocrat (a nephew of Prince Orlov) and Court Chamberlain, who was not a member of the delegation. In his memorandum he savagely criticised the actions of the Ministry of Interior and of the Editing Commissions, and demanded that the bureaucracy be " bridled," and elective representatives of the nobles summoned, in whom only, in his opinion, the supreme authority should seek support.

Alexander's ire, provoked by the sharp expressions of that memorandum, was reflected in his attitude towards the addresses of the delegates, although these were drawn in a loyal and correct tone. The delegates who had signed the addresses were reprimanded by their respective Governors,[2] and their comments in most cases passed unnoticed. In the end this incident, which served as a beginning for the development of an oppositional movement among the nobles and a certain part of society, proved beneficial to the Editing Commissions and to the outcome of their work, because it strengthened Alexander's sympathy with them and their activities.

After the departure of the delegates of the first summons, the second period of the work of the Editing Commissions began. They revised their projects so as to include some of the suggestions of the first delegates and some of the projects that had arrived from other provinces, although they did not find it necessary to make any essential changes in their original plans. But before the work came to an end, an event took place which seemed to threaten the reform with disaster.

On February 6, 1860, Rostovtzev died after a three months' illness caused by overwork and nervous strain. Count Panin, the Minister of Justice, was appointed to the post of chairman of the Editing Commissions. He was a rabid routinist-bureaucrat and thorough conservative, and an outspoken opponent of the programme of action of the Editing Commissions. This appointment aroused general astonishment and indignation. Herzen used a black border in printing in the *Bell* the news of Panin's appointment, and declared despondently that the tone of the reign had changed. He invited the members of the Commissions to resign, if there was a drop of citizen-blood in them.[3] Miliutin shared the same view, and only the

[2] On February 20, 1860, Unkovsky was banished to the province of Viatka, for a sharp protest against the restriction of free discussion, decreed by the Minister of Interior.— Tr.

[3] A contemporary describes in the appearance of Panin at the sessions of the Editing Commissions. In came " an enormous awkward being, with arms as long as those of an orang-outang. This being fiercely and seriously glared at every one over his spectacles, and listened to the names of those whom he met, as they were read out to him by Bulgakov. Some of the representatives were honoured by his shaking

persistent persuasions of Grand Duchess Yelena prevented him from carrying out his intention of resigning. Alexander II explained his motive in reply to the amazed question of his aunt Yelena: "You do not know Panin; his only conviction is the exact fulfilment of my orders." Alexander forbade Panin to make any changes in the policy of the work established by Rostovtzev. Yet his appointment revived the hopes of the serf-holders and of the enemies of the Editing Commissions. The delegates of the second summons, who belonged mostly to the committees of the black-soil and the Western provinces and who advocated a landless liberation of the peasants, arrived at Petrograd with the intention of throwing over the projects of the Commissions with the aid of Panin. They were disappointed: Panin endeavoured formally to keep his promise to the Tzar, and did not assist the delegates. The delegates criticised the projects of the Editing Commissions, especially the ideas of allotting land to the peasants and of the formation of peasant-communities and *volosts* independent of the land-owners; they did not scruple about arguments, and went to any length to discredit the work of the Commissions from the conservative point of view, ascribing the projects republican, socialistic, and communistic principles. Thus the criticism of those delegates differed in principle from that of the delegates of the first summons. The Editing Commissions had no difficulty in disproving those exaggerated accusations. But after the

hands with them, but the majority had to be satisfied with a slight and even slighting nod."

James Mavor, in quoting the above statement in his *An Economic History of Russia*, adds that Panin was proprietor of 21,000 serfs, his income was 136,000 rubles, his interests were bound up with the maintenance of peasant-bondage, his political views were those of a conservative of conservatives.

At the first rumour of Panin's appointment, Herzen wrote in his *Bell*: "What? Panin, Victor Panin! That lanky madman who has destroyed the last vestige of justice in Russia by his formalism! Ha! Ha! Ha! This is a mystification."— TR.

departure of the delegates, when the third, codificatory, period had begun for the Commissions, the group of members led by Miliutin had to live through a hard time.

Count Panin carefully but persistently endeavoured to promulgate in the Commissions some of his views which seriously threatened to cripple the work. Other members of the Commissions, who secretly sympathised with the aspirations of the delegates of the second summons, renewed the struggle with the group of Miliutin, Cherkassky, Samarin, and Soloviov. The conflict assumed a quite bitter character; at one session Panin stated that Miliutin expressed mistrust in his, Panin's, words, and with another member, Bulygin, Miliutin came on the verge of fighting a duel. Panin's main purpose consisted in striking out the expression "perpetual" in the clause granting allotments to the peasants; he pretended to oppose that expression from the juridical point of view, but he evidently intended to create a basis for the realisation of the desires of those provincial committees which had tried to prove, with the aid of Posen, that by the sense of the Rescripts the allotments were to belong to the peasants for the temporary Obligatory period only. Panin failed in his attempt, in spite of all his endeavours, which went so far as falsifying the journals of the sessions, as Miliutin proved. Owing to the steadfast defence of that point by Miliutin and his friends, all that Panin could attain was the substitution of the word "permanent" for the word "perpetual," its equivalent in fact.

Although Panin's opposition was thus frustrated, Miliutin and his friends had to yield several more or less substantial points during the third period (and partly during the second) of the work of the Commissions. Those compromises consisted in some diminution of allotments in certain districts; in some raise of the *obrok* norm in the black-soil provinces, where it had been originally proposed to be one ruble lower than in the non black-soil provinces. and finally in the permission of an *obrok*-revision after twenty years, i.e., of the transvaluation of the obligations in accordance with the changed prices on grain in those estates where the fields were given to the peasants in perpetuity. Yielding to that last change, on which the Tzar himself had insisted, Miliutin hoped that no Minister of Interior would ever undertake the readjustment of the *obroks* in the non-redeemed estates. Indeed, no revision of the *obroks* took place in 1881, but instead obligatory redemption was introduced in all those estates where there still remained temporary Obligatory peasants.

On October 10, 1860, the Editing Commissions were closed after having worked without rest for about twenty months, and having prepared projects of sixteen various acts with explanatory memoranda, indices, etc. The printed reports of the departments, the journals of the sessions of the Commissions, the summaries of the projects of the provincial committees, and other works of the Editing Commissions filled eighteen enormous volumes, besides six volumes of statistical information about all estates having more than one hundred serfs, and three big volumes of comments by the delegates of the provincial committees, also published by the Commissions.

CHAPTER XXII

FROM the day of the closing of the Editing Commissions in October of 1860, the work began in the Main Committee. It lasted two months; irreconcilable contradictions among the members appeared which placed Grand Duke Constantine, who had been appointed chairman of the Committee in place of Prince Orlov, in a very difficult position. No majority could be formed on certain questions; there were only ten members, and they broke into three or four groups, and not one of them had an absolute majority.

The main question concerned the methods and norms of the land-allotments for the peasants. At the discussion of this question an obstinate group was formed under the leadership of M. N. Muraviov, Minister of State Domains, who was joined in all questions by the Chief of Gendarmes, Prince V. A. Dolgorukov, and in most cases by Minister of Finance, A. M. Kniazhevich, and for some time also by the Court Minister, Count V. F. Adlerberg, who later, however, withdrew from the coalition. This group had endeavoured to establish the norms of the allotments and their valuation as recommended by the provincial committees, but seeing the impossibility of carrying out that point of view they attempted to have those questions transferred to the decisions of local authorities, permitting the Main Committee to define only the general principles of the reform. The project presented by them was prepared by the new star of the aristocratic party, the hope of the serfholders and feudalists — P. A. Valuiev, who had not long before exchanged his post of Governor for a position in the Ministry of

State Domains, and who was appointed Minister of Interior after the publication of the Act of February 19.

But that group was not able to get a majority in the Main Committee; on the side of the projects accepted by the Editing Commissions were four votes, but they had no absolute majority either, as Prince Gagarin who desired a landless liberation of the peasants, and Count Panin who opposed many of the Commissions' decisions, stuck stubbornly to their opinions. After many efforts on the part of Grand Duke Constantine to win over Panin, the latter joined the majority (five against four), having succeeded in decreasing the norms of the allotments in numerous districts from one-quarter to one-half of a desiatin. Thus the work of the Main Committee came to an end after two months, and the decisions of the Editing Commissions suffered no fundamental changes.

The Tzar was present at the last session of the Main Committee, and by invitation, all members of the Council of Ministers. The Tzar thanked the Editing Commissions for their good work, and declared that in transferring the matter to the State Council he would not tolerate any procrastination in the final discussions, and then and there he appointed February 15 as the last day for the examination of the question, so that the abolition of bondage might be enacted before the beginning of field-works. " This," said Alexander, " I desire, I demand, I command! "

The members of the State Council were given ten days for getting acquainted with the question, and on January 28, 1861, Alexander II opened the sessions with a long and vigorous speech in which he reviewed the whole course of the peasant-question during the preceding reigns and in his own time, and repeating his demand for a rapid examination of the question in the State Council, he said: " Different views on the work presented before you may exist. I shall willingly listen to all opinions, but I have the right to demand one thing: that putting aside your personal interests, you act not as landowners, but as State dignitaries endowed with my confidence." At that he reiterated his desire to have the matter accomplished by the middle of February.

Indeed, the members of the State Council had finished the examination of the whole matter by February 17. The Tzar gave his resolution on each question, joining the opinion of the majority at one time, and that of the minority, at another. Not seldom he agreed with the opinion of eight against thirty-five, in order to sustain the decision of the Editing Commissions (which he succeeded on all points).

The project passed the State Council with only one new amendment, made by Prince Gagarin, who having been defeated in all his attempts to carry through a landless liberation, proposed that in cases of mutual agreement the landowner might give the peasants one-fourth of the allotment determined by the law, gratuitously, whereupon all their obligations to one another would be cancelled. The State Council unanimously approved of the amendment, and it was confirmed by the Tzar. Thus originated the so-called " quartered," or in the expression of the people, " beggarly," " charity " allotments. The peasants were frequently tempted with the possibility of receiving a gratuitous allotment, no matter how small it might be; this caused a spread of land-dearth among the peasants, particularly in the Steppe-provinces, where there was so much land in 1861 that the peasants were not very eager to assert their proprietorship of it.

On February 19 the Tzar signed the Act and the solemn manifesto which was written by the Metropolitan of Moscow, Filaret. At first the writing of the manifesto was entrusted to Y. Samarin, but his project was found unsuitable, and it was turned over as material to Filaret, who performed the work reluctantly, in view of his opposition to the way in which the reform was carried out.

Let us analyse the Act of the 19th of February. The new legislation concerning the peasants was very cumbersome — there were seventeen acts and special rules. First came the " *General* act concerning the peasants freed from bondage "; besides general introductory articles the act defined the legal position of the liberated peasants and their administrative organisation which was to be alike everywhere. Of a similarly general character was the act concerning *redemption,* i.e., the methods and conditions under which the allotments were to be redeemed. The act about *house-serfs* also had a general significance. They were to be freed completely and gratuitously two years after the publication of the Act, without getting anything from their masters. Equally general was the nature of the act concerning *local institutions for peasant-affairs,* by the aid of which the new legislation was to be put into practice, namely: Peace-Mediators and their District-Conferences, and Provincial Boards for Peasant Affairs. In regard to the economic side of the question several *local* acts were issued regulating the different conditions. One act was issued for the peasants of Great Russia, White Russia, and New Russia, where the communal — *obshchina* — system was in existence; a special Little Russian act was issued for the peasants of the provinces Poltava, Chernigov, and part of Kharkov; a local act was also issued for the Southwestern provinces, and a local act for the Lithuanian provinces of Vilna, Kovno, Grodno, and Minsk; in each case the acts were to fit the peculiar local agricultural conditions that had taken form in the historical process.

Special acts were issued also for 1) small serf-owners who were permitted to sell their estates to the Government, in case the conditions of the emancipation were disadvantageous for them; for 2) peasants performing obligatory work in landowners' factories; 3) peasants in mountain and salt-works; 4) peasants in the Region of the Don Army; 5) peasants and house-serfs in the province of Stavropol (the only Cau-

casian province subjected to peasant-reform at that time);
6) peasants in the Bessarabian Region where personal bondage
had been abolished even before its annexation to Russia; finally
a special act was issued for 7) Western Siberia; in Eastern
Siberia there had been no bondage-right. Considering that
the number of articles in every act exceeded one hundred, we
may get an idea of the gigantic legislative and codificatory
work performed by the Editing Commissions.

The chief significance of the Great Reform has been its
legal aspect; in this respect the fall of bondage has been the
most important event in all the modern history of Russia.
Contemporaries and especially participators of the reform were
fond of saying that by the Act of February 19 the people were
for the first time brought on the historical arena in Russia.
At any rate we may say that the whole status of the people has
fundamentally changed with the introduction of the reform.
Whatever the material consequences of the reform have been,
one cannot deny the enormous importance of the fact that men
were no longer permitted to sell other men or to transfer them
from field work to house service, i.e., to a state of domestic
slavery. The peasants got rid of the unlimited interference in
their life, which the landowners had exercised even to the extent of arranging marriages among them.

From the generally human point of view the legal significance of the reform has been colossal, but we must observe
here that the abolition of serfdom, having freed the peasants
from personal and legal subjection to the landowners, has not
equalised the peasants with the landowners in their civil rights:
the reform has transferred them from the class of bonded
peasants *not into the class of fully able citizens, but into the
class of the so-called tributary orders.* This vestige of the
general binding of all orders, on which the Muscovite state
had been based, has continued to exist. The legal position
of the tributary orders consisted in their being taxed by the

Government per capita, not according to their income; the tax had to be paid by the group as a whole, by *mutual guarantee,* which bound every one to the group in which he was registered, by the aid of a special *passport system.* Every tributary order was responsible for all its members, and for this reason the Government was obliged to allow such groups a certain authority over its members, the right to keep them forcibly within the group. As long as the " mutual guarantee " system and the per capita tax existed there could not be any full rights of separate classes in Russia, or actual equality of all citizens before the law; those under the burden of the tributary system had no freedom of movement or of profession, for in order to be transferred from one group into another one had to obtain a verdict of dismissal. One limitation logically resulted another, and the traces of that bondage are still noticeable in Russia.

Another article in the General Act stated that during the first nine years after the publication of the Act the temporary Obligatory peasants could not refuse their allotment and had to perform obligations for it; their personal freedom was thus definitely limited. One should have in mind that the men who worked out the peasant-reform of 1861 did not profess the liberal views of the men of the end of the eighteenth or of the beginning of the nineteenth century, whose starting point were the rights of human personality, the ideology of the Declaration of Rights of Man and Citizen. The members of the Editing Commissions desired primarily the security of the welfare of the people and of the State. They undoubtedly were well disposed towards the peasants and sincerely wished to improve their life in a fundamental way, but since they acted for *welfare,* and not for *personal freedom* in the proper sense of the word, it is natural that at times questions of welfare prevailed against questions of personal liberation. As a result of that attitude came the beneficial part of the reform — the liberation of the peasants with land, but the same circumstance conditioned the element of guardianship which was considered necessary to introduce for the time of the organisation of the freed peasants.

The reasonable apprehension that the emancipated peasants might again fall under the power and even bondage of the landowners, resulted in the *administrative organisation* established for the peasants. The peasantry was organised in autonomous social units, of which the smallest was a village community. Economically the communities had considerable independence; in "communal" villages the taxation was determined by the peasants according to the size of individual allotments, which in their turn were determined by the general assembly of the village community. That general assembly could tax the members with dues for various spiritual, mental, or moral needs, and for social exigencies.

Originally it was intended that while the village-communities should have complete management of the economic part, the *volost* was to be another unit of the local administration, not connected hierarchically with the economic unit; but in the end the *volost* was placed above the village community in many administrative matters. The elected village functionaries, the Elders, had to submit in police questions to the *volost*-chiefs and the *volost*-boards, and together they were subordinate to various police and administration authorities of the district, whose orders they had to fulfil without dispute, under the fear of disciplinary penalties which could be inflicted by the Peace Mediator at his own initiative or upon complaints of various officials. In the end the persons elected by the village-autonomy became virtually petty agents of the district-police; although chosen by the village communities and *volosts* they were responsible not to their electors, but to the "authorities." This circumstance undermined the principle of self-government at its root.

We have seen that those defects in the administration were decisively attacked by the delegates of the first summons. The Editing Commissions, fearing the ferule of the landowners over the peasants, objected to having the *volost* represented by all classes and remaining independent from the district administration; but they fell into another extreme, and subjected the village communities to bureaucratic arbitrariness.

In the *economic* respect the Editing Commissions considerably deviated from the recommendations of the provincial committees, particularly in regard to the norms of the allotments, the norms of the peasants' obligations for those allotments, and the question of redemption and compensation. According to the Act, the peasants were to *retain approximately those allotments which they had been using in their bondage-state.* But the Commissions regarded the fact that in some places the landowners gave their peasants larger allotments than were needed (because in the industrial, non black-soil provinces land was of small value); while in other regions the landowners gave their peasants such small allotments that the peasants could neither subsist on them nor be able to eke out the assessed *obrok.* In view of this the Editing Commissions worked out special norms for the regulation of existing conditions. In every region there was to be a *maximal norm;* if peasants on a certain estate were in possession of more land than was limited by that norm, the landowner had the right to let them use the whole land for additional obligations or he could demand the cutting off of the surplus. On the other hand *minimal norms* in the measure of one-third of the maximal norms were established. Where the peasants' allotments were below that minimum, the landowner was obliged to add land for the completion of the norm.

In respect to the maximal norms, the size of which naturally determined the minimal norms, Russia was divided into three regions: the non black-soil, the black-soil, and the steppes. In the non black-soil region there were seven possible grades of norms, from three and a quarter to eight desiatins, so that there could be maximal allotments of three and a quarter, three and a half, four, five, six, seven, and eight desiatins. In the black-soil region were five grades: three, three and a quarter, three and a half, four, and four and a half desiatins; in the region of the steppes were four grades: six and a half, eight and a half, ten and a half, and twelve desiatins. In establishing these norms the Editing Commissions increased about twice the norms recommended by the provincial committees. In the course of the Commissions' work they had to take into account the considerations and protests of the delegates, and decrease many norms by one-quarter, one-half, and even by whole desiatins. Later the bargaining affair between Grand Duke Constantine and Panin further reduced the size of the norms. But after all the insufficiency of the peasants' allotment was due not so much to the diminution of the original norms recommended by the Editing Commissions, as to the fact that *in the best cases the peasants received those allotments that had been in their possession during the bondage state, and those allotments required only half of their labour, and could not therefore yield enough for their subsistence and for the fulfilment of the obligations.*

In respect to the *obligations* of the peasants, the Editing Commissions subdivided Russia into four regions: non black-soil, industrial (i.e., of the *obrok*-system); non black-soil (of the *barshchina*-system); black-soil (all of *barshchina*); and the steppe region. The maximal, or full, *obrok*, which corresponded to the maximum norm of the allotment, was in the non black-soil industrial region nine rubles per soul, and ten rubles in the more advantageous places, as those in the vicinity of the Capitals or in the province of Yaroslavl. In the other regions the norm was originally estimated to be eight rubles all over, but in view of the protests of the delegates and of some of the members of the Commissions, the *obrok* in the black-soil region had to be raised to nine rubles.

The " full " *obrok* could be levied only on maximum allotments in a given region; smaller allotments were assessed with lower *obroks,* but the diminution of the *obroks* was not made proportional to the diminution of the size of the allotment. A special *gradational system* was accepted for the estimation of additional desiatins, so that if a peasant had seven desiatins in a region of an eight desiatin-norm, his nine rubles *obrok* was diminished not by one-eighth, but only by fifty-six and two-thirds copecks. In regions where under the bondage-system the peasants had allotments below one-third of the maximal norm, additional allotments required *obroks* almost twice above the norm. For this reason the peasants preferred in such cases " beggarly " gratuitous allotments to additional land, where for one-third allotment they had to pay two-thirds *obrok.* There were many disturbances in places where landowners refused to yield to the peasants' demand for gratuitous " quarterly " allotments.

From the aforesaid we can see what were the allotments received by the peasants after the liquidation of the bondage, and what were their obligations. Their allotments were equal approximately to one-half of the amount of their earning capacity, for in the best cases they received only that land which they possessed under bondage and which required only three days' work in a week, the rest of the time being given to *barshchina.* In order to utilise their labour power, the peasants had either to rent the other half of the land from the landowner, or to hire themselves to the landowner, or to look for some side work which would enable them to pay the taxes and the *obroks* and to buy such necessaries as their own property could not supply them with. With the growing density of the population the dearth of land was felt more and more, rent rose higher and higher, and the peasant grew poorer and poorer;

for this reason *in the most fertile part of Russia the misery of the peasants is at the present time the greatest.* The peasants of the black-soil regions, particularly rich in soil, as in the provinces of Tula or Tambov, live in worse poverty than the peasants of the provinces of Tver or Yaroslavl, where the land yields little, but where they earn from industrial occupations.

By the Act of February 19 the peasants received the land in " perpetual," or as Panin insisted — in " permanent " utilisation. By *voluntary agreements* with the landowners they could eventually redeem their obligations, and receive the land in personal possession. Not the land but the obligations were redeemed. *Compulsory redemption* was rejected both by Alexander and Rostovtzev who consented only to redemption by mutual agreement. Yet, as one could have foreseen, the majority of the landowners *had* to seek redemption. In the non black-soil provinces they wished it themselves; in the black-soil provinces, especially in the *barshchina*-estates, the position of the landowners grew unbearable, for with the abolition of their authority over the peasants the latter performed their *barshchina* very inadequately and evasively, so that those estates deteriorated considerably. The landowners in the black-soil regions began to hope for redemption as the only way to settle with their bondmen. On the whole the redeeming operation was realised more rapidly than one could have expected, and it was delayed only in cases where the peasants were unwilling to meet the offers of the landowners.

Such was the economic side of the reform of February 19 for the peasants and for the landowners. For the gentry proper the results of the liquidation of bondage were not alike in all regions. In the black-soil provinces, after the hard *barshchina*-period, the landowners retained most of their land, were able to get cheap labour in view of the dense population and the absence of non-agricultural occupations. Besides, they received a compensation which they could employ either for the improvement of their estates or for the extinction of their debts. If they were not inclined to manage their estates, they could profitably rent their land, since the rentals were very high on account of the insufficient allotments of the peasants.

But in the non black-soil industrial region the landowners, having received their compensation, severed in most cases all connections with their former possessions; only a few remained on their estates, and endeavoured to continue agricultural pursuits. It was difficult to obtain labour hands from a population that catered to industrial occupations, and the majority of the landowners sold out their estates, and employed their capital for industrial purposes, if they did not waste it otherwise. Thus with the abolition of serfdom industry received new capital.

In conclusion let us say that the chief significance of the abolition of bondage has lain not only in the enormous economic consequences which it bore for the peasantry, gentry, and industry of the country, but still more in the fundamental change wrought by it in the legal conditions of the Empire. Only after the abolition of serfdom did all those great reforms that were promulgated during the Sixties become possible. Only then could the road for the judiciary reform be cleared. During the bondage-system the whole administrative structure was based on class-principles, with the prevalence of the gentry; the landowner was the caretaker of everything on his estate, and the Central authority had confidence in the management of the " gratuitous chiefs-of-police " (Nicolas's expressed idea of the rôle of the nobles. Tr.) Now had the bureaucratic method been feasible, everything should have been rebuilt from top to bottom; but the bureaucracy did not possess sufficient power for such a grandiose transformation. Hence the abolition of serfdom resulted in the introduction of local self-government, in one way or another. Moreover, the Government seemed to prefer a self-government with no class limitation to that of the aristocratic gentry whose oligarchic pretensions at that moment were more disquieting than democratic principles.

Such were the results for the country of the fall of bondage.

CHAPTER XXIII

IN the preceding chapters I have expounded more or less fully the entire course of the peasant-reform, and in the last chapter I analysed the Act of February 19. Now I shall endeavour to illustrate the influence of those labours on the development of public thought in various circles, to trace the differentiation of political views and tendencies that had taken place in this connection in the press, and to clarify in passing the influence of the press on the course of the peasant-reform and the attitude of the Government towards the press. Finally I intend to sketch the programme for the reorganisation of various sides of the State life, that had been definitely formulated among governmental circles, and also those social demands which were expressed in 1861 or about 1861 in the progressive press and in declarations of various social institutions.

We have observed that the position of the press in 1855 was very difficult in respect to censorship-conditions. As a matter of fact, all social and political questions were nearly unmentionable for the press; at the same time one should note that after the oppression which the Russian public had experienced during the long reign of Nicolas, particularly during his last seven years, the public's activity and thought were so stultified that it was hardly ready for active participation in the great work that stood before the country.

In spite of the unanimous consciousness of the need for fundamental reforms, the public indicated very timidly and vaguely the ways for the realisation of those reforms. The public was as devoid of a definite plan for practical reorganisations, as was the Government at the beginning of the reforms. We

have seen that the public regarded the new Tzar very optimistically, and that optimism almost bordered on apathy; everything was expected from the higher spheres. This condition
was strengthened by the difficult position of the press in regard
to censorship, the absolute impossibility of expressing with some
freedom views and opinions on social and political questions,
even for those few persons who had such. Even in those
memoranda which had circulated widely and had been presented to the Government, and which were not restricted by
censorship, the demands were expressed very moderately, as we
may see from their formulation in Chernyshevsky's programme
of 1856, which has already been mentioned.

The position of Herzen was quite exceptional not only in
view of his freedom from the censor's oppression, but because
by preparation and equipment he knew contemporary Russia
exceptionally well, so that in some matters he appeared almost
as a prophet. Thus as early as 1853, before the beginning of
the crisis of Nicolas' system, which had opened the eyes even
of ordinary persons, Herzen predicted that the fall of bondage
was "necessary, inevitable, unavoidable," and that it would
occur in the nearest future. Even then Herzen declared his
radical programme for the solution of the peasant-question,
and demanded not only the liberation of the peasants, but
their liberation with all the land which under the bondage-
régime they had been using. Upon the accession of Alexander
II, Herzen decided to found an organ for the expression of
immediate problems of Russian national and social life. In
1855 he began to publish his pamphlets *Polar Star,* and upon
the establishment of the Unofficial Committee on peasant
affairs, Herzen undertook the publication of a bi-weekly, soon
transformed into a weekly paper — the *Bell.* The *Bell*
acquired a great importance; Katkov told Herzen during his
visit to London that the *Bell* lay on Rostovtzev's desk as a
source of information on the peasant-question. It revealed

with an unaccustomed straightforwardness all the sores of
Russian national and social life, pilloried abuses and unsavoury
actions of individual officials mercilessly, and appeared as a
constant menace to the higher functionaries, and as an institution which pushed on the Government and the public, without
letting them stop.   Herzen was often reproached — especially
by Chicherin, in an article published in the *Bell* — for his nerv-
ousness, passionateness, for the unevenness of his judgments, for
his frequent leaps from praising the Government to sharply
condemning its activity.   Herzen replied that his platform was
immutable, that he always stood on the side of the one who
liberated, and as *long* as he liberated.   To a great extent the
leaps in the *Bell's* attitude towards the Government were due
to the vacillating policy of the latter which in all questions —
except that of peasant-reform — as in the question of the press
or the universities, hesitated and now moved ahead, now retreated.   At any rate, until 1858 Herzen's *Bell* was the only
organ where the opinions of the Russian progressives could
be freely expressed, and in this respect he performed a great
service by his stimulating influence on the Government, and
by his activity for the formation of a public opinion in the
country.

As to the periodicals published in Russia, their tendencies
and programmes began to differentiate from the year 1858, when
the press was permitted to discuss the peasant-question, and
when the provincial committees were opened; these, although
closed for the public, did not keep their activity in secret,
and gave food for discussion in the provinces and in the
Capitals.

The *Contemporary,* directed by Chernyshevsky and Dobroliubov, was the first to move sharply to the left.   The *Contemporary* was published, as in the time of Nicolas, by Panaiev
and Niekrasov, but they were not the influential leaders of the
organ.   After the death, in 1848, of its leading contributor,

Bielinsky, in the period of suffocating reaction all the
best literary forces of that time, the so-called writers of the
Forties, who professed the views of Bielinsky in his last years,
were united in the magazine.   But the writers who expressed
the aspirations of the best part of Russian society in the Forties
were liberals, not radicals.   Alongside with them, however,
began to appear in the pages of the *Contemporary* representatives of the young generation, at first in the person of
Chernyshevsky, who being older than Dobroliubov, Pisarev,
and the other Men of the Sixties, had begun his career in the
Fifties; then in the person of young Dobroliubov who began
to write in 1857 at the age of twenty, and manifested at once
unusual gifts and an extraordinary independence of views.
In 1858 Chernyshevsky took over the department of economics
and peasant-problems, and gave Dobroliubov the position of
literary critic, which in the " thick " magazines of that time
had a great importance, as it included all publicistic discussions
and much wider tasks than the title implied.   The manager of
the critical department occupied a rôle similar to that of the
leader in a chorus, or that of the first violin in an orchestra,
and such was the rôle of young Dobroliubov who did not long
remain under the instructorship of Chernyshevsky, but soon
became his equal colleague and friend.   By his views he was
an heir not only to Bielinsky and to the radical critics of the
Forties, but he proceeded further, and appeared as the first
herald of populistic (*narodnichestvo*) principles and ideals in
Russian critique.

The young leaders of the *Contemporary* soon collided with
the representatives of the older generation on the magazine:
Turgeniev, Grigorovich, Goncharov, and other novelists of the
Forties, who were joined by the recently discovered Tolstoy.

Dobroliubov soon began to feel dissatisfied with the development and tendency of Russian Progress, and with ardent
passion he expressed his impatience and discontent.   He

considered that timid and moderate Progress as treading on one and the same place; he spoke with contempt of the evasive and vague revealments of Russian sores and abuses in the press. Both he and Chernyshevsky were bitterly disappointed in the nobles whose class egoism was manifested in the activities of the provincial committees; Chernyshevsky, who in February, 1858, praised Alexander, and in April wrote complimentary notes about the liberal landowners, changed his tone by the end of the year. About that time a pause came in the press-discussion of the peasant-question. When in April, 1858, Chernyshevsky published in the *Contemporary* a continuation of his article " On New Conditions of Village Life," and quoted at length Kavelin's project which in 1856 circulated freely and was known to the Government, that article appeared very dangerous in the eyes of the Government by its advocating the transfer of the land to the peasants through redemption. The Main Committee considered it an impertinence, and by its request a circular was issued forbidding the discussion in the press of the questions of redemption and *votchina*-authority. The circular and the persecution of Kavelin made a depressing impression on the *Contemporary* and on the other representatives of the progressive press. Katkov (then a liberal) demonstratively discontinued the department on peasant-questions in his *Russian Messenger;* the publishers of *Village Well-Being,* a magazine started by the Slavophiles mainly with Koshelev's money, were about to close it forever. This did not last long, however. We know that the Government's views changed in regard to the redemption question; in the fall of 1858 it permitted again a more or less free discussion of the peasant-problem. Then (at the end of 1858 and particularly early in 1859) Chernyshevsky began to write extremely virulent articles against the selfishness of the landowners, their greedy aspirations and extraordinary appetites, which he had been shown by the works of the provincial committees. He recommended such radical ways for the solution of the problem that they appeared absolutely inacceptable to the Government and as spelling utter ruin for the landowners.

At the same time Dobroliubov reached the apogee in his attacks on the weakness and vagueness of the liberalism of the nobles, and on the cowardice and mildness of Russian progressives. Such were his articles on Shchedrin's *Provincial Sketches,* and on Goncharov's *Oblomov.* When Herzen read his famous " What is Oblomovism? " he thought the *Contemporary* had gone too far, and that it required restraint. During 1859–1860 articles appeared in the *Bell* that warned the *Contemporary,* and defended the liberalism of the nobles from the attacks of Chernyshevsky and Dobroliubov. Thus the *Contemporary* occupied in 1858–1859 a position more radical than that of Herzen's paper.

The main representative of the liberal, or rather the liberal-democratic current was Katkov's *Russian Messenger* which sided with the views of Unkovsky and the Tver liberals. Katkov was at that time perhaps the most consistent and firm upholder of liberalism, and an opponent of any governmental ferule. To a certain degree the same tendency was pursued by Kraievsky's *Annals of the Fatherland,* but the editor, Dudyshkin, was a weak publicist, and had no influence. Druzhinin's " thick " monthly, *Library for Reading,* intended to become an organ of English constitutional Toryism, so to speak, i.e., it hoped to create an enlightened conservative party which would endeavour to promulgate certain liberal reforms and then instead of constantly moving forward, reduce its tasks to the conservation of the positions won. That magazine lacked talents, and was unable to play the rôle it had intended to.

The Slavophile views were expressed in a periodical *Russian Discourse* which appeared irregularly. In 1857 the Slavophiles issued a newspaper *Rumour,* but the censorship conditions were then very hard, and the paper was discontinued by the end of the year. Ivan Aksakov, who was forbidden in 1852 to be editor or even to publish his writings, received a permission in 1859 for a newspaper, *Sails,* but his tone was so sharp that publication was stopped on the second number.

In general the Slavophiles occupied a quite peculiar position. On one hand, they appeared as conservatives *par excellence,* and even as reactionaries; in some respects they wished to turn Russia back to pre-Petrine times. In their eyes Peter's reforms which had drafted Western civilisation upon Russian life were a distortion of Russia's natural peculiarities, and they demanded a return to ancient times. The Slavophiles idealised the old ages, when the Government did not interfere with social, communal, or private life, and advocated Orthodoxy and Autocracy as necessary foundations of Russian life. They understood under Orthodoxy a church free from external influence and service to the state, and absolutely rejected the official Orthodoxy of the present. In regard to Autocracy they stood on the platform expressed by Constantine Aksakov in his letter to Alexander II: *The power of authority belongs to the Tzar, but the power of opinion — to the people.* In this respect their views were quite radical; for instance, they demanded not an alleviation of the position of the press, but complete freedom of speech, and in religious questions they demanded unlimited freedom of conscience and creed. They did not admit in private or communal life any regulation or interference on the part of the state. They expressed their ideas sharply and radically, and for this reason were unable to promulgate them through the press. Their only successful attempt was the magazine *Village Well-Being,* published for one year at the *Library for Reading,* with the co-operation of Koshelev, Samarin, and Cherkassky. It printed articles exclusively on peasant-problems, mostly written by progressive members of the provincial committees. Chernyshevsky and Dobroliubov admitted that outside of the *Contemporary* the *Village Well-Being* was the only honest publication, although they often opposed its views. In Moscow another magazine appeared devoted exclusively to the peasant-question, the *Landowners' Journal,* edited by Zheltukhin; most of its articles were written by representatives of black-soil provinces, and therefore advocated landless liberation of the peasants. Professor Vernadsky's magazine, *Economical Indicator,* stood in principle for the interests of big landownership, and advocated pure Manchesterism. It was an academic publication, and the public knew about it only from Chernyshevsky's sharp attacks upon its articles.

During that period, between 1859 and 1861, when the process of the differentiation in the tendencies of the press took place, the freedom of the press grew in spite of the unrelenting censorship; newspapers and magazines became bolder and widened the sphere of their interests, so that by 1861 the press actually discussed all social and political questions of the day. We must say that the very contingent of the questions had expanded considerably. During the first five years of Alexander's reign the public consciousness made big strides, and had gained initiative and definiteness of purpose. In connection with the peasant reform there emerged concomitant questions concerning local self-government, judicial reorganisation and jury-trials, publicity and freedom of speech, and numerous other questions regarding culture, education, and the satisfaction of the economic and industrial needs of the rejuvenated country. Those questions were formulated in projects of provincial committees, in speeches and addresses of delegates to the provincial assemblies in 1860, and were echoed in the press.

In *Voices from Russia* Herzen published parallel with the *Bell* memoranda and projects which could not be published in Russia; there we may see the growth and development of the plans for reorganisation. In the end of 1860 appeared the ninth and last number of *Voices from Russia,* in which alongside with the "Political Will" written by Rostovtzev before his death for Alexander, was published an unsigned memorandum about the desirable course of the peasant-reform. The publishers of the *Bell* asserted that had the Editing Commissions followed the direction of the author of that memorandum, Russia would have had a true, not pseudo-liberation of the peasants. The *Bell's* admonition came too late, for the Commissions had been already closed. The *Bell* expressed, however, its general satisfaction with the activity of the Commissions, and even said a good word about the deceased Rostovtzev whom it had pursued for years.

The memorandum, which for some considerations I am inclined to ascribe to N. A. Serno-Solovievich, had at the end a programme which formulated the views of the most progressive groups of that time.

"In conclusion," wrote the author, "let us indicate the main demands of public opinion, demands not only perfectly legal, but very moderate, for they are practised in all somewhat enlightened states:

1. The liberation of the peasants with land.
2. Equality of all before the courts and the law.
3. Complete separation of the judiciary power from the administrative; jury-courts.
4. Reorganisation of the police.
5. Responsibility of all administrative organs, beginning with the ministers.
6. Right of verification of the collection and expenditure of taxes.
7. Right of control over the issue of new laws.
8. Freedom of conscience and creed.
9. Freedom of the press.
10. The abolition of the Contract-Monopoly, and the re-

vision of the laws oppressing commerce, industry, and national labour.

11. Abolition of civil ranks.

12. Full amnesty for all sufferers for political convictions.

" The last eleven points are a natural consequence of the first — the abolition of serfdom. In foreign words, it is a constitution; in Russian — it means a regulated order."

As a matter of fact, there was no constitution in the programme; neither a representative government, nor legal guarantees are mentioned there, but it offers a broad liberal, and in some features, radical reorganisation of the state. From that plan we can see how far public opinion outgrew the programmes of the Government.

Such were the *desiderata* of the progressive groups at the moment of the fall of bondage. The fact that those demands had outgrown the offers of the Government brought about new relations between the public and the Government of Alexander II, relations quite different from those that existed at his accession. Now there was no longer the older perfect and unanimous confidence in the Government; on the contrary, the governmental activity aroused scepticism and mistrust, in spite of its progressive tendencies and desire to place the public initiative before that of the Government. At the moment of the emancipation of the peasants, the *entente cordiale* which had existed between the public and the Government at the beginning of the reform, vanished entirely. The declaration of freedom in March, 1861, dissatisfied not only the radical circles of society, but first of all — the peasants.

CHAPTER XXIV

WHILE the reform was in preparation the peasants had patiently awaited for four years the decision of their fate. Many times during that period when the enemies of the reform tried to frighten Alexander with probable peasant disturbances, the Tzar did not believe them, pointing out their general calmness. Until the moment of the publication of the Act there reigned an unusual calm among the peasants. But as soon as the Act was solemnly declared from church pulpits, and copies of it were given out to every landowner and every village community, there began that fermentation among the peasants which the enemies of the reform had long before predicted.

In the majority of the districts no measures were taken for the proper explanation of the Act to the peasants. Only in a very few places which had enlightened governors, such as Artzimovich of Kaluga, care was taken to help the peasants orient themselves in the sense of the Act. But even in such places the publication of the Manifesto aroused misunderstandings on the part of the landowners and the peasants. The peasants had patiently waited four years expecting that in the end they would receive " full freedom," which meant in their eyes the immediate fall of the landowners' power, and the granting to the peasants without any compensation not only of the lands which they had been using under the bondage-order, but also of the land of the landowners to whom the Tzar would pay " salary " for it. When the Act of February 19 was issued, and the peasants saw that for an indefinite time the

65

obligations were retained — *barshchina* or *obrok* —, that in some cases their land might be diminished, that they had to be bound to their masters until the redemption was accomplished, that redemption could be realised only upon mutual agreement by both sides,— the peasants came to the conclusion that it was not at all the freedom which they had been expecting; they decided that the Tzar could not have given them such a freedom, that the landowners had concealed the " real freedom " and published a " forged freedom." On this basis a number of disturbances and riots arose. Foreseeing the possibility of such events, the Government had commissioned to all provinces prominent generals who were given the power of governor-generals for extraordinary cases; at the slightest sign of disturbances these special authorities had the right to employ all means for the suppression of the unrest, including the right to command military forces, and charge at the people. Thus it came to pass that when the peasants, considering the declared freedom as " forged," and at times trying to read into the Act of February 19 what they had been hoping for, refused to perform *barshchina* and pay *obrok* and other obligations to the landowners, the Generals displayed their power in one way or another. Where the Generals happened to be better disposed or more reasonable, or where the peasants were more peacefully inclined, peace was restored by mere persuasion. But in a number of places bloodshed took place. In the village of Bezdna, province of Penza, the peasants, led by a fanatical defender of the people's rights, their fellow-villager, Anton Petrov, were greatly disturbed; in the end General Apraksin ordered the troops to fire at them, which resulted, according to the greatly underrated official figures, in fifty-five dead and seventy wounded. The students of the Kazan university, under the leadership of the young Professor Shchapov, had a requiem served for the dead of Bezdna. Alexander personally dictated a resolution by which the monks who had officiated at that mass were to be exiled to Solovki, and Shchapov was to be brought to Petrograd. It was the first instance of the manifestation of dissatisfaction on the part of the democratic layers of the people, and of corresponding repressions on the part of the Government.

At that time a significant change had taken place in the upper spheres, in the very department which was to carry through the reform. As a concession to the landowners who were grieved by the peasant reform, Minister of Interior Lanskoy and his closest assistant, Miliutin, were dismissed from their posts, although in a gracious manner: Lanskoy was granted the title of Count, and Miliutin was promoted to the rank of Senator, with the right to go abroad. Valuiev, who had been known as an opponent to the reform and to the character of the work of the Editing Commissions, was appointed Minister. During the discussion of the question in the Main Committee he assisted the enemies of the project of the Editing Commissions, Minister of State Domains Muraviov, and Chief of Gendarmes Dolgorukov, for whom he worked out a special memorandum.

Now Valuiev declared that he considered his task " the strict and exact realisation of the acts of February 19, but in a conciliatory way." As a matter of fact he soon revealed his purpose of working into the hands of the landowners, not scrupling even about twisting and misinterpreting the law. The carrying through of the reform was placed in the hands of Peace Mediators, their District Conferences, and Provincial Peasant Boards. Before his dismissal Lanskoy had sent out an important circular to the Governors, instructing them about the selection of adequate persons as Peace Mediators. He pointed out that since the Governors were to appoint the Mediators from among nobles recommended by the nobles themselves, they should be very cautious in the selection, admitting to that post only persons known for their sense of justice and friendliness towards the peasants, and who would be apt to enjoy the confidence of the peasants.   Indeed, the best inclined Governors, whose numbers were considerably increased during Lanskoy's administration, had made a successful selection of Peace Mediators.   In general one must say that the Peace Mediators of the first summons had left an excellent memory as just and devoted workers.   In view of their quite independent position — they could be dismissed only after a trial by the order of the Senate which confirmed their appointments — they were not subordinate to the provincial or central authorities, and were in a position to follow the law and decide cases according to their conscience.   In many places they came into collision with the interests of big and influential landowners; the latter complained to Valuiev who came out in their defence, but he suffered a decisive fiasco, owing to the energetic resistance of the Peace Mediators to the attempted pressure on the part of the Government.   Irritated by his failure, Valuiev launched a special campaign against the Mediators, attempting to force their subordination through the Provincial Boards.   Failing in bringing them under his influence or discharging them, he tried to decrease their number through the Provincial Boards, under the pretext of economy, naturally leaving out of the staff the most stubborn of them.   But the Peace Mediators were willing to sacrifice their material interests, and they declared that if it was a question of economy they were ready to receive a half or a third of their salary, provided their number remained intact, as otherwise they would not be able to accomplish the work within the appointed two years.   Thus Valuiev failed even in his last stratagem.   It was much easier for him to press upon the Governors, for they depended upon him to a great extent, and as a matter of fact those Governors who had honestly followed the Act of February 19 were either dismissed or " promoted " against their will to the Senate.   After all, however, the Act of February

19 was carried out in most cases in its correct way, thanks to the firmness of the Peace Mediators.

Yet in spite of this the changes in the spheres, which appeared to all as a sign of concessions to the reactionaries, the substitution of Lanskoy by Valuiev, Valuiev's policy, and also the bloody events and the suppression of the disturbances in the spring of 1861 — all these contributed to the general indignation of the *intelligentzia,* reflected partly in the tendencies of the press.

About that time the most radical organs were joined by another magazine, the *Russian Word,* founded in 1859 by Count Kushelev. During its first two years it had no significance, but from 1861 Pisarev, the twenty-year-old publicist who appeared in the literary arena with as much brilliance and force as Dobroliubov, set its tone. Dobroliubov died in November, 1861, at the age of twenty-five, having inscribed his name indelibly in the history of Russian literature. While the *Contemporary* was a political and social organ *par excellence,* and represented in those questions the most radical groups of the public, the *Russian Word* was the organ of the Nihilists, using that term in the sense introduced about that time by Turgeniev (in his novel, " Fathers and Children ").

One of that generation, still living with us, Prince P. A. Kropotkin, characterises that movement as " the struggle for individuality "; the foremost purpose was the liberation of the individual from the aged conventions and prejudices, from the chains of family, society, and religion. Pisarev considered the spread of natural science and the dissemination of the conclusions of science one of the main means leading to that aim, supposing not without reason that it would be the best weapon in the struggle with the prejudices and superstitions that had entangled the old order of Russian life. He attacked all authorities mercilessly, and for this reason, although he paid little attention to political questions, considering that the liberation of personality should in itself be a panacea against all evils in life, his destructive tendencies and passionate struggle with all sorts of authorities appeared more dangerous in the eyes of the Government than the socialistic tendencies of the *Contemporary*. The propaganda of the *Contemporary* and of the *Russian Word* began to arouse the apprehensions not only of the Government, but also of the moderate progressives among the social workers of that time.

As to the nobles, they were divided as before into two wings. One represented the oligarchic-pro-serfdom group, who now, after the abolition of serfdom, were mainly occupied with the question of the compensation which the gentry desired to receive from the Government in order to maintain its prevalence in the country. The representatives of that current saw such a compensation in the expansion of the political rights of the nobles only, without a corresponding expansion of the rights of other classes, for which reason we may call that current oligarchical. The other wing of the oppositional gentry represented a liberal-democratic current, largely based on the ideology of the progressive nobles who had manifested their ideas in the declarations of the Tver provincial committee, during the assemblies of the nobles in 1859, and through their delegates in the Editing Commissions. Their ideas were at that time popular largely among wide strata of the nobles-landowners in the industrial non black-soil provinces. Later N. K. Mikhailovsky gave them the characteristic name of " repentant nobles."

The oligarchic current found considerable support in the Ministry of Interior, whose head, Valuiev, was ready to extend some compensation to the nobles. Acting in this direction, he tried on one hand to change the projected *zemstvo*-self-government to accord with more aristocratic principles, and on the other hand he declared himself in 1863 in favour of granting the nobles some participation in the Government, if not of a legislative, at least of a consultative character. During the Polish uprising Valuiev presented a report to the Tzar, in which he asserted that in view of the loyal and patriotic sentiments of the Russian nobility, they should be given an advantage over the Polish nobility who were soliciting the restoration of the Constitution of 1815.

The views of the liberal-democratic group soon found a brilliant expression in the famous Tver incident which took place early in 1862.

The oppositional current of the liberal-democratic character was manifested in 1861, as it had been since the very beginning of the peasant-reform, most acutely in the province of Tver where the most conscious representatives of that movement were found. After the emancipation of the peasants the Russian nobles prepared to demand the organisation of land-credit for the nobles. The nobility of Tver considered that question inflated, properly speaking, conditioned by the fact that the peasant-reform had not been solved by paying the landowners at once the compensation sum which would be sufficient for the hiring of labour and for reasonable improvements. But if meliorative credit was to be considered necessary, it was necessary not only for the nobles, but for all agriculturists, of all classes, including the peasants. The Tver nobles regarded the discussion of that question possible only in conjunction with the other needs of the moment, which originated in the questions aroused, but not solved, by the peasant-reform. The Tver assembly found the following reforms necessary for the establishment of a regulated and well organised private credit: 1) The reorganisation of the financial system of the State in the sense that it should depend upon the people, not upon lawless wilfulness; 2) the establishment of independent and public courts; 3) the introduction of full publicity in all branches of the administration, without which there could be no confidence in the Government, and consequently in the firmness of the existing order of the State; 4) the abolition of antagonism among classes. Upon the realisation of these reforms, the question of credit, in the opinion of the Tver nobles, would be solved by itself, without the interference of the State and without the aid of the State treasury. The resolution of the Tver nobility further declared: " The nobles, being profoundly convinced of the necessity of doing away with inter-class antagonism, and desiring to dismiss every possibility of being reproached for forming an obstacle to the common good, declare before all Russia that they abdicate from all their class-privileges . . . and do not consider an infringement of their rights the obligatory allotment of the peasants with land in property, with the compensation of the landowners by the aid of the State."

The concluding point of that resolution was of particular significance, for it corresponded perfectly with the ideas of the most radical groups of the *intelligentzia,* as expressed by Chernyshevsky in his " Letters with no address," written by him a few weeks after the Tver assembly, but published only in 1874 in the periodical *Forward* issued abroad by Lavrov.

" The realisation of these reforms," declared the resolution of the Tver nobility, " is *impossible by means of governmental measures,* as our social life has been managed until now. Even supposing the full readiness of the Government for promulgating the reforms, *the nobles are deeply convinced that the Government is not in a position to accomplish them. The free institutions towards which these reforms lead must emanate from the people, otherwise they will be only a dead letter, and will place the public in a still more tense position.* For this reason the nobles *are not appealing to the Government with a request* for carrying out these reforms, but, considering its *incompetency* in this matter, they are merely indicating the road which it should enter for the salvation of itself and of the public. *This road is an assembly of men elected by the whole nation, without difference of class.*"

On such a radical platform the nobility now stood! In accordance with those resolutions an address was dictated to Alexander. It reiterated the need for an obligatory redemption, and in regard to the question of the class privileges, the nobles wrote: " By virtue of class privileges the nobles have been exempt until now from the fulfilment of the most important social duties. Sire, we consider it a deadly sin to live and make use of the benefits of the social order at the expense of other classes. The order of things is unjust, under which the poor man pays a ruble, while the rich man does not pay a copeck. This could have been tolerated only under the bondage-system, but now it puts us in the position of parasites, utterly useless to our country. We do not wish to enjoy any longer such a disgraceful privilege, and we do not accept the responsibility for its further existence. We most loyally beg your Imperial Majesty to allow us to take over part of the State taxes and obligations according to our status.

" Besides property privileges we enjoy the exclusive right of supplying men for the administration of the people; at present we consider the exclusiveness of this right lawless, and we beg that it be extended to all classes."

Indicating further the lack of mutual understanding between the Government and the public, the representatives of the latter thus concluded their requests:

" The general disorder serves as the best proof that the reforms demanded by the most urgent needs can not be realised in a bureaucratic way. *Even we do not pretend to speak for the whole nation, in spite of the fact that we stand nearer to it,* and we firmly believe that good intentions are in themselves insufficient not only for the satisfaction, but even for the indication of the national needs; we are convinced that all reforms remain unsuccessful because they are being undertaken without the opinion and the knowledge of the people.

" *The summons of men elected by all Russia* is the only

means for a satisfactory solution of the problems aroused, but not solved, by the Act of February 19."

Compare these resolutions and their tone with the declaration of Unkovsky, or with the resolutions of the same Tver nobility in 1859, and you will see how far during a year and a half that nobility had shifted to the left, and how much more aggressive its democratic tone had become. They emphasised that the question did not so much concern the promulgation of liberal reforms and the improvement of the existing order of things, as the way in which those reforms should be carried out, and to how great an extent the representatives — not of society, but of the people proper, would participate in carrying them out.

When the resolutions and the address were made public, Valuiev, who had constantly upheld the privileges and rights of the nobles, dared not even raise the question of the legality of such resolutions. Formally the nobles were entitled to the right of expressing their opinions about their needs, and although the declaration concerned the fundamental reorganisation of the order of the state, still it could be construed as emanating from the discussion of the position and needs of the nobility. But Valuiev found a way for punishing, if not the Tver nobles as a whole, at least those of their representatives of the most progressive elements, who had been elected Peace Mediators by the nobles and confirmed by the Senate. Those Peace Mediators were the initiators of the whole affair, and after the transmission of the address to the Tzar they came together at the regular Provincial Assembly of Peace Mediators, and declared that since the nobles had formulated their views, the assembled Mediators would in their further activity be guided not by the orders of the Government, but by the views of the public. In this case one could certainly find infringement of the order and of the service-duty. Valuiev utilised that circumstance, had the thirteen Peace Mediators who signed the declaration arrested, brought to Petrograd, and imprisoned in the fortress of SS. Peter and Paul. After a confinement of five months they were tried by the Senate and sentenced to two years' imprisonment with the deprivation of certain rights and privileges. The Governor-General of Petrograd, Prince Suvorov, interceded, however, before the Tzar, and the accused were set free; they were deprived of certain service-rights, but these were restored to all who later petitioned for them.

The Tver movement was echoed in other places. In general the idea of the need of constitutional guarantees and a representative order spread widely among the nobility and the *intelligentzia*. Herzen supported that idea in his *Bell* in special articles, and through the project of a general address proposed by Ogarev. One must say that Ogarev's address was considerably less democratic in its demands than that of the Tver nobility, due to the fact that Ogarev had intended to unite for signing the address different layers of the nobility, even the section which was more oligarchically than democratically inclined. Turgeniev, a close friend of the publishers of the *Bell,* disapproved of Ogarev's project, indicating that the *Bell* was wrong in attacking the Act of February 19, since the peasantry had accepted the Act as a symbol of their freedom and would consider its opponents their enemies. He objected both to the contents of the address and to the timeliness of the moment for its presentation. He recommended the working out of an adequate address for the moment when the statutes concerning the *zemstvo*-self-government would be published; by that time it appeared certain that Valuiev would in a great measure distort the projects of the Editing Commissions regarding local self-government.

Other persons of the liberal-democratic camp regarded the address with similar hostility. Kavelin, for instance, pointed out that the country had not as yet prepared the necessary elements for the realisation of a constitutional order, that the constitution would exist only on paper, or would become aristocratic, the more so since the matter was considered from the point of view of recompensing the landowners for their losses on account of the peasant-reform. Kavelin, as many others among the *intelligentzia* and among governmental circles, looked upon the *zemstvo* as a school for the preparation and training of political workers; he considered well organised local self-government as the only way out for the moment.

Samarin occupied a nearly similar position. He protested in a letter to Ivan Aksakov, the publisher of the newspaper *Day,* against the movement of writing constitutional addresses. Aksakov did not publish that letter for fear that Samarin would make many unnecessary enemies among the public; besides, Aksakov predicted that the addresses would have no success. It is curious that Samarin did not come out from the customary Slavophile opposition to any constitution, but, like Kavelin, claimed that *at that moment* the people were not ripe for a constitution, that " we cannot yet have a popular constitution, while a non-popular constitution, i.e., a rule of the minority acting without authority in the name of the majority, is a lie and a fraud." He argued that under such a constitution centralisation would develop, and Petrograd would stifle Russia. In his opinion Russia needed at that moment various liberatory reforms, the liberation of the public from the despotism of the administration, an independent judiciary, absolute religious toleration, freedom of the press, the reorganisation of the taxes in a direction favourable for the people, the development of education, the limiting of the unproductive expenditures of the Treasury and the Court — all these measures Samarin considered realisable under an autocratic régime.

We have seen what the tendencies of the peasants, of the nobility, and of the *intelligentzia* were in 1861. I wish to touch now upon the characterisation of the commercial-industrial *milieu*. The merchants and manufacturers of that period presented that "dark kingdom" which Ostrovsky depicted so strongly in his comedies (Dobroliubov wrote in this connection his famous critical article, "Dark Tzardom"). But even in that *milieu* there appeared many flashes of progressive ideas, and aspirations to get out of the darkness.

Even during the Crimean Campaign an extraordinary enlivenment took place in the commercial-industrial circles. The war contracts, the new issues of assignations which artificially inspired business-transactions, the liberal perspectives of the new reign — all these combined to account for the appearance of numerous undertakings, trade-companies, stock companies, etc. The Government, in contrast to the oppressions of the preceding reign, regarded them liberally, from the *laissez-faire* point of view. The spread of the movement was caused by the issue of large quantities of money by the Treasury, as I have mentioned; besides, by some strange financial combination, the Government decided at that moment to decrease the interest paid on deposits in governmental credit-institutions; naturally the deposits were withdrawn, and their owners tried to boom new undertakings in order to invest their capital. Still greater enlivenment was expected from the building of new railroads and from the completion of those already begun.

Commercial and industrial activities had developed suddenly with extraordinary force, out of proportion to the needs and actual possibilities of the moment; the flourishing of commerce and industry in a country which was utterly drained by the war, and had been economically bleeding, was abnormal and could not endure long: indeed, after about three years after the war a number of failures took place. Many undertakings which had attracted savings of long years began to collapse, because their conception had not been in accord with the actual needs of the country. Failures were enhanced by the universal industrial crisis of 1857–1858, brought about by changes in the means of production. Although the building of railroads began at that time, the Government gave the work over to foreign capitalists, so that Russian capitalists were forced to invest their capital in more or less ephemeral undertakings.

Naturally the very fact of transferring such colossal undertakings as the building of railroads into the hands of foreigners aroused dissatisfaction and opposition among industrial circles, and their aggravation grew under the influence of the crisis and the fall of the course of the paper-money. Hence we may understand the alliance that was manifested in the years of the crises between the oppositional merchants and the radical *intelligentzia,* and the sympathy which the commercial-industrial circles began for the first time to show for various organs of the progressive press.

The majority of the conscious representatives of the commercial-industrial circles sincerely welcomed the peasant-reform both because they had always been antagonistic towards the nobles, and also because capitalistic undertakings could not exist without a sufficient amount of free labour, and the abolition of serfdom undoubtedly promised a considerable amount of such labour in the near future.

The abolition of bondage, combined with the building of new roads of communication, created an advantageous conjuncture for Russian capitalism. Hence the conscious elements among the industrialists were progressively inclined and sympathised with the early liberal measures of the Government; but they soon grew disappointed in the activity of the Government, which in many cases was directed against their interests. From the end of the Fifties individual representatives of the commercial-industrial class began to appear, who astonished their contemporaries with their unexpected independence and enterprise not only in commercial but also in social affairs. For instance, Kokorev, a famous contractor who had manifested great enterprise and thoughtfulness in the peasant-question, actively interfered with the redemption-question, and was the first to point out those means which could be undertaken to aid the Government, in case it should decide to choose the road of obligatory redemption. Kokorev was closely connected with all the progressive and liberal representatives of the public and the press, and enjoyed a great prestige in the Moscow liberal circles. Katkov and Pogodin, and even Herzen in his *Bell,* praised him greatly. During the time of the first censorship-repressions in 1858, when the press was forbidden to discuss redemption and other problems, and the liberal Moscow censor, N. F. Kruze, was discharged the Moscow authors collected about fifty thousand rubles, not without the aid of Kokorev, for Kruze. The progressive merchants even in the provinces willingly contributed money for educational purposes, as for woman-gymnasia, and in other ways manifested their sympathy with enlightenment and progress.

CHAPTER XXV

THE Government watched with great alarm the development of the general opposition and radicalism; it was particularly worried by the revolutionary proclamations which appeared in 1861, some of which were printed abroad, and some, in Russia. The revolutionary spirit in those proclamations grew very rapidly; the first widely distributed sheet, the *Great Russian,* in whose composition Chernyshevsky, Serno-Solovievich, and other persons of the *Contemporary* circle took part, still stood on a liberal-democratic platform, and its contents were not as sharp as the resolution of the Tver nobility. But as early as the fall of 1861 there appeared a proclamation, "To the Young Generation," ascribed to the poet M. L. Mikhailov, which alongside with extremely naïve demands, such as the complete abolition of any police, secret as well as open, definitely threatened the Dynasty, declaring that if the Dynasty would not carry through the reforms that were needed, the question of its deposition would arise; it further asserted that Russia was in need not of a monarch, but of an elected, salaried Elder, who would serve the people — thus manifesting a republican spirit, although the establishment of a republic was not put forth as a practical task of the near future.

In 1862 appeared a proclamation, "Young Russia," which appealed directly for a bloody revolution, social as well as political, and which was written in an unusually ferocious, Marat-like tone. It divided all Russia into two parts: the party of the people, and the party of the Emperor, and as all those who did not sympathise with the revolution were considered as belonging to the party of the Emperor, they were to be slaughtered and exterminated everywhere; the axe and fire were advocated with enthusiasm. The author of that proclamation was a young student, Zaichnevsky, who was soon caught distributing the "Golden Charter" in the state of his father (a general), and was exiled to Siberia. The proclamation produced a grave impression, although the matter was not so serious, coming as it did from two young men behind whom there was no party. The Government also attributed to it an exaggerated importance, the more so since at that time numerous conflagrations occurred in Petrograd, which threw the population into a panic. It undoubtedly was the work of incendiaries who announced their purpose in advance, and devastated whole quarters. Some ascribed the conflagrations to students, some to Poles, but it is curious that not one of the incendiaries was caught. That it was the work of young revolutionists, is hard to believe; that Polish emissaries did the work appeared more probable subsequently, when in 1863 the cynic proclamation of General Mieroslavsky was discovered which recommended similar extreme measures for the increase of disturbances in Russia, since general unrest was considered an important prop for the success of the Polish insurrection. But no definite facts have ever been discovered for the confirmation of such propositions. Prince Kropotkin suggested in his memoirs that the conflagrations in many places (the city of Simbirsk and other Volga towns were burned) were the work of the reactionary party, as provocative acts. If his suggestion is correct, one must admit that the work was cleverly carried through, as the guilt for the conflagrations was in the end laid at the doors of Russian or Polish revolutionists, and this circumstance produced a natural rift in the progressive ranks. It doubtless served as the first cause for the turning away of a considerable part of Russian society from progressive aspirations, owing to the terrorising influence of such revolutionary actions.

The Government in its turn reacted upon those occurrences very severely. In the first place it began to arrest all who distributed the proclamations, and soon caught their alleged authors. M. L. Mikhailov, the author of "To the Young Generation," was arrested. The Government began to persecute those who had any relations with Herzen abroad, although before it had regarded visits to Herzen quite liberally (among those visitors had been persons of high standing in the Court circles). In 1861–1862 many such persons were arrested; among them were representatives of the progressive press: Chernyshevsky, Serno-Solovievich, and soon after, Pisarev (for writing a ferocious article for an underground publication). The Senate, before which they appeared for trial, sentenced them severely, often disregarding the law, and being guided exclusively by inner conviction. Chernyshevsky was sentenced to fourteen years of hard labour for the alleged authorship of a proclamation, "To the Landowners' Peasants"; the accusation was based on the testimony of a spy, and partly on the basis of a comparison between the handwriting of a certain note with Chernyshevsky's other manuscripts, although he argued that at least one-half of the letters of that note did not correspond with his characters. Serno-Solovievich was also sentenced to hard labour, and Pisarev was sentenced to two and a half years' imprisonment in the fortress; as a matter of fact he spent there four and a half years, for his preliminary imprisonment was not counted as a part of his penalty.

Not satisfied with these arrests, processes, and banishments, the Government pounced upon those organs in which the revolutionary tendencies had been expressed, or whose personnel had been compromised. The *Contemporary* and the *Russian Word* were discontinued for eight months. At the same time Aksakov's *Day* was discontinued, naturally only for its sharp tone, because Aksakov took no part in the revolutionary movement, and was hostile towards the revolutionary, and particularly the Nihilist, tendencies. After four months the *Day* was restored under the responsible editorship of Samarin, and then from the New Year Ivan Aksakov was again permitted to edit it, without any changes in the personnel or in the tendency of the paper. But the discontinuation of the *Contemporary* and the *Russian Word,* and the elimination of their leaders, had decisively influenced their further fate.

The main consequence of those events was the split in the ranks of progressive society. The public mood was characteristically expressed during the Petrograd conflagrations in the words of a liberal to Turgeniev: " Look what your Nihilists are doing: they are setting Petrograd on fire." The view that the " Nihilists " had become a menace and a danger not only to the Government, but to the very public, was shared by many. A sharp argument arose between the liberal *Russian Messenger* and the radical *Contemporary* and the Nihilistic *Russian Word.* When Katkov (the editor of the *Russian Messenger*) was criticised by Herzen for a virulent article, " To which Party Do We Belong? " in which he derided all existing parties, the *Russian Messenger* opened a ruthless campaign against the *Bell* and Herzen, ignoring his services in the matter of the peasant-reform. The quarrel between them grew particularly bitter in 1861, when Herzen, partly under the influence of Ogarev and later of Bakunin, who fled from Siberia and came to London, began to support the leaders of the Polish movement. He carried on definite negotiations with the Poles, and agreed under certain conditions to support their struggle against the Russian Government; in the eyes of Katkov and his readers this appeared as national treason, the more so since in the ardour of his campaign against the governmental repressions in Poland, Herzen published articles encouraging Russian officers and soldiers to desert their army and fight against the Government for the Polish cause.

All these manifestations of unrest made a very strong impression abroad, especially among circles connected with Russian finances through holding Russian securities. The foreign rumours about the approaching revolution in Russia, which threatened the position of her finances abroad, alarmed the Government; in a circular to all Russian ambassadors Prince Gorchakov, Minister of Foreign Affairs, interpreted the internal events in a way intended to calm the foreign bourses. In his customary picturesque manner Gorchakov wrote: " The expanse of the sea, as Racine says, cannot be calm. Such is the condition here. But the equilibrium is getting restored. When the billows rise, as they now have all over, it would be naïve to assert that the sea will immediately calm down. The main task is to put up dams where danger threatens the public peace and the interests and existence of the State. Toward this are directed our cares, *without deviating from the way which our august Tzar has chosen from the very day of his accession. Our motto is — neither weakness, nor reaction.* Russia begins to understand this motto. It requires time to have it acclimatised also in Europe, but I hope that the most prejudiced minds will be convinced of what is evident."

The Note was intended to quiet European circles interested in Russian financial conjunctures, by persuading them that in the first place there was no revolution as yet, and secondly that no reaction would follow, but reforms would be carried through for the peaceful continuation of Russia's social and economic life.

In the meantime the Polish movement developed *crescendo,* and in 1863 an armed uprising broke out in Warsaw.

The policy of Marquis Velepolsky had been carried on in Poland. He was a very distinguished statesman, but did not, however, win the sympathy of the dominating Polish parties. He tried to realise the policy recommended in 1858 by another Polish statesman, State-Secretary Enoch, who, inspired perhaps by Velepolsky, asserted that if Russia desired the pacification of Poland she should seek support in the middle class which was economically connected with Russian interests. For the satisfaction of the political demands of that group of the Polish population, Velepolsky proposed a series of more or less liberal reforms inclined mainly towards the restoration of national independence within the limits of the Kingdom, and of such institutions as were composed of local men; as a result of the re-establishment of Polish loyalty to the Tzar it was proposed to reintroduce the Constitution of 1815.

The Russian Government approved of that policy, but it did not satisfy either of the two predominating active revolutionary parties. One of them, the White, composed of the nobility, aspired further politically than Velepolsky (for the restoration of the Poland of 1772), while in the social respect it did not sympathise with the bourgeois-democratic reforms proposed by the latter. The other party, the Red, using demogogic means, demanded more radical reforms than those recommended by Velepolsky, and also required the restoration of the territory of 1772.

Velepolsky, in the capacity of Polish Minister of the Interior, had a number of collisions with the Russian vice-rois who were changed four times during two years (1861–1862). Finally Grand Duke Constantine was appointed to the post (at his own request), and he promoted Velepolsky to the position of Chief of the Civil Administration, which was equivalent to the post of a prime-minister. But by that time Velepolsky, on account of the struggle he had to carry on with both the aristocratic and the democratic parties, was greatly discredited in the eyes of the population.

In his struggle with his internal enemies Velepolsky closed up the " Agricultural Society " which was the centre of the active organisations of the nobles, and, on the other hand, desiring to moderate or somehow avert revolutionary actions on the part of the revolutionary Democrats, he declared a recruitment in the cities only, hoping in this way to eliminate all the young men of the lower urban classes, who formed the chief support of disturbances and of revolutionary street-riots in the cities. But his attempt to carry out that measure in Warsaw served as a signal for an open revolt.

The first act of the revolt was the annihilation of the sleeping unarmed Russian soldiers in the barracks. That circumstance aroused many in Russia against the Poles, including Aksakov, and particularly Katkov, who up to that time advocated the satisfaction of Velepolsky's demands — the granting of some independence to Poland within the limits of the " Congressuvka," i.e., the present ten Polish provinces (before 1915. Tr.) Aksakov had considered it desirable for the sake of her dignity for Russia to withdraw her troops from Poland and allow the Poles to take care of themselves. But after the treacherous slaughter of the Russian soldiers many Russian organs published indignant articles against Poland.

The irritation against Poland became still greater when the European Powers attempted to interfere in the matter, and even threatened armed intervention. The " skirmisher " in that case appeared to be, as before the Crimean Campaign, Napoleon III, who maintained active connections with the Polish emigrants. The threats of foreign intervention aroused an unexpected outburst of patriotism in Russia. A mass of patriotic addresses was sent by nobles, merchants, peasant- and town-societies, and even by Schismatics. The address of the last-named was composed by Katkov; it was he who inserted the famous phrase: " In the novelties of thy reign our antiquity is felt. . . ."

Those addresses greatly encouraged the Government and having produced a certain impression abroad helped it to repulse with dignity the attack of the foreign diplomatists. But at the same time the patriotic movement, merged with the anti-Nihilistic current and with the opposition to the revolutionary manifestations that took place in Petrograd in 1862, not only deepened the schism in the ranks of the *intelligentzia*, but produced a considerable shifting of all social elements to the right, so that the radicals remained isolated and weakened. Katkov, who had gone far to the right from the position he occupied in 1861, was triumphant and the hero of the day.

The prestige of Alexander's government was restored, and it was no longer afraid of the liberal and radical opposition which had completely lost its influence. The change in the public mood was expressed among other ways in the fall of the *Bell's* circulation: from two and a half to three thousand it fell to five hundred, and although it existed for five years, its circulation never rose above that number. Its existence became hardly noticeable.

In view of the conditions that had solidified during 1862–1863, a supposition might have risen that the triumphant reaction would discontinue the realisation of the proposed reforms. This did not take place, however. *The Government remained as before directly interested in the promulgation of the reforms.* Without some of them it could not technically administer the country, while others were necessary for the support and development of the cultural and economical life of Russia. In this respect the lesson taught by the Crimean Campaign still preserved its significance. Besides, the Government had to fulfil the programme announced by Gorchakov to the financial circles of Western Europe. The Government was to show its loyalty to the slogan: "Neither weakness nor reaction," and indeed, it undertook to continue the reforms even before the suppression of the Polish uprising. But now the democratic basis which appeared to unite in 1861 the Tver nobility and the *Contemporary* and Aksakov's *Day* was to a great extent eliminated from those reforms which were worked out in a purely bureaucratic way: in the depths of governmental chanceries, of special committees and commissions. True, the projects were given wide publicity and were discussed by competent persons and in the press, but not in the mood in which the peasant-reform was carried out.

Of the subsequent reforms the first was the financial, which resembled Speransky's Plan of 1809. During the years 1862–1866 V. A. Tatarinov, one of Alexander's most honest and able assistants, after a careful study abroad of various financial systems, had undertaken important measures for the regulation of the financial administration. His measures were first of all directed towards the eradication of the abuses which flourished in all departments in regard to the squandering of sums without any adequate accounting. Tatarinov had centralised the state economy in the hands of the Ministry of Finances which was to be responsible before the State Comptroller for all income and expenditures, and was to prepare a yearly budget-scheme for the approval of the State Council; up to 1862 the budget had not had any publicity. At the same time the so-called "single cash" system was established, by which all individual treasuries at various departments were abolished, and every copeck of income or expenditure had to pass through the Ministry of Finance, which also directed the assignations for single departments in accordance with the state budget. Tatarinov was placed at the head of the State Control, and that department was reorganised so that it might control the carrying out of the budget and also the fiscal accounts at the Capital and in the provinces. Local Controlling Chambers were formed, independent of the administration — of the governors and of the chiefs of separate departments.

Alongside with these reforms for the improvement of the financial apparatus another important measure was undertaken — the establishment of the State Bank; on one hand it supplanted the old credit-institutions which proved quite clumsy for the developing economic life, and on the other hand it was to encourage and finance commercial-industrial undertakings.

Finally, in 1863, the wine-contracts were abolished. The beverage income had constituted the lion share of the budget; the Government had been wavering between two systems for exploiting it, the direct fiscal monopoly of the manufacture and sale of the beverages, or the system of contracts. The abuses of the first system forced Kankrin to prefer the system of contracts which had been abolished by Guriev. But the system of contracts demoralised the officials just as much, as the contractors bribed the whole local administration, so that it was a generally known fact that every local official received two salaries — one from the Government, and another, larger than the first, from the contractors. The Government tolerated that system, being aware of the insufficient salary it paid its functionaries. In 1863 the sale of wine was permitted to all; every vessel of wine or vodka was taxed with a special excise, and every wine-house with a special license-tax. The taxes were collected by local excise institutions, whose personnel was well remunerated and consisted of educated persons.

Parallel with these financial reforms some inprovements were made in the personnel of the financial administration. In place of incapable ministers, like Brock and Kniazhevich, the young and capable M. K. Reitern, whose appointment aroused great hopes among society, now stood at the head of the Ministry. Those hopes were ultimately disappointed, but he did introduce some improvement in the management of the finances. The honest, gifted, and energetic administrator, K. K. Grote, was at the head of the new Excise Department.

Next to financial reform came that of the universities, in 1863. During the first years of the new reign the oppressions introduced in the reign of Nicolas were removed, and although the old statute of 1835 remained intact, the students enjoyed actual freedom and independence; the old Curators were supplanted with humanistic and enlightened persons who permitted them to have their organisations and meetings, and publish their own periodicals free from censorship. Private persons, unclassified students, and even women, were admitted into the universities. The awakened society, not too rich in intellectual forces, placed great hopes in the university youth, and the position of the students was quite honourable. They were flattered by such an attitude, and became imbued with social aspirations; they took active part in establishing Sunday Schools, popular libraries, and similar educational institutions.

In 1860, Pisarev, a new prophet of the young generation, appeared. He demanded that youth be allowed to speak in public, to write and publish their thoughts, in order " to shake up with their original scepticism those stale objects, that dilapidated junk " called " general authorities." " This is the final word of our young camp," wrote Pisarev,—" what can be broken, we should break: whatever will stand the blow — is of use; whatever will be smashed to pieces — is rubbish; at any rate, smash right and left; no harm may come out of this."

The spirit of criticism, self-will, and youthful pugnaciousness toward the professors was not slow in appearing. It became customary in the classes to applaud, to whistle, to hiss. Various demands were presented to the professors. In 1861 one of the first revolutionary proclamations, the one composed by Mikhailov, was directly addressed " To the Young Generation." In Kazan, as I have mentioned, after the Bezdna catastrophe the students led by the young Professor Shchapov had a demonstrative mass served for the souls of the peasants killed by the soldiers. At the convocation of the Petrograd university, February 8, 1861, the students created a scandal when the address announced by Kostomarov about the recently deceased Constantine Aksakov was forbidden by the Minister.[1]

---

[1] To this day Russian revolutionary students are fond of a song which has a refrain about the *nagaika*, i.e., the Cossack-whip:
" Ah, little nagaika, little nagaika, my little nagaika —
Thou danced on our backs on February the Eighth."— Tr.

In a word, the university showed, as a correct barometer, to use Pirogov's expression, the stormy tendencies that had accumulated by that time among society.

The Government, alarmed, attempted to check this movement by strict measures. The weak, human Minister Kovalevsky was dismissed, and his place was taken by an extreme obscurantist, Admiral Putiatin, recommended by Count Stroganov, the same Stroganov who was Curator in Moscow during the Forties, and who now stood at the head of the reactionary government circle. Under the chairmanship of Stroganov special temporary rules were worked out for the universities and were sanctioned by the Tzar on May 31, 1861. These rules forbade all embryos of corporative life among the students, even the uniform dress; [2] they forbade the issue of poverty-certificates, the exemption of poor students from tuition fees and any gathering without the permission of the authorities. Curator Delianov, who was then a liberal and had attempted with the aid of Kavelin and other popular professors to work out in co-operation with student-delegates reasonable and feasible regulations, was discharged immediately after Kovalevsky, to be supplanted by General Philipson, formerly Attaman (chieftain) of the Cossack troops. In the fall, when the new rules were to be put into practice, grandiose student-riots took place, which resulted in mass-expulsions from the University, in a procession of the students through the city towards the home of Curator Philipson, in a collision with the troops near the University buildings, and in the imprisonment of three hundred students in the fortress. Simultaneously the Moscow students rioted and marched on the streets. But there the police instigated the common people against them, by spreading a rumour that the nobles made

[2] During the last two reigns, however, the wearing of a uniform has been made obligatory for students, under the threat of penalty for being discovered in civilian garb. The motive for this policy has been the Government's desire to facilitate for its agents the task of recognising "suspicious" elements on the street and in public places.— Tr.

disturbances because they desired the re-establishment of serf-dom. The students were cruelly beaten up, many were arrested, and later expelled from the University. Alexander II was at that time in Crimea with the Empress, who was ill. He was greatly alarmed by these occurrences, hastened back to Petrograd, and expressed his dissatisfaction both with the actions of Count Putiatin and with those of the Petrograd Governor-General Ignatiev. The former gave way to A. V. Golovnin, who was recommended by Grand Duke Constantine, and proved to be one of the most enlightened and well-intentioned Ministers of Education in Russia; Ignatiev was supplanted by the human and good-hearted Prince A. A. Suvorov, who treated the youth very sympathetically. Golovnin at once began to work out a new statute. Professor Kavelin, dismissed with four other professors a short time before for having protested against the measures of Putiatin, was now commissioned to go abroad for the study of university conditions in various countries. Prominent scholars, professors, and administrators took part in the preparation of the new statute.

The project worked out in the Ministry was printed and sent out to various competent persons in Russia and abroad. The press took active part in the discussion of the question. The opinion of Stroganov about the transformation of the universities into exclusive aristocratic institutions was rejected by all. The general views were divided between two systems. One was represented by the historian Kostomarov and by Baron Korf, and it advocated the view that universities were to give the students only knowledge, while education proper should be implanted at home and in the lower schools. The other system was represented by the friends and disciples of the late Granovsky — Chicherin, Kavelin, Katkov, and other liberal professors, who insisted that the universities should have a general educational mission for the young generation. Kavelin brought from abroad the unanimous opinion of foreign authorities in favour of a corporative constitution for the universities. The project was presented to the State Council, after a preliminary discussion by a special commission under the chairmanship of Count Stroganov. The progressive principles were considerably modified and curtailed in that commission, and in such a form it passed the State Council and was sanctioned by Alexander II on June 18, 1863.

The new statute restored the university-autonomy within the limits of the statute of 1804, although it preserved some paragraphs of the statute of 1835, which concentrated a considerable discretionary power in the hands of the Curator. The Statute greatly limited the entrance of outsiders. The corporation of professors received autonomy in the form of a self-governing council of the faculties, but the students were allowed no legal opportunity for the organisation of their own social and academic life. Yet as long as Golovnin remained at the head of the Ministry, his liberal policy contributed to the establishment of some order and peace in the universities.

The secondary schools were also reformed at that time. The gymnasia were divided into classic and " real "; in the first Greek was added to the instruction of Latin, and the preparation was intended mainly for the universities; the " real "-gymnasia were to prepare their students chiefly for higher technical schools. The Statute was sanctioned November 19, 1864, but its realisation was hampered by lack of funds and of Greek instructors.

Here we should say a few words about the secondary schools for women. Before the accession of Alexander no open schools for women had existed; they were taught either at home or in some closed Institutes which were organised according to an antiquated system dating back to the days of Catherine. When, on the basis of the emancipation-movement, the struggle for individualism began, the woman-question became one of the most burning problems. In the press, at provincial assemblies, in university circles — everywhere was discussed the necessity of emancipating woman from her dependent and secluded position. In 1859 schools began to open for women in cities where the inhabitants were able to collect from voluntary contributions a more or less sufficient sum. Those woman-gymnasia, at first of four grades, and later of six, were placed under the patronage of the Empress Maria Alexandrovna, and their management was conducted not by the Ministry of Education, but by the Department of the Institutions of Empress Maria (formed by Nicolas I after the death of his mother, Maria Feodorovna, the widow of Paul I). The chief administrator of the woman-gymnasia was the enlightened and distinguished pedagogue, N. A. Vyshnegradsky. The programme of those schools was slightly shorter than that of the " real "-schools.

With the emancipation of the peasants arose the urgent need for the organisation of primary education which up to that time had existed only in a few estates of rich and philanthropically inclined landowners, and partly among the State-peasants. In some places church-parish schools appeared to exist, but in the prevailing majority of cases they existed only on paper. The question about popular schools had been discussed very actively among the *intelligentzia* from the end of the Fifties. With the aid of Professor Pavlov numerous Sunday Schools supported by students, progressive army-officers, women of wealthy families, and so forth, were established in Kiev in 1859 and then in many other cities. During the years of stormy opposition, 1861–1862, in several places the Sunday Schools became the arena for largely naïve political propaganda, which resulted in the Government's decree in 1862, closing all Sunday Schools until the issue of special rules concerning them.

At the same time the idea persistently circulated among society about founding special societies for the spread of learning among the people. One of the projects belonged to I. S.

Turgeniev. Special Committees of Learning were established at the Free Economic Society in Petrograd and at the Agricultural Society in Moscow; those committees were of great use in the work of popular education both through collecting money for schools and through publishing and distributing popular books.

With the appointment of Golovnin as Minister of Education his Ministry began to work on a statute for primary education. Two projects were presented before the State Council, one of which proposed the management of the primary schools by the Ministry of Education, and the other recommended the organisation of local committees in the provinces and districts for the maintenance of those schools. The Chief of the Second Department of H. M.'s Chancery, Baron Korf, suggested to the State Council that it hand over the management of the projected schools to the proposed *zemstvo*-institutions. The State Council decided to organise special councils in the provinces and districts, into which representatives of the *zemstvo* were to be invited. The Statute was sanctioned June 14, 1864.

CHAPTER XXVI

THE abolition of serfdom, as I have already mentioned, caused many changes in the existing system of local administration which had been closely connected with the bondage-right. The landowner had been the sole and unlimited representative of the administrative power on his estate, and most of the police and judiciary positions in the district and provincial administration had been filled by nobles. Such a system could be tolerated only under bondage conditions, but when the Crimean Campaign had revealed the sores in the old order of things, the Government saw the necessity of reorganisation to improve the national and social life of the country through the participation of all capable and living forces of society. Such were the principles expressed by Miliutin, chairman of the commission for the reform of the local administration, in a memorandum presented to and approved by the Tzar at the very beginning of the reforms. Miliutin's plan was: *To give local self-government more confidence, more independence, and more unity.* Declarations of some of the provincial committees, particularly of the non black-soil industrial provinces, followed, emphasising and developing the suggestions of the delegates of the first summons which had indicated the necessity of establishing self-government on an all-class basis, in accordance with the new civil order of the country now liberated from bondage. On those foundations Miliutin's commission prepared the first sketch of the *zemstvo*-institutions.

The same commission was to work out a general police-reform and the organisation of new Peace-institutions for carrying out the peasant-reform. Its work was far from completed, when Lanskoy and Miliutin were dismissed, and the new Minister, Valuiev, assumed the chairmanship of that commission. We know that Valuiev was opposed to the principle of class-equality, and strove to support and strengthen the prestige and power of the nobility, which had been shaken by the abolition of serfdom. Yet he dared not set aside the principle of class-equality altogether, but he tried to give the nobles prevalence in the zemstvo-institutions, by lowering the census for nobles in comparison with that of landowners of other classes, and by increasing the number of delegates from private estates over the number of delegates from peasant-communities. But his amendments were rejected by the State Council, owing to their criticism by Baron Korf who pointed out that they would arouse dissatisfaction and irritation among the public. Although the representation of the population was finally based on a curial system, still it was more just and democratic than the one suggested by Valuiev. Valuiev had intended to give electoral rights to nobles who possessed land equal in size to fifty maximum-peasant-allotments of a given region, while the census for landowners of other classes was to be equal to one hundred such allotments. The State Council instituted a uniform census for all categories — the equivalent of one hundred allotments.

The electors of the zemstvo-delegates were divided into three curiæ: 1) the curia of private landowners, 2) the curia of village-communities, and 3) the curia of townspeople whose participation in the elections required the possession of real estate in the town of a certain value (three thousand and six thousand rubles), or membership in a merchant-guild, or the possession of commercial-industrial establishments with a turnover of not less than six thousand rubles yearly. For the number of delegates to be sent by each curia to the district-zemstvo-assembly Valuiev had intended to institute a preference in favour of the private landowners, proposing that while the village-communities should elect one delegate from every four thousand allotments, the private landowners should be entitled to one delegate from a tract of land equivalent to only two thousand allotments. The State Council equalised all curiæ to a requirement of three thousand allotments for the election of one delegate, and of an equivalent amount of property for townspeople. It was further decided that the total number of delegates elected by one curia could not exceed the total number of delegates elected by the other two curiæ combined.

The structure of the *zemstvo*-institutions was proposed in the following way. The *zemstvo* organs of the province as well as of the district were divided into those of arrangement and of execution. The first were instituted as *zemstvo* assemblies of delegates elected by the curiæ; the number of the delegates to the district-assembly varied according to the size of the district, from fourteen to over a hundred; the provincial assemblies were composed of provincial delegates elected by the district assemblies. The presidents of the district-assemblies were marshals of district nobility, and presidents of the provincial assemblies — provincial marshals of nobility. The district assemblies were to manage economic affairs of the district, the provincial — the economic matters that concerned the whole province. The district-assemblies were made completely independent of the provincial. The assemblies of both categories were to convene once every year for the determination of a general plan of management, for the confirmation of the budget with the right to tax real estate and the commercial-industrial establishments within their region, and finally for the election of executive organs which managed the entire business, and for the examination and approval of the yearly accounts presented by those executive organs, called *Zemstvo*-Boards, provincial and district, each composed of a chairman and several members. The delegates were to be elected for three years, and the

Boards had to be elected for the same term by the assemblies. As to the competency of the *zemstvo*-institutions, Miliutin, not wishing to expand the circle of affairs under their jurisdiction too much, insisted that in their sphere only they enjoyed full independence from the local administration-authorities, and were subject only to the Senate, while the Governors simply had the right of supervising the legality of their transactions. At first it was proposed to hand over to the *zemstvo* all those matters that had been managed before the Emancipation by the local administration, of which the most important were: the construction and maintenance of roads of communication, matters of public welfare, i.e., hospitals and asylums, and alimentary affairs. Upon the suggestion of Baron Korf, the power of the *zemstvo* was expanded to include caring for the spread of local education, for the construction of churches and of prisons, for the development and organisation of medical and veterinary aid in the districts and provinces, and in general for the benefits and needs of the local population, of the village-interests, commerce and industry.

Such were the general features of the structure and powers of the all-class local self-government organs created by the act of January 1, 1864.

They were introduced at first only in thirty-three provinces, and even there gradually, beginning in the year 1865. By the first of January, 1866, they were introduced in nineteen provinces, by January 1, 1867 — in nine more provinces, totaling twenty-eight; during 1867, in two more, and after January 1, 1868, in four more; the Bessarabia Region was included in the *zemstvo*-provinces.

The public and the press placed great hopes in the *zemstvo*-self-government and many exaggerated its significance, although the Act in itself aroused much criticism. Most pessimistic was the opinion of I. Aksakov who refused to see in it any self-government, but considered it as one of the forms of calling elected *zemstvo*-men to the service of the State. He greeted only the principle of class-equality put through in the *zemstvo*-act. The most optimistic view was expressed by K. D. Kavelin in a series of articles which appeared in Korsh's *St.-Petersburg News*. He saw in the *zemstvo*-institutions a necessary and excellent school for the preparation of men of all classes for participation in state-affairs under the future representative order; he ardently appealed to all progressive and enlightened persons to take part in the new institutions.

However, the *zemstvo*-institutions had to begin their activity under very unfavourable circumstances, for in 1866 reaction was triumphant throughout Russia. They were regarded with hostility by all governmental organs — local and central, and were soon limited in their right of taxing commercial and industrial establishments; then the publicity and accessibility of *zemstvo*-assemblies was restricted, and the freedom of their discussions limited, in view of which many precious and worthy *zemstvo*-workers soon lost interest in the work, and withdrew from the personnel of the *zemstvo*-boards and assemblies.

Chronologically, the next capital reform of the Sixties was brought about in the judiciary, through the issue of new statutes on November 20, 1864. To grasp the enormous importance of that reform, one must remember what the old courts and court-proceedings had been in the pre-reform days. " Black in the courts with black injustice," thus on the eve of the Crimean Campaign the poet-patriot of the Slavophil camp — A. S. Khomiakov, characterised Russia. " The old court! " I. S. Aksakov who had served personally on many pre-reform judiciary institutions, wrote in the Eighties — " at the very memory of it my hair stand up on end, a frost rasps my skin! . . ."[1]

From the time of Catherine the judiciary remained un-

[1] From his editorial in the news-paper *Russ*, February 15, 1884.

changed, although the need for its fundamental reorganisation had been admitted by Alexander I and by Nicolas I, and during those two reigns a number of memoranda, and projects were prepared on the question by such men as Speransky, Nicolas Turgeniev, Dashkov, Bludov, and others. They were unable to shake the firmly established " justice," as long as the bondage system existed, and the nobles prevailed in all grades of state-service and in all state-institutions, central and local. Even under Alexander II the measures undertaken for the improvement of the judiciary at the beginning of his reign enjoyed no success until after the fall of bondage. The judiciary reform progressed in a rapid tempo only after 1861, when it was decided to have no historical connection with the previous structure, but to begin anew, on the basis of new principles founded on juridical science and on the experience of civilised countries. The chief vices of the old order were the class-differentiation of the cases, the multitude of court-instances, the complete dependence of the court on the administration, the archaic inquisitorial process in criminal cases, the secrecy of the proceedings, the declaration of the verdict without arguments of the parties or attorneys, the ignorance of the judges and their meagre remuneration which was the cause of flagrant bribery and abuses, and — in a word — the domination of force over justice and truth. In truth it was an " abomination of desolation in the holy place " (Aksakov).

After the abolition of serfdom and the appointment of Zamiatnin instead of Count Panin to the post of Minister of Justice, the work of the fundamental reform was entrusted to a special committee of enlightened and brilliant jurists. An extremely perseverant and devoted person, State-Secretary of the State Council, S. I. Zarudny, was the life of the work. The main principles were worked out and confirmed by the Tzar in 1862, and a hurried preparation of judiciary statutes on the basis of juridical science was begun. Into the foundation of the new structure were laid the principles of non-class composition of the courts, equality of all citizens before the law, absolute independence of the court from the administration, for which purpose judges were appointed for life, received large salaries, and were chosen from among enlightened and juridically-educated persons.

Trials were to be open and public, with the active participation of both sides; accusations were to be formulated and supported by the procurator, while the interests of the defendant were to be upheld by a sworn attorney. The number of instances was considerably shortened: two for civil cases, and one for common criminal cases. A jury court was established, the jurymen to be chosen in turn from a list of full right citizens who had reached a certain age. The jury system was copied from the English courts. Only in case the jury court acted against the established forms or order of proceedings, or if the law was incorrectly applied by the judge, could the parties appeal to the Senate which, if it found the complaint just, might order a new trial of the case by the same or another court, but at any rate by a new jury. Unfortunately from the very beginning cases of state-treason, of certain official misdemeanours, and also press-cases were eliminated from the competency of the juries, and the general and political importance of the latter was thus diminished.

The independence of the judges was somewhat curbed by the fact that although they could not be removed from office by the authorities, there still remained the system of rewards and presentation of ranks and orders, so that the administration (the minister of justice) had some power over the more pliable judges. Later, during the period of reaction, the Government tried to shake the principle of the permanence of office of judges, and to increase the number of cases eliminated from the jurisdiction of juries (from 1866 on).

Alongside with this general judiciary reform which aspired

indeed for a "fast, just, and merciful" court (the words of Alexander II), there were introduced justices of peace for petty cases, elected by the *zemstvos* and by municipal *dumas*.

One may say without hesitation that in spite of the restriction of some of the principles originally instituted, the judicial reform was the most radical and in principle the most consistent of all the great reforms of the Sixties.[2]

Unfortunately the new courts as well as the *zemstvo*-institutions began to operate in 1866 at the beginning of a period of prolonged reaction, which mutilated and distorted the judicial statutes of Alexander II, through the so-called "novelles," i.e., partial modifications and amendments which were subsequently enacted as permanent laws.

The last of the great reforms of the Sixties was the new legislation about the press, issued in 1865 in the form of "Temporary Rules." Nowhere during the first ten years of Alexander's reign did the Government and the Tzar show so much vacillation as in the question of censorship regulation and the position of the press. In any case, the liberation of the press from censorship appeared to the Government as the most dangerous of the reforms which it considered necessary

[2] Maxime Kovalevsky (recently deceased), the greatest authority on Russian institutions, illuminates the impotence of the Russian juries in his article on the "Reforms of Alexander II":

"Not every person is allowed to become a member of the jury; to enjoy this privilege a man must be a land-proprietor possessing not less than one hundred desiatins, or real property valued at five thousand rubles. . . . No wonder that our jurymen show, as has been said, a great severity in judging all offences against property. The requirements of the law have been even increased during the reign of Alexander III, and the growing class of proletarians has been in this way more and more deprived of any participation in the performance of this civil duty. At the same time the Government has kept in its own hands the power of eliminating from the lists any class of people it considers untrustworthy. . . ." M. Kovalevsky, *Russian Political Institutions.*— TR.

to introduce. As early as 1855 Valuiev, later one of the most persistent and cunning oppressors of the press, asserted in his famous memorandum, " A Russian's Meditation," that before all other reforms it was necessary to grant some freedom to the press. Indeed, at the very beginning of the reign the Buturlin-Committee was abolished, and Baron Modest Korf, one of its leaders and initiators, became one of the most consistent liberals in the governmental circles. New magazines were permitted to appear with widened programmes and with the right to discuss political and social questions. Upon the rescript of November 20, 1857, the press was permitted to discuss the peasant-question and the abolition of bondage. Soon, as we remember, there came a pause, a change in the Government's mood, but it passed in a few months. In 1859 Alexander II said to the censor, Academic Nikitenko, that he was opposed to oppression of the press, but that he could not allow any " evil tendencies. . . ."

Actually the freedom of the press grew and developed until the year of 1861, when it manifested in its radical organs an outspoken revolutionary tendency. The progress made in the development of the public thought in six years — from 1855 to 1861 — was unbelievable. At that time the stupid obscurantist Putiatin was supplanted by the liberal Golovnin, who began to work on a new censorship-statute, and at the same time tried to influence diplomatically the editors of the magazines. But in the governmental spheres a reaction had already begun, and Minister Valuiev obstructed Golovnin on every step, and complained of his levity toward the press. The matter of repressions and punitive measures against the press was transferred to Valuiev, while Golovnin continued to manage the general censorship and to work on the reform in the commission of Prince D. A. Obolensky. Then came the conflagrations of 1862, and new rules concerning " warnings " and " discontinuations " of periodicals were issued for the restraining of the press. Those rules were at once applied to the radical Petrograd magazines and to the non-radical, but too sharp, *Day* of Aksakov. Upon the request of Golovnin the whole censorship question was transferred to the Ministry of Interior, where a new commission for its solution was formed under the chairmanship of the same Obolensky. That commission regarded the issue of a new censorship statute untimely and dangerous; instead it introduced in 1865 as an experiment " temporary rules," which continued to exist without considerable changes for forty years.

According to those rules preliminary censorship was abolished for books of a certain volume (not less than ten sheets for original, and not less than twenty for translated books); for periodicals the question of exemption from preliminary censorship was left to the discretion of the Minister of Interior, and for the first time it was decided to introduce that freedom only in Petrograd and Moscow. The permit for publication of new periodicals was also left to the discretion of the Minister of Interior; among the punitive measures those introduced by the temporary rules of 1862 were retained.

Such was the extremely moderate freedom granted to the press by the reform of 1865. Of all the reforms of the Sixties this was undoubtedly the most parsimonious and cautious. Yet on September 1, 1865, the progressive papers, appearing for the first time without preliminary censorship, expressed their joy in eloquent, grateful articles. Soon, however, they were bitterly disappointed.

The low spirits, the prostration and the even reactionary mood, into which certain circles of society had fallen after the revolutionary outbreaks of 1862 and after the Polish revolt, had gradually passed away under the influence of the renewed progressive activity of the Government. In circles of the nobility constitutional aspirations again appeared, though in a more reserved tone, and far less democratic than the Tver declarations of 1862. The assembly of nobles at Moscow in the year 1865, mostly aristocratically-oligarchically inclined, accepted an address to the Tzar, edited by Katkov. In that address they begged the Tzar "to crown the edifice of his reforms" with the summons of representatives of the Russian land, by which they understood mainly the representatives of the nobles. Alexander II regarded that address unfavourably, and in a rescript to Valuiev he indicated that the right of initiative in State reorganisations belonged to the Tzar alone, and that such addresses on the part of the nobles might only hinder him in carrying out the reforms he had decided on.

The radical part of the public was at that time, as we have seen, completely deranged; yet partly under the influence of the practical ideals pointed out in Chernyshevsky's novel, " *What is to be done?* " various circles and associations began to arise among the young generation which purported to fulfil the ideals preached in that novel. One enterprising Moscow circle, led by Ishutin, was preparing for a broad and definite propaganda of communistic ideas, but before it had time to start its activity, one of its members, a cousin of Ishutin, Karakozov, an unbalanced and probably abnormal fellow, decided against the persuasions of his comrades to assassinate Alexander II. Karakozov came to Petrograd, and fired a pistol at the Tzar, when the latter was entering his carriage after a stroll with his daughter in the Summer Garden. The bullet missed its mark, because a commoner, Komissarov, who happened to stand near by, pushed Karakozov's hand.[3] That event made an indelible impression on Alexander and on the public, and the reactionaries and enemies of the democratic reforms made skilful use of that impression. The period of reforms came to an end before some of them had been carried out; the municipal reform was accomplished in 1870, and that

[3] Komissarov was promoted to the rank of nobleman by the Tzar. — Tr.

of universal military service, in 1874. A stubborn and lasting reaction began in April, 1866, and lasted with a few short pauses till 1905. The reforms which had been accomplished suffered mutilation during that reaction; not only radicals, but even the liberally inclined social groups underwent various persecutions and restrictions. This circumstance did not, however, destroy either the great historical significance of the promulgated reforms, or the preparation and internal development of that socio-political process which forms the contents of Russian history in the nineteenth century, and has not as yet been completed. The importance of the great reorganisations of the period of reforms is such that the dividing line they have placed between the pre-reform and post-reform Russia is impassable and ineraseable; no reaction in the Government's and social circles could have returned Russia to her pre-reform position. The reaction which started in 1866 brought much evil to the country: it disturbed the peaceful course of the development of society and of the people; by driving all opposition into the " underground " it provoked an underground revolutionary movement which acquired a more and more irreconcilable and terroristic character; but the reaction was powerless to restore the old régime, for that régime was irrevocably destroyed with the abolition of serfdom and with the development of democratic ideas among the public. The reaction could cripple and distort the new order, but it could not bring back the old.

The democratic principles of the new all-class order have found a favourable soil in the Russian people. In a short time they became so deeply rooted that they proved strong enough to stand a half century-long attack at the hands of the reaction which came immediately after their declaration. The country would perish, and the great State become disrupted because of internal dissensions and a lasting, decomposing struggle, rather than give up those principles; during fifty years, whenever the reaction weakened through internal or external causes, the inner course of the socio-political process manifested its rights at once and developed with a multiplied force along the road indicated during the period of the great reforms of the Sixties.

PART THREE

CHAPTER XXVII

THE attentate of Karakozov, on April 4, 1866, produced a shocking impression upon Alexander and upon the public. They refused to believe that the attempt was planned and carried out by an individual, and they ascribed it to the work of some powerful and fiendish organisation, of some unknown secret society. General M. N. Muraviov, famous for the cruelty and ruthlessness with which he had suppressed the recent Lithuanian uprising,[1] was appointed head of the committee for the investigation of the affair; but in spite of his vigorous efforts to reveal the alleged conspiracy, and in spite of his unscrupulous actions and orders which terrorised the peaceful citizens, especially college-students and authors, no conspiracy against the life of the Tzar was discovered. The insignificant circle of Ishutin at Moscow had nothing to do with regicide ideas; as a matter of fact the members of that circle tried to dissuade Karakozov from his intention, and considered him mad and abnormal. But the Government made use of the existence of that circle, and of the fact that Karakozov had belonged to it, to throw a shadow of suspicion upon the tendencies of the young generation, upon the state of affairs in the universities, and upon the direction of the Ministry of Education which was then managed by the enlightened and liberal A. V. Golovnin. The court circles did not miss the opportunity to utilise the impressions of those events upon Alexander, and they directed their reactionary blows first of all at the Ministry of Education, even before Muraviov's investigation had come to an end.

[1] In the revolutionary parlance he has been known as the "Hangman."— TR.

Karakozov's attentate took place on April 4, and on April 5, during the session of the Committee of Ministers, the Super-Procurator of the Holy Synod, Count D. A. Tolstoy, attacked as not sufficiently Russificatory the policy of Golovnin in the Northwest; this partial criticism soon became a general attack, ind Golovnin, convinced that he had lost the Tzar's confidence, was forced to resign and leave his place to Count Tolstoy.

Tolstoy had by that time a thoroughly established reputation. In 1859 he made known his pro-serfdom ideas in a sharp criticism of the works of the Editing Commissions; Alexander said of that criticism, that its author either did not understand anything about the peasant-question, or was a person of evil intentions. This did not prevent Tolstoy from becoming Super-Procurator of the Synod in 1864, and Minister of Education in 1866, with definite reactionary plans.

If Muraviov did not succeed in discovering a conspiracy against the life of the Tzar, he and his friends from among the court-reactionaries succeeded in connecting the unrest and fermentation in the minds of the young generation with the policy of the Ministry of Education and with the tendencies of the radical press. The *Contemporary* and the *Russian Word* were closed forever; the attitude of the Government towards the young generation was characteristically expressed in the Imperial rescript on the name of Prince P. P. Gagarin, President of the Committee of Ministers, dated May 13, 1866. "Providence has willed," the rescript read, "to reveal before the eyes of Russia what consequences we may expect from aspirations and ideas which arrogantly encroach upon everything sacred, upon religious beliefs, foundations of family life, property right, obedience to the law, and upon respect for the established authorities. My attention is now turned to the education of the youth. I have given instructions to the end that the education be directed in the spirit of religious truths, of respect to right of property, and of keeping the fundamental principles of public order, and that in all schools there should be forbidden the open or secret teaching of those destructive conceptions which are hostile to all conditions of moral and material well-being of the people." The rescript invited the parents to co-operate with the Government in its activity; it further indicated the necessity for guarding the existing order of things from all sorts of destructive attempts emanating from certain pernicious organs of the press, and from private persons (some of whom occupied State positions, the rescript declared). " It is necessary," the paper concluded, " to put a stop to the repeated attempts for arousing hostility among various classes, particularly against the nobility and the landowners, in general, in whom the enemies of public order naturally see their direct opponents."

The reaction that began in 1866 affected not only the Ministry of Education; after the resignation of Golovnin other resignations followed. Prince V. A. Dolgorukov, Chief of the Gendarmes, resigned, among others. He could not be suspected of liberalism, but after the event of April 4, he admitted that he was too old for his position. He was supplanted by a young court-general, Count P. A. Shuvalov, who soon became the soul of the reaction in governmental spheres; he was joined in the Committee of Ministers by Valuiev and by Minister of State Domains, General Zelenoy. They formed a very influential triumvirate. Prince A. A. Suvorov, the human and tactful governor-general of Petrograd, was also dismissed and succeeded by General Trepov who was appointed Supreme Chief of Police in the Capital; he had already manifested his abilities as Supreme Chief of Police in the Kingdom of Poland.

Shuvalov, Valuiev, and Zelenoy presented a project to the Tzar about the strengthening of gubernatorial powers; although that project contradicted to the recently promulgated liberal reforms, and in spite of the opposition of Minister of Justice

Zamiatnin and Minister of Finance Reitern, Alexander admitted the necessity of the measure, owing to the fact that Shuvalov constantly disturbed him with reports about the unrest in the provinces. Although it required legislative sanction, the measure was passed in an administrative order, in the form of an act of the Committee of Ministers, confirmed by the Tzar. Persons of judiciary ranks, whose independence had not long before been established by the new statutes, were ordered in a special circular to present themselves before the governor of their province whenever he demanded this, and to regard the governor as the representative of the monarchical authority. Thenceforth not one official could occupy his position without the consent of the governor; to this rule were subject the Controlling Chambers which had just opened, and even the *zemstvo*-institutions, although the latter were recognised by the law as non-governmental, but " public " institutions. Such were the first symptoms of the reaction in 1866.

Here we should note that the event of April 4, 1866, and the white terror perpetrated by M. N. Muraviov, which followed it, had a tremendous influence not only on governmental circles, but also upon the public. Some journalists, like Katkov, who now passed definitely to the side of the reaction, furiously attacked the Nihilists and the seditious Poles. For these Katkov found even Muraviov's measures not sufficiently severe. Others, like Niekrasov, were so frightened that they were ready to make the most undignified compromises with Muraviov. This, however, did not save Niekrasov's magazine from being discontinued. Still others, like Dostoievsky, were not only sincerely terrified by the event, but held society responsible for it. On the whole an extreme mental confusion reigned, which naturally was utilised by the Government. Under such unfavourable circumstances the new courts and the *zemstvo*-institutions had to begin their activity.

Yet, we have already observed, in spite of the new

tendency of the Government the reaction was not in a position to set Russia back to her pre-reform position. The reforms accomplished could be distorted, but not recalled. Moreover, during this reactionary period the Government was forced to proceed with carrying out the reforms in various departments of national life and administration which had been planned in the preceding years. It had to complete the arrangement of the peasant-affairs by expanding the Act of February 19 upon the State (formerly Fiscal) peasants, to introduce the principles of self-government in municipalities, and finally to accomplish the great reform in the matter of military service, and a series of reforms within the army. Alongside with these it had to pursue a progressive financial and economical policy in order to help the development of the country, although such a policy hardly harmonised with the new reactionary course in the affairs of internal administration and education.

For these reasons Alexander II was obliged to retain such advocates of progress as Dmitri Miliutin in the Ministry of War, as Grand Duke Constantine at the head of the Navy and of the State Council, as Tatarinov at the post of State Comptroller, and as Reitern in the position of Minister of Finance, while he saw Tolstoy succeed Golovnin, and the formation within the Committee of Ministers of the reactionary triumvirate of Shuvalov, Valuiev, and Zelenoy. In a word, life in Russia did not stop or regress during that heavy period of governmental and to some extent public reaction, but it continued, as we shall see, to develop and progress, although under the yoke of repressions and reaction that development had frequently assumed morbid and mutilated forms. The foes of progress could do nothing more, in the face of the uncontrollable process of the internal growth and development of the national organism, than put sticks into the wheels and hinder the process as much as they could.

In 1866 the peasant-reform was completed by spreading the

fundamental principles of the Act of February 19 to the numerous categories of the State peasants. Still earlier — in 1863 — the reform was applied to the *Udielny* peasants. The name *udielny* (appanage) was used in the Act of the Imperial Family, issued under Paul in 1797, for the peasants who were ascribed to estates of members of the Imperial family. By the time of the peasant-reform there were about eight hundred and fifty thousand *Udielny* peasants of the male sex. Upon Alexander's request the Ministry of the Court issued in 1858 a special ukase, equalising the *Udielny* peasants in their personal rights and administrative management with the State peasants; this measure at once abolished personal bondage in the Imperial estates. As to the land-allotments of those peasants, a special commission in the Ministry of the Court discussed their conditions for two years after the emancipation act of 1861, and as a result the position of the *Udielny* peasants was made considerably better than that of the landowners' peasants. In the pre-reform period the *Udielny* peasants possessed larger " basic " portions than other categories, and besides they made use of various additional portions out of the " reserved " lands of the Imperial estates. The application of the Act of February 19 to those peasants would have put them in a much worse condition than before. Count Adlerberg, Minister of the Court, disagreed with the Main Committee, which suggested that the *Udielny* peasants relinquish their additional, reserved portions, in view of the fact that their " basic " allotments were quite satisfactory in comparison with the allotments of the landowners' peasants; he worked out a project which was approved by the Tzar and enacted as a law on June 26, 1863, by which the peasants reserved all their former allotments, while those whose allotments were below the maximum portions of the landowners' peasants, received additional land. Thus the maximal norms of the allotments of the landowners' peasants were taken as minimal norms for those of the *Udielny* peasants. At the same time the obligations remained unaltered (they were comparatively light. Tr.), and the *obrok*-payments at once began to be counted as redemption-payments, to be completed in forty-nine years; the peasants were directly acknowledged as proprietors of their allotments.

As to the numerous categories of the State peasants, it was decided to apply the Act of February 19 to them also. Before the formation of the Ministry of State Domains under Count Kiselev, during the reign of Nicolas I, the possession of the State lands had no order or regulation. In some places Fiscal peasants were in possession of enormous tracts of land, which they were actually unable to cultivate; while in other places they owned not more than half a desiatin per soul, and were obliged to rent land from neighbouring landowners or even peasants. During the Forties Kiselev founded Cadastral commissions which were to equalise the allotments of the Fiscal peasants throughout the empire, and in cases where it was impossible to allot the peasants sufficient land, they were to be transplanted to other free State lands, and pay *obrok*. Another task of the commissions was to work out a just system of *obroks,* in accordance with the agricultural and industrial conditions of different allotments. After almost twenty years of work, those commissions succeeded in establishing more regulated conditions for the Fiscal peasants in the provinces of European Russia; in provinces where land was scarce the minimum of the peasants' allotments was eight desiatins per soul — a quite satisfactory amount in comparison with the allotments of the landowners' peasants, while in provinces where land was abundant the peasants received as much as fifteen desiatins per soul. Thus even under Kiselev (1837-1856) the State peasants were considerably provided with land. As to taxes, the Cadastral commissions estimated them not according to the size of the allotment, but according to the income of the peasants, since in many provinces the peasants were occupied with industry more than with agriculture. In the end the *obroks* of the State peasants were considerably smaller than those of the landowners' peasants.

When the general peasant-reform began, Kiselev had already left his post, and was succeeded at first by Sheremetiev, then (from 1857) by M. N. Muraviov, the most vicious and clever serfholder among Alexander's ministers. Fearing that the prosperity of the State peasants would bring about the enactment of better laws for the landowners' peasants, Muraviov decided to make the condition of the State peasants worse. With this aim he undertook in 1859 a revaluation of the *obrok*-assessments; he claimed that the State land alloted to the peasants belonged to the State, not to the peasants, and their *obroks* were not taxes, but rental fees. The new *obroks* were increased on the whole fifty per cent., in some places, eighty per cent. When the ukase of March 5, 1861, was issued, ordering the introduction of the emancipatory reform in the State domains, Muraviov prepared a project which was very unfavourable for the State peasants. Fortunately, however, some defenders of their rights were found among the members of the Main Committee and the question fell into the hands of N. A. Miliutin, who succeeded in frustrating Muraviov's attempts, and in making the State peasants hereditary owners of those allotments which were given to them by the Cadastral commissions. We have seen that those allotments were larger than even those of the *Udielny* peasants, let alone those of the landowners'. As to the obligations, in spite of their considerable increase owing to the efforts of Muraviov in 1859, they were still smaller than the *obroks* instituted for the landowners' peasants.

In the legal and administrative respects the *Udielny* and State peasants — the latter by the ukase of January 18, 1866 — were to enjoy the general system instituted for the landowners' peasants. This equalised the entire Russian peasantly legally and administratively. Yet the final settlement of the

State peasants was delayed a few more years after 1866, owing
to the fact that the Cadastral commissions had not completed
all their work by that time, and in single provinces special
enactments had to be carried through between 1867 and 1872.
Thus the land question of the landowners' and of the *Udielny*
peasants was settled much earlier than that of the State peasants, and the allotments of the latter were not at once considered their property; they had to redeem them later at considerably raised norms.

We get the following picture of Russian landownership in
the Seventies of the nineteenth century from the official data of
the Central Statistic Committee, issued in 1878 for forty-nine
provinces of European Russia, not including Finland, Poland,
and the Caucasus. The entire land in those forty-nine provinces was estimated as three hundred and ninety-one million
desiatins, in round figures; this included one hundred and fifty
million desiatins of fiscal lands, i.e., lands not allotted to the
peasants, but at that moment the property of the State,— which
formed thirty-eight and a half per cent. of the entire territory.
Lands of the Imperial family, after the allotment of the
Udielny peasants, occupied seven and four-tenths million desiatins, or two and two-tenths per cent. of the whole territory;
in private property of landowners of all classes were ninety-
three million desiatins, i.e., twenty-three and seventy-eight
hundredths per cent.; of the latter the land belonging to nobles
proper toward the end of the Seventies amounted to only
seventy-three million desiatins, while lands owned by non-
nobles, by commoners, among whom were also rich peasants
who bought property outside of their communities, amounted
to twenty-million desiatins. The amount of lands owned by
churches, cities, monasteries, and other institutions reached eight
and a half million desiatins. Finally the total amount of the
peasant-allotments was one hundred and thirty million desiatins,
i.e., thirty-three and four-tenths per cent. of the territory of

the forty-nine provinces — considerably more than the amount of land in private ownership.

Professor L. V. Khodsky published a book in the Eighties, devoted to the study of the position of the peasants after the Reform and of the material well-being of separate peasant-classes. Before this, in 1876, Professor Yanson undertook the same task, and endeavoured to estimate the allotments and obligations of the peasants on the basis of quite unsatisfactory figures. Later we shall have to deal with his calculations and conclusions, but at present, for the general picture of land-ownership in Russia, I shall quote Professor Khodsky's figures, because they are based on the data of the Central Statistic Committee, published in 1878. Khodsky had figured out that out of ten million six hundred and seventy thousand State and *Udielny* male peasants, five million four hundred thousand, or fifty per cent., were given generous allotments; three million eight hundred thousand, or thirty-five per cent., were given sufficient allotments, and one million four hundred and fifty-five thousand, or thirteen and seven-tenths per cent., were given insufficient allotments. Professor Khodsky employed the terms " generous," " sufficient," and " insufficient," conditionally. He indicated that the maximal allotment of the landowners' peasants was equal to one-half of the amount of land the peasant was capable of cultivating, considering that he did not receive that portion for which he had to work three days *barshchina* in the pre-reform days. In regard to the State peasants, Khodsky figured on the basis of the reports of the Cadastral commissions, and in view of the absence of *barshchina* among them, that the average allotment of the State peasants was sufficient for a tolerable existence, and absorbed the whole working capacity of the individual; hence he regarded the allotments that were above that average norm as *generous*. Out of these considerations Khodsky concluded that fifty per cent. of the State and *Udielny* peasants were allotted *generously*, and thirty-

five per cent.— *sufficiently*. By *sufficiently* Khodsky understood, not quite consistently, the allotments that were to be
classed between the maximal norm of landowners' allotments and the average norm of the State allotments. This
second class appeared far from uniform, because the
peasants whose allotment approached the maximal norm of
the landowners' allotment received, as we have seen, only
one-half of what they were capable of cultivating, while
those whose possessions were near the average norm of the
allotments of the State peasants, received indeed a more or less
sufficient portion. For this reason Khodsky considered in the
province of Samara, for instance, those who received more than
ten desiatins as generously endowed, while in the category of the
sufficiently endowed he included those who received from three
to ten desiatins — a quite variegated category. Finally, Khodsky found that the allotments below that norm were absolutely
insufficient, and in this category he figured thirteen per cent.
from among the State and *Udielny* peasants.

As to the landowners' peasants, whose number was approximately equal to the total number of the State and *Udielny*
peasants (there were about ten million State, and about eight
hundred and fifty thousand *Udielny* peasants — altogether
about ten million six hundred thousand souls, while the number
of landowners' peasants was also about ten million six hundred
thousand),— Khodsky found among them only thirteen per
cent. *generously* allotted, i.e., whose portions were above the
average norm of the State peasants. Then four million six
hundred thousand and twenty-five, or forty-three and a half
per cent., were allotted *sufficiently,* and finally forty-two per
cent.— four million four hundred and sixty thousand — received absolutely *insufficient* allotments. If we put all the
categories of the peasants together, we find that of the total
of twenty-one million two hundred and seventy-eight thousand
male souls there were six million nine hundred thousand *gen-*

erously alloted, mainly from among the State and *Udielny* peasants; they formed thirty-two per cent., i.e., *less than one-third* of the total mass.   Eight million four hundred and thirty thousand, or about forty per cent., were *sufficiently* allotted with those limitations of that term which I have observed. Finally five million nine hundred thousand, or about twenty-eight per cent., i.e., *more than one-fourth,* were allotted *insufficiently.*

On the whole this treatment of the peasants was quite liberal, if we compare the general dimensions of peasant ownership with those of private landownership of that day, and do not take into account the enormous tracts of fiscal landownership which consisted in the main of remote and unarable land, of which only four million desiatins were utilised as *obrok*-paying assets, while the remaining one hundred and forty-six million desiatins were situated chiefly in the northern provinces, and consisted of forests, water, and marshes, which greatly increased the total amount of fiscal landownership, but, in view of their climatic and soil-conditions, did not form a part of the utilisable land-fund.

This is, in general features, the picture of the peasants' landownership, as it appeared soon after the realisation of the Reform.   In another chapter we shall analyse the changes and defects that had eventually been revealed in that system.

CHAPTER XXVIII

WE shall now examine the immediate economic and social results of the peasant-reform, which have directed the general current of Russian life until recent times.

Historians who have studied this question — like Professor Miliukov in his book, "Studies in the History of Russian Culture," and those who have quite recently investigated the data connected with this question — like M. Oganovsky in his work, "Studies in the History of Agrarian Relations in Russia," published in 1911,— agree that the first immediate, and at the same time the most conspicuous, consequence of the peasant-reform was the extraordinary rise of the growth of the population. P. N. Miliukov arrives at this conclusion after an examination of past centuries; he justly indicates that the growth of the population had been checked for a long time, and that at the beginning of the eighteenth century, in the period of Peter's stormy activity, his wars and expensive reforms and constructions, the population of Russia, especially of her central regions, had absolutely decreased. We may fairly presume the same to have been true during the Troubled Time, at the end of the sixteenth and the beginning of the seventeenth century. Miliukov supposes therefore that beginning perhaps with the sixteenth century down to the second quarter of the eighteenth century, there had been no increase in the population, since the entire surplus was swallowed up by the enormous sacrifices which the people had to make for the creation of the Russian state and for territorial aggrandisement. Miliukov gives the following figures for the central provinces, i.e., for the Petrine province of Moscow which embraced the future provinces of Kaluga, Tula, part of Riazan, part of Nizhni-

Novgorod, Kostroma, Vladimir, and part of Tver: In 1678 there were thirty-nine persons per square verst, in 1724 — somewhat less than twenty-nine persons, and only in 1858, on the eve of the peasant-reform, did the density of the population again reach that of the middle of the seventeenth century, i.e., thirty-nine and four-tenths per verst. At first glance there appears indeed an enormous leap in the growth of the population during the last forty years of the nineteenth century. In the Petrine province of Kiev Miliukov estimated in 1678 eleven and four-tenths per square verst, in 1724 — eleven and two-tenths, while in 1858 the density of population there reached forty persons per square verst, and in 1897 — fifty-seven,— a growth not only in the post-reform time, but even before the Reform. P. N. Miliukov brings analogous figures for other parts of European Russia, which seem to prove that although the growth of the Russian population has progressed quite rapidly since Peter, its most rapid progress was manifested after the Reform. Most of the later investigators are inclined to share this view, among them the above mentioned Oganovsky who cites Miliukov's figures and diagrams in support of his opinion of the great significance of the increased growth of the population after the Reform.[1]

If we should take into account, however, the data of all the census that took place in Russia during the nineteenth century, we shall see that the growth of the population changed somewhat differently from the way Mr. Oganovsky suggests. Thus, if we trace the numbers from the fifth " revision " (census), at the very end of the eighteenth century, to the cen-

[1] It seems that the first investigator of the peasantry to have categorically claimed the "extraordinary" growth of the population after 1861, was P. P. Semionov, in his introduction to the Census materials issued in 1882. To a considerable extent his conclusion was shared by P. B. Struve, in his famous early work, *Critical Notes on the Question of Russia's Economic Development*, Petrograd, 1894. In his later work, *The Bondage Economy*, published in 1913, Struve rejected his former point of view.

sus of 1897, i.e., for one hundred years, we shall find that at
the beginning of that period the population of Russia was about
thirty-six million of both sexes, including (approximately) the
population of the conquered provinces, or twenty-nine million
without the latter. The next, sixth, " revision " took place
before the war, in 1811, and showed that the population had
increased in fourteen years from thirty-six to forty-one million.
By the seventh " revision," taken immediately after the war
of 1812, the *general* population of the Russian Empire had
increased to nearly forty-five million, but one must observe
that this number included the population of the annexed territories — the Kingdom of Poland (about three million), the
Grand Duchy of Finland (over one million), the region of
Bessarabia (about three hundred thousand), and the dominion
of the Caucasus where it was impossible at that time to get any
figures as to the number of the people. Excluding these territories, we see by the calculation of Academic Herman [2] that
without Poland, Finland, and Bessarabia, but including the
Caucasian portion and Siberia, Russia had in 1811 a male
population of eighteen million eight hundred thousand in round
figures, which within four years diminished by nearly a million.
Considering that the annual increase of the population in the
preceding years exceeded one per cent., the increase during the
four years should have been approximately eight hundred thousand, whereas there was a loss of nearly one million, i.e., in
general the human loss caused by the Napoleonic wars was over
one and a half million male persons. After the wars the population began to grow again, in spite of the existence of bondage;
as in the case of other countries, slavery did not lead to the
diminution of the population. Indeed, during the Thirties and
the Forties the numbers increased greatly, and by the ninth

[2] In accepting the data of Herman, I have corrected the important
errors included in his table published in *Mémoirs de l'Academie des
Science de St. Petersbourg, 1820,* page 456.

" revision " we see that in 1851 there were sixty-eight million as against forty-five million in 1815, i.e., in thirty-six years the population increased more than one time and a half, in spite of the fact that there were no territorial acquisitions during that time, and that those years included the cholera epidemic of 1848, when owing to the ignorance of means for combating the disease about one million people perished; besides, there were a number of famines on account of failure of crops (1820–1821, 1833, 1839–1840, 1843–1846, 1848). In the short period of seven years, from the ninth " revision " to the tenth, in 1858, the population again increased considerably, reaching seventy-four million, in spite of years of misery, including the Crimean Campaign which cost at least half a million lives.

Thus we see that under bondage the *general* population grew quite noticeably. True, the number of bonded peasants not only did not increase, but diminished between the eighth and ninth, and ninth and tenth " revisions," but this shows merely that even during the bondage system there was a considerable number of peasants who had changed their status — through liberation of single villages (the number of which was quite considerable after 1804), through redemption of persons or families, through the purchase of estates from landowners by the State, under Kiselev (about fifty-four thousand souls), through flights and forced exiles to Siberia. But the most considerable loss of bondmen was due to the recruitments which took place every other year, and at times every year, requiring from five to ten men out of every thousand. Between the eighth and tenth " revisions " the recruitments diminished the number of bondmen by not less than one and a half million.[3]

[3] From 1834 the recruitments took place each year alternately in one-half of the empire, taking five to ten men from every thousand. During the war of 1853–1856 seventy men were recruited from every thousand, which depleted the ten million bondmen by not less than seven hundred thousand. One should also bear in mind that the re-

Thus we may come to a well founded conclusion that the number of the bonded peasantry diminished not because of the decrease of the *natural* growth of the population, but merely because a considerable part of the bondmen were then assigned to different classes of the people.

I am bringing out these facts in order to limit the optimistic conclusions which are apt to spring from the superficial comparison of the numbers of the peasants before and after the emancipation. If we take the whole first half of the nineteenth century, it will indeed appear that the growth of the population during that period was smaller than during the second half of the century — on account of the Napoleonic wars and epidemics; but after the Napoleonic wars, in spite of two cholera epidemics and numerous crop failures, the relative growth of the population was almost as large as after the Emancipation. In my opinion the increase of the population in the years following the Napoleonic wars was one of the main causes which, alongside with a number of other economical conditions that undermined the system of bondage-land-ownership, prepared the fall of bondage.

A priori considerations lead the investigators of the post-reform to another idea — that after such an event as the emancipation of the peasants from bondage there must have taken place in a large degree the *distribution* of the population among less populated fertile provinces, on the one hand, and its movement into cities — on the other. The latter especially, since with the abolition of serfdom it appeared possible to bring about those conditions which create in all countries a normal development of capitalism (the increase of the labour supply on the market, and the transition of natural wealth into money-wealth on a large scale). Some historians have followed these

cruits were men between the ages of twenty-five and thirty-five, i.e., the most fecund producers of children, which fact decreased the number of births in the years following recruitments.

a priori considerations, and accordingly interpret the figures given by the statistic data. But if we should follow the statistic material furnished by the " revisions " and censuses, and by the data collected at various times by the Central Statistic Committee, we shall see that in this case also the *a priori* considerations are not justifiable.

A detailed study of the growth of population in single provinces will show us that in the regions where the peasants immigrated before and after the Reform, i. e., in the provinces where the population had particularly increased during the nineteenth century, a considerable part of that increase, and in some provinces the main part, took place in the pre-reform time. A comparison between the growth of the population from 1797 to 1897 in the southeastern and southern provinces with its growth in the central, particularly in the non black-soil provinces, will show a colossal difference. Whereas in the province of Yaroslavl the increase for the whole century was seventeen per cent., in those of Vladimir and Kaluga, thirty per cent., in those of Kostroma, Tver, Smolensk, Pskov, and even the *black-soil* Tver, fifty to sixty per cent.,— in the province of Astrakhan the increase was one thousand and seven hundred and fifty per cent., in that of Ufa — one thousand two hundred per cent., in that of Samara and in the Region of the Don Army — one thousand per cent., in that of Kherson — one thousand per cent., in Bessarabia — eight or nine hundred per cent., in that of Tavrida (Crimea) — four hundred per cent., in that of Yekaterinoslav — three hundred and fifty per cent., and so forth. These figures indicate a considerable outflux of the population from the centre to the peripheries. Among the central and northern non black-soil provinces only those of Moscow and Petrograd show during that time an increase of one hundred and fifty per cent. for that of Moscow, and five hundred per cent. for the province of Petrograd, an increase explained wholly by the growth of the urban population in the capitals. From the table and cartograms at the end of this chapter you can observe that the process of the migration from the centre to the peripheries had taken place in a considerable measure, and in some cases largely, in the pre-reform period.

Approximately the same may be said concerning the growth of the urban population in Russia. P. N. Miliukov, in his work on the history of Russia culture, gives very interesting figures about the growth of the urban population for the last two and a half centuries. In the middle of the seventeenth century, in 1630, the urban population numbered two hundred and ninety-two thousand, or two and four-tenths per cent. of the entire population. About one hundred years later their number increased only to three hundred and twenty-eight thousand, or two and a half per cent. of the total population; we must remember that this was in the time of Peter, when the numbers of the people diminished greatly. By the fourth " revision," made in 1782, we had already eight hundred and two thousand urbanites, or three and one-tenth per cent. of the total population. The fifth " revision," in 1796, the starting point for the study of the population movement in the nineteenth century, shows one million three hundred and one thousand — four and one-tenth per cent. of the total population. For the sixth " revision " Miliukov gives the figures of one million six hundred thousand, or four and four-tenths per cent.; for the " revision "— three million and twenty-five thousand, or five and eight-tenths per cent.; for the ninth " revision," in 1851, three million four hundred and eighty-two thousand — five per cent.;[4] for 1858 — six million, or nine and two-tenths per cent. of the total. Then Miliukov takes at once the census of 1897, and shows the number of the urban population as sixteen million two hundred and eighty-nine thousand, almost thirteen per cent. of the entire population.

[4] Miliukov gives the wrong percentage — seven and eight-tenths.

The general conclusion that one may draw from these figures is that the urban population increased after the Reform
not only absolutely but even relatively, although Miliukov himself finds the present proportion of the urban to the general
population very unfavourable, in comparison with other countries of a higher culture. As a matter of fact, the figures used
by Miliukov require considerable corrections. Those he employs for the pre-reform time (except the figures for 1858,
evidently) denote the numbers of the so-called *city classes,*
the merchants and commoners (*mieshchanie*) combined, whereas
the census of 1897 gives the number of all the *city inhabitants,*
not only of the merchants and commoners. From the data
of the Economy Department we can see that in 1847 the entire urban population of Russia equalled four million seven
hundred thousand persons, of whom there were two million
three hundred thousand commoners, or fifty per cent., about four
and a half per cent. were merchants, about five and a half per
cent. nobles and other privileged persons, about one-half per cent.
— clergy. All these categories formed sixty-one and a half per
cent. of the total number of city inhabitants, while the remaining thirty-eight and a half per cent. were marked in the category
of " others." Professor Ditiatin, who has made a special study
of the history of Russian cities in the nineteenth century, explained that the " others " denoted " factory workers, labourers,
drivers, and other categories of workingmen almost all whom
belonged by their origin and ascription to the *peasant-class."*

Indeed, we witness a similar phenomenon at present: in Moscow and Petrograd an enormous portion of the population is
ascribed to the peasants in spite of the fact that for years and
decades they have lived in the cities, engaged in commerce or
industry. By the end of the Forties nine per cent. of the Petrograd population were commoners, and five per cent.— merchants,
while the remaining eighty-six per cent. belonged to non-urban
classes.

Hence it is evident that the city-classes and the city-inhabitants are not synonymous; the figures given by Miliukov for the city-classes of the pre-reform days can not be compared with the figures of the city-population as a whole, given by the census of 1897, which included nobles and peasants and persons of various ranks who lived at that time in the cities.

If we should take for a basis of the city contingent of the population the data of the Economy Department, taken in the forties, quoted and illuminated by Professor Ditiatin, we shall have to multiply the figures [5] quoted by Miliukov for the pre-reform time at least one time and a half, if not more, and then the picture will be quite different. It will appear that the growth of the city population proceeded consistently, gradually, very slowly, and has increased little after the Reform. One must note, however, that in regard to the population of the capitals and of some big industrial centres, it grew considerably more rapidly after the Reform than before it.

Thus you can see that the *a priori* considerations about the effect of the peasant-reform on the growth of the population, on its distribution through the empire, on the growth of the cities and, in general, on the preparation of the capitalistic order, are not quite correct, and should be regarded with great caution. Upon a close study of the figures and relations, we see that the transformation of the economic status after the Reform has been accomplished more slowly and gradually than one might have expected.

The reasons for this fact are quite simple. During the first years after the Reform Russia was in a very depressed economic state. On one side the peasants found themselves burdened with almost intolerable payments; on the other side, the land-owners were unable to cope successfully with the new condi-

[5] I do not know where Miliukov has taken his figures for the population in 1858, but they evidently express the entire city population, not only the city-classes.

tions produced by the revolution. The landowners lacked the resources required for the new form of agricultural management which demanded not only hired labour, but also a complete new inventory — implements and cattle, for under the bondage system the peasants had cultivated with their own implements and cattle the land of their masters. Not having their own inventory, the landowners of the black-soil provinces were not infrequently forced to rent the larger part of their estates to the emancipated peasants.

In the non black-soil, industrial provinces, the conditions of the landowners were in this respect still worse. With a few exceptions they were unable to meet the new conditions, and their estates were either ruined or sold out; since the peasants did not have the money for the purchase of the much needed land, the estates were sold to merchants or to single rich peasants who treated it like birds of prey, cut out forests and even gardens, and then themselves sold the ravaged estates to peasants.

Such was the situation in the field of agriculture. Curiously enough, in the years immediately following the Reform, we find no improvement in the industrial field either. We know that the merchants and factory owners had expected that the emancipation of the peasants would increase the supply of labour, from among the freed peasants, especially since their allotments were not sufficient. But such was not the case in the first years after the Reform. A great number of factories, especially iron-foundries and cloth-factories, were still Possessional, i.e., they depended on bonded labour. As soon as their working men were liberated, they began to abandon the factories in crowds, in their desire to get away from the hateful places of their long suffering and slavery. For this reason many factories were forced either to close up or to lessen their production in the first years after the Reform.

Tugan-Baranovsky, in his book, *Russian Factories,* sets forth curious figures about the Kuvshinsky works, for instance.

In 1857 that foundry produced four hundred and seventy-
nine thousand puds of cast-iron, in 1862 — three hundred and
thirteen thousand puds, and even in 1868, seven years after
the Reform, it produced only three hundred and fifty-three
thousand puds. Such was the general situation in the Urals.
All the Ural foundries gave in 1860 fourteen million five hundred thousand puds, in 1861 — only fourteen million two hundred thousand puds, in 1862 — ten million four hundred thousand, in 1863 somewhat more — eleven million four hundred
thousand, in 1867 — twelve million four hundred thousand
puds, and only about 1870 did the total reach the first norm,
and soon thereafter began to exceed it. In the seventies the
iron-production was considerably larger than in the pre-reform
days; it took the iron manufacturers ten years to orient themselves in the new circumstances. The cloth-factories also required five to six years before they could adapt themselves to
the new conditions.

It is curious to observe that a similar situation existed for
the cotton-mills, although they had instituted hired labour long
before the Reform, and had therefore expected an improvement in the labour conditions. It happened that England was
going through a severe commercial-industrial crisis at that time,
which raised the prices of cotton-yarn (a considerable part of
the Russian cotton-mills still depended on English yarn). For
this reason their conditions had also somewhat deteriorated in
the first years after the Reform.

These circumstances which resulted from or coincided with
the peasant-reforms, affected the state of internal commerce
in Russia. A clear illustration is furnished by the figures of
the turnover of the Nizhni-Novgorod fair. Fairs had a greater
significance at that time than now when they are giving way
before the modern methods of wholesale trade. In 1860 the
turnover of the Nizhni-Novgorod fair was one hundred and
five million rubles, in 1861 — ninety-eight million rubles, in

1862 — one hundred and three million rubles, and only in 1864 did it exceed the turnover of 1860, reaching one hundred and eleven million rubles, after which it continued to increase.

Such were the post-reform economic conditions in Russia. The state of industry was far from flourishing, and the way was still far to a developed capitalistic order.

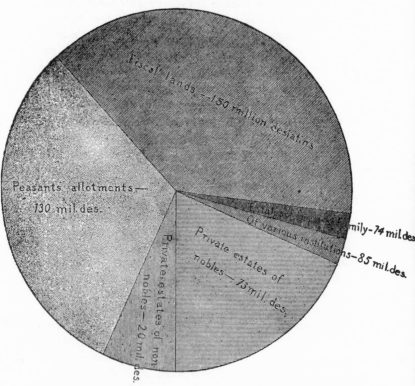

DISTRIBUTION OF LAND-OWNERSHIP BY CATEGORIES
IN 49 PROVINCES IN THE YEAR 1878.

DENSITY OF THE POPULATION IN VARIOUS PROVINCES

Provinces in order of density of population in 1797	Per sq. mile of 1797 by revision (both sexes)	Place of province in order of density	Per sq. mile by revision of 1858 and data of 1863 (both sexes)	Place of province in order of density	Per sq. mile of 1897 by census (both sexes)	Place of province in order of density	Percentile increase of density for 100 yrs.	Notes
Tula	1600	1	2048	3	2378	5	ab. 50%	} Owing to Moscow.
Moscow	1586	2	2572	1	4064	1	150	
Kursk	1400	3	2160	2	2776	3	100	
Kaluga	1340	4	1647	8	1760	14	130	
Yaroslavl	1234	5	1430	13	1486	19	17	
Riazan	1176	6	1850	4	2220	7	100	
Oriol	1170	7	1775	5	2314	6	100	
Vladimir	1062	8	1356	14	1604	17	30	
Penza	1003	9	1674	7	2040	11	100	
Simbirsk	952	10	1306	16	1654	15	72	} Partly owing to Kharkov.
Kharkov	932	11	1760	6	2286	2	200	
Smolensk	928	12	1110	18	1440	20	ab. 60	
Nizhni-Novgorod	916	13	1340	15	1618	16	60	
Tambov	860	14	1644	9	2170	8	75	
Voroniezh	840	15	1580	11	2085	10	150	
Pskov	762	16	858	21	1316	21	150	
Kazan	752	17	1431	12	1926	12	60	
Kostroma	624	18	709	25	884	28	150	
Tver	582	19	856	22	940	25	50	
Saratov	504	20	1122	17	1566	18	60	
Petrograd	480	21	1610	10	2768	4	200	} Owing to Petrograd.
Yekaterinoslav	396	22	1013	20	1820	13	500	
Viatka	356	23	806	23	1097	23	350	
Novgorod	283	24	450	28	592	29	200	
Kherson	272	25	1070	19	2156	9	700	} Partly owing to Odessa.
Tavrida (Crimea)	238	26	534	27	1272	22	400	
Perm	149	27	368	29	476	30	200	
Orenburg	82	28	209	31	360	31	340	
Samara	82	29	572	26	933	26	1000	V
Ufa	82	30	780	24	1090	24	1200	
Don Region	81	31	326	30	892	27	1000	
Vologda	72	32	129	32	177	33	118	ab.
Olonetzk	14	33	105	34	127	34	70	
Astrakhan	14	34	130	33	256	32	1750	
Arkhangelsk	13	35	19	35	23	35	75	

CHAPTER XXIX

COMBINED with the depressed economic state of the country was a similar state of the national finances. After the Crimean Campaign, during the whole reform-period, and in the post-reform years, the Government was in very difficult circumstances. One of the main causes was the fall of the course of the paper-ruble. After the money-reform of 1843 and until the Crimean Campaign the position of the Russian finances was quite satisfactory. Owing to Kankrin's reform the amount of credit-money in circulation was very moderate: in 1854 three hundred eleven million rubles, and their course stood at par in view of the presence of a metallic fund of one hundred and twenty-three million rubles, which allowed a free exchange of the paper money. The war required new issues of paper-money, the amount of which reached in 1858 the sum of seven hundred and eighty million rubles, while the metal-reserve had fallen to one hundred and nineteen million rubles, i. e., below the one-sixth norm which Kankrin considered necessary for the uninterrupted maintenance of free exchange; hence the Government was forced to refuse redemption. Naturally the course of such unredeemable money fell continually during the years immediately following the Crimean Campaign.

At the same time the Government was eager to see the development of private credit and of private capitalistic undertakings; with this view it lowered the interest paid for deposits in fiscal credit-institutions — to direct the deposits to private enterprises. The deposits began to flow out rapidly, descending in ten years to two hundred million from over one billion rubles.   In the pre-reform time the Government made free use of that fund, and borrowed from it for its needs, so that in the end the debt of the Government to the saving institutions exceeded five hundred million rubles.   When the deposits began to be withdrawn more rapidly than it had been expected, the Government was forced to contract new loans on heavy conditions, and yet it did not cover the entire debt; it still owed the credit-institutions one hundred and sixty million rubles.

The course of the paper-money fell not only because of the superabundant issue of such money and the diminution of the metal-fund, but also because of Russia's extremely unfavourable balance of trade at that time, in view of her insignificant export and large import soon after the war.   This unfavourable trade balance was enhanced by the fact that after the abolition of the rule forbidding Russians to go abroad, which was introduced in the reign of Nicolas, the number of Russian travellers abroad became very large, and they withdrew enormous quantities of money from their country.

The situation resembled that after the Treaty of Tilsit and during the Continental System, early in the nineteenth century.   Under such difficult conditions the Tzar appointed in 1862 the comparatively young M. K. Reitern as Minister of Finance, after two absolutely incapable ministers — Brock and Kniazhevich.   Reitern's ability had been demonstrated through his activity in the financial sub-commission of the Editing Commission, which worked out the plan of the redemption-operation.

Reitern's immediate task consisted in raising the course of the paper-ruble, while his remote ideal was the transition to a permanent metal standard.   However we may regard such a plan of political economy, which is reduced to one exclusive problem, we must say that at his very start Reitern committed a big blunder. In order to raise the course of the paper-money he attempted to make it redeemable by contracting a loan of fifteen million pounds sterling, i.e., about one hundred and fifty million rubles, which at once increased the metal-fund, and allowed the Government to announce that it was ready to redeem the credit-money. But at this Reitern made a naïve mistake: he declared that until a certain date the paper-ruble would be exchanged at a certain rate, after a certain time — at a higher rate, then at a still higher, and so forth — calculating that the course of the ruble would constantly rise owing to the redemption. He did not take into account the numerous speculators who hastened to buy out the credit-bills while the rate of exchange was low, to present them for redemption when the rate was promised to be the highest. This mad speculation absolutely paralysed the possible success of the measure; to this was added the Polish revolt, and the expected intervention of foreign powers, the fear of which forced the Government to spend a part of the reserve fund for military preparations. Soon Reitern was not in position to continue the redemption-operation, and the course of the paper-ruble fell lower than before. Although the number of credit-bills in circulation had decreased from seven hundred and eighty million to seven hundred million rubles, the metal-fund had also shrunk from one hundred and nineteen million to fifty-five million rubles, which formed only about one-twelfth of the total amount of credit-money, and was thus less than one-half of the moderate fund considered by Kankrin as indispensable.

Reitern's first big error was masqued, however, by the Polish revolt and by the military preparations which absorbed large sums of money; his reputation did not suffer, and he remained at his post sixteen years. His next activity was directed to the raising of the country's productive powers, after he saw his " heroic " measures for the raise of the paper-course fail. He understood that in order to increase the export of the Russian chief commodity — grain, it was necessary to build railroads; toward this he directed all his efforts. Owing to the fact that he enjoyed the confidence of Alexander II, Reitern was the actual manager in this matter, in spite of his frequent conflicts with the Minister of Communications.

The history of railroad building presents one of the most cardinal parts of the history of the development of capitalism in Russia, and its study is of great importance for the clear understanding of the course of the transformation of Russian social life after the abolition of serfdom. We have seen the difficult conditions of the embryonic capitalism immediately after the Emancipation; and we all know that the development of a net of railroads is the most powerful nerve in the evolution of capitalism in every country.

The first Russian railroad was the Tzarskoselsky (from Petrograd to Tzarskoie-Selo. Tr.), twenty-five versts long, built in 1837 by private means without any subsidies or guarantees on the part of the Government; the railroad was to remain the property of its builders for an indefinite time. The construction lasted two years, and cost comparatively little — forty-two thousand rubles per verst, including all the necessary buildings. The exploitation of that railroad convinced the Government of the practicability of railroads in Russia, and it undertook the construction of the Petrograd-Moscow line, subsequently called, the Nicolaievsky. At the head of the fiscal undertaking stood Minister of Communications Kleinmichel, one of Arakcheiev's generals; although it is generally testified that personally he was honest, the construction of the railroad was connected with flagrant abuses. True, it was firmly built, especially the depots, bridges, etc., but it cost one hundred and sixty-five thousand rubles per verst, as against forty-two thousand rubles of the Tzarskoselsky railroad. The construction of the Nicolaievsky railroad lasted nine years; the bonded peasants were driven in hordes to the works, and the workers perished in large numbers.

These were the only railroads built during the reign of Nicolas. True, in 1851, the Government decided to construct the Warshavsky (Petrograd-Warsaw) Railroad, again by fiscal means, in spite of the lesson it had learned, but until 1853 only a small portion was constructed, at the expense of eighteen million rubles, and the breaking out of the war caused the work to cease for lack of funds. After the Crimean Campaign the Government of Alexander II, which had just experienced the horrors of want of roads, when the ammunition had to be transported to Sevastopol on horses, and the troops had to march there on foot, determined to consider as one of its first tasks the construction of roads. But in view of the bitter lesson taught by the fiscal management of the building of the Nicolaievsky railroad, and in accordance with the principles of its new economic policy, the Government decided to hand the matter over to private companies, limiting its own rôle to general initiative and to encouragement of private enterprisers. Added to these considerations was the plan for attracting capital and metal-money into Russia, for which reason foreigners were allowed to head the undertaking. Although among the founders was one Russian banker, Stiglitz, most of them were foreigners; even the office of the Company was not in Petrograd, but in Paris. A joint-stock company was formed, under the title, Main Company of Russian Railroads; it issued stock, with the Government's guarantee for five per cent. income on that capital, besides other privileges, as, for instance, that the company should retain ownership of the roads for ninety-nine years. Yet the founders of the company did not furnish any cash capital, but only underwrote it; special " obligations " had to be issued for the construction of the roads. Owing to the fact that the founders had squandered a considerable part of the stock-capital, the building of the roads proceeded with great difficulties and at high cost — about one hundred thousand rubles per verst.

The Main Company was to complete, first of all, the War-shavsky line, then to construct the line Dünaburg-Riga, next the Moscow-Nizhni-Novgorod line, and finally, the Moscow-Sevastopol line. It had been planned in that way to connect the fertile Volga provinces, part of New Russia, and the central black-soil provinces, with a Baltic port through Moscow, while Moscow would in her turn be joined with the Black Sea (Sevastopol). But the Main Company completed only the Warshavsky road and the line to Nizhni-Novgorod, while the Dünaburg-Riga was not finished by the stipulated time, and the Moscow-Sevastopol railroad was not even begun. Only part of the capital was subscribed abroad, but the larger portion of the stock and obligations the company sold and realised in Russia, so that in the end the hopes of the Government for the influx of foreign capital were not fulfilled; the reverse came to pass, and the whole enterprise, conducted as it was rapaciously in means and methods, proved unfortunate in all respects.

In view of this failure, particularly after it appeared that owing to the high cost of the construction the profitableness of the railroads was doubtful, the more so since the movement of freight on the Warshavsky road was not large, the dividend expectations of the stockholders were not realised, and the Government had to pay out considerable sums on the basis of its guarantee. Not only was the Russian public disappointed in the results of the undertaking, but the Government itself felt almost despondent, and in 1861 it cancelled its first agreement with the Main Company, insisted upon the transfer of the main office from Paris to Petrograd, and that the management should include four members appointed by it; the company was released from its obligation to construct the remaining two railroads.

In spite of this failure, Reitern and the new Minister of Communications, Melnikov, decided to continue the work; in Reitern's opinion the construction of railroads was unconditionally necessary for his basic task — the development of the country's productive powers, in general, and the raise of the course of the Russian money, in particular, by way of increasing the grain-export. Melnikov prepared a quite purposeful plan for the further development of the railroad net; to construct the Moscow-Sevastopol line, the lines Odessa-Kiev and Kiev-Moscow, to complete the Dünaburg-Riga road, to continue it through Riga-Libava (Libau), and to connect that road with Oriol, i.e., with a central point for export commodities, particularly agriculture products; Oriol was to be joined with Tambov and Saratov. On the other hand a line was to be built from Kiev, or from some point on the Odessa-Kiev line, towards the Austrian border, for strategic reasons, and a line from Yekaterinoslav to the Grushevsky coal-mines in the Don Region, in order to provide the new roads with mineral fuel, in case the forests along their course would not furnish them with sufficient fuel.

The plan was apparently well made, but it was very difficult to begin its realisation. Reitern still preferred private capital for the undertaking; he expected an influx of Russian and foreign capital; besides he pointed out that since a considerable part of the construction would have to be done by the aid of loans, it was important that those loans be a private matter, although with the Government's guarantee, lest the contracting of new loans should harm the national credit. On the other hand, Melnikov considered that since private construction had been compromised, the work should be done by fiscal means; he recommended the establishment of a strict supervision, to eliminate thievery. Melnikov's view was defeated, and a hunt for private concessionaires began. It appeared that the heads and members of the Main Company, who had filled their pockets with Russian money, had spread rumours abroad about the extreme difficulty of constructing railroads in Russia, asserting in addition that the whole enterprise was unprofitable. For this reason no capital could be attracted on the Continent. The Government tried to find willing capitalists in England, and offered them extraordinary privileges, such as ninety-nine years of proprietorship, a guarantee of five per cent. profit for the entire capital, gratis sites for depots at Sevastopol, Moscow, and other places, and even its readiness to establish porto-franco at Sevastopol, i.e., the Government was willing to promulgate measures which would have undermined its own financial policy.

Fortunately the English proved too slow, and let pass the final date announced by the Government; owing to that delay only the concession did not take place. Then Melnikov suggested that temporarily at least the construction of some of the projected roads be commenced by fiscal means. The Kiev-Balta railroad was built in this way, and it appeared that thanks to Melnikov's personal honesty and strict watchfulness, the cost was only a little over fifty thousand rubles per verst.

An important rôle in the history of Russian railroads was played by the concession given to a Russian contractor, Derviz. In 1866 he undertook to build the Riazan-Kozlov line which connected through Riazan, Moscow, and through the latter — Petrograd, with the most fertile region; the enterprise proved very profitable, and yielded eight per cent. dividend the first year. It completely changed the state of the Riazan-Moscow line which began to pay twelve per cent. dividend. These circumstances, discovered after 1866, aroused the appetites of Russian capitalists, and improved the chances of Russian railroads abroad. Many high personages, or persons with high connections, began to seek concessions; even many zemstvos.

Reitern's propositions were examined by a special committee under the chairmanship of a member of the State Council,

Chevkin, and with the participation of N. A. Miliutin; the committee decided that the further construction of railroads was a most vital question for Russia. Miliutin argued that in the next ten years (1865–1875) at least five thousand versts of railroads should be built. Although Miliutin's calculation was considered optimistic in 1865, it was greatly exceeded, because owing to the concession-fever which began after the success of the Riazan–Kozlov line, between 1865 and 1875 were built not five thousand, but twelve thousand more versts, so that by 1875 Russia was in possession of a net of seventeen thousand versts, which connected the most productive regions with ports and with the coal region of the Don, and allowed a wide export of internal products abroad.

Thus we may say that the plans of railroad construction were finally well realised; but as to the question of its cost for the Treasury and the country, and as to whether the work was done at all conscientiously, we must say that not only was the cost of the construction excessively large, and enormous capital fell into the pockets of the " *gründers,*" but there were numerous other unpardonable abuses, with which many high personages were connected.[1]

Particularly strange appeared the episode of selling the Nicolaievsky railroad to the Main Company. Reitern decided to form a special railroad-fund for the encouragement of private capitalists; the Nicolaievsky line was not very profitable (owing to its high cost), he proposed to sell it, as well as other unprofitable State property, and to use the money for the railroad-fund. We can understand these considerations, but the subsequent course of the affair is beyond comprehension. A solid company of Moscow capitalists, headed by Koshelev, offered to buy the line on very advantageous conditions, but it was sold to the Main Company, which had begun its career with

[1] Kornilov generally uses the term "high personages" for members of the Imperial family.— Tr.

fraud, compelled the Government to pay out an enormous sum as "guarantee," managed its affairs badly, and still owed a large debt to the Government. Some explain that outside of ordinary graft in the matter, the sale of the road to the Main Company was motivated by the desire of the Government to give it a chance for settling with its creditors, primarily with the Treasury. A quite extraordinary consideration!

Thus was accomplished the construction of the railroads which have been a powerful factor in the development of Russian capitalism.

Outside of this activity Reitern worked hard for the creation and popularisation of private credit. In the pre-reform time, and shortly after the reform, until the opening of the Imperial Bank in 1860, Russia had no organised private credit. Reitern was not satisfied with the exclusive activity of the Imperial Bank, and decided to encourage the establishment of private banks. The question was vividly discussed in the press and in financial circles. With the aid of the Ministry of Finance a number of societies were formed from among private capitalists for various forms of private credit. Reitern was also interested in the question of general agrarian credit, but in this respect he acted timidly, fearing that in view of the instability of prices on land there might be great abuses.

His immediate task in the field of national finances, in the narrow sense of the word, was his struggle with deficits in the State-budget. The budget had grown less considerably than one might have expected by the perspectives pictured during the reform-period. At the beginning of Reitern's administration it amounted to three hundred and fifty million rubles, and by the end of his service, in 1878, i.e., after fifteen years, it increased only to six hundred million rubles (in paper-money). We should add that in spite of such a moderate growth of the budget, in spite of the constant economising in the expenditures of various departments, even in the reorganisation of the army, which was found indispensable after the Crimean Campaign, every budget brought a deficit, and Reitern was continually fighting with individual ministers for the diminution of expenditures.

Only about the years 1873–1874 did he succeed in reducing the deficit to zero, and in 1875 in having the income exceed the expense. He then began to save up for a reserve fund which he considered necessary for a transition to a metal-currency. Just when his last dream seemed realisable to him, it vanished — at the outbreak of the war in 1877.

The same considerations which forced the Government to support capitalism, to prepare and encourage its development, compelled it to carry through several other important reforms during that reactionary period.

It is instructive to note in this respect that Reitern, a person who did not share the liberal aspirations of his progressive contemporaries, was forced, however, in 1866 to enter into a stubborn battle with his most reactionary colleagues in the Committee of Ministers, and first of all with the Chief of Gendarmes, Count Shuvalov, in which battle he almost lost his post. In one of his posthumous notes, issued by his heirs in 1910 as supplements to Kulomzin's biography of him, we read: "In 1866, after the attentate of Karakozov, the appointment of Shuvalov, the resignation of Golovnin,— a regular baiting began against me from different sides, instigated by Shuvalov. He was joined by Valuiev, and together they opened a pseudo-liberal campaign, i.e., they tried to produce an impression of liberalism on the public, at the same time adhering relentlessly to absolutism. The enclosed memorandum had put an end to their attacks against me. . . ."

We can hardly agree with calling the policy of Shuvalov-Valuiev " pseudo-liberalism "— as a matter of fact it was undoubtedly a reactionary policy which at times used very thin liberal phrases as a subterfuge, but this is immaterial; what interests us is the memorandum presented by Reitern to the Tzar on September 16, 1866, about which the author says that it had put an end to the attacks against him — so convincing did its contents prove for Alexander II. That memorandum is therefore of considerable significance for the characterisation of the Government's mood at that moment, and for the under-standing of the circumstance that in spite of the reigning re-action certain reorganisations were carried through which had not been accomplished during the reform-period. In that memorandum Reitern wrote:

"Your Imperial Majesty has obliged me to report to you about the present financial difficulties, and about the measures which should be undertaken for the improvement of the financial and economic conditions of the country.

" The financial and economic state of a country is complex; its roots abide not only in fiscal measures and in purely economic conditions, but in phenomena of general national development. If, on one side, it is doubtless that lack of frugality, a bad administration, and ill-considered and op-pressive fiscal measures are bound to derange the finances, and then the economic state of a country,— it is, on the other side, also true that during certain epochs of national development financial difficulties appear as an inevitable result of circum-stances, as a symptom of the process that is going on within the social organism."

Reitern further analysed the situation in which Russia found itself at the beginning of Alexander II's reign — which is again quite characteristic for a memorandum written at that time by a *minister of finance.*

" Russia came out from the Crimean Campaign tired of the gigantic struggle, with drained finances and exhausted money-funds, crippled by an issue of four hundred million credit-bills. The moral authority of the Government was shaken; the war revealed numerous defects of our administration, both military and civil; it shook the dominating position which Russia had occupied in Europe since the Vienna Congress; as a consequence of this came the fall of our authority abroad, and mistrust for the power and ability of the Government — within the Empire.

" Even if the Government," he further wrote, " had wished after the Crimean Campaign to return to the traditions of the last forty years, i.e., to a relentless opposition to all modern aspirations, it would have met insurmountable obstacles, if not in an open, at least in a passive resistance which might in time have shaken even the loyalty of the people — the broad basis of the monarchical principle in Russia. For the happiness of Russia your Imperial Majesty has chosen a different road. History of all nations proves that revolutions may be forestalled only by timely reforms which give the people in a peaceful way that which they seek in revolutions, i.e., the elimination of the outgrown forms and of the inrooted abuses. The reforms which will immortalise the reign of your Imperial Majesty did not touch only the surface of the social order, as most reforms undertaken voluntarily by governments do. Courageously and consistently you approached the root of the evil, and laid a correct foundation for the structure of civil order. Millions of our people have been called to civilism, without being divorced from the soil; the system of administrative graft which had been officially tolerated and even encouraged has fallen with the contracts (i.e., of the beverage), and now there is a possibility for an honest administration; the great principle of the separation of the judiciary from the administration has been strictly carried through in the reorganised courts — without it the sense of justice cannot develop among the citizens. Finally, in the field of local *zemstvo* affairs the principle of self-government has been laid.

" These and many other reforms have already deeply changed Russia, and I venture to say, for the best, but they have not had time to become ripe, and have aroused in certain minds extreme and deplorable tendencies." "In a word, the reforms are so broad, they have so thoroughly affected the depth of our state-structure and social life, that much time, much labour, many sacrifices will be required before Russia will emerge from her transitional state, and will be firmly established on new, rational foundations. Only then will the economic development find a stable basis, confidence and credit will be restored, and there will be found a solid ground for finances, which does not exist at present. . . ."

Such were the frank declarations of the Minister of Finance who had directly connected the reforms which were accomplished, and those that were to be promulgated in the future, with the financial well-being of the State. Naturally those were the most substantial arguments in favour of reforms, that could at that moment produce an impression on Alexander.

At the very end of his lengthy memorandum, after the exposition of his financial principles and plans, Reitern wrote:

"With such a course of action one may hope that in a few years the economic forces of Russia will grow stronger; the reforms which form the glory of your Majesty's reign will not have to be stopped in their development on account of want of means, but on the contrary they will yield abundant fruit, and Russia will finally emerge from the transitional and restless period which naturally and inevitably follows revolutions in the civil and economic order, stronger and richer than ever."

This memorandum, in spite of the reactionary mood of Alexander, supported by Shuvalov and other retrogrades, was accepted by him graciously, and had not only put an end to attacks against Reitern, as the latter believed, but it enabled him to develop the financial policy which was quite progressive for that moment, and did not at all harmonise with the general reaction of the Government.

Out of similar considerations other reforms were carried

out: municipal, which were connected in the beginning with certain reforms projected by the Ministry of Interior back in the Forties, and then a whole series of important reorganisations in the sphere of the military department, the urgent necessity of which was demonstrated by the unfortunate Crimean Campaign, but the realisation of which was delayed mainly because of the poor state of Russian finances at that time.

CHAPTER XXX

SO far I have not spoken about the municipal reforms and the development of the cities, in general, because there has been little to say on the subject. The status of the cities remained almost without change throughout the first half of the nineteenth century, indeed, till the end of the Sixties, so that municipal self-government instituted by Catherine had not only not developed, but had come to a standstill and was decaying. To give a clear picture of the cities and the city-life in Russia during the earlier part of the nineteenth century, I shall quote some statistics gathered from official sources in an article by Professor Ditiatin, one of the best scholars in the field of the pre- and post-reform municipal life. Those statistics were taken three times during the nineteenth century — in 1825, in 1852, and in 1867, and on each occasion they showed the same picture of a stagnant, motionless city-life.

We see by the tables of 1825 that out of forty-two provincial capitals — including such cities as Odessa, administratively equivalent to provincial capitals — only in two, Odessa and Vilno (both hardly Russian cities), did stone-buildings prevail over wooden houses; in Odessa, by the way, stone was cheaper than wood. In Petrograd there were twice as many and in Moscow two and a half times as many wood as stone-buildings. In other provincial capitals the proportion was still worse: one out of five, in one place, one out of seven, in two cities, one out of eight, in three, one out of ten, in two, and finally, in Samara, there was one stone-building for every seven hundred and eighty-four wooden ones.

The same picture was presented by the figures of 1852 and

of 1867.   Such, in spite of the quite broad self-government that
was granted to them by Catherine in 1785, were the poverty
and backwardness of the cities.   By that charter the population
of the cities was divided into six classes; all of them were
admitted to the election of a general *duma,* the delegates of
which elected from among themselves an executive of six members.   Paul I abolished that Statute before it had time to
become fairly rooted; beside his tendency to undo all that his
mother had undertaken, he pointed out that the city-charter,
taking up the liberties and rights of the citizens, contradicted
the autocratic order which he intended to guard so jealously.
Alexander I restored the charter, but it continued to exist
merely on paper.   From the investigations of the Ministry of
Interior we see that not only in small towns, but even in large
provincial cities, even in the Capitals, municipal institutions
were a myth.   We find, for instance, that such an institution
as the Assembly of Delegates, which was to keep the registration books of the voting citizens, did not exist even in Petrograd
and Moscow, so that the elections of the general *dumas* and
of the city-mayors were evidently performed by casual persons
whose voting rights nobody examined.   Never more than one-
tenth, and more often only a twentieth of the voters made use
of their privilege.   The percentage of the voters differed
according to classes; Professor Ditiatin shows that only one-
half to one-tenth per cent. of the commoners entitled to vote
took part in the elections of the city-mayor of Moscow in the
Forties.   Moreover, the revision of the Ministry of Interior
during the Forties proved that the general *dumas* seldom existed
in reality; such was the case in Moscow early in the nineteenth
century.

It thus appears that the city-inhabitants had failed to make
use of the privileges granted them by the law.   The revision
discovered that instead of the legal institutions there existed in
the towns various forms of peculiar chanceries, completely sub-

jected to the local police, which did not tax the population, but begged the well-to-do to give contributions for the miserable maintenance of the town-administration. Thus did reality differ from the lofty phrases of Catherine's legislation.

I see one explanation of the fact in the general relationship between the authorities and the subjects; the omnipotent guardianship manifested on the part of the representatives of the authority, i.e., the police, deprived all reasoning persons from the desire to take part in pseudo-self-government. A greater importance had the circumstance that according to Catherine's legislation the self-government was given no power for levying taxes; it was to seek means for the required expenditures, i.e., it was allowed to collect contributions for paving the streets or putting up lanterns. Naturally no sensible citizen had any taste for such self-government.

When some symptoms of economic development in Russia appeared in the Forties the Government became somewhat alarmed at the deplorable state of the cities. The Minister of Interior, L. A. Perovsky, a quite enlightened man, instructed the young and gifted N. A. Miliutin, who then occupied the post of Chief of the Economy Department, to investigate the matter. In co-operation with such intelligent men as Yuriy Samarin, Ivan Aksakov, and others, Miliutin made a thorough study of the conditions and needs of Russian cities, and presented the material to the Minister of Interior for the preparation of a new statute for municipal government. Owing to Miliutin's energy a new statute was worked out for Petrograd, which was sanctioned by Nicolas, in spite of the fact that the Forties were the years of cruel reaction; evidently the Government had no apprehensions of unrest on the part of the hapless, harmless city *duma*.

By that statute the general municipal *duma* which had not existed in reality was restored. Miliutin, well intentioned, but inexperienced, ascribed the backwardness of municipal affairs to lack of culture among those strata of the population, which were expected to take care of them; therefore he decided to instill into municipal self-government the most cultured and enlightened forces of the country — the nobles. The *duma* was to be elected by six orders, of which the first was the order of hereditary nobles who had some connection with the city; next followed personal nobles and officials, merchants, commoners, and the order of *tzekh*-artisans who belonged to the class of commoners; every order could elect from one hundred to one hundred and fifty representatives, so that the dimensions of the *duma* were quite majestic — over five hundred members. It is astonishing that Nicolas I acquiesced in the establishment of such a representative body. The *duma* was to elect a special, executive *duma* for the actual management of all affairs. Properly speaking, the new statute differed little from that of Catherine; it was rather a well-intentioned attempt to re-establish or to call to life that which had been instituted by law. The attempt did not succeed; the nobles who lived in Petrograd showed no interest in the municipal affairs, and besides, since the *duma* had no right to levy taxes it was utterly impotent. Yet with the appearance of progressive tendencies among society the Government became uneasy about even this form of self-government. At the end of the Fifties the Governor-General of Petrograd, Ignatiev, expressed alarm at the dimensions of the *duma* as instituted by Miliutin in 1846. The Government was afraid of the repetition of the Western European events of 1848 when in almost all big centres the social movement emerged from the city-halls. The similarity was of course only external, yet it alarmed the Government to such an extent that the municipal statute was revised by the State Council, the number of the *duma*-members was reduced to two hundred fifty, and the very elections of the delegates were made not direct, but through special assemblies of electors, called by class-curiæ.

Such was the situation when other Russian cities, moved by the general liberal spirit and manifestation of initiative after the Crimean Campaign, began to petition in the end of the Fifties and early in the Sixties for the expansion to them of the Petrograd municipal statute. In 1863 the Government introduced that system in Moscow and Odessa; at the same time, trying to meet the general desire, the Tzar ordered on July 20, 1862, the working out of a new municipal statute for the Empire.

Valuiev, who was then Minister of Interior, sent out a circular to the governors, in which he requested them to form special commissions from among the representatives of the public for the discussion and clarification of the question. Five hundred and nine local commissions were formed; all of them presented their considerations and desires which were not based on any experience, but were imbued with liberal aspirations, and justly connected the poor state of the cities with the existing order of things; yet they did not go beyond generalities, and did not even express a definite demand that first of all municipal self-government should have the right of self-taxation, without which nothing could be done.

On the basis of the presentations of the commissions the Ministry of Interior worked out in 1864 a general project which, with the conclusions of Baron Korf, the Chief of the Codificatory Department, was presented to the State Council on March 31, 1866. But a few days later Karakozov's attentate took place, which resulted in general confusion and reaction. The project remained motionless for two years, and finally was returned to Timashov, the new Minister of Interior, more reactionary than Valuiev. In 1869 Timashov presented it to the State Council, without substantial changes. The State Council sent it back to the Ministry of Interior, demanding that representatives of the city-communities take part in the discussion of the project. Six provincial mayors and two from the Capitals were invited into a special commission for such discussion. The commission proved very conservative and opposed to the principle of all-class-representation in city government; fearing that the democratic elements would numerically prevail against the more well-to-do classes, the commission introduced the so-called *Prussian Class-System,* according to which the tax-payers were divided into three separate curiæ. The first curia consisted of the highest tax-payers, who subscribed one-third of all taxes; their number was of course very small. Those who paid the second third of the taxes, formed the second curia, and finally all the small tax-payers who filled the last third, formed the third curia. Each curia had an equal number of delegates, so that one-third of the city-*duma* represented a few wealthy people, one-third represented the middle class, and only one-third — the multitude of small tax-payers.

On June 18, 1870, the statute became a law. Its main defects were its distortion of the all-class-principle, and the insufficient amount of independence it afforded the municipal self-government. True, the city-*dumas* were made independent of the local administration, and were made subject directly to the Senate, while the governors were instructed only to watch the legality of the enactments of the *dumas.* But actual independence is connected with the power of taxation, and in this respect the rights of the *dumas* were very limited. They were permitted to tax only certain incomes, and to a limited amount, so that they received very meagre means for their expenditures; but at the same time they were charged with the fulfilment of many obligations which were by their nature fiscal rather than local, as, for instance, the up-keep of the police,[1] or the partial up-keep of the civil administration of the city. As a result, the funds of the municipal self-government did not suffice for the satisfaction of such cultural needs as popular education and

[1] All Russian police are in *national* service.— TR.

medical care. The limitations and restrictions promulgated in the municipal statute were more considerable than those introduced into the *zemstvo*-statute by the law of November 21, 1866. We shall see later how the municipal self-government has developed in actual life.

Let us turn now to the important reforms in the Ministry of War, which I have mentioned. The question of the reorganisation of the army, and the radical reformation of all the defensive means of the country loomed up gravely after the Crimean Campaign which had proved the general backwardness of Russia in comparison with civilised countries, and the inadequate conditions of her defence, in spite of her numerical strength. But such reforms as the equipment of the army with modern ammunition, or the laying out of good roads, required immense sums of money and in view of the poor financial conditions after the war, these reforms, obvious as their need appeared, had to be postponed. The first two years after the war were occupied by the release of a considerable part of the army which amounted in 1856 to two million two hundred thousand; it was reduced to one and a half million. It was intended to reduce the army further, but the international complications of 1859, and later the Polish insurrection of 1862–1863, which threatened the intervention of foreign Powers, forced the Government to carry through an additional mobilisation, and to keep five military corps on the western frontier.

Another circumstance which blocked the work of reorganisation was the presence at the head of the Ministry of an ordinary Nicolaievan general, Sukhozanet, a firm man, but one utterly unfit for any reformatory activity. Not until 1861 was he supplanted by D. A. Miliutin, brother of N. A. Miliutin, in whom Alexander had finally found the right person to carry through the reform. D. A. Miliutin had been a professor in the Academy of the General Staff, and later Chief of the Staff of the Caucasian army, and thus, in addition to distinguished personal gifts, he combined a theoretic with a practical preparation.

Miliutin began by mitigating the service for the soldiers. Up to that time the term of service was twenty-five years of what was generally considered equivalent to hard labour. Even the bonded peasants looked upon military service as the severest and most degrading punishment; the soldiers naturally felt quite humble, and considered themselves no better than criminals, a circumstance that had considerable bearing upon the spirit of the army. Miliutin reduced the term to sixteen years; abolished corporal punishment which had been widely practised before; he further endeavoured to change the attitude of the officers toward their subordinates — in general he tried to elevate the soldier to the dignified position of the defender of his country. He reorganised the management of the Ministry of War along more reasonable and economical lines; he proposed the abolition of separate army-staffs in time of peace and of such big units as corps, so that the largest military unit became a division (four regiments). The minister of war was given greater authority, but on the other hand the military administration was somewhat decentralised, being divided into Military Districts, the commanders of which appeared to be quite independent authorities in time of peace, combining the authority of corps-commanders with that of military governor-generals in relation to the army. The next important reform was the reorganisation of the military judiciary along more humane principles, the same as were laid as the foundation of the judiciary reforms of 1864; owing to the fact that Miliutin stood at the head of the work, and to the absolute confidence Alexander had had in him, the reform of the military judiciary was spared the mutilations which the civil judiciary suffered during the years of reaction. Alongside with this one should consider the reform of the military schools which were reorganised from exclusive caste-institutions into military gymnasia, with a higher educational programme. Higher Junker-schools were assigned for special military training and for the preparation of military specialists; among these were the Pavlovsky, Alexandrovsky, Constantinovsky, and Nicolaievsky Schools. This reform contributed greatly to the higher educational level of the military contingent, and to the mitigation of martial customs, in general.

But the chief military reform carried out by Miliutin was the radical change in the very system of the military obligation, the complete abolition of the recruitments which lay heavily on the people, and the introduction of a most democratising principle into Russian life. Throughout Europe the introduction of universal military service was taking place at that time; that system was important not only by virtue of the conditions of equality which it established in accordance with the new order of society instituted everywhere during the nineteenth century, but it appeared considerably more adequate also in the technical, military, and economic respects.

The military reorganisation which was carried through in Prussia after the Treaty of Tilsit by the talented General Scharnhorst served as the prototype of that system. In view of Napoleon's prohibition of maintaining more than forty thousand men in actual service, Scharnhorst hit upon the clever idea of subjecting the whole nation to a military training, by making the service-term very short, and registering every soldier upon the completion of his actual service into the reserve. Thus in case of war the forty thousand men could be rapidly multiplied many times, through mobilising the reserves. On this idea was based the acceptance of universal military service by most of the European Powers during the first half of the nineteenth century. But while the mobilisation of the reserves was quite feasible for Prussia, in view of her small size, good roads of communication, and the comparatively high culture of the population,— it was almost impossible in the Russia of the first half of the nineteenth century. For this reason Alexander I was forced to turn to the unfortunate idea of Military Colonies; for the same reason Russia kept under Nicolas I, as at present, an army of one million, although the population was three times smaller than now.

With the development of railroad-building in the Seventies there arose a possibility for the reorganisation of the army along general European lines. Miliutin presented his plan for the reform to Alexander; it was approved, passed by the State Council, and became a law on January 1, 1874.

By the new statute recruitments were abolished, and universal service equal for all classes took their place. While before men had been recruited from the age of twenty to thirty-four and were often fathers of families, the new law called only for men of the age of twenty for a term of six years, after which time they were registered as reserves for nine years, and remained assigned to the militia till the age of forty. All classes enjoyed equal privileges. Miliutin granted exemption of the first degree to only sons of parents, or only grandsons of grand-parents, or only brothers-supporters of orphan-minors. The exemption of the second degree was granted to those who had brothers younger than eighteen. Exemption of the third degree was granted to those who followed immediately brothers in active service, even if there were other brothers-supporters in the family.

The non-exempted, if found healthy and capable of service, were assigned as recruits, in the order of lot-numbers they drew, until they filled the amount required every year from a given district. If the number of the non-exempt was not sufficient for the completion of the required contingent, those of the third-degree and, next, of the second-degree-exemption were called upon, again in the order of the lots drawn. But the men of the first degree exemption could be called to service only by a special Imperial summons.

Privileges were granted to persons of education. University men had to serve half a year, instead of six years; those who had a secondary education had to serve two years; graduates of Municipal or District schools, or of four-grade-gymnasia — three years. Finally, those who had a primary education served four years. Men of a university or secondary education were permitted, besides, to enter the army as volunteers, in which case the term of their service was further reduced to one half.

Such were the fundamental features of Miliutin's reform which has proved to be one of the most important factors in the democratisation of Russian society; at the same time it was one of the most humane reforms of the reign of Alexander II, having actually abolished military bondage.

In 1875 Miliutin introduced new rules for the training of soldiers, which concerned not only military subjects, but began with general reading. In regard to literacy, the contingent of the army had improved by virtue of the fact that it was composed of men of higher classes after the promulgation of the new statute; until the reform of 1874 the number of literate in the army amounted to thirteen per cent., while in 1874 the percentage rose at once to twenty. Owing to the rules of 1875, almost every recruit went back home able to read and write, so that in Miliutin's hands the army had become a considerable surrogate of schools, the number of which was quite insufficient in Russia.

Curiously enough, during the discussion of that reform in the State Council, the educational privileges and other liberal articles of the reform were opposed by those ministers who should have upheld them. Minister of Education, Count Tolstoy, denied the desirability of granting special privileges for men of a university education, and Count Pahlen, Minister of Justice, opposed the subjection of cases about evading military service to juries; Miliutin, a military general and Minister of War, had to defend the liberal principles from the attack of those who might have been expected to take a different stand. Enjoying the full confidence of Alexander, Miliutin was in a position not only to have his reform passed through the State Council, but, unlike the other reform-ministers of Alexander II, to *see it carried out into life,* since he was not dismissed like Lanskoy or his brother, Nicolas, but remained minister of war to the very end of Alexander's reign.

CHAPTER XXXI

OF a totally different character was the activity of the Minister of Education, Count D. A. Tolstoy, outspokenly reactionary and directed plausibly against Nihilism, but in fact against any liberal and democratic ideas. His policy was in complete accord with the reactionary mood of the Government, which took form after Karakozov's attempt on the Tzar.

In general we may say that Count Tolstoy and Miliutin were two persons who brilliantly characterised the two contradictory sides, the two irreconcilable, almost mutually exclusive, tendencies of the reign of Alexander II. It may appear astonishing that for fifteen years after 1866 those two great political actors remained among the co-workers of Alexander II, and that both had evidently enjoyed his full confidence. We may explain it by the fact that in Alexander himself there was going on a constant conflict between two opposed principles. On one side he was fully aware of the necessity for promulgating progressive reforms which would radically alter the former order, but on the other side he was under constant repression and fear of the growing revolutionary movement which he considered it necessary to combat rigorously. We have seen that after the reactionary tendencies of the Government had become quite definite, still the peculiar conditions of the new life, the technical and economic needs of the State, powerfully demanded the continuation of the reforms, and such reforms as the municipal and the military were carried out after 1866.

Count Tolstoy consistently and incessantly represented those reactionary tendencies and demands, under the onslaught of which Alexander found himself after 1866. As a matter of fact, Tolstoy was not an enemy of education; he was neither like the mystic clericalist Golitzin of the time of Alexander I, nor like the savage obscurantist Shirinsky-Shikhmatov at the end of the reign of Nicolas I. In his personal tastes and fondness of Classicism Tolstoy resembled externally rather Count Uvarov, to whom Russia owes a considerable advance in education in spite of his boast that he would hold back her general development for fifty years. But undoubtedly Tolstoy was less clever and educated than Uvarov, and at the same time more consistent and perseverant in the promulgation of his ideas, for Uvarov was, properly speaking, first of all a man of compromise, and ever calculating about his career. Yet, unlike Uvarov, Tolstoy has left behind him the reputation of having been unreservedly a foe and extinguisher of enlightenment.

As I said, Tolstoy was not an enemy of education proper, but he was a constant, consequential, and vicious enemy of the people, and as minister he obstinately and persistently trampled the most sacred rights and interests of the *people* for the sake of the interests and prerogatives of that ruling *class,* to which he belonged. For this reason he appeared to be one of the most ardent advocates of that political and social order with which those prerogatives were connected. Of all the ministers of Alexander none equalled Tolstoy in his persevering and uncompromising upholding of the reactionary principles. We have seen that Reitern wrote that Shuvalov and Valuiev carried on a pseudo-liberal policy, while actually it was reactionary. Nobody could have said this about Tolstoy; he was an open and outspoken reactionary, and of all the ministers of Alexander II he was the only one who *openly declared himself opposed to the reforms of the Sixties.* He never compromised with his views like Valuiev who appeared liberal during the period of liberalism and reactionary during the period of reaction. Tolstoy was a convinced reactionary; he

sharply criticised the peasant-reform in a memorandum which
aroused the indignation of Alexander, and was appointed Minister of Education as an acknowledged reactionary, at the time
when the Tzar considered such a reactionary necessary for that
post.

In his activity Tolstoy found support in the theoretic principles with which he was furnished by the prominent publicists
of the time — M. N. Katkov and P. M. Leontiev, the editors
and publishers of the *Russian Messenger* and the *Moscow
News*. Katkov, as we know, had then become a most rabid
opponent of the Nihilistic tendencies which developed at the
end of the Sixties; on the other hand, being opposed to the
separatistic tendencies which began to manifest themselves in
some of Russia's borderlands, particularly in the Western
provinces, he grew more and more reactionary after the Polish
insurrection, and especially after the attentate of Karakozov.
During the epoch of reforms he was known as a liberal of the
English calibre; he still preserved a portion of his Anglomania,
but it turned conservative and even reactionary. Tolstoy
shared Katkov's Anglomania, and intended to transplant the
English system of education, which appealed to him on account
of its aristocratic character. But while the English aristocratic system was in full accord with the established political
order (where the aristocracy was a constitutional factor,
although a conservative one) and has guarded the acquired
rights and liberties of the people from the absolutism of the
kings, the aristocracy which Katkov and Tolstoy aspired to
implant in Russia was to suppress the interests of the people
under the wing of the autocracy. This difference between
English and Russian aristocracy was well observed and indicated by Prince A. I. Vassilchikov in a memorandum published
in 1875 in Berlin, called a *Letter to the Minister of Education,
Count Tolstoy, from Prince A. Vassilchikov*. On the whole,
we must say that although Tolstoy's system undoubtedly had

certain aristocratic tendencies, in the most unattractive sense of that word, yet his main and most essential idea consisted in the struggle with Nihilism which had rapidly developed in Russian society, and to which was ascribed an important revolutionising influence. It was from that point of view that Katkov also criticised the former system of popular education.

By Nihilism was then understood the spread of the materialistic point of view, which in its turn was connected with the popularisation of the latest conclusions of natural science among broad circles of the *intelligentzia* and the college youth, owing to the efforts of Pisarev and other publicists of the *Russian Word,* the chief organ of the Nihilists. Tolstoy and Katkov held accountable for the spread of such a *Weltanschauung* among students the system of education which allowed hours to the study of natural science, of history, of rhetoric, and similar subjects which train the pupils in " senseless highbrowiness," in " water-grinding," in acquiring " premature, hasty conclusions "; in short they opposed such studies as helped to develop independent thinking, demanding instead a system which would train the young minds exclusively in the acquisition of exact information, and prevent them from excessive reasoning which led to Nihilistic ideas and materialistic teachings. They considered ancient languages, and next — mathematics, as the most important studies in secondary schools. Such were the basic principles of Russian Classicism, theoretically elaborated by Katkov, and put into practice by Tolstoy.

From the very first Tolstoy favoured that system, but he found its realisation quite difficult; financial conditions did not permit any considerable expenditures, there was a dearth in instructors of Latin, and particularly of Greek, and besides he was aware of the opposition his plan was bound to meet not only on the part of the public, but even among the upper bureaucratic circles, even among the members of the State Council, where the discharged reform-ministers succeeded in creating a liberal atmosphere and sympathy with the ideas of the former progressive Minister of Education, Golovnin. Tolstoy had to move his plan slowly. At first he sent out a circular to all District Curators, asking them to point out the defects of the existing system of education. Next he founded a new high institution, the Philological Institute, which was to prepare instructors of ancient languages; later he reorganised along these lines the Lyceum founded by Bezborodko in Niezhin. At the same time he engaged in active negotiations with foreign institutions, especially Austrian, where there were many Slav philologists who might easily learn Russian and become instructors of ancient languages in Russian gymnasia. A considerable number of such instructors soon flowed in from Galicia and Bohemia.

In 1871, i.e., five years after his appointment, Tolstoy decided to bring his plan to the front. He presented a carefully worked out memorandum to the Tzar, recommending classic education as a means for combating Nihilistic tendencies among the youth, the evil influence of which Alexander had pointed out in his rescript to Prince Gagarin, in 1866. Alexander regarded the general tendencies of Tolstoy's report favourably, but since he himself had no classic education, he ordered a commission of experts to discuss the matter. Among the members of the special commission were Valuiev, Troinitzky, Tolstoy, some specialists from his ministry, and Count S. G. Stroganov. Tolstoy found it necessary to prepare himself for the occasion, and he took lessons in Greek from a director of a gymnasium.

The commission rapidly worked out a detailed plan for the new statute, and presented it to a special committee of the State Council, among whom were all ministers who had charge of some schools, the former Ministers of Education — Kovalevsky and Golovnin, former Minister of Justice, Count Panin,— D. A. Miliutin,— fifteen members altogether. Of them nine members sided with Tolstoy, while six vigorously opposed his plan; those who pleaded most energetically against it were D. A. Miliutin, then Admiral Count Lietke, the former tutor of Grand Duke Constantine, former Minister Golovnin, Academic J. K. Grot, and to the general surprise — Count V. N. Panin. Miliutin and Golovnin pointed out that the classic system was considered dead even in England and Prussia, which countries Tolstoy used as models for his plan, and that *real*-schools were being opened there on equal rights with classic gymnasia, so that the parents might be free to choose. Miliutin also denied the connection between a *real* system of education and Materialism and Nihilism; he indicated that all the actors of the French revolution, the Materialists at the end of the eighteenth century, were brought up on Classicism. Tolstoy won in the special committee.

But at the general session of the State Council, where the discussion was customarily purely formal, as the members accepted the project prepared by some special department or committee, something unusual occurred on this occasion. Moved by one of the strongest human feelings — parental love, to use the expression of Prince Vassilchikov, the State Council rejected Tolstoy's project by twenty-nine votes against nineteen. But Alexander joined the minority, and on May 15, 1871, Tolstoy's project became law.

In the new Classic gymnasia forty-nine hours a week were assigned for the study of Latin, and thirty-six hours for Greek. The students were to gain a thorough knowledge of the grammatical and syntactical peculiarities of the ancient languages, and to be capable of rapidly translating under dictation difficult passages from Russian into Latin or Greek. Then the amount of mathematics taught was considerably enlarged, while the hours of the instruction in Russian language and rhetoric were greatly decreased; the instruction in Church-Slavic was introduced at the expense of Russian. Natural science was eliminated, the hours for history, geography, and modern languages were contracted, and the study of modern languages was declared of secondary importance.

At the same time the whole educational system in the gymnasia was changed. The pupils were to be trained in such a way that they should appear ultra-disciplined and absolutely obedient; espionage was encouraged under the form of " special confidence " and " frankness " on the part of the pupils towards their instructors. The Pedagogic Councils lost all authority, and the entire power was concentrated in the hands of the directors; the latter, as well as the inspectors, were appointed largely (70–80 per cent.) from among instructors of ancient languages.

Alongside with this the *real*-gymnasia were abolished; in their place were founded *real*-schools, with a six years' course (the gymnasia had an eight years' course), intended to give the students a special, technical or industrial, education, which in the opinion of Katkov and Tolstoy would satisfy the educational needs of the higher industrial classes. Subjects of general education and development were eliminated from the *real*-schools as well as from the classical gymnasia. In place of ancient languages the *real*-schools required an enormous amount of drawing — forty hours a week. A considerable amount of mathematics was required, and a very moderate dose of natural science which, according to instructions, was to be taught not scientifically, but " technologically," whatever this term might have meant. Thus the main object of the schools was frankly considered not the elevation of the level of knowledge and enlightenment, but the substitution for matters of general education of subjects designed to discipline the mind.

At the time of the discussion of the project it was vigorously attacked by the progressive press, such as *European Messenger, Petrograd News, Voice* (the radical organs, *Contemporary,* and the *Russian Word,* had already been discontinued). But when it was presented to the State Council, Tolstoy obtained an Imperial order prohibiting the discussion of the plan by the press.

Tolstoy had intended to reorganise in a corresponding spirit the higher educational institutions, but in spite of his repeated efforts in that direction, he never succeeded in radically changing the university statute of 1863. He was forced to be satisfied with issuing additional rules periodically, with the aim of further restricting the liberties of the students and of the professors. During his administration numerous disturbances occurred among the students, particularly grave in the years 1869, 1874, and 1878. Tolstoy made use of those disturbances for preparing the reform of the universities, and worked in that direction upon the mood of Alexander. But in spite of the co-operation of Katkov he failed to accomplish his aim. The elements of the new statute he prepared were ultimately put into practice by his successor, Delianov, in 1884, at a more opportune conjuncture.

Tolstoy's interference with the gymnasia for women, which belonged to a different department (the Institutions of Empress Marie), was of such a nature, especially in regard to the limitation of the instruction of natural science, that the distinguished pedagogue, Vishnegradsky, who was at the head of those schools, was forced to resign. Tolstoy was opposed to higher education for women. Before 1863 women had forced themselves into the universities as " free-hearers," or unclassified students; but the commission which discussed the statute of 1863 rejected the clause about admitting women into universities. Then a group of progressive women, under the leadership of Mesdames Trubnikov, Stasov, and Philosophov, began a series of intercessions for the organisation of higher education for women. Tolstoy finally had to yield, and permit public lectures for both sexes, to be read by university professors; one weighty reason for his consent was the fact that

Russian women, deprived of higher education at home, filled the universities of Switzerland, where they easily fell under the influence of socialistic and anarchistic propaganda, to the mortification of the Government. Thus the Alarchinsky Courses were opened, the majority of whose students consisted of women. Similar courses, especially for women, were opened in 1870 in Moscow, under the name of Lubiansky; they acquired the character of a school of natural sciences, *par excellence;* one year later they were joined by a historico-philological department. As to Petrograd, it was only in 1878 that Professor Bestuzhev-Riumin succeeded in opening private courses for women, with a physico-mathematical and a historico-philological department. A special society was organised for the finding of means for the support of those courses, and owing to the energy of that society and of the persons who stood at the head of that institution, those courses have developed into Higher Courses for Women, which are still in existence.

Tolstoy refused to allow women to study medicine, but D. A. Miliutin, as Minister of War, opened in 1872 medical courses for women at the Nicolaievsky Hospital. In 1881, Minister of War Vannovsky found the existence of the courses at a military hospital out of place, and they were closed. Only in 1897 were they reopened in the form of the now existing Medical Institute for Women.

Such was the fate of the secondary and higher schools under Count Tolstoy. We should note that Miliutin's military gymnasia were at that time the only schools of a general educational character.

Tolstoy's attitude was as negative towards primary as towards secondary and higher education. By the statute of Golovnin, of 1864, the Ministry of Education left the founding of primary schools to the initiative of private persons, societies, cities, *zemstvos,* and other institutions. The Ministry obliged itself only to supervise the order of instruction in those schools; it was to spend for the support of primary schools, one hundred thousand rubles the first year, two hundred thousand the second year, and three hundred thousand rubles during the third year. Actually only the first assignation took place, in 1864; in the following years money for schools was expended only for the western borderland, with the view of fighting Polonism. The one hundred thousand rubles assigned for the Russian provinces were to be distributed among the thirty-four School Councils which existed in the *zemstvo*-provinces, so that it would make three thousand rubles for each province. But even that meagre sum was given a different direction by Minister Tolstoy who either used it for organising some Ministerial Schools, or for the foundation of Teachers' Institutes, or of Seminaries for teachers of primary schools.

The *zemstvos* have played the main rôle in opening primary schools, although by the statute of 1864 they were not obliged to engage in that activity, except for the clause added through the initiative of the *zemstvos* of Petrograd and Nizhni-Novgorod, and owing to the support of M. A. Korf. According to this the *zemstvos* were allowed to care for the finding of means for the spread of primary education in *zemstvo*-provinces and districts. From the very start the *zemstvos* interpreted that clause broadly, and considered it one of their chief obligations to care for the dissemination of popular education in Russia. In view of the meagre means in their possession, they were at the beginning rather unsuccessful in their attempts to encourage the opening of schools by village-communities.

According to the statute of 1864 there were Provincial and District School Councils. The Provincial Councils were poorly constructed. Golovnin had to combat the aspirations of the Ecclesiastical Department for the management of popular education; he was forced to compromise and to decree that the Provincial Council was to be presided over by a bishop, and its membership to consist of the governor, two representatives of the Ministry of Education, and two members of the *zemstvo*. Since the bishop and the governor were absorbed in their own affairs, the Provincial Councils were clumsy, dead institutions. The District Councils consisted of one representative of the Ministry of Education (usually the principal of the local District-school), one representative of the Ministry of Interior (who was preferably to be elected from among the local gentry), and two members from the *zemstvo*. They were permitted to elect their own president, and he was generally one of the *zemstvo*-members. The District Councils were inclined to work hand in hand with the *zemstvo*, and this greatly strengthened the position of the latter in its educational policy.

When Tolstoy was appointed Minister of Education in 1866, he sharply criticised the existing state of affairs, and immediately prepared a project for the installation in every province of a special ministerial inspector who would guard the school-business from falling into "ill-intentioned" hands. In 1869 the inspectors were installed, and one year later Tolstoy had the audacity to claim in his report to the Tzar that the activity of the School Councils and of the *zemstvo* was "good for nothing," and that only the inspectors were performing their duties properly. Even a superficial glance at the situation was sufficient to prove that one inspector for a whole province was actually unable to get acquainted with the state of affairs, and was in fact impotent in regard to the supervision of the schools.

Striving to take the management of primary education out the hands of the School Councils, Tolstoy obtained in 1871 a new Imperial decree, instructing the inspectors to interfere with the appointment of teachers by the Councils. This was in violation of the statute of 1864, which placed the *zemstvo*-institutions outside of the jurisdiction of the administration; complaints against the Provincial Councils could be brought only before the Senate. The conflict between the *zemstvo* and the Ministry of Education was sharp and relentless. Tolstoy saw the necessity of changing the statute, in order that he might usurp the management of the primary schools. In 1873 he presented a plan for a new statute, by which directors of People's Schools were to be appointed at the head of the Provincial Councils, and at the head of the District Councils — inspectors of those Schools, which posts (of directors and inspectors) were to be established in every province and district. The reformed Councils were to be subordinate to District Curators.

Although this reform was approved by the Emperor, it was strongly opposed by the State Council. Tolstoy unexpectedly came into collision with a strong wing of the nobility who were indignant at his attempts to place popular education in the hands of the bureaucracy. That sentiment found access to Alexander, and on December 25, 1873, Tolstoy received an Imperial rescript, in which his attention was called to the fact that the supervision of the schools was to be intrusted in the provinces to the first order — the nobility. Accordingly Tolstoy had to alter his plan, and place at the head of the Provincial Council the provincial Marshal of Nobility, and at the head of the District Council — the District Marshal of Nobility. In many places the Marshals were on the side of the *zemstvo,* it should be noted. The number of inspectors was increased to two for every province, instead of one; Tolstoy could not install more inspectors on account of financial difficulties.

The conflict between the Ministry of Education and the *zemstvo* was continued in the Eighties, under Minister Delianov. During Tolstoy's administration the struggle assumed bitter forms. The representatives of the *zemstvo* had to defend the popular schools from the bureaucratic encroachments of the inspectors who tried to restrict and curtail the education of the peasants' children. After the issue of the law concerning universal military service, the *zemstvo*-members of the School Council had to perform the function of examiners for those who sought the educational privilege of the fourth degree, i. e., of primary education. This rôle enabled the *zemstvo*-members to manifest more vigorously their opposition to the policy of the Ministry of Education.

The friction between the *zemstvo* and the agents of the Ministry of Education finally grew so keen that in certain provinces, where the representatives of the Ministry were particularly aggressive in their endeavour to limit the participation of the *zemstvo*-members in the school management, the *zemstvo* refused to vote money for the schools. In 1879 the Tver *zemstvo* resolved to discontinue all money appropriations for popular education. It is not known what the end would have been had not the epoch of the " heart dictatorship " come, and had not Loris-Melivov obtained the dismissal of Count Tolstoy in 1880. Only then were the *zemstvos* enabled to breathe more freely, under the more liberal ministers, A. A. Saburov and Baron Nicolayi (both of them did not keep their positions for a long time: Saburov from the end of 1880 till the spring of 1881, and Baron Nicolayi from May, 1881, to May, 1882).

CHAPTER XXXII

WE shall now examine the sphere of activity of the *zemstvo*-institutions and their means and powers. The organs of the *zemstvo*-self-government were instituted for the management of local affairs, in districts and provinces, and for the satisfaction of local needs by the aid of the means that were given them and of the certain administrative authority which was granted them by the law. The entire field of their activity was indicated in the second article of the statute of 1864. It comprised first of all various so called *zemstvo*-obligations: to maintain in good order the roads, to lay out new roads when necessary, to manage the so-called *zemsky*-post, i.e., the post-horses and stations for internal communication in the districts, to take charge of the alimentation of the people, of "public welfare," in the broad sense of the word, including care of cripples, poor, and of corresponding philanthropic institutions; it also included care for the development of local commerce, industry, and particularly agriculture, and for the insurance of property; also care for public health, i.e., local medical-sanitary activity, for popular education in the provinces and districts, for the erection of churches, and for the up-keep of penitentiaries.

Most of these tasks were performed even in the pre-reform time by various bureaucratic or class-institutions which used for the purpose certain *zemsky* taxes and also "natural obligations" borne by the people by the order of provincial and district authorities. The law of 1851 divided the *zemsky* obligations and taxes into *State* and *provincial;* the income from those taxes amounted to four million four hundred and fifty thousand rubles in 1814, and fifty years later — to twenty-three million nine hundred thousand rubles; of the latter sum nineteen million were classified as State-taxes, and only four million eight hundred thousand — as provincial. At the institution of the *zemstvos* the entire *zemsky* State taxes, which formed, as we have seen, three-fourths of the pre-reform revenue, were retained for the central organs of the Government. The *zemstvos* were permitted to obtain means through self-taxation, i.e., by levying provincial and district taxes on real-estate and commercial-industrial institutions. They also received about nine million rubles which had been collected for the maintenance of various philanthropic institutions; in the thirty-three provinces, where *zemstvos* had been instituted at that time, there were in all seven hundred and eighty-five such asylums, for which the population paid yearly a little over four hundred thousand rubles, an average of twelve to thirteen thousand rubles per province. The *zemstvos* received also nine million rubles which had accumulated as alimentary capital.

The pre-reform revenues proved insufficient for the needs of the *zemstvos*. In 1865, when nineteen *zemstvos* were installed in provinces, their budget reached five million six hundred thousand rubles; in 1867, when there were twenty-eight *zemstvo*-provinces, the budget rose to ten million three hundred and nine thousand, in 1868 to fourteen million and a half, in 1871 to twenty-one and a half million, in 1876 to thirty and a half million, and towards the eighties, in spite of the drainage of the Russo-Turkish war, the *zemstvo*-budget reached thirty-six million rubles. Thus in 1880, sixteen years after the publication of the *zemstvo*-statute, the *zemsky*-taxes increased more than sixteen times over those of the pre-reform period; yet compared with the growing needs of the people, the collected revenue was far from sufficient.

From the very beginning the *zemstvos* encountered very unfavourable conditions; besides the reaction in governmental circles, which impeded their activities, they were greatly embarrassed by the general economic and financial conditions. The situation of both the landowners and the emancipated peasants immediately after the Reform was sucn that it was practically impossible to assess land. Prince A. I. Vassilchikov wrote at that time:

" The Russian land is poor, for it, the land — literally the soil, is paying above its capacity, above its productivity . . . because for centuries agriculture has been burdened more than any other branch of national labour with high taxes . . . because the land squeezes out of the poorest tax-payers most of the taxes for the satisfaction of those State needs which least concern the poor tax-payers. . . ."

Unable to tax the over-burdened land any more, the *zemstvos* tried to meet their requirements by assessing heavily industry and commerce. But Minister of Finance Reitern saw in this policy a danger to his plans of protecting big industry, and owing to his initiative a new law was issued on November 21, 1868, making it possible for the *zemstvo* to assess only the immovable property of factories and foundries, and commercial patents and license — not more than ten to twenty-five per cent. of their fiscal assessments. This at once put the *zemstvos* in a difficult financial position, and caused the first friction between them and the Government, which has continued to grow keen, assuming at times such extreme forms as the temporary closing of the *zemstvo* institutions (in the province of Petrograd).

The enormous needs of popular education, of public health, etc., required immense sums of money, and the *zemstvos* had to solve the grave problem of how to obtain the necessary sums without taxing the population beyond endurance. Prince Vassilchikov furnished curious figures about the *zemsky* taxes before the Reform; of the total sum of thirty-five million five hundred and ninety-eight thousand rubles, thirty-five million were collected from one hundred and nine million desiatins of peasants' land, five hundred thousand rubles from seventy million desiatins of landowners' land, and thirty-six thousand rubles from one hundred and thirteen million desiatins of fiscal land. Thus fiscal land paid *zemsky* taxes one thousand times less, and the landowners' land seventy times less per desiatin than the peasants' land. The *zemstvos* had to regulate the payment of the taxes, and we see from the budget of 1868 what a radical change they wrought in that field: Of the nine million seven hundred thousand rubles of land-assessments, four million eight hundred thousand rubles were levied on landowners', and Imperial lands — seventy-five million desiatins altogether, while an almost equal sum was collected from the seventy million desiatins of peasants' land.

Another difficulty of the *zemstvos* consisted, and still consists, in the regulation according to which they must first of all cover the so-called *obligatory* expenses — pre-reform items; these do not include such needs as public health, education, agricultural or industrial improvements. From the budget of 1868 we see that eighty-two and eight-tenths per cent. were spent on the *obligatory* items plus maintenance of *zemstvo*-boards; only eight per cent. could be spent on public health, and five per cent. for popular education.

We must note that on the whole the early *zemstvo*-workers manifested high idealism and disinterestedness; they stood above class-interests, and honestly strove for the betterment of the peasants' conditions in every respect. If the results of their ardent work were not brilliant, we should not overlook the most obvious causes: lack of funds, and the opposition of the Government.

After Karakozov's attempt on the Tzar's life, the relation between the Government and the *zemstvo* grew rapidly worse. A series of new rules was issued in quick succession, limiting the rights and publicity of the *zemstvo*-institutions, and subor' dinating them to the local administration, to wit the governors. The growing restrictions, and the systematic ignoring of *zemstvo*-pleas and declarations by the Ministry of Interior, affected the attractiveness of the *zemstvo*-activity, and drove away many disappointed devoted workers. In their place came new types of members who demonstrated not only narrow class-interests, but often base selfish aspirations. During the railroad-delirium, the *Gründer*-spirit found expression even among *zemstvo*-institutions, and the altruistic service of the early workers gave place to seeking for a portion of the " public pie." During the dark period not many idealists were capable of retaining their fighting posts in an atmosphere of depression; only exceptional personalities could continue the hard struggle against the reaction, and devote themselves to modest, but productive culture work against heavy odds. Under such circumstances progressive tendencies could be preserved, naturally, only in a few provincial and district *zemstvos*.

CHAPTER XXXIII

L ET us cast a glance at the new courts, and at the press freed from preliminary censorship at the end of the sixties and during the first half of the seventies.

Properly speaking, the new judiciary statutes were enacted as early as November 20, 1864. But the question of their installation was subjected to a lengthy discussion, at first by the Committee of Ministers, then by a special committee, and lastly by the State Council, after which a decree was issued concerning the introduction of the statutes into practice. The Government's hesitation was due to two serious reasons: lack of funds (nine million rubles were assigned for the reform), and lack of adequately prepared men for the occupation of the new judicial posts which were to be held for life. Fortunately the Government rejected the proposed compromise — to withdraw the life-tenure principle, which measure, instituted at the very introduction of the new statutes, would have dealt them a death-blow. As to the financial difficulties, two suggestions were made; Prince Gagarin, President of the Committee of Ministers, proposed introducing the new courts simultaneously throughout the Empire, but in view of lack of means, limiting their personnel. This would have taxed the energy of the new institutions, and would have affected the speed of the court decisions; yet it had been solemnly promised that the new courts would be " speedy, just, and merciful." The other plan was offered by Minister of Justice Zamiatnin, and called for the installation of the new courts for the time being in only two districts, that of Petrograd and that of Moscow. The Tzar ordered a special commission to examine both opinions; the majority accepted Zamiatnin's plan, against a minority of the most ardent friends of the reform, who, headed by Senator Zarudny, insisted that it would be better to postpone the installation of the new courts altogether, if it was impossible to carry out the reform simultaneously throughout the Empire. We may rejoice now that the opinion of the minority did not triumph, for who knows what would have become of the new statutes during the reactionary period, had they not been promulgated in 1866?

The State Council approved the opinion of the majority, and decreed that the new institutions be opened on April 17, 1866, in both Capital districts. Karakozov's attempt on the Tzar on April the 4th, encouraged the reactionaries to suggest the postponement of the opening of the new courts, but Alexander remained firm in his decision. The courts were opened on the date set.

In spite of all apprehensions the personnel of the new courts was extraordinarily successful. Minister Zamiatnin had spent much of his time in seeking out distinguished and honest workers among the old courts, and he filled the four hundred new positions in the districts, which ranked from coroners to senators of the cassational departments, with brilliant men. From the very start the trials in the new courts, in spite of the novelty of the proceedings, passed smoothly and successfully. The public interest might be compared perhaps only with the interest shown in the sessions of the first State *Duma;* the gallery was always filled with eager crowds who could not control their enthusiasm, and cheered in spite of the admonitions of the presiding judge.

The press also warmly greeted the new courts. Here is what Katkov wrote at that time:

"With this reform an entirely new principle is entering into our life, which will place a conspicuous border-line between the past and the future, and which will be reflected *in everything.* . . . Its influence will not be limited to the judiciary institutions proper, but like a keen element it will invade everything, and will lend to all a new significance, a new power. Justice, performed publicly and with the participation of jurymen, will become a living social force. An independent court, not subject to administrative control, will elevate and ennoble the social milieu, for through it the character of independence will be imparted to all manifestations of public life. . . ."

In 1867, after the courts had demonstrated their adequacy, Katkov wrote:

" In truth, one can hardly believe that such an important matter, so dissimilar to our former order, has been so firmly and successfully implanted from the basic idea to the minutest details in a short time. *History will not forget a single one of the names of those connected with this great work of the civic rejuvenation of Russia."*

Now we can hardly believe that those words belonged to Katkov, who eventually became one of the most vicious enemies of the new courts, and accused them of taking part in the general sedition. But then it was the " honey-moon " of the reform, to use the expression of J. V. Hessen; as a member of the new courts, the now famous A. F. Koni, expressed himself then, all the workers put into their activity their *first love.* The idyl of the honey-moon could not last very long, considering the reactionary conditions.

First of all the keen dissatisfaction of the Government, especially of Valuiev, was aroused by the verdicts of the courts concerning cases of violating censorship regulations. Such cases began to appear in 1866. The first, in which A. S. Suvorin, then a liberal, was tried for his book, " All Sorts," passed comparatively safely for the new courts: the author was sentenced to a light penalty, and the book was withdrawn from circulation. But in the very next case, against Pypin, editor of the *Contemporary,* and Y. G. Zhukovsky, author of the article " The

Cause of the New Generation," the Crown court (not a jury) found no guilt, and acquitted them. Valuiev was utterly enraged, declared the verdict impossible, and requested the dismissal of Motovilov, the president of the court, in defiance of the principle of life-tenure. Alexander remained, however, within the limits of the law, perhaps because the verdict was decided while Motovilov was on a furlough. The case ended with the procurator appealing to the higher cassation, and the Judicial Chamber sentencing Pypin and Zhukovsky to one week's arrest; as to the magazine itself, the *Contemporary* had been in the meantime stopped forever by an Imperial decree.

Another celebrated case was that of Protopopov, a petty clerk who was accused of having insulted one of his superiors, a vice-director of the department. To Valuiev's horror, the jury found Protopopov irresponsible, on the basis of a diagnosis by experts, and acquitted him as having acted in a moment of mental derangement. The reactionary press, especially the *Tiding,* began to attack the revolutionism of the courts.

Early in 1867, when the Petrograd *zemstvo* held public discussions concerning the new law which limited the power of taxation by the *zemstvo,* one of its members, M. N. Liuboshchinsky, Senator of the Cassational department of the Senate, delivered an indignant address; upon Valuiev's report, Alexander in a moment of rage decided to discharge the Senator. But Minister Zamiatnin tried to convince him that such a step would be a direct infringement of the law, and to his great displeasure Alexander, perhaps for the first time in his life, came to see that even his power might have some limit. The Senator retained his post, but Minister Zamiatnin and his Deputy, Stoianovsky, were dismissed as suddenly as had been Lanskoy and Miliutin in 1861, upon the publication of the peasant-reform. In the selection of a successor the Tzar followed the suggestion of Chief of Gendarmes Count Shuvalov, who recommended a person who was foreign to justice and had had his experience in a different sphere,— Count K. I. Pahlen, at that time Governor of Pskov, and before vice-director of the Police Department; so utterly unprepared was he in the work of his new department, that the management of the Ministry of Justice had to be temporarily intrusted to Prince Urusov, Chief of His Majesty's Second Chancery, while Pahlen underwent preparatory instruction. Soon, however, Pahlen came out with self-confident criticism of the statutes, the guardianship of which he had just assumed.

Even before he entered upon his duties Pahlen held a consultation with the Moscow members of the procurature, trying to find support among them for the reactionary measures he was about to introduce. By way of experiment he expressed his opinion concerning the dangerousness of granting life-tenure to young men appointed as coroners, since there remained no way for correcting errors in such appointments. Pahlen found no sympathy among the members of the Moscow procuracy, who testified unanimously to the excellent personnel of the coroners. Yet he insisted on his notion, and as it was still considered premature to abolish one of the cardinal principles of the new statutes — that of life-tenure, the Minister used a roundabout way, and received the Imperial permission to appoint not coroners, but officials to " act in their place "; the latter, of course, might be discharged. This roundabout way has become firmly established in the Ministry of Justice; to this day there are persons who have been " acting " coroners for twenty years and more.

By the Statutes the Procurator is the representative of the Government's authority, and is directly subordinate to the Minister of Justice (who has the title of Procurator-General); he does not enjoy the life-tenure privilege. But as the procurators were also general guards of the law and defenders of the citizens from illegal encroachments of the administration, it is evident that for the worthy fulfilment of their function they had to be conscious of their independence from local administration; this consciousness could be the easier cultivated since the young procurators were to be selected from the minor judiciary personnel, the coroners, who had the life-tenure privilege. Hence one may understand how the actual deprivation of coroners of that prerogative might affect the personnel of the procurators. Bear in mind that the judiciary statutes were a sort of Habeas corpus act for Russia; for the first time they asserted that no one could be punished without due court-proceedings. Yet at the same time it was stated that the administrative authorities were to take legal measures for prevention of crimes. When the Statutes were discussed by the commission, Unkovsky, the former Marshal of the Tver Nobility, published an article in which he pointed out the danger of administrative measures for prevention of crime, since officials were not responsible for their actions; he insisted that in order to maintain the significance of the civil guaranties it was necessary to establish responsibility of officials for their actions against private persons. His idea was not accepted.

For this reason the guarding of private rights was left to the procurators; one can readily see the importance of the selection of their personnel, and of the establishment among them of a tradition of independence from the administration. But Pahlen throughout his administration endeavoured to bring up the procurators in the bureaucratic spirit, and to make them follow hints from higher up. They were instructed not to counteract the local administration, but on the contrary, to work in accord with the governors. This naturally was reflected in the local application of the Statutes. As the activity of the new courts grew there appeared considerable punitive activity on the part of administrative authorities and institutions, particularly severe and frequent in regard to the peasants; these were classed as "measures for prevention of crime." It was up to the procurators to struggle against such abuses of the police and administration. During Pahlen's administration the personnel of the procurators, and consequently the judiciary personnel as a whole, fell very low, since the further career of the procurators consisted in being promoted to the Judicial Chamber and the Senate.

During the same time a long series of so-called *novelles* was issued — additions and modifications of the laws, which actually distorted their principles. As early as 1866, after the process of Pypin and Zhukovsky, Valuiev insisted upon the exemption of press-cases from District-Courts, and their direct trial by Judicial Chambers. In 1871, when the first symptoms of the spread of the underground revolutionary movement had become manifest, after the Nechaiev-process, Pahlen and Shuvalov carried through a radical reformation of the order and proceedings of cases concerning State crimes; namely, all such cases were to be investigated in their first stage not by coroners, but by officers of the gendarmerie with the participation of procurators. The investigations were to be submitted through the procurator of the Judicial Chamber and the minister of justice to the Tzar who might direct the case in one of these three ways: either order regular court-proceedings (such a direction had almost never occurred, except in cases when the inevitability of a severe verdict appeared certain), or the Tzar might order to drop the case, or the third, most frequent, way — that of solving the case administratively, i.e., by exile into more or less remote provinces. That administrative method was motivated by a most hypocritical consideration — the desire to mitigate the punishment for young political criminals; the hypocrisy of that motive was soon shown when the administration demanded not the mitigation, but the hardening of punishments for belonging to revolutionary societies, which demand was satisfied by a special law issued in 1874.

The very order of the proceedings in political cases had been changed time and again. At first they were subject to Judicial

Chambers, then to special sessions of the Senate, and by the *novelle* of 1878, they were again entrusted to Judicial Chambers, owing to the fact that by that time the Government had prepared an obedient contingent of judges among the members of the Judicial Chambers. In the same year those cases were transferred to Military Courts, under the provision that they should apply Article 279 of the Military Code, which gave a death sentence for nearly all cases; by a special circular, in 1887, the military courts were directly forbidden to employ measures of punishment other than death, and if they found special reasons for the mitigation of the verdict they were to petition about the commutation of the sentence at its confirmation.

The fact that the Government decided to make use of the military courts at quite a late date, in spite of the growing reaction and revolutionary movement, was due to the reorganisation of those courts by Miliutin; as long as he remained at the head of the Ministry of War, the Government feared the courts of his department more than the civil courts manipulated by Pahlen.

Among other reactionary changes in judiciary circles was the limitation of the rights of attorneys in matters of internal organisation; by the law of 1874 their order was declared subject to District Courts and Judicial Chambers. Finally, clouds began to gather over the most important side of the new institutions — the juries. The Ministry of Justice had collected material alleged to prove the immense number of acquittal-verdicts declared by juries in cases of doubtless guilt. A persistent campaign was launched not only to exempt a series of cases from the jurisdiction of juries — this had been already done to a considerable measure before — but to abolish jury-courts altogether. Count Pahlen's opposition to the juries was moderated, however, after he had read the memorandum written on that question in 1878 by A. F. Koni, who had been presiding judge of the Petrograd District Court for many years, had gathered large material of statistic data and personal observations, and convincingly proved the wrongness of the prevailing opinion concerning the jury courts. The campaign against the juries was postponed till the Eighties.

Turning now to the position of the press, we observe that all the publications which appeared on September 1-st, 1865, abounded in praise for the Government's measure which had abolished preliminary censorship, although they were aware of the difficulties which the new statute promised for them. Ivan Aksakov wrote in his *Day:*

" At last to-day's issue appears without preliminary censorship. To-day, starting to write an editorial, we know that we shall read it in print just as we wrote it down; to-day we are not obliged to comply with the taste, valour, and *Weltanschauung* of the ' gentlemen having command of the barriers and turnpikes.' . . . To-day the nightmare, in the form of the censor, will not disturb our work, will not oppress our spirit, stifle our mind, and hold back our pen, and we are granted an unprecedented, an unheard of right: *not to lie, not to quibble,* to speak not in a falsetto, but in our own, natural voice."

The joy was of short duration. The press soon came to see that the power of the administration was not curbed by the new law. By the " temporary rules " of 1865 a monthly magazine appearing without " preliminary censorship " still had to be presented two days before its publication to the censor who might delay its release or cut out certain articles or pages. The provincial magazines and newspapers remained for a long time under censorship, except the Kiev paper, the *Kievite.* Soon the Government had press-cases exempted from regular court-proceedings, and made broad use of the administrative penalties permitted by the Statute. In the first place there were the " warnings "; after 1865, a newspaper or magazine having received two warnings and deserving a third one, was to be stopped for a period of from two to eight months; the counting of the warnings did not begin every year, but might hang, like the sword of Damocles, for years over a publication. The censor had another means for affecting the material conditions of the press: he could forbid the printing of private advertisements, besides imposing heavy money-penalties.

When in 1868 Valuiev was displaced by Timashov, the position of the press became still more difficult during the ten years of the latter's administration. A number of *novelles* were issued regarding the press rules. On June 14, 1868, a rule was illegally carried — through the Committee of Ministers instead of the State Council — by which a publication could be forbidden, on account of pernicious tendencies, to sell its issues to non-subscribers. In 1871 magazines were ordered to be presented to the censor not two, but four days ahead of publication; also books that were published without preliminary censorship were to be presented to the censor one week before their publication. In 1873 the minister of interior was given the right to forbid the discussion of certain internal or foreign questions in the press; it was then that the reform of the secondary schools, which had been the burning problem of the day, was not allowed to be touched in print. A publication which disobeyed that rule could be stopped without warning for a period not over three months. For forty years those "temporary rules" raged over the Russian press, swollen by additional restrictions issued by Timashov, and later (in the Eighties) by Tolstoy.

A few words about the conditions and the tendencies of the press during that time. The Slavophiles, in spite of their loyal convictions, in spite of their profession of the three basic principles of the Russian order — Autocracy, Orthodoxy, and Nationality — still suffered restrictions in the spread of their ideas and opinions. Yuriy Samarin was forced to publish Khomiakov's writings abroad, in 1867, and there he began to publish his *Russia's Borderlands.* Upon the appearance of the first issue of that publication, Samarin received an Imperial reprimand. The fate of Ivan Aksakov was no better. After many adventures he brought his paper, the *Day,* to a natural death, in 1866; when he attempted in 1867 to publish a new magazine, *Moscow,* a shower of various and frequent penalties fell upon him. During one year the magazine was stopped three times, after a series of warnings, and finally upon the presentation of Timashov, the Committee of Ministers resolved to stop its publication forever. True, the Senate permitted Aksakov to contest the ministerial decision, and he even won the case before the Senate, but since the senatorial decision was not unanimous, the case was transferred into the State Council, where it was finally resolved to discontinue the *Moscow.* Without awaiting the outcome of his contest, Aksakov began to publish a daily, the *Muscovite,* but it met with such a number of penalties that he had to stop it by the end of the year. Thus from 1868 the Slavophiles actually had no organ of their own. True, in 1872 Koshelev founded the magazine *Discourse,* but its pages were open to writers of different tendencies; after the confiscation and burning of two issues of that magazine, it also was discontinued at the end of the first year. Strakhov's *Dawn* was also partly inclined toward Slavophilism. It was published from 1870 to 1871, and actually expressed the views of the " Men of the Soil." [1]

As to the radical press, we have seen that in 1866 the *Contemporary* and the *Russian Word* were stopped forever by an Imperial order, and for a year and a half nobody dared renew their traditions. Only by the end of 1867 Blagosvietlov attempted to continue the work of the *Russian Word,* and founded a magazine *Action,* in which Pisarev, Shelgunov, Zaitzev, and other contributors to the *Russian Word,* took part.

[1] Dostoievsky was one of the " Men of the Soil "; their ideas may be defined as reactionary *Narodnichestvo.*— TR.

Pisarev, however, soon had a disagreement with Blagosvietlov, was drowned, in 1868, and with him disappeared the chief force of the movement; Zaitzev soon emigrated abroad. Shelgunov, who was far from being an adequate exponent of the Nihilistic views, remained the only representative of Pisarev's ideas.

The traditions of the *Contemporary* were restored in 1868 in the *Annals of the Fatherland,* which Niekrasov rented from Kraievsky, and edited together with Yeliseiev and Saltykov. Of the former members of the *Contemporary,* Pypin, Zhukovsky, and Antonovich did not join the new publication. The new *Annals of the Fatherland* began to demonstrate populistic (*Narodnichestvo*) views, which became so one-sided during the Seventies that the magazine rejected all political ideals for the near future, and labelled the Constitutional idea " a fad of the nobility " (for which it did not pay to break lances), asserting that the only question of the moment was the improvement of the conditions of the masses. In 1866 a weekly, the *Week,* appeared under the editorship of Dr. Conradi and his gifted wife; although officially the publication had no party allegiance, it undoubtedly promulgated ideas of *Narodnichestvo,* and one of its main contributors was P. L. Lavrov, the founder of that doctrine, about whom we shall speak again.

Katkov's *Russian Messenger,* and *Moscow News,* the daily which he edited together with Leontiev, inclined more and more to the right. Katkov mercilessly attacked the Nihilists, Separatists, and all non-Russians, especially the Poles. But he was still somewhat liberal in respect to judicial independence and to local self-government, and even in his chauvinistic and Russificatory ideas he was still not the typical rabid reactionary of the Eighties. The newspaper *Tiding,* organ of the selfdom-advocates and of the oligarchic-constitutional nobles, had to discontinue publication in 1869 for lack of subscribers and in view of governmental persecutions. A few years later Prince

Meshchersky, editor of the *Citizen,* resolved to revive the views of the *Tiding,* and to this day [2] he appears as the representative of the aristocratic aspirants, and as a relentless enemy of the democratic order which came as a result of the reforms of the Sixties.

Of the daily papers the *Moscow News,* as long as it did not become completely reactionary, was the most influential and widely read during the Sixties and Seventies. But its prestige began to be rivalled by that of the Petrograd liberal paper, *Voice,* especially after its powerful articles against Tolstoy. The influence of the *Voice* became still greater when in 1871 the historian Bilbasov became its editor; its liberal tendencies were tinted occasionally with Slavophile hues, as in the articles of A. D. Gradovsky and of Prince A. I. Vassilchikov.

Until the middle of the Seventies the *Petrograd News,* published by the Academy of Science, but rented and edited by V. F. Korsh, occupied an important place. Owing to its attacks against Tolstoy the paper suffered persecution, and in 1875 the Academy of Science was requested to withdraw it from Korsh, and lend it to more yielding hands. The forces which had been grouped around Korsh were distributed between two publications, the *Bourse Gazette* of Poletika, which existed till the end of the Seventies, and the *New Time* (*Novoie Vremia*), founded in 1876 by Suvorin, then an extreme liberal. Suvorin did not preserve his liberalism, however, and soon began to turn to the right and to vacillate.[3] In the latter half of the Seventies the *Russian News* (*Russkiya Viedomosti*) began to gain influence as an organ of the moderately liberal democrats; it has been inspired by young professor-economists, headed by A. I. Chuprov and A. S. Posnikov.

[2] Meshchersky died in 1914.— TR.

[3] To this day the *Novoie Vremia* is the weathercock of the official policies. It still preserves the epithet given it by the satirist Saltykov-Shchedrin —" the ' What is your request? ' paper."— TR.

The public was in a quite depressed mood after 1866. Only once, in 1870, did symptoms of life appear among society,— in connection with the announcement of important military and zemstvo-reforms, and with the victory of Russian diplomacy in abrogating the limitations imposed by the Treaty of Paris, in 1856, upon Russian navigation in the Black Sea. The general mood was well illustrated in the address to the Tzar presented by the duma of Moscow; it was edited by the Slavophiles, greeted the Government's return to reformatory activity, and expressed hope for further liberal steps in respect to freedom of press, of conscience, and of the Church. After the assurances of loyal rejoicing on the occasion of the diplomatic victory, the address went on:

" Whatever trials may threaten us now, they will — we are certain — not find Russia unprepared, but will find her closely concentrated around Your throne.

" With greater faith than in the past does Russia now look at her future, aware of a constant spiritual revival. Every one of Your great reforms which have been accomplished, or are being accomplished, or are eagerly awaited, has served as a source of new power for the country as well as for Your Majesty. No one is so entitled to the gratitude of the people, as You, Sire, and to none has the nation shown such gratitude. . . . From you alone the nation expects the fulfilment of your beneficent promises, and first of all — *freedom of opinion and the printed word,* without which the national spirit withers, and there is no room for sincerity and truth in the relations to the Government; *freedom of the Church,* without which the preached sermon is impotent; finally, *freedom of religious conscience* — the most precious treasure for man's soul.

" Sire! Internal and foreign affairs are mutually connected. The pledge of our success in the foreign region lies in the power of national self-consciousness and self-respect. . . . Confidence on the part of the Tzar in his people, reasonable self-restrain in freedom and honesty in loyalty on the part of the people, a mutual, unseverable bond between the Tzar and the people based on the accord of aspirations and beliefs — herein is our power, our historical mission. Yes, Sire, we shall conclude with the words of our ancestors in their reply to your first crowned forebear, in 1642: "*Your will* we are ready to serve with our wealth and with our blood, but *our thought* is what it is."

The address was edited by Ivan Aksakov, Prince Cherkassky, and Yuriy Samarin. But the Slavophiles were once more convinced that the Government desired not honest loyalty, but slavish obedience. The Minister of Interior found that the address abounded in such impossible expressions that it could not be presented to the Tzar. . . .

After this the last signs of social life were extinguished, and the public, tired by its struggle and disappointed in its attempts, began to stagnate in a prostration which lasted till the second half of the Seventies.

CHAPTER XXXIV

I N one of the previous chapters I outlined the external process of the distribution of landownership, as it took form after the expansion of the peasant-reform in 1866 upon the State-peasants. Now I intend to examine the contents of the internal process, the outcome of which depended upon many material and non-material factors.

By the Act of February 19, the redemption of peasant-allotments was based, under normal conditions, upon mutual agreement between the landowners and the peasants. The landowners were allowed to demand redemption against even the desire of the peasants, but in such cases they received not full compensations, but only eighty or seventy-five per cent. of the full amount. Moreover, by the Act of February 19, only *obrok*-estates might be redeemed, while *barshchina*-estates had first to pass to the *obrok* system, after which the landowners might demand redemption which was estimated by the capitalisation of the *obrok*.

We have already observed that on the *barshchina*-estates the productivity of the peasants after the Reform had considerably fallen, since the emancipated peasants had become aware of the fact that the landowners no longer exercised their former authority; in many places the peasants refused to be transferred from *barshchina* to *obrok*. In 1862 a number of declarations by the gentry concerning the necessity of introducing obligatory redemption appeared. Outside of the sharp declarations of the Tver nobility, which had a political character, there had been petitions of a purely business character, as for instance, the petition of the nobles of the province of Kazan, where the majority of the peasants were on *barshchina,* and where the landowners felt helpless and were being rapidly convinced of the necessity of bringing their peasants to redemption.

In 1863 the Government issued an additional law by which *barshchina*-estates might be directly redeemed upon the request of the landowners who were to receive from the Redeeming Institution only eighty and seventy-five per cent. of the compensation sum. In the meantime peasants of many places, particularly in the southeastern and in the southern New Russia provinces, actually fled from redemption, in spite of the fact that they did not have to make any additional payments and that their debt by the compensation arrangement equalled only three-fourths or four-fifths of the capitalised *obrok.* The peasants refused redemption in view of the absence of side earnings in those regions.

Then the Government was forced to make use of the additional clause introduced by Prince Gagarin, concerning the so-called " quarterly " or " beggarly " allotments. Wherever the peasants were unwilling or unable to pay for the land they were allowed to demand free " quarterly " allotments. The entire southeast of Russia and part of the eastern provinces, as Ufa, the southern part of Perm, part of Voronezh, all of Tambov, Samara, and part of Saratov, appeared to be the region of the greatest expansion of those " beggarly " allotments.

In view of the fact that during the first years after the Reform most of the redemption cases were accomplished upon the demand of the landowners (more than sixty-five per cent.), and since because of this the latter received incomplete compensation, they in their turn made broad use of their right to " cut off " the allotments of the peasants within the limits of the established maximal norm. Those " cut-offs " had in many places a great importance in that they not only diminished the property of the peasants in size but in that they greatly deteriorated it qualitatively, and often placed the peasants in complete economic dependence upon the landowner because the latter intentionally cut off such necessary parts of the land as the meadow or the pasture land. In non-black-soil provinces where the land requires manuring the peasants could not exist without raising cattle, and they could not keep cattle without having the meadows and pastures, so that they were compelled to rent those " cut-offs " at such prices as the landowners were pleased to name.

These conditions affected the general state of agriculture very unfavourably in the first years after the Reform. On one side the peasants owing to the " cut-offs " fell in many places into complete economic bondage to the landowners. On the other side the landowners also depended to a great extent upon the peasants, being forced to conduct their estates by free hired labour; although owing to the greater freedom of movement after the Reform outside labourers appeared, still the landowners preferred to deal with their former serfs. In the non-black-soil provinces industry was well developed, and the landowners had great difficulty in finding labourers for their estates. They were forced to sell out their property.

A different economic conjuncture was in the black-soil provinces. There the peasants received very small allotments and at the same time in most of those places they could find no side-earnings. They were forced either to hire themselves as labourers to the landowners or to rent land from the latter.

We should note that at that moment the black-soil provinces were splendidly situated in respect to raising grain. Since the end of the Forties after the abolition of the Corn laws in England and under the influence of the growing concentration of the population of Western Europe in cities, the demand for Russian grain increased, and agriculture had come to be very profitable; after the Reform to this was added the building of railroads which was so planned as to facilitate the export of grain from the most fertile provinces to sea-ports.[1]

Under this influence the cultivation of the soil in the fertile provinces grew very rapidly after the Reform. During the Sixties the area of cultivated land in European Russia equalled eighty-eight million eight hundred thousand desiatins; twenty years later one hundred and six million eight hundred thousand desiatins were under cultivation, and in 1887 one hundred seventeen million desiatins. We must not forget that in the non-black soil provinces the landowners abandoned their estates, so that the amount of land under cultivation did not increase throughout the Empire. In the black-soil provinces the cultivated area increased unequally; in the central black soil provinces it increased only by five per cent.; in the middle Volga provinces during the twenty years following the Reform the area increased by thirty-five per cent.; in the Little Russian provinces — by thirteen per cent., while in New Russia it increased by ninety-eight per cent., and in the Southern Trans-Volga region by three hundred and sixty-five per cent.

These figures do not show an increase in the landowners' estates at all. In spite of the increase of prices on grain, which rose during those twenty years by fifty to eighty per cent.; in spite of the fact that the landowners had received an enormous capital in the form of compensation sums, and that during the Eighties a number of Agrarian banks were opened — the landowners did not invest those funds in agricultural improvements, but spent them in various ways, and preferred to rent their

[1] The export of grain from Russia which was very unsteady in the first half of the nineteenth century, but had not reached even thirty million puds before 1845, rose to fifty-one million puds between 1846–1850; in the next five years, 1850–1885, it fell to forty-five million, on account of the war; between 1856–1860 it rose to sixty-nine million, between 1861–1865, to seventy-six million, between 1876–1880, to two hundred and fifty-seven million puds per year, and so forth.

land to the peasants, making use of the growth of rental prices. So that on the whole landowners' estates decreased.

This is explained by the fact that at the moment of the liberation of the serfs the landowners did not have their own inventory, and that their estates were deep in debt. Of the five hundred and eighty-eight million rubles which the landowners were to receive as compensation during the first ten years after the Reform about two hundred and sixty-two million rubles was retained for the extinction of their debts to the Treasury, and the remaining three hundred and twenty-six million rubles were paid in bonds, the course of which was quite low, so that the actual sum equalled only two hundred and thirty million rubles. The indebtedness of the landowners' estates continued to grow; by the end of the Sixties the new debt was equal to two hundred and thirty million rubles, by the beginning of the Eighties it reached four hundred million rubles and by the end of the Eighties it exceeded six hundred million rubles. A general view of the first twenty years after the Reform will show the following process:

In the North landowners' estates deteriorated; they were either sold or transformed into industrial units. In the Southern provinces landowners retained their possessions, but they rented a considerable part of their land to peasants. During the Eighties in European Russia, excepting Poland, Finland, and the Caucasus, there were sixty-eight million desiatins under cultivation, of which forty-seven million and three hundred thousand desiatins belonged to peasant-allotments, about twelve million desiatins were rented by the peasants from the landowners, and only eight million seven hundred thousand desiatins belonged to private landowners. Thus we see that eighty-seven per cent. belonged to the peasants, and only twelve and eight-tenths to private landowners.

In respect to the black-soil provinces we must come to the conclusion that although the landowners retained the land they did not improve or expand the cultivation of their estates, and in the meantime their indebtedness continued to grow, so that during the Nineties a wholesale liquidation of landowners' estates took place with the aid of Peasant and Gentry banks. The statistic data about the sale of landowners' estates show that the average sale of their land between 1859–1875 equalled five hundred seventeen thousand desiatins yearly; between 1875–1879 seven hundred and forty-one thousand desiatins yearly; at the beginning of the Nineties — seven hundred and eighty-five thousand desiatins yearly. The yearly average of the sales has continued to grow, and reached one million desiatins by the beginning of the twentieth century, while in 1906 (when special conditions existed) seven and one-half million desiatins of landowners' property was offered for sale.

The distribution of the land by classes during that time had changed in the following way; in 1877 the nobles possessed 77.8 per cent. of the entire area of private landownership, the merchants — 12.2 per cent., commoners — two per cent., peasants — seven per cent., and all " other " private owners — one per cent. In 1887, ten years later, we get the following figures: nobles 68 per cent., merchants — 13 per cent., commoners — 2.9 per cent., peasants — 12 per cent., and " others " —2.3 per cent.

While the merchants have been buying the land from the nobles not for agricultural, but for industrial or speculative purposes, the peasants bought land mainly for direct cultivation. Most of their purchases during that period were accomplished not by communities or societies, as it was in the next period, but by individuals. During the Sixties the peasant purchases equalled ninety-one thousand desiatins annually, during the Seventies — two hundred and three thousand desiatins, during the Eighties — four hundred and thirty-eight thousand desiatins. In many cases peasant-buyers were land speculators like the merchants.

It thus appears that the peasants triumphed all along the line; their possessions expanded, they bought land, increased the size of rented land. We must not forget, however, that they aspired for an increase of property because, owing to the limited allotments which were given them by the Act of February 19, they had no other way out. The dearth of land in the black-soil region was felt by the peasants particularly during the first years after the Reform. While the prices of grain doubled, the rental prices increased by three hundred and even by four hundred per cent., which was due not only to the rise of grain prices on the international market, but also to the extension of railroads to such places as Kozlov, Morshansk, Saratov, Penza, Kursk, Oriol, Kharkov, New Russia, and so forth. The sale of grain became very lively near the new railroad centres, and the peasants were tempted to produce more of it. But in view of the enormous rental prices most of the peasants were in the long run ruined, and furthermore, the excessive cultivation of the soil caused the exhaustion of the black soil.

The economic conditions of the peasants on their own allotments were no better, because they were greatly burdened with all sorts of payments. In 1872 Minister of State Domains Valuiev, collected interesting material about their condition in various parts of Russia. Putting aside the official conclusions we may derive valuable information from the work of such independent investigators as Professor Yanson, or as Prince Vassilchikov. From such data we learn that the sum of all direct taxes and payments which lay on the rural population in 1872 was two hundred and eight million rubles, of which only thirteen million rubles fell upon private landowners; the rest, about two hundred million rubles, fell upon peasants' land. Among those taxes were the State *zemsky* tax, local *zemsky* taxes, redemption payments, and in some places — *obrok* payments. In all, the peasants paid ninety-five million rubles of land assessments.

Then followed the per capita tax of forty-two million rubles, which was paid exclusively by peasants — altogether ninety million rubles of various non-land payments. These did not include the natural obligations which were performed only by peasants, and which we may roughly estimate as equivalent to several tens of millions rubles. Thus, not counting the natural obligations, the ninety and one-half million peasants paid about two hundred million rubles of taxes, i.e., an average family paid thirty rubles. Such payments were doubtless unbearable for the ordinary peasant.

We should add that these taxes were unequally distributed among the peasants themselves. The landowners' peasants had to pay fifty-four million rubles for their allotments of thirty-three and one-half million desiatins, while the State-peasants had to pay only thirty-seven million rubles for their seventy-five million desiatins. The general picture of the heavy and unproportional taxation to which the peasantry was subjected appeared early after the Reform. As early as 1867 there was a grave failure of crops in the province of Smolensk, which was followed by a famine; Valuiev, then Minister of the Interior, at first denied the existence of the famine and asserted that there were sufficient alimentary reserves for the satisfaction of the peasants' needs, but investigators who were appointed discovered that the reserves were not sufficient, and that the peasants not only had to eat various substitutes for bread, like bark, lime, etc., but that they actually died from starvation. The Government became alarmed and appointed a special commission under the chairmanship of the Heir (the future Emperor Alexander III) for the relief of the starving peasants.

Three years later another failure of crops occurred; it affected mainly the southeastern provinces which had been considered the granary of all Russia and even of Europe; in the province of Samara it lasted three years and resulted in a famine of enormous dimensions. It became clear to the Government that it was necessary to lighten the burden of the over-taxed peasants on one side, and on the other to bring an end to their landlessness in the black-soil provinces. Yet the Government continued to act very slowly, and allowed the conditions of the peasants to grow worse. During the Seventies some local administrators attempted to explain away the misery of the peasants by their own bad morals. For instance, Klimov, the Governor of Samara, expressed it as his opinion before the Committee of Ministers in 1873 that the peasants spent all their income on drink and hence starved when the crops failed. The State Comptroller, A. A. Abaza, pointed out that Klimov's information about his own province was incorrect; Abaza indicated that the province of Samara paid more than three per cent. of the general sum of taxes collected in Russia, while its excise payments equalled only one and one-half per cent. of the total excise revenue, thus definitely proving to the Governor of Samara that his province was one of the most sober in Russia. The exhaustion of the black-soil belt of Russia in the Nineties was certain beyond a doubt. During the famine years of 1892–1893 I had to gather statistic data about starving peasants, and I personally saw a large number of impoverished villages in the central black-soil provinces; for instance in the province of Tula seventy-five per cent. of the peasants' houses had their stoves built without chimneys, for the sake of economy in fuel which consisted of wood or straw; the ceilings in those houses were absolutely black with soot, and in damp weather they dripped black mud. A large number of houses in such villages were uncovered; only the rafters remained on the roof, since the straw was removed and given to the cattle. According to the data I collected it appeared that by the beginning of the Nineties in some villages about fifty per cent. of the peasants had no horses, while of the remaining fifty per cent. about forty-five per cent. owned one horse, and only five to six per cent. possessed two or more horses.

If the Government was slow in undertaking serious measures for the improvement of the unbearable position of the peasants, the public saw even during the Seventies that the status of the peasantry was doomed to slide downward. Among the writers who made use of the statistic data gathered by the Government commissions were two distinguished investigators whom I have already mentioned — Y. E. Yanson and Prince A. I. Vassilchikov. Professor Yanson had definitely expressed the conclusions which he drew from his investigations in his book, *A Statistic Investigation of the Peasant-Allotments and Assessments.* He set forth the economic insecurity of the peasant, his poor nourishment, bad physical and moral conditions of living, large number of sickness and high death rate; he named as the causes of such conditions poor soil, insufficient allotments, and finally the heaviness of taxation. He recommended the lowering of land taxes, the transplanting of peasants into unoccupied provinces, the facilitation of land acquisition by the migrating peasants, and finally the revision of the system of taxation. Most of his recommendations were put into practice early in the Eighties.

Prince A. I. Vassilchikov differed from Yanson in that he considered the main cause of the miserable conditions of the peasants not the insufficiency of their allotments, but the terrible taxation system which paralysed the beneficial results of the reform of February 19. Quoting the epigraph of Taine, in his characterisation of the position of the peasants in France before the Revolution of 1789 — *quand l'homme est miserable, il s'aigrit; mais quand il est à la fois propriétaire et miserable, il s'aigrit encore d'avantage* — Prince Vassilchikov found the condition of the French peasants of that time quite analogous to the position of his contemporary Russian peasants, and he warned the Government that the tax system was bound to bring the small landowners to desperation and to such outbursts of popular indignation as were manifested during the French Revolution.

The opinions of Prince Vassilchikov and Professor Yanson were in a large measure shared by most of the writers of that time; this attitude was expressed back at the end of the Fifties and early in the Sixties by Chernyshevsky, and later by Serno-Solovievich and others. During the Sixties a quite definite and persistent opinion about the defects of the economic order that was established by the peasant Reform was formed among the progressive Russian *intelligentzia;* the spread of that opinion gave rise to the movement of *Narodnichestvo* in literature and in life.

CHAPTER XXXV

THE pessimistic conclusions of Yanson and Vassilchikov did not surprise the representatives of the *intelligentzia* who were familiar with the critical views of Herzen, Chernyshevsky, Dobroliubov, and other publicists of the *Contemporary* or the *Bell*. Radical public opinion regarded the Governmental activity with mistrust and suspicion. From the very beginning of the Sixties the formation began of the so-called *Narodnichestvo* [1]-school in Russian literature. Already in 1860–1861 the first productions appeared of such writers as Nicholas Uspensky, Naumov, Levitov, Rieshetnikov, and a number of others who brilliantly described the difficult position in which the people found themselves at the moment of emerging from the bondage system. The above-mentioned writers could do it the easier since by their origin they were close to the people; they were the commoner-writers who were then entering Russian literature which until that time had been created chiefly by nobles. In an article " Is It Not the Beginning of a Change? " dedicated to Nicholas Uspensky, Chernyshevsky indicated that phenomenon.

Those *Narodniki*-writers had tasted in their personal life of the misery which oppressed the people. In their description of the real state of the masses they worked largely upon the public conscience, upon the conscience of the most susceptible minds, particularly of the young generation. There loomed up the question of the duty of the *intelligentzia* before the people, for it

[1] *Narod* — means: people. The derivatives are numerous. *Narodnichestvo* — the doctrine of going " to the people." *Narodnichesky* — the adjective. *Narodnik* — an adherent of the doctrine.— TR.

appeared clear to those idealists that every intellectual body is enabled to enjoy the benefits of culture only at the expense of the people; this brought about the problem of paying back to the people the debt which lay upon the shoulders of the *intelligentzia*. Such was the sentiment not only of the commoners who came from the ranks of the people, but of numerous representatives of the nobility — those whom a few years later N. K. Mikhailovsky named " Repentant Nobles."

When in 1861 student disturbances took place in connection with some questions regarding the liberation of the peasants, when Putiatin and Ignatiev exaggerated the event and tactlessly ravaged the University of Petrograd, and hundreds of young men were expelled and thrown into fortresses and barracks, Herzen wrote in his *Bell,* addressing those expelled students:

" Where shall you go, youths, from whom knowledge has been shut off? Shall I tell you, Where? Give ear, for even darkness does not prevent you from listening,— from all corners of our enormous land, from the Don and the Ural, from the Volga and the Dnieper, a moan is growing, a grumbling is rising,— this is the first roar of the sea-billow, which begins to rage, pregnant with storm, after a long and tiresome calm. *V narod!* To the people! — that is your place, O exiles of knowledge. Prove to those Bistroms [2] that out of you will emerge not clerks, but soldiers, not mercenaries, but soldiers of the Russian people! "

That slogan: *V narod!* To the people!, which was used by Herzen on a particular occasion, was caught up by the *narodnichestvo*-literature, and was powerfully reflected in the minds of the young.

[2] Bistrom was the General who commanded the soldiers during the quelling of the student disturbances in 1861; he told his soldiers that the disturbers were " clerks " dissatisfied with the liberation of the peasants.

True, in the following years, under the influence of the collapse of the progressive *intelligentzia,* which took place in 1862 after the Petrograd conflagrations, under the influence of the Polish insurrection which aroused reactionary mood, but mostly under the influence of that current which under the leadership of Pisarev received the name of Nihilism, and put forth more selfish questions — of the struggle for individuality (i.e., for the liberation of one's intellectual personality from all religious, social and other chains and prejudices) under the influence of those circumstances the Russian *intelligentzia* had somewhat deviated from the *Narodnichestvo* aspirations and from the tendencies which began to develop in literature after the peasant Reform.

But during the second half of the Sixties the *Narodnichestvo* movement again came to the front, enhanced by the new rules issued by Minister Tolstoy in 1867, which severely restricted University life; the young generation felt oppressed, insulted, and removed from the honourable place to which it was elevated by Dobroliubov, Pisarev, and other literary leaders of the radicals. In place of problems of internal struggle for individuality and for the liberation of one's personality there inevitably rose before them the question of the necessity of acquiring first of all more tolerable external conditions. That thought necessarily pointed towards social problems.

At the same time we have seen that in 1868, in connection with the famine in the province of Smolensk, the question about the misery of the peasants rose before the public for the first time. The young generation were deeply affected by the pictures of the sufferings of the people, and a strong fermentation was going on among the University students during 1868–1869. Grave disturbances took place, in which the students protested against the Government, and in the result masses of them were excluded from the University and from the Medical Academy, and were transported to their homes. The surging young mass was thus scattered throughout Russia, where it came in contact with society, and at once began to propagate the very ideas which they had been punished for holding. The year 1869 and those immediately following saw the beginnings of new, revolutionary and radical-*Narodnichesky* currents among Russian youth.

As if to meet the new currents an article written by P. L. Lavrov in the magazine *Week* appeared, which was a successful formulation of the tasks which were placed before society by the new circumstances. Lavrov, who was quite moderate during the Sixties and had been opposed by the radical organs, especially by Pisarev, had moved considerably to the left. In spite of his maturity — he was then a retired Colonel of forty — Lavrov was inclined to evolution, and constantly moved forward, trying to preserve his bond with the younger generation and with their problems. In 1868 in his articles written from exile under the transparent pseudonym of Mirtov,[3] he formulated those general problems which in his opinion were then before the Russian *intelligentzia.* He wrote:

" The development of the individual physically, mentally and morally, the embodiment of truth and justice in social forms, this short formula embraces everything that may be considered Progress."

On the basis of that formula Mirtov wrote a series of articles under the title of " Historical Letters," in which he indicated the conditions for the achievement of the purpose. He put forth the obligations of every " critically thinking individual," whose rôle he saw in paying the price of Progress.

" A civilised minority," he wrote, " who do not strive to be civilising in the broadest sense of the word, bear responsibility for all the sufferings of their contemporaries, which they could have removed, had they not limited their rôle to that of

[3] *Lavr* — means: laurel. *Mirt* — myrtle.

representing and conserving civilisation, but had taken upon themselves also the rôle of moving it ahead."

"The embodiment of truth and justice in social forms," as the aim of human activity, and the obligation of striving for the achievement of that aim, gave the young generation a basis for its conduct which it needed gravely at that moment, and which Pisarev could not furnish.

Later the sociological teachings of Mikhailovsky gave a brighter and stronger expression to the task outlined by Lavrov, but the latter was undoubtedly the first Russian thinker to place that task before the public. So much did his formula suit the moment that even Shelgunov, the leader of the *Action* and promulgator of Pisarev's ideas, greeted the appearance of Lavrov's articles in book form, and although he disagreed with some of the latter's views, he warmly recommended the book to the public as "an extraordinary phenomenon in Russian literature."

The formula of Lavrov was so broad that it was taken up by representatives of various platforms. Since "the embodiment of truth and justice in social forms" might be achieved in various ways, the formula was accepted by revolutionaries as well as by peacefully inclined *Narodniki* who limited their activity to cultural development of the country, particularly of the village.

A formula, politically more definite, although in substance analogous to that of Lavrov, was announced abroad at that time by the most distinguished representative of the Russian emigration, M. A. Bakunin. In 1868 a Russian magazine was founded in Geneva, the *Cause of the People,* under the editorship of N. I. Zhukovsky; in the first issue Bakunin placed before the progressive Russian youth a number of tasks required, in his opinion, by the moment. The first point of his programme completely corresponded with the formula of Lavrov, with the only difference that Bakunin was more definite.

First of all was placed the task of liberating one's personality from any bonds, but it was definitely indicated that only the individual who had thrown off all religious beliefs and had become atheistic, might be considered free, so that Atheism was put forth as the cornerstone of personal evolution. The second point of the programme called for the "embodiment of truth and justice in social forms," but it pointed out definitely that by truth and justice was meant a certain social order in which was to be attained not only the social and economic liberation of the people through the abolition of all *hereditary* property, transferring the land to agricultural communes, and the factories, capital and means of production — to labour-associations, granting equal rights to women, abolishing marriage and family, and submitting all children to a public education: all these Bakunin considered realisable only in case the work began from the complete annihilation of the State. Anarchism was the typical feature of Bakunin's programme. According to him, as long as mankind will live and develop under forms of state, economic and social freedom will be impossible, for whatever the form of government — whether a constitutional monarchy or a democratic republic — any state organism is based on compulsion and hence inevitably leads to inequality and domination of one social group or class over others.

The sharp and irreconcilable formulation of the question by Bakunin appealed to the aroused youth more than the vague and abstract formula of Lavrov. During the winter of 1868–1869 Bakunin's programme was the subject of lively discussion among students. The question rose whether it was worth while to study. According to Bakunin all study, all knowledge, were at that time waste of the people's sources; the transfer of knowledge and culture to the people was impossible as long as the people were not free, in Bakunin's sense of the word; hence until that moment it was not worth while to study. Bakunin recommended leaving the universities, going to the people, and raising them — not in the sense of imparting knowledge and ideas to them, but in the direct sense of rebelling against the existing order of things, since until that order were overthrown and annihilated no proper social development was possible.

Soon a new herald of revolutionary ideas appeared among the young generation, who went further than Bakunin. It was the twenty-three-year-old Niechaiev, a teacher in a primary school, and an unclassified student at the University. He had a magnetic influence not only upon the young people, but upon all who came in contact with him. Among his followers was the forty-year-old writer, Pryzhov, who admitted that he had never met such a winning personality. Niechaiev soon fled abroad, and there he produced such an impression on Bakunin that the latter was ready to submit to him, and even tried to win Herzen to his side, but the latter brusquely turned away. Bakunin succeeded, however, in converting Ogarev and for a time, Herzen's children, whom he persuaded after the death of their father (January, 1870) to hand over to Niechaiev the public money which had been in their trust.

Upon the young generation Niechaiev had a hypnotising effect. In his extreme ambition he intended personally to manage the whole movement; he did not scruple about spreading mystifying rumours and using dishonest means for the achievement of his purpose. Bakunin finally became utterly disappointed in him. Niechaiev put into the foundation of his political system the principle of extreme jesuitism. In his opinion a revolutionist was justified in ignoring all moral principles, in deceiving, killing, and robbing; for the sake of holding the organisation in a firm grip, Niechaiev allowed himself to compromise his coworkers, to steal their letters or documents, and to terrorise them in other ways.

This harmonised with the structure of his organisation which was borrowed from Babeuf and his followers. It consisted of a hierarchy of " fives "; each group of five knew only one superior from the next " five," and at the very top was the mysterious " committee," which was itself a myth, since Niechaiev was the actual head of all the " fives." In one of the Moscow " fives " which consisted of Uspensky, Pryzhov, Nicolaiev, Kuznietzov, and Ivanov, Niechaiev observed that Ivanov began to regard him critically. He ordered the other members of the " five " to kill Ivanov, as a spy, calculating that the crime, once committed, would throw those who had taken part in it into slavish subjection to him. He succeeded in his plan; the student Ivanov was murdered. But the affair was disclosed, and served as the basis for the Process of the Niechaievians, in which eighty-seven persons were tried, thirty-three sentenced to various penalties, while many of the acquitted were later exiled in the administrative order.

When Bakunin gained a clear view of the personality of Niechaiev and his system, he did his best to disavow any connection with him and to denounce him publicly. But the evil had been done: Niechaiev's organisation, " The Tribunal of the People," had produced a deep impression upon the contemporary public, and that episode had greatly harmed the reputation and development of the revolutionary movement. In 1872, one year after the trial of the Niechaievians, Dostoievsky, himself a former revolutionist, wrote a novel " Demons " (" The Possessed "), with the Niechaiev affair as its basis. But Dostoievsky generalised that monstrous phenomenon, and applied it to the whole movement, which naturally aroused great indignation in radical circles; it was adequately expressed in an article of a young writer in the *Annals of the Fatherland*, N. K. Mikhailovsky, who, without attempting to defend Niechaiev and his system, protested at the same time against Dostoievsky's general slander of the revolutionary movement.

About the same time, in the early Seventies, the circle of the

Chaikovtzy, who were grouped around a young university graduate, N. V. Chaikovsky, a new movement, in contrast to that of Niechaiev, arose among the young generation. In his *Memoirs of a Revolutionist* Prince Kropotkin describes the origin of that circle and of similar circles.

" In all cities, in all the ends of Petrograd, appeared circles of ' self-development.' There the works of philosophers, economists, and of the young school of Russian historians were carefully studied. The reading was accompanied with endless discussions. The aim of all those readings and discussions was to solve the great problem which stood before the young men and women: *In what way could they be most useful for the people?* Gradually they came to the conclusion that there existed only one way: *One must go to the people and live their lives.* Young men began to depart for villages as physicians, assistant-surgeons (*feldshers*), school-teachers, *volost*-clerks. In order to be still closer to the people, many became hard day-labourers, blacksmiths, woodchoppers. Girls began to undergo examinations as school-teachers, midwifes, nurses, and flocked by the hundreds to villages where they devoted themselves unreservedly to the service of the poorest part of the population. None of them had as yet any thought of revolution, of any revolutionary reorganisation of society after some definite plan. They merely wanted to teach the people how to read and write, to enlighten them, to help them in some way to get out of darkness and misery, and at the same time to learn from the people themselves, *their* ideal of a better social life."

These memoirs were written several decades after that epoch, and many of them have become, so to speak, chronologically merged; there might have been perhaps some chronological aberration. We may therefore take Kropotkin with some reservations. We may point out that many members of the circles were revolutionists from the very beginning; another prominent *Chaikovetz*, L. E. Shishko, tells us in his memoirs that when still a junker he professed revolutionary ideas. Many others entered the circles with definite revolutionary ideas. But at any rate even the political processes at the end of the Seventies assure us that numerous *Narodniki* who " went to the people " in the middle of the Seventies were imbued with most peaceful intentions. Here is the testimony of S. I. Bardin, a woman defendant in the Process of Fifty, tried in 1876:

" I belong, gentlemen, to the category of those who are known among the young people as peaceful propagandists. Their task is to instil into the consciousness of the people ideals of a most perfect and most just social order, or to clarify for them ideals which are unconsciously inrooted in them; to point out to them the defects of the present order, in order that the errors might be avoided in the future; but when that future will come, we do not state, and we cannot state, since its ultimate realisation does not depend upon us. I think that it is quite a distance from such propaganda to instigation for riots. . . . We are accused of being political revolutionists; but if we aspired for a political *coup d'état* we should have acted differently; we should not have gone to the people whom it is necessary to prepare and develop, but we should have sought to bring together the dissatisfied elements among the educated classes. . . . But the truth of the matter is that we have in no way aspired for a *coup d'état*. . . ."

It is certain that in the early Seventies the aims of the *Chaikovtzy* were not revolutionary, but peaceful, cultural. In their desire to come in contact with the people they put on peasant garments, tried to appear " common," and at the same time endeavoured to disseminate among the masses and the *intelligentzia* general knowledge and their own social views. Among them were men of various political views, and many who were not at all interested in political questions. Among the books which they spread were: Marx' " Capital," the first volume of which had been translated into Russian (1872), articles by Chernyshevsky, Dobroliubov, Mirtov's " Historical Letters," Flerovsky's " The Position of the Labouring Class," and his " ABC of Social Sciences." The Censorship Committee forbade those books, and even burned some of them. Then the *Chaikovtzy* were forced to deviate from the legal path of action, and they began to print in an underground way small, thin brochures. For this purpose they established a printing place, with the aid of Ippolit Myshkin, a governmental stenographer in Moscow.

The propagation of Socialistic, or to be exact, Anarchistic ideas among Petrograd workingmen occupied a considerable place in the early activity of the *Chaikovtzy*. Foremost in this respect was Prince P. A. Kropotkin, a former Imperial Page, a well educated military officer who served not in the Guard, but in Siberia, whither he was attracted by his desire to investigate that little known region. In 1871 he lived abroad, and frequented German workingmen-circles. It was the moment of the split in the International, owing to the difference of opinion between Marx and Bakunin. The two men were mutually exclusive both in questions of programme and of tactics. While Marx aspired for the establishment in the remote future of an ideal social order through socialising the means of production and the realisation of Socialism by the aid of a *state,* and placed before the proletariat a definite task of capturing the authority of the State, and even, if necessary, instituting a dictatorship — Bakunin first of all denied the State, and considered that every person or group of persons who wished to improve the condition of the masses economically and socially, would have to fight the State as their main enemy. The conflict between the two leaders ended in the expulsion of Bakunin from the International, but his cause was upheld by many sections, especially in Latin countries, and the International perished in the internecine strife. Kropotkin, who happened to find himself in the thick of those dissensions, decisively took the side of Bakunin; he also thought that the liberation of the working masses was possible only upon the abolition of the State and the establishment in its stead of federative unions, starting with the smallest socialistic or communistic units.

Then Kropotkin joined the circle of the *Chaikovtzy,* and began to propagate these ideas actively in this and also in other circles of revolutionary youth, which began to form at that time. Those students who had been expelled from higher institutions, especially in 1869, prepared revolutionary cadres in the provinces among senior gymnasia students, among their younger brothers and sisters, seminarists, etc.; so that parallel with the circle of the *Chaikovtzy* there appeared a number of other, revolutionary, organisations. The revolutionary mood affected even men of mature age. Thus Kovalik, President of the Conference of Peace Mediators in Mglinsk, gave up his position, and devoted all his time to the organisation of revolutionary circles; in a short time he went through several provinces, and established more than ten revolutionary organisations. He soon made close connections with another known organiser, a Penza landowner, Voinaralsky, who contributed all his fortune — about forty thousand rubles, to the cause, and actively organised circles. I have already mentioned Ippolit Myshkin, who made use of his position as governmental stenographer for maintaining an illegal printing machine at his Moscow home for the publications of the *Chaikovtzy.*

At the same time considerable revolutionary cadres were being prepared abroad. Part of the expelled students went there. Especially large was the number of girl students who went abroad, on account of the difficulties of procuring higher education at home; from the early Seventies Zurich swarmed with Russian girls, and even married women — often fictitiously married. Girls frequently at that time contracted fictitious marriages with persons whom they might never meet again, in order to free themselves from parental guardianship. In the Zurich " Colony " there were some wealthy members; the Colony purchased a home for eighty thousand francs, where they had meals and daily lectures, addresses, readings, and so forth. Lavrov was a permanent lecturer at the Colony, and became the editor of the revolutionary publication, *Forward*.

He had by that time accepted in a certain sense Bakunin's programme, except that he considered the federative-anarchic order an ideal of the remote future and hence recommended a long road of propaganda and peaceful preparation of the masses for the future uprising and revolution. Bakunin, as an ardent, irreconcilable revolutionary Anarchist, naturally rejected Lavrov's way, and advocated immediate action, organisation of revolts, considering even a small revolt as the best propaganda. He proclaimed therefore *propagande par le fait,* and his numerous followers were called Bakunists-parlefaitists.

The intensive activity of the Lavrists and of the Bakunists alarmed the Russian Government. It demanded that by January 1, 1874, the students come back to Russia, threatening those who might come after that date with many difficulties; on the other hand it indicated its intention of organising higher education for women. Indeed, we may believe that owing to the threatening dimensions of the Zurich Colony the Government did not oppose the opening of courses for women at Petrograd and Moscow. The students resolved to take the Government's notice as a signal for going " to the people "; they went back, but not with the intention of studying; they marched " to the people."

Together with the revolutionary cadres that had been formed at home, the *Narodniki* from abroad were scattered among the people. Most of them decided to act peacefully, in the beginning at least, and to limit their activity to propaganda of social ideas. They acted very clumsily, having had no experience or preparation, taking no precautions against the police, and failing to conceal their identity under the transparent peasant-guise. Two or three months after the beginning of that movement, the Government started an investigation of the propagandists; Count Pahlen prepared an extensive memorandum concerning the matter. In the month of May many of the young idealists were imprisoned. Some of them were soon released, but many were kept two and three and four years; those arrests gave the basis for the big Process of 193, which took place in 1877.

From the memorandum of Count Pahlen we may judge approximately the dimensions of the movement: during two or three months seven hundred and seventy persons were arrested in thirty-seven provinces — six hundred and twelve men and one hundred and fifty-eight women. Two hundred and fifteen persons were imprisoned, and the rest were set free. Many propagandists were not caught, and one must assume higher figures than the official ones for those who went " to the people." Among those apprehended were Kovalik, Voinaralsky, a number of girls from noble families, like Sofia Perovsky, V. N. Batiushkov, N. A. Armfeld, Sofia Leshern von Herzfeld; there were daughters of merchants, like the three sisters Kornilov, and persons of all ranks and classes, from Prince Kropotkin to common workingmen.

Pahlen stated with horror that society not only did not resist the movement, but even assisted it financially and otherwise. He could not understand that the public did not sympathise with the Government's reactionary policy, and therefore welcomed any expression of opposition.

For the *Narodniki* the movement " to the people " proved a failure; not only because they were soon arrested, but because they did not come into contact with the people. The peasants shunned them, and in some places betrayed them to the police. The *Narodniki* who were not imprisoned began to think of a firmer organisation. Two attempts were made in 1876 to organise the revolutionary forces. In Moscow a group of peaceful *Narodniki*-propagandists was formed, who figured in the Process of Fifty, in 1877. Among them were L. N. Figner, V. I. Alexandrov-Nathanson, Dzhabarti, and several workingmen, one of whom, Peter Alexeiev, delivered at the trial an ardent speech which made a profound impression. Of a greater importance was the attempt to bring together the Petrograd revolutionary *Narodniki* in the society which subsequently became known under its historical name " Land and Freedom " (*Zemlia y Volia*). At the head of that society were Mark Nathanson, his wife Olga, Alexander Mikhailov, and the remnant of the *Chaikovtzy* and those *Narodniki* who had not yet been arrested.

The basic principle of the programme of " Land and Freedom " was the assumption that only an *economic revolution from the bottom* might bring about a final and complete change from the existing order to a juster social organisation *harmonising with the ideals of the people*. Therefore they based their operations on the people proper, and divided their activity into the following branches: (1) *organising activity* — the creation of a fighting squad among the people, which would concentrate all the material and spiritual forces of the revolution, and could start a general uprising at the right moment. But since even Bakunin acknowledged before his death (1876) that it was necessary to engage in preparatory work, the party proposed (2) *agitational activity* — *passive* (sending petitions, strikes, refusal to pay taxes, etc.), and *active* (riots and uprisings), which was employed only in one place with the aid of forged manifestoes — in Chigirin (the case of Stefanovich and Deich); (3) *establishment of regular connections with the existing organisations among the people* (Schismatists and Sectants); (4) *propagation of revolutionary Narodnichestvo*

among society, young people, and city workingmen. According
to Aptekman, these four points exhausted the tactics-programme
of " Land and Freedom."

Alongside with this programme a definite constitution was
worked out, by which the original Petrograd group was to be
the nucleus of the organisation, and the members of which
could recommend outside elements. From the nucleus the
" administration " of the society was formed; it had a " heavenly chancery "— for the fabrication of false passports; there
were separate groups for propaganda among students and workingmen, and a special, *disorganising,* group for the application
of armed force against the Government and traitors. Finally
for direct propaganda and organisation of the people there existed the most important and numerous group of the " rustics "
(*derevenshchiki*). The " disorganising " group gradually increased, by force of circumstances, and formed a basis for the
terroristic party, " Will of the People," about which we shall
have to speak later.

The first manifestation of the " Land and Freedom " society
was expressed in a demonstration in front of the Kazan Cathedral in Petrograd, on December 6, 1876, in which thousands of workingmen were to take part; the speaker was a
young man, G. V. Plekhanov, now leader of the Russian So-
cial-Democrats. Only two or three hundred persons gathered, however, and were easily scattered by janitors and petty
merchants, organised for the occasion by the police. Twenty
men were arrested, tried a month and a half later, and severely punished; some were sentenced to hard labour for five
or ten years, while the minimum penalty was exile.

The most numerous group of that society, the " rustics,"
made persistent efforts to establish firm connections with the
peasants. Taught by the bitter experience of 1874, they were
more cautious and tactful, and no longer appeared an easy prey
of the police and of the ignorant, treacherous peasants. But in

the end they were forced to the conclusion that the people were hopelessly unprepared for the acceptance of their ideas, and that no success of their work was even thinkable until the people were more developed. They could only, therefore, either abandon all revolutionary plans and turn into peaceful *Kulturträger* for life, or — abandon the village, and begin the work " from the other end." The difficulties which they had to go through, the rude persecutions on the part of the Government, the growing indignation against the despotism of the administration — were bound to direct the minds of the *Narodniki* toward the second alternative. It appeared necessary to acquire first of all elementary conditions of social life which would allow free intercourse with the people. Circumstances developed in such a way that the number of " rustics " began to decrease, while the " disorganising " group grew and became at the end of the Seventies the famous " Executive Committee," which originated among Kiev revolutionists, but soon attracted all the active revolutionary forces, and made the terroristic struggle with the Government the main issue, pushing the *Narodnichestvo*-dreams and ideals to the background.

CHAPTER XXXVI

ALONGSIDE with the growth of revolutionary tendencies among the young generation, with the accretion of dissatisfaction on the part of liberal *zemstvo*-circles, elements of discontent and exasperation had accumulated during that post-reform period of Russian history in various parts of the vast Empire, provoked by insulted and persecuted national feelings. Under the influence of the Russificatory policy carried on in the crudest forms in the borderlands there arose and developed morbidly sharpened national interests and feelings.

The Ukrainophile movement appeared in Little Russia, and grew and strengthened, thanks to the persecution of the Little Russian language which had been inaugurated by Nicolas and renewed during the Sixties and Seventies in connection with the chauvinistic tendencies that prevailed in the ruling spheres and among a part of the public and the press after the suppression of the Polish uprising. Katkov turned patriot and chauvinist, and attacked all non-Russian nationalities for the aspirations of cultural self-expression and alleged political separatism. His persecution of the Ukrainophiles caused the Government to appoint a special commission, of Minister of Education Tolstoy, Minister of Interior Timashov, Chief of Gendarmes Potapov, and a renowned Kiev chauvinist, Yusephovich. The commission investigated, among other things, the activity of the Southwestern branch of the Geographical Society, found its work in the field of Little Russian poetry connected with Ukrainophilism, and had it closed in 1875. At the same time persecutions of the Little Russian language began: all publications and stage productions in that language were forbidden. Professors Dragomanov (historical philologist) and Zieber (economist) of the University of Kiev were dismissed (after they refused to resign) by the " Third point," which deprived them forever of the right to occupy an official position. The ethnographer Chubinsky was banished from Kiev, while Dragomanov and Zieber preferred to migrate abroad.[1]

The Polish question at that time was no less acute. Before the uprising the governmental policy was based at first on the principles suggested by Marquis Velepolsky, and later on the views of N. A. Miliutin and Y. F. Samarin, who distinguished between the question of Russian domination in Poland proper, and that of Russian prevalence in the Northwest and Southwest, where the task was to combat the influence of Polonism upon those Russian or Lithuanian regions. The Kingdom of Poland was to be absolutely free to employ the Polish language and develop its own culture. But that policy changed rapidly after the removal of Miliutin, who was stricken with apoplexy in 1866, and the management of Russian affairs in Poland fell into the hands of Prince V. A. Cherkassky, whose heavy character and brusqueness made the relations with Polish society acute; from that time the Russian policy in the Kingdom of Poland began to be governed by the same principles that had been applied to the Western region.

Compulsory instruction of Russian was demanded at first in secondary, and later also in primary schools; elementary education became very difficult, since the Poles naturally were unwilling to give money for Russian schools and send their children there as long as they were not allowed to be taught in their native tongue. During the Seventies and Eighties (under Curator Apukhtin) the restrictions had reached such an

---

[1] There exists an opinion that Dragomanov did so upon the advice of Prince Dundukov-Korsakov, Governor-General of Kiev, who was friendly disposed toward him.

extent that even religious instruction was not permitted in Polish, owing to which in the majority of schools such instruction was entirely discontinued during that time. All trade-signs had to be either in Russian or in both languages.

In the Seventies the question concerning the Kholm region, which was solved in recent years by the Third *Duma,* came to the front. A large portion of that population were not Poles, but Ruthenians, i.e., Little Russians, who had formerly belonged to the Orthodox creed; under Polish dominion their faith was modified, in that while they preserved Orthodox traditions they also acknowledged the supremacy of the Pope. During the Seventies the question arose about the reconversion of those *Uniates* to the Orthodox church, as had been done under Nicolas I in the Northwest. But the administration acted in that case rudely, hastily, and violently; a number of atrocities, riots, and repressions took place; hussars and cossacks were sent to aid the " voluntary " conversion to the Orthodox faith, and the reunion of the *Uniates* acquired the character of a real scandal. It is obvious that such a policy could not have aroused any good feelings towards the Government on the part of the oppressed nationalities; it enhanced the general opposition which existed under the influence of economic factors and of the growing reaction.

The general discontent caused by this stubborn reaction and by senseless repressions was complicated during the Seventies by difficulties in foreign affairs. By that time the old Eastern question had ripened.

For twenty years after the Crimean Campaign the Russian military authorities, especially on the frontiers, had been trying to restore the prestige which the Russian army had lost in Crimea, if not in Europe — at least in Asia. Two years after that war Russian territory began to increase steadily all along the Eastern Asiatic frontier. In 1858 Governor-General Muraviov of Eastern Siberia annexed to Russia the entire left bank of the river Amur, together with the vast region Ussuriysk, to the south of the mouth of Amur down to Vladivostok; the Chinese government had no power to resist, and Muraviov accomplished the great conquest with the aid of a few hundred soldiers. In 1860 the annexation was officially confirmed in Pekin.

Simultaneously the conquest of the Caucasus was completed, in the form of the " pacification " of the stubborn mountaineers. The decisive blow was delivered in 1859, by the capture of the village Gunib and the surrender of Shamil, the spiritual head and military leader of the mountain tribes. By 1865 the entire Caucasus and Trans-Caucasia, to the Turco-Persian frontiers, were parts of the Russian Empire.

Alongside with this there went on throughout the Sixties a constant pushing forward of the Russian border into the depth of Central Asia, at the expense of the Khanates. Russia had from old carried on commercial relations with those Khanates, but their subjects, who consisted of wild steppe raiders, had continually harassed the Russian borderland, robbing and carrying away not only cattle, but often men, women, and children, whom they sold into slavery. The numerous attempts of the Government to check the raiders had failed mainly because of the topographic difficulties. Under Peter the Great a military expedition under the command of Prince Cherkassky-Betovich moved far into those lands, but perished after a temporary success. In 1839 during Nicolas' reign Governor-General Perovsky of Orenburg undertook a winter expedition against Khiva; the snow-storms of the winter proved not less disastrous than the heat of the summer in those regions. In 1853 Perovsky succeeded in pushing the Russian military posts to the shores of Syr-Daria, and built there a considerable fort, later named after him.

At the same time the frontiers to the south of Siberia and the Steppe Region continued to be moved southward. In 1854

the border line extended along the river Chu from the city
Vierny to Fort Perovsky, enforced by a series of military posts.
Wild hordes from Bokhara and Kokland tried to break through
that line, and those raids gave the Russian commanders a pretext for pushing the raiders farther inland.   In 1864 Colonel
Cherniaiev captured Tashkent, in Kokand.   The Government
approved of his action, annexed the region of Tashkent, and
two years later formed there the Turkestan Governor-General-
ship.   This led to further collisions with Bokhara and Kokand,
again without any official order from above.   England looked
with alarm upon the aggressive movements of the Russians towards South Asia; remembering since the days of Napoleon
the fantastic Russian plans of penetrating India through Asiatic
mountains and steppes, the British Government asked the Russian Chancellor where his Government intended to stop.
Gorchakov replied that the Emperor did not have in mind the
aggrandisement of Russian territory, but the strengthening and
improvement of the frontier.

In the end a formal war broke out with Bokhara and
Kokand, in which both of them were discomfited, and in 1868
the Russians took the city of Samarkand, the burial place of
Tamerlan,— a sacred place with which there is connected a belief that whoever possesses it will possess all Central Asia.
Governor-General Kaufman of Turkestan impressed the half-
savage Eastern tribes with his cruel conduct, and firmly established the Russian prestige.   Making use of an uprising in
Kokand, he sent an army there under the command of Skobelev,
who conquered the Khanate and had it annexed to Russia under the name of Fergan Region.   General Kaufman's next step
was to undertake a campaign against Khiva, in 1873; the Khan
was forced to give up more than half of his possessions, to
free all his slaves, and to become a dependent vassal of Russia,
as his neighbour, the Emir of Bokhara, had become before.

Thus was the conquest of all Central Asia accomplished, to

the great indignation and natural apprehension of the English who saw that between the Russians and India lay only the lands of the Turcomen and Afghanistan, and that the Russian invasion of India was no longer as fantastic a dream as it had appeared at the beginning of the nineteenth century.

While the British apprehensions were reaching their apogee in regard to the " Russian peril " in Asia, the state of affairs in the Near East had grown very acute.   In 1874 the insurrection in Bosnia and Herzegovina broke out, chiefly because of the unbearable taxation system of the Turkish government. Other nationalities on the Peninsula were restless, and the situation grew alarming.   The uprising in Herzegovina made Austria uneasy, as she feared that Bosnia and Herzegovina she coveted would unite with Serbia, and avoid her grip; her Foreign Minister Andrashi urged a collective intervention on the part of the European Powers, and in January, 1876, the Sultan had to yield to the demand of six Powers to conclude an immediate armistice with the insurrectionists, and to undertake a series of radical reforms in the general administration and taxaton of the provinces which had revolted.   But the Herzegovinians declared that they would not lay down their arms until the European Powers gave them sufficient guarantees that the Sultan would keep his promise.   Turkey refused to satisfy the demands of the insurgents; a religious movement against Christians arose among the Mohammedans; the Sultan was accused of submitting too much to foreign influence.   He was forced to send hordes of savage Bashi-Bazouks for the suppression of the restless Christians, and those irregulars committed bloody massacres in Bulgaria, in which, according to the investigation of a British diplomat, twelve thousand Bulgars of both sexes were slaughtered.   At the same time the French and German consuls in Saloniki were murdered.   The indignation against Turkey became general in Europe.

The semi-independent states of Serbia and Montenegro de-

clared war against her, and masses of Russian volunteers filled
their armies. Although the commander of the Serbs was General Cherniaiev, the conqueror of Tashkent, they proved poorly
prepared and equipped, and the Turks delivered them a number of crushing defeats. Seeing that Serbia was on the verge
of the abyss, and that she was threatened by massacres similar
to the Bulgarian atrocities, Russia demanded of Turkey the immediate cessation of war activities and the conclusion of an
armistice. That demand was supported by other European
Powers, although Austria, in her desire to see Serbia decisively
beaten by the Turks, hesitated for some time.

In 1876 a memorandum was issued in Berlin, in which the
Powers demanded of the Sultan the immediate introduction of
the promised reforms in the Christian dependencies of Turkey,
the enlargement of the territory of Serbia and Montenegro,
and the appointment of Christian governors in Bulgaria, Bosnia,
and Herzegovina. England, however, refused to join the other
Powers; encouraged by this circumstance, Turkey declined the
demands of the Berlin memorandum. When the European
Powers sent their fleet for a demonstration at Saloniki, the British fleet was sent plausibly to assist Turkey.

In the meantime by a court revolution Sultan Abdul-Aziz
was deposed and strangled; his successor, Murad V, proved
half-witted, and was supplanted by Abdul-Hamid, who remained on the throne till the revolution of 1908. A conference was called in London for the peaceful solution of the
acute situation; Turkey consented to a six weeks' armistice
with Serbia and Montenegro. Confident in the support of
England, the Turkish plenipotentiaries at the conference allowed themselves, we may say, to mock at the European Powers: They declared that the Sultan had resolved to grant his
people a constitution, hence no changes in the internal or foreign affairs could be made without the consent of their parliament. This reference to a constitution which had not existed

exasperated all the diplomats, even those of England. Russia sent an ultimatum to Turkey threatening war unless the Turkish Government accepted immediately the project prepared by the European Powers. Turkey declined, and in April, 1877, Emperor Alexander declared war.

Alexander II did not take this step with an easy heart; he was well aware of its importance, of the financial difficulties connected with the war; he saw clearly that it might easily become an all-European conflagration, and the still more dangerous possibility of Russia being forced to fight against Austria, England, and Turkey, with the other Powers neutral. The head of the Russian diplomats, Prince Gorchakov, had become somewhat senile by that time — he was about eighty years old — and his policy was extremely wavering. Alexander himself wavered considerably; he was compelled to wage war against his desire, by the bellicose mood in the Court-circles and by the public opinion created by the Slavophiles. The pro-Slav sentiment at home and abroad was so general that the Emperor could not remain behind his people in the eyes of the world, and had to take decisive measures in defence of the Slavs.

In vain Reitern tried to dissuade Alexander from plunging the country into war. In 1875 he had succeeded in attaining a budget without deficit, and even in saving up a metal reserve of one hundred and sixty million rubles; but even before the war unfavourable circumstances had begun to threaten the course. A considerable failure of crops in 1875 had been complicated by a drought which hampered the navigation in some of the water-ways that were of great importance for the transportation of grain to ports. The seventeen thousand versts of railroads were still not generally profitable, and the Government had to pay guaranteed income. The course of the ruble began to fall under the influence of the unfavourable balance of trade (owing to the decrease in exported grain), of the forced payments of railroad-guaranties, of the outflow of foreign capital in view of the alarming international affairs, and of a panic on the Moscow bourse, caused by the bankruptcy of a large bank. Reitern's plans began to quaver, and the war threatened them with complete ruin. For a partial mobilisation in 1876, intended as a demonstration against Turkey, the Government had to contract a loan of one hundred million, and Reitern sharply remarked to the Tzar that in case of war Russia might go bankrupt.

When the war broke out, it appeared that beside the fact that it was necessary to issue masses of paper-money, which destroyed all Reitern's efforts to restore the course of the paper-ruble, Russia was unprepared in every other respect. Miliutin's reforms in the army were only two years old, the new order had not as yet been working well, and it took six months to draw even moderate forces towards the Turkish frontier.

Ambassador Ignatiev gave assurances that Turkey was decaying, and that very small forces would be required for its defeat. It was criminal optimism. The Russian army was not only insufficient, but inefficient. The staff was extremely bad. Grand Duke Nicolas, the Tzar's brother, was made commander-in-chief, although he lacked elementary strategic ability; he appointed as Chief of the Staff General Niepokoichitzky, who was senile and had no plan for the campaign. After their brilliant crossing of the Danube, the Russian armies were scattered; individual commanders accomplished heroic feats, but in view of the lack of concerted action, the army was threatened more than once with disaster. Had Suleiman-Pasha obeyed orders and joined forces with the brave Osman-Pasha, the Turks would have succeeded in cutting off the advance-forces of Gurko's army.

With all the blunders of the Turks and miraculous escapades of isolated Russian troops, the war lasted throughout 1877 and part of 1878. After the capture of Plevna (with the aid of the Roumanian army, under the command of Prince, later King, Carol) the Russians crossed the Balkans, occupied Adrianople, and appeared before Constantinople in January, 1878. It was then that Alexander received a telegram from Queen Victoria, asking him to stop, and conclude an armistice. Although Alexander had promised England even before the war that he would not occupy Constantinople, Lord Beaconsfield had the parliament vote six million pounds for military expenses; war seemed inevitable. But Turkey was exhausted and forced to ask for peace; in the middle of January, 1878, the Adrianople armistice was signed, and soon after diplomatic negotiations began in San Stefano, where Ignatiev successfully represented Russia. In March the peace was signed, in which all Russian demands were satisfied; Serbia and Montenegro were enlarged, and Bulgaria became a semi-independent principality, with a territory reaching to the Ægean Sea. In Asia Russia was to receive the conquered Kars and Batum, with their environs. Part of Bessarabia which went to Roumania in 1856 was restored to Russia, and Roumania was compensated with Dobrudja.

Lord Beaconsfield immediately protested against any territorial changes being made in Turkey without the participation of the Great Powers who had signed the Treaty of Paris, in 1856. Under the threat of war with England and Austria, Alexander was forced to consent to a congress of European representatives in Berlin, presided over by Bismarck. At that Congress the conditions of the peace were substantially changed: the possessions of Serbia, Montenegro, and especially Bulgaria, were diminished; part of Bulgaria, to the south of the Balkans, was separated as a Turkish province under a Christian governor. Beaconsfield protested also against Russia's territorial acquisitions, but he succeeded only in changing Batum from a military port into an open port for all nations.

The humiliation at Berlin, coupled with the inadequate

management of the campaign, and with the theft and graft which were discovered in the matter of provisioning the army — aroused the indignation and opposition of wide circles in Russia, not only of radical and revolutionary layers, but of the most loyal society, as the Slavophiles. When rumours concerning the concessions wrested from Russia at the Berlin Congress had reached Moscow, Ivan Aksakov delivered a thundering speech at the public session of the " Slav Society," in which he said:

" Shall we admit even a particle of truth in all those letters and telegrams which are circulating every day, every hour in all tongues, to all corners of the world, disgraceful news about our concessions? Not once denied by the Government, this news, spreading among the people, scorches them with shame, stings their conscience, oppresses them with bewilderment."

He went on describing in strong terms the humiliating conduct of the Russian diplomats, the significance of the concessions for the independence of Bulgaria and of other Slav nationalities on the Balkan peninsula, for the political preponderance of treacherous Austria, and for the fall of Russian prestige among the Slav nations. Aksakov repeated several times that he refused to believe that those actions of the diplomats were approved by the " supreme authority," and he finished his remarkable speech with the following words:

" The people are raging, grumbling, indignant, disturbed with the daily news from Berlin, and await, like a blessed tiding, the resolution of the Throne. Russia awaits and hopes. Its hope shall not be belied, for the Tzar's words: ' The sacred cause will be brought to its end,' shall not be broken. Loyal duty commands us all to hope and trust, but loyal duty commands us also not to keep silent in these days of lawlessness and untruth which are building up a wall between the Tzar and the land, between the thought of the Tzar and the thought of the people. Is it indeed possible that in answer there will sound from above a grave word: *'Hold your peace, O honest lips! Speak but you, O flattery and falsehood!'*"

When Alexander heard about that speech, he was so enraged that in spite of Aksakov's position in society, and his age, he ordered him banished from Moscow.

Still greater was the excitement among the liberal *zemstvo*-men and among the revolutionary circles, especially in the South, where the people were nearer to the war zone, and had been able to see better the abuses and disorders in the commissariat, and where the Ukrainophile movement had been quite widely spread. The conviction of the necessity of a constitutional order in Russia became particularly widespread among Kiev society. That conviction was strengthened by the fact that in Bulgaria, which from an oppressed, wild, and uncivilised country was transformed into an independent Principality, a constitutional order was immediately established; this could not have taken place without the consent of Alexander; hence the hopes of the Russian patriots and liberals were encouraged. From the South the constitutional movement spread throughout Russia.

The revolutionary movement had by that time taken on sharp forms. The non-political aspirations of the *Narodniki* underwent a change under the repressive measures of the Government which prevented them from carrying on their peaceful, cultural work among the people; after the attempt of Viera Zasulich to shoot Chief of Police Trepov for flogging a political prisoner,[2] the revolutionary movement became a keen political

---

[2] The Government was so confident that the process of Zasulich would lower the reputation of the revolutionists in the eyes of the public, that it allowed her to be tried by a jury. To its horror the jury declared Viera Zasulich not guilty, in spite of the fact that she did not deny her actual shooting at Trepov with the intention of killing him. Upon leaving the court, Zasulich was almost arrested by gendarmes who had intended to deal with her " in the administrative order," but the crowd protected her, and soon after she fled abroad. She is still active in the revolutionary propaganda.— TR.

struggle. It had become evident that under the existing political conditions it was impossible to carry on any social propaganda; moreover, the masses were not at all sympathetic with such a propaganda; the *Narodniki* began to seek means for the improvement of political conditions. After an armed uprising in Odessa and the execution of Kovalsky, Stepniak-Kravchinsky murdered Chief of Gendarmes Mezentzev in daylight on the streets of Petrograd, and was not caught.

The Government appealed to the public for co-operation in its struggle against the " sedition." At that time *zemstvo* workers of several southern provinces had united, and held some conferences in Kiev and Kharkov which were attended by liberal elements of the public. They attempted to make a temporary agreement with the revolutionists, and persuade them to discontinue their terroristic activity in order to enable the liberals to try peaceful means of persuasion with the Government. Their attempt failed. Yet the *zemstvo* men decided to call the attention of the Government to the fact that in its struggle with the revolution it had been employing measures which infringed upon the interests and rights of society as a whole, and that as long as the Government ignored the just demands of the public and did not respect the inviolability and elementary rights of peaceful citizens, the representatives of society were unable to give it any assistance. Similar resolutions were planned by many *zemstvo* assemblies, in response to the invitation of the Government for co-operation. At the provincial assembly of the Chernigov *zemstvo*, I. I. Petrunkevich delivered a characteristic speech in which he pointed out all the abuses of the autocracy, the bigoted measures of Tolstoy, the absence of freedom of press and of speech, and ended with the resolution that under such conditions society was unable to come to the assistance of the Government.

The Government hastened to forbid the discussion of such questions at *zemstvo* assemblies, so that only a few of them had time to publish their declarations. The resolution of the Tver assembly was as follows:

" The Emperor, in his care for the Bulgars, liberated from the Turkish yoke, has found it necessary to grant them true self-government, inviolability of personal rights, independence of the judiciary, and freedom of press. The *zemstvo* of the province of Tver ventures to hope that the Russian people who have borne all the burdens of the war with such readiness, with such unreserved love for their Tzar-Liberator, will be granted the same benefits, which alone will enable them to enter, in the words of the Tzar, on the way of gradual, peaceful, and legitimate development."

The Marshals of Nobility were notified through a circular that they would be held responsible by the Minister, if they let such resolutions pass. Yet the movement in the *zemstvo* circles did not calm down, but continued to grow. In 1879 and 1880 there were many secret *zemstvo* assemblies, the most imposing of which took place in Moscow. The Government began to punish the active members of the movement. Petrunkevich was arrested and banished to the province of Kostroma.[3]

At the same time, as we have seen, the activity of the revolutionary Socialists grew more extreme and drastic. From 1878 a series of terroristic acts took place, with the view of wresting elemental political freedom from the Government. In 1879 the party " Land and Freedom " had a conference at Voronezh, for the discussion of new ideas and the revision of their programme. A preliminary conference was held at Lipetzk by the extreme wing of the party, the leader of which was a prominent revolutionist from Odessa, Zheliabov; it decided to form

[3] I. I. Petrunkevich is at present a prominent leader of the Constitutional Democrats, and an untiring *zemstvo* worker. He was elected to the First *Duma*, and at the first session demanded amnesty for all political prisoners.— TR.

a special " Executive Committee " for terroristic actions against the Government. The majority of the Voronezh conference approved of the Lipetzk resolution; a small group of *Narodniki*, led by Plekhanov, separated from the majority, declaring themselves in favour of the former programme and tactics which placed social propaganda before political struggle. The party of " Land and Freedom " split in two: the larger organisation of the " Will of the People " (*Narodnaia Volia. Narodovoletz, Narodovoltzy* — members of the party), which concentrated its chief forces on a systematic terroristic struggle with the Government, though retaining some *Narodnichestvo* ideals in their programme; and the smaller and less influential group, the party of the " Black Partition " which continued to advocate the old *Narodnichestvo* views in full. The field of action remained in the hands of the " Will of the People," which during the next two years performed a number of terroristic acts that shook the governmental organisation.

CHAPTER XXXVII

THE economic and financial difficulties were very acute after the war; Minister of Finance Reitern, who had been opposed to the war, resigned upon its conclusion, not wishing to cope with the complicated situation. At the same time the gulf between the Government and the people grew deeper and wider, signified by the development of the *zemstvo* oppositional movement, and by the conversion of the revolutionary *Narodniki* to active terroristic activity.

The terroristic attempts of the "Will of the People" were directed chiefly against the life of the Tzar; he was systematically besieged by a small, but energetic group who organised nets of mines, exploded bridges, trains, and buildings, risking their own as well as many other lives. The revolutionists strongly believed that the murder of the Tzar would serve as a signal for a general uprising of the people. The bewildered Government, finding no support in the people whose needs and rights it did not consider, undertook convulsive repressive measures which made the conflict more acute and resolute, and rendered the life of peaceful citizens as unbearable as under the conditions of a siege.

After the attentate of Soloviov in 1879 and a number of other attempts on the life of the Tzar, it appeared clear to all that the Government was unable by repressive measures alone to eradicate the revolution and establish peace in the country. Some of the higher administrators and members of the Court began to look for other means. Governor-General Loris-Melikov of Kharkov, appointed after the attentate of Soloviov, experimented with a new policy in his region; continuing to suppress the revolutionists, he at the same time endeavoured to win the sympathies and respect of the population by a human and decent management of public affairs. Parallel with this, Count Valuiev, President of the Committee of Ministers at that time, began to inspire the Emperor with the idea of trying to regain the confidence and co-operation of society, by allowing its representatives to participate in affairs of the State; for this purpose he dug out the project he had prepared back in 1863. Grand Duke Constantine, then President of the State Council, also presented his plan for a representative order, drawn up by his request in 1866 by Prince Urusov.

While those projects had been discussed in court circles, throughout the country administrative despotism reigned arousing general discontent and exasperation. The revolutionists organised a daring explosion in the Winter Palace, on February 4, 1880. The explosion took place just at the moment when the entire Imperial family were to take their seats at the dining table, to entertain the Prince of Bulgaria, Alexander Battenberg. The carefully planned slaughter of the whole family failed only because the train of the Bulgarian Prince was late, and the dinner took place half an hour behind the scheduled time.

This event proved to all, and first of all to Alexander himself, the danger of the situation, in which the revolutionists were better informed and more efficient than the costly, enormous police organisation. New views concerning the internal policy began to dominate among the higher circles. A week before the explosion the Emperor called a conference for the discussion of Valuiev's plan. The Heir, Tzesarevich Alexander, who took part in the discussions, expressed himself definitely against the constitutional plans suggested by Valuiev and Grand Duke Constantine, thus demonstrating early the political beliefs which he later professed throughout his reign. At the conference called by the Tzar after the explosion the

Tzesarevich suggested the establishment of a supreme investigating commission, with large authority, similar to the commissions instituted in 1862 after the Petrograd conflagrations, and in 1866 after the attentate of Karakozov. The Tzar at first regarded his son's plan negatively, but at the conference which took place on the next day, with the participation of several governors-general who happened to be in the Capital, Alexander II declared that he intended to make use of the Heir's plan for the formation of a dictatorial institution, under the name of the Supreme Commanding Commission, which should have extraordinary power for the suppression of sedition, and should at the same time seek a way out of the untolerable position of the moment. At the head of the commission Alexander placed Loris-Melikov, the only governor-general who had shown energy not only in suppressing the revolution, but also in winning the sympathy of the population. By a special ukase all administrative authorities, including the ministers, were subjected to the commission under the command of Adjutant-General Loris-Melikov.

To the public at large Loris-Melikov was known as a prominent Caucasian general who won glory in the War of 1877–1878 by the capture of Kars, and later during the spread of the black-plague in the province of Astrakhan, as an energetic administrator. In the South he was known as Governor-General of Kharkov. Immediately upon his appointment, February 14, 1880, Loris-Melikov issued a proclamation to the inhabitants of Petrograd, in which he declared that while firmly endeavouring to eradicate the criminals who attempted to shake the existing order, he at the same time desired to reassure the peaceful and well-intentioned elements of the public.

" Upon the support of the public," he wrote, " I look as upon the main power which may assist the Government in the restoration of a normal course of national life, from the disturbances of which the interests of the public suffer mostly."

Most of those who knew Loris-Melikov personally, testify to his straightforwardness, honesty, sincerity, true liberalism, readiness to meet loyal public demands even to the extent of allowing society some participation in the affairs of the State. It is a mistake, however, to consider him a constitutionalist who intended to introduce any Western form of government. He openly opposed the establishment of any representative institution, considering the moment inopportune; he advised that affairs be regulated by a series of administrative and legislative measures, to restore the institutions created by the reforms of the Sixties and destroyed during the reaction, and in that work of improving the conditions caused by the reaction he intended to admit in one form or another the representatives of the people to participate.

The fundamental task of Loris-Melikov was to suppress the revolution. He decided to centralise the repressive authority, and with this view abolished the Third Department of His Majesty's Chancery, instituted with the aid of Benckendorff by Nicolas I, and had all police affairs concentrated in the hands of the Minister of Interior. At the head of the Police Department he placed the former procurator of the Petrograd Judicial Chamber, V. K. Plehve,[1] who was instructed to bring the procurature in close connection with the activity of the police, thus furthering the work of Pahlen — of rendering the procurators dependent upon the administration. The new Dictator, as he was called, expanded his repressive measures upon not only revolutionists, but all persons opposed to the Government. At the very beginning of his " dictatorship of the heart," he exiled N. F. Annensky, the famous writer and statistician, to Siberia. He rejected the petition of the Borozna *zemstvo* to allow Petrunkevich to return to the province of

[1] Minister of Interior during the present reign; perpetrator of the Kishinev massacre of 1903, and of other atrocities; assassinated in 1904.— TR.

Chernigov; Petrunkevich was permitted, however, to change his abode from the province of Kostroma to that of Smolensk. At the same time Loris-Melikov consistently carried through his ideas concerning guarding the rights of the *peaceful* citizens. It was his intention to restore in full measure the *zemstvo* and judicial statutes of 1864, and to abolish all restrictions and distortions which had followed them. He then insisted on the dismissal of Minister of Education, Count Tolstoy, and supplanted him with the liberal A. A. Saburov, who endeavoured during the short term of his administration to return to the principles of Golovnin. His next step was to discharge Minister of Finance General Greig, who was both incapable and reactionary; in his place was appointed A. A. Abaza, a friend of N. A. Miliutin and one of the circle of Grand Duchess Yelena Paulovna. Abaza's first measure was to abolish the heavy salt-tax; he undertook a number of measures for the promulgation of liberal financial reforms, which were partly carried out during the following reign.

Loris-Melikov had considerably improved the conditions of the press. A number of new organs began to appear during his dictatorship: The *Country,* edited by L. A. Polonsky, the *Order,* edited by M. M. Stasiulevich, *Russian Thought,* edited by Yuriev, a friend of Koshelev. For the twelfth time Ivan Aksakov was permitted to raise his voice — in the Slavophile publication, *Russ,* which existed for several years. The *zemstvo* workers were finally allowed to have their own organ, established in Moscow by the means of Koshelev, under the title *Zemstvo;* it appeared for two years under the editorship of Scalon, and manifested a very liberal, if not radical, tendency. Allowing the press to discuss political questions and to criticise governmental measures, Loris-Melikov insisted upon one restriction: the press was not permitted to mention or discuss constitutional problems, in order that it might not arouse false hopes. Such restrictions were announced not in the form of circulars, but were indicated to the editors in personal conversations with the Dictator.

The Supreme Commanding Commission was closed six months after its institution, upon the report of Loris-Melikov who found no further need of extraordinary authority for the struggle with the sedition. He was appointed Minister of Interior, and at that post he continued his activity in the former spirit. Enjoying the full confidence of the Tzar, he at the same time kept up direct connections with progressive and democratic circles of the public, particularly of the *zemstvo*, and eagerly tried to realise many of the desiderata expressed by public men in private memoranda and conversations.

After a study of the peasant-question through various *zemstvo* presentations, he came to the conclusion that fundamental reforms, which would be a direct continuation of the Reform, were required for the satisfaction of the crying needs of the peasants. He considered among other urgent needs the revision of the taxation system, and the reorganisation of the legal and administrative status of the peasants. The latter question Loris-Melikov decided to hand over for a preliminary discussion to the *zemstvos*, and by a circular to the governors, December 22, 1880, he directed them to permit the discussion of the question at provincial and district *zemstvo* assemblies.

This policy of establishing a certain harmony between the Government and the representatives of the people was tremendously successful, and even such radical *zemstvos* as that of Tver regarded Loris-Melikov's activity with full approval. In an address to him, written in 1880, the Tver *zemstvo* said:

" In a short time you have been able to justify the confidence of the Tzar, and many hopes of the public. You have introduced straightforwardness and good-will into the relations of the Government and the people. You have wisely recognised the lawful needs and desires of the public."

In the end the Tver *zemstvo* expressed its belief that " the deplorable past would not return, and a happy future was opening for our dear country." Since the establishment of the *zemstvos* no other high functionary has been honoured with such a sincere public approval, neither before nor after Loris-Melikov.

On the part of the revolutionists, however, the activity of Loris-Melikov not only did not meet with approval, but aroused irritation and alarm. The revolutionary circles were in a state of temporary disorganisation, owing to the arrest of a prominent member of the "Executive Committee," Goldenberg, the slayer of Governor Prince Kropotkin of Kharkov in 1879; the clever tactics of the gendarmes brought Goldenberg not only to complete repentance, but made him betray the names of most of his comrades. For a time the organisation was forced to discontinue its activity, for fear of falling an easy prey to the well informed police. Loris-Melikov mistakenly interpreted the temporary lull in the terroristic acts as the decision of the "Will of the People" to give up that activity. In their underground publications the revolutionists sharply condemned his policy as that of "the fox's tail"; they logically feared that the "dictatorship of the heart" would isolate them from the fascinated public.

Loris-Melikov understood that in order to maintain the good-will of the public he had to allow some outlet for the desires progressive circles manifested to take part in State affairs. In his report to Alexander II, presented on January 28, 1881, he reiterated his opinion about the untimeliness and impossibility of granting the people constitutional institutions; yet he insisted on the necessity of satisfying the desire of the advanced representatives of the people for State activity. He suggested following the practice of the Editing Commissions in inviting public men to co-operate in working out national reforms; alongside with capable officials he wished to invite *zemstvo* workers, professors, publicists, and other competent persons. For the first time he proposed appointing two preliminary commissions in Petrograd; an *administrative* one, for the general reorganisation of the administration, and a *financial* commission, for questions of taxation, etc. The plans for those commissions were to be brought before the *General* commission, which was to consist of the members of the preliminary commissions, and also of local experts invited for the purpose, who were to be elected by *zemstvos,* or by municipal self-governments. Finally the plans were to pass from the *General* commission to the State Council, into which were to be invited ten to fifteen elective persons, as representatives of public opinion.

You can readily see that it is erroneous to call Loris-Melikov's plan *constitutional,* as it has been widely known. Yet his moderate plan might have been a step forward in the formation of an understanding and co-operation between the public and the Government; its realisation might have brought about a constitution in a peaceful way, while the present constitution had to be wrested through a revolution, and the people were not organically prepared for it.

On the whole we may say that the policy of Loris-Melikov was not unsuccessful; but the fact that he regarded somewhat optimistically the results of his system in regard to the suppression of the revolutionary organisations, played a tragic rôle. The revolutionists had concentrated all their forces to deliver the Government a telling blow; they disregarded Loris-Melikov as a nonentity, but renewed their attempts to kill Alexander II. Petrograd, one may say, was undermined; in many places, where the passage of the Imperial carriage might be expected, the street or bridge was mined. After numerous attempts the revolutionists resolved that mines did not bring any results, in view of the difficulty of establishing the exact moment of the Emperor's passing by; they decided to make use of hand-bombs. One week before March 1, Zheliabov "sounded a call," as they expressed it in the parlance of the "Will of the People," i.e., he asked for volunteers to appear on the streets with bombs in their hands. The bombs were prepared by the talented chemist, Kibalchich. In the end of February Zheliabov and Trigoni were arrested; Sophia Perovsky, who was still unarrested, decided not only not to drop the matter, but to hasten its accomplishment. On March 1, Alexander II, disregarding the warnings of Loris-Melikov, who had succeeded twice in keeping the Tzar from Sunday rides, rode out to inspect the troops, then to the Mikhailovsky Palace (now Museum of Alexander III), the residence of Grand Duchess Yelena, whence he was to return to the Winter Palace. The revolutionists, led by Sophia Perovsky, manœuvred on the streets, shifting positions, and making sure not to miss their victim. The circumstances of the catastrophe are too well known to be retold here.[2]

[2] When the Imperial carriage turned on the Catherinian Canal, Sophia Perovsky waved her handkerchief, as a signal to her comrades who were scattered at various corners of the adjacent streets. One of them, Rysakov, flung a bomb wrapped in cotton at the cortège; the bottom of the carriage was smashed, a number of the escorting Cossacks were wounded and thrown from their saddles, but the Tzar was not injured. The coachman suggested to drive on to the Palace, but Alexander approached the wounded Cossacks and the imprisoned, half dead Rysakov. "Thank God, I am untouched," he said in answer to anxious inquiries of his entourage. "It's too soon to thank God," shouted another terrorist, Grinevitzky, who came close to the Tzar, and threw a bomb at his feet. The explosion was heard throughout the city. A number of persons were wounded, among them Grinevitzky. The Emperor suffered severe wounds; one leg was shattered to the top of the thigh, the other severed to the knee; the abdomen was torn open; the face was terribly disfigured; the right hand was lacerated, pieces of the Tzar's wedding-ring having been driven into his flesh. He could barely whisper to Grand Duke Mikhail: "Quick home, to Palace, there die." At the Palace his legs were amputated; he died about an hour and a half later, without regaining consciousness.

On the 16th of April the death sentence was executed upon the participators of the assassination — A. J. Zheliabov, Sophia Perovsky, U.

Thus was brought to a sudden end the system of measures planned by Loris-Melikov. Alexander III, as you might have concluded from his stand at the conference before the explosion in the Winter Palace, showed no promise of becoming a liberal monarch.

Kibalchich, T. Mikhailov, and N. Rysakov. Grinevitzky had died of his wounds before the trial, and the execution of Jessie Hanfman was postponed because of her pregnancy.— TR.

CHAPTER XXXVIII

EMPEROR ALEXANDER III was the second son of Alexander II; his elder brother, Tzesarevich Nicolas, died from tuberculosis in 1865. Until that year Alexander was brought up as an ordinary Grand Duke, whose career was to be mainly military; after the death of his brother care was taken to broaden his education. A number of prominent professors were invited to him, among them the historian S. M. Soloviov, and K. P. Pobiedonostzev, who was destined to play such an important rôle in the future. At that time Pobiedonostzev was not reactionary; on the contrary, he had taken part in the preparation of the judicial reform, and was one of the most brilliant of Russian jurists. Other more or less progressive professors were employed, but the young Tzesarevich did not form any liberal ideas and principles as a result of his education. In his personal and family life he presented an original exception in the Court circles. He early married the bride of his late brother, the Danish Princess Dagmar, and after his marriage led a private life, occupied himself with music and Russian history; it was he who founded the " Imperial Russian Historical Society," of which he was the first president.

Partly because of his mode of life, and still more perhaps because society had little information about him, a legend grew up that Alexander was a liberal. We have seen that he had manifested his conservatism some months before his accession, and promised no sympathy for liberal reforms.

On March 2, 1881, at the reception of the members of the State Council and other high dignitaries, who took the oath,

Alexander III declared that he hoped to follow the policy of his father; this was apparently a promise of a human and liberal reign. Then in a circular note of March 4, sent to Russian representatives abroad, it was announced that the new Emperor, ascending the throne at such a difficult moment, desired to preserve peace with all Powers, and concentrate all his attention on internal affairs. The note too made a favourable impression on the public.

In the meantime a question arose concerning the project of Loris-Melikov, which had been approved by Alexander II on the morning of his assassination; the late Tzar had ordered a conference for March 4 at the Winter Palace, for the discussion of the method of the opening of the projected commissions. Alexander III at first considered that project as a legacy from his father, which would give the finishing touch to his reign. He called a special meeting of the Committee of Ministers, to which was invited Count S. G. Stroganov, leader of the Court conservatives, to decide whether the opening of the commissions should be announced to the public or not. The conference took place on March 8, and two conflicting, mutually excluding tendencies appeared — a progressive, to which belonged Loris-Melikov, Minister of Finance Abaza, Minister of War D. A. Miliutin, and Grand Duke Constantine, head of the Navy Department and President of the State Council, and a reactionary group which was represented first of all by K. P. Pobiedonostzev, not long since a member of Loris-Melikov's Supreme Commanding Commission. In 1880 Pobiedonostzev was appointed, upon the presentation of Loris-Melikov, Super-Procurator of the Holy Synod, in place of Count D. A. Tolstoy; he was tutor to Alexander and his elder brother, and enjoyed the confidence of the Tzar. At the conference he was supported by Count Stroganov who had been invited at his suggestion, and by former Minister of Interior, Makov. An intermediary position was maintained by Grand Dukes Vlad-

imir and Mikhail; of the ministers, Minister of Justice Na-
bokov was inclined liberally, but supported Loris-Melikov
hesitatingly, while Count Valuiev, President of the Committee
of Ministers, who had appeared in 1880 with *quasi*-constitu-
tional projects, showed little support of Loris-Melikov's project
at the conference, because of his hatred for the former Dictator and for Grand Duke Constantine.

At the conference it appeared that Alexander III sympathised with the reactionaries, and was impatient with the
liberal members; he was impressed by the passionate speech
of Pobiedonostzev which opened with the phrase: *" Finis
Russae,"* and predicted disasters and revolutions in case of the
acceptance of Loris-Melikov's project. Alexander remarked
that Emperor Wilhelm I had definitely advised his late father
of the danger of a constitutional régime for Russia, and urged
him, in view of the rumours about the Tzar's intention of
granting a constitution, to withdraw it, if it was not too late,
and if it was — to curtail it as much as possible; Alexander
referred also to the Danish ministers who regarded the influence
of the constitutional institutions pernicious for Denmark.

No decision was immediately arrived at. Alexander continued to hesitate for some time. He was loath to disobey the
last will of his father, the more so since some of the Court
liberals informed him of the grave mood of the country, and
counselled a liberal course as the only means for restoring calm
in the land. On the other hand, Pobiedonostzev tried to persuade the Tzar of the absence of constitutional aspirations
among the wide circles of society, and drew to his support
Katkov and Ivan Aksakov. Katkov represented at that time
the extreme reactionaries, and openly hinted in his *Moscow
News* that the revolutionary movement emanated not from
the country, but that it " had built a nest on the threshold of
the supreme power," referring to Loris-Melikov and other
liberals at the court. Aksakov was deeply shocked by the event

of March 1. He came soon after to Petrograd, and delivered a passionate speech at the Slav Society, in which he attacked not only the revolutionists, but all the tendencies of Western liberalism. Pobiedonostzev succeeded in persuading Alexander that Katkov and Aksakov represented the public opinion of the country, and he was secretly commissioned to draw up a manifesto. On April 29, 1881, to the complete surprise of Loris-Melikov and the other ministers the significant manifesto appeared, which was intended to put an end to further vacillations. In one place it read:

" In the midst of our great grief God's voice commands us to stand courageously at the helm of the government, relying upon Divine Providence, *with faith in the power and truth of the Autocracy which, for the benefit of the people, we are called upon to strengthen and guard from any encroachments."*

Those words were naturally interpreted as a clear indication from above that the principle of autocracy was to be the cornerstone of the governmental policy, and that no constitutional expectations would not be realised. Immediately upon the publication of the manifesto Loris-Melikov, Abaza, and Miliutin resigned. Yet, in spite of the defeat of the progressive elements, the programme of the new reign was still not quite reactionary, as it may be seen from the personnel of ministers selected by the Tzar. As Minister of Interior N. P. Ignatiev, a Slavophile, was appointed. He expected, together with Aksakov, to be able to bring about the summoning of a *Zemsky Sobor* (assembly of men of the land), of a consultative character. N. C. Bunge, a man of conservative views, but a sincere friend of the reforms of the Sixties, a convinced democrat who strove to alleviate the lot of the people, took the place of Abaza as Minister of Finance. In place of Saburov, who had resigned some time before, Alexander appointed Baron Nicolayi, who immediately began to carry out Golovnin's policy, and actively opposed Pobiedonostzev.

The manifesto of April 29 promised to strengthen and continue the great reforms of the preceding reign. This motive was emphasised in the circular of the new Minister of Interior, Ignatiev, sent out on the very day of his appointment, May 6, 1881. He indicated that the Government would take measures for the establishment of close relations with the people, and for the participation of local men in the affairs of the State. The circular further stated that the rights of *zemstvos* and the municipal institutions would remain intact, on the basis of the Act of 1864. The peasants were warned against false rumours, and were promised that not only would their rights and liberties be guaranteed, but that measures would be taken for the lightening of their burdens (mainly the taxes), for the satisfaction of their needs (particularly of land), and for the improvement of the rural administration and structure.

Thus we see that the régime was as yet far from reactionary. Ignatiev's circular resembled the programme of Loris-Melikov; one month after its issue Count Ignatiev began to carry out his promise about allowing local men to take part in State affairs. In June, 1881, the first session of " informed men " was summoned by the Government for the discussion of such important questions as the lowering of redemption payments, the regulation of peasant migration, the beverage question — which involved both the problem of combating drunkenness and of regulating the revenue.

At the same time the Government raised the question of redemption; there still remained one-seventh of the estates, or one million four hundred thousand peasants who paid *obroks,* as " temporary-Obligatory." Loris-Melikov had pushed the question ahead, and in January, 1881, the State Council determined to introduce obligatory redemption of the *obroks* in those estates where a voluntary redemption had not been started. At that time reactionary agitation began to appear on the part of the nobles who considered compulsory

redemption an infringement of the sacred rights of property.
In the State Council that view was voiced by former Minister
of Interior Timashov, and later it was expressed in resolutions
of many assemblies of the nobles (of Tambov, Moscow, and
others), which impressed Alexander III in spite of the arguments of Ignatiev. The agitation of the nobles brought no
fruit, however, and the reform was carried out safely.

Then a series of new enactments began, which were known
as the reforms of Bunge, although a considerable part of them
had been prepared in the period of the " dictatorship of the
heart." The first problem was to ameliorate the conditions of
the freed peasants by lowering the redemption payments. The
session of the " informed men " who assembled in June of 1881
worked out, together with representatives of the Government,
a law by which all allotments received a reduction of one ruble
from every payment, and five million rubles, to be distributed
by the *zemstvos,* were assigned for lowering the payments in
especially burdened provinces; the total sum of reductions
amounted to twelve million rubles. It is worth noting that
in some provinces, very few indeed, reactionary voices against
the lowering of the payments rose from the nobility, although
that reform was carried on at the expense of the Treasury.

The next reform promulgated by Bunge was the abolition
of the per capita tax. Bunge in his financial policy was a follower of Reitern, and had also striven primarily for the raising
of the course of the ruble and for the establishment of a firm
balance of the budget. Hence his protectionism, and economy
in expenditures. Yet he determined to do away with the detrimental per capita tax, which necessitated " mutual guarantee,"
and thus limited freedom of movement and of occupations
among the peasants. But the abolition of that tax meant a
loss of forty million rubles in yearly revenue; Bunge had to
fill that gap in some way, for Russian finances were still in a
deplorable state since the war with Turkey. Part of the loss

was retrieved through an increase of the liquor tax, which affected mainly the drinking portion of the population, and the rest of it Bunge had to recover by taxing the better situated and less burdened peasants. The land-taxes of the State peasants were raised by forty-five per cent. The abolition of the per capita tax was accomplished in two terms: In 1883 and 1884 it was removed from the most burdened peasants, and in 1886 — from the rest.

Bunge also made a serious attempt to regulate the collection of taxes, which the police had accomplished in the crudest and most cruel ways, compelling the peasants at times to sell their crops in advance in order to pay the taxes. Bunge appointed tax-inspectors who were to collect taxes, and also to gather information concerning the paying capacity of the population, with a view to further regulating the tax-system.

CHAPTER XXXIX

AMONG the measures directed against the dearth of land we should mention three: The establishment of a Peasant-bank, to aid the peasants with credit for buying land; the facilitation of renting fiscal lands; and the regulation of migration. All those tasks had been definitely outlined during the " dictatorship of the heart."

The Government assigned five million rubles a year for the Peasant-bank; in spite of the meagre sum, its activity during the first three years, while Bunge remained Minister and while the first personnel of the bank administration, selected by Bunge, was in power, was regulated by considerations of comparative needs of the peasants to whom loans were made. But later the activity of the bank changed; the Government became alarmed at the number of tax-delinquents, and began to sell with zeal the lands of peasants who were in arrears; as a result the activity of the bank was reduced by the end of the Eighties to insignificant transactions and occasional irrational land-purchases by well-to-do peasants. After ten years of its existence it had assisted the increase of peasant landownership by one and a half per cent, i.e., by scarcely twelve hundredths per cent. annually, whereas the previous assistance of private credit-institutions had increased the peasant landownership by three-tenths per cent. annually.

The growing rent rates had become the burning question in the progressive press, in governmental circles, in the second session of the " informed men." The general desire was for the regulation of the fiscal and private renting prices and conditions of rent. But the State Council had expressed on several occasions its fear of arousing false hopes among the peasants by agrarian reforms from above; in this case it allowed the regulation of rents only on fiscal domains, which amounted to several million desiatins. In 1881, when Loris-Melikov was still in power, Ignatiev, then Minister of State Domains, carried through a law, by which fiscal lands were to be rented primarily to peasants of respective districts; this measure at once raised the amount of fiscal land rented to peasants from twenty-three to sixty-six per cent. In 1884 the law of 1881 was somewhat restricted; the term of rent was shortened from twenty-four to twelve years, and land could be freely rented only by peasants who lived within twelve versts of it.

The migration question was an old one. During the serfdom-system peasants were either transported by their masters to new estates, or fled from their owners into free lands, where they settled with the actual, although unofficial, knowledge of the Government. The migration of Fiscal peasants went on more regularly since the days of Kiselev; they were often helped by the Government in various ways. Between 1831 and 1866 the migration of Fiscal peasants averaged nine thousand persons annually, while in certain years the number reached twenty-eight thousand.

By the Act of 1861 peasants were not allowed to leave their allotments during the first nine years without the consent of the landowner. Nevertheless they migrated in enormous masses to less remote parts of Siberia or to the borderlands of European Russia; few made use of the privileges offered in the regions of Amur and Ussuriysk. By the end of the Seventies official estimates of such "wilful" migrators totalled forty thousand per year. Special rules were issued on June 10, 1881, restricting the migration, and requiring the permission of the Ministers of Interior and of State domains in every case. The rules were not put into practice, and the illegal migration continued. The second session of "informed men," called by

Ignatiev in September, 1881, criticised the restrictive rules, and recommended that the Government assist the migrators in every way. Their recommendation was not heeded until July, 1889, when in spite of the reigning reaction under D. A. Tolstoy as Minister of Interior, the State Council passed a law by which migration was facilitated and aided.

Under Bunge protective laws concerning workingmen were issued for the first time. By the law of 1882 the working time of women and children was limited, the conditions of their work were placed under the official supervision of Factory Inspectors. The latter institution was further developed in subsequent laws, issued in 1884, 1885, 1886.

Bunge made the first attempt to shift the burden of taxes upon the shoulders of the wealthy. In 1882 a law was issued about an inheritance-tax, and in 1885 — a tax on bonds was instituted.

Such were the not unimportant, although purely palliative measures of the Government early in the Eighties for the improvement of the economic conditions of the masses.

The question of the reorganisation of the rural administration was handed over to the *zemstvos* for discussion, by the circular of Loris-Melikov of December 22, 1880. The *zemstvos* did not arrive at an unanimous opinion, however, and it was left for the Government to institute in the fall of 1881 a special commission under the chairmanship of State Secretary Kokhanov, Deputy-Minister under Loris-Melikov. Into the commission entered those Senators who had been commissioned by Loris-Melikov to inspect certain provinces and report the results of their revisions, some of those who participated in the original preparation of the reform of local administration, and, as expert-members, various *zemstvo* workers. The commission appointed from its midst a sub-commission, headed by Kokhanov, which was to work out the reform. After two and a half years the sub-commission presented a plan for important reforms in the entire local administration, on the basis of the principle of *classlessness*. But the completion of the work of Kokhanov's sub-commission (the end of 1884) coincided with the absolute triumph of the reaction in governmental spheres, when Tolstoy had become Minister of Interior. Tolstoy decided to liquidate the work of Kokhanov's commission, and in order to do it in " good form," he invited into the commission such " informed men " as would undoubtedly reject its conclusions; without Kokhanov's knowledge several governors and a number of reactionary nobles were appointed as members, who naturally disagreed with the views of the sub-commission.

The collapse of Ignatiev's régime took place, properly speaking, in May of 1882, one year after his appointment as Minister. His fall was caused by the same Pobiedonostzev who a year before had brought about the fall of Loris-Melikov. Pobiedonostzev made use of Ignatiev's suggestion that a *Zemsky Sobor* be summoned during the coronation in Moscow; that *Sobor* was to consist of nearly three thousand persons, and presented a quaint assembly, similar to neither the legislative nor consultative institutions of any civilised country. The project was prepared by some Moscow Slavophiles, presented to the Tzar, and had gained his approval, when Pobiedonostzev appeared on the stage. He succeeded in persuading Alexander III to discard once and for all the system of concessions to public opinion. Ignatiev was informed that his project could not be accepted, and resigned. His place was taken by the same Count D. A. Tolstoy, who in 1880, at the request of Loris-Melikov and to the joy of all thinking Russia, had been dismissed. Only from that moment did the course which Alexander III followed to the end of his days, begin to appear distinctly.

CHAPTER XL

IN the two preceding chapters I have characterised the first two brief but significant periods of the reign of Alexander III, which had a preludial, transitory, hence hesitating character. With the collapse of Ignatiev's ministry and the appointment of Tolstoy began the reign of reaction, the true epoch of Alexander III. Simultaneously with the dismissal of the Slavophile ministry of Ignatiev were discarded the secret societies which had existed at the Court, the "Holy Squad," and the "Voluntary Guard," in whose midst were discovered constitutional tendencies and circles organised by the young Count Shuvalov, with the aid of Court Minister Count Vorontzov-Dashkov.

After the coronation, safely celebrated in Moscow in May, 1883, the Government, with the aid of the traitor Degaiev, and owing to the internal decay of the revolutionary organisation, succeeded in capturing the remnants of the "Will of the People." Tolstoy was given full authority thereafter. But even Tolstoy had to spend many efforts and considerable time on the final liquidation of the heritage of the "heart dictatorship"; for three more years Bunge remained at his post; the Kokhanov-Commission continued its work for two more years, and its activity had to be annulled by a special effort on the part of the Government, described in the last chapter.

First of all Tolstoy restored the reactionary tendency in his old department — the Ministry of Education, which he had managed for sixteen years under Alexander II; Baron Nicolayi was supplanted in May, 1882, by Delianov, formerly a liberal, but now obsequiously obedient to Pobiedonostzev and Tolstoy.

In 1884 a new University Statute was worked out according to the ideas of Katkov, Leontiev, and Liubimov, concerning which Katkov announced his famous triumphant outcry: "Rise, Gentlemen: the Government is coming, the Government is returning." By the new Statute the University Councils were deprived of all vestiges of autonomy, and the Ministry was enabled to introduce its own programme in the departments of law and philology; it resembled the régime of Shirinsky-Shikhmatov. The students were to be handled with "porcupine gloves," to use a Russian expression; no corporative organisations of students were to be tolerated, and at the first attempt to protest they were to be reduced to soldiers.

The secondary schools were to preserve all the features of Tolstoy's Classical system, and at the same time regain the class-character which they bore during the reign of Nicolas. Delianov sent out a circular in which he urged the elimination of children of lower ranks from secondary schools.

Pobiedonostzev insisted upon handing over primary education into the hands of the Ecclesiastic department; this did not take place because the nobles, although reactionary, were unwilling to relinquish their control of popular education, and because of lack of funds. In an enormous majority of cases the zemstvos refused to transfer their schools to the Ecclesiastic department, and the Government could not afford to take them by force and maintain them at its own expenses. But the lowest type of the schools, the so-called Reading and Writing Schools, which were established by the peasants themselves, were given over to the Ecclesiastic department, by the law of June 13, 1884, carried through by Pobiedonostzev with the aid of Delianov.

The reactionary tendencies of the nobles received support and encouragement from Tolstoy, and they were reflected chiefly in the fate of the peasant-question and in the reform of the zemstvo administration. Whenever the interests of the nobles were threatened, the reactionaries began to spread rumours about unrest and sedition among the peasants, in the form of expectation of a " black " partition of the land. Those rumours, undoubtedly inflated, produced a strong impression upon the Tzar, and in his Coronation speech to the *volost*-chiefs he sounded a warning to the peasants — not to listen to " sedition " talk, but to obey " their " Marshals of Nobility.[1]

On the occasion of the centenary jubilee of the Nobility Charter, in 1885, a special Bank of the Nobility was opened, with the view of supporting landowners by means of loans. In the manifesto issued in connection with that event a wish was expressed that *" the Russian nobles preserve a dominant place in military leadership, in affairs of local administration and courts, in spreading exemplary rules of faith and loyalty and sound principles of popular education."*

In their address of thanks the nobles, especially the reactionally circles, such as the nobility of the province of Simbirsk, voiced by Pazukhin, indicated that they put their hopes in the firm hand of the Government, the force of which would allow them to live peacefully in the villages. The Government replied that it would direct its legislation in that spirit. Thus the liberal ideas of Bunge and Ignatiev came to an end. Pazukhin symbolised the new régime; he it was who received the authority to liquidate all the work and the projects of the Kokhanov-Commission. He published an article in 1885, in which he voiced the sentiments of the most reactionary elements of the nobility. He considered the reforms of the Sixties, particularly those of the *zemstvo* and of the courts, the source of all evils in the country, since they destroyed the principle of class-differences.

[1] That speech was reprinted during the present reign, and widely distributed through the Empire, especially in rural public places.— Tr.

" If," he wrote, " in the reforms of the former reign we see a great evil in the destruction of the class-organisation, it is the task of the present reign to restore what has been destroyed."

No wonder that in view of such tendencies among the nobility, rumours began to circulate in the villages of the approaching restoration of the bondage-system.

Count Tolstoy was greatly pleased with the views of Pazukhin; he appointed him Chief of his Chancery, and commissioned him to work out a project of the " restoration." As a result of that work appeared the statute of July 12, 1889, concerning *Zemsky* Chiefs, and the statute of June 12, 1890, concerning *zemstvo* institutions. The principle of both statutes was to create a " firm local authority," concentrated in the hands of the nobles. The *Zemsky* Chiefs, appointed from among the nobles, were to enjoy enormous power over the peasants and their organs of self-government. By the Statute of 1890 the *zemstvo* institutions were completely deprived of that portion of independence from the Government, which was granted to them by the Statute of 1864. Tolstoy reduced the *zemstvo* boards to organs of the Ministry of Interior, subject at every step to the governor; the presidents of the boards were to be appointed by the Government. Pazukhin's ideas concerning the necessity of reviving class-spirit found expression in the revision of the electoral system for the *zemstvos*. The modified rules gave the nobles a complete predominance. The number of peasant-delegates was greatly reduced; the *volosts* could elect only candidates for delegates, and the governor appointed delegates from among them. The *zemstvo*-assemblies were actually, by the Statute of 1890, transformed into assemblies of the nobles. We must say, however, that Tolstoy died before he carried through his entire plan; his successor, I. N. Durnovo, possessed neither Tolstoy's talent, nor his character and influence, and the State Council passed his original project with certain changes, which retained some semblance of self-government for the *zemstvos*.

During that period the mutilation of the judiciary statutes went on *crescendo*. The jury institution suffered most of all. Besides, by the law of July 12, 1889, one of the fundamental principles of the statutes — that of separation of administrative and judiciary authorities — was destroyed: The *Zemsky* Chiefs were to perform both administrative and judiciary functions; Justices of Peace were discarded.

Naturally the press was further restricted during that time. Tolstoy issued in 1882 " temporary rules," in addition to the rules of 1865 and the " additions " of Timashov. By those rules organs which had been temporarily stopped after three warnings, might reappear only on condition of their being presented to the censor on the eve of publication, not later than at eleven P. M. This caused the discontinuation of liberal dailies which could not of course exist under such conditions. Another rule established a special Areopagus of four Ministers — of Education, Interior, Justice, and the Super-Procurator of the Synod, who might stop any publication for pernicious tendencies, and even forbid the editor of such a publication to edit at any time in the future. Heavy penalties were showered upon the press, prohibition of private advertisements, of retail sale, etc.

During the last two or three years of Tolstoy's régime the number of those penalties had diminished, and it might appear that the Government had loosened the reins; but as K. K. Arseniev remarks, the diminution of the number of penalties was due to the fact that liberal organs had either disappeared or had been placed in such a position that they could not say anything offensive. Only a very few liberal organs, such as the *European Messenger, Russian Thought, Russian News,* lived through the difficult period, with the sword of Damocles constantly hanging over them.

Particularly difficult during that gloomy period was the position of non-Russian nationalities. In spite of the law of May 3, 1883, which promised toleration for Schismatists and Sectants, Pobiedonostzev persecuted the dissenters severely, even furiously. Even such pure, moral sects as Tolstoyans, Dukhobory, Stundists, were persecuted, and at times deprived of their children. In 1894 the Stundists were forbidden to assemble in their houses of prayer.

In harmony with this were the measures against the Uniates in the West and in Poland, and in some cases against Lutherans in the Baltic provinces. Jingo Nationalism had reached its apogee. Jews and Poles were persecuted most of all; Lamaites, Kalmycks, and Buriats also suffered persecution and were not allowed to build temples and perform worship.

Jews in particular suffered from restrictions. By the " temporary rules " of May 3, 1882, they were forbidden to live even within the Pale of Settlement — outside of cities and small-towns (*miestechki*) ; they were forbidden to buy real estate in villages. In 1887 Rostov-on-the-Don and Taganrog with its district were exempted from the Pale; thus the Pale of Settlement was reduced. In 1891 Jewish artisans who had the right to settle outside the Pale, were driven out from Moscow; about seventeen thousand of them were rudely exiled. In 1887 a percentage for Jewish children entering schools was introduced. In 1889 an end came to granting Jews the rank of Sworn Attorney; they had to remain Assistant-Attorneys to the end of their days.

The Poles were restricted in their rights of occupying governmental positions in Poland and in the Western provinces, but in other parts of the Empire they suffered no special oppressions.

The reactionary spirit was reflected also in the army. The humanistic principles implanted by Miliutin had gradually disappeared. The Government tried to bring up the officers in the spirit of caste distinction. Thus the penalty for duels was reserved only for civilians; military officers were exempt from it. The military schools, reorganised into gymnasia by Miliutin, were once more turned into Cadet Corps, and Minister of War Vannovsky endeavoured to revive the spirit of exclusive institutions of the time of Nicolas I.

CHAPTER XLI

THE only breach in the reactionary wall of Alexander III's government was Bunge's handling of the financial policy. He remained at his post until January 1, 1887, in spite of the intrigues and insinuations that persued him in the Court circles and in the reactionary press. He resigned, under the pretext of old age, and was supplanted by I. A. Vyshnegradsky, a learned technologist and practical financier, who had had experience as professor in the Technological Institute and in the Mikhailovsky Academy of Artillery, and also as a speculator on the bourse. In his financial-economic policy he did not demonstrate any broad views or foresight; like most of the Russian ministers of finance in the nineteenth century, he considered raising the course of the paper-ruble the paramount aim. The main and immediate task of the Ministry under Vyshnegradsky had become the accumulation of large money reserves in the Treasury, and the broad participation in foreign stock-exchange operations with the aid of those reserves, with the view of effecting a pressure upon the foreign money market, and thus raising the course of the ruble. Alongside with this, the protectionist tariff policy had reached its apogee in 1891.

Big industry had become the pet child of the Ministry of Finance. Upon the complaints of large manufacturers, Bunge's workingmen-laws were revised in favour of the capitalists; the factory-inspectors were restricted in their activity, so that independent and conscientious inspectors soon resigned, and that institution began to deteriorate. The Ministry protected the home industry in every way by a special customs tariff and by special railroad-rates; artificial favourable conditions were created for manufacturers, at the expense of the interests of other classes of the people, particularly the rural population, who felt the effect of the tariff of 1891 in the rise of prices on such important commodities as iron and agricultural implements.

As I have described in a previous chapter, the peasantry grew impoverished and ruined, and was naturally losing its buying capacity. This affected the internal market, for such commodities as, for instance, cotton fabrics. The manufacturing industry sought compensation in the markets of Central Asia, but those were not sufficient; by the end of the reign of Alexander III a new idea originated — to push the market to the Far East. In this connection appeared the idea of building the Siberian railroad, the question of an outlet to the Pacific Ocean, of the acquisition of an ice-free port in the Far East, and all that policy which brought to the development of the Russian Far East undertakings that culminated in the Russo-Japanese war.

A few words concerning the railroads. By the end of the reign of Alexander II the net of railroads amounted to twenty-two and a half thousand versts, and for the thirteen years of Alexander III's reign it grew to thirty-six thousand six hundred and sixty-two versts. The old policy of Reitern was followed in building the roads so that they would aid the hauling of raw materials to ports, in order to increase the exports and thus improve the money course; on the other hand, the Ministry granted special low rates for manufacturers of the industrial Central provinces. For the latter purpose a special department was instituted at the Ministry of Finance — the Tariff Department, at the head of which was placed a young man, S. Y. Witte, destined subsequently to play an important rôle in the history of Russia. Another feature of the new railroad policy, in contrast to that of Reitern, was the increase of fiscal ownership of railroads. During the reign of Alexander III the verstage of fiscal railroads increased by twenty-two thousand versts, while that of private roads diminished by seven thousand six hundred versts, in spite of the building of new private railroads: the Government continually redeemed old roads.

Such were the features of the financial policy which prepared and deepened the acute state of Russian socio-economic conditions at the beginning of the twentieth century. Those conditions developed alongside with the crisis lived through by the people after the famine of 1891–1892, when failure of crops caused misery and starvation in twenty provinces, mostly in the black soil region. That crisis formed, we may say, the finishing touch to the general picture of Russia as seen at the end of the reign of Alexander III, and appeared at the same time as a powerful factor for bringing about the grave changes of the subsequent years.

In his foreign policy Alexander III was undoubtedly original and independent, and bent his own line. In 1882 the senile head of Russian diplomats, the class-mate of Pushkin, Prince Gorchakov, died; his place was taken not by another distinguished statesman, but by a modest official, State-Secretary Giers, who was in fact not so much a minister as a private secretary of Alexander in the sphere of foreign policy.

During the first half of his reign foreign conjunctures did not develop favourably for Russia; she was constantly threatened by war, on the part of Austria or England, and there appeared various international complications, partly in connection with Eastern affairs. The conquest of Central Asia, begun in the Seventies, was continued and completed, to the growing alarm of England.

By the plan of General Skobelev, to a considerable extent realised by himself, the last stronghold of the Turcomen, Geok-Tepe, was to be destroyed, in order to bring the Russian frontier to Afghanistan, and in one point even to the northern border of British India. After energetic efforts and stubborn conflicts, Skobelev finally succeeded in capturing Geok-Tepe, subduing the savage tribes, and approaching Afghanistan and British territory; after some bloody battles with the Afghans, the last point of that portion of Central Asia — Merv — was captured by the Russians. Alexander III was able to furnish adequate answers to the interpellations of the British diplomats, and to avert war with England.

Another danger threatened from Austria; Bismarck did his best to involve Russia in a war with Austria, so that he might have a free hand to deal with France; he also tried to embroil Russia in the Balkans, where Serbia and Roumania ascribed their failures at the Congress of Berlin to Russia, and where Bulgaria was going through internal dissensions. Alexander III, who personally disliked Germans, yet held up the traditional friendship of his dynasty with the Hohenzollern House, and disregarded the machinations of Bismarck. The exasperating affairs in Bulgaria, the Principality which was created by Russia and maintained by her, brought Russia to the verge of intervention and probable war with Austria; but in that case also Alexander III disappointed Bismarck, withdrew his army-officers from Bulgaria, and left the Bulgars to themselves. Alexander III, aware of his isolated position in Europe, asserted that Russia was not in need of any alliances; on one occasion he demonstratively raised a toast to his *only* friend in Europe — the Prince of Montenegro.

In the second half of Alexander's reign a possibility was opened for Russia to establish better international relations. In 1887 Bismarck nearly succeeded in instigating war between Germany and France; a personal letter from the Tzar to Emperor Wilhelm I restrained the latter from declaring such a war. This served as the beginning of the *rapprochement* between Russia and France; in 1889 a union was signed between them, and made public after the solemn declaration by Wilhelm II of the Triple Alliance of Germany, Austria, and Italy.

The Russo-French alliance served as an important factor in the international policy of the end of the nineteenth century; it certainly brought an end to Bismarck's aspirations to crush France. Alexander III, even during his life-time, was justly called the Tzar-Peacemaker by many historians and publicists.

SELECTED BIBLIOGRAPHY

I. GENERAL WORKS

BEAZLEY, SIR CHARLES RAYMOND, NEVILL FORBES, and G. A. BIRKETT: *Russia from the Varangians to the Bolsheviks.* Oxford, 1918. xxiv, 601 p.

KLIUCHEVSKII, V. O.: *A History of Russia.* London, N. Y., 1911–31. 5 v.

MILIUKOV, P. N., CHARLES SEIGNOBOS, and L. EISENMANN: *Histoire de Russie.* Paris, 1932–3. 3 v.

MILIUKOV, P. N.: *Outlines of Russian Culture.* Philadelphia, 1942. 3 v.

MIRSKY, DMITRII S.: *Russia, a Social History.* London, 1931. xix, 312, xxi p.

PARES, SIR BERNARD: *A History of Russia.* 3d ed. rev., N. Y., 1937. xxiii, 570 p.

PLATONOV, S. F.: *History of Russia.* N. Y., 1925. vii, 435 p.

POKROVSKII, MIKHAIL N.: *Brief History of Russia.* N. Y., 1933. 2 v.

STÄHLIN, KARL: *Geschichte Russlands von den Anfängen bis zur Gegenwart.* Stuttgart, 1923–39. 5 v. in 6.

VERNADSKY, GEORGE: *A History of Russia.* Rev. ed., New Haven, London, 1933. xix, 413 p.

II. CATHERINE II AND PAUL I

ADAMCZYK, THERESIA: *Fürst G. A. Potemkin; Untersuchungen zu seiner Lebensgeschichte.* Emsdetten, 1936. vi, 127 p.

273

ANTHONY, KATHARINE: *Catherine the Great.* N. Y., 1925. 3–331 p.

BIL'BASOV, V. A.: *Geschichte Katharina II.* Rev. ed., Berlin, 1900. 2 v.

BLEASE, WALTER LYON: *Suvorof.* London, 1920. xxiii, 366 p.

BRÜCKNER, ALEXANDER: *Katharina die Zweite.* Berlin. 1883. vi, 642 p.

CATHERINE II. *Memoirs.* N. Y., London, 1927. ix, 3–337 p.

DREIFUSS, JEROME: *Catherine and Potemkin; an Imperial Romance.* N. Y., 1937. viii, 343 p.

JACOBY, JEAN: *Souvarov, 1730–1800.* Paris, 1935. 352 p.

R. R.: *Kaiser Pauls I Ende. 1801.* Stuttgart, 1897. 188 p.

RADISHCHEV, A. N.: *Reise von Petersburg nach Moskau (1790).* Leipzig, 1922. 188.

REDDAWAY, W. F., ed.: *The Documents of Catherine the Great.* Cambridge, Eng., 1931. xxxii, 349 p.

SOLOVEYTCHIK, GEORGE: *Potemkin: a Picture of Catherine's Russia.* London, 1938. xv, 17–349 p.

WALISZEWSKI, KAZIMIERZ: *Paul the First of Russia, the Son of Catherine the Great.* London, 1913. v, 495 p.

——: *The Romance of an Empress, Catherine II of Russia.* N. Y., 1894. viii, 458 p.

III. ALEXANDER I AND NICHOLAS I

CAULAINCOURT, ARMAND AUGUSTIN LOUIS: *Mémoires du Général de Caulaincourt.* Paris, 1933–8. 3 v.

CUSTINE, ASTOLPHE LOUIS LÉONARD, COMTE DE: *La Russie en 1839.* Paris, 1843. 4 v.

CZARTORYSKI, ADAM, PRINCE: *Memoirs of Prince Adam Czartoryski and His Correspondence with Alexander I.* 2d ed., London, 1888. 2 v.

HAXTHAUSEN-ABBENBURG, AUGUST, FREIHERR VON: *The Russian Empire, Its People, Institutions and Resources.* London, 1856. 2 v.

HERMANT, ABEL: *Madame de Krüdener, l'amie du tzar Alexandre Ier (1764–1824)*. Paris, 1934. 220 p.

LACROIX, PAUL: *Histoire de la vie et du règne de Nicolas Ier, empereur de Russie*. Paris, 1864–73. 8 v.

MAZOUR, ANATOLE G.: *The First Russian Revolution, 1825; the Decembrist Movement, Its Origins, Development, and Significance*. Berkeley, 1937. xviii, 324 p.

NICHOLAS, GRAND DUKE: *L'Empereur Alexandre Ier; essai d'étude historique*. St. Petersburg, 1912. 2 v.

PALÉOLOGUE, GEORGES MAURICE: *Alexandre Ier, un tsar énigmatique*. Paris, 1937. 315 p.

SCHIEMANN, THEODOR: *Geschichte Russlands unter Kaiser Nikolaus I*. Berlin, 1904–19. 4 v.

TURGENEV, NIKOLAI I.: *La Russie et les Russes*. Paris, 1847. 3 v.

VERNADSKY, GEORGE: *La Charte constitutionnelle de l'Empire Russe de l'an 1820*. Paris, 1933. viii, 283 p.

IV. ALEXANDER II, ALEXANDER III AND NICHOLAS II

BARING, M.: *A Year in Russia*. London, 1907. xi, 319 p.

BRANDES, GEORG: *Impressions of Russia*. N. Y., 1889. x, 353 p.

CLEINOW, GEORGE: *Aus Russlands Not und Hoffen*. Berlin, 1906. vii, 318 p.

DIXON, W. H.: *Free Russia*. N. Y., 1870. 359 p.

DOLGORUKOV, P. V.: *La Verité sur la Russie*. 2d ed., rev. and enl., Leipzig, Paris, 1861. 2 v.

ECKARDT, J.: *Modern Russia: Russia under Alexander II*. London, 1870. viii, 388 p.

GILLIARD, PIERRE: *Treize Années à la cour de Russie*. (*Péterhof, septembre 1905–Ékaterinbourg, mai 1918*). Paris, 1922. vii, 264 p.

GURKO, V. I.: *Features and Figures of the Past; Government and Opinion in the Reign of Nicholas II*. Stanford University, 1939. xix, 760 p.

HÖTZSCH, OTTO E.: *Russland; eine Einführung auf Grund seiner Geschichte von 1904 bis 1912*. Berlin, 1913. xviii, 550 p.

KOKOVTSOV, VLADIMIR N.: *Out of My Past; the Memoirs of Count Kokovtsov, Russian Minister of Finance, 1904–1914, Chairman of the Council of Ministers, 1911–1914*. Stanford University, 1935. xx, 615 p.

KOVALEVSKII, M. M.: *La Crise russe; notes et impressions d'un témoin*. Paris, 1906. ii, 304 p.

KOVALESKII, V. I., ed.: *La Russie à la fin du 19ᵉ siècle*. Paris, 1900, xx, 989 p.

KULCZYCKI, LUDWIK: *Geschichte der russischen Revolution*. Gotha, 1910–14. 3 v.

LEROY-BEAULIEU, ANATOLE: *The Empire of the Tsars and the Russians*. N. Y., 1893–6. 3 v.

LEVIN, ALFRED: *The Second Duma: a Study of the Social-Democratic Party and the Russian Constitutional Experiment*. New Haven, 1940. viii, 414 p.

LOWE, CHARLES: *Alexander III of Russia*. N. Y., 1895. viii–xii, 370 p.

MILIUKOV, P. N.: *Russia and Its Crisis*. Chicago, London, 1906. xv, 3–589 p.

NIKOLAEVSKY, BORIS J.: *Aseff, the Spy; Russian Terrorist and Police Stool*. N. Y., 1934. xii, 307 p.

NOVIKOV-PRIBOI, A. S.: *Tsushima*. London, N. Y., 1936. xxi, 425 p.

PARES, SIR BERNARD: *Russia and Reform*. London, 1908. xiv, 576 p.

POBIEDONOSTSEV, K. P.: *L'Autocratie russe; mémoires politiques, correspondance officielle et documents inédits relatifs à l'histoire du règne de l'empereur Alexandre III de Russie (1881–1894)*. Paris, 1927. 665 p.

——: *Reflections of a Russian Statesman*. London, 1898. xi, 271 p.

STEAD, W. T.: *Truth about Russia*. London, N. Y., 1888. vii, 464 p.

STEINMANN, FRIEDRICH, and ELIAS HURWICZ: *Konstantin Petrowitsch Pobjedonoszew, der Staatsmann der Reaktion unter Alexander III*. Königsberg, Berlin, 1934. viii, 281 p.

STUPPERICH, R.: *Die Anfänge der Bauernbefreiung in Russland*. Berlin, 1939. 214 p.

TERESHCHENKO, SERGIEI: *La Guerre navale russo-japonaise*. Paris, 1931. 512 p.

URUSOV, PRINCE S. D.: *Memoirs of a Russian Governor*. London, N. Y., 1908. vii, 180 p.

VRBA, RUDOLF: *Die Revolution in Russland; statistische u. sozial-politische Studien*. Prague, 1906. 2 v.

WALLACE, SIR DONALD MACKENZIE: *Russia*. Rev. and enl. ed., London, N. Y., 1912. x, 788 p.

WITTE, SERGIEI: *The Memoirs of Count Witte*. Garden City, N. Y., and Toronto, 1921. xi, 445 p.

V. THE WORLD WAR, 1914–1917

BADAEV, A. E.: *The Bolsheviks in the Tsarist Duma*. N. Y., 1932. xv, 250 p.

BUCHANAN, SIR GEORGE: *My Mission to Russia, and Other Diplomatic Memoirs*. Boston, 1923. 2 v.

CHURCHILL, WINSTON S.: *The Unknown War; the Eastern Front*. N. Y., 1931. xv, 396 p.

FLORINSKY, MICHAEL T.: *The End of the Russian Empire*. New Haven, London, 1931. xvi, 272 p.

GANKIN, OLGA H., and H. H. FISHER: *The Bolsheviks and the World War; the Origin of the Third International*. Stanford University, 1940. xviii, 856 p.

GOLDER, FRANK A.: *Documents of Russian History 1914–1917*. N. Y., London, 1927. xvi, 663 p.

GOLOVINE, NICHOLAS N.: *The Russian Army in the World War*. New Haven, 1931. xix, 287 p.

GURKO, VASILII: *Memories and Impressions of War and Revolution in Russia, 1914–1917*. London, 1918. xvi, 347 p.

KOROSTOVETS, VLADIMIR: *Seed and Harvest*. London, 1931. 387 p.

Letters of the Tsar to the Tsaritsa, 1914–1917. London, N. Y., 1929. xv, 324 p.

Letters of the Tsaritsa to the Tsar, 1914–1916. London, 1923. xliii, 478 p.

MOSOLOV, A. A.: *At the Court of the Last Tsar; Being the Memoirs of A. A. Mosolov, Head of the Court Chancellery, 1900–1916*. London, 1935. vii, 272 p.

PALÉOLOGUE, GEORGES MAURICE: *L'Écroulement du tsarisme*. Paris, 1939. 158 p.

PARES, SIR BERNARD: *The Fall of the Russian Monarchy; a Study of the Evidence*. N. Y., 1939. 5–510 p.

La Chute du régime tsariste; interrogatoires des ministres, conseillers, généraux, hauts fonctionnaires de la cour impériale russe par la Commission extraordinaire du gouvernement provisoire de 1917. Paris, 1927. 7–577 p.

RODZIANKO, M. V.: *The Reign of Rasputin: an Empire's Collapse; Memoirs*. London, 1927. xiv, 292 p.

SUKHOMLINOV, V. A.: *Erinnerungen*. Berlin, 1924. xxxi, 526 p.

VI. SPECIAL REGIONS OR PEOPLES

BADDELEY, JOHN F.: *The Russian Conquest of the Caucasus*. London, N. Y., 1908. 518 p.

DUBNOV, S. M.: *History of the Jews in Russia and Poland, from the Earliest Times to the Present Day*. Philadelphia, 1916–20. 3 v.

KRAHMER, GUSTAV: *Russland in Mittel-Asien*. Leipzig, 1899. vi, 221 p.

KRAUSSE, ALEXIS S.: *Russia in Asia; a Record and a Study, 1558–1899*. London, N. Y., 1899. xii, 411 p.

LOBANOV-ROSTOVSKY, PRINCE: *Russia and Asia*. London, 1933. viii, 334 p.

McCORMICK, FREDERICK: *The Tragedy of Russia in Pacific Asia*. N. Y., 1907. 2 v.

PRICE, M. P.: *Siberia*. London, N. Y., 1912. xviii, 308 p.

SCHUYLER, EUGENE: *Turkistan; Notes of a Journey in Russian Turkistan, Khokand, Bukhara and Kuldja*. N. Y., 1877. 2 v.

SHOEMAKER, M. M.: *The Great Siberian Railway from St. Petersburg to Pekin*. N. Y., London, 1903. viii, 243 p.

SKRINE, F. H.: *The Expansion of Russia, 1815–1900*. Cambridge, Eng., 1903. vii, 386 p.

TREVOR-BATTYE, A.: *A Northern Highway of the Tsar*. Westminster, 1898. xiv, 256 p.

WRIGHT, GEORGE FREDERICK: *Asiatic Russia*. N. Y., 1902. 2 v.

VII. INTERNATIONAL RELATIONS

BOUDON, ADRIEN: *Le Saint-Siège et la Russie; leurs relations diplomatiques au xixᵉ siècle*. Paris, 1922. xv, 580 p.

CHURCHILL, ROGERS PLATT: *The Anglo-Russian Convention of 1907*. Cedar Rapids, Ia., 1939. ii, 365 p.

CLAUSEWITZ, GENERAL CARL VON: *Der Feldzug 1812 in Russland und die Befreiungskriege von 1813–15*. 3d ed., Berlin, 1906. 494 p.

CLYDE, PAUL HIBBERT: *International Rivalries in Manchuria, 1689–1922*. 2d ed. rev., Columbus, 1928. xv, 323 p.

KORFF, BARON SERGIEI ALEKSANDROVICH: *Russia's Foreign Relations during the Last Half Century*. N. Y., 1922. 227 p.

LANGER, WILLIAM LEONARD: *The Franco-Russian Alliance*. Cambridge, London, 1929. v–ix, 455 p.

LARIVIÈRE, CHARLES DE: *Catherine II et la révolution française d'après de nouveaux documents*. Paris, 1895. xxxiii, 396 p.

LEROY-BEAULIEU, A.: *La France, la Russie et l'Europe; les*

questions actuelles de politique étrangère en Europe. 2d ed., Paris, 1888. iv, 367 p.

LEVINE, ISAAC DON, ed.: *The Kaiser's Letters to the Tsar*. London, 1920. xviii, 281 p.

MICHON, GEORGES: *The Franco-Russian Alliance, 1891–1917*. London, 1929. 340 p.

MOSELY, PHILIP E.: *Russian Diplomacy and the Opening of the Eastern Question in 1838 and 1839*. Cambridge, 1934. v, 178 p.

NEKLIUDOV, A. V.: *Diplomatic Reminiscences before and during the World War, 1911–1917*. N. Y., 1920. xiii, 541.

NOLDE, BARON BORIS: *L'Alliance franco-russe; les origines du système diplomatique d'avantguerre*. Paris, 1936. 704 p.

——: *Die Petersburger Mission Bismarcks, 1859–1862. Russland und Europa zu Beginn der Regierung Alexander II*. Leipzig, 1936. viii, 214 p.

PALÉOLOGUE, GEORGES MAURICE: *Guillaume II et Nicolas II*. Paris, 1935. 249 p.

PURYEAR, VERNON: *England, Russia and the Straits Question, 1844–1856*. Berkeley, 1931. xvi, 481 p.

ROSEN, ROMAN ROMANOVICH: *Forty Years of Diplomacy*. London, N. Y., 1922. 2 v.

SAVINSKY, A.: *Recollections of a Russian Diplomat*. London, 1927. 11–316 p.

SAZONOV, SERGIEI: *Fateful Years, 1909-1916; the Reminiscences of Serge Sazonov*. N. Y., 1928. 327 p.

SCHREINER, GEORGE ABEL, ed.: *Entente Diplomacy and the World War; Matrix of the History of Europe, 1909–1914*. N. Y., London, 1921. xxxii, 762 p.

SIMPSON, JAMES YOUNG, ed. and transl.: *The Saburov Memoirs; or Bismarck and Russia; Being Fresh Light on the League of the Three Emperors, 1881*. Cambridge, Eng., 1929. ix, 304 p.

STIEVE, FRIEDRICH, ed.: *Der diplomatische Schriftwechsel Iswolskis, 1911–1914*. Berlin, 1925–6. 4 v.

TAUBE, BARON M. DE: *La Politique russe d'avant-guerre et la fin de l'empire des tsars (1904–1917).* Paris, 1928. 412 p.

VANDAL, ALBERT: *Napoléon et Alexandre Ier. L'alliance russe sous le premier empire.* Paris, 1898–1903. 3 v.

VIII. ECONOMIC DEVELOPMENT

ANSPACH, ALFRED: *La Russie économique et l'œuvre de M. de Witte.* Paris, 1904. xviii, 394 p.

ANTSYFEROV, ALEKSEI N.: *Russian Agriculture during the War.* New Haven, 1930. xvii, 394 p.

KOVALEVSKII, MAKSIM M.: *Le Régime économique de la Russie.* Paris, 1898. 362 p.

MAVOR, JAMES: *An Economic History of Russia.* 2d ed., rev. and enl., London, Toronto, N. Y., 1925. 2 v.

MILLER, MARGARET S.: *The Economic Development of Russia, 1905–1914, with Special Reference to Trade, Industry and Finance.* London, 1926. xviii, 311 p.

NOLDE, BARON BORIS E.: *Russia in the Economic War.* New Haven, 1928. xvi, 232 p.

OWEN, LAUNCELOT A.: *The Russian Peasant Movement, 1906–1917.* London, 1937. xix, 267 p.

RAFALOVICH, ARTHUR: *Russia: Its Trade and Commerce.* London, 1918. ix, 461 p.

ROBINSON, GEROID TANQUARY: *Rural Russia under the Old Regime; a History of the Landlord-Peasant World and a Prologue to the Peasant Revolution of 1917.* London, N. Y., 1932. x, 342 p.

TEGOBORSKI, LUDWIK: *Commentaries on the Productive Forces of Russia.* London, 1855–6. 2 v.

TUGAN-BARANOVSKII, M. I.: *Geschichte der russischen Fabrik.* Berlin, 1900. vi, 626 p.

TURIN, SERGEI PETROVICH: *From Peter the Great to Lenin: the History of the Russian Labour Movement.* London, 1935. xii, 216 p.

WITTSCHEWSKY, VALENTIN: *Russlands Handels-, Zoll-, und Industriepolitik von Peter dem Grossen bis auf die Gegenwart.* Berlin, 1905. x, 392 p.

ZAGORSKY, S. O.: *State Control of Industry in Russia during the War.* New Haven, London, 1928. xix, 351 p.

IX. LAW AND GOVERNMENT

CHASLES, PIERRE: *Le Parlement russe. Son organisation, ses rapports avec l'empereur.* Paris, 1910. vii–xv, 218 p.

GRIBOVSKII, VIACHESLAV M.: *Das Staatsrecht des Russischen Reiches.* Tübingen, 1912. xi, 197 p.

HOWARD, B. DOUGLAS: *Prisoners of Russia; a Personal Study of Convict Life in Sakhalin and Siberia.* N. Y., 1902. 389 p.

KENNAN, GEORGE: *Siberia and the Exile System.* N. Y., 1891. 2 v.

KORKUNOV, N. M.: *General Theory of Law.* 2d ed., N. Y., 1922. xxviii, 524 p.

KOVALEVSKII, MAKSIM M.: *Russian Political Institutions; the Growth and Development of These Institutions from the Beginnings of Russian History to the Present Time.* Chicago, 1902. ix, 299 p.

VASILIEV, A. T., and FÜLOP-MILLER, RENÉ: *The Ochrana: the Russian Secret Police.* Philadelphia, London, 1930. 305 p.

X. EDUCATION

HANS, NICHOLAS: *History of Russian Educational Policy (1701–1917).* London, 1931. vii–xiii, 255 p.

IGNATIEV, P. N., D. M. ODINETZ, and P. J. NOVGORODTSEV: *Russian Schools and Universities in the World War.* New Haven, 1929. xxvi, 240 p.

LEARY, DANIEL BELL: *Education and Autocracy in Russia from the Origins to the Bolsheviki.* Buffalo, N. Y., 1919. 5–127 p.

XI. SOCIAL AND INTELLECTUAL LIFE

AKSAKOV, SERGIEI T.: *A Russian Gentleman*. London, 1917. ix, 209 p.

BRESHKO-BRESHKOVSKAIA, EKATERINA K.: *Hidden Springs of the Russian Revolution: Personal Memoirs*. Stanford University, 1931. xxi, 369 p.

CARR, EDWARD HALLETT: *Michael Bakunin*. London, 1937. x, 501 p.

CHERNYSHEVSKII, NIKOLAI G.: *What's to be Done?* Boston, 1886.

ELNETT, MRS. ELAINE: *Historic Origin and Social Development of Family Life in Russia*. N. Y., 1926. xi, 152 p.

FIGNER, VERA N.: *Memoirs of a Revolutionist*. London, 1929. 318 p.

HECKER, JULIUS F.: *Russian Sociology; a Contribution to the History of Sociological Thought and Theory*. London, 1934.

HERZEN, ALEKSANDR I.: *My Past and Thoughts, the Memoirs of Alexander Herzen*. London, 1924–7. 6 v.

KOYRÉ, ALEXANDRE: *La Philosophie et le problème national en Russie au début du xixe siècle*. Paris, 1929. 213 p.

KRAVCHINSKII, S. M. /STEPNIAK/: *Underground Russia; Revolutionary Profiles and Sketches from Life*. N. Y., 1883.

KROPOTKIN, PETR A.: *Memoirs of a Revolutionist*. Boston, N.Y., 1930. xiv, 502 p.

LABRY, RAOUL: *Alexandre Ivanovič Herzen, 1812–1870*. Paris, 1928. 431 p.

MASARYK, THOMAS GARRIGUE: *The Spirit of Russia; Studies in History, Literature and Philosophy*. London, N. Y., 1919. 2 v.

MAZOUR, ANATOLE G.: *Outline of Modern Russian Historiography*. Berkeley, 1939. ix, 130 p.

MILIUKOV, P. N.: *Le Mouvement intellectuel russe*. Paris, 1918. 445 p.

PALÉOLOGUE, GEORGES MAURICE: *Les Précurseurs de Lénine.* Paris, 1938. 247 p.

QUÉNET, CHARLES: *Tchaadaev et les Lettres Philosophiques; contribution à l'étude du mouvement des idées en Russie.* Paris, 1931. 440, lxviii p.

SACKE, GEORG: *W. S. Solowjews Geschichtsphilosophie; ein Beitrag zur Charakteristik der russischen Weltanschauung.* Berlin, Königsberg, 1929. xvi, 138 p.

SAVINKOV, BORIS V.: *Memoirs of a Terrorist.* N. Y., 1931.

STEINBERG, I.: *Spiridonova, Revolutionary Terrorist.* London, 1935. xxii, 313 p.

STREMOUKHOV, DMITRII: *Vladimir Soloviev et son œuvre messianique.* Paris, 1935. 351 p.

XII. RELIGIOUS HISTORY

CONYBEARE, FREDERICK C.: *Russian Dissenters.* Cambridge, 1921. x, 370 p.

CURTISS, JOHN S.: *Church and State in Russia; the Last Years of the Empire, 1900–1917.* N. Y., 1940. ix, 442 p.

FRERE, W. H.: *Some Links in the Chain of Russian Church History.* London, 1918. xvi, 200 p.

GRASS, K. K.: *Die russischen Sekten.* Leipzig, 1905–14. 2 v. in 3.

LATIMER, ROBERT SLOAN: *Under Three Tsars; Liberty of Conscience in Russia, 1856–1909.* London, 1909. xii, 244 p.

MAUDE, AYLMER: *A Peculiar People, the Doukhobors.* N. Y., 1904. xi, 338 p.

PALMER, WILLIAM: *Notes of a Visit to the Russian Church in the Years 1840, 1841.* London, 1882.

PALMIERI, AURELIO: *La Chiesa russa: le sue odierne condizioni e il suo riformismo dottrinale.* Florence, 1908. xv, 759 p.

PIERLING, PAUL: *La Russie et le Saint-Siège, études diplomatiques.* Paris, 1896–1912. 5 v.

INDEX

Abaza, A. A., II: 204, 243, 250, 252
Abdul-Aziz, II: 230
Abdul-Hamid, II: 230
Act, of February 19, II: 43, 44, 45, 46, 52, 55, 65, 66, 68, 74
Action, II: 191, 211
Adrianople, II: 233
Afghanistan, II: 229, 270
Agricultural Society, II: 85
Aksakov, Constantine, I: 289, 292, 293, 306; II: 61
Aksakov, Ivan, I: 253, 295, 302, 303, 305, 306; II: 11, 29, 61, 76, 83, 86, 99, 153, 189, 191, 195, 234, 235, 251, 252
Alexander I, I: 52, 57, 62, 64–220, 223, 224, 225, 229, 230, 231, 232, 237, 238, 245, 260, 269, 283, 285, 293; II: 152, 160, 164
Alexander II, I: 231, 246, 263, 267, 293, 301, 310; II: 3–250, 260, 268
Alexander III, II: 240, 241, 249–271
Amur, II: 227, 257
Annals of the Fatherland, I: 291, 301, 302; II: 192, 214
Arakcheiev, I: 155, 170, 175, 176, 177, 178, 179, 180, 186, 201, 211, 238, 242, 270; II: 139, 230
Arseniev, K. K., II: 264
Arzamas, I: 196, 239, 284
Asia, II: 226, 229, 233
Asia, Central, I: 63, 171, 183, 220; II: 227, 228, 268, 269, 270
Asia, East, II: 226
Asia, South, II: 228

Assignations, I: 59, 108, 109, 170; II: 77
Assignational Bank, I: 47
Austria, I: 60, 61, 128, 138, 158, 159, 161, 163, 174, 253, 297, 300, 307; II: 233, 234, 269, 270, 271

Bagration, I: 151, 152, 154, 156
Bakunin, I: 289, 290, 303; II: 211, 212, 213, 214, 217, 219, 221
Balkans, II: 233, 234, 270
Barclay de Tolly, I: 151, 152, 154, 155, 169, 170
Barshchina, I: 27, 28, 53, 203, 254, 255, 262, 264; II: 13, 15, 19, 21, 36, 45, 50, 51, 52, 68, 197
Battenberg, Prince A., II: 240
Beccaria, I: 20, 23, 111
Bell, The, II: 22, 27, 38, 56, 60, 63, 65, 75, 79, 207, 208
Benckendorff, I: 196, 239, 245, 247, 248, 249, 297; II: 242
Berlin, Congress of, II: 233, 234
Bestuzhev-Riumin, I: 204, 205
Beverage reform, I: 274, 275
Bezpopovtzy, I: 296
Bibikov, I: 263; II: 5, 12
Biblical Society, I: 187, 189
Bielinsky, I: 289–293, 301–305
Black Partition, II: 238, 264
Bogoliubsky, Prince Andrey, I: 8
Bogrov, II: 330
Bondage-question, I: 13, 14, 21, 65, 94, 102, 254, 255, 257, 258, 301; II: 10–56, 62, 78, 96
Boyars, I: 13, 41

i

Bulgaria, II: 229, 230, 233, 234, 237, 240, 270
Bunge, Minister, II: 252, 254, 255, 256, 258, 260, 261, 267
Buturlin Committee, II: 4, 6, 104
Byzantium, I: 34, 39

Cantonists, I: 176, 190
Carbonari, I: 197, 198
Carol, King, II: 232
Catherine II, I: 23–49, 51, 52, 54, 55, 58, 59, 67, 68, 69, 72, 80, 81, 86, 90, 95, 97, 101, 104, 105, 111, 132, 143, 144, 179, 191, 199, 213, 214, 269, 283; II: 151, 152, 154
Caucasus, II: 158, 210, 227
Cause of the People, II: 211
Censorship, Statutes, I: 160, 192; II: 55, 60, 62, 103, 105
Chaadaiev, I: 285, 286, 287, 289, 292
Chaikovsky, N., II: 215–221
Cherkassky, Prince, II: 15, 32, 40, 61, 195, 217
Chernyshevsky, II: 7, 22, 27, 57, 58, 59, 72, 80, 82, 106, 207
China, I: 171, 267
Citizen, The, II: 193
Classicism, I: 281; II: 164, 166, 168
Clergy, I: 33, 54
Collectors of Russian Soil, I: 12
Collegia, I: 43, 52, 90, 91, 95
Colonisation, I: 24, 25, 104, 105, 108
Committee, Code, I: 44; of December 6, I: 245, 246, 249, 258, 260, 280; Main, II: 34, 35, 37, 42, 43, 116, 118; of Ministers, I: 104, 109, 179, 180, 181, 242; II: 146; Secret, I: 259, 260; II: 17, 18; Scholastic, I: 189, 191;

Unofficial, I: 83–95, 109, 114, 246; II: 56
Compensation, see Redemption
Constantine, Grand Duke (brother of Nicholas I), I: 23, 167, 205, 224–227, 231, 250; (brother of Alexander II), II: 30, 42, 43, 50, 168, 240, 250, 251
Constantinople, I: 72
Contemporary, The, I: 291, 301, 302, 303; II: 22, 27, 82, 83, 112, 169, 183, 184, 191, 192, 217
Continental System, I: 66, 123, 125, 126, 128, 137, 140, 144, 147, 148, 183, 215, 216, 220, 223, 266; II: 137
Course of paper-money, I: 108, 109, 125, 137, 182, 271; II: 12, 71, 78, 136, 137, 138, 139, 231, 232
Crimean Campaign, I: 224, 252, 308, 310; II: 1, 6, 9, 136, 140, 146, 147, 148, 150, 154, 157, 226
Czartoryski, Prince Adam, I: 70–73, 83–91, 111, 116–118, 127, 160

Dawn, The, II: 191
Day, The, II: 76, 82, 105
Decembrists, I: 198, 233, 235, 236, 239, 245, 260, 283, 289
Degaiev, II: 260
Delianov, Minister, II: 91, 170, 174, 260, 261
Depositki, I: 276, 277
Derzhavin, I: 86, 93, 94, 97, 99, 102, 106, 128
Diet, Polish, I: 165, 166, 193, 194, 202, 209, 211, 250
Dnieper Russ, I: 8, 10, 11, 18
Dobroliubov, II: 207, 211, 217
Dolgorukov, Prince A. M., II: 42, 59, 60, 67, 69
Dolgorukov, Prince V. A., II: 113

Dostoievsky, I: 308; II: 114, 191, 214
Dukhobory, I: 106, 294, 296; II: 265

Economical Indicator, II: 62
Editing Commissions, II: 31, 33, 34, 35, 38, 39, 41, 43, 46, 47, 49, 50, 112, 137
Education, II: 89–95, 113, 116, 164–175, 261, 334
Elizabeth, Empress, I: 26, 37, 44, 47, 51
England, I: 60, 61, 78, 85, 100, 107, 114, 116, 122, 123, 126, 137, 140, 146, 159, 161, 163, 170, 183, 219, 220, 231, 266, 307; II: 143, 227, 230, 233, 269, 270
European Messenger, I: 98, 143, 285; II: 169, 264

Figner, Viera, II: 221
Finland, I: 23, 25, 123, 129, 136, 148, 151, 173, 206, 216, 219; II: 200
Fletcher, Ambassador, I: 12
Forward! II: 72, 219
Fotiy, Archimandrite, I: 210, 242, 294
Forties, Men of, II: 6
France, I: 60, 113, 114, 128, 131, 134, 148, 149, 161, 216, 251, 252, 253, 299, 307
Free Agriculturists, I: 101, 102, 133
Free Economic Society, I: 187
Freemasonry, I: 163, 184, 196
French ideas, I: 37, 38, 39, 284, 289
Friend of Enlightenment, I: 99

Gagarin, Prince P. P., II: 16, 43, 44, 112, 167

Gagarin, Prince A., II: 167, 181, 197
Geok-Tepe, II: 269, 270
German ideas, I: 39, 283, 284, 290, 291
Germany, I: 25, 104, 158, 159, 195; II: 270, 271
Giers, II: 269
Godunov, Boris, I: 16
Gogol, I: 302, 303
Golden Horde, I: 9, 10
Golitzyn, Prince A. N., I: 188, 189, 193, 210, 211, 225, 245, 246
Golovnin, II: 92, 95, 104, 111, 112, 167, 168, 171, 172, 243, 252
Goncharov, II: 58
Gorchakov, II: 9, 84, 228, 231, 269
Great Russian, The, II: 80
Grinevitzky, II: 247, 248
Gruzia, I: 142, 169, 171, 181, 182, 211, 270, 271, 272, 274
Guriev, Minister, I: 142, 169, 171, 181, 182, 211, 270, 271, 272, 274

Hanfman, Hessie, II: 248
Hegel, I: 286, 290, 291
Herzegovina, II: 229, 230
Herzen, I: 283, 289, 290, 291, 293, 296; II: 7, 8, 56, 75, 79, 82, 83, 207, 208, 213
Hetæriæ, I: 197
Hohenzollern, II: 270
Holstein-Gotorp, I: 147
Holy Alliance, I: 163, 187, 209
Holy Synod, see Synod
Hungarian Uprising, II: 1

Ignatiev, Minister of Interior, II: 154, 208, 232, 233, 252, 253, 254, 257, 259, 260, 261
Ikonobortzy, I: 296
India, II: 228, 229
Industry, I: 21, 27, 67, 128, 183,

184, 226, 267, 268, 269, 271, 273;
II: 77, 78, 133, 134, 268
Intelligentzia, I: 5, 34, 36, 37, 48,
223, 279, 282, 285, 289, 302, 303,
309; II: 22, 69, 72, 75, 76, 166,
206, 207, 209, 210, 216
Interregnum, I: 16; II: 23, 32, 123
Inventory Regulations, I: 259, 263,
264; II: 5, 18
Italy, I: 60; II: 271
Ivan Kalita, I: 9
Ivan III, I: 9, 10, 16
Ivan IV, I: 10, 16, 57

Jesuits, I: 163, 187
Jews, I: 104–107, 118, 120, 206;
II: 265
Judiciary reform, II: 101, 102;
curbing of, II: 181–186, 187, 189

Kankrin, I: 169, 186, 212, 214, 261,
269, 270, 271, 272, 274, 275, 276,
277, 278, 279, 309; II: 89, 136,
138
Karakozov, II: 106, 111, 112, 146,
155, 163, 165, 179, 182
Karamzin, I: 57, 98, 99, 113, 128,
142, 143, 144, 156, 178, 191, 194,
211, 215, 219, 226, 236, 237, 238,
239, 241, 242, 243, 245, 253, 279,
308
Katkov, I: 289, 290; II: 59, 60,
86, 87, 106, 114, 165, 166, 169,
170, 182, 183, 192, 224, 236, 251,
252, 261
Kaufman, General, II: 228
Kavelin, II: 27, 59, 75, 91, 92
Khodsky, Professor, II: 120, 121
Khomiakov, I: 284, 287, 292, 306,
307; II: 190
Khlysty, I: 296
Kholopy, I: 17
Kibalchich, II: 247, 248

Kievite, The, II: 190
Kireievsky, I: 284, 286, 287, 292
Kiselev, I: 173, 174, 179, 260, 261,
262, 263, 279, 301, 309; II: 117,
118, 257
Kluchevsky, I: 7, 8, 12, 13
Kokhanov, II: 258, 259, 260, 261
Kochubey, I: 72, 78, 83, 85, 86, 88,
95, 103, 105, 136, 139, 173, 178,
243, 245, 246, 249
Komissarov, II: 106
Koni, A., II: 183, 189
Korf, Baron M. A., I: 264, 304,
306
Koshelev, I: 292, 306, 307; II:
61, 144, 197, 243
Kovalevsky, M., I: 13; II, 103
Kovalevsky, N., II: 303
Kropotkin, II: 69, 81, 215, 217,
218, 220
Krüdener, Baroness, I: 162, 163,
187, 210
Kutuzov, I: 118, 149, 150, 154, 155,
156, 157, 158

La Harpe, I: 42, 68, 70, 71, 73, 74,
75, 77, 82, 87, 91, 115, 163, 164,
229, 290
Lamennais, I: 302
Lancasterian Schools, I: 200
Land, distribution of, II: 42, 43,
44, 49, 50
Land and Freedom, II: 221, 222,
237, 238
Landowners, see Nobles
Landowners' Journal, II: 62, 96,
97
Landownership, II: 119–122
Lanskoy, II: 10, 14, 16, 22, 27, 67,
97, 162, 184
Lappo-Danilevsky, I: 31, 32
Lavrov, II: 192, 210, 211, 212, 219
Leibach, Congress, I: 202, 231, 285
Leontiev, II: 165, 192, 261

Levshin, II: 11, 13, 15, 17, 18, 22, 29
Lipetzk, Congress, II: 237, 238
Lomonosov, I: 36, 111
Loris-Melikov, II: 175, 239, 241–259
Lovers of Nature, society, I: 196, 197
Lovers of Wisdom, society, I: 284, 292

Magazine for Lovers, I: 99
Magazine of Russian Letters, I: 99
Magnitzky, I: 190, 192, 211, 237, 242
Maistee, de Joseph, I: 189, 190
Malta, Order of Knights, I: 55, 60, 61
Martinists, I: 38
Masons, I: 38, 172, 196
Mavor, James, I: 13
Merchants, I: 30, 31, 34, 182; II: 77, 78, 79
Merezhkovsky, I: 42, 63
Meshchersky, Prince, II: 193
Metternich, I: 163, 164, 209, 217, 253
Mezentzev, II: 236
Mikhailovsky, N. K., II: 208, 211, 214, 267
Military Colonies, I: 175, 176, 178, 201, 210, 213, 217, 237, 242, 247; II: 160
Miloradovich, I: 186, 201, 226, 227, 232
Miliukov, P. N., I: 7, 12, 16, 38, 40; II: 123, 124, 129, 130, 131, 283, 303, 307, 319, 326, 333
Miliutin, D. A., II: 157–171, 184, 189, 250, 252, 266
Miliutin, N. A., I: 301; II: 28–40, 67, 97, 99, 118, 144, 153, 155, 157, 225, 243

Ministers, Committee of, see Committee
Ministries, establishment of, I: 91, 94, 95
Mnemozina, I: 284
Molokane, I: 100, 294, 296
Mongols, I: 8, 12
Montesquieu, I: 20, 38, 101, 106
Monthly Writings, I: 37
Mordvinov, Admiral, I: 87, 88, 89, 100, 128, 129, 140, 144, 181, 182, 187, 243, 244, 274
Moscow, I: 8, 9, 12, 41, 42, 96
Moscow Almanach, I: 293
Moscow Mercury, I: 99
Moscow Messenger, I: 284, 288
Moscow News, II: 165, 192, 193, 251
Moscow Observer, I: 99
Moscow Telegraph, I: 284, 285
Motley, I: 38
Muraviov, Alexander, I: 196, 197
Muraviov-Apostol, Matvey, I: 197, 205
Muraviov-Apostol, Sergey, I: 197, 202, 204, 228
Muraviov, Mikhail (Imperial tutor), I: 69, 111
Muraviov, Mikhail (Decembrist), I: 145, 199
Muraviov, Gov.-Gen. of Amur, II: 226, 227
Muraviov, M. N., II: 18, 23, 24, 42, 67, 111, 112, 118
Muraviov, Nikita, I: 197, 200, 205, 207, 208, 219, 233, 236
Muscovite, The, I: 288, 292, 293, 307; II: 191
Mutual Guarantee, I: 9; II: 47, 254
Myshkin, Ippolit, II: 217, 218

Napoleon I, I: 60, 61, 66, 114–171, 197, 215, 216, 217, 230

Napoleon III, II: 9, 86
Narodnichestvo, II: 191, 192, 206, 207, 209, 221, 223, 238
Narodniki, II: 207, 211, 216, 219, 220, 221, 223, 235, 236, 238, 239
Narodovoltzy, I: 208; II: 238
Nathanson, Mark and Olga, II: 221
Nicolas I, I: 181, 192, 212, 223–310; II: 1, 3, 4, 140, 153, 154, 160, 161, 162, 224, 226, 227, 242, 261, 266
Nicolayi, Baron, II: 192, 252, 260
Niechaiev, II: 213, 214, 216
Niekrasov, II: 114, 192
Nihilism, II: 69, 83, 114, 163, 165, 166, 167, 168, 192, 209
Nobles, I: 20, 21, 30, 33, 34, 54, 136, 141, 155, 184, 185, 186, 255, 256, 257, 258, 264; II: 13–21, 23–40, 71, 73, 78, 97, 197–201, 208, 262, 267
Northern Messenger, I: 100
Northern Society, I: 205, 207, 208, 227, 243
Novikov, I: 38, 52, 196, 213
Novoie Vremia (New Time), II: 193
Novosiltzev, I: 73, 78, 83, 85, 88, 89, 90, 111, 119, 127, 131, 160, 161

Obligatory redemption, II: 41, 79
Obligatory, transitory period, II: 25, 26, 27, 28, 33, 35
Obrok, I: 21, 28, 103, 262, 240; II: 33, 35, 40, 41, 51, 66, 117, 118, 196, 197, 202, 253
Ogarev, II: 75, 210
Old Servers, I: 77, 78, 79, 87, 90, 94
Osterman-Tolstoy, I: 152, 153
Ostsee Statute, II: 12

Pahlen (regicide), I: 74, 78, 79
Pahlen, K. I., II: 161, 185, 187, 189, 220, 242
Pale of Settlement, I: 100
Panin, Nikita, I: 33, 51, 75, 78, 79, 80
Panin, V. N., II: 38, 39, 40, 43, 50, 167, 168
Paris, Treaty of, II: 9, 233
Paskevich, I: 233, 245, 264, 299, 300; II: 2, 32
Paul I, I: 27, 38, 50–63, 69, 70, 75, 76, 77, 78, 79, 80, 81, 84, 96, 97, 104, 105, 107, 108, 109, 114, 128, 177, 214, 220, 224, 228
Pavlov, Professor, I: 283, 289
Pazukhin, II: 262, 263
Peasants, I: 14, 17, 21, 26, 28, 33, 53, 54, 185, 186, 254, 258, 259, 260, 264; II: 10–54, 286–289; disturbances of, II: 66
Peasants, Economical, I: 28; Fiscal, I: 28, 54, 102, 104, 211, 246, 260, 261, 262; Obligatory, I: 262, 263; II: 41, 46, 47, 253; Possessional, I: 28; II: State, I: 28, II: 115, 116, 117, 118, 119, 257; Udielny, II: 116, 117, 118, 119
Peace-Mediators, II: 67, 68, 69, 74
Periodical Publications, I: 100
Permanent Council, I: 81, 85, 90, 94, 110
Perovsky, Sophia, II: 220, 247
Persia, I: 58, 62, 114, 123, 138, 140, 273
Pestel, I: 197–219, 234, 236, 260, 283
Peter, the Great, I: 11, 15, 16, 17, 19, 24, 31, 35, 36, 37, 38, 41, 42, 43, 45, 46, 94
Peter III, I: 32, 147
Petersburg, I: 16
Petrashevsky, I: 302, 304, 306

Petrograd News, II: 169, 193
Petrunkevich, I: 1; II: 236, 237, 242, 243
Pisarev, II: 166, 191, 192, 209, 210, 211
Plehve, II: 242
Plekhanov, II: 222, 238
Pnin, I: 99, 100
Pobiedonostzev, II: 249, 250, 251, 252, 259, 260, 261, 265
Pogodin, I: 284, 288, 292, 293, 307
Poland, I: 8, 10, 15, 16, 72, 75, 105, 116, 120, 124, 147, 159, 160, 161, 163, 165, 167, 172, 173, 193, 205, 206, 211, 216, 219, 250, 267, 268, 272, 273; II: 9, 81, 83, 84, 85, 86, 87, 200, 225, 265
Polevoy, I: 284, 285, 303
Poll-Tax, I: 17, II: 255
Polonism, II: 172, 225
Popovtzy, I: 296
Population, growth of, II: 123–131
Polar Star, The, II: 8
Posen, M. P., II: 15, 26, 32, 33, 34, 40
Possessed, The, II: 114
Possessional Factories, I: 183, 184, 256, 267; II: 132
Potiomkin, Prince, I: 52
Potocky, Count Severin, I: 93, 97, 111, 139
Press, conditions of, II: 55, 61, 62, 103, 104, 105, 186–194
Princes, dissensions of, I: 8, 12
Prussia, I: 68, 115, 117, 118, 120, 121, 124, 126, 131, 148, 158, 159, 161, 174, 253, 300, 308; II: 159, 168
Pugachov, I: 27
Pushchin, I: 201
Pushkin, I: 186, 239, 240, 284, 285; II: 269
Pypin, II: 183, 184, 187, 192

Radicalism, II: 80, 81, 83, 106
Radishchev, I: 35, 52
Railroads, II: 78, 139–146, 268, 269
Rastopchin, I: 128, 155, 157
Recruitments, I: 16
Redemption, II: 25, 27, 28, 32, 33, 41, 45, 59, 71, 79
Reform, results of, II: 123, 134
Reglament, Peter's, I: 92, 93, 94
Reitern, II: 114, 115, 137–178, 231–239
Rescript, to Nazimov, II: 18, 20, 21
Rhenish Confederation, I: 120
Romanovs, I: 41
Rosenkreizer, I: 38
Rostovtzev, I: 228; II: 15, 16, 27, 28, 31, 32–38
Roumania, II: 233, 270
Rousseau, I: 38
Runich, I: 101, 102, 190, 211, 237, 242
Russia, consolidation of, I: 9, 15, 18, 23
Russia's Borderlands, II: 191
Russian Discourse, II: 60
Russian Justice, I: 205
Russian Messenger, I: 192; II: 27, 60, 83, 165, 192
Russian News, II: 193, 264
Russian Thought, II: 243, 264
Russian Word, II: 69, 82, 83, 112, 166, 169, 191
Ryleiev, I: 201, 208, 227, 234; II: 16
Rysakov, II: 247, 248

Sails, II: 61
Saltykov, I: 67, 179
Saltykov-Shchedrin, I: 305; II: 192, 193
Samarin, Yuriy, I: 289, 292, 295,

305, 306; II: 14, 29, 30, 40, 44,
61, 75, 152, 190, 191, 195, 225
San-Stefano, II: 233
Sardinia, I: 307; II: 1
Schad, Professor, I: 185, 191
Scharnhorst, I: 174
Schelling, I: 283, 284, 286, 290
Schilder, I: 51, 151, 178, 251
Schismatics, I: 40, 41, 55, 107, 294,
295, 297; II: 221, 265
Schwarz (XVIII c.), I: 38, 196,
213
Schwarz, Colonel, I: 202
Scythian Plan, I: 150
Secret Expedition, I: 80
Sectants, I: 105, 107, 293, 294, 296,
297; II: 221, 265
Semionovsky Guards, regiment, I:
196, 197, 202, 209, 285
Senate, I: 42–45, 81, 86, 90, 91, 92,
93, 94, 135, 166, 214; II: 82,
174, 184, 188, 190
Serbia, II: 229, 230, 233, 270
Serving Class, I: 13, 16
Seven Years' War, I: 46, 47
Shamil, II: 227
Shcherbatov, Prince, I: 33
Shelgunov, II: 191, 192
Sherwood, I: 211
Shevchenko, I: 306
Shevyrev, I: 284, 288, 292
Shishkov, I: 99, 128, 145, 155, 162,
168, 172, 211, 242, 249, 279, 281
Shuvalov, P. A., II: 113–115, 146,
149, 164, 184, 187
Skoptzy, I: 296
Slavophiles, I: 284, 286, 287, 289,
292, 293, 302; II: 59, 60, 61, 76,
190, 191, 193, 194, 195, 231, 233,
252, 260
Slavs, settlement of, I: 7
Son of the Fatherland, I: 192, 195
Southern Society, I: 196, 204, 205,
211, 228
Spain, I: 147, 160

Speransky, I: 109, 110, 130–144,
148, 154, 165, 166, 172, 178, 181,
182, 190, 192, 195, 226, 237, 243,
245, 246, 247, 253, 260, 270
Spirit of Journals, I: 185, 192
Stankevich, I: 289, 290
State Council, I: 136, 139, 141, 143,
166, 178, 180, 182, 187, 201, 225,
226, 232, 233, 260, 263; II: 43,
44, 88, 93, 95, 98, 143, 154, 155,
160, 161, 162, 166, 167, 168, 170,
174, 181, 182, 186, 191, 240, 249,
250, 254, 258, 264
Stein, Baron, I: 161
Steingel, Baron, I: 236
Stepniak-Kravchinsky, II: 236
Storch, Academic, I: 25, 53, 97,
106, 185, 230
Stroganev, I: 73, 82, 83, 85, 91,
103, 109, 110, 127
Struve, P. B., II: 124
Student-disorders, II: 91, 92
Sturdza, I: 189, 190, 191
Sumarokov, I: 37
Suvorin, A., II: 183, 193
Suvorov, General, I: 60, 61
Surovov, Gov.-Gen., II: 75, 92,
113
Sweden, I: 8, 11, 13, 18, 123, 138,
146, 148, 149, 216
Synod, Holy, I: 48, 225, 234; II:
250, 260
Szlachta, I: 161

Tacitus, I: 101
Talleyrand, I: 131, 132, 159
Tariffs, I: 31, 59, 61, 107, 170, 182,
183, 215, 220, 268, 269, 270, 271;
II: 267, 268
Tashkent, II: 227, 230
Tatarinov, II: 88, 115
Tatishchev, I: 36
Taxes, I: 15, 17, 108, 141, 271,

272; II: 73, 76, 156, 202, 203, 204, 205, 206, 254, 255, 258
Telescope, The, I: 284–287, 295
Tiding, The, II: 192, 193
Tilsit, Peace of, I: 126; Treaty of, I: 126, 128, 129, 130, 137, 146, 159, 174, 215, 216, 218, 223
Tolstoy, Dmitri, II: 112, 115, 161–175, 190–265
Trepov, Feodor, I: 113, 235
Trigoni, II: 248
Triple Alliance, II: 271
Troshchinsky, I: 77, 80, 81, 109, 130
Troubled Time, see Interregnum
Trubetzkoy, S. P. (Decembrist), I: 201, 205
Tugan-Baranovsky, I: 31, 184, 266; II: 133
Tugendbund, I: 197, 199, 200
Turcomen, II: 229, 269
Turgeniev, Nicolas, I: 186, 196, 200, 201, 203, 205, 236; II: 101
Turgeniev, Ivan, I: 305; II: 58, 75
Turkestan, II: 227, 228
Turkey, I: 15, 18, 23, 43, 47, 121, 123, 124, 129, 138, 140, 146, 148, 149, 210, 250, 251, 252, 260, 274, 307; II: 229, 230, 231, 232, 233, 234
Tver, I: 10, 12; Resolution of, II: 71–74
Tyaglo, I: 15

Ukrainophiles, II: 224, 235
Ulozhenie, I: 82, 254
Uniates, II: 226, 265
Union of Salvation, I: 197, 198, 199, 201, 204
Union of Welfare, I: 199, 200, 201, 202, 203, 227
United Slavs, society, I: 196, 205
Universal Service, II: 159

University Councils, I: 112, 187
University Statutes, I: 112, 187, 282; II: 93, 261
Unkiar-Skelessi, Treaty of, I: 252
Unkovsky, II: 24, 25, 36, 37, 60, 74, 186
Uspensky, N., II: 207, 214
Ussuriysk, II: 227, 257
Uvarov, I: 185, 191, 195, 239, 249, 253, 279, 280, 281, 285, 286, 288, 304; his formula, II: 164

Valuiev, II: 42, 67, 68, 70, 74, 75, 97, 104, 106, 113, 115, 146, 155, 164, 167, 183–187, 202, 203, 240, 251
Vannovsky, Minister, II: 171, 266
Vassilchikov, I: 186, 196, 203, 211, 214, 245, 251
Vassilkov, I: 204
Vassily III, I: 10
Velepolsky, Marquis, II: 82, 83, 84, 85, 86, 225, 226
Vellansky, I: 283
Venevitinov, I: 284, 290
Viazemsky, Prince, I: 284
Viazmitinov, I: 97, 192
Vienna, Congress, I: 159, 162, 253; II: 9, 148
Village Well-Being, II: 59, 61, 62
Vishnegradsky, I. A., II: 267
Vishnegradsky, N. A., II: 94, 170
V Narod! II: 208
Voice, II: 169, 193
Voices from Russia, II: 62
Voinaralsky, II: 218, 220
Volkonsky, S. G., I: 198, 204, 205, 243
Voltaire, I: 38
Vorontzov, A. A., I: 85, 86, 87, 116
Vorontzov, M. S., I: 186, 216
Vsevolod Big Nest, I: 8

Week, The, II: 192, 210
Western heresies, I: 40
Wilhelm I, II: 251, 270
Wilhelm II, II: 271
Will of the People, II: 222, 238, 239, 245, 247, 260
Winter Palace, I: 87, 94, 127; II: 240, 250
Witgenstein, I: 151, 152, 197, 198, 199
Witte, II: 268

Yakushkin, I: 197, 198, 201
Yankovich de Mirievo, I: 37, 111, 280
Yanson, Professor, II: 120, 202, 205, 206, 207

Yaroslav, I: 206
Yelena, Grand Duchess, II: 15, 30, 38, 243, 247
Ypsilanti, I: 210
Yushnevsky, I: 203, 204

Zamiatnin, II: 101, 114, 181, 182
Zarudny, II: 101, 182
Zasulich, Viera, II: 235
Zavadovsky, I: 81, 82, 110, 136
Zemsky Chiefs, introduced, II: 263
Zemsky Sobor, I: 41
Zemstvo, II: 96–103, 143–148, 157, 171–180, 183, 194, 224, 235–264
Zheliabov, II: 237, 246, 247
Zhukovsky, Vassily, I: 232, 242; II: 3, 4